Natural Language Generation

NATO ASI Series

Advanced Science Institutes Series

A Series presenting the results of activities sponsored by the NATO Science Committee, which aims at the dissemination of advanced scientific and technological knowledge, with a view to strengthening links between scientific communities.

The Series is published by an international board of publishers in conjunction with the NATO Scientific Affairs Division

A	Life Sciences	Plenum Publishing Corporation
B	Physics	London and New York
C	Mathematical and Physical Sciences	D. Reidel Publishing Company Dordrecht, Boston, Lancaster and Tokyo
D	Behavioural and Social Sciences	Martinus Nijhoff Publishers Dordrecht, Boston and Lancaster
E	Applied Sciences	
F	Computer and Systems Sciences	Springer-Verlag Berlin, Heidelberg, New York
G	Ecological Sciences	London, Paris and Tokyo
H	Cell Biology	

Series E: Applied Sciences – No. 135

Natural Language Generation

New Results in Artificial Intelligence, Psychology and Linguistics

edited by

Gerard Kempen

Department of
Experimental Psychology
University of Nijmegen
The Netherlands

1987 **Martinus Nijhoff Publishers**
Dordrecht / Boston / Lancaster
Published in cooperation with NATO Scientific Affairs Division

Proceedings of the NATO Advanced Research Workshop on "Natural Language
Generation", Nijmegen, The Netherlands, August 19-23, 1986

Library of Congress Cataloging-in-Publication Data

NATO Advanced Research Workshop on Natural Language
    Generation (1986 : Nijmegen, Netherlands)
    Natural language generation.

    (NATO ASI series. Series E, Applied sciences ;
no. 135)
    "Published in cooperation with NATO Scientific
Affairs Division."
    "Proceedings of the NATO Advanced Research Workshop
on Natural Language Generation, Nijmegen,
The Netherlands, August 19-23, 1986"--T.p. verso.
    Includes index.
    1. Linguistics--Data processing--Congresses.
I. Kempen, Gerard, 1943-   . II. North Atlantic
Treaty Organization. Scientific Affairs Division.
III. Title. IV. Series.
P98.N27 1986   410'.28'5   87-14043
ISBN 90-247-3558-0

ISBN 90-247-3558-0 (this volume)
ISBN 90-247-2689-1 (series)

Distributors for the United States and Canada: Kluwer Academic Publishers,
P.O. Box 358, Accord-Station, Hingham, MA 02018-0358, USA

Distributors for the UK and Ireland: Kluwer Academic Publishers, MTP Press Ltd,
Falcon House, Queen Square, Lancaster LA1 1RN, UK

Distributors for all other countries: Kluwer Academic Publishers Group, Distribution
Center, P.O. Box 322, 3300 AH Dordrecht, The Netherlands

Printed in The Netherlands

Contents

I   Pragmatic Aspects

II   Generation of Connected Discourse

III   Generator Design

IV   Grammars and Grammatical Formalisms

V   Stages of Human Sentence Production

VI   Aspects of Lexicalization

vi

Preface		ix
Authors and Participants		xi

I   Pragmatic Aspects **1**

1. Some pragmatic decision criteria in generation — 3
    Eduard H. Hovy
2. How to appear to be conforming to the 'maxims' even if you prefer to violate them — 19
    Anthony Jameson
3. Contextual effects on responses to misconceptions — 43
    Kathleen F. McCoy
4. Generating understandable explanatory sentences — 55
    Domenico Parisi & Donatella Ferrante
5. Toward a plan-based theory of referring actions — 63
    Douglas E. Appelt
6. Generating referring expressions and pointing gestures — 71
    Norbert Reithinger

II   Generation of Connected Discourse **83**

7. Rhetorical Structure Theory: description and construction of text structures — 85
    William C. Mann & Sandra A. Thompson
8. Discourse strategies for describing complex physical objects — 97
    Cecile L. Paris & Kathleen R. McKeown
9. Strategies for generating coherent descriptions of object movements in street scenes — 117
    Hans-Joachim Novak
10. The automated news agency: SEMTEX — a text generator for German — 133
    Dietmar Rösner
11. A connectionist approach to the generation of abstracts — 149
    Kôiti Hasida, Shun Ishizaki & Hitoshi Isahara

III   Generator Design **157**

12. Factors contributing to efficiency in natural language generation — 159
    David D. McDonald, Marie M. Vaughan & James D. Pustejovsky
13. Reviewing as a component of the text generation process — 183
    Masoud Yazdani
14. A French and English syntactic component for generation — 191
    Laurence Danlos
15. KING: a knowledge-intensive natural language generator — 219
    Paul S. Jacobs

IV	**Grammars and Grammatical Formalisms**	**231**

16. The relevance of Tree Adjoining Grammar to generation
Aravind K. Joshi — 233
17. Notes on the organization of the environment of a text generation grammar
Christian Matthiessen — 253
18. A formal model of Systemic Grammar
Terry Patten & Graeme Ritchie — 279
19. Generating answers from a linguistically coded knowledge base
Simon C. Dik — 301
20. A computer model of Functional Grammar
Kwee Tjoe-Liong — 315
21. Utterance generation from semantic representations augmented with pragmatic information
Harry Bunt — 333

V	**Stages of Human Sentence Production**	**349**

22. Exploring levels of processing in sentence production
Kathryn Bock — 351
23. Incremental sentence production, self-correction, and coordination
Koenraad De Smedt & Gerard Kempen — 365
24. A theory of grammatical impairment in aphasia
Herman Kolk — 377

VI	**Aspects of Lexicalization**	**393**

25. Stages of lexical access
Willem J.M. Levelt & Herbert Schriefers — 395
26. Where do phrases come from: some preliminary experiments in connectionist phrase generation
Karen Kukich — 405
27. The generation of tense
Veronika Ehrich — 423
28. Perceptual factors and word order in event descriptions
Giovanni B. Flores d'Arcais — 441
29. Metacomments in text generation
Bengt Sigurd — 453

Name Index — 463

Preface

The chapters of this book are edited versions of all 29 papers presented at the *Third International Workshop on Natural Language Generation,* which took place in Nijmegen, The Netherlands, from August 19-23, 1986. The Workshop was attended by virtually all leading researchers in the area of natural language generation, and their contributions address many different issues from all three relevant disciplines: computer science (artificial intelligence), psychology, and linguistics. However, I grouped the chapters along the lines of content rather than discipline. One of the rewarding experiences during the Workshop was the discovery that traditional boundaries between disciplines play hardly any role in the study of natural language generation.

Part I deals with *pragmatic aspects of language generation*: dialogue partner modeling (Hovy, Jameson, McCoy, Parisi/Ferrante) and referential communication (Appelt, Reithinger). Part II discusses the *generation of connected discourse* : rhetorical structure (Mann/Thompson), descriptions of objects, events and situations (Paris/McKeown, Novak, Rösner), and abstracts (Hasida/Ishizaki/Isahara). Part III is devoted to *generator design* issues (McDonald/ Vaughan/Pustejovsky, Yazdani) and implemented generation systems (Danlos, Jacobs). Various types of *grammars and grammatical formalisms* are presented in Part IV: Tree Adjoining Grammar (Joshi), Systemic Grammar (Matthiessen, Patten/Ritchie), Functional Grammar (Dik, Kwee), and Discontinuous Phrase-Structure Grammar (Bunt). Section V concentrates on *human sentence production* in its many varieties (Bock, De Smedt/Kempen, Kolk). Finally, Part VI addresses *lexicalization* issues: problems related to accessing and selecting lexical items and related linguistic units in language generation (Levelt/Schriefers, Kukich, Ehrich, Flores d'Arcais, Sigurd).

I owe considerable debt to the following persons and institutions:
— Mrs. Dr. A.D. Wolff-Albers (Deputy Director General for Science Policy, Ministry of Education and Science, The Hague) for her stimulating opening address.
— Dr. Joachim Laubsch and Dr. Douglas Appelt, who organized the two predecessors of this Workshop (at the University of Stuttgart and at Stanford University, respectively).
— Dr. Anthony Jameson (Department of Psychology, University of Nijmegen) for checking and correcting the English of most of the chapters written by non-native speakers, and for his creative editorial advice.
— Mrs. Nettie Theyse for the pleasant, competent and continuous secretarial assistance before, during and after the Workshop.
— Mrs. Nettie Theyse and Ms. Jolanda Ariëns for accurately preparing the camera-ready copy from text files submitted through electronic mail or on various sorts of diskettes.
— The technical and administrative staff of the Department of Psychology of the University of Nijmegen for their invaluable support.
— The participants of the Workshop who reviewed prefinal versions of the papers published here.
— IBM Nederland N.V. and BSO (Bureau voor Software Ontwikkeling) for generous financial contributions.
— The NATO Scientific Affairs Division for the ARW grant (Advanced Research Workshop) and for efficient organizational backing.

Nijmegen, March 1987

Gerard Kempen

Authors and participants

Gert Anbeek
Océ-Nederland
Postbus 101
5900 MA Venlo
The Netherlands

Douglas E. Appelt
Artificial Intelligence Center
SRI International
Menlo Park, CA 94025
USA

J. Kathryn Bock
Dept. of Psychology
Psychological Research Building
Michigan State University
East Lansing Michigan 48824
USA

Harry Bunt
Dept. of Language and Informatics
University of Tilburg
Postbus 90153
5000 LE Tilburg
The Netherlands

Stephan Busemann
Technische Universität Berlin
Institut für Angewandte Informatik
Franklinstrasse 28/29
D-1000 Berlin 10
West Germany

Walter Daelemans
AI Laboratory
Vrije Universiteit Brussel
Pleinlaan 2
1050 Brussel
Belgium

Laurence Danlos
LADL, Université de Paris 7
2, Place Jussieu
75221 Paris
France

Simon C. Dik
Institute for General Linguistics
University of Amsterdam
Spuistraat 210
1012 VT Amsterdam
The Netherlands

Veronika Ehrich
Max Planck Institute for Psycholinguistics
Wundtlaan 1
6525 XD Nijmegen
The Netherlands

Donatella Ferrante
Istituto di Psicologia del CNR
Via dei Monti Tiburtini 509
00157 Roma
Italy

Giovanni B. Flores d'Arcais
Max Planck Institute for Psycholinguistics
Wundtlaan 1
6525 XD Nijmegen
The Netherlands

Angela Friederici
Max Planck Institute for Psycholinguistics
Wundtlaan 1
6525 XD Nijmegen
The Netherlands

Kôiti Hasida
Machine Inference Section (ETL)
1-1-4 Umezono, Sakura-mura, Niihari-gun
Ibaraki 305
Japan

Eduard Hovy
Yale University
Dept. of Computer Science
10 Hillhouse Avenue
New Haven, CT 06520
USA

Hitoshi Isahara
Machine Inference Section (ETL)
1-1-4 Umezono, Sakura-mura, Niihari-gun
Ibaraki 305
Japan

Shun Ishizaki
Machine Inference Section (ETL)
1-1-4 Umezono, Sakura-mura, Niihari-gun
Ibaraki 305
Japan

Paul S. Jacobs
General Electric
Corporate Research and Development
P.O.Box 8
Schenectady, NY 12301
U.S.A.

Anthony Jameson
University of Nijmegen
Dept. of Psychology
Montessorilaan 3
6525 HR Nijmegen
The Netherlands

Aravind K. Joshi
Dept. of Computer and Information Science
University of Pennsylvania
Philadelphia, Pennsylvania 19104
USA

Gerard Kempen
University of Nijmegen
Dept. of Psychology
Montessorilaan 3
6525 HR Nijmegen
The Netherlands

Ritchard Kittredge
Linguistique
Université de Montreal
C.P. 6128
Montreal H3C 3J7
Canada

Herman Kolk
University of Nijmegen
Dept. of Psychology
Montessorilaan 3
6525 HR Nijmegen
The Netherlands

Tanya Korelsky
Linguistique
Université de Montreal
C.P. 6128
Montreal H3C 3J7
Canada

Karen Kukich
Bell Communications Research
435 South Street
Morristown, NJ 07960
USA

Kwee Tjoe-Liong
Alpha-Informatics
University of Amsterdam
Herengracht 286
1016 BX Amsterdam
The Netherlands

Joachim Laubsch
Hewlett-Packard Computer Research Center
1501 Page Mill Road
Palo Alto, CA 94304
USA

Willem J.M. Levelt
Max Planck Institute for Psycholinguistics
Wundtlaan 1
6525 XD Nijmegen
The Netherlands

Donald Mackay
Dept. of Psychology
University of California
Los Angeles, CA. 90024
USA

William C. Mann
USC/ISI
4676 Admiralty Way
Marina del Rey, CA 90291
USA

Domenico Parisi
Istituto di Psicologia del CNR
Via dei Monti Tiburtini 509
00157 Roma
Italy

Christian Matthiessen
USC/ISI
4676 Admiralty Way
Marina del Rey, CA 90291
USA

Terry Patten
2408 Ulrich Rd. N.W.
Calgary, Alberta T2N 4G5
Canada

Kathleen F. McCoy
Dept. of Computer and Information Science
University of Delaware
Newark, DE 19711
USA

James D. Pustejovsky
Computer Science Dept.
Brandeis University
Waltham, MA 02254
USA

David D. McDonald
Dept. of Computer and Information Science
University of Massachusetts
Amherst, MA. 01003
USA

Norbert Reithinger
Universität des Saarlandes
Fachbereich Informatik
Im Stadwald 15
6600 Saarbrücken
West Germany

Kathleen R. McKeown
Columbia University
Dept. of Computer Science
New York, NY 10027
USA

Graeme Ritchie
Dept. of Artificial Intelligence
University of Edinburgh
80 South Bridge
Edinburgh EH1 1HN
Scotland

Hans-Joachim Novak
IBM Deutschland GmbH
LILOG
Schloszstrasse 70
7000 Stuttgart
West Germany

Dietmar Rösner
Universität Stuttgart
Institut für Informatik
Herdweg 51
D-7000 Stuttgart 1
West Germany

Cecile Paris
Columbia University
Dept. of Computer Science
New York, NY 10027
USA

Herbert Schriefers
Max Planck Institute for Psycholinguistics
Wundtlaan 1
6525 XD Nijmegen
The Netherlands

Klaus Schubert
BSO
Kon. Wilhelminalaan 3
Postbus 8348
3503 RH Utrecht
The Netherlands

Bengt Sigurd
Lund University
Helgonabacken 12
22362 Lund
Sweden

Koenraad De Smedt
University of Nijmegen
Dept. of Psychology
Montessorilaan 3
6525 HR Nijmegen
The Netherlands

Sandra A. Thompson
Department of Linguistics
University of California at Santa Barbara
Santa Barbara, CA 93105
USA

Marie M. Vaughan
Dept. of Computer and Information Science
University of Massachusetts
Amherst, MA. 01003
USA

Masoud Yazdani
Dept. of Computer Science
University of Exeter
Stocker Road
Exeter EX4 4QL
UK

Michael Zock
1, Rue Albert Guilpin
94250 Gentilly
France

PART I

Pragmatic Aspects

Chapter 1

SOME PRAGMATIC DECISION CRITERIA IN GENERATION

Eduard H. Hovy

ABSTRACT

When you compare the language produced by people to the text produced by existing language generation programs, one thing becomes immediately clear: people can say the same thing in various ways to achieve various effects, and generators cannot. People vary the content and form of their text when they want to convey more information than is contained in the literal meanings of their words. This information expresses the speaker's perception of the pragmatic aspects of the conversation, and, in particular, of his interpersonal goals toward the hearer. Making a program do this requires identifying the choice points in the grammar at which this information can be incorporated and defining criteria by which to make the choices. However, since the pragmatic concerns are too general to be used by a generator, these criteria cannot reflect them directly. Speakers require strategies that are specifically tailored to the concerns of producing language. A number of such intermediate strategies, here called rhetorical goals, are described in this paper. These rhetorical goals activate appropriate strategies that give rise to the stylistic differences in the text that enable the speaker to communicate additional information. To illustrate these ideas, the generator PAULINE produces stylistically appropriate text from a single representation under various 'pragmatic' circumstances.

1. THE PROBLEM

It is straightforward to write a language generation program that produces impressive text by associating a sentence template (or some equivalent general grammatical form) with each representational item and then using a grammar to realize the template into surface form. Such a program, however, is not sensitive to anything but the input items, and therefore produces the same output to all hearers in all circumstances.

When we produce language, we tailor our text to the hearer and to the situation. This enables us to include more information than is contained in the literal meanings of our words; indeed, the additional information often has a stronger effect on the hearer than the literal content has. This information is carried in both the content and the form of the text. The various ways of expressing a single underlying representation are governed by rules that all language users, speakers and hearers, use to make reasonably accurate predictions about the speaker, his goals, the hearer, and the conversational circumstances. Thus, for example, in Wodehouse (1979, p. 37), when the butler Jeeves says to his master Wooster

'The scheme I would suggest cannot fail of success, but it has what may seem to you a drawback, sir, in that it requires a certain financial outlay.'

and Wooster paraphrases this to a friend as

'He means... that he has got a pippin of an idea, but it's going to cost a bit.'

we understand that the former is urbane, formal, and perhaps a little smug, while the latter is young and trendy. By making Jeeves's text highfalutin and Wooster's slangy, the author has communicated far more than simply fifty-odd words.

In order for generators to produce pragmatically appropriate text, they must have some means of representing relevant characteristics of the hearer, the conversation setting, and their interpersonal goals. These are the *pragmatic* concerns. In addition, they must contain choice points in the grammar that enable the topic to be said in various ways. These are the *syntactic* concerns. Finally, they require criteria by which to make the decisions so that the choices accurately reflect the pragmatic aspects and convey appropriate additional information. These are called here the *rhetorical* concerns.

Some work has been done on the computer generation of pragmatically appropriate language. The effect of the hearer's knowledge on the selection of speech act was studied by Cohen (1978); on text planning by Appelt (1981); the explanation generator of Swartout (1981) had a switch distinguishing between programming and medical expert users; a theory of how speakers bias their text in evaluative situations such as job interviews was developed by Jameson (in this volume). In addition, much related work on the structure of discourse uses some pragmatic information, for example, Grosz & Sidner (1985).

This paper describes how the program PAULINE (Planning And Uttering Language In Natural Environments) produces stylistically appropriate text from a single representation under various settings that model pragmatic circumstances. It first describes the program's pragmatic settings and syntactic choices; this is followed by a description of the way these can be linked using a set of intermediate-level goals. Finally, the generation of an example under five settings is described.

2. PRAGMATICS AND RHETORICAL GOALS

Though there has been much discussion about what pragmatics as a field of inquiry is all about (see, for example, Carnap, 1938; Morris, 1938; Grice, 1957; Katz, 1977; Gazdar, 1979; Searle, 1979; and Levinson, 1983), no generally accepted scheme has emerged yet. Gazdar (1980) lists pragmatic constraints on sentences; Bühler (1934) names some pragmatic aspects of conversation; Jakobson (1960) extends this list. In the tradition of systemic grammar (e.g. Halliday, 1976), interesting recent work on pragmatics can be found in Fawcett (1980) and Gregory (1982). Therefore, as its pragmatic characterization of the conversation, PAULINE was simply given a list of features that are similar to many of the aspects commonly discussed. The justification of these features is that they are the kinds of features necessary to make a generator of this type work. The following is PAULINE's characterization of the **conversation setting:**

Conversational Atmosphere (setting):
  - **time** — *much, some, little*
  - **tone** — *formal, informal, festive*
  - **conditions** — *good, noisy*

Speaker:
  - **knowledge of the topic** — *expert, student, novice*
  - **interest in the topic** — *high, low*
  - **opinions of the topic** — *good, neutral, bad*
  - **emotional state** — *happy, angry, calm*

Hearer:
- **knowledge of the topic** — *expert, student, novice*
- **interest in the topic** — *high, normal, low*
- **opinions of the topic** — *good, neutral, bad*
- **language ability** — *high, normal, low*
- **emotional state** — *happy, angry, calm*

Speaker-Hearer Relationship:
- **depth of acquaintance** — *friends, acquaintances, strangers*
- **relative social status** — *dominant, equal, subordinate*
- **emotion** — *like, neutral, dislike*

In addition, PAULINE can have the following **interpersonal goals**:

Hearer:
- **affect hearer's knowledge** — *teach, neutral, confuse*
- **affect hearer's opinions of topic** — *switch, none, reinforce*
- **involve hearer in the conversation** — *involve, neutral, repel*
- **affect hearer's emotional state** — *anger, neutral, calm*
- **affect hearer's goals** — *activate, neutral, deactivate*

Speaker-Hearer Relationship:
- **affect hearer's emotion toward speaker** — *respect, like, dislike*
- **affect relative status** — *dominant, equal, subordinate*
- **affect interpersonal distance** — *intimate, close, distant*

Though the pragmatic aspects of conversations help determine the speaker's text, most do not do so directly, since they are too general to be attuned to the requirements of language production. (Invariably, attempts to write down rules that relate pragmatic aspects to generator production decisions become bogged down in minutiae and produce rules with very little credibility. For example, what is the effect on sentence length if the speaker is socially dominant over the hearer? Or if the speaker wants to be friendly, should she[1] make active or passive sentences?)

The solution proposed here is that speakers use a number of other goals that act as intermediaries between, on the one hand, the speaker's interpersonal goals and other pragmatic aspects of the conversation, and, on the other, the syntactic decisions a text producer has to make. These goals will be called *rhetorical goals*. Rhetorical goals achieve their results by causing characteristic stylistic effects on the text. Through style, the speaker can communicate additional information that the hearer can interpret and respond to.

Classifying all the possible styles of text is an impossible task, since one can imagine text characteristics that fit almost any adjective. But certain features of text — such as formality and force — are generally accepted as stylistic. A study of some of the major handbooks of good writing (Weathers & Winches, 1978; Birk & Birk, 1965; Payne, 1969; Hill, 1892; Loomis, Hull & Robinson, 1936; Baker, 1966; Cowan & McPherson, 1977; Strunk & White, 1959; Willis, 1969) indicates that the authorities agree on a few such common broad-based features in their discussions of style. These features they describe in terms of the characteristics of finished paragraphs of text. However, this descriptive approach is of very little use in a theory of language production, since it never makes clear why and how style is formed out of words; nor does it indicate any systematicity behind the classification of stylistic features.

In contrast to such descriptions, a functional approach is to describe style in terms of the decisions a generator has to make. The production of a sentence involves a large number of decisions (in the form of selecting from a set of alternatives). These decisions range from tasks with relatively large effect on the text, such as topic selection and organization into phrases and sentences, through sentence and clause organization, to relatively low-level tasks such a word

---

[1] For the sake of simplicity, female pronouns will be used throughout

choice. Whatever the nature of the generator and the implementation of the grammar, all generators have to perform these decisions. (The simplest generators, of course, perform them by having only one available option.) PAULINE makes the following types of decisions:

- **topic collection**: collect aspects of the topic and related items as sentence topics
- **topic organization**: find appropriate groupings and interpretations of candidate topics; find appropriate ways to juxtapose topics in phrases
- **sentence organization**: for each topic, select appropriate subject, pre-sentence clauses, verb, predicate clauses, etc., and order them
- **clause content and organization**: determine and order the contents of clauses and noun groups
- **word choice**: select appropriate words and phrases

Different styles are produced by varying these decisions systematically in appropriate ways. Thus, with respect to the syntactic concerns of generation, the techniques for achieving stylistic (i.e., rhetorical) goals are defined in terms of the effects they have on the generator decisions. Examples are given later.

On the other hand, the relation between the rhetorical goals and the pragmatic aspects of the conversation is not so clear-cut. Pragmatic-based generation would be simple if each rhetorical goal reflected one and only one interpersonal goal or conversational aspect. In this case, each rhetorical goal would simply be a repository for the generator-specific knowledge required to express its pragmatic partner. But the pragmatic aspects of conversations are not independent; they influence each other. This fact necessitates the existence of rhetorical goals as entities distinct from pragmatic features. To see why, note that a single rhetorical goal can express opposite pragmatic aspects under different conditions. For example, if the speaker has the goal to make the hearer feel close to her, she may activate the rhetorical goal to be humorous (say, by choosing funny words and by selecting funny topics). Usually this will work well, but it will backfire if the hearer has just heard of her mother's death. In this case, an appropriate rhetorical goal is the goal to be serious and slightly formal — which, under normal circumstances, would tend to alienate her. Hence, combinations of rhetorical goals act in concert to produce pragmatic effects; for example, low **formality**, high **force**, and high **partiality** *together* have an effect on text that is distinctly pragmatic and clearly distinguishable from the text produced when these values are inverted: the former could be characterized as *no-nonsense*, the latter as *blather*.

Rhetorical goals, then, are the ways the speaker's pragmatic goals can index (and can determine the application of) his stylistic techniques, which control decisions of the realization process. PAULINE uses the following rhetorical goals, with values as indicated:

- **simplicity** (*simple, normal, complex*): Simple text has short sentences and easy words
- **verbosity** (*terse, normal, verbose*): Terse text uses few words and short phrases
- **formality** (*highfalutin, normal, colloquial*): Highfalutin language is used for speeches and toasts
- **force** (*forceful, neutral, quiet*): Forceful text is energetic and driving
- **floridity** (*dry, neutral, flowery*): Flowery text contains unusual words
- **timidity** (*timid, reckless*): Willingness to consider including opinions
- **partiality** (*impartial, implicit, explicit*): How explicitly opinions are stated, if **timidity** allows
- **detail** (*details, interpretations, both*): Too many details can be boring to non-experts
- **color** (*facts only, with color*): Colorful text includes examples and idioms
- **personal reference** (two ranges, for speaker and hearer): Amount of direct reference to the interlocutors
- **openmindedness** (*narrow-minded, openminded*): Willingness to consider new topics
- **flightiness** (*flighty, stuck*): Tendency to search for new topics to switch to when openminded

Since some styles exhibit the features of a number of the above, simpler, styles taken together, such composites can be defined in terms of the simpler styles. Using the above goals as building blocks, PAULINE has been given, in addition, the following rhetorical goals:

- **haste** (*pressured, unplanned, somewhat planned, planned*): When there's not much time, you must speak fast
- **respect** (four values): Being arrogant, respectful, neutral, or cajoling
- **aggression** (*aggressive, neutral, placating*): Aggressive text is forceful and explicitly partial
- **incitement** (*inciting, normal, calming*): Practised by politicians and union leaders

Of course, it is impossible to list all possible styles. Every speaker has an idiosyncratic set of techniques, often tailored to particular hearers, for using language to achieve her interpersonal goals. The claims made here about text styles are: *function* — they are the expression of rhetorical goals, which in turn serve the speaker's interpersonal goals in the text; and *method of definition* — they are defined as constraints on the decisions the generator has to make. The advantages of defining and using rhetorical goals are obvious. Not only do they seem intuitively plausible, but they enable one to make explicit, collect, and organize many generator decisions and design characteristics that most generators have left implicit or avoided altogether.

Briefly stated, PAULINE works in the following way: it is given a topic, opinions, and values for the pragmatic features of its 'conversation', including the hearer's sympathies and relationship to the speaker. It uses these values to activate the appropriate rhetorical goals. Then it proceeds to collect sentence topics, to organize them, and to produce text. Whenever the program encounters a decision point, it queries pragmatic strategies which use the activated rhetorical goals as criteria to pick one of the available options. (The options are produced when the possibilities of the language, as contained in the syntactic specialists and the planning knowledge, are applied to the piece of representation under consideration.) The queries are analogous to Mann's *choosers* (Mann, 1983). Using the selected option, the program proceeds with further planning and realization until the next decision point is encountered. The program also monitors the number of times each rhetorical goal is satisfied by a decision.

In PAULINE, rhetorical planning and realization are interleaved processes, where the interleaving takes place at the decision points. PAULINE's approach differs from the traditional planning paradigm, in which one or more initial goals are transformed, after a hierarchical goal-plan expansion cycle, into a series of steps that are executed by some agent. In the generation process, this approach takes the form of building up and associating generator instructions with increasingly detailed parts of the input topics until, eventually, enough instructions have been assembled to realize each part of the input as one or more words (see Appelt, 1981).

Of course, planning all the way down to the actual details of word choice requires that the planner have access to as much syntactic knowledge as the realization component itself. This obviates the need for a realization component. This model is unrealistic, however: we don't start speaking only when we have planned out the full utterance. When we start speaking, we have usually made some decisions and have postponed others; that is, we have some vague notion about what topics we want to cover, and maybe even of the desired slant and a particular phrase we want to use; we leave the details — especially the syntactic details — for later, real-time, consideration. This suggests that the planner assemble only a partial set of generator instructions — enough for the realization component to start working on — and then continue planning when the realization component requires further guidance. Thus, as argued in Hovy (1985) and in McDonald & Pustejovsky (1985), the solution is to interleave planning and realization.

Of course, when a number of rhetorical goals are activated, certain of their strategies are likely to make conflicting suggestions at decision points. This conflict can be dealt with in various ways. One way is simply to 'average out' conflicting suggestions (say, two suggestions for 'long sentences' cancel out two for 'short sentences'). Another is to use the values to make decisions in proportion to the number of activated strategies, for example by making every third sentence short. This is the reason to monitor the satisfaction of rhetorical goals. Another way is to order the goals in importance and use strategies accordingly. PAULINE's strategies use an implicit ordering.

3. A WORKED EXAMPLE

The rest of the paper briefly describes PAULINE's generation of an example under five pragmatically different scenarios. First, the five texts are presented. The next section describes the rules that serve four relevant rhetorical goals. The subsequent sections describe how PAULINE uses these rules to perform a series of tasks that transform the input representation into the various texts. Finally, a summarized analysis of the five examples is given.

The conversation topic represents the outcome of a hypothetical primary election between the politicians Carter and Kennedy during the 1979 race for the Democratic nomination for President. In the primary, Kennedy narrowed Carter's lead; however, both candidates gathered some delegates in preparation for the final nomination election. The episode is defined in a property-inheritance network (such as described in Charniak, Riesbeck & McDermott, 1980), using about 80 elements of a representation scheme similar to Conceptual Dependency (Schank, 1972, 1975; Schank & Abelson, 1977).

In **case 1**, PAULINE must simply inform an *acquaintance* of the outcome of the primary and of the current status of both candidates. Neither interlocutor has opinions about the topic; both have the usual knowledge of the electoral process. The conversation is *informal* and unhurried (**time** is *much*). In this case, the program says

> **Case 1.**
> CARTER AND KENNEDY WERE THE CANDIDATES IN A PRIMARY IN MICHIGAN ON 20 FEBRUARY. CARTER LOST TO KENNEDY BY 335 VOTES. AT PRESENT, KENNEDY HAS A BETTER CHANCE OF GETTING THE NOMINATION THAN BEFORE. CARTER IS ALSO CLOSER TO GETTING THE NOMINATION THAN BEFORE. BOTH CARTER AND KENNEDY WANT TO GET THE NOMINATION.

In **case 2**, PAULINE is sympathetic to Kennedy, while the hearer, the program's knowledgeable sibling Sue (*expert*), supports Carter. The siblings are *friends* and the distance is *intimate*. To Sue, using the same input, PAULINE says

> **Case 2.**
> WELL, SO CARTER LOST THE PRIMARY TO KENNEDY BY 335 VOTES

Case 3 is similar to case 2, but the hearer is a *friend* and social *equal* (say, a colleague, Bill) who is not as expert as Sue. The conversational tone is *informal*. PAULINE has the time to prepare its text well, in order to try to convince Bill that Kennedy is going to win. It says

> **Case 3.**
> KENNEDY DIMINISHED CARTER'S LEAD BY GETTING ALL OF 2185 VOTES IN THE PRIMARY IN MICHIGAN. IN A SIMILAR CASE, CARTER DECREASED UDALL'S LEAD IN A PRIMARY IN 1976, AND HE EASILY TROUNCED UDALL TO BE NOMINATED BY 2600 DELEGATES. I AM REAL GLAD THAT KENNEDY IS NOW CLOSER TO GETTING THE NOMINATION THAN BEFORE.

In **case 4**, PAULINE is a Carter supporter and is speaking formally; say, making a speech at a debate. The audience is presumed to support Kennedy. In this case, the program says

> **Case 4.**
> I AM PLEASED TO INFORM YOU THAT CARTER HAS IMPROVED HIS CHANCES OF WINNING THE NOMINATION. AT THE PRESENT TIME,

CARTER HAS MANY MORE DELEGATES THAN HE HAD IN THE PAST;
ALSO, CARTER HAS MANY MORE THAN KENNEDY DOES.

Finally, in **case 5**, PAULINE is a Carter supporter and is speaking to its boss, an irascible Kennedy man. Since they are making a long-distance telephone call, the program is under some time *pressure*. What's more, the program is *distant* to its boss and does not want to anger him (desired emotional effect is *calm*). To its boss, the program says

Case 5.
...
nothing!

Note that PAULINE's texts are all based on a fairly small set of locutions. To make it generate widely different versions of the central theme would be easy: the program would simply have to discriminate to one of a number of greatly different sentence forms (however they are represented) and then fill it in. But this would defeat the point: it would prove nothing beyond the fact that PAULINE uses relevant pragmatic aspects in its discrimination process. In this work, the question is more subtle: *how is additional information implicitly encoded in text?* In other words, how can the same phrases and words be selected, rearranged, and juxtaposed in order to convey different information? When this question has been answered, the correct way of using greatly different sentence forms will be answered too.

3.1. Rules for setting rhetorical goals

After setting up the scenario, PAULINE activates values for each of its 18 rhetorical goals. Four will be discussed here and used in the example: **RG:formality**, **RG:partiality**, **RG:detail**, and **RG:haste**.

Formality. The level of textual formality expresses both the perceived distance between the interlocutors and the tone, or level of formality, of the atmosphere. Usually, a close relationship and an informal atmosphere are reflected in informal text. The level of formality is most apparent when it is inappropriate or is suddenly changed. When the speaker becomes less formal she signals a perceived or desired decrease in the interpersonal distance, since this permits the selection of more intimate topics and the use of more personal phrases and words. However, being too informal for the occasion seems cheeky or irreverent. Conversely, if she becomes more formal she indicates the opposite, perhaps after taking offense or disliking the topic. Being too formal seems cold.

PAULINE uses the following rules to set a value for **RG:formality**:

1. set **RG:formality** to
   - *colloquial* when the **depth of acquaintance** is marked *friends*, or when the **relative social status** is marked *equals* in an **atmosphere (tone)** marked *informal*
   - *normal* when the **depth of acquaintance** is marked *acquaintances*
   - *highfalutin* when the **depth of acquaintance** is marked *strangers*

2. then, reset **RG:formality** one step toward *colloquial* if: **desired effect on interpersonal distance** is marked *close*, that is, if the speaker wants the hearer to feel closer to her; or if **tone** is marked *informal*, that is, if the conversation occurs in a relaxed, friendly atmosphere

3. or reset **RG:formality** one step toward *highfalutin* if: **desired effect on interpersonal distance** is marked *distant*, that is, if the speaker wants to increase the emotional distance between herself and the hearer; or if **tone** is marked *formal*, that is, if the speaker wants to establish a serious tone for the conversation, or if she is making a speech at a formal occasion

4. and invert the value of **RG:formality** if **desired effect on hearer's emotion toward speaker** is marked *dislike*, since inappropriate formality is often taken as an insult; or if **desired effect on hearer's emotional state** is marked *angry*, that is, if the speaker wants to anger the hearer. (The contrapositive of these two rules provides the default rule: to make the hearer like you, select an appropriate level of formality.)

Using these rules, PAULINE's value for **RG:formality** is *highfalutin* in case 4 (the speech) and *colloquial* in the other four cases.

Partiality. The rhetorical goal **RG:partiality** controls how strongly the program injects its opinions into the text. Many speaker goals to affect hearers depend on the communication of their sympathies. Natural languages contain a large number of linguistic techniques for injecting affect into text — emphasizing or evading topics they like or dislike and phrasing them appropriately. PAULINE has a number of these techniques. It also has rules to determine its opinions about any piece of the topic that govern the combination of affects and their propagation along the relationships among representation elements. These techniques and rules are discussed in Hovy (1986). (Also see Goody, 1978, and Lakoff, 1977, on politeness.)

In general, since her sympathies and antipathies reflect so accurately the speaker's disposition toward the world, any opinion with which the hearer disagrees implies distance between them — perhaps even censure on the part of the speaker. Thus, if the speaker's opinion agrees with the hearer's, expressing it will tend to make them closer; when it disagrees, expressing it may cause fights. Partiality for a topic can be expressed explicitly, in sentences that state the speaker's opinion, or implicitly, using techniques such as phrasal juxtaposition and stress words. The rules PAULINE uses are based on the affect rule given in Hovy (1986), which can be paraphrased as 'When the affects disagree, explicit partiality produces distance, dislike, and anger, so that implicit partiality is more effective; when the affects correspond, the effects are inverted'. Worked out in detail, the rules are:

1. set **RG:partiality** to *explicit* if the speaker's and hearer's **affects for the topic agree** and **desired effect on hearer's emotion toward speaker** is marked *like*; or **desired effect on interpersonal distance** is marked *close*; or **tone** is marked *informal*
2. set **RG:partiality** to *implicit* if the speaker's and hearer's **affects for the topic agree** and **desired effect on interpersonal distance** is marked *distant*, since being lukewarm about the agreement with the hearer separates them; or **speaker-hearer relative social status** is marked *dominant*, for the same reason; or **desire to involve hearer** is marked *repel*, that is, if the speaker does not want make the hearer too involved in the conversation
3. otherwise, set **RG:partiality** to *impartial* if their **affects agree**, or if their **affects disagree** and **desired effect on hearer's opinion** is marked *none*; or **hearer's knowledge level** is marked *expert* and **speaker's knowledge level** is marked *student* or *novice*, and **desired effect on hearer's emotion toward speaker** is marked *respect* or *like*, since when the speaker cares about an expert hearer's opinion of her, she will not want to exhibit her partiality and lack of knowledge
4. set **RG:partiality** to *explicit* if the speaker's and hearer's **affects for the topic disagree** and: **desired effect on hearer's opinion** is marked *switch*; or **desired effect on hearer's emotional state** is marked *anger*; or **desired effect on hearer's emotion toward speaker** is marked *dislike*; or **desired effect on interpersonal distance** is marked *distant*
5. otherwise, set **RG:partiality** to *implicit* if their **affects disagree** and: **desired effect on hearer's opinion** is marked *switch*; or **desire to involve hearer** is marked *involve*; or **relative social status** is marked *subordinate* (that is, the hearer is subordinate)

Using these rules, PAULINE's value for **RG:partiality** is *impartial* to the acquaintance (case 1), *explicit* in the speech (case 4), and *implicit* in the other three cases.

Detail. Rather than presenting a number of candidate topics one at a time, the speaker may be able to find a single interpretation (a high-level concept) which subsumes them. Saying the interpretation instead results in concise and elegant text, since many low-level constituent parts and affectively sensitive parts are implied and need not be said explicitly.

What is the appropriate value for **RG:detail** in a given set of circumstances? The answer can be summarized thus: If the speaker can trust the hearer to make the high-level interpretations herself, then all she need give her are the details. In the Carter-Kennedy example, if the hearer is a political pundit then clearly the details are better, since she can draw the conclusion without difficulty, and, in addition, she has precise numerical information. If, in contrast, the hearer has only minimal knowledge about or interest in the nomination procedure, then the interpretation (that Kennedy narrowed Carter's lead by a small amount) is better, since it doesn't burden her with details and require her to do the interpretation herself. And, if the hearer is interested and has some knowledge (say, she is a student of the political process), or if she is knowledgable but unlikely to make the right interpretation (say, she supports the wrong candidate), the speaker must ensure that the hearer understands how she is expected to interpret the facts. So she must be told the details and the interpretations. In addition, painful details can be avoided by saying interpretations. PAULINE uses the following strategies:

1. set **RG:detail** to *details* if the **hearer's knowledge level** is marked *expert*, or if the **hearer's interest level** marked *high*
2. otherwise, set **RG:detail** to *all* (details and interpretations) if the **hearer's knowledge level** is marked *student* or *novice*, or if the **time** marked *little*. Also check that the hearer's sympathies and antipathies for the central topic indicate that she will make the right interpretation.
3. otherwise, set **RG:detail** to *interpretations* to ensure that painful aspects (the details, the interpretation, or the inferences used to make it) can simply be left out, if the **speaker's opinion of the topic** differs from the **hearer's opinion**, and **depth of acquaintance** is marked *strangers*, or **relative social status** is marked *subordinate*, or **desired effect on hearer's emotion toward speaker** is marked *like*, or **desired effect on interpersonal distance** is marked *close*, or **desired effect on hearer's emotional state** is marked *calm*
4. otherwise, set **RG:detail** to *interpretations*

Using these rules, PAULINE's value for **RG:detail** is *all* in case 3 (the friend), *interpretations* in case 5 (the irascible boss), and *details* in the other three cases.

Haste. Haste refers to the amount of time the speaker allows herself to produce sentences. The more time available, the less pressure on the speaker, the more effort she can spend in making the text appropriate and striking. Thus **RG:haste** affects the decision points where the speaker can take short-cuts. (The degree of speaker haste is one of the factors that makes spoken text different from written text.)

Ideally, the speaker should completely plan out the text, testing each topic, phrase, and word for affective and pragmatic suitability. However, the situation and the hearer do not always afford the speaker enough time. For example, the speaker's level of haste must increase when she is making a long-distance telephone call, or when she is socially subordinate to the hearer and must ensure that she is entertaining enough for the hearer to continue the conversation. (See Straker, 1980, for similar effects of relative social status on generation.) Based on such considerations, PAULINE's activation rules include:

1. set **RG:haste** to *pressured* if: **time** is marked *little*, the **relative social status** is marked *subordinate*, and the **depth of acquaintance** is marked *acquaintances* or *strangers*
2. set **RG:haste** to *unplanned* if: **relative social status** is marked *subordinate* and the **depth of acquaintance** is marked *acquaintances* or *strangers* ; or if **time** is marked *little*
3. set **RG:haste** to *highly planned* if: **time** is marked *much* and the **speaker-hearer depth of acquaintance** is marked *friends*
4. otherwise, set **RG:haste** to *somewhat planned*
5. then, reset **RG:haste** one step toward *highly planned* if: **hearer's knowledge level** is marked *expert* and the **speaker's knowledge level** is marked *expert* or *student*

Using these rules, PAULINE's value for **RG:haste** is *pressured* to the boss in case 5, *highly planned* to the friend in case 3, and *somewhat planned* in the other cases.

3.2. Candidate sentence topic collection

The episode representation consists of about 80 elements, of which the central element represents the primary election. It has two outcomes, respectively representing the number of votes Carter and Kennedy received; since Kennedy won, his outcome is greater than Carter's. Both candidates also have a total number of committed delegates; these numbers are greater than the numbers of committed delegates they had before the primary. Finally, both Carter and Kennedy have the goal to win the primary and the goal eventually to win the nomination. Of course, the former goals are subgoals of the latter; also, they are in mutual opposition.

After PAULINE's pragmatic setting and interpersonal goals have been set, it is given as input topic the element representing the primary. From this element, the program has to search for additional relevant sentence topics. The program has three topic collection plans (similar to the schemas in McKeown, 1982): the RELATE plan is used in case 1 (speaking to an acquaintance), where the interlocutors do not hold different affects for the topic; the CONVINCE plan is selected in the other cases (see Hovy, 1985). The plan's steps are applied to the representation in order to suggest candidate topics. In case 5, speaking to the boss under *pressured* **RG:haste**, PAULINE has to say each candidate topic as soon as it is found; in the other cases, it can apply all the plan steps and collect the candidates before planning. In cases 2 and 3, the candidates are the topics that support a pro-Kennedy argument: Kennedy's and Carter's outcomes and Kennedy's current delegate count. In cases 4 and 5, they are Carter's delegate count, including the facts that it is larger than it was and is still larger than Kennedy's.

3.3. Sentence topic organization

After it has collected candidate topics and before it says them, PAULINE can perform a number of organization tasks: it can test its opinion of the candidate topics for affective suitability; examine the possibility of grouping them together under a single overarching interpretation; reorder the candidates for maximum effect; and cast them into multi-predicate phrases to make clear their individual roles in the text and their mutual relationships. When PAULINE speaks to its boss (case 5), the candidates it collects all oppose his sympathies. Since **RG:partiality** is *implicit*, the program is required to mitigate such sensitive topics (by using appropriate phrases or saying an overarching interpretation that implicitly contains them). However, these are time-consuming tasks, and it can only do this when **RG:haste** permits. The value *pressured* does not allow PAULINE to do more than test the candidates for affective suitability; hence, in this case, PAULINE cannot say *anything*!

In case 3 (speaking to the friend), however, PAULINE has more time to perform the planning tasks. In particular, the collected facts (Carter was and still is ahead but Kennedy won the primary) match the pattern defining the high-level interpretation *narrow lead*. Indexed under the interpretation, following the description of memory organization in Schank (1982), the program finds two remindings: Hart narrowing Mondale's lead in 1984 (but still losing the nomination), and Carter narrowing Udall's lead in 1976 (and eventually winning). Since **RG:detail** is not set to *details*, the program is allowed say the interpretation; also, the value *planned* allows time to select the appropriate reminding (by mapping the equivalent role fillers and checking affects) and to cast all this in suitable phrases. (In addition, the newly created interpretation is added to memory; when PAULINE generates the story a second time, the interpretation is immediately found and can be said.)

In case 2, when speaking to its expert sibling, PAULINE's goal **RG:detail** calls for low-level details, and so it doesn't search for interpretations but simply says the outcomes. Similarly, to the acquaintance in case 1, the program organizes its details *impartially* by alternating topics with opposing affects. And in case 4, since it doesn't find interpretations indexed off the Carter-supporting topics it collected, the program simply orders them and casts them into phrases.

3.4. Sentence organization

When organizing the parts of a sentence, PAULINE must select the subject, select which adverbial clauses to say before the subject, select a verb that doesn't require inappropriate aspects (for example, preferring 'win', without direct object, over 'beat', when defending Carter), and order the predicate clauses. The relevant strategies for producing *highfalutin* text call for

1. including adverbial clauses to lengthen sentences
2. selecting options that place these clauses at the beginnings of sentences
3. avoiding elision, even though it may be grammatical, in sentences like 'Joe got more than Pete (did)'

while *colloquial* text is made by the opposite strategies. In case 4, when PAULINE addresses the hostile audience, it includes the clauses 'I am pleased to inform you' and 'at the present time', the latter before the sentence subject instead of after it, as well as the extra verb 'does'.

For explicit or implicit **RG:partiality**, sentence organization strategies are the following (for more detail see Hovy, 1986):

1. include clauses expressing the speaker's opinion (when partiality is explicit)
2. include appropriate adverbial and adjectival descriptive clauses and words (explicit and implicit)
3. include stress words (explicit and implicit)

In cases 2, 3, and 4, PAULINE includes the clauses 'I am glad that', 'I am pleased to inform you that', and the stress words 'many', 'all of', and 'easily'.

Finally, *pressured* **RG:haste** corresponds to *explicit* partiality and more forceful and simpler text (as defined by **RG:force** and **RG:simplicity**). PAULINE includes fewer clauses in sentences and makes short sentences (obviating the search for relations between topics or for simple conjunctions to make long sentences).

3.5. Word choice

The strategies for *highfalutin* text include:

1. select formal phrases and words, when they are so designated in the lexicon
2. if syntactically possible, do not pronominalize a concept, unless nothing new can be said about it
3. select nominal forms of verbs and adverbs
4. do not select popular idioms, slang, and contractions

To produce explicit and implicit partial text, the program selects nouns and verbs that carry affect as described in Hovy (1986).

3.6. The examples analyzed

In summary, the following tables present the effects of different values of the four rhetorical goals on the decisions and thus on the final text. Brackets indicate the words affected by the decision listed on the same line.

Case 1 (to an acquaintance): *colloquial, impartial, details, somewhat planned*

text	decision	rhet. goal value
Topic: central topic	RELATE plan	
[ ] CARTER AND KENNEDY WERE	no clauses before	*colloquial*
THE CANDIDATES IN A PRIMARY		
[IN MICHIGAN] [ON 20 FEBRUARY].	clauses after subject	*colloquial, planned*
Topic: result	RELATE plan	
CARTER [LOST]	neutral verb	*impartial*
TO KENNEDY BY [335] VOTES.	neutral details	*impartial, details*
Topic: outcome with good affect for Kennedy	RELATE plan	*impartial*
AT PRESENT, KENNEDY		
HAS A BETTER CHANCE		
OF [GETTING] THE NOMINATION	informal word	*colloquial*
THAN [ ] BEFORE.	elide *he had*	*colloquial*
Topic: outcome with good affect for Carter	RELATE plan	*impartial*
CARTER IS ALSO CLOSER	separate sentence	*colloquial*
TO [GETTING] THE	informal word	*colloquial*
NOMINATION THAN [ ] BEFORE.	elide *he was*	*colloquial*
Topic: actors' goals (twice)	RELATE plan	
BOTH CARTER AND KENNEDY [WANT]	informal verb	*colloquial*
TO [GET] THE NOMINATION.	informal verb	*colloquial*

Case 2 (to an expert sibling): *colloquial, implicit, details, somewhat planned*

text	decision	rhet. goal value
Topic: results with good affect for Kennedy	CONVINCE plan	*implicit, planned*
[WELL, SO] CARTER LOST THE	informal, to sibling	*colloquial*
PRIMARY TO KENNEDY BY [335] VOTES.	details	*details*
Topics: outcomes with good affect for Kennedy	CONVINCE plan	*details*
...	suppressed due to	
	hearer knowledge	

Case 3 (to a friend): *colloquial, implicit, all* (details and interpretations), *planned*

text	decision	rhet. goal value
Topic: results with good affect for Kennedy	CONVINCE plan	*implicit*
[ ] KENNEDY	no clauses before	*colloquial*
[DIMINISHED] CARTER'S [LEAD]	interpretation	*all, planned*
BY [GETTING]	informal verb	*colloquial*
[ALL OF]	stress word	*implicit*
[2185] VOTES	details	*all*
[IN THE PRIMARY] [IN MICHIGAN].	clauses after subject	*colloquial*
Topic: reminding	indexed off interp	*planned*
IN A SIMILAR CASE, CARTER	reminding	*implicit, planned*
DECREASED UDALL'S LEAD IN A		
PRIMARY IN 1976, AND HE [EASILY]	stress word	*implicit*
[TROUNCED] UDALL TO BE	stress verb	*implicit*
NOMINATED BY [2600] DELEGATES.	details	*all*
Topic: outcome with good affect for Kennedy	CONVINCE plan	*implicit*
[I AM REAL GLAD THAT]	informal opinion	*colloquial, explicit*
KENNEDY IS [NOW] CLOSER TO	clause after, informal	*colloquial*

| [GETTING] THE NOMINATION THAN | informal verb | *colloquial* |
| [ ] BEFORE. | elide *he was* | *colloquial* |

Case 4 (making a speech): *highfalutin, explicit, details, somewhat planned*

Topic: results with good affect for Carter	CONVINCE plan	*explicit*
	none	
Topic: outcome with good affect for Carter	CONVINCE plan	*explicit*
[I AM PLEASED TO INFORM YOU]	formal opinion	*highfalutin, explicit*
THAT CARTER HAS [IMPROVED HIS	formal phrase	*highfalutin*
CHANGES] OF WINNING THE		
NOMINATION.		
Topic: outcome with good affect for Carter	CONVINCE plan	*explicit*
[AT THE PRESENT TIME], CARTER	clause before, formal	*highfalutin*
HAS [MANY] MORE DELEGATES THAN	stress	*explicit*
[HE HAD] IN THE PAST;	no elision	*highfalutin*
[ALSO], CARTER HAS	long sentence	*highfalutin, planned*
[MANY] MORE THAN	stress	*explicit*
KENNEDY [DOES].	no elision	*highfalutin*

Case 5 (to the boss): *colloquial, implicit, interpretations, pressured*

| Topic: results and outcomes for Carter | CONVINCE plan | *implicit* |
| | no time for mitigation | *pressured* |

4. CONCLUSION

The question 'why and how is it that we say the same thing in different ways to different people, or even to the same person in different circumstances?' is interesting from a number of pespectives. From a cognitive perspective, it helps shed light on speakers' goals and personal interrelationships in conversations; from a linguistic perspective, it raises interesting questions about the information content of language; and from an engineering-AI perspective, it helps provide principled reasons by which a program that can realize the same input in various ways can make its selections.

As described in this paper, the answer deals with the pragmatic nature of communication — a big and complex field of study. In order to begin to study how pragmatics is used in generation, a number of rather crude assumptions about plausible types of speaker goals and the relevant characteristics of hearers and of conversational settings must be made. The specific pragmatic features used by PAULINE are but a first step. They are the types of factors that play a role in conversation; no claims are made about their eternal veracity. Similarly, the strategies PAULINE uses to link its pragmatic features to the actual generator decisions, being dependent on the definitions of the features, are equally primitive; again, no strong claims are made about their existence in people in exactly the form shown. However, in even such a simple theory as this, certain constraints emerge, and these constraints, I believe, hold true no matter how sophisticated the eventual theory is. The constraints pertain primarily to the organization of pragmatic information in a generator: the fact that pragmatic and interpersonal information is too general to be of immediate use; the resulting fact that intermediate strategies, here called rhetorical strategies, are required to run a generator; the fact that, in a model of generation that incorporates these goals, rhetorical planning and realization are interleaved processes, where the interleaving takes place at the choice points. (This view supports the standard top-down planning-to-realization approach, as well as a bottom-up approach, in which partially realized syntactic options present themselves as opportunities to the rhetorical criteria, at which point further planning can occur.)

Of course, this suggests further work to be done. In particular, the ways that the components of text style (a) help create pragmatic effects and (b) are actually incorporated in sentences should be studied. With this in mind, the kinds of interpersonal and situation-specific perceptions and goals that speakers use when speaking should be investigated. Perhaps, one day, the study of pragmatics will cease to be ad hoc (i.e., pragmatic) and become scientific!

5. ACKNOWLEDGEMENTS

This work was supported in part by the Advanced Research Projects Agency monitored by the Office of Naval Research under contract N00014-82-K-149. Thanks to Larry Birnbaum for discussions, to Rod McGuire for the initial idea, to Jeff Grossman for some programming help, and to Tony Jameson for very detailed comments and helpful suggestions.

6. REFERENCES

Appelt, D.E. (1981) *Planning Natural Language Utterances to Satisfy Multiple Goals*. Ph.D. dissertation, Stanford.

Atkinson, J.M. (1982) Understanding Formality: the Categorization and Production of 'Formal' Interaction. *British Journal of Sociology*, *33*, 86-117.

Baker, S. (1966) *The Complete Stylist*. New York: Crowell.

Birk, N.P. & Birk, G.B. (1965) *Understanding and Using English*. New York: Odyssey Press.

Bühler, K. (1934) *Sprachtheorie*. Jena: Fischer.

Carnap, R. (1938) Foundations of Logic and Mathematics. In: O. Neurath, R. Carnap & C.W. Morris (Eds.) *International Encyclopedia of Unified Science*, Vol. 1, 139-214.

Charniak, E., Riesbeck, C.K. & McDermott, D.V. (1980) *Artificial Intelligence Programming*. Erlbaum: Hillsdale, NJ.

Cohen, P.R. (1978) *On Knowing What to Say: Planning Speech Acts*. Ph.D. dissertation, University of Toronto.

Cowan, G. & McPherson, E. (1977) *Plain English Rhetoric and Reader*. New York: Random House.

Fawcett, R.P. (1980) *Cognitive Linguistics and Social Interaction*. Heidelberg: Julius Groos Verlag.

Gazdar, G. (1979) *Pragmatics: Implicature, Presupposition, and Logical Form*. London: Academic Press.

Gazdar, G. (1980) *Pragmatic Constraints on Linguistic Production*. In: B. Butterworth (Ed.) *Language Production*, Vol. 1. London: Academic Press.

Goody, E. (Ed.) (1978) *Questions and Politeness: Strategies in Social Interaction*. Cambridge: Cambridge University Press.

Gregory, M. (1982) Towards 'Communication' Linguistics: a Framework. In: Benson, J.D. & Greaves, W.S. (Eds.) *Systemic Perspectives on Discourse*, Vol. 1.

Grice, H.P. (1957) Meaning. In: D. Steinberg & L. Jacobovits (Eds.) *Semantics: an Interdisciplinary Reader in Philosophy, Linguistics, and Psychology*.

Grosz, B.J. & Sidner, C.L. (1985) Discourse Structure and the Proper Treatment of Interruptions. In: *Proceedings of IJCAI'85*. Los Angeles: California.

Halliday, M.A.K. (1976) *Halliday: System and Function in Language*. (Selected papers, edited by G.R. Kress), Oxford University Press.

Hill, A.S. (1892) *The Foundations of Rhetoric*. New York: Harper & Brothers.

Hovy, E.H. (1985) Integrating Text Planning and Production in Generation. In: *Proceedings of IJCAI-85*. Los Angeles: California.

Hovy, E.H. (1986) Putting Affect into Text. In: *Proceedings of the Eighth Conference of the Cognitive Science Society*, Amherst, Mass.

Irvine, J.T. (1979) Formality and Informality of Speech Events. *American Anthropologist, 81*, 773-790.

Jakobson, R. (1960) Language and Poetics. In: T. Sebeok (Ed.) *Style in Language*. Cambridge, Mass.: MIT Press.

Katz, J.J. (1977) *Propositional Structure and Illocutionary Force*. New York: Crowell.

Lakoff, R. (1977) Politeness, Pragmatics, and Performatives. In: *Proceedings of the Texas Conference on Performatives, Presuppositions, and Implicatures*. Austin, Texas.

Levinson, S.C. (1983) *Pragmatics*. Cambridge: Cambridge University Press.

Loomis, R.S, Hull, H.R. & Robinson, M.L. (1936) *The Art of Writing Prose*. New York: Farrar & Rinehart.

Mc Donald & Pustejovsky. (1985) Description-Directed Natural Language Generation. In: *Proceedings of IJCAI-85*. Los Angeles: California.

McKeown. (1982) *Generating Natural Language Text in Response to Questions about Database Structure*. Ph.D. dissertation, University of Pennsylvania.

Mann, W.C. (1983) *An Overview of the Nigel Text Generation Grammar*. Information Sciences Institute Technical Report no RR-83-113.

Morris, C.W. (1938) Foundations of the Theory of Signs In: O. Neurath, R. Carnap & C.W. Morris (Eds.) *International Encyclopedia of Unified Science, vol. 1*.

Payne, L.V. (1969) *The Lively Art of Writing*. Chicago: Follett.

Schank, R.C. (1972) 'Semantics' in Conceptual Analysis. *Lingua, 30*, 101-139.

Schank, R.C. (1975) *Conceptual Information Processing*. Amsterdam: North-Holland.

Schank, R.C. & Abelson, R.P. (1977) *Scripts, Plans, Goals and Understanding*. Erlbaum: Hillsdale, NJ.

Schank, R.C. (1982) *Dynamic Memory: A Theory of Reminding and Learning in Computers and People*. Cambridge: Cambridge University Press.

Searle, J.R. (1979) *Expression and Meaning*. Cambridge: Cambridge University Press.

Straker, D.Y. (1980) *Situational Variables in Language Use*. University of Illinois (Urbana) Technical Report no 167.

Strunk, W. jr & White, E.B. (1959) *The Elements of Style*. New York: Macmillan.

Swartout, W.R. (1981) *Producing Explanations and Justifications of Expert Consulting Programs*. Massachusetts Institute of Technology Technical Report LCS-TR-251.

Weathers, W. & Winchester, O. (1978) *The New Strategy of Style*. New York: McGraw-Hill.

Willis, H. (1969) *Structure, Style, and Usage (The Rhetoric of Exposition)* . New York: Holt, Rinehart and Winston.

Wodehouse, P.G. (1979) *Carry On, Jeeves*. New York: Penguin.

Chapter 2

HOW TO APPEAR TO BE CONFORMING TO THE 'MAXIMS' EVEN IF YOU PREFER TO VIOLATE THEM

Anthony Jameson

ABSTRACT

This chapter discusses a dialog system designed to illuminate certain familiar features of everyday dialogs which in most contexts are difficult to model precisely: 1. When deciding what information to offer to a listener, a speaker must make some assessment of the desirability of the impact that the information would have on the beliefs and judgments of the listener. 2. A speaker may be biased toward the presentation of certain types of information, even if this bias is not in the interest of the listener. 3. Listeners often interpret informative statements by considering what the speaker might have said but did not say; and the speaker can take this fact into account when deciding what to say. 4. A listener may hold an incorrect assumption about the dialog goals of the speaker; and the speaker may consider such a misconception desirable and attempt to behave in accordance with it. 5. The extent to which a speaker can achieve noncooperative dialog goals such as these depends on the constraints placed by the contributions of the other dialog participants. 6. Some dialog contributions are intended primarily to convey a certain image of the speaker's dialog motivation, even if they do not refer to it explicitly. 7. Speakers must often deal with the above considerations when uncertain of the beliefs that the listener has or while simultaneously addressing several listeners who have differing beliefs. 8. A speaker who has assumptions about the listener's values may try to avoid letting the listener recognize the content of these assumptions.

1. INTRODUCTION

Much of the research on computer models of language generation can be seen as addressing the question 'Exactly what must a speaker (or a corresponding computer program) do in order to adhere to Grice's (1975) conversational maxims?' In particular, explicit references to these maxims will be found in a number of the chapters in the present volume. These chapters remind us of the variety of specific problems that must be solved if a system is to generate utterances which are not only true but also clear, relevant, and appropriately informative. They also illustrate how difficult it is to develop methods of achieving these goals which have any degree of generality.

Since it is such a challenging task to get a computer program to exhibit even what for human speakers is the most straightforward cooperative dialog behavior, one can easily lose sight of a number of intriguing issues which would remain open even if this problem had already been solved completely.

First, the conversational maxims are not important mainly as a sensible set of criteria which a cooperative speaker should strive to satisfy; more interesting is their role in the interpretation of utterances. If the listener assumes that the speaker accepts the maxims, the listener will often draw conclusions which go well beyond the conventional meaning of the speaker's utterances.

A second rather obvious point is that it is often not the speaker's purpose to provide for 'a maximally effective exchange of information' (Grice, p. 47). A look at Hovy's chapter in this volume will remind one of the variety of goals that speakers pursue, some of which require them to construct their utterances according to principles which are incompatible with the conversational maxims. For example, if the speaker's goal is to persuade rather than to inform, he or she may refrain from verbalizing certain types of information which a purely cooperative speaker would consider relevant and important. (See also, e.g., Schwitalla, 1979.)

Even in such cases, if the listener is aware of the criteria according to which the speaker's utterances are being generated, he or she can draw correct conclusions from them which go beyond their conventional meaning. In other words, noncooperative principles of generation can play the same role in interpretation as the maxims do, as long as the listener is aware of their nature.

But a noncooperative speaker may manage to *appear* to be conforming to the maxims even though this is not the case. The listener is then likely to draw some substantive conclusions which are incorrect (cf. Grice, 1975, p. 49). The most obvious situation of this sort is where the speaker is lying but is assumed to be telling the truth; but similar effects can occur whenever there is a discrepancy between actual and apparent dialog goals. (Since the pattern is much more subtle and interesting when all utterances are strictly truthful — at least to the best of the speaker's knowledge — the phenomenon of lying will not be considered further in this chapter.)

It might at first seem a formidable task to construct a computer model which can help to bring issues such as these into sharper focus, given the difficulty of realizing even more straightforward cooperative dialog behavior. The contribution of the present chapter is to show that this can in fact be done if (a) one restricts oneself to a certain type of dialog situation in which the basic problem of how to conform to the usual maxims is exceptionally easy to solve and (b) one is willing to concentrate only on the question of what information the system is to convey, abstracting away from all of the issues involved in the formulation of text in a specific natural language.

1.1 Evaluation-oriented dialog

The especially tractable type of dialog referred to may be called *evaluation-oriented dialog*. Perhaps the most familiar examples are the exchanges that take place between a person who is considering buying a certain product and another person who provides information about its virtues and defects. Another type of situation in this category is the personnel selection interview, in which an interviewer attempts to determine the suitability of a given candidate for a particular position.

What these two situations have in common, in their purest form, is the nature of the goals pursued by the two participants. We will assume that one participant, to be called the *Evaluator*, is interested only in obtaining information about a certain *Object* (or person) which will help the Evaluator to make an evaluative judgement or decision about it. The other participant, the *Informant*, has the goal of supplying the Evaluator with relevant information about the Object (which may happen to be the Informant herself, as in the personnel interview situation).[1] Just how objective and cooperative the Informant tries to be can vary from one case to the next, as the reader can readily imagine on the basis of these two examples.

The present chapter will be built around a discussion of the dialog system Imp, which takes the role of the Informant in an evaluation-oriented dialog. The system is not restricted to any

---

[1] To facilitate exposition, we will arbitrarily assume that each Evaluator is male and each Informant female.

particular topic area, but it does have to be supplied in each case with a good deal of domain-specific information, to be described below. For the examples used in the present chapter, this information was supplied by a young woman who had recently been interviewed for a position as a typesetter in a small printing firm.[2]

The Imp system is quite small in scale, embodying only a few key principles, yet its behavior can be quite complex, since all of these principles may interact simultaneously to produce a given utterance. The degree of complexity in any particular case depends mainly on certain parameters which define the system's dialog motivation, its sophistication, and other aspects of the dialog situation. In the interest of clear exposition I will begin by discussing the simplest possible situation. Later, a sequence of more interesting situations will be defined, each of which introduces one or more new complications for the system to deal with.

For each of the five situations in this sequence I will first state the assumptions which define the situation and sketch the characteristic dialog behavior which one would expect in such a situation. I will then describe how Imp is equipped to deal with this type of situation and discuss some specific examples of its behavior in the personnel interview domain. Finally, I will comment on the generalizability of the ideas embodied in the system, especially to types of dialog other than evaluation-oriented dialog, and call attention to some questions which the model raises but does not answer.

2. SITUATION 1: GENERATING AN INFORMATIVE MONOLOG

2.1 Assumptions

We will assume in the first four situations that the Informant in effect has the opportunity to generate an unconstrained monolog about the Object. For example, a personnel interviewer, as Evaluator, might say to the job applicant 'Tell me about yourself.' In this first situation, we assume that the Informant is motivated to produce in the Evaluator an unbiased and sufficiently definite picture of the Object. The only reason why she might withhold any information is the fact that mentioning it did not seem to be worth the effort.

2.2 Characteristic behavior

Consider the case of the personnel selection interview. There are certain questions about an applicant which are of such great importance for a selection decision that a cooperative informant would be almost certain to volunteer information concerning these topics, even if the information offered was not particularly unusual. Where matters of less overriding importance are concerned, the Informant would be inclined to make some comment only if the truth about herself deviated in some important way from what the Evaluator would be likely to expect a priori. Finally, there are obviously a great many facts about any job applicant which would have such slight impact for a personnel decision that they would be passed over in silence no matter how much they deviated from the norm.

---

[2]   The system was originally developed and tested in quite different domains, e.g., a situation where an Informant was offering a room for rent to the Evaluator (cf. the earlier brief account in Jameson, 1983). For the present domain, once the domain-specific information had been elicited and entered, the examples discussed here were run without modification of this information. The present version of the system is implemented in the object-oriented language Orbit (De Smedt, in press).

2.3 Realization in Imp

2.3.1 Representation of values and expectations

Even in this simple situation, in order to behave appropriately in the role of the Informant, Imp
must be able to make some reasonable assumptions as to the properties which the Evaluator
would consider desirable or undesirable in the Object, and as to how likely he thinks they are to
be present.

A convenient representation for such assumptions is a data structure which may be called an
evaluation form. This representation is reminiscent of the sort of rating form which is often
found in practical situations for the systematic evaluation of objects or persons (e.g., papers
submitted to conferences, or applicants to universities). In Imp the evaluation form consists of a
set of *items*, each of which concerns some evaluation-relevant aspect of the Object. Twelve
items were supplied by our example Informant, one of which is reproduced in Figure 1.

Item: Family Situation

Possibilities:

		Value	Probability
A.	Married without children.	-35	.15
B.	Married with children.	-20	.05
C.	Living together.	-10	.35
D.	Steady relationship, not living together.	0	.25
E.	No steady relationship.	10	.20

Formulations:

	Possibilities left open	Effort
I am married.	A B	50
I am not married.	C D E	50
I have <number> children.	B C	50
I don't have any children.	A D E	50
I live alone.	D E	50
I have a boyfriend.	C D	75
I am married and I don't have children.	A	100
I am married and I have <number> children.	B	100
I am living with my boyfriend.	C	100
I have a boyfriend but we don't live together.	D	100
I don't have any steady relationship.	E	100

Figure 1. An item from the evaluation form assumed by the Informant of the examples

Each individual item is a sort of multiple-choice question accompanied by a scoring key. An
item specifies several conditions, or *possibilities*, which are defined in such a way that exactly
one of them must be realized by any Object. With each possibility, two numbers are associated:

(a) a *value*, i.e., a number of points which may be assigned to the Object if it satisfies the condition; and (b) a *probability*, i.e., an estimate of the likelihood that a randomly chosen Object will fulfill that condition.

The item shown in Figure 1 reflects, among other things, the Informant's belief that her prospective employer would be disappointed to hear that she was married, especially if she did not (yet) have children. Such assumptions on the part of the Informant may be based on experience with other Evaluators, on her own reasoning, or on some combination of the two; they may be realistic or wildly inaccurate. Neither the origin nor the degree of accuracy of the assumptions embodied in the evaluation form is important in the context of the Imp model.

If the Evaluator were actually to use an evaluation form to evaluate the Object, he would attempt, for each item, to determine which of the possibilities was realized by the Object. If he succeeded, he would add the corresponding value to his rating of the object. If the information available was not sufficient to rule out all possibilities but one, he would use the probabilities specified for the remaining possibilities to estimate how many points the Object deserved for the item.[3]

Imp in effect acts as if it expected that the Evaluator would fill in the evaluation form on the basis of the information that the system provided. Although this assumption is obviously very seldom true, it captures some essential aspects of the judgment process and it has appealingly concrete implications for the way the Informant ought to behave.

2.3.2 Information concerning possible formulations

In order to be able to volunteer information relevant to a given item, the system must have an idea of what comments might conceivably be made which are germane to that item. Since Imp is intended to be domain-independent and concerned only with the pragmatic aspects of natural language generation, it possesses no methods for generating entirely new formulations on its own. It must be provided, for each item, with a list of possible formulations. For example, Figure 1 shows a number of things that can be said about a female applicant's family situation. The meaning of such a formulation, for Imp, is simply the set of possibilities which are consistent with the formulation on a straightforward interpretation.

Note that it is only the more complex and/or awkward formulations that are sufficiently precise to rule out all but one of the five possibilities distinguished. In order to be able to take into account the idea that some propositions require more effort to express than others do, the system must be provided with a rating of the relative complexity of each possible formulation. This may be a function of the intrinsic complexity of the proposition being expressed, or it may depend on the concepts available in the particular language being used.[4] Although any method of ranking possible formulations in this respect is likely to be largely arbitrary, it is essential to capture at least the most striking differences of this sort among formulations — cf. McCawley (1978) and the maxims in Grice's (1975) categories of Manner and Quantity.

It is convenient to view silence as a special sort of comment which can be made about any item, which (when interpreted straightforwardly) is consistent with all possibilities, and which involves no effort.

---

[3]   The reader may notice that this sort of use of an evaluation form only makes sense if the items are independent of each other, in the sense that knowing what possibility is realized for one item cannot affect one's assessment of the probabilities associated with another item. A simple way of avoiding such dependencies is to mention within a single item any properties of Objects which are substantially correlated. This is why, for example, the distinctions 'married vs. single' and 'children vs. no children' are not captured in separate items.

[4]   For example, the concept *boyfriend* is more awkward to express in English than in some other languages. Winograd (1977) mentions a different sort of example, noting that whether a speaker conveys a vague or a precise impression of the temporal aspects of a given event can depend on the options offered by the language's system of tense and aspect.

2.3.3 General strategy

The system's general strategy is to consider each item in the form in turn and to decide what, if anything, is worth saying about it. That is, it must choose for each item, from among the possible comments for that item which are true of the Object in question, the one comment (possibly silence) which is the most worth making, i.e., the one whose benefits most clearly justify the degree of effort involved.

2.3.4 Assessing the desirability of an impression change

How can one quantify the notion of the benefits which result from the production of an informative comment? Relevant suggestions have been contributed, e.g., by Grewendorf (1981), Harrah (1963, chap. 11), and Hintikka (1975), but none of these approaches yields a quantitative index which takes into account both the likelihood and the importance of the states of affairs which are consistent with the comment.

The key concept in Imp for doing this is that of an *impression*. At any given moment and for any given item, the Evaluator is assumed to have an impression of the Object with respect to the item. The nature of the impression depends on which possibilities the Evaluator (still) thinks might be realized by the Object. Before the Informant has said anything about a given item, the Evaluator's impression concerning it will be relatively indefinite, since all of the possibilities must be considered (although some are less likely than others). If the Informant makes a certain comment concerning the item, in general one or more possibilities can be eliminated, so that the impression will become more definite. It is this sort of *impression change* that Imp views as a potentially desirable consequence of the production of a comment. To be able to quantify the desirability of a given impression change, Imp operationalizes the concept of an impression in terms of a probability distribution, determined by the values and the probabilities associated with the possibilities which have not yet been eliminated from consideration.

Figure 2 shows graphically the impression that the Evaluator is assumed to have initially concerning the 'Family situation' item. It also shows the impressions that would remain after each of two possible comments that the Informant might make.

The distinction between a relatively positive and a relatively negative impression can now be captured in terms of the mean, or *expected value* of the probability distribution in question; for example, in Figure 2 the first comment rules out the three least desirable possibilities, and as a consequence the expected value rises; it would actually rise more sharply if it weren't for the fact that the two least desirable possibilities are considered relatively improbable to begin with.

A second important property of an impression is the degree of *uncertainty* associated with it. This can be quantified in terms of the standard deviation of the probability distribution. In general, the greater the number of possibilities that have not yet been eliminated, the greater the degree of uncertainty associated with an impression (this is illustrated in Figure 2); but the standard deviation captures this concept better than a mere count of the remaining possibilities would, since it is sensitive to the relative likelihoods of the remaining possibilities and the differences in their values.

In terms of these concepts, one way in which an impression change can be desirable is when the expected value of the new impression is closer to the actual value of the Object (i.e., the value associated with the possibility which is actually realized). After all, a discrepancy between the expected value and the actual value means that the Evaluator has an inaccurate picture of the Object; a cooperative Informant will strive to reduce or eliminate such discrepancies.

The desirability of an impression change also depends on the extent to which uncertainty is reduced. After all, since the items associated with considerable uncertainty will presumably be the ones that the Evaluator is most anxious to hear about, a comment on such an item will in general be appreciated; but this will only be the case if the comment is sufficiently specific to reduce the amount of uncertainty considerably.

Initial impression:

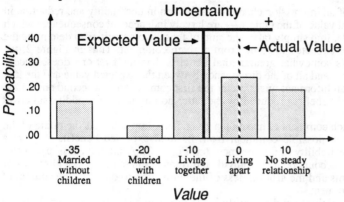

Impression after comment "I live alone":

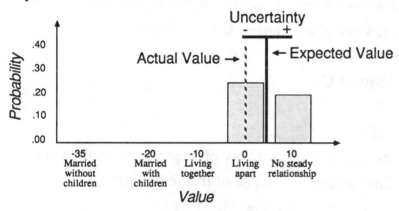

Impression after "I have a boyfriend, but we don't live together":

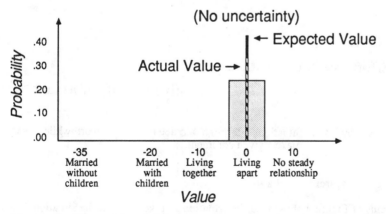

Figure 2. Illustration of the concepts of an impression and its associated expected value and uncertainty.

These two properties of an impression change — reduction in uncertainty and reduction in discrepancy from the actual value of the Object — are largely independent consequences which can be considered desirable. Imp simply takes the sum of these two quantities to determine the total benefit which can be expected to result from a given comment. Thus in Figure 2, the second comment produces somewhat greater total benefits than the first one does, since it reduces all of the uncertainty and all of the discrepancy between the expected value and the true value. But it is likely that an Informant might prefer the first comment to the second one on the grounds that the additional benefits produced by the latter do not justify the additional effort involved.

In finally deciding which comment to make on a given item, Imp subtracts the rating of the effort associated with each possible comment from its total expected benefits to yield a quantification of the net desirability of the comment (cf. Figure 3). A 'talkativeness' parameter is also required to take into account both the individual differences in the general willingness of speakers to make comments and the arbitrariness of the units used to quantify the amount of effort associated with a comment.

The comment with the highest net desirability is the one which is actually made. In many cases the most desirable comment will simply be silence (which, as can be seen from the above definitions, always has a net desirability of zero), since the benefits that would be brought about by the other possible comments are less than the associated cost in terms of effort.

Net desirability of a comment C on an item I =

    Benefits of C

   — Costs of C

Benefits of C =

    Reduction of uncertainty of impression concerning I

  + Shift in expected value of this impression

      toward true value (Situation 1)

      or in desired direction (Situations 2 - 4)

Costs of C =

    Effort associated with C / Talkativeness of Informant

Figure 3. Formulas used by Imp in Situations 1 through 4 to determine how worthwhile it is to make a given comment.

2.4 Examples of the system's behavior

The first two columns of Figure 4 show what information Imp volunteered in Situation 1 on each of the twelve items in the evaluation form. The way in which all of the comments are connected into a single long sentence, which is rather unnatural in this situation, will be discussed in connection with Situation 5. As far as the choice of comments is concerned, the criteria discussed above result in a reasonable selection: The comment on Item 1 is considered worthwhile mainly because of the importance of the item, i.e., the large amount of uncertainty initially associated with it. The other four items about which something is said are less important, but the possibility realized is in each case either the most or the least desirable one.

The two comments which would perhaps be least likely to come from any real job applicant are the ones on Items 3 and 4, which reveal exceptionally unfavorable facts about the applicant. The way most job applicants are motivated, of course, this would be considered a good reason *not* to say anything about these items. In Situation 2, such considerations will be taken into account.

2.5 General issues raised

It will have struck the reader that Imp's specific method of choosing comments embodies a number of arbitrary decisions. For instance, there are alternatives to the use of the standard deviation as a way of capturing the concept of uncertainty. But more interesting than such details are the basic features of the model, which are generalizable to other types of dialog.

The goals of reducing uncertainty and correcting inaccuracies make sense for a cooperative speaker in virtually any context, for example in task-oriented dialog. Although in the Imp model these two goals are arbitrarily assumed to be equally important, it is interesting to consider the conditions under which one of them may be given more weight than the other one.

In any case, the idea that the benefits of saying something may or may not be 'worth the effort' is also very general. While it is not easy, and may seem unnatural, to quantify the benefits and the costs of an utterance, consideration of the examples discussed above is sufficient to show that the factors involved are a matter of degree and that they can reinforce or compensate each other in determining what is said. The pragmatics of generation in even a simple situation such as this can thus not be understood fully without an account of how these basically quantitative assessments are made and combined.

3. SITUATION 2: POSITIVE OR NEGATIVE BIAS

3.1 New assumptions

In this situation we will allow the possibility that the Informant is not attempting to be as cooperative as possible but rather has the goal of creating in the Evaluator an especially favorable (or unfavorable) overall impression of the Object. We continue to assume, however, that the Informant restricts herself to strictly truthful factual comments which are not explicitly evaluative.

3.2 Characteristic behavior

Within these constraints, positive or negative bias on the part of the Informant can only be reflected in her selection of comments from among the set of possible truthful comments about the Object. The simplest consequence of, say, positive bias is that some aspects of the Object that an objective Informant would comment on are not mentioned at all, since any truthful comment could only make a poor impression. An alternative to remaining completely silent about a given topic is to make a vague comment on it which leaves open certain possibilities which are more favorable than the one which is actually realized.

	Comments Chosen		Pragmatic Interpretations Expected (after comments in third column)	
Item	Situation 1 (objective bias)	Situations 2 - 4 (positive bias)	Situation 3 (positive projected bias)	Situation 4 (objective projected bias)
1. Amount of work experience	I'VE BEEN WORKING FOR ABOUT A YEAR AND A HALF	I'VE BEEN WORKING FOR MORE THAN A YEAR	1. Between 1 and 2 years experience.	[No pragmatic interpretation possible - see discussion in text.]
2. Variety of work experience			2.	
3. Complexity of previous work	BUT MY WORK HAS BEEN PURELY ROUTINE		3. Not especially challenging work.	Not especially challenging work.
4. Vocational training	AND UNFORTUNATELY I NEVER RECEIVED ANY VOCATIONAL TRAINING		4. No higher-level vocational training.	Usual amount of vocational training.
5. Work-related hobbies			5.	
6. Reason for changing jobs	BUT THE REASON I WANT TO LEAVE MY PRESENT JOB IS THAT I'M LOOKING FOR MORE CHALLENGING WORK	AND THE REASON I WANT TO LEAVE MY PRESENT JOB IS THAT I'M LOOKING FOR MORE CHALLENGING WORK	6.	
7. Nonvocational schooling	AND I WENT TO UNIVERSITY PREPARATORY SCHOOL	AND I WENT TO UNIVERSITY PREPARATORY SCHOOL	7.	
8. Plans for future education			8.	
9. Family situation			9.	
10. Place of residence			10.	Does not live especially far away.
11. Frequency of previous job changes			11.	
12. Nature of position ultimately desired			12.	Is not aiming for position unattainable in this company.

Figure 4. Monologs produced by Imp in Situations 1 through 4.

3.3 Realization in Imp

The Imp system includes a parameter 'bias' which can take the values 'Objective' (as assumed implicitly in Situation 1), 'Positive', or 'Negative'. The effect of this parameter is on the way in which possible comments are rated in terms of their expected impact on the Evaluator's impressions. Recall that in Situation 1 an impression change was rated relatively desirable if the expected value of the impression moved closer to the true value for the Object. When the bias is positive, what is desirable is simply that the expected value should *increase*, or at least decrease as little as possible, regardless of the actual value of the Object. Specifically, the extent of the anticipated increase in expected value is added to the anticipated reduction in uncertainty to determine the benefits to be derived from making the comment (cf. Figure 3). A consequence is that a possible comment which would cause a marked decline in the Evaluator's impression is unlikely to emerge as the most desirable comment on that item. Note, however, that the presence of bias need not affect the goal of reducing uncertainty: If a comment would greatly reduce uncertainty, it may be selected even if it causes a slight downward impression shift.

3.4 Examples of the system's behavior

The third column of Figure 4 shows that Imp's behavior with respect to three items is different when it has a positive bias. Specifically, the comments made in Situation 1 on the routine nature of the Informant's previous work and her lack of vocational training are not made here, because their net desirability is less than that of silence: They eliminate all uncertainty, but their downward shift in expected value is now weighted negatively.

For Item 1, the Informant's fairly precise specification of her amount of work experience is replaced by a vague statement which requires the same amount of effort. The latter comment is now preferred because the positive discrepancy between the expected value of the impression it will leave and the actual value is now considered desirable.

3.5 General issues raised

The phenomenon of bias is obviously not restricted to evaluation-oriented dialog. Though less easily formalizable in other domains, it also occurs, for instance, in speeches or texts which attempt to change the listener's standpoint on a particular issue. By abstracting away from almost all problems involving natural language directly, the Imp model focusses attention on simple selectivity as a mechanism of bias, as opposed, say, to rhetorical techniques involving particular expressions (cf. Hovy, 1986 and this volume).

Whatever the particular benefits the speaker may expect from a biased selection of information, they must somehow be assessed and weighed against other considerations in the general way summarized by Figure 3. There are several plausible variants on this formula which would lead to somewhat less subtle manifestations of bias than those seen in the version of Imp described above. For instance, a biased speaker may attach less weight, or none at all, to the basically cooperative goal of reducing uncertainty, aiming only for impression shifts in a particular direction. Another possibility is that such a speaker may increase her general talkativeness in order to compensate for the fact that she is, because of her selectivity, producing fewer utterances.

4. SITUATION 3: ANTICIPATING THE PRAGMATIC INTERPRETATION OF COMMENTS

4.1 New assumptions

When anticipating the impact that a given comment would have on the Evaluator, the Informant has up to now assumed that each comment would be interpreted on the basis of its conventional meaning: The only possibilities which the Evaluator was expected to rule out were the ones which were incompatible with a straightforward interpretation of the comment. We will now take into account the fact that the Evaluator may rule out further possibilities by taking into account the fact that the Informant has chosen *not* to say certain things which she might well have said, i.e., by deriving what may be called a *pragmatic interpretation* of a comment. Such an interpretation is based on the following reasoning schema: 'Possibility P is consistent with the meaning of the Informant's comment C; but then again, if P were the possibility that was realized, the Informant would surely have said something like D instead of C; therefore, P must not be realized'.[5] We also assume that the Informant is sophisticated enough to realize that her comments will be interpreted in this way and to take this fact into account where it is relevant.

4.2 Characteristic behavior

A consequence of these assumptions is that the Informant no longer takes it for granted that she can manipulate the impressions of the Evaluator quite as easily as in Situation 2. For example, if our job applicant chooses to remain vague (or to say nothing at all) about a particular item, she will recognize that the interviewer will not continue to entertain the possibility that she rates especially high on that item. In some cases, in fact, her vagueness may be interpreted so negatively that it will gain her nothing at all.

4.3 Realization in Imp

In this situation, the way in which Imp initially searches for an appropriate comment on an item is the same as in the previous situations. After the most desirable comment has been determined, however, the system attempts to anticipate whether the Evaluator would be likely to give it a narrower pragmatic interpretation: For each of the possibilities which are compatible with the comment's conventional interpretation, Imp considers what comment it would have made if that possibility had been realized. If it sees that it would have found some alternative comment to have been much more desirable in that case, Imp concludes that this possibility will be eliminated by the Evaluator. The possibilities which would not be ruled out in this way are the ones which Imp assumes will continue to be entertained by the Evaluator. (This strategy is summarized in Figure 5 to facilitate comparison with the more general strategy used in Situation 4.)

4.4 Examples of the system's behavior

In the fourth column of Figure 4, the cases are noted in which Imp expects the Evaluator to make a pragmatic interpretation which differs from the straightforward interpretation. For Item 1, the vague comment about the Informant's amount of work experience ends up being interpreted in about the same way as the more precise comment produced in Situation 1. In this instance, therefore, Imp's positive bias did not result in the creation of a more positive impression.

The other two pragmatic interpretations are of silence (Items 3 and 4). In both of these cases the most desirable possibility for the item in question is ruled out. Note that the resulting

---

5   This schema is more general than Grice's (1975, p. 50) conception of the way in which a conversational implicature is 'worked out' by the listener. The notion of conversational implicature presupposes, among other things, (a) that the speaker is observing the cooperative principle and (b) that the interpretation made by the listener depends on the listener's recognition of the speaker's expectation that the listener will make that interpretation. By contrast, a pragmatic interpretation in the sense defined here could be made by a listener who was eavesdropping on a speaker who was being blatantly uncooperative.

impressions are here more positive than the ones that resulted in Situation 1 from Imp's objective comments, since it is the *least* desirable possibilities which are actually realized.

4.5 General issues raised

Although all of the concrete examples in this chapter concern evaluation-oriented dialog, it should be noted that none of the ideas introduced in Situation 3 refer to any specific features of this type of dialog. They are applicable, rather, in any context where one is able to quantify the net desirability of producing a particular comment. (This is largely true of the later situations as well.)

The strategy summarized in Figure 5 should best be viewed as but one representative of a class of strategies whose use presumably depends on both situational factors and the inclinations of the speaker. For instance, in the present situation Imp anticipates the pragmatic interpretation of a comment only in order to be able to keep track of what the Evaluator believes; but it would also be possible to go further, allowing the anticipated pragmatic interpretation to determine which comment was produced in the first place.

A general point which is illustrated by the performance of Imp in this situation is that communication is sometimes more efficient if the speaker is biased and the listener takes this into account than when the speaker attempts to be as objective as possible. The reason is that the way in which a biased person decides what to say is in some respects simpler, as can be seen in the formula of Figure 3. It is therefore sometimes easier for the listener to imagine what the speaker would have said under different circumstances and thus to arrive at an accurate pragmatic interpretation.

To select a comment on a given item:

1. Find the comment on that item with the greatest net desirability.

   (assuming a conventional interpretation and given your bias)

2. Anticipate the Evaluator's pragmatic interpretation of this comment. I.e., for each possibility P which is consistent with its conventional meaning:

   Would some other comment rate much higher if P were the possibility actually realized?

   (given your projected bias)

   If so, eliminate this possibility from the pragmatic interpretation.

3. If no possibilities remain (i.e., the comment is inconsistent with your projected bias) then:

   Reject this comment.

   Return to Step 2, using the comment with the next greatest desirability.

4. Make a note of the possibilities that remain, as the ones that the Evaluator will continue to reckon with.

5. Verbalize the comment.

Figure 5. Basic strategy used by Imp to select comments in Situations 3 through 5. (The shaded portions are not applicable in Situation 3.)

5. SITUATION 4: DIVERGENCE OF PROJECTED BIAS FROM ACTUAL BIAS

5.1 New assumptions

In Situation 3, the Informant implicitly assumed that the Evaluator had a remarkable degree of awareness of the specific way in which she selected her comments. After all, when anticipating the Evaluator's pragmatic interpretation in the way described above, the Informant is considering what the Evaluator will think that she, the Informant, would have said under various circumstances. In reality, of course, the Evaluator may make various kinds of false assumptions about the Informant's dialog goals and/or the specific evaluation standards that she ascribes to him. In the present situation, we will allow for the possibility that the Evaluator incorrectly assesses the nature of the Informant's bias — or at least, that the Informant thinks that he does so. In other words, in addition to having an *actual bias,* the Informant now assumes that she has a certain *projected bias* which the Evaluator ascribes to her. In this situation we also assume that the Informant will not attempt to change the nature of the projected bias, but on the contrary will attempt to behave in such a manner that the Evaluator will continue to ascribe this bias to her.

5.2 Characteristic behavior

The most frequent pattern of this sort is presumably the one where the Informant has a positive or negative bias but attempts to maintain an image of objectivity. A more drastic discrepancy is sometimes found in people who attempt to convey a favorable impression of themselves while appearing to be self-deprecating.

When the Evaluator bases a pragmatic interpretation on a correct assumption about the Informant's bias (as implicitly assumed in Situation 3), his interpretation will in general be both more precise and more realistic than a literal interpretation of the comment would be. When the Evaluator's assumption is incorrect, however, his pragmatic interpretation can be entirely inaccurate. For example, if he assumes objectivity, he will often interpret silence on an item as ruling out both the most desirable and the least desirable possibilities; but if the Informant is positively biased, the least desirable possibility may happen to be the one that is realized. In this situation, then, the Informant will sometimes notice that her comments are causing the Evaluator to draw false conclusions.

It can now also occur that the Informant cannot make the comment that she would in principle consider most desirable, because it would be inconsistent with her projected bias. For example, an exceptionally vague comment may sound rather strange coming from a supposedly objective Informant, if there is no reason for such an Informant not to be more precise, whatever the truth about the Object might be. This means that an Informant who is sophisticated enough to anticipate pragmatic interpretations should recognize that such a comment would betray her bias.

5.3 Realization in Imp

In addition to its actual bias parameter, Imp has a projected bias, which can take either the same value (as implicitly assumed in Situation 3) or a different one. The actual bias determines the system's initial choice of a comment on a given item, whereas the projected bias is consulted when the system anticipates the pragmatic interpretation that the Evaluator would give to the comment (cf. the shaded portions of Figure 5).

The most important consequence of a discrepancy between the actual and the projected bias is that the possibility actually realized can be ruled out in the course of pragmatic interpretation. This happens in those cases in which an Informant with the projected bias would clearly prefer some comment different from the one actually made.

5.4 Examples of the system's behavior

In the right-hand column of Figure 4, we can compare the pragmatic interpretations expected in this situation with those of the previous situation. Note that, for three items on which the Informant says nothing, the Evaluator is now expected to rule out the least desirable possibility, reflecting his faith that the Informant would have said something if this possibility had been realized (Items 4, 10, and 12). This faith is, of course, not justified: In the case of Item 4, for which the least desirable possibility is in fact realized, the resulting pragmatic interpretation is inaccurate.

Since the vague comment about previous work experience (Item 1) is inconsistent with the projected objectivity, Imp on second thought decides not to produce it at all, substituting the more precise comment of Situation 1.

5.5 General issues raised

The sort of distinction made here between actual and projected bias is in principle applicable to all of the other parameters that contribute to the selection of comments. The importance of 'projected talkativeness', for instance, is shown by the fact that a job applicant who had few positive things to say about herself might try to come across as a 'quiet type', so that her reticence would not give rise to much in the way of pragmatic interpretations.

In fact, the points illustrated in this situation are by no means specific to evaluation-oriented dialog; they are applicable to any sort of parameter which affects the generation of informative utterances: When the listener makes a false assumption about the value of such a parameter, he or she runs the risk of drawing some incorrect conclusions about matters of fact. And some — though not all — of the utterances that the speaker would be most inclined to produce would betray the discrepancy between the actual and the apparent values of the parameter.

6. SITUATION 5: RESPONDING TO SPECIFIC QUESTIONS OF THE EVALUATOR

6.1 New assumptions

We will now assume that an actual dialog takes place. The Evaluator asks the Informant questions which may be quite open or very specific. The Informant responds to these questions in accordance with normal dialog conventions, but she may also take the opportunity to volunteer additional relevant information which falls outside of the scope of the question as strictly interpreted.

6.2 Characteristic behavior

The behavior of the Informant in this situation consists of direct answers to questions plus some occasional brief monologs (Figure 6 shows some examples of Imp's behavior in this situation). The generation of comments which were not explicitly solicited is governed to a large degree by the same principles that we saw in the first four situations. In addition, however, the Informant is constrained by the fact that the Evaluator has chosen to focus attention on certain topics. In general, any unsolicited comments should be related to the questions asked; but even quite indirectly related information may be appreciated by the Evaluator if it is sufficiently beneficial in terms of reducing uncertainty and correcting inaccurate impressions (cf. Siklossy, 1978).

	Type of Question	Natural Language Formulation	Formulation of Answer	Commentary on Answer
1.	Focussing on general topic "Personal situation"	Tell me something about your personal situation.	I LIVE HERE IN AMSTERDAM	No mention of family situation; not important enough.
2.	Yes-no question on item "Family situation"	Do you have children?	NO IN FACT I LIVE ALONE	Additional information volunteered because of the focus on the item - but still not detailed enough to rule out all possibilities.
			AND BY THE WAY THE REASON I'M CHANGING JOBS IS THAT I'M LOOKING FOR MORE CHALLENGING WORK	Comment on indirectly related item.
3.	Focussing on single item "Complexity of previous work"	How challenging has the sort of work been that you've done up to now?	UNFORTUNATELY IT HAS BEEN PURELY ROUTINE	Some comment other that silence obligatory here.
			BUT BY THE WAY I'VE BEEN WORKING FOR ABOUT A YEAR AND A HALF AND I WENT TO UNIVERSITY PREP SCHOOL	Comments on indirectly related items.
4.	Yes-no question on item "Variety of previous work"	Did you get a good deal of experience in different departments?	NO BUT I SUBSTITUTED OCCASIONALLY IN OTHER DEPARTMENTS	A minor point - but mentioned because of focus on very specific topic.
5.	Yes-no question on item "Vocational training"	Did you graduate from the MTS? [= higher-level graphic training]?	NO	An objective Informant would here definitely add that she had received no vocational training.
6.	Unexpected yes-no question on same item	But of course you did get some vocational training, didn't you?	NO	
			I GUESS I'D BETTER BE GOING - GOODBYE	Canned expression for case where discrepancy between actual and projected bias has been exposed.

Figure 6. Example dialog conducted with Imp in Situation 5. (The actual bias is positive and the projected bias is objective.)

A feature of the Informant's behavior which becomes particularly salient in this situation is that her successive comments are often formulated using connectives and/or sentential adverbs which express the relationship between them. The appropriateness criteria for this sort of use of sentential adverbs and connectives are more a matter of semantics than of pragmatics. (Van Dijk, 1981, chap. 6, investigates the pragmatic use of some of the same word.) Still, they are of interest in the present context because of the ways in which the use of such words depends on some of the same characteristics of impression changes that are so important in determining the selection of comments in the first place.

A third difference between this situation and the previous ones is that it is now more dangerous for the Informant consciously to allow the Evaluator's pragmatic interpretation to yield an inaccurate impression about a given topic. If the Evaluator for some reason later asks a question about the topic concerned which forces the Informant to disclose the truth, the Informant's behavior will be revealed to have been inconsistent with her projected bias.

6.3 Realization in Imp

6.3.1 Types of question handled

Imp is capable of responding to three representative types of question about the Object. Each type creates a somewhat different context for the application of the basic principles introduced in the first four situations. The problem of analysing the natural language input is sidestepped completely: When entering a question, one must specify its type and the topic, item, and/or possibilities that it refers to.

Type 1: Request for Comments on a General Topic. A *topic* is viewed in Imp as a set of (one or more) items which are related in content. For example, the topic introduced by the first question in Figure 6, the applicant's personal situation, comprises the items 'Family situation' and 'Place of residence'. Imp treats a question of this type as an invitation to produce a monolog, which may in principle touch on any item in the evaluation form; but the monolog focusses primarily on the topic introduced in the question. The way in which this focussing is accomplished is the same for all three types of question; it will be discussed below.

Type 2: Request for Some Comment on a Particular Item. This is basically a special case of the first type of question, with the topic focussed on comprising only a single item; but a question is only assigned to this category if it is formulated in such a way that some real comment (as opposed to just silence) is obligatory. Imp accordingly eliminates silence as a candidate comment for the focal item, with the result that it may have to say something which it would have preferred to leave unsaid (cf. the third question in Figure 6).

Type 3: Yes-No Question on a Particular Item. The system in effect assumes that general dialog conventions require an answer of 'Yes' or 'No' to any yes-no question, regardless of the desirability of the anticipated impact of the answer on the Evaluator's impressions (cf. the answers to the last three questions in Figure 6). Such an answer will in general rule out at least one of the possibilities remaining for the item, but often more than one possibility will be left; in this case, the system may consider it worthwhile to add a further comment on the same item, especially inasmuch as the item has been focussed on specifically. Whether it does so or not, it may proceed to comment on other items, taking into account their relation to the focal item.

6.3.2 Role of Dialog Focus in the Selection of Optional Comments

The system presupposes that a question of any of these three types focusses attention on some topic (as defined above). The distinction between *broad* and *specific* topics can be quantified in terms of the total uncertainty initially associated with the items that fall under the topic. In this way, we can account for the fact that an Evaluator who asks how varied the applicant's work experience has been will seem to be zooming in on a relatively specific and unimportant topic: The values associated with the various possibilities for this topic differ less than do the values associated with more important items.

The first principle that Imp uses in taking dialog focus into account is the following: When the Evaluator focusses attention on a relatively specific topic, the prospective benefits (as defined in Figure 3) of making a comment on one of the items within this topic should be multiplied by a certain *magnification factor*. The degree of magnification is a function of the specificity of the topic. This principle has the natural consequence that even a fact which is of very little importance in itself may be mentioned spontaneously if the Evaluator has focussed attention on a specific topic which includes it. (See, e.g., the comment after the fourth question in Figure 6. The first two exchanges also illustrate the effects of focussing on topics with different degrees of specificity.)

A similar principle is applied to items which do not fall directly within the topic of the question but which nonetheless are related to it in some way. For example, the item 'Reason for changing jobs' is related to the topic 'Family situation' in that there is a broader topic which covers both of them — namely the issue of the applicant's motivation for working at this company (cf. the comment made on the second question in Figure 6). We may call the most specific topic which covers both a given item and the topic of the question the *common topic* which relates the two. The magnification factor used for comments on items outside the scope of the question is a function of the specificity of this common topic. As a consequence, the less an item has to do with the question topic, the less its associated benefits will be magnified; in the extreme case where an item has nothing in common with the question topic (aside from the fact that both concern the desirability of the applicant), no magnification at all occurs.

But even this use of a lower magnification factor for items outside of the question topic does not do justice to the fact that commenting on such an item involves forcing the Evaluator to shift his attention from the topic that he asked about to a different one. For example, a remark about the applicant's amount of work experience was considered well worth making in the monologs of Situations 1 through 4, where it did not benefit from any magnification; yet an Evaluator would presumably find it quite irritating if it were offered in response to the first question in Figure 6, concerning the applicant's personal situation. To take this consideration into account, Imp multiplies the prospective *costs* of any comment outside of the question topic by a factor which is a function of the relation between the specificity of the question topic and that of the common topic.

These considerations are all taken into account in the formula sketched in Figure 7.

Net desirability of a comment C on an item I
after a question focussing on topic F =

$$\text{Benefits of C (as defined in Figure 3)}$$
$$\text{X \quad Specificity of common topic for I and F}$$

$$- \quad \text{Costs of C}$$
$$\text{X \quad Specificity of F} \Big/ \text{Specificity of common topic for I and F}$$

Figure 7. Summary of the effects of dialog focus on Imp's assessment of the desirabililty of making a given comment

6.3.3 Selection of sentential adverbs and connectives

The rules which Imp applies in choosing words such as *unfortunately* and *but* with which to preface its comments make heavy use of the concepts introduced so far. Since these concepts can be quantified in a natural manner within the context of evaluation-oriented dialog, we can attempt here to define the conditions for the appropriate use of these words with considerably more precision than is possible in general (see Weydt, 1979, for an example of a more qualitative analysis of one such word).

The crucial quantity is the *change in expected value* which the comment is expected to produce with respect to the item it concerns. This quantity is multiplied by the appropriate magnification factor, as defined in the previous section. The word *unfortunately* is chosen if this change in expected value is in the negative direction and its size exceeds a certain threshold. The other expressions used reflect a relation between two successive changes in expected value: If both changes are in the same direction, the second comment is prefaced by *and* or *in fact*, the latter being chosen only if the second comment concerns the same item as the first one. *But* is used if the second of two successive changes is in a different direction than the first one. In addition, *fortunately* is inserted after *but* if the second change is in the positive direction, if the two comments concern the same item, and if the magnified size of the change exceeds a certain threshold.

In the occasional cases in which the system considers it worthwhile to make a comment which departs fairly radically from the question topic, it prefaces the comment with the words *by the way*. Exactly when this is appropriate is a function of the ratio between the specificity of the topic of the question and that of the common topic which relates the question and the comment.

Finally, if the system is asked a question which it must answer directly with a statement which will presumably not result in any change at all in the impressions of the Evaluator, it adds an expression of surprise such the word *why* (as in 'Why no!'; cf. Lakoff, 1973). The idea is that the Evaluator should already have known (or inferred) the answer to the question which he asked.

6.3.4 Consequences of failure to maintain a consistent image

A particularly interesting and complex question concerns what an Informant should do if her projected bias has been exposed (cf. Harrah, 1963, chap. 13 for a discussion of related issues). Imp does not at present embody an answer to this question. When this situation occurs, the system in effect simply admits that its actual bias is different from what it appeared to be and gives up (see the end of the dialog in Figure 6).

6.4 General issues raised

The general points made about the role of dialog focus in the spontaneous offering of information apply very generally to information-providing dialogs. What is specific to evaluation-oriented dialog is the way in which the notion of the degree of specificity of a topic can be quantified. It is much more difficult to capture this concept quantitatively for other types of dialog motivation; but, as one can see by examining the above examples, this variable must be quantified in some way and combined with the other variables discussed so far if natural dialog behavior is to be produced.

Imp's handling of connectives and sentential adverbs is not intended as a balanced contribution to the study of the semantics of these expressions. Among other limitations, it takes into account only the evaluative implications of statements (as in 'She is young [positive] *but* inexperienced' [negative]), whereas other implications can also influence the use of such expressions (as in 'She is young *and* [as one might therefore expect] inexperienced'). What the Imp model shows is that (a) the dependence on evaluative implications can only be understood given a reasonable quantification of the changes in the listener's evaluations, such as that made possible by the concept of the expected value of an impression; and (b) the impact of such a change depends on the extent to which the topic concerned has been focussed on in the dialog.

Regarding the general issue of maintaining a given projected dialog motivation, Imp helps to bring some of the processes involved into focus. For instance, the model clarifies why even a speaker who is quite willing to mislead the listener on a given issue may feel compelled to volunteer the truth about it simply because some *related* topic has been asked about.

Finally, it should be pointed out that implemented dialog models can help users to transfer their theoretical understanding of dialog processes into more appropriate dialog behavior. For instance, it is an instructive exercise for a user to take the role of the Evaluator and to try to pose a sequence of questions which will lure the system into a situation in which the discrepancy between its actual and projected dialog motivation will be exposed (as at the end of Figure 6). The possibility of engaging in such exercises constitutes one of the motivations for modelling the ethically questionable sort of behavior introduced in Situation 4.

7. MORE COMPLEX SITUATIONS

It may have struck the reader that several important questions have not been treated in connection with the above situations. How, for example, can an Informant intentionally *change* her projected bias? And how must her behavior be adapted if she has considerable uncertainty about the expectations of the Evaluator?

These and related questions have been addressed in extensions of the Imp model which handle several additional situations. Although detailed discussion of these situations must be left to a later paper, a brief summary of the main ideas may be of interest here as a complement to the exposition in the previous sections.

7.1 Situation 7: establishing a projected bias

In this situation, the Informant assumes, as in previous situations, that she has a certain projected bias; but she also has a *desired projected bias*. As long as these differ, she attempts to select her comments in such a way as to change her projected bias. This goal takes precedence over her goal of creating a certain kind of impression about the Object. This is reasonable, since once she has achieved this goal the new projected bias will influence the Evaluator's pragmatic interpretation of all of her subsequent comments. A similar situation can often be recognized in tendentious communications which begin with disclaimers such as 'I have nothing against foreign workers as a group, mind you, but . . . ' We assume, however, that the Informant makes no explicit claims about her bias but rather attempts to achieve her goal solely by exploiting the freedom she has in choosing what information to convey about the Object.

Specifically, the Imp system continues to rate the desirability of the various possible comments according to the same criteria as in the previous sections. When anticipating pragmatic interpretations, the system naturally rules out any comments which would seem inconsistent with the desired projected bias. More importantly, it rules out any comment which is *consistent* with its current projected bias. It thus chooses the most desirable (or least undesirable) comment which will force the Evaluator to change his assumption about the Informant's bias.

To illustrate, if the initial actual and projected biases are both positive and the desired projected bias is objective, the ideal comment for the Informant to offer first is a mildly negative one such as 'I've changed jobs several times in the past few years'. The comment should preferably not be strongly negative, since this would create an unfortunately poor impression of the Object; but it must be sufficiently informative so that an objective Informant might consider it worth making in the given dialog context. The price the system has to pay, in terms of the evaluation of the Object, in order to change its projected bias depends largely on factors beyond its control. For example, the Informant is lucky if the Evaluator's first question zooms in on some relatively unimportant topic on which the Informant can plausibly volunteer (but is not obliged to supply) some tidbit of negative information.

7.2 Situation 7: addressing more than one Evaluator

Many new questions arise if an Informant is speaking to two (or more) Evaluators at the same time, especially if they are assumed to have different evaluation criteria. For example, a job applicant may be interviewed by the two directors of a company, one of whom appears to value independence and creativity whereas the other seems to be more interested in conformity and reliability. We assume in this situation that the Informant aims to maximize the average desirability of the impressions she creates in the two Evaluators.

A very similar situation can arise if there is only one Evaluator but the Informant is quite uncertain as to what standards he will apply. One simple but reasonable strategy for coping with this type of ambiguity is to think of two (or more) configurations of standards — e.g., the creativity-oriented and conformity-oriented configurations mentioned above — which, taken together, seem representative of the range of possible Evaluators. By acting as if she were speaking to both of these possible Evaluators at once, the Informant can produce utterances which are likely to be at least reasonably appropriate no matter what the criteria of the Evaluator actually happen to be.

The way the Imp system handles this situation is a straightforward generalization of its treatment of Situation 5. It in effect ascribes a separate evaluation form to each Evaluator. When assessing the desirability of a comment, Imp averages its expected beneficial effects on the impressions of the two Evaluators.

When anticipating the pragmatic interpretation of the comment deemed most desirable, Imp considers each Evaluator separately, since their pragmatic interpretations may differ; and it actually verbalizes the comment only if it turns out to be consistent with Imp's projected bias for each of the Evaluators.

An example of the sort of phenomenon that emerges in this situation is given by Imp's behavior when it attempts to make a good impression on both the creativity-oriented and the conformity-oriented interviewer and expects both of them to ascribe to it a positive bias. On items for which the Evaluators' criteria are in conflict (e.g., 'Complexity of previous work'), Imp tends to remain silent, since any beneficial impact that a comment would have on one Evaluator would be roughly cancelled by its undesirable impact on the other one. But when anticipating the Evaluators' pragmatic interpretations of its silence, Imp recognizes that the two Evaluators are likely to form two different interpretations of the silence, each of which is worse than the initial impression according to the respective Evaluator's criteria, since each one is likely to rule out one or more of the possibilities that he would value most highly. In other words, by trying to please both Evaluators at once, Imp not only fails to make a particularly good impression on either one of them, but actually causes them to draw conclusions which are on the whole unjustifiably negative. This paradoxical result (which may be worthy of contemplation by politicians) underscores one of the general points raised by Situation 3: It may be advisable for an Informant to take the likely pragmatic interpretation of a comment into account when rating its desirability, not just when checking whether the comment is consistent with her image.

7.3 Situation 8: discrepancy between actual and projected assumptions about the Evaluator's values

There are many situations in which a speaker has certain assumptions about the interests and beliefs of the listener but prefers not to let these assumptions become known. Suppose, for example, that an employer is in fact looking for a reliable worker to perform routine tasks but, to make the job seem more attractive, describes it as if it involved challenging work. A job applicant who is aware of the true nature of the work and nonetheless wants the job may find it diplomatic to play along and appear to accept the employer's characterization of the work. In this situation, then, the Informant determines what she would like to say on the basis of her *actual* model of the Evaluator, but she must ensure that her utterances are consistent with her *projected* model of him.

Imp handles this situation by using one evaluation form to rate the desirability of possible comments and a second one to anticipate pragmatic interpretations. This latter, projected evaluation form also determines the selection of connectives and sentential adverbs. A typical result is the remark 'Unfortunately, the work I've done up to now has been purely routine', which Imp generates in the expectation that the Evaluator, as it were, will scarcely be able to conceal his delight.

As in Situation 7, it is by no means always possible for the Informant to find comments which simultaneously satisfy its different dialog goals so neatly. In particular, this is much easier if the projected bias is objective. When it is positive, for example, an ostensibly negative comment such as the example just given cannot be made, since it would be inconsistent with the Informant's image. This situation, then, shows that the projection of objectivity can bring benefits which are more subtle and less familiar than those that we saw in the earlier situations.

8. CONCLUDING REMARKS

It is fitting to conclude this chapter with a biased evaluation of the contribution made and an attempt to anticipate a possible misinterpretation. Persons who have been exposed to the Imp system briefly are sometimes inclined to dismiss the model as being restricted to a certain idealized type of dialog and as attempting to reduce the complexities of human conversation to a few arithmetic operations. This evaluation appears to be based on the assumption that the way the model handles Situations 1 and 2 constitutes the core of its contribution. In reality, as noted in the Introduction, the simplest versions of the model are best viewed as laying the foundations required for the developments introduced in the later sections — developments which are not specific to evaluation-oriented dialog and whose formalization in the computer model is largely independent of the specific assumptions and techniques introduced in the first two situations.

In short, the very assumptions and restrictions which at first seem to forebode triviality in fact permit us to model some of the inexhaustible subtleties of human dialog which — as researchers on language generation can all too easily forget — were the real topic of Grice's analysis of conversational maxims.

ACKNOWLEDGMENT

The author is indebted to Eduard Hovy for thoughtful comments on an earlier draft of this chapter.

REFERENCES

De Smedt, K. (in press) Object-oriented programming in Flavors and CommonORBIT. In: R. Hawley (Ed.) *Artificial intelligence programming environments*. Chicester: Ellis Horwood.

Grewendorf, G. (1981) Pragmatisch sinnvolle Antworten. Ein entscheidungstheoretischer Explicationsvorschlag. In: D. Krallmann & G. Stickel (Eds.) *Zur Theorie der Frage*. Tuebingen: Narr.

Grice, H. P. (1975) Logic and conversation. In: P. Cole & J. L. Morgan (Eds.) *Syntax and semantics, Vol. 3: Speech acts*. New York: Academic Press.

Harrah, D. (1963) *Communication: A logical model*. Cambridge, MA: MIT Press.

Hintikka, J. (1975) Answers to questions. In: J. Hintikka (Ed.) *The intentions of intentionality and other new models for modalities*. Dordrecht: Reidel.

Hovy, E. H. (1986) Putting affect into text. *Proceedings of the Eighth Annual Conference of the Cognitive Science Society*. Hillsdale, NJ: Erlbaum.

Jameson, A. (1983) Impression monitoring in evaluation-oriented dialog: The role of the listener's assumed expectations and values in the generation of informative statements. *Proceedings of the Eighth International Joint Conference on Artificial Intelligence.* Karlsruhe.

Lakoff, R. (1973) Questionable answers and answerable questions. In: B. B. Kachru, R. B. Lees, Y. Malkiel, A. Pietrangeli, & S. Saporta (Eds.) *Issues in linguistics: Papers in honor of Henry and Renee Kahane.* Urbana: University of Illinois.

McCawley, J. D. (1978) Conversational implicature and the lexicon. In: P. Cole (Ed.) *Syntax and semantics,Vol. 9: Pragmatics.* New York: Academic Press.

Schwitalla, J. (1979) Nonresponsive Antworten. *Deutsche Sprache, 7,* 193-211.

Siklossy, L. (1978) Impertinent question-answering systems: Justification and theory. In: *Proceedings of the 1978 ACM National Conference.*

Van Dijk, T. A. (1981) *Studies in the pragmatics of discourse.* The Hague: Mouton.

Weydt, H. (1979) 'Immerhin'. In: H. Weydt (Ed.) *Die Partikeln der deutschen Sprache.* Berlin: de Gruyter,

Winograd, T. (1977) A framework for understanding discourse. In: P. A. Carpenter & M. A. Just (Eds.) *Cognitive processes in comprehension.* Hillsdale, NJ: Erlbaum.

Chapter 3

CONTEXTUAL EFFECTS ON RESPONSES TO MISCONCEPTIONS

Kathleen F. McCoy

ABSTRACT

In this work I attempt to specify the content and structure of corrective responses to misconceptions in enough detail to be used by the tactical component of a language generation system. I define a process model which specifies how various aspects of the discourse context, as well as a model of the user, can affect the generated text.

When a misconception is judged important in the discourse, a corrective response may include information that refutes the faulty reasoning believed to have led to the misconception. I present schemas that capture the structure and content of such extended responses, and associate each schema with a distinguished structure in the user model. The user model itself is enriched with a new notion of object perspective, which reflects aspects of the discourse context that affect the response. A response to a misconception can thus be formulated by examining the enriched user model for one of the distinguished structures, and then instantiating the associated schema.

1. INTRODUCTION

In this chapter I discuss a process model for correcting misconceptions that allows contextual information to be taken into account in identifying the appropriate structure and content of the corrective response. The model accounts for a wide range of behavior found in human responses to misconceptions.

When a human conversational partner is faced with a query that reveals a misconception, there is a wide range of responses s/he might give depending both on the context in which the misconception occurs and on beliefs about the person exhibiting the misconception. At one end of the spectrum is a misconception that is trivial with respect to the current discourse goals of the participants. This misconception is likely to illicit no response. For example, imagine a brother and sister at the local aquarium. The brother is looking for the whale.

(1)   B. I can't find the whale. I looked in the 'large aquatic fish' tank, but it isn't there!
       S. It's in the tank around the corner.

Even if the brother's misconception about the correct classification of whale was detected by his sister, the misconception was deemed unimportant to his goals and was ignored by his sister.

At the other end of the spectrum is a misconception that is central to the goals of the conversational participants. It is likely that this misconception will not only be corrected, but enough detail will be included in the response to remedy the faulty reasoning that led to the misconception. Imagine a session of high school biology where animal classification is the subject under discussion.

(2)   T.   How do you think whales are classified?
      S.   Whales are fish.
      T.   No, they are mammals. You may have thought they were fish because they are fin-
           bearing and live in the water. However, they are mammals since (while fish have
           gills), whales breathe through lungs and feed their young with milk.

Notice in this case the corrective response can be seen as consisting of three parts: (1) a denial
of the incorrect information, (2) a statement of the correct information, and (3) justification for
the denial/correction given. In this instance the justification is in the form of a concede/override
pair. The similarity between whales and fish found in attributes that they have in common is
conceded. This similarity is likely to be the source of the misconception. Next, however, this
conceded information is overridden with attributes that make whales mammals and not fish.

We see from these examples that the current discourse goals are important in deciding how
much of a response to give to a misconception. It might seem reasonable to conclude that if a
misconception is trivial with respect to the discourse goals it should be ignored as in dialogue
(1). If it is important it should merit a 'full' response as in dialogue (2). Further analysis
reveals, however, that the discourse goals alone are not enough to specify the form of the
correction. For instance, different preceding dialogues may cause a very important
misconception to be corrected with different 'full' responses. Imagine, once again, being back
in biology class discussing the classification of various sea animals. The class has just finished
discussing sharks — those rather large fish that many people are afraid of.

(3)   T.   OK — that is one kind of sea animal we have classified. What about whales — does
           anyone know how they might be classified?
      S.   Whales are fish too.
      T.   No, whales are not fish, they are mammals. You may have thought they were fish
           since they are like the fish, sharks, in that both are large aquatic creatures and both
           scare people. However, whales are mammals since (while fish have gills), whales
           breathe through lungs and feed their young with milk.

Note that, as was the case above, this response can be seen as consisting of the deny, correct,
justify triple, but the justification is different in this case. Here the likely source of the
misconception is seen as a similarity between whales and some subset of fish — the sharks. It
is this similarity that is conceded and then overridden by attributes that make whales mammals
and not fish.

The conclusion that might be drawn at this point is that the discourse goals determine how
much of a response to give, but do not completely specify the content of the response. The
actual justification must be supplied by other means. Further study reveals examples that seem
to refute even this conclusion however. In the following example an obviously important
misconception is responded to with less than a full response. Once again, imagine being in
biology class classifying aquatic animals:

(4)   T.   OK, so we know that mammals breathe through lungs and feed their young with
           milk... Now, we have been discussing whales and we know that even though they
           live in the water, they don't breathe underwater like fish do. They must come to the
           surface and take in air through their lungs. In addition, their young are born alive and
           are fed by their mother's milk. How do you think whales should be classified?
      S.   As fish?
      T.   No, as mammals!?!

Despite the obvious importance of this misconception, the teacher is somewhat at a loss to
include much more in her response than the denial of the wrong information and a statement of
the correct information. This is because s/he has just given the student all of the information
s/he feels is needed to have the student draw the correct conclusion. Yet the student still exhibits

the misconception. S/he can think of nothing more to say at this point in order to correct the misconception.

This paper presents a computational strategy that accounts for the variability in these responses. It is hypothesized that these effects can be explained by having both discourse factors and a model of the person with the misconception (henceforth called the user) come into play during the generation process. The discourse factors that are involved include the discourse goals, a new notion of *object perspective*, and a record of past focus (the attentional state of the user). The discourse goals of the conversational partners are used to determine what *gross level strategy* (or rough response) to use in responding to the misconception. Once the gross level strategy has been determined, it must be expanded into a finer specification of the response. Critical to this expansion is an analysis of the user model which has been highlighted with object perspective to reflect the domain orientation elicited by the conversation so far. The expansion may also be influenced by the attentional state of the discourse.

The next section discusses the overall picture of the correction process with an emphasis on where discourse goals come into play. First the gross level correction strategy is introduced. In the section following that, the processes involved in elaborating the gross level strategy are discussed. Particular attention is paid to motivating and elaborating a set of fine level correction strategies that are triggered by particular aspects of the user model. Section 4 describes how these processes are affected by object perspective. The final section contains some concluding remarks.

2. GROSS LEVEL STRATEGY

This work is done in the context of a natural language interface to a database or expert system. I view this interface as consisting of several modules. This work concentrates on the misconception corrector module which is responsible for correcting a misconception that has been detected by some other module of the interface. I am assuming that a *misconception* is a discrepancy between what is in the system's knowledge base and what the user apparently believes (as exhibited through the conversation). When such a discrepancy is detected, the system assumes that its own model is correct. Consequently the job of the misconception corrector is to bring the user's knowledge into line with the system's knowledge.

When a misconception is input to the misconception corrector, the first decision that must be made is how much, if any, of a correction to attempt. As was seen in the examples, the information included in a response can range from nothing (ignoring the misconception) to a 'full' misconception response containing (1) a denial of the incorrect information, (2) a statement of the correct information, and (3) justification for the correction given. The decision about which of these three parts to include in the response is a decision about the *gross level strategy* of the response. The gross level strategy, then, is some subset of {*deny, correct, justify*} which will be given to the strategy elaboration component (discussed below) for further analysis.

I claim that the gross level strategy can be chosen on the basis of the relationship of the current discourse goals to the misconception. If the misconception is peripheral to the discussion, the null set will be chosen and the misconception will be ignored. As the misconception is judged more important, larger subsets of the three identified pieces may be chosen. For a misconception judged very important, a full three part strategy will be specified.

This gross level strategy decision will be passed to a component which is responsible for elaborating the strategy and for generating the specification of the actual response. Figure 1 contains a schematic diagram of the picture so far.

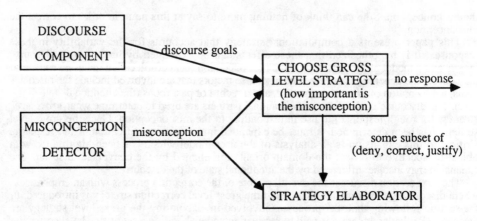

Figure 1. Discourse Goals Affect Response

Notice that this process model seems to contradict some of the examples shown in the previous section since it seems unable to explain dialogue (4). Recall that in that example the misconception was deemed to be very important to the conversational goals and thus this model would predict that the choose gross level strategy component would request that a full response including justification for the correction be given. Despite this, the response contains no justification. We will see in the next sections, however, that even though the gross level strategy may request a full response, the strategy elaborator may be unable to fulfill the request. In such a situation, less than a full response may be given to an obviously important misconception.

3. ELABORATING GROSS STRATEGY: USER MODEL ANALYSIS

Once a gross level strategy has been chosen, it must be elaborated into an actual response. Input to the elaborator will be some subset of deny, correct, justify. The specification of the response must be elaborated so that it contains enough detail so that it can be input to a tactical component such as McDonald (1980) or Derr & McKeown (1984) and translated into actual English text. Elaborating the denial and correction are fairly straightforward. They can be filled in using information from the system knowledge base. The most interesting question has to do with elaborating the justification.

To date, misconception responses that contain justification have been generated in an almost canned fashion. Traditionally only intelligent tutoring systems (see for example, Stevens & Collins, 1980; Brown & Burton, 1978; and Woolf, 1984) have been concerned with such responses. These systems have, for the most part, dealt with misconceptions by relying on an *a priori* listing of misconceptions and response specifications. This approach has several problems. Only two of these will be mentioned here; discussion of others can be found in McCoy (1985). First, systems that rely on *a priori* listings of misconceptions are totally at a loss when faced with a novel misconception since they have no ability to reason about the misconceptions themselves. Second and perhaps more important to this discussion, a reliance on an *a priori* listing severely hampers the ability of a system to provide responses that are context sensitive. The few systems that handle contextual effects do so by allowing discourse factors to affect the way in which the content of the response is presented. The content of the response itself, however, is unaffected by discourse context. The approach is therefore at a loss to account for two different justifications being given to the same misconception, such as found in dialogues (2) and (3). One of my objectives has been to develop a method for generating responses to misconceptions that takes contextual information into account.

In order to gain insight into how context-dependent justifications might be generated, I undertook a study of transcripts of humans responding to misconceptions. The analysis revealed that, in many circumstances, the justification included in a response took the form of refuting faulty reasoning that might have led to the misconception in the first place. Very often the justification would re-enforce that part of the reasoning that was correct, while correcting that part of it that was wrong.

It might seem that this discovery is not very enlightening since the kinds of faulty reasoning one might use to come to a misconception are seemingly infinite. However, further transcript analysis showed that for a particular kind of misconception (e.g., a misclassification) a limited number of kinds of faulty reasoning were corrected in misconception responses. Moreover, one could abstract out a regularity in the justification contained in responses that were aimed at correcting a particular kind of faulty reasoning.

The transcript analysis concentrated on two types of misconceptions: misclassifications (classifying an object wrong) and misattributions (giving an object a property it does not have). For each type of misconception, a small number of (fine-level) response strategies were identified based on the justification included in the response. These fine-level response strategies were appropriate elaborations to a request for a ' full' misconception response from the gross level strategy component.

Given that a characterization of response strategies was found, one must decide on the criteria for using a given response strategy to respond to a particular misconception by a particular user. Since each response strategy refutes a particular kind of faulty reasoning, it would make most sense to use a strategy when a model of the user indicates evidence for the reasoning it refutes. By characterizing this evidence in a domain-independent fashion in terms of configurations of a user model, we can choose an appropriate strategy by doing an analysis of the user model that looks for one of the pre-identified configurations. If one matches the user model, then the corresponding strategy can be instantiated.

This process will be illustrated by examples of misclassifications. Before going into the examples, I will lay out my assumptions about the kind of knowledge available.

— The system's model of the world contains an object taxonomy with attribute/values attached to the objects.
— The user's model of the world contains the same kinds of things (i.e., an object taxonomy and object attributes). Thus, these are the things about which the user may have a misconception. In addition, since the system's knowledge base contains the same kinds of things, these are the kinds of information that may be included in a response to a misconception. Saying the user's model of the world contains the same kinds of things as the system knowledge base is not saying anything about the content of the user's model. These two models may be quite different in content.
— The system has available to it a model of the user (that is, a model of the user's model of the world) which is in the same form as its own knowledge base. It is assumed that this model starts out as a model of some canonical user and is updated as the conversation progresses.

In the following analysis I am assuming that the gross level strategy component has deemed the misconception important and thus requests elaboration of a full deny, correct, justify response. Thus the 'fine-level' strategies shown here will correspond to elaborations of all three pieces of the gross level strategy. Examples of responses for which the gross level strategy requested a full response are found in dialogues (2), (3), and(4) of section one. Each one of these responses correspond to a different correction strategy — each refutes a different kind of support for the misconception. I will therefore take each one of these in turn, abstract out the underlying strategies, indicate the kind of support the strategy refutes, and illustrate user model configurations that would explain their use. In the end, the process model of the strategy elaboration component should be clear.

Let us consider the response in dialogue (2) at a somewhat more abstract level. The content can be abstracted into the following:

MISCONCEPTION = X *is-a* Y
RESPONSE =

1. X *is-NOT-a* Y
2. X *is-a Super-Type*(X)
3. X is like Y because both share *attributes-of*(X) $\cap$ *attributes-of*(Y)
4. BUT X has *attributes-of*(X) — *attributes-of*(Y)
5. WHILE Y has *attributes-of*(Y) — *attributes-of*(X)

1 and 2 correspond to the denial of the incorrect classification and statement of the correct classification of the misclassified object. It is the justification contained in 3 - 5 that is of interest to us here. We see from the rule that the justification in the response hinges on the attributes that the objects have. First attributes that X and Y (Whales and Fish) have in common are offered as a similarity X and Y have. Attributes that refute the misclassification are offered in 4 and 5. These are attributes that are disjoint between the two objects.

This rule basically tells us what things from the knowledge base should be included in the response (e.g., the correct classification, intersecting and disjoint attributes, etc.). In order to generate an English response like the one in dialogue (2), we must not only capture the response's content, we must also capture its rhetorical force. That is, we must specify the communicative role played by each piece of the response so that it can be reflected in the surface text. For instance, we not only need to know that sentences 4 and 5 list attributes of objects X and Y respectively, but we need to know that these attributes are meant to override false conclusions that might be drawn from what was communicated in 3. The specification of the communicative role is done by specifying a *rhetorical predicate* for each proposition in the response.

McKeown describes rhetorical predicates as being 'the *means* which a speaker has for describing information' (McKeown, 1982). They can be thought of as describing the structural relationships that hold among the propositions in a response. These structural relationships must be reflected in the surface structure of the response, and thus must be specified by a text generator in order for an appropriate surface structure to be generated.

Other work on text structure (e.g., Reichman, 1981; McKeown, 1982; Mann & Thompson, 1983; Mann, 1984) has described schemas/grammars/models of the text in terms completely devoid of the *content* of what is to be said. These researchers have abstracted the communicative roles played by propositions in a wide range of texts used for a common discourse purpose (such as describing an object or arguing a point). McKeown showed how such 'rhetorical schemas' could be used in text generation by attaching a 'semantics' to each rhetorical predicate that indicated the kind of knowledge from the knowledge base that could be used to fill that role. A particular rhetorical schema was chosen based on the purpose of the discourse; the semantics were used to decide what information from a pool of possibly relevant knowledge to include in the discourse; a focusing mechanism was used to arbitrate between choices.

Perhaps because the kind of generation being done here has a much narrower goal, it was found that the model for the generation process outlined above was not the most effective for this task. In the more general case addressed by previous researchers, the only thing that could be abstracted from the analyzed texts was the rhetorical force of the propositions involved. Because of the more restricted goals of the text being generated here, not only can the rhetorical force of the text be abstracted, but some information about the content of the text can be abstracted. In fact, the content of the responses to misconceptions was just as important (and constrained) as the choice of rhetorical predicates. This was evidenced by the rule given above capturing an abstract specification of the content of responses like that found in dialogue (2). Because of this, a decision was made to employ schemas which contained both kinds of information. Thus in terms of a McKeown-like model, the schemas are responsible both for assigning the rhetorical force of each proposition in the text and for determining what knowledge from the knowledge base is relevant. As a result, the choice of what schema to use is a more complicated one. It is based not only on the purpose of the discourse (e.g., to correct the user's misconception) but also on beliefs about the user.

A schema which captures the strategy used in dialogue (2) is shown below. This schema contains both rhetorical predicates (derived from the work of Reichman, 1981; McKeown, 1982; Mann & Thompson, 1983; Mann, 1984; and from my own transcript analysis) and a specification of what information from the knowledge base is to be included (derived from the rule shown above). It is termed the *like-super schema* for reasons given below. It may be used to respond to an OBJECT being misclassified as a POSITED when it is really a REAL.

```
((deny (classification OBJECT POSITED))
 (state (classification OBJECT REAL))
 (concede (share-attributes    OBJECT
                               POSITED
                               ATTRIBUTES1))
       (override (share-attributes    -----
                               POSITED
                               ATTRIBUTES2))
       (override (share-attributes    OBJECT
                               REAL
                               ATTRIBUTES3)))
```

Notice how this schema captures both content and communicative roles.[1] The first line of the 'like-super' schema indicates that the propositional content of the first statement is an object classification and that it should be communicated as a denial. Thus this line expands the 'denial' given in the gross level strategy to specify what information should be denied. The second line expands the 'correct' specified in the gross level strategy. The remainder of the schema is concerned with expanding the 'justify'. The content part of the schema indicates what kind of information from the knowledge base can be used; the communicative role indicates *how* it should be used.

It is the communicative role of a proposition that is crucial for determining the actual surface form of the response. For example, the concede predicate is responsible for the 'you may have thought' which precedes the intersecting attributes in the surface structure. The 'however' and 'while' in the last sentence of dialogue (2) can be explained by the override predicate.[2]

So far we have abstracted a response strategy and shown how the vocabulary used to write down the strategy affects the wording used to realize it. Before this information can be used by a system, we must address the question: under what circumstances is it appropriate to use this schema in response to a misclassification?

Since the schema concedes a similarity between the misclassified object and the posited superordinate, it would be appropriate to use the schema when there is evidence that such a similarity may have led to the misconception. This might be the case when, according to the model of the user, the user believes that the misclassified object and the posited superordinate are similar to each other. In such a situation it is likely that the user reasoned as follows: 'I don't know how to classify this object, but I do know about a class of objects called posited. I also believe that object is a lot like posited. Therefore, it is reasonable that object is a member of that class.' Using the like-super strategy in this situation will assure the user that s/he was right in noting the similarity between object and posited (thus that aspect of his/her world model is correct) but indicate that the similarity is not enough to conclude that the object should be

---

[1] These schemas differ in another important way from schemas previously seen. The ordering of the propositions is not fixed by the schema. The surface ordering of the response is dependent on discourse factors not considered here. In fact, preceding discourses can be constructed that make almost all possible orderings of the propositions in the schema seem natural.

[2] It should be noted that the dialogues here were not generated by a system. They are simply meant to illustrate the points.

classified as a posited. In fact, the object is a real because of other properties that the strategy lists.

Dialogue (3) contains a full response containing a different kind of justification. The difference can be most clearly seen by abstracting it into the following rule:

MISCONCEPTION = X *is-a* Y
RESPONSE =

1. X *is-NOT-a* Y
2. X *is-a Super-Type*(X)
3. ∃Z (Z *is-a* Y ∧ X is like Z because both have *attributes-of*(X) ∩ *attributes-of*(Z))
4. HOWEVER X *is-a Super-Type*(X) because X has *attributes-of(Super-Type*(X)) — *attributes-of*(Y)

Note that this strategy is very similar to the one above in that it contains reference to a similarity due to intersecting attributes. The big difference here is that above a reference was made to a similarity between the posited superordinate and the misclassified object. Here the similarity between some *descendent* of the posited superordinate and the misclassified object is mentioned as a possible source of the misconception. As was the case above, the content rule is not sufficient to specify the response. The rhetorical force is also needed. The following schema captures the content of the above rule with the appropriate rhetorical force.

```
((deny (classification OBJECT POSITED))
 (state (classification OBJECT REAL))
 (concede (similarity
              OBJECT
              DESCENDENT
              (share-attributes   OBJECT
                                  DESCENDENT
                                  ATTRIBUTES1)))
 (override (share-attributes   OBJECT
                               REAL
                               ATTRIBUTES2)))
```

Since this schema calls for refuting the similarity between the misclassified object and a descendent of the posited superordinate, it would be appropriate to use when such a similarity led to the misconception. Evidence for this being the case would be found in a user model that indicates the user believes such a similarity exists. Finding the similarity suggests that the user may have reasoned as follows: 'I don't know how to classify the object, but I do know how to classify this other object — it is a descendent of posited. Since the descendent of posited and the misconception object are similar to each other, perhaps they are classified in the same way'. In such a situation, the above schema would refute this faulty reasoning while still confirming the correct (but misleading) information that may have led to the misconception.

The last strategy that must be accounted for is the one found in dialogue (4). At first glance it may appear that the model as so far developed cannot account for this case. Despite the obvious importance of this misconception, the response contains no justification for the correction. But surely the Gross Level Strategy Chooser faced with this misconception would have specified that a full response be given. How can a less than full response be explained? One explanation for this is that the gross level strategy did specify that the justification be included, but the strategy elaborator was unable to expand the specification into a response because all of its justifications are triggered by pre-identified configurations of the user model and none of these matched the current model of the user. In that situation the elaborator would be unable to figure out what may be supporting the misconception and thus could not refute it. This seems to be the case with the teacher in dialogue (4). You can imagine the teacher thinking, 'There is no explanation for this misclassification... I don't know what is being used to support it, so I can give no justification'. The teacher would be left with only the straightforward denial and correction in her response.

In sum, the general model for the gross level strategy elaborator is one that contains several modules — a module for each different kind of misconception. We looked at the misclassification module. Within each module is a specification of how to expand each possible element of the gross level strategy. In order to expand the justification, an analysis of the user model must be done which looks for certain pre-identified configurations. The user model configurations identified in this section were based on object similarity. If one of the identified configurations is matched, then the corresponding justification schema is used. So, for misclassifications, the user model analysis might proceed as follows: If the user model shows that the user thinks that the misclassified object and the posited superordinate are similar, then use the like-super schema to generate the justification. If the user model indicates that the user thinks that the misclassified object and some descendent of the posited superordinate are similar, then use the like-some-super schema to respond. If neither of the above are true, then generate no justification; include only the denial and correction in the response.

4. THE HIGHLIGHTED KNOWLEDGE BASE

The model described so far seems to predict that a misconception by a particular user (or two users for which the system has the same user model) will always be corrected in the same way. The plausibility of the dialogues given in Section 1 show that this prediction is suspect. The model given so far can still be used and the contextual effects can be explained if the user model analysis described in the preceding section (1) takes into account the attentional state of the discourse (Grosz & Sidner, 1985), and (2) works on a user model that has been highlighted by *object perspective*.

The user model analysis must take the attentional state of the discourse into account in order to avoid telling the user facts that s/he is already attending to. For instance, there was no reason for the teacher in dialogue (4) to include anything in the corrective response that was included in the preceding monologue because it was already included in the attentional state of the dialogue participants. Re-mentioning such things should have no effect. Since her only choices of justification did re-mention things already attended to, none of them were chosen.

Aside from the attentional state of the discourse (which basically contains entities and attributes that have been explicitly mentioned), the preceding discourse serves to highlight certain aspects of the domain. I claim that the user model analysis must therefore not use a regular semantic network representation of the user such as one represented by a KL-ONE representation (KL-ONE, 1982; see Brachman, 1979 for a survey of several other systems that fit this description). Rather, it must use a model of the user that has been highlighted from the previous discourse. I introduce object perspective as a mechanism for modeling this highlighting affect. User model analysis done on a model of the user highlighted by object perspective can account for examples like in dialogues (2) and (3) where two different responses were given to the misconception 'whales are fish' due to the preceding discourse.

The preceding dialogue causes a certain orientation to be taken on the domain. In that orientation certain objects and attributes become important while others are suppressed. When processing (like assessing object similarity) is done on a knowledge base, it must take this orientation into account. The result is that a similarity assessment may come out quite differently depending on the orientation. For instance, one view you might take of a building is as someone's home. Under this perspective the building is probably seen as somewhat similar to an apartment. On the other hand, the same building might be viewed as an architectural work. Under this 'architectural work' perspective, it is similar to other buildings with the same kinds of architectural features — perhaps an office building down the street. The building is not seen as similar to the apartment. To model this intuitive notion, we need a means of highlighting the knowledge base and a metric of object similarity that is sensitive to this highlighting.

Notions of object perspective have been introduced in the past. Grosz (1977); Bobrow & Winograd (1977) and Tou, Williams, Fikes, Henderson & Malone (1982) have defined object perspective through a limited inheritance mechanism. Instead of an object inheriting attributes from all of its superordinates as is normally done, an object in the generalization hierarchy inherits attributes only from the superordinate 'in perspective'. For instance a particular building might either inherit attributes from the superordinate 'architectural work' or from the superordinate 'home', depending on which superordinate is in perspective. While this notion seems to capture perspectives for individual objects, it fails to capture the feeling of an orientation being taken on an entire domain. (See McCoy, 1985, for additional problems.)

McKeown & Matthews (1985) have defined another notion of perspective which seems to capture more of the intuitive feeling. In McKeown et al.'s work, 'perspectives' are actually 'chunks' of the generalization hierarchy. Both objects and attributes 'disappear' in some perspectives. For instance, the 'architectural works' perspective of a domain would just include those attributes and objects that are important in that perspective. So, for instance, buildings with special architectural features would be included, but apartments would not. This notion is closer to the intuitive one mentioned above, but is subsumed in a simpler notion of object perspective that I will define here.

First, instead of tying perspective into the generalization hierarchy of objects as has been done in the past, the new notion of perspective is independent of that hierarchy. 'Perspectives' which can be taken on the objects in the domain will be defined and will sit in a structure which is orthogonal to the generalization hierarchy.

Second, a number of perspectives can be defined for any domain of discourse and *any* given domain object may be viewed from any one of several perspectives defined for that domain.

Third, each perspective comprises a set of attributes with associated salience values. It is these salience values that dictate which attributes are highlighted and which are suppressed.

Fourth, one such perspective is designated *active* at any particular point in the discourse.[3]

This notion of object perspective works as follows. An object or group of objects is still said to be viewed through a perspective. In particular, any object which is accessed by the system is viewed through the current *active* perspective. However, instead of dictating which attributes an object inherits, the active perspective affects the salience values of the attributes that an object possesses (either directly or inherited through the generalization hierarchy). The active perspective essentially acts as a filter on an object's attributes — raising the salience of and thus highlighting those attributes which have a high salience rating in the active perspective, and lowering the salience of and thus suppressing those attributes which are either given a low salience value or do not appear in the active perspective.

This notion of perspective serves to explain how, when certain attributes and objects are mentioned, other attributes become highlighted. Perspectives capture 'precompiled' feelings of 'similar' attributes all becoming important together even though not all of them are explicitly mentioned. This is explained by a single perspective that rates all of the attributes highly salient becoming active by mention of a few of the key attributes.

It is obvious how this notion affects attribute importance, but it also affects object importance. The importance of an object in a discourse may be determined by the salience values given to the attributes it possesses.

$$importance(X) = \sum_{X \ has\text{-}a \ P} salience(P)$$

The idea is that the whole becomes highlighted by having its parts highlighted. Thus, during a discussion in which the active perspective highlights many attributes having to do with home, all objects that have many of those attributes will become highlighted. Objects having none of these attributes (like office buildings) will be suppressed.

In order for this notion of object perspective to be beneficial, processes that access the knowledge base must be sensitive to the highlighting. One of these processes that is important to correcting misconceptions is the assessment of object similarity. Tversky (1977) introduces a

---

3   Saying that exactly one perspective is active is actually a simplification. It may be the case that a number of perspectives can be active. In this case the resulting 'active perspective' will be some function of the individual active perspectives. The exact nature of this function is an open research question.

metric of object similarity that is sensitive to the salience values of the attributes the objects possess. His metric can therefore be used with the salience values assigned by object perspective to yield similarity ratings that change with perspective. Tversky's metric is based on intersecting and disjoint attributes of the objects involved. A simplified version of his metric is shown here:

$$s(a,b) = f(A \cap B) - f(A - B) - f(B - A)$$

where a and b are the objects and A and B are the attributes of a and b respectively. The function f returns a salience value for each attribute involved. Basically the metric says that the similarity of a and b is the sum of the salience values of the attributes they have in common, minus the sum of the salience values of the attributes that are disjoint between them. If we use object perspective to fix the salience values, then two objects will be seen as similar in a perspective that highlights attributes that they have in common, and as not similar in a perspective that highlights attributes that are disjoint between them.

In defining a knowledge base for a particular domain, the system designer must not only define the object taxonomy as before, but must also define the perspectives that can be taken on the domain. One perspective we might imagine defining for the fish-mammal domain would be the 'body-characteristics' perspective. In this perspective attributes like 'fin-bearing', 'have-gills', and 'breathe-through-lungs' would be given high salience and thus highlighted. Other attributes would be suppressed by this perspective. Another perspective that might be defined is the 'common-people's-perception' perspective. This perspective might highlight attributes like 'large-aquatic-creatures' and 'scare-people'. Other attributes, like 'have-gills' and 'fin-bearing' would be suppressed by this perspective.

Consider how the user model analysis would proceed given the misconception 'whales are fish' under the two different perspectives. First, suppose that the 'body-characteristics' perspective is active. The user model analysis first calls for a test on the similarity of whales and fish. Since this perspective highlights properties common to whales and fish, the similarity metric will return a positive reading and the like-super strategy will be used to respond generating a response like that found in dialogue (2).

On the other hand, suppose the 'common-people's-perception' perspective is active. Since this perspective highlights attributes that are disjoint between whales and fish, the similarity metric will return a negative reading and the like-super strategy will not be applicable. User model analysis will then look for descendants of fish that are similar to whales. Shark is a descendant of fish and since the active perspective highlights attributes common to sharks and whales, the applicability conditions for the like-some-super schema hold and it will be instantiated generating a response like that found in dialogue (3).

5. CONCLUSIONS

In this paper I have described a two-stage process model for responding to misconceptions. The model takes contextual information into account in several places. In the model, detection of a misconception triggers the first component, which determines the importance of the misconception with respect to the discourse goals of the participants. This component is responsible for choosing the gross level strategy for the response. The gross level strategy which is represented as a (possibly improper) subset of the rhetorical predicates deny, correct, justify indicates how detailed a response is desirable. A gross level strategy represented by the null set indicates that ignoring the misconception is preferable, while one represented by the full set indicates that a full response should be generated.

The gross level strategy is passed to a second component which uses it as an outline for generating the response. This component is responsible for elaborating the response, filling in the details about the content and structure of what is to be generated. When the gross level strategy requests justification to be included, the strategy elaborator analyzes the user model looking for structures that might indicate support for the misconception. Associated with each structure is a schema used to generate justification that refutes the found support.

The elaborator is made context sensitive by taking into account the attentional state of the participants and by operating on a user model which has been highlighted by object perspective. Object perspective serves to model the orientation to the domain which is taken by the discourse participants. The orientation serves to highlight certain aspects of the domain beyond those explicitly mentioned in the dialogue.

REFERENCES

Brown, J.S. & Burton, R.R. (1978) Diagnostic models for procedural bugs in basic mathematical skills. *Cognitive Science, 2,* 155-192.

Brachman, R. (1979) On the epistemological status of semantic networks. In: N. Findler (Ed.) *Associative Networks: Representation and Use of Knowledge by Computer.* New York: Academic Press.

Bobrow, D.G. & Winograd, T. (1977) An overview of KRL, a knowledge representation language. *Cognitive Science, 1,* 3-46.

Derr, M.A. & McKeown, K.R. (1984) Using focus to generate complex and simple sentences. In: *Proceedings of COLING84,* Stanford.

Grosz, B. (1977) *The Representation and Use of Focus in Dialogue Understanding.* Technical Report 151, SRI International, Menlo Park Ca.

Grosz, B. & Sidner, C. (1985) Discourse structure and the proper treatment of interruptions. In: *Proceedings of the 1985 Joint Conference on Artificial Intelligence,* Los Angeles.

KL-ONE (1982) *Proceedings of the 1981 KL-ONE workshop.* Technical report 4842, BBN, Boston Ma.

Mann, W.C. (1984) Discourse structures for text generation. In: *Proceedings of COLING84,* Stanford.

Mann, W.C. & Thompson S.A. (1983) *Relational Propositions in Discourse.* Technical Report ISI/RR-83-115, ISI/USC.

McCoy, K.F. (1985) *Correcting Object-Related Misconceptions.* PhD. Thesis, University of Pennsylvania.

McDonald, D.D. (1980) *Natural Language Production as a Process of Decision Making Under Constraint.* PhD. Thesis. MIT.

McKeown, K. (1982) *Generating Natural Language Text in Response to Questions about Database Structure.* PhD. Thesis, University of Pennsylania.

McKeown, K., Wish, M. & Matthews, K. (1985) Tailoring explanations for the user. In: *Proceedings of the 1985 Conference on Artificial Intelligence,* Los Angeles.

Reichman, R. (1981) *Plain Speaking: A Theory and Grammar of Spontaneous Discourse.* PhD. Thesis, Harvard University. BBN Report no. 4681.

Stevens, A.L. & Collins, A. (1980) Multiple conceptual models of a complex system. In: P.A. Federico, R.E. Snow & W.E. Montague (Eds.) *Aptitude, Learning, and Instruction.* Hillsdale, N.J.: Erlbaum:

Tversky, A. (1977) Features of similarity. *Psychological Review, 84,* 327-352.

Tou, F., Fikes, R., Henderson, A. & Malone T. (1982) Rabbit: an intelligent database assistant. In: *Proceedings of AAAI-82,* Pittsburgh.

Woolf, B. P. (1984) *Context Dependent Planning in a Machine Tutor.* PhD. Thesis, University of Massachusetts.

Chapter 4

GENERATING UNDERSTANDABLE EXPLANATORY SENTENCES

Domenico Parisi
Donatella Ferrante

TABLE OF CONTENTS

1. Introduction
2. Explaining a third party's actions
3. Explaining events
4. Conclusion

1. INTRODUCTION

An important component of a language generation system is being able to produce explanatory sentences and texts. Operationally an explanatory sentence can be defined as a sentence which is an appropriate answer to a *why*-question:

(1) Q: Why did John go out?
     A: He wanted to buy a packet of cigarettes

Explanatory talk, of course, goes beyond producing appropriate answers to *why*-questions. What we may also want to call explanations are responses to requests for definition and clarification of terms, concepts, or ideas, or to questions about conclusions reached, methods followed, and so forth — all of which are usually not formulated as *why*-questions. Howewer, for the purposes of the present paper, we will restrict our attention to giving explanations as answers to *why*-questions.

Even within this restricted subclass we must distinguish between explanations of human (and perhaps, animal) actions — e.g. John's going out — versus explanations of events — e.g. a house's falling down —, explanations of the system's own actions versus explanations of other people's actions, and so forth. The reason for making all these distinctions is that a proposed solution for one type of explanation may not be appropriate for other types. (For a discussion of some of these topics, see Wilks, 1977.) In the present paper we will deal separately with explanations of third party's actions (not the system's own actions; section 2) and explanations of events (section 3).

2. EXPLAINING A THIRD PARTY'S ACTIONS

Answering a *why*-question could be viewed as just a particular instance of answering wh-questions — i.e. questions about *who, what, where, when, how*, etc. — without posing special problems. Let us assume that a system's knowledge is represented as a network of nodes and arcs, with nodes representing the entities that the system has knowledge about and the network around each node representing the knowledge about the entity corresponding to the node. Generating an answer to a wh-question can be conceived as a procedure composed of two parts. The first sub-procedure identifies a node (or nodes) in the knowledge network on the basis of the constraints provided by the question. For example, the question *Who is sleeping in the living room?* requires the system to identify one or more nodes on the basis of knowledge items such as (a) 'is a person', (b) 'is currently sleeping', (c) 'the sleeping takes place in the living room'. Once the node or nodes have been identified, the second sub-procedure directs the system to construct a linguistic expression for some additional knowledge that is found attached to the node or nodes, e.g. *John*.

From this point of view *why*-questions are not different from other kinds of wh-questions. The question *Why did John go out?* directs the system to identify a node in the network on the basis of the following constraints: (a) the node represents an event or fact causing another event or fact — this derives from the meaning of the word *why*; (b) the second event is that John goes out. Once this particular node has been found, the system selects some knowledge attached to the identified node and expresses this knowledge with the sentence *He wanted to buy a packet of cigarettes*.

This account of how *why*-questions are answered could be extended to cases where the knowledge about the identified node is not directly found attached to the node but must be inferred. In any case, the account might be judged as basically correct.

The problem appears to be more complex if we look at answering *why*-questions from a different perspective. Considered from the point of view of the person who has posed the question, answers to *why*-questions can be understandable or not understandable (we might also say: good or bad, or relevant or not relevant answers), with various degrees of understandability in between. Consider question (1) again:

(1)   Why did John go out?

with the following list of potential answers:

(2)   A. He wanted to buy a packet of cigarettes
       B. He wanted to go to Piazza Venezia
       C. He wanted to rub his nose
       D. He wanted to raise his left arm

For the system that generates any of these answers they may be all correct answers in the sense that each answer is based on the system's knowledge, whatever that knowledge may be. However to me, answer A is a good answer to question (1), but answers B-D are bad answers, with perhaps different degrees of badness among them. Now, if we want to construct a system that is able to generate answers to *why*-question the system must be able to generate not any kind of answers but only good answers, that is, answers that prove to be understandable or relevant for the user.

In order to generate good answers to *why*-questions the system

— must possess a model of the user's knowledge store
— must be able to test a potential answer against the model and on the basis of this test conclude that the answer is a good or a bad one.

In other words, to generate good answers the system must try to understand its own potential answers using the user's knowledge store (or, more correctly, its model of the user's knowledge store). This implies that an important component of a sophisticated sentence generating system is a sentence understanding subsystem. (The role of user modelling in generating appropriate behavior is a widely studied topic in human-computer interaction. McKeown, Wish and Matthews (1985) have investigated how knowledge of the user's goals can help in generating explanations tailored to the user.)

We propose that to decide if a potential answer to a *why*-question is an answer which is understandable to the user the system must check if the answer satisfies three criteria. In order to explain these criteria we will have first to introduce some preliminary notions.

We assume that part of the knowledge contained in the user's knowledge store is practical knowledge, i.e. knowledge about goals that people have and about ways to reach such goals. The basic unit of such a knowledge is a 3-element structure connecting an action (A) node, a goal (G) node, and a condition (C) node.

(3)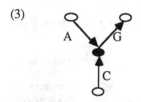

The action node represents an action that must be done to reach the goal represented by the goal node, and the condition node represents a condition that must be satisfied for the action to lead to the goal.

Basic units of practical knowledge are connected together in that an action node can be shared by more than one unit and the same holds for goal nodes and condition nodes. Moreover, the goal node of one unit can simultaneously be the condition node or the action node of another unit yielding complex, plan-like structures.

(4)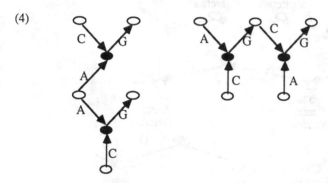

Some goal nodes, however, are not means to further goals, and these we will call 'terminal' goals. For example, the goal of 'having the chicken roasted' has the higher goal of 'eating the chicken'. Hence, 'having the chicken roasted' is a non-terminal goal. Even 'eating the chicken' can be considered as non-terminal since it has the further goal of 'eliminating hunger'. However, 'eliminating hunger' has no further goal and it is a terminal goal.

A terminal goal is a goal which is taken for granted, a goal that one does not usually ask why it is pursued. No one will ask why John is trying to eliminate his hunger. However, even non- terminal goals can be taken for granted, and this happens if they are univocally connected to a specific terminal goal. Thus, no one will ask why John is eating the chicken if this leads univocally to the single terminal goal of eliminating hunger.

Having defined these few notions we will try to apply them to the task of evaluating the goodness of a potential answer to a *why*- question. We assume that when the system generates — on the basis of its own knowledge store — a potential answer to a *why*-question, the question and the answer activate two distinct nodes in the system's model of the user's knowledge store. For example, the pair:

(5) Q: Why did John go out?
A: He wanted to buy a packet of cigarettes

activates the node of 'John's going out' (question node, or Q- node) and the node of 'John's buying a packet of cigarettes' (answer node, or A-node). At this point the system proceeds to applying the following criteria to what has been activated.

I.   Is the Q-node, in my model of the user's knowledge store, linked to the A-node by a sequence of action-goal or condition-goal links?
II.   Is the A-node, in my model of the user's knowledge store, a terminal goal node or, if not, is the A-node univocally linked to a terminal goal node?

By applying these criteria the system is able to give an appropriate goodness rating to the potential answers generated by its own knowledge store.

Let us go back to the various possible answers to question (5) and examine how the answers satisfy these criteria. We will assume that the system's model of the user's knowledge store includes the knowledge items depicted in (6). The filled node represent practical knowledge units. They are linked to action, goal, and condition nodes by A, G, and C links. 'Go out' is an action to the goal of 'be outside'. 'Be outside' is a condition for a number of different goals, among them 'buy cigarettes' and 'go to Piazza Venezia'. 'Buy cigarettes' has the goal of 'have cigarettes', which in turn is a condition for the terminal goal of 'smoke'.

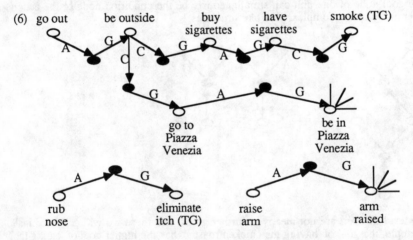

(6)

'Go to Piazza Venezia' is an action to the goal of 'be in Piazza Venezia', which in turn is a condition for a number of different goals. 'Rub nose' is an action to the goal of 'eliminate itch', which is a terminal goal. On the other hand, 'raise arm' has the goal of 'arm raised', which is a condition for a number of different goals.

Given question (1) the Q-node is 'go out'. The A-node in the case of answer A is 'buy cigarettes'. The path linking the two nodes satisfies criterion I. 'Go out' is linked by an action/goal link to 'be outside', and this node is linked by a condition/goal link to 'buy cigarettes'. Furthermore, 'buy cigarettes' even if not a terminal node, is linked univocally to a terminal node: 'smoke'. Hence, if (6) is the user's knowledge store, answer A will be perfectly acceptable to the user.

We now turn to answer B, where the A-node is 'go to Piazza Venezia'. This node is linked to the Q-node by adequate action/- or condition/goal links, hence criterion I is satisfied. However, 'go to Piazza Venezia' is not a terminal node by itself and it is not linked univocally to a terminal node, hence criterion II is not satisfied. Answer B is not a good answer to question (1).

For answer C the A-node is 'rub nose'. This univocally leads to a terminal goal node (criterion II) but it is not appropriately linked to the Q- node (criterion I). Therefore, answer C is not a good answer either. Finally, the A-node of answer D, 'raise arm', violates both criterion I and II, and therefore answer D appears to be the worst answer of all.

Consider now a possible further answer to question (1):

(7)   E. It was very sunny outside

which of course is a good answer to question (1). To deal with this answer we must assume that the knowledge store includes the additional items in (8). In other words, 'be sunny' is a condition that, together with the further condition of 'be outside', leads to reaching the terminal goal of 'get sun'. This example shows that a unit can have multiple conditions associated to it. It also shows that the A node can be a goal node (as it would be if the answer were *To get some sun*) but also a condition for an appropriate (criterion II) goal node.

(8)

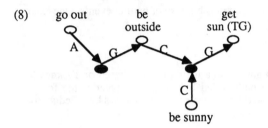

Another possible answer to the question *Why did John go out?* is the following:

(9)   F. He wanted to smoke

This answer satisfies both criterion I and II, given the knowledge store (6). *To smoke* is a terminal goal and it is connected by an appropriate chain of links to the Q-node. However, (9) is not a particularly good answer to question (1) unless one assumes additional knowledge. This indicates that the two criteria so far defined are not sufficient for evaluating all kinds of answers.

Consider that if one must go out in order to smoke there might be at least two different reasons for that: one is that the person has no cigarettes and he must go out in order to buy some, the other is that smoking is prohibited inside and the person must go outside. In other words, the knowledge store (6) includes the additional unit (10).

(10)

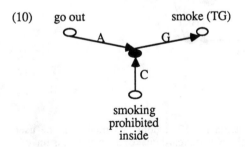

Now it appears that a third criterion for the goodness of an answer to a *why*-question is something like this:

III.   The path linking the A-node to the Q-node in the user's knowledge store must be the same path linking the A-node and the Q-node in the system's knowledge store.

This criterion requires to go back to the process by which an answer to a *why*-question is originally generated by the system using its own knowledge store. In one case the system may know that the cause of John's going out is John's desire to smoke given that he has run out of cigarettes; in another case the system may know that it is John's desire to smoke given that smoking is prohibited inside. The path used to generate the answer *He wanted to smoke* can be the one or the other, according to the knowledge actually present in the system's store. However, assuming that the user's store includes both (6) and (10) there is no guarantee that the user will go through the same path from the Q-node to the A-node as the actual path followed in that particular occasion by the system — and this violates criterion III.

3. EXPLAINING EVENTS

Why-questions can be asked not only of human actions but also of natural events. One example is the following:

(11) Why did the house fall down?

In this case too a system that generates an answer to a *why*- question based on its knowledge store must check that the answer can be understood by the user. Consider the following alternative answers to question (11) based on different states of the system's knowledge store:

(12) A. There was an earthquake
      B. Someone in the house wanted to cook
      C. Someone in the house laughed

While answer A is perfectly understandable, answers B and C are not. (B) can be understood but only with a lot of thinking and cleverness; (C) cannot be understood at all.
   Knowledge about causal relations between events can be represented as units constituted by a causal node linking two event nodes. We can therefore represent the user's knowledge store as follows, with the filled nodes representing causal relationships:

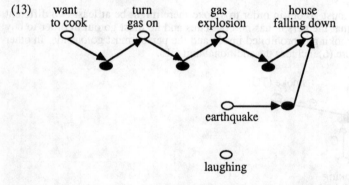

If the system checks the three potential answers in (12) against its model of the user's knowledge store, i.e. (13), it will discover that the A-node (earthquake) in answer A is linked to the Q-node by a single causal link. This provides a perfectly understandable answer. On the other hand, the A-node in answer B (wanting to cook) is linked by a whole sequence of causal links to the Q-node. In this case the answer will be understood by the user but with some effort. Finally, the A-node in answer C (laughing) is not linked by causal links to the Q-node, and in this case the answer cannot be understood at all.

This suggests a first criterion for the goodness of answers to *why*-questions about natural events. (In analyzing what makes explanations of natural events understandable we have relied on Castelfranchi, Devescovi & Burani, 1982.)

I.   The A-node must be linked by causal links to the Q-node, and the answer will be better the smaller number of causal links.

This principle explains why *Someone in the house turned the gas on* (two causal links) would be a better answer than *Someone in the house wanted to cook* (three causal links) and why *There was a gas explosion* (one causal link) would be an even better answer.

Consider now a second set of answers to a *why*-question about a natural event:

(14)   Q: Why did John die?
        A: A. He ate poisonous mushrooms
           B. He ate toxic food
           C. He ate toxic tomatoes
           D. He ate mushrooms
           E. He ate tomatoes

Answers A, B, and C appear to be perfect answers. The fourth answer, *He ate mushrooms*, is less understandable. The fifth, *He ate tomatoes*, requires substantial thinking to be understood. We can assume (15) to be the system's model of the user's knowledge store (square nodes indicate class/subclass relations with arrows going from subclass to class.)

(15)

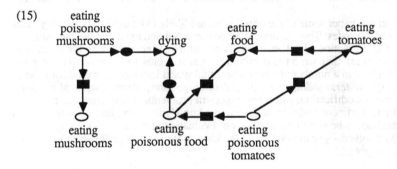

On the basis of (15) the user knows that dying can be directly caused by eating poisonous mushrooms or by eating poisonous food. However, (15) also includes knowledge about class/subclass relations (indicated by square nodes). The user knows that eating poisonous mushrooms is a subclass of eating mushrooms, that eating poisonous tomatoes is a subclass of eating toxic food, that eating toxic food is a subclass of eating food, and finally that eating tomatoes is a subclass of eating food.

Given (15) and the goodness ratings of the various possible answers to question (14), we can identify some additional criteria for the goodness of answers to *why*-questions. Such answers are perfectly good if

II.   The A-node is linked by one or more subclass/class links and then by a causal link to the Q-node

The previously defined Criterion I applies to answers A and B in (14). Criterion II applies to answer C — all perfectly good answers. On the other hand, answers are less good if

III.   The A-node is linked by one or more class/subclass links and then by a causal link to the Q-node.

This applies to answer D, *He ate mushrooms*, that we saw is less good than the first three answers. And finally, a even less good answer — but still understandable with some effort — results if

IV.   The A-node is linked by alternating subclass/class links and class/subclass links, and then a causal link, to the Q-node.

This is the case for the last answer in (14), *He ate tomatoes*, which is the worst answer in the whole set.

4. CONCLUSION

Answers to *why*-questions must be good answers, that is answers which are not only true answers in terms of what the answer generating system knows but also answers that can be understood by the user who has posed the question. In order to check if a potential answer to a *why*-question is a good answer, the system must consult its model of the user's knowledge store on the basis of the following procedure:

Step 1   The question and the answer activate their corresponding nodes in such a model, respectively, the Q-node and the A-node

Step 2   The shortest path connecting the Q-node and the A-node in the network is identified.

Step 3   The identified path is examined in terms of a number of well defined criteria and the answer is judged 'good' if these criteria are satisfied and 'bad' if they are not satisfied.

We have indicated in this paper some of the criteria that are likely to be used in evaluating paths between Q-nodes and A- nodes. These criteria may be corrected and extended but they seem to be pointing in the right direction. Another interesting feature of the procedure for generating good explanatory answers that we have outlined is that it seems to be basically the same procedure that is involved in a number of cases where real world knowledge is used for solving problems of language *understanding*. Semantic disambiguation, identification of pronoun antecedents, noun noun modification, and other important problems of language understanding all appear to require that pairs of nodes be activated in a knowledge store, that the shortest path between the activated nodes be identified, and various evaluation operations — varying with the type of problem to be solved — be conducted on the knowledge located on this path (see Parisi and Castelfranchi, to appear).

ACKNOWLEDGEMENT

We thank Cristiano Castelfranchi and Gianni Romano for useful discussions on the topics of this paper. This research is supported by 'Strategic Project: Expert Systems' of the Italian National Research Council.

REFERENCES

Castelfranchi, C., Devescovi, A. & Burani, C. (1982) *Understanding causal relations*. Paper presented at the Conference on Language, Reasoning, and Inference, Edinburgh.

McKeown, K.R., Wish, M. & Matthews, K. (1985) Tailoring explanations for the user. *IJCAI-85*, 794-798.

Parisi, D. & Castelfranchi C. Disambiguation in a lexically based sentence understanding system. In: S.L.Small, G.W.Cottrell & M.K.Tanenhaus (Eds.) *Lexical ambiguity resolution in the comprehension of human language*.

Wilks, Y. (1977) What sort of taxonomy of causation do we need for language understanding? *Cognitive Science, 1*, 235-264.

Chapter 5

TOWARD A PLAN-BASED THEORY OF REFERRING ACTIONS

Douglas E. Appelt

TABLE OF CONTENTS

1. What is referring?
2. Fundamentals of the model
2.1 A formal language
2.2 Sincerity, helpfulness, and competence
2.3 Mental representation of objects
2.4 Identification constraints
3. The referring schema
4. Implications for language generation
5. Summary and conclusion

Much recent work in the field of natural-language generation has been performed within the paradigm of viewing language as action that is planned with the intention of achieving the speaker's goals (Appelt, 1985; Cohen & Perrault, 1979). According to this view, language generation is a planning problem, in which various aspects of the utterance are planned because the generator reasons that they will have the intended effect on the hearer's mental state.

One of the reasons for the success of this approach is that the speech-act characterization of sentential utterances is relatively straightforward. Cohen & Levesque (1985) illustrate how it is possible to develop a theory of the effect of utterances given the propositional content of the utterance and its mood. Although there are a number of representational and semantic difficulties to be overcome, the problem is straightforward because our intuitions are fairly clear about what the effects of sentential utterances should be. For example, if a speaker utters a declarative sentence with propositional content P, it is clear that, barring exceptions, he intends that the hearer believe P. This is not to say that declarative utterances are always intended literally, but that there is an analysis that accounts for the 'normal' use, and a systematic account of exceptions can be provided that applies when certain preconditions of the 'normal' use are mutually believed by the speaker and the hearer to have been violated.

Our intuitions suggest that the propositional act of referring should also be accounted for by such an analysis. Referring is an action about which one can say that a speaker succeeds or fails. But precisely what is it that a speaker succeeds or fails at? It is the answer to this question toward which this chapter is directed.

1. WHAT IS REFERRING?

Before we can present a theory of referring, we must first specify what referring is. This question has occupied several generations of philosophers of language, and it is unlikely that anything close to a consensus will emerge in the forseeable future. For example, Donnellan (1966) has argued that using definite descriptions attributively does not constitute referring at all, since in such cases the speaker 'does not have any particular object in mind'. For Searle (1979), in contrast, there is no significant difference between referential and attributive uses, as

far as referring is concerned. Because it is impractical to wait for a consensus on this issue, we
select a philosophical position that appears promising as a foundation for a computational
model. No harm is done as long as we have clearly stated our philosophical prejudices.
We therefore define referring from an intuitive standpoint as follows:

> *Definition.* An agent is referring when he has a mental representation of what he
> believes to be a particular object, and he intends the hearer to come to have a mental
> representation of the same object, at least in part through the use of a noun phrase
> that is intended to be a linguistic representation of that object.

Note that, according to this definition, specific indefinite noun phrases function as referring
expressions. Also, some definite noun phrases are not referring expressions: for example,
superlatives that occur within the scope of a modal operator (e.g. *John wants to drive the fastest
car in town*). The reader should also bear in mind that having a mental representation of an
object has few epistemological consequences. A hearer can have a mental representation of 'the
thing the speaker is talking about' without knowing what that object is, or without being able to
pick it out.

I will also briefly mention a distinction that can be the cause of much confusion if it is not
noted. In generating and interpreting noun phrases, it is desirable to distinguish between
internal and *external* perspectives with respect to the discourse. According to the internal
perspective, theorists seek to provide constraints on relations among noun phrases, and they
need not concern themselves with the question of what objects (if any) correspond to those
noun phrases. Examples of internal-perspective theories include Discourse Representation
Theory (Kamp, 1984) and Webber's (1983) theory of discourse models. Using Webber's
terminology, noun phrases *evoke* discourse entities and subsequently *access* them. Webber was
trying to account for how anaphoric noun phrases are linked in a discourse. Therefore the
central problems that she addressed are how discourse entities are evoked and accessed; the
question of how the hearer interprets the relationship between an evoked discourse entity and
some individual in the world is left as an open problem. The theory says nothing about the
differences in processing of two sentences such as *'The woman over there* has five children'
and *'The average woman* has 1.8 children'. Both noun phrases introduce discourse entities that
can be accessed anaphorically by other expressions, although only in the former case is the
hearer expected to identify some individual the speaker has in mind, and hence it is the only one
that fits the definition of referring given above.

The internal perspective is essential to understanding the syntax and semantics of natural
language. However, once we consider language as a means by which rational agents can
achieve goals, the external perspective becomes indispensable. After all, it makes a great deal of
difference to an agent attempting to achieve some goal that the hearer understands that he (the
speaker) has a particular object in mind, and furthermore that the hearer is then able to identify
it. Any system that combines linguistic and nonlinguistic actions, and that is capable of
cooperative behavior, must be able to talk about objects. It must understand when a noun
phrase has a referent in the real world and when it does not, when knowledge of the referent is
required and when it is not, when knowledge of the referent is presupposed and when it should
be actively sought.

2. FUNDAMENTALS OF THE MODEL

A precise description of referring requires a model of how individual entities are represented to
agents, and a formal language in which to state the beliefs and goals of agents and how they are
affected by various actions. We adopt a dynamic modal logic whose semantics is very similar to
Cohen & Levesque's (1985) formal system. We provide here a gloss of the various modal
operators, predicates, and functions relevant to the theory of referring, and direct the reader
desiring more information on the logic and its semantics to Cohen & Levesque's article.

2.1 A formal language

Modal operators:
— **Bel**(A, P): agent A believes that P.
— **MB**(A, B, P): A and B mutually believe P.
— **Goal**(A, P): agent A has goal P.
— **After**(E, P): after the occurrence of event E, P is true.

Predicates:
— Done(E): Event E has *just* occurred.
— Holds(d, x): d is a predicate of one argument, which is true of the individual x.

Terms and functions:
— Do(A, E): the event of A's performing an action of type E.
— $e_1; e_2$: the event e_1, followed immediately by the event e_2.
— p?: an event that terminates if and only if p is true (e.g., Done(p?; Do(*Agent, Act*)) means that p was true immediately prior to *Agent's* doing *Act*).
— t_u: A shorthand notation for the time at which the utterance u occurred. It is assumed that every situation has a discrete 'time stamp'.
— cont(np): the descriptive content of np (a noun phrase).

2.2 Sincerity, helpfulness, and competence

Both this theory of referring and Cohen & Levesque's theory of speech acts rests on a common core of definitions and axioms. Frequently, it is necessary to refer to properties of sincerity, helpfulness, and competence on the part of the speaker and hearer. These concepts are given a precise meaning in terms of the formal theory as follows.

Sincerity: A is sincere to B with respect to P if whenever A has the goal of B believing P, he believes P himself. That is:

1 sincere $(A, B, P) \overset{def}{=} (\text{Goal}(A, \text{Bel}(B, P))) \supset \text{Bel}(A, P))$.

Helpfulness: A is helpful to B with respect to P if whenever A believes B's goal is to get A to bring about P, A adopts the goal P:

2 helpful $(A, B, P) \overset{def}{=} (\text{Bel}(A, \text{Goal}(B, \text{Goal}(A, P)) \supset \text{Goal}(A, P))$.

Competence: A is competent with respect to P if, whenever A believes P, P is actually true:

3 competent $(A, P) \overset{def}{=} (\text{Bel}(A, P) \supset P)$.

2.3 Mental representation of objects

An *individuating set* is the formal entity corresponding to the intuitive notion of an agent's mental representation of an object. Individuating sets are composed of intensional objects called *intensional object representations (IORs)*. A relationship of denotation can hold between each IOR and some individual in the world. An individuating set for an agent A is a maximal set of IORs, all believed by A to denote the same object. The set is *maximal* in the sense that if any two IORs are believed to be denoting the same object, they must belong to the same individuating set. The function IS(z) maps an IOR z into its associated individuating set. The

IORs themselves are either *perceptual IORs, discourse IORs,* or *functional IORs.* Perceptual IORs are mental representations of objects that result from perceptual acts, and denote the object perceived. The function $\Pi(a, t, i)$ maps an agent a, an instance of time t, and an individual i onto a perceptual IOR. A discourse IOR is an IOR resulting from an agent a using a noun phrase with a descriptive content cont(np) at time t ($\Delta(a, t, \text{cont}(np))$) and denotes the individual to which the speaker intends to refer, if such an individual exists. Functional IORs are the values of functions whose arguments are also IORs. For example, a function *father-of* may map IORs denoting persons into IORs denoting their fathers.

An individuating set is the result of an agent's beliefs, not a mirror of what is actually the case. It is certainly possible to have an individuating set of IORs that do not denote anything real (e.g. a child's representation of Santa Claus). Moreover, an agent may possess two distinct individuating sets for the same object (e.g., Oedipus's representation of his mother and his wife), or he may possess a single individuating set that, as a matter of fact, contains two IORs denoting different objects. If all is well, and there actually is an object corresponding to all the IORs in the set, we say that the *referent* of the set is that object. In the formalism adopted here, the function Ref(i) maps an individuating set i onto its referent if it exists. That is:

$$\text{Ref}(i) = \begin{cases} x & \text{if } \forall z \; z \in i \supset \text{denote}\,(z, x) \\ undefined & \text{otherwise.} \end{cases}$$

For the sake of notational clarity, 'RefIS(x)' is often used to represent 'Ref(IS(x))'.

The goal of a speaker's referring act is that the hearer have an individuating set whose referent is the same as the referent of a certain individuating set of the speaker's. The individuating set makes it possible to state what one agent wants another to believe without stating the goal in terms of some common vocabulary of standard names. However, individuating sets are motivated independently by a number of considerations. First, the concept of individuating sets provides a solution to several problems that are raised by the referential/attributive distinction (Kronfeld, 1981, 1985). Second, psychological experiments (Anderson, 1978; Ortony & Anderson, 1977) suggest that there are in fact structures in memory that encode the information contained in individuating sets.

2.4 Identification constraints

Although one may say that an agent who has complied with the definition of referring given above has referred to something, that does not mean that his communicative goals are satisfied. Every speech act entails a literal goal and conditions of satisfaction. For example, if a speaker requests that a hearer close the door, his literal goal is satisfied if the hearer understands that the speaker wants him to close a particular door. The relevant condition of satisfaction of this request is that the door actually be closed, and the hearer must decide whether to comply with the request. The definition represents the *literal goal* of a referring act, but says nothing about its conditions of satisfaction.

The condition of satisfaction of a referring act is that the hearer *identify* the referent of the speaker's referring expression in some manner that is appropriate to the current situation. Identification in the context of referring is a *pragmatic* notion, not an epistemological one. Referent identification in conversation does *not* necessarily mean knowing who (or what) the referent is. In general, the requirements for referent identification can be characterized in terms of *constraints that apply to the relevant individuating set*. These constraints are called *identification constraints*.

Because these constraints depend on details of the situation and the particular communicative act being performed, it is impossible to give a general characterization. However, identification constraints are generally *inferred*, not explicitly communicated. For example, if a speaker says 'Replace the small round yellow piece of rubber', it is impossible for the hearer to comply with the request unless he can perceive the object that the speaker wants replaced. Therefore, successful identification entails perceiving the referent, and this condition can be expressed as a constraint on the relevant individuating set, namely, that it contain a perceptual IOR. In other situations identification may only require making an anaphoric connection. In the case of an utterance like 'I met *an old friend* yesterday', there may be no applicable identification constraints at all. The relevant individuating set contains a single discourse IOR meaning something like 'whichever person the speaker meant by saying "an old friend"', which is sufficient for pragmatic identification.

Note that there are at least two ways in which the hearer can fail to recognize the hearer's intentions with respect to a referring act: He may fail to apply the right identification constraints, or having recognized an identification constraint, he may be unable to satisfy it.

3. THE REFERRING SCHEMA

The following schema is the cornerstone of the above-stated theory of referring. This schema states what is true of the hearer's beliefs about the speaker's and hearer's beliefs as a result of using *np* as a referring expression.

4   Referring Schema:

MB(S, H, sentence (U) $\wedge$ constituent-of(NP, U) $\wedge$ potential-refexp(NP)) $\supset$
After(Do(S, Utter(S,U)),
        Bel(H, **MB**(S, H,
            Goal(S, **Bel**(H,
                $\exists z$ RefIS(Δ (S, t_u, cont(NP)))) = $z \wedge$
                Goal(S, **Bel**(H, Holds(cont(NP), RefIS(Δ(S, t_u, cont(NP)))))))))))).

The referring schema states that if the speaker and hearer mutually believe that U is a sentential utterance and NP is both a constituent of U and a potential referring expression,[1] then the speaker has the goal that the hearer believe two things: first, that the speaker has an individuating set representing the individual corresponding to his utterance of NP, and second, that the speaker wants the hearer to believe that the descriptive content of NP is true of the individual represented by his individuating set.

Moreover, if indeed it is mutually believed that the speaker has a particular object in mind when he uses the noun phrase, it should also be mutually believed that the speaker intends the hearer to have a representation of that object. But in a typical Gricean fashion, once the hearer recognizes this intention, he *does* have such a representation, namely 'whatever object the speaker is talking about'. The following *activation axiom* captures this fact:

5   Activation Axiom:

MB(S, H, $\exists x$ RefIS(Δ(S, t_u, cont(np)))) = x) $\supset$
        MB(S, H, RefIS(Δ(S, t_u, cont(np)))) = RefIS(Δ(H, t_u, cont(np))))).

Note that, if the consequent of (5) is satisfied, the speaker has succeeded in inducing in the hearer a mental representation of the object he (the speaker) has in mind, at least in part through the use of a noun phrase that is intended to be a linguistic representation of the same object. This is the intuitive definition of the literal goal of referring given earlier. In the terms of the formalism, the definition can be stated as follows:

---

[1]   It is presupposed that there is a theory that identifies a noun phrase as a potential referring expression based strictly on its syntactic and semantic properties. For example, a referring noun phrase cannot be an indefinite complement of a copula, and it cannot be within the scope of a modal operator.

6   $\mathbf{MB}(S, H, \exists x \, [\text{RefIS} \, (\Delta \, (S, \, t_u, \, \text{cont(np)})) = x \wedge \text{Ref IS} \, (\Delta \, (H, \, t_u, \, \text{cont(np)})) = x].$

The goal of making (6) true is the *literal goal* of a referring act. For any referring action, (6) follows from (4) and (5) *provided* that the hearer believes that it is mutually believed that the speaker is sincere and competent with respect to the proposition that there is an individual represented by his individuating set.

Of course, satisfaction of this literal goal is only the first step. Now the hearer is expected to find out what identification constraints apply and whether the newly created individuating set representing the referent satisfies those constraints. The second conjunct of the referring schema is directed toward this end. Note that if one ignores the first conjunct of the referring schema, the effect of a referring action is expressed as follows:

7   $\mathbf{Bel}(H, \mathbf{MB}(S, H,$
          $\mathbf{Goal}(S, \mathbf{Bel}(H,$
                    $\mathbf{Goal}(S, \mathbf{Bel}(H, \text{Holds(cont(NP)}, \text{RefIS}(\Delta(S, \, t_u, \, \text{cont (NP)})))))))))$.

This means that the hearer believes that it is mutually believed that the speaker wants him to believe that the speaker wants him to believe that the description used in the referring expression holds of the referent of the speaker's individuating set. But, because this is the configuration of goals about beliefs that characterizes an informing action (Cohen & Perrault, 1979), it is proper to say that the speaker *informs* the hearer that the description is true of the thing he is talking about.

If this informing action is successful, then the hearer should have the knowledge he needs to satisfy the identification constraints. Just as in the case of the utterance of a declarative sentence, the informing act will be successful only if the conditions of the speaker's sincerity and competence are mutually believed with respect to the description. If the hearer does not believe the speaker is competent with respect to the referring description (perhaps he believes that nothing satisfies the description), the identification constraints can still be satisfied. Goodman (1983) discusses the details of a process by which identification can proceed in such circumstances. The important feature of this analysis is that sincerity and competence conditions apply separately to the existence of a referent and the description used to refer to it. It is possible for the hearer to believe the former, and even satisfy the relevant identification constraints, without believing the latter.

4. IMPLICATIONS FOR LANGUAGE GENERATION

If an utterance planning system is to plan referring expressions, it must employ a theory of what referring is, and how it achieves the effects it is supposed to have. Although knowing the Referring Schema and Activation Axiom does not provide everything necessary to design a planner that produces referring expressions that satisfy multiple goals, it provides some important principles to guide such a design. For example, it makes some specific predictions about why an utterance may fail to achieve certain effects: sincerity and competence conditions may not be satisfied, either with respect to existence of the referent or to a potential description of the referent, or the speaker may not be able to reason that the hearer can formulate an appropriate plan to satisfy relevant identification constraints given a potential referring description.

This analysis provides a justification for the action subsumption strategy followed by KAMP (Appelt, 1985). Referring actions can subsume informing actions because they are, in an important sense, informing actions. A referring description can subsume an informing action if it is possible for the hearer to satisfy the applicable identification constraints without knowing the description. KAMP used a single identification constraint applicable to every situation: a hearer can identify the referent if he knows a standard name for the individual the speaker is referring to. Because analysis of identification constraints increases the range of situations to which the analysis of referring applies, it is possible to apply action subsumption strategies in situations in which such strict referent identification is not required. For example, a specific individual may be introduced by an indefinite description, and informing acts that provide additional information about the individual may be subsumed by the description. Consider 'I met someone yesterday. He was an old friend from high school', and 'I met an old friend from high school yesterday'. The description can freely subsume informing actions in this situation because there are no identification constraints that need to be satisfied.

5. SUMMARY AND CONCLUSION

This chapter has presented a formal model of referring. It has been shown that referring, like other speech acts, has a *literal goal* and *criteria for success*. Satisfaction of the literal goal establishes mutual belief concerning the speaker's intention to refer to a particular object. The referring act succeeds when the object is identified correctly according to context specific criteria.

An important feature of this analysis is that most parts of it are independently motivated. The theory of speech acts and rationality was developed by Cohen & Levesque for reasons other than accounting for referring actions; individuating sets are motivated independently of this analysis, and the referring schema can be justified independently of its role in showing how referring expressions are used for informing. This analysis lays a necessary foundation for progress in language generation research based on planning.

ACKNOWLEDGMENTS

The research reported in this chapter was supported by the National Science Foundation under grant DCR--8407238. This research was conducted by the author in cooperation with Amichai Kronfeld, who is responsible for many of the good ideas reported herein but none of the errors. The author is grateful to Harry Bunt for providing many helpful comments on the preliminary version of this paper.

REFERENCES

Anderson, J.R. (1978) The processing of referring expressions within a semantic network. In: *Proceedings of TINLAP-2*.

Appelt, D.E. (1985) *Planning English Sentences*. Cambridge: Cambridge University Press.

Appelt, D.E. (1985) Some pragmatic issues in the planning of definite and indefinite noun phrase. In: *Proceedings of the 23rd Annual Meeting of the Association for Computational Linguistics*.

Cohen, P.R. & Levesque, H. (1985) Speech acts and rationality. In: *Proceedings of the 23rd Annual Meeting of the Association for Computational Linguistics*.

Cohen, P.R. & Perrault, C.R. (1979) Elements of a plan-based theory of speech acts. *Cognitive Science, 3*, 117-212.

Donnellan, K.S. (1966) Reference and definite description. *Philosophical Review, 75*, 281-304.

Goodman, B. (1983) Repairing miscommunication: relaxation in reference. In: *Proceedings of the National Conference on Artificial Intelligence of the American Association for Artificial Intelligence*.

Kamp, H. (1984) A theory of truth and semantic representation. In: Groenendijk, et al., (Eds.) *Truth, Interpretation, and Information*. Dordrecht: Foris.

Kronfeld, A. (1985) *Reference and Denotation: The Descriptive Model*. Technical Note 368, SRI International Artificial Intelligence Center.

Kronfeld, A. (1981) *The Referential-Attributive Distinction and the Conceptual-Descriptive Theory of Reference*. PhD thesis, University of California, Berkeley.

Ortony, A. & Anderson, R. (1977) Definite descriptions and semantic memory. *Cognitive Science, 1*, 74-83.

Searle, J. (1979) Referential and attributive. In: *Expression and Meaning: Studies in the Theory of Speech Acts*. Cambridge: Cambridge University Press.

Webber, B.L. (1983) So what can we talk about now? In: M. Brady & R. Berwick (Eds.) *Computational Models of Discourse*, Cambridge, Mass.: MIT Press.

Chapter 6

GENERATING REFERRING EXPRESSIONS AND POINTING GESTURES

Norbert Reithinger

ABSTRACT

Among other things, a natural language generator which is embedded in a dialog system should take the user's input into account. In this way, the output generated will be better adapted to the user's needs. Consequently, the generator and the other components of the system should share knowledge bases whenever possible. In this chapter, preliminary considerations pertaining to the generation component of XTRA — a natural language access system to expert systems — are presented. The generator is fully integrated into the system and shares its knowledge bases. The advantage of this structure is demonstrated for the generation of certain referring expressions. Apart from linguistic reference — e.g. pro-words — extralinguistic pointing gestures can be employed both by the user and the XTRA system as well. Finally, the integration of pointing gestures in the generation component is discussed.

1. INTRODUCTION

If the environment in which a natural language (NL) generator is to be embedded consists mainly of communication between a computer system and a human user, a stand-alone generator will not produce communicatively adequate output. In communicative situations, for instance, the output of the generation system should take into account discourse entities introduced by the dialog partner (Karlin, 1985), even if the input was not NL (e.g., in an expert system with a menu-based interface).

This is even more true in an environment where the input of the computer system is also NL. Here, the generator should refer to the words and phrases the dialog partner has used. Therefore, the generator must have access to the system's knowledge bases, especially to those which contain knowledge about the context. Consequently, the generator and the embedding system should use the same knowledge bases whenever possible, e.g. lexicon and context memories. Otherwise, communication will require more or less complicated interfaces between the knowledge bases of the generator and those of the other components of the system.

In this article, we present preliminary considerations dealing with the generation component of the system XTRA (eXpert TRAnslator). The goal of the project XTRA is to develop an NL access system for expert systems that facilitates the user's interaction with the expert system. The communication between the user and the system is not limited to natural language. The system also presents on the screen graphic objects which relate to the domain of the expert system to which XTRA provides natural language access. These graphic objects can be forms or blueprints, for example. In this kind of communicative situation, real-life consultations where dialog partners are able (and inclined) to point at a sheet or copy are simulated (cf. Schmauks, 1986a). In the dialog with XTRA, either dialog partner can use pointing gestures to refer to entities on the screen. This is simulated by means of the mouse as a pointing device. Conversely, the generator also should be able to point at the screen by means of a mouse-cursor if that type of response is likely to be understood better by the user of the system. The domain of the expert system currently connected to XTRA consists of an assistance system which helps to fill out an 'annual withholding tax adjustment form', which is visible on the screen.

As stated above, one goal of the system's structure is the common use of the knowledge bases by all system components. For example, only one lexicon containing morphological, syntactic and semantic information should exist within the system. Both the analysis components and the generator should use this lexicon. Also, knowledge that is built up dynamically (such as contextual knowledge) should have the same structure, regardless of whether it was built up in the analysis or in the generation process.

In the following section we will briefly describe certain knowledge bases of the system. The way the knowledge bases — and especially contextual information — are used for the generation of pro-words and pointing gestures is presented in the third section.

2. KNOWLEDGE BASES IN XTRA

2.1 Declarative knowledge bases

As stated above, the knowledge bases presented are also used by the other components of the system. A description of their use in the analysis of the input is given in (Kobsa et al., 1986). The declarative knowledge bases of the system are the lexicon, the functional semantic structure (FSS), the conceptual knowledge base and the form hierarchy. The lexicon will not be discussed here. The FSS and the conceptual knowledge base will be implemented in a KL-ONE-like network representation formalism (Brachman & Schmolze, 1986).

Example structures[1] of the FSS, the conceptual knowledge base and the dialog sequence memory (DSM, see section 2.2) for the short dialog

> (1) U: Ich arbeite in Völklingen.
>   I work in Völklingen.
> (2) S: Fahren Sie dorthin mit dem Auto?
>   Do you drive there by car?

are shown in Figure 1. The conceptual layer of the FSS is omitted and only the individualized FSSs for the sentences are presented. The links in the graphical presentation of the referential objects (see section 2.2) to the FSS and the individualized part of the conceptual knowledge base have been replaced by the names of the corresponding nodes.

The FSS describes formal semantic relationships between propositions, phrases, and words in the input string. Concepts of the FSS are semantic categories for words and phrases, which can be annotated with, e.g., certain syntactic features such as number or gender, or the corresponding word stems. Concepts are linked to the functional roles which exist between two concepts, e.g. semantic deep cases. For example, the concept of the individualization PERSON-ACTIVITY-1 contains the structural description of words which describe the activity of a person. A necessary semantic case is AGENT. In the example, the role for LOCATION is inherited from the root node — called *FSS* — which is linked to the roles for free attributes.

With an FSS description we do not resolve references to objects of the 'real world'. Instead, this is carried out by the referential-semantic interpretation. It determines which individualizations of the conceptual knowledge base are denoted by the FSS of a sentence, or it creates new individualizations if descriptions of new objects or events were in the FSS.

---

[1] The examples present a provisional state of affairs.

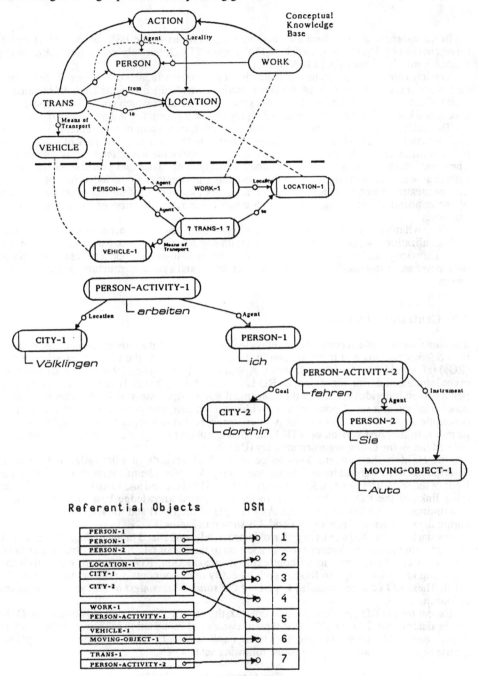

Figure 1. Conceptual knowledge base (top), FSS (center) and DSM (bottom) of sentences 1 and 2

In the example above, there are two individualizations in the FSS for the object which represent the city Völklingen, namely, CITY-1 and CITY-2, but only one individualization in the conceptual level, namely, LOCATION-1.

The form hierarchy represents the hierarchical geometric structure of the form. In the graph, each node represents a region of the form. Nodes of embedded regions are subordinated to nodes of the region that contains them. Also presented are links which connect concepts of the conceptual knowledge base to corresponding regions of the form (cf. Allgayer, 1986).

The analysis of a user's input is a two-step process, consisting of intrasentential semantic analysis and referential-semantic interpretation. In the first step, an FSS of the input is individualized, and in the second step, the conceptual representation of the input is determined. Then, the inference processes of the conceptual knowledge base and probably of the expert system as well start working. During this procedure, new entries to the individualized section may be created, resulting in, for example, a marking of those parts of the individualized section of the conceptual knowledge base which contain the representation of the content of the response.

The 'what-to-say' component of the generator uses the parts marked to select individualizations which must be verbalized with regard to the contextual conditions, e.g. the user's knowledge and the phrases already used. The 'how-to-say' component creates an FSS of the answer as an intermediate structure, selects words and syntactic structure, and inflects the words.

2.2 Contextual knowledge

The data structure which connects the individualized section of the conceptual knowledge base, the FSS-descriptions and their position in the current dialog, is the set of referential objects (ROs) (cf. von Hahn, Hoeppner, Jameson & Wahlster, 1980; Habel, 1984). For each object or event introduced during the dialog, an RO is created. An RO basically consists of two parts: a pointer to an individualization in the conceptual knowledge base which describes this object conceptually and a set of pointer pairs. Within such a pair, one pointer is directed to an FSS description of the RO. The second pointer connects this description to the dialog context memory. In this first version of XTRA, the dialog context memory consists of a sequentially ordered list — the dialog sequence memory (DSM).

The DSM is the dynamic knowledge base which records in what order and by what descriptions RO's were addressed during the dialog. After the identification of an object in the input or the verbalization of an RO, an entry in the DSM is created and linked to the RO. Via the other links of the RO, its description in the conceptual knowledge base and its semantic descriptions in the FSS can be found. An example of the DSM and the ROs that are built up during the processing of sentences 1 and 2 is shown in Figure 1.

As stated above, RO's exist only for objects already verbalized in the dialog. But in XTRA another communication channel exists in addition to the use of NL. Since the objects shown on the screen can be referred to without explicit introduction, RO's for them exist from the beginning of each dialog. An RO for such an entity does not contain pointers to FSS's or the DSM. These RO's can be classified as parts of the *situational context* of the system (Rochester & Martin, 1977).

Except for the RO's in the situational context, the set of FSS's and their position in the DSM can be determined for each RO. This type of contextual information is known as the *explicit verbal context*. Not covered by the RO's is the *implicit verbal context*. A common example for the use of implicit context is given by the following sentences:

Joan left her house. *The* door slammed behind her.

The noun phrase *the door* is used here with a definite article, thus indicating that the object referred to was already introduced. In order to find the referent, one cannot simply search through the RO's, but has to look at the implicit context of the previous phrases. In our example the listener has to infer from the house which is explicitly mentioned to a part of it, namely, the door. In order to create noun phrases with correct determiners (Grosz, 1977), a natural language system has to anticipate that such inferences may be drawn by the user.

3. GENERATING REFERRING EXPRESSIONS

3.1 Types of referential expressions

In this section we will show how the DSM of XTRA will be used to generate certain classes of referring expressions. First of all, the conditions will be considered under which a generator can use referential expressions. The reference can be directed backward to objects already mentioned, or it can be directed forward to objects that will be introduced later on in the discourse. We limit ourselves to *backward*, or *anaphoric references*. *Forward*, or *cataphoric references* present problems that differ from those dealt with here.

The simplest form of backward reference to an RO is to repeat the phrase most recently used to refer to this RO. If a generator operates in this manner, the output is awkward and violates many conversational maxims. In natural languages many different degrees of reference can be verbalized and, depending on the actual situation, descriptions can be condensed. For example, consider the use of pronouns vs. the use of complex noun phrases.

To avoid communicative inadequacies, the generator needs criteria for the decision procedure that creates references. One criterion is the 'distance' of the backward reference. If a reference refers to objects in the previous sentence, different words will be used compared with a reference to facts or events verbalized in an earlier dialog step. Also, the focus of attention plays an important role. References to objects in the focus of the hearer's attention must be treated differently than those which refer to objects outside of the focus. One therefore needs a model of the user and focus of attention (Sidner, 1983) or a context model (Reichman, 1985).

Because, so far, there is no user modeling or focusing algorithm in XTRA, the generator is limited to the DSM as the sole contextual knowledge base. The DSM mainly contains information about the verbalization sequence of objects and events. But even with the DSM, some interesting applications of contextual knowledge can be shown.

According to their surface structure, expressions which refer to objects and events which have already been introduced can be roughly divided into two groups:

— reference with pro-words and
— reference with definite noun phrases (NP's)[2]

As a supplement to linguistic reference, XTRA offers the possibility of referring to objects by means of pointing gestures. Some considerations about the generation of pro-words and pointing gestures in XTRA are presented in the following two sections.

3.2 Referring by use of pro-words

Pro-words are restricted in their referential power. Only pronouns in the first and second person have fixed referents in two-person dialogs. The other pro-words can only be used to refer to objects or events which were used in the current local context. In all other cases, one has to use definite noun phrases. In the first version of the generator, the local context will be limited to the current and the previous sentence. As the development of XTRA progresses, it we intend to replace this simple model with a context-space model, similiar to that of Reichman (Reichman, 1985). Until then, we believe that the limited model will generate acceptable linguistic output.

The considerations presented here are restricted to cases in which pro-words are not obligatory for syntactic reasons. The basic algorithm is an adaptation of Wong's (1975) pronominalization algorithm to the knowledge bases of XTRA. A rough sketch of its basis

---

2   Prepositional phrases (PP's) are treated here in the same way.

ideas will be given with reference to the conditions for the generation of the pro-adverb *dahin* (*there*) in the example dialog of sentences 1 and 2 (see Figure 1 for the knowledge bases).

During the analysis of the input, the individualizations WORK-1, PERSON-1 and LOCATION-1 are created. The individualization ?TRANS-1? in the conceptual knowledge base is created by the inference engine of the system. It indicates that the system needs this information in order to solve its task. The question marks indicate that a question is to be generated as the surface speech act. The answer's FSS is PERSON-ACTIVITY-2.

The surface realization of the individualization CITY-2 without the use of a dialog memory depends on the role it is linked to. In the example it is a GOAL role. The corresponding syntactic structure is a PP. It can be replaced by an adverbial phrase consisting of the pro-adverb *dorthin* because the RO which is verbalized by this phrase arose last in element 2 of the DSM and no phrase which belongs to the FSS class CITY arose between them in the DSM.

The generation of an adverb for the RO LOCATION-1 (Völklingen) would not be possible if sentence 1 read as follows:

> (1a) U: Ich arbeite *in Völklingen* und wohne *in Saarbrücken*.
>   I work *in Völklingen* and live *in Saarbrücken*.

Given this utterance, *dorthin* in sentence 2 would refer to *Saarbrücken*, which is the last CITY. The user might be able to conclude from the communicative situation that, from home, a person normally goes to work by car. Therefore the user could presumably resolve the reference. But since references should be resolvable without major inferences, this type will not be produced by XTRA's generator. Hence, the decision to generate an adverbial phrase instead of a PP for an RO is based on the last occurrence of the RO's semantic class in the DSM. If the last occurrence of this class in the DSM is linked to the identical RO, a pro-adverb can be generated.

The selection of the appropriate adverb depends on the functional role between the FSS description of the RO and the governing expression. For example, if a *causal* relationship exists between the object to be generated and the verb of the clause of which the object is a part, the adverbs *deswegen* or *deshalb* can be generated. An algorithm for the selection of the proper pro-adverb is given in (Reithinger 1984).

The selection of pronouns is performed in a similar manner. For German, the situation sometimes arises that two pronouns with the same inflected form which are not coreferential[3] are used in a sentence, e.g.,

> (3) U: *Die Gesellschaft* hat mir *die Dividenden* überwiesen.
>   *The company* remitted me *the dividends*.

> (4) S: Hat *sie₁* *sie₂* schon versteuert?
>   Did *they* already pay the tax on *them*?

In sentence 4, there are two identical pronouns. Yet German speakers can assign sie_1 to the phrase *Die Gesellschaft* as a singular term and sie_2 to *die Dividenden* as a plural expression. The criteria for the correct identification can be syntactic and/or semantic. In this example, the system can use two identical pronouns because the role/role-filler structures in the FSS are identical for the corresponding RO's and because the verb is inflected in the singular form. The knowledge bases of XTRA are rich enough to provide this information to the generator. To avoid possible confusion, however, the system will not generate such constructions.

If a phrase is to be verbalized in the center field of a German sentence — that is between the finite part of the verb-complex and its other parts (e.g. participles) — the location of a phrase depends a great deal on whether it contains given or new information (Duden, 1984). The use of a pro-word indicates that the phrase in question contains no new information; it will therefore be placed — in front of the NP's and PP's — in the center field.

---

[3] Coreferential pronouns in German sentences generally differ in their inflected forms.

3.3 Generating pointing gestures

3.3.1 Introduction

In XTRA, referent specification is not only possible with verbal descriptions but also by means of pointing gestures. A description of the gestural input analysis is given by Allgayer & Reddig (1986). XTRA's generator will also use this kind of referent identification. For example, in a domain with technical terms, a user will be able to identify parts of a blueprint more easily if the system points at these parts instead of describing them in natural language (cf. Appelt, 1985). This is also the case for the first application domain of XTRA, in which a tax form is to be filled out. The user can resolve the combination of a gesture and a NL expression (Sentence 5a, Figure 2) more easily than the complex description of the location in Sentence 5b.

Werbungskosten

Fahrten zwischen Wohnung und Arbeitsstaette

Aufwendungen fuer Fahrten mit eigenem

		Letztes amtl.Kennzeichen		
PKW	Motorrad/ Motorroller		Moped/ Mofa	Fahrrad

Arbeitstage je Woche	Urlaubs-und Krankheitstage	Erhoehter Kilometersatz wegen Koerperbehinderung			
		von mindestens 70 v.H.		von mindestens 50 v.H. und Gehbehinderung	

Arbeitsstaette in (Ort u.Str.)		benutzt an Tagen	einfache Entf. (km)	Staendig wechselnd Einsatzstellen von-bis

(5a) Sie müssen "Völklingen" hier eintragen.
You have to write "Völklingen" here.

(5b) Sie müssen in der Region "Werbungskosten" in der Spalte "Arbeitsstätte" "Völklingen" eintragen.
You have to write "Völklingen" under the column reading "Arbeitsstätte" in the section "Werbungskosten".

Figure 2. Reference with gestural output vs. linguistic reference

In its responses, the generator has to refer to regions of the form which can be pointed to. This will be achieved by means of a special mouse-cursor. Regions of the form itself will not be highlighted, framed, or otherwise emphasized. This is due to the philosophy of the system: The form on the screen simulates a passive entity like a sheet of paper. The form can only be changed through entries in its value regions.

3.3.2 Special features of pointing at a form

Pointing gestures, as employed by humans, do not generally denote an unambiguous referent. In our system, however, there are particular limitations which simplify the task of recognizing and generating a pointing gesture (Schmauks, 1986a, 1986b). The limitations are due to two important factors: the *structure* of the space that is pointed at, and the *type* of pointing. The forms are only two-dimensional and consist of regions which do not overlap. Therefore, the problem of ambiguity between possible referents is narrowed down greatly. Problems may arise only if the region which the system has to point at consists of other regions. Since forms also have a fixed orientation the problem of having to first define directions does not arise.

The (simulated) pointing gesture is *tactile*, that is, the object the gesture refers to is always touched with the pointing device. Thus, the pointing gesture can be very precise, even if the corresponding description of a conceptual object on the form consists of subregions. Consequently, from the generator's point of view, there are only three possible referents for every pointing gesture:

— the *region* of the form
— the *entry* in a value region
— the *concept* of which the region is an instance.

In most cases, the system is able to refer unambiguously because it can generate a sufficiently precise expression together with the pointing gesture. Whether or not such a gesture can be generated depends on the form hierarchy. If there is a link between the conceptual representation and the hierarchy, a gesture is possible. The type of expression correlated with the gesture depends on the object of the conceptual knowledge base that is to be verbalized.

A purely linguistic description of the location of a *region* of the form is a PP. If the system generates a gesture to refer to it, it has to generate a referential adverbial phrase that links the gesture to the sentence. In this case we use the local adverbs *hier, da* and *dort*[4] as expressions correlated with the gestures.

With regard to pointing actions in three-dimensional space, the choice between those adverbs often depends on the (real or imagined) distance between the speaker and the object in question. In the case of form deixis, the adverbs do *not* denote increasing distance because all regions the system and the human partner can point to are within the *field of action* of both (Schmauks, 1986). Instead, their use can indicate a *sequence*, e.g.,

(6) Sie müssen *hier, da* und *dort* etwas eintragen.
You have to insert something *here, there* and *there*.

or a *contrast*, e.g. as in sentences 9 and 10 of Figure 3.

A pointing gesture to an *entry* in the form is correlated with the demonstrative expressions *dieser* (this) or *jener* (that). They can occur with or without a correlated NP, e.g.,

(7) *Dieser* Eintrag ist falsch, *jener* nicht.
This entry is wrong, but *that one* isn't.

Again, the two different forms can indicate a sequence of or a contrast between two referents. If the system has to generate the *description of a concept* which has an associated region on the form, no pointing gesture will be generated in order to specify this region. The location of the region on the form can be part of the description, whose content depends on the decisions of the 'what-to-say' part of the system. Because this is a reference to a region, it can be generated in the manner described above.

3.3.3 Limitations

As a device of nonverbal reference, the additional possibility of pointing poses some problems. Humans are usually multi channel agents. They take advantage of this feature during the production and understanding of speech and gestures. One person can speak and point, while the other listens and pays attention to the gestures. The first person, on the other hand, visually checks whether the recipient is really attentive to the gestures and explicitly demands the addressee's attention if he or she is not.

Of these channels, XTRA lacks an important one, namely real visual input. The user's audio-input channel is also excluded, though it would be possible to connect XTRA to a speech synthesizer. But lacking this possibility, the 'listener' has to read the text from a screen. Hence,

---

[4] The english translation of *hier* is *here*; *da* and *dort* both mean *there*. The choice between *da* and *dort* is not simple and can be made, e.g., for stylistic reasons or in order to distinguish between two distant locations.

the messages reach the user only via his/her visual channel which is used for both natural language as well as for the pointing gesture.

If the response of the system contains more than one pointing gesture, the relation between a gesture and the correlated linguistic expression will cause problems. For example in the sentence

(8) Sie müssen *dieses* und *dieses* addieren und das Ergebnis *da* eintragen.
You must add up *this* and *this* and enter the result *there*.

the proper sequence of pointing gestures is important. But the user probably cannot keep track of it, and the system cannot notice this. As a result, the sentence may not be understood. Currently we are investigating the proper simulation of those gestures empirically. In the first version, the generator will be limited to only one pointing gesture per response. If it contains exactly one pointable RO, this will cause no problems. If more than one RO associated with a region in the form is to be verbalized in a single response, the generator will use the following heuristics. Because descriptions of locations are usually very complex, it will prefer to use a pointing gesture for a RO which describes a location on the form. If more than one such description is to be verbalized, the generator will use the DSM. For the most recently mentioned location, it will generate the word *hier* (*here*). The pointing gesture will then remain available for the introduction of a new description, verbalized only with the word *da* (*there*).

A short example is given in Figure 3. The arrow represents the moment the user pointed at the screen.

The above mentioned pro-words — linking natural language and the pointing gesture — can also be used anaphorically. The generator will avoid conflicts between the two possible interpretations by preferring the use of a pro-word as deictic expressions correlated with a pointing gesture. In these situations, anaphoric references which would use the same words will have to be replaced by other expressions.

4. CONCLUSION

In this chapter, some basic concepts of the NL access system XTRA — and especially its generator — have been presented. An important one is the common use of knowledge bases by both the analysis components of the system and the generator. The advantage of this structure has been demonstrated for the generation of some classes of referring expressions within a limited context model. The use of pointing gestures as an extralinguistic device for generating references has also been discussed.

Since certain structural considerations concerning focus, focus shifting, and user modeling have not yet been completed, the generation of definite and indefinite noun phrases has not been dealt with in this article. The requirements and implications of this knowledge with respect to answer generation are still under discussion.

We have begun with the implementation of the first prototype of the generator on a Symbolics LISP machine. The other components of XTRA are being developed concurrently. Requirements that arise during the development of the generator will be integrated as far as possible into the overall structural design of the system.

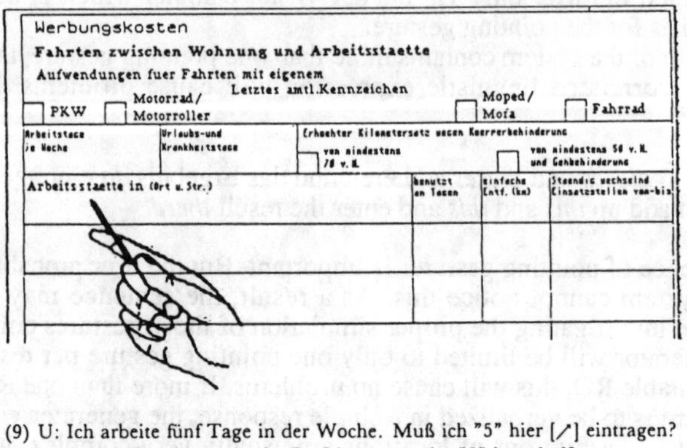

(9) U: Ich arbeite fünf Tage in der Woche. Muß ich "5" hier [/] eintragen?
    I work five days a week. Do I have to write "5" here [/]?

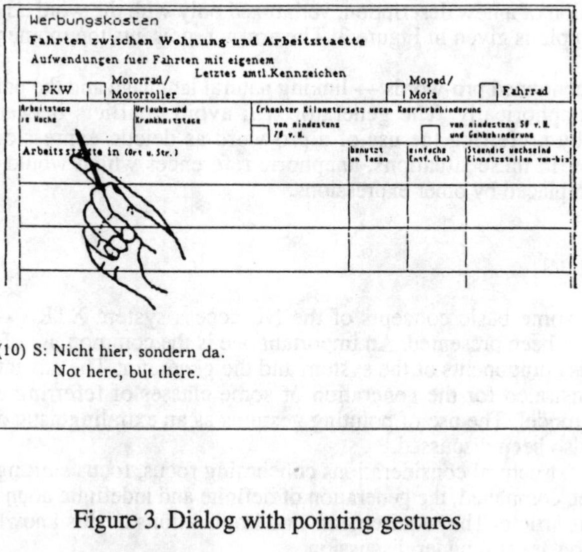

(10) S: Nicht hier, sondern da.
     Not here, but there.

Figure 3. Dialog with pointing gestures

ACKNOWLEDGEMENTS

The work presented here is being supported by the German Special Collaborative Program on AI and Knowledge-Based Systems (SFB 314) of the German Science Foundation (DFG), project NL1: XTRA: A Natural Language Access System to Expert Systems. I would like to thank D. Appelt for various helpful suggestions, J. Allgayer, C. Kemke, A. Kobsa, C. Reddig, and G. Retz-Schmidt for their comments on earlier versions of the paper, W.Finkler for the preparation of the drawings and especially D. Schmauks, who introduced me to the secrets of pointing gestures.

5. REFERENCES

Allgayer, J. (1986) Eine Graphikkomponente zur Integration von Zeigehandlungen in natürlichsprachliche KI-Systeme. In: Hommel, G. & Schindler, S. (Eds.) *GI—16. Jahrestagung*. Berlin: Springer-Verlag.

Allgayer, J. & Reddig, C. (1986) Processing Descriptions Containing Words and Gestures — A System Architecture. In: Rollinger, C.R. (Ed.) *GWAI/ÖGAI 86*. Heidelberg: Springer Verlag.

Appelt, D.E. (1985) *Planning English Sentences*. Cambridge: Cambridge University Press.

Brachman, R.J. & Schmolze, J.G. (1985) An Overview of the KL-ONE Knowledge Representation System. *Cognitive Science, 9*, 171-216.

Duden (1984) *Duden — Die Grammatik*. Mannheim: Bibliographisches Institut.

Grosz, B. (1977) *The Representation and Use of Focus in Dialogue Understanding*. Ph.D. Thesis. University of California, Berkeley.

Habel, C. (1984) Zur Repräsentation der referentiellen Struktur. In: Rollinger, C.-R. (Ed.) *Probleme des (Text-)Verstehens — Ansätze der Künstlichen Intelligenz*. Tübingen: Niemeyer.

Hahn, W. von, Hoeppner, W., Jameson, A. & Wahlster, W. (1980) The Anatomy of the Natural Language Dialog System HAM-RPM. In: Bolc, L. (Ed.) *Natural Language Based Computer Systems*. München: Hanser/Macmillan.

Karlin, R.F. (1985) *Romper Mumbles*. Report MS-CIS 85-41, Department of Computer and Information Science, University of Pennsylvania, Philadelphia.

Kobsa, A., Allgayer, J., Reddig, C., Reithinger, N., Schmauks, D., Harbusch, K. & Wahlster, W. (1986) Combining Deictic Gestures and Natural Language for Referent Identification. In: *Proceedings of the 11th International Conference on Computational Linguistics*. Bonn, West Germany.

Reichman, R. (1985) *Getting Computers to Talk Like You and Me*. Cambridge, MA.: MIT Press.

Reithinger, N. (1984) *Antwortgenerierung für das Erlanger Spracherkennungssystem*. Diploma Thesis, University of Erlangen-Nürnberg.

Rochester, S.R., Martin, J.R. (1977) The Art of Referring: The Speaker's Use of Noun Phrases to Instruct the Listener. In: Freedle, R.O. (Ed.) *Discourse Production and Comprehension*. Norwood, NJ.: Ablex.

Schmauks, D. (1986a) *Formulardeixis und ihre Simulation auf dem Bildschirm. Ein Überblick aus linguistischer Sicht*. Memo No. 4, Sonderforschungsbereich 314, Department of Computer Science, University of Saarbrücken.

Schmauks, D. (1986b) *Form und Funktion von Zeigegesten: Ein interdisziplinärer Überblick*. Memo No. 10, Sonderforschungsbereich 314, Department of Computer Science, University of Saarbrücken.

Sidner C.L. (1983) Focussing in the Comprehension of Definite Anaphora. In: Brady, M. & Berwick, R.C. (Eds.) *Computational Models of Discourse*. Cambridge, MA.: MIT Press.

Wong, H.K.T. (1975) *Generating English Sentences from Semantic Structures*. Technical Report No. 84, University of Toronto.

PART II

Generation of Connected Discourse

RHETORICAL STRUCTURE THEORY: DESCRIPTION AND CONSTRUCTION OF TEXT STRUCTURES

William C. Mann
Sandra A. Thompson

ABSTRACT

Rhetorical Structure Theory (RST) is a theory of text structure that is being extended to serve as a theoretical basis for computational text planning. Text structures in RST are hierarchic, built on small patterns called schemas. The schemas which compose the structural hierarchy of a text describe the functions of the parts rather than their form characteristics. Relations between text parts, comparable to conjunctive relations, are a prominent part of RST's definitional machinery. Recent work has put RST onto a new definitional basis. This paper details the current status of descriptive RST, along with efforts to create a constructive version for use as a basis for programming a text planner.

1. THE ROOTS OF RHETORICAL STRUCTURE THEORY

Rhetorical Structure Theory (RST) has been developed as a basis for text generation, specifically for planning large texts of diverse kinds. It currently exists in a well elaborated form as a descriptive theory, and in a more rudimentary form as a constructive theory based on the descriptive theory.[1] This paper presents an overview and status report, showing the predominant general cases and passing over some of the details and exceptions. (Other papers attempt a much more precise account.)

2. PRINCIPAL MECHANISMS OF DESCRIPTIVE RST

RST describes a text by assigning a *structure* to it. Prior to analysis, a text is broken into *units* of a size that is convenient for the analyst's purposes. (Independent clauses are normally the smallest units; however, larger units may be chosen for larger texts.) These units function as terminal nodes in an RST structure — which is a tree that covers the entire text. In this way an RST structure resembles a conventional sentence structure, but the resemblance is superficial.

---

[1] Rhetorical Structure Theory was initially defined by the authors and Christian Matthiessen; Barbara Fox, Cecilia Ford, and others have made important contributions. It has been influenced significantly by Grimes (1975) and McKeown (1985). Mann & Thompson (1986), Mann (1984) and Mann & Thompson (1985) are our principal earlier papers on RST. Mann & Thompson (1987) describes its relations to other theories in some detail. William C. Mann is with the Information Sciences Institute of the University of Southern California, where RST was initially developed; Sandra A. Thompson is with the Department of Linguistics of the University of California at Santa Barbara. The support of the National Science Foundation and the Air Force Office of Scientific Research are gratefully acknowledged; the opinions in this paper are solely the authors'.

The RST analysis is built out of instances of *schemas*, diagrammed in Figure 1. Each schema indicates how a particular unit of text structure is decomposed into other units. The vertical line points to one of the *text spans* which the schema covers, called the *nucleus*. The other spans are linked to the *nucleus* by relations, represented by labelled curved lines; these spans are called *satellites*. The schema definitions do not constrain the order of spans; the analysis of a particular text is drawn using the left-to-right order of the text whenever possible. A schema is defined in terms of one (occasionally two) relations. For example, the *Evidence schema* is defined as a schema of applications of the *Evidence relation*.

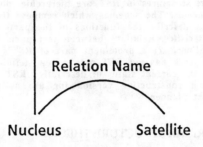

Figure 1. The Generic RST Schema

We illustrate RST structures with Figure 2, which shows an analysis that we have published elsewhere (Mann 1984). The text is a 9 sentence article from a political magazine.[2] The analysis contains 12 applications of 8 different schemas: Evidence, Antithesis, Justify, Elaboration, Concessive, Conditional, Circumstance and Motivation/Enablement. Two particular regions are highlighted: the applications of the Evidence schema. Note that there are two Evidence satellites in the upper region: Multiple satellites are allowed in schema applications. This schema covers (decomposes) the text span consisting of units 1 through 13. The nucleus is the span consisting of unit 1, and the two satellites are the spans of units 2 through 9 and 10 through 13.

A schema application is valid if the relation definitions of which it is composed all apply to the appropriate text spans, with the same nucleus span in every case. An analysis of a text

---

[2] The full text is: I don't believe that endorsing the Nuclear Freeze Initiative is the right step for California CC. Tempting as it may be, we shouldn't embrace every popular issue that comes along. When we do so, we use precious, limited resources where other players with superior resources are already doing an adequate job. Rather, I think we will be stronger and more effective if we stick to those issues of governmental structure and process, broadly defined, that have formed the core of our agenda for years. Open government, campaign finance reform, and fighting the influence of special interests and big money, these are our kinds of issues. Let's be clear: I personally favor the initiative and ardently support disarmament negotiations to reduce the risk of war. But I don't think endorsing a specific nuclear freeze proposal is appropriate for CCC. We should limit our involvement in defense and weaponry to matters of process, such as exposing the weapons industry's influence on the political process. Therefore, I urge you to vote against a CCC endorsement of the nuclear freeze initiative. (signed) Michael Asimow, California Common Cause Vice-Chair and UCLA Law Professor (used by permission).

consists of a set of schema applications which collectively decompose the text into either terminal units or spans further decomposed in the analysis.[3]

The heart of RST is the relation definitions. In past work we have relied on open descriptive relation definitions (Mann 1984). More recently we have developed a new style, in which a relation definition consists of four fields:

1. *Constraints on the Nucleus*
2. *Constraints on the Satellite*
3. *Constraints on the combination of Nucleus and Satellite*
4. *The Effect*

We can see how it works in the definition of the Evidence relation used above. Informally, these are the values of the fields in the definition of the Evidence relation:

1. *Constraints on the Nucleus (the* claim *):*
   The reader possibly does not already believe the claim.
2. *Constraints on the Satellite (the* evidence *):*
   The reader either already believes the satellite or will find it credible.
3. *Constraints on the combination of Nucleus and Satellite:*

   Comprehending the evidence will increase the reader's belief in the claim.[4]
4. *The Effect:* The reader's belief in the claim is increased.

Each of the fields specifies particular judgments that the text analyst must make in building the RST structure. Given the nature of text analysis, these are judgments of plausibility rather than of any sort of certainty. In the case of the Effect field, the analyst is judging whether it is plausible that the writer desires the specified condition.[5]

This is a more explicit form of definition than we had used before. It is still based on judgments, necessarily, but since it provides a checklist of affirmations it makes it easy to identify the claims underlying a particular analysis.

An RST analysis is simply a set of schema applications for which:

1. one schema application decomposes the text as a whole, yielding smaller spans,
2. the others decompose the spans yielded by other applications, and
3. the analyst affirms the judgments involved in the relation definitions of the schema applic -
   ations.

Note that since every definition has an Effect field, the analyst is effectively providing an account for the whole text of a plausible reason the writer might have had for including each part.

---

[3] There is no absolute requirement that the spans covered by a schema application be adjacent, but in practice it is virtually always so.

[4] Belief is treated as a degree concept. This is not a central feature of the definitions, but it helps explain certain text features, e.g. why people provide multiple lines of evidence. All of the judgments of the reader's states and reactions are necessarily from the analyst's view of the writer's view, since they are based on the text.

[5] Plausibility is a threshold concept, based on a degree scale and a conventional way of dividing the scale to provide a binary judgment.

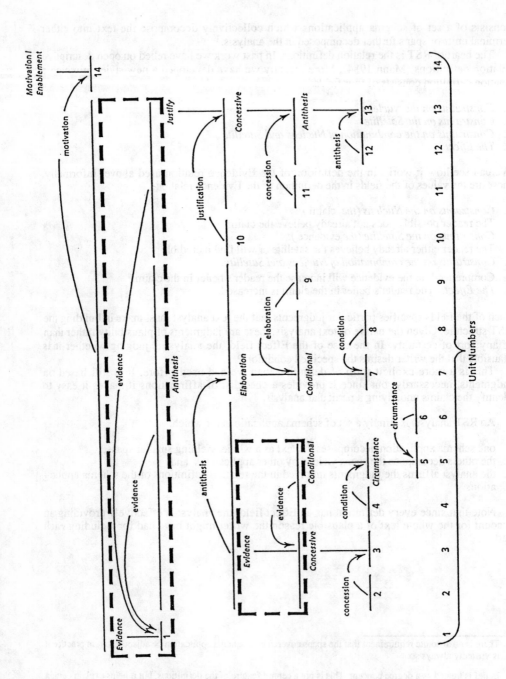

Figure 2. RST Diagram of an Advocacy Text

3. AN ACCOUNT OF A TEXT

To see how this works, we analyze the text of the second highlighted Evidence schema from Figure 2. The text is:

> 2. Tempting as it may be,
> 3. we shouldn't embrace every popular issue that comes along.
> 4. When we do so
> 5. we use precious, limited resources
> 6. where other players with superior resources are already doing an adequate job.

The first constraint says that the reader possibly does not already believe the claim, units 2 and 3. This is plausible, since the reader may have a popularity-contest view of how to choose what to support. The second constraint says that it is plausible that the reader believes units 4 through 6 or will find them credible. The third and most crucial constraint is that (in the writer's view) comprehending the evidence (in this case an apparent waste of resources) will increase the reader's belief in the claim (that we should not support every popular issue). The final constraint, based on the Effect field, is that the writer wants it to be the case that the reader's belief in the claim is increased.

Since in the role of analyst we affirm that all of these constraints are fulfilled, the Evidence relation holds between these two spans. The analysis of the entire text is constructed similarly.

4. NUCLEARITY

What is nuclearity? Why is the terminology of nucleus and satellite appropriate for consistent use with a variety of relations? The discussion of nuclearity so far simply uses 'nucleus' and 'satellite' as span labels in definitions. But they represent a much more pervasive and significant regularity.

As RST was being developed, a pattern in the way relations appear in text became evident. The principal features of the pattern are these:

1. Relations are nearly all asymmetric. (For example, if A is serving as evidence for B, B is not at the same place serving as evidence for A.)
2. There is a characteristic difference across relations in how the two spans function:

> a. One span is more prominent than the other.
> b. One span is more essential to the text than the other.
> c. For schemas with multiple relations, there is a single core span that all of the other spans are related to.
> d. The identity of the prominent and essential span can be predicted from the relation itself. It is not conditional on the content of the spans or their context.

The prominent and essential core span is called the nucleus, and the remaining spans the satellites. The identity of the nucleus is part of the relation definition. The use of the terminology reflects the fact that the pattern described above is predominant in texts.

5. OTHER RELATIONS

The set of relations is not closed. Depending on one's purposes and the kind of text in view, relations can be added, subdivided and otherwise manipulated. Still, they are not an open category like Noun, subject to unconstrained overt invention. The set of rhetorical relations is more like the set of conjunctions (than like the set of nouns) in that it is reasonably stable for any particular purpose, yet flexible enough to bend to a new task. They seem to be somewhat language-specific and culture-specific, certainly in frequency if not in occurrence.

We are currently developing a reasonably precise exposition of descriptive RST (Mann & Thompson 1987). It will include definitions (in the style illustrated and exemplified for Evidence in Section 2 above) for the following relations:

Circumstance	Solutionhood
Elaboration	Background
Enablement	Motivation
Evidence	Justify
Volitional Cause	Non-Volitional Cause
Volitional Result	Non-Volitional Result
Antithesis	Concession
Condition	Otherwise
Interpretation	Evaluation
Restatement	Summary
Sequence	Contrast

Other definitions which have not been fully developed are: Means, Comparison, Contribution, and Disjunction.

6. RELATIONAL PROPOSITIONS: THE PHENOMENON

In a previous paper we identified a phenomenon called Relational Propositions (Mann & Thompson, 1986a). It is an assertion-like effect in which the assertions are not expressed explicitly in clauses. Often there is no explicit signal at all, yet the assertion is effectively communicated by the text. For example, here is an extract from a letter to the editor of BYTE magazine (diagrammed in Figure 3). The writer is praising a program which computes federal income tax, published in a previous issue of the magazine:

1. The program as published for calendar year 1980 really works.
2. In only a few minutes, I entered all the figures from my 1980 tax return
3. and got a result which agreed with my hand calculations to the penny.

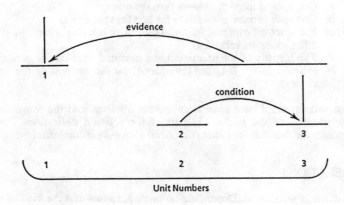

Figure 3. RST Diagram of the Program Testimonial

We would posit an Evidence relation with unit 1 as nucleus and units 2 through 3 as satellite. The relational proposition of this text says that this experience (entering the figures and getting a result which agreed with hand calculations), is a suitable basis for believing that the program really works. The text conveys this idea of evidence, but does not express it explicitly. (The previous examples did not express it explicitly either. Evidence is one of several relations for which explicit expression is rare.) In fact, this proposition is essential to the coherence of the text. Suppose we alter the text by adding another sentence so that the proposition about evidence is not affirmed:

> 'The program as published for calendar year 1980 really works. In only
> a few minutes, I entered all the figures from my 1980 tax return and got
> a result which agreed with my hand calculations to the penny. **But that
> doesn't suggest in any way that the program works.**'

The resulting text is obviously incoherent: we no longer know what the writer is saying. This supports our view that the natural (coherent) text crucially relied on and conveyed the proposition of evidence. Several other kinds of support for this view are described in Mann & Thompson (1986a). More generally, we find that *every relation in an RST structure conveys some relational proposition*. The conveyed propositions are essential to the coherence of the texts in which they arise.

There is an interesting and complex relationship between the relational propositions and the various forms that express such information, especially the conjunctions. Unfortunately, it has not yet been well studied.[6] This raises a point that is important for discourse theory as a whole. *Expression of implicit propositions is not an occasional side-effect that accompanies the clausal propositions of a text. Rather, they are an inevitable and essential component of text communication.* [7]

How can we know what relational proposition arises from any particular relation in the structure of a text? This is a problem on which we are currently working. The preliminary answer is that the relational proposition can be identified generically at the time that the corresponding relation is defined. Furthermore, the relational proposition does not constrain the definition; rather it is derivable from the other parts of the definition. We are not yet confident that this is the complete story, but it is at least approximately correct.

We should note that the phenomenon of relational propositions has significant added consequences for text generation:

1. Relational propositions are an expressive resource, a means for achieving brevity.
2. Explicit clausal expression of a proposition which is also conveyed as a relational proposition produces an excessively repetitive text.
3. Since relational propositions can be conveyed without clausal material, a text generator must be specially designed to control what propositions are conveyed.

7. CONSEQUENCES OF DESCRIPTIVE RST

The most important finding in RST-based studies of text is that virtually all small published texts in our culture have RST analyses. Since the definitions and conventions of RST are restrictive enough that there is no a priori reason why so many texts should have analyses, this is a genuine finding. This is an advance in that it shows what relations are essential in composing text, and how they can be arranged. And it demonstrates that relational linking is

---

[6]   But see Martin (1983) and Brée & Smit (1986); much more work is needed.

[7]   Mann & Thompson (1985) develops the idea that the relational propositions described in Mann & Thompson (1986a) do in fact arise from the RST discourse structure of the texts in which they occur.

comprehensive (spanning the whole text) and pervasive (linking on every scale down to small units).

A companion study (Thompson & Mann, 1987), provides strong evidence that the relations of RST structure and the relations of clause combining are one and the same set. Thus RST is informative about phenomena of clause combining, conjunction and related issues of form and function. In the clause combining area, another companion study shows the close relationship between RST and hypotaxis (Matthiessen & Thompson, 1986).

RST also yields guidance for work in knowledge representation. The relations of RST reflect a set of distinct kinds of knowledge that are given special treatment in text organization. It is therefore essential to represent these in the knowledge notations underlying a general text comprehender or generator.

8. CONSTRUCTIVE RST

RST was created so that it could be the basis of an autonomous computational text planner. Satisfying this goal requires more than just a descriptive theory; it also requires an approach to synthesis of structures, i.e. constructive RST. Constructive RST is in a much more rudimentary state than the descriptive theory, but enough has been done to be described.

We have chosen not to work with stored fixed combinations of RST schemas. We do not have genre-specific or task-specific text structures as a starting point. In this way our work is very different from McKeown's (1985) work, and so some of the strengths of her system are more difficult for us to achieve.[8] Instead, we are developing a text planner that uses the individual RST schemas as its building blocks.

One of the principal problems in developing a general approach to text planning is to manage the complexity of the task. It is necessary to factor the task into manageable parts so that, to a close approximation, independent issues are treated independently, and issues which are not of central interest are distinguished from those which are primary.

One approach to creating a factoring of issues is the 'method of oracles' described below.

There are very many intellectual problems that come up in text planning. Some of these are not essentially problems of text planning, but nevertheless they are of a kind which must be solved if one is to plan text. These problems must be factored out in order to make progress on text planning.

For example, the following sorts of questions come up inside our text planner:

1. If I say X, will the reader believe it?
2. What do I know that is evidence for X?
3. Does the reader have the prerequisite knowledge to comprehend a straightforward statement of X?
4. If the reader wants to do X, will he be able to do it?
5. If X is suggested as an action for the reader to perform, will he want to do it?
6. Do I have the right to present X at this point in the text?
7. Does the reader know of a particular apparent refutation for X, which I believe is not a genuine refutation of X?

These are not centrally questions about methods for structuring text. Rather they are concerned with the information resources used by a text structuring method. Answering them (and many others like them) is essential to creating certain kinds of texts.

To factor such questions out of the text planning algorithm we use the method of oracles, familiar to many through Robin Cohen's thesis (1983) on argument recognition. Each such question is assigned to an opaque 'black box,' called an Oracle, which is responsible for answering it. Nothing is claimed about how the answers are produced. The claim for the non-

---

[8] See Mann & Thompson (1986b) and Mann (1984) for comparisons of the two lines of work.

Oracle portion of the algorithm is that *if the Oracles answer their assigned questions correctly, the algorithm will function correctly.*

Many of the Oracles' questions are very difficult. For some there are no programs that even come close to implementing an answering process. Is this sort of text generation therefore hopeless? Not at all. Even though the general case is unapproachable, many of the Oracles have restricted forms that are suitable for implementation. For example, in a system with internalized proofs, the question 'What do I know that is evidence for X?' might be approached by searching in the proof of X.

Currently, text generation is severely limited by the state of the art of knowledge representation. For many kinds of knowledge there are no strong precedents for how to represent them. Such kinds of knowledge cannot yet be expressed in computer-produced text. The Oracles that appear particularly difficult to implement are generally those for which there are unsolved problems of knowledge representation. From one point of view this is fortunate: the kinds of texts we cannot plan are the kinds for which our machines have little to say.

9. A STRUCTURED TEXT PLANNING PROCEDURE

We have a draft procedure which is able to plan many varieties of texts. It is entirely a human-executed procedure. We test it by simulating the process of generating small natural texts. With ourselves representing the Oracles (about 30 of them), we can reliably produce structures which are identical to, or acceptable for, structures of actual texts. We have identified an unmarked ordering for all of the relations; we use it exclusively.

The 'input' for this procedure is a statement of the writer's goal, in terms of the intended effect of the text, which is a description of the state to be achieved. For example, an intended effect might be: 'The reader wants to buy our disks' or 'The reader knows what kind of object a Response Unit is.'[9] The 'output' for this procedure is an RST structure, with propositions identified with each of the terminal nodes of the structure, and underlying speech acts to be performed relative to those propositions. This information is chosen so that, with minor supplementation, it is sufficient to specify sentences to be generated by a functional grammar. In a more complex system, some clause combining methods external to the RST planning (but relying on it) may be used before the information reaches the grammar. The method is a top-down, goal-pursuit method.

Much of the complexity of texts, and thus much of the action in text planning, comes because the reader is not ready to receive and accept what the speaker wants to convey. A large part of the method is devoted to consulting a model of the reader (hidden under the Oracles) and providing the support - such as evidence, background, concessions and motivation - to make the pursuit of the text goal effective. The method as it stands reflects the need for an elaborate model of the reader and many kinds of processes that manipulate it.

The method is not yet sufficiently developed to justify documenting it publicly. However, to give an indication of the sorts of issues being considered, Figure 4 shows a fragment of it, about 5% of the whole. The figure shows 3 oracles, with the Belief Oracle being used twice. This fragment encodes essentially the same commitments about the writer's viewpoint that are represented in the definition of the Evidence relation.[10]

Several kinds of text planning activity are not included in the structure planning method. We have not yet incorporated provisions for skilled use of clause combining, manipulation of thematic structures or the interactions of text structure with lexical choice. Both descriptive and constructive RST are being extended and refined. Constructive RST is being readied for application in a paragraph planner.

---

9 The goals are not in terms of intended actions by the speaker, e.g. 'Tell the superclass and part composition of a Response Unit.' Such goals might be appropriate as part of a process control mechanism, but they do not relate directly to the function of the text.

10 The emphasis on evidence in this paper is presentational. The work is in fact much more evenly distributed.

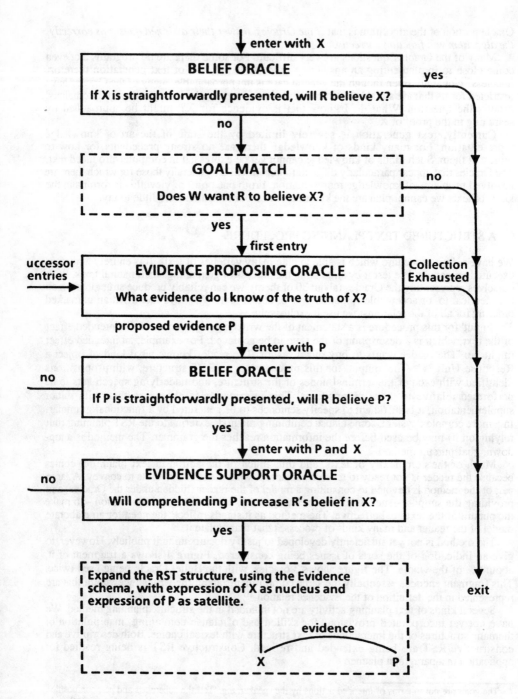

Figure 4. A Portion of the RST Structure Construction Method

10. CONCLUSION

The status of RST has advanced beyond the level indicated by available papers and reports. Descriptive RST has been developed to the point at which it can raise interesting issues about discourse and communication. The nature of coherence, the communicative potential of multisentential texts, the functions of conjunctions and the nature of clause combining are some of these areas. Given the current definition methods, an RST structure for a text is necessarily a declaration of a functional account of every part of the text, a plausible effect of each part and its role in the text as a whole. Since so many texts have RST structures, descriptive RST is an interesting new tool for text analysis.

Constructive RST has been developed enough to pass rudimentary tests of effectiveness. It can mimic part of the generation of natural texts, producing appropriate structures given suitable extra-textual information. However, it is definitely only a partial solution to the problem of designing an implementable text planner for large innovative texts.

REFERENCES

Bree, D.S. & Smit, R.A. (1986) Linking propositions. In: *Proceedings of the 11th International Conference on Computational Linguistics*, (COLING86), Bonn.

Cohen, R. (1983) *A computational model for the analysis of arguments*. Ph.D. thesis, University of Toronto.

Grimes, J.E. (1975) *The Thread of Discourse*. The Hague: Mouton.

Mann, W.C. (1984) Discourse Structures for Text Generation. In: *Proceedings of the 1984 Coling/ACL Conference*, Stanford.

Mann, W.C. & Thompson, S.A. (1985) Assertions from discourse structure. In: *Proceedings of the Eleventh Annual Meeting of the Berkeley Linguistics Society*, Berkeley.

Mann, W.C. & Thompson, S.A. (1986a) Relational propositions in discourse. *Discourse Processes, 9,* 57-90.

Mann, W.C. & Thompson, S.A. (1986b) Text generation: The problem of text structure. In: *Proceedings of the 11th International Conference on Computational Linguistics*, (COLING86), Bonn.

Mann, W.C. & Thompson, S.A. (1987) Rhetorical structure theory: A theory of text organization. In: L. Polanyi (Ed.) *Discourse Structure*. Norwood, N.J.: Ablex.

Martin, J.R.(1983) Conjunction: the logic of English text. *Forum Linguisticum*.

Matthiessen, C. & Thompson, S.A. (1987) The structure of discourse and 'Subordination'. In: Haiman & Thompson (Eds.) *Clause combining in grammar and discourse*. Amsterdam: Benjamins.

McKeown, K.R. (1985) *Studies in natural language processing. Volume 2: Text generation: Using discourse strategies and focus constraints to generate natural language text.* Cambridge University Press: Cambridge.

Thompson, S.A. & Mann, W.C. (1987) *Antithesis: A Study in Clause Combining and Discourse Structure*. Paper accepted for publication.

Chapter 8

DISCOURSE STRATEGIES FOR DESCRIBING COMPLEX PHYSICAL OBJECTS

Cecile L. Paris
Kathleen R. McKeown

ABSTRACT

In past work, discourse strategies, identified through analyses of naturally occurring texts, have been used in computer systems to guide a generation system in deciding what to say. In this paper, we describe the use of discourse strategies to guide the generation of descriptions of physical objects. In particular, we present a new type of strategy, the process strategy, which provides directives on how to trace the underlying knowledge base. Since the system has a set of possible strategies that can be used to generate descriptions of physical objects, we identify how a strategy can be selected based on information about the user and show how a system can combine several strategies in a single description so that it chooses the most appropriate strategy at each point in the generation process.

1. INTRODUCTION

In previous work, researchers (e.g., McKeown, 1982, 1985; Mann, 1984; McCoy, 1986; Kukich, 1985; Weiner, 1980) have identified and formalized the structure of naturally occurring texts for particular goals or situations as discourse strategies. These strategies have been employed in computer systems to guide the generation process in deciding what to say and how to organize it. One commonality of strategies presented in the past is that they impose a structure on the knowledge base which is used to produce text. That is, the structure of the generated text is based on an abstract characterization of patterns occurring in many texts and is not dependent on the structure of the underlying knowledge base. We term this type of strategy a declarative strategy.

By examining texts which describe physical objects, we found that they exhibit a type of structure that differs from that captured in the discourse strategies previously formalized. In this paper, we present a new type of strategy that encodes this new structure. The key characteristic of this strategy is that it consists of directives on how to trace the underlying knowledge base to select textual content. We term this type of strategy a procedural strategy. The structure of the text produced by a procedural strategy mirrors the structure of the knowledge base in ways dictated by the strategy. In contrast, texts produced by declarative strategies mirror the abstract pattern represented in the strategy, not the knowledge base. Both types of strategies are important, and a generation system can produce a greater variety of texts if it can make use of both. We show how a procedural and a declarative strategy can be used in combination to produce a single description of a complex physical object.

2. DECLARATIVE STRATEGIES IN NATURAL LANGUAGE GENERATION

Declarative discourse strategies are typically composed of rhetorical predicates. Rhetorical predicates are the means available to a speaker to present information, and characterize the structural purpose of a sentence. They have been discussed by a variety of linguists (Grimes 1975, Shepherd 1926) and computational linguists (Hobbs 1978, 1980, McKeown 1982, Mann 1984) who have also referred to them as coherence or rhetorical relations. Researchers construct declarative strategies by analyzing naturally occurring texts. The main method used in such text analysis is to decompose a text into propositions (or clauses), classifying each proposition as a predicate. The combination of predicates appearing in texts with the same discourse structure is identified as a discourse strategy. A few predicates, based on Grimes's and Shepherd's definitions, are shown in Figure 1.

---

1. **Identification**: Description of an object in terms of its superordinate.
   Example: This bear is a koala bear.

2. **Constituency**: Description of the sub-parts or sub-entities.
   Example: The telephone consists of a transmitter, a receiver and a housing.

3. **Attributive**: Associating properties with an entity.
   Example: Beth's teddy bear is black and white.

4. **Cause-effect**: A cause-effect relationship between two events or relations.
   Example: The soundwaves strike the diaphragm and cause it to vibrate.

5. **Comparison**:
   Example: The loudspeaker works in the opposite way to the microphone.

6. **Elaboration**:
   Example: The diaphragm was originally invented by Thomas A. Edison.

7. **Renaming**:
   Example: The current goes through the coil, called the 'primary coil'.

Figure 1. Rhetorical predicates used in this analysis

In earlier work on text generation, McKeown (1982) found that certain combinations were associated with discourse purposes such as providing definitions, comparisons, and des - criptions. Mann (1984) identified a large number of rhetorical nucleus/satellite combinations found in a variety of texts. Similarly, McCoy (1986) identified combinations of rhetorical predicates that are appropriate for correcting different types of user misconceptions.

As an example, consider the constituency strategy which McKeown found could be used both to provide definitions and to describe the type of information available in a knowledge base. It can be characterized by the following four steps and is represented formally as shown in Figure 2.

1. Identify the item as a member of some generic class
2. Present the constituents of the item to be defined
3. Present characteristic information about each constituent in turn
4. Present additional information about the item to be defined.

{Identification (description of an object in terms of its superordinate)}[1]
Constituency (description of sub-parts or sub-types.)
Attributive* (associating properties with an entity) / Cause-effect*
{ Depth-identification / Depth-attributive
  { Particular Illustration / Evidence}
  { Comparison ; Analogy}   }+
  { Attributive / Explanation / Attributive / Analogy }

Figure 2. The Constituency Schema

3. TWO STRATEGIES FOR DESCRIBING COMPLEX PHYSICAL OBJECTS

In this work we are investigating strategies for describing physical objects. This work is part of the RESEARCHER project which must eventually be able to produce natural language descriptions of physical objects. RESEARCHER is a program that reads patent abstracts written in English and creates a permanent long term representation containing a generalization hierarchy learned from the concepts described in the texts (Lebowitz, 1983, 1985). The abstracts describe complex physical objects in which spatial and functional relations are emphasized. Being able to provide descriptions of the physical objects it has learned about is thus an important component of the program. Furthermore, since the knowledge base contains several different kinds of information (spatial, functional, and attributive) and the amount of information is very large and detailed, a generation program needs to choose among many facts about an object. As a result, deciding what to include in a description is not trivial.

Our goal was to characterize the different strategies used to describe physical objects. We studied various natural language texts describing complex objects, and compared their organizational strategies.[2] We began by analyzing the different texts using methods developed by other researchers (Hobbs, 1978, 1980; McKeown, 1982; Mann, 1984). We decomposed paragraphs by identifying the rhetorical predicates of each proposition in an attempt to find consistent structures for the texts.[3] This type of analysis showed one prevalent type of description: description in terms of the sub-parts of the object being described.

This type of description can be characterized by the constituency structures posited by McKeown (1985) as they provide details about the sub-parts of an object and their properties (attributes). The following is a description for a telephone from Collier (1962):

> The hand-sets introduced in 1947 consist of a receiver and a transmitter in a single housing available in black or colored plastic. The transmitter diaphragm is clamped rigidly at its edges to improve the high frequency response. The diaphragm is coupled to a doubly resonant system — cavity and an air chamber — which broadens the response. The carbon chamber contains carbon granules, the contact resistance of which is varied by the diaphragm's vibration. The receiver includes a ring-shaped magnet system around a coil and a ring shaped armature of anadium Permendur. Current in the coil makes the armature vibrate in the air gap. An

---

[1] We are using McKeown's notation:'{}' indicate optionality, '/' indicates alternatives, '+' indicates that the item may appear 1-n times, and '*' indicates that the item may appear 0-n times. Finally, ';' is used to represent the fact that a proposition could belong to either classification.

[2] We studied texts from encyclopedias and high school physics textbooks. We analyzed twenty examples from each encyclopedia and textbook, each example containing several paragraphs.

[3] More details and examples are given in (Paris, 1985).

attached phenolic-impregnated fabric diaphragm, shaped like a dome, vibrates and sets the air in the canal of the ear in motion.

However, many texts could not be characterized using the analysis methods of earlier work. No known declarative strategy consistently accounted for the other type of descriptions. Moreover, identifying the rhetorical predicates of the sentences did not provide insights into a useful structure. Instead, we found that the main strategy used in these descriptions was to trace through the process that allows the object to perform its function. We captured this structure in the *process strategy* and have developed a precise formulation of it, consisting of directives rather than predicates. The process strategy and the constituency schema together accounted for all the texts analyzed.

4. THE PROCESS STRATEGY

The process strategy dictates how to trace the knowledge base in order to produce a process description. A process description is embodied in the links connecting events contained in the knowledge base (usually causal links). The process strategy thus dictates how to follow the links in the knowledge base in order to trace through the process. Although we will describe the process strategy in terms of our domain, we believe it can be used in any domain where processes occur. The process strategy is dependent on the knowledge base only to the extent that the knowledge base needs to have information about processes, which is frequent. Given different knowledge bases with other types of links, the implementation of the strategy (the functions which retrieve the information from the knowledge) would have to be adjusted to reflect the changes, but the process strategy would remain unchanged. Unlike other existing strategies, this new strategy does not impose a structure on the underlying knowledge base, but, on the contrary, follows it closely.

In this sense, the process strategy is similar to the strategy used by people to describe their apartments (which we term the apartment strategy), as identified by Linde & Labov (1975). The apartment strategy follows the lay-out of the apartment being described, as if the speaker were taking an imaginary tour through the apartment. The speaker may either start by describing a main hall and then describe the rooms off that hall, or may go from one room to the next if they lead to each other. The apartment strategy, however, was never formalized as part of a generation system to produce text. Furthermore, the apartment strategy provides a physical description and not a functional one.

Like the apartment strategy, a process trace can be seen as following a sequence of events (called the main path) in the knowledge base, going from a start state to a goal state. For example, in a description of a physical object, this chain of events describes the object's function from the beginning (start state) to the end (goal state), thus providing an explanation of that process. The apartment strategy, however, results in a complete description of the apartments (with branching points and backtracking), in that every room was generally included.[4] This is not the case for the process strategy, where not every causal link will be included. In a complex knowledge base, we can expect to have many links branching out of the main path. These links include both side links and substeps. To keep the process explanation coherent, a process trace cannot follow every causal link base that may branch out of the main path. Therefore the process strategy needs to dictate which side links to include in the text, which to ignore, and when to include a side link it has chosen to include.

In order to use the process strategy, we must first limit the part of the knowledge base to be traced through. To do this, we identify the main path of links from the start to the goal. Given the main path, the process strategy then decides what to include in the description as the program traces along the path. It makes decisions based on the type of side-links or substeps it encounters. The next sections describe the different types of links that may exist, how a

---

4   Even though every room was included in the lay-out of the apartment, they were not all described at the same level of details. Furthermore, closets were not necessarily included.

program can identify the main path, and, finally, other choices the process strategy needs to make.

4.1 Identifying the main path and different kinds of links

Process information consists of links between events in the knowledge base that may express different relations between events. For example, in our domain, we have three types of relations expressed in links:

— Control links: these links indicate causal relations between events, such as *cause-effect, enablement,* or *interruptions,* such as 'X interrupts Y'.
— Temporal links: these links indicate temporal relations between events, such as 'X happens *at the same time* as Y'.
— Analogical links: these indicate analogies between events, such as 'X is *equivalent to* Y', or 'X *corresponds to* Y'.

Because these links represent relations between events, they could all be mentioned in the process description. However, as they express different relations, it is possible to rank them by order of importance. This ranking helps the strategy decide which links to include when it has to choose among several. For example, in our domain, the most important links to describe process are control links, as they represent causality between events.

4.2 The main path

The main path represents the chain of events from the start to the goal. In our knowledge base, the main path describes the sequence of events that are performed in order for an object to achieve its function.

Consider, for example, the subset of our knowledge base (representing the loudspeaker) shown in Figure 3.[5] In this figure and the other figures in this paper, each labelled box represents an object. Each box is a frame containing information about the object, but, for clarity, we only show the labels here. The boxes are connected with non-directed arcs that represent the parts hierarchy. So, for example, the 'loudspeaker' is shown to have an 'armature', a 'permanent magnet', an 'air gap' and a 'diaphragm'. The directed arcs between objects represent the relations among the objects. For example, the 'coil' is 'wound around' the 'permanent magnet' and the 'current' 'varies'. Furthermore, some of these relations can be broken up into substeps (e.g., 'varies' can be decomposed into 'increases' and 'decrease'). These substeps are also shown in the figure. Finally, the different types of links between events are shown with arcs between relations. The thick directed arcs between relations represent the main path, that is the main sequence of events that occur when the object (the loudspeaker) performs its function, namely:

— The varying current causes the field of the electromagnet to vary.
— The varying field causes the diaphragm to vibrate.
— The diaphragm vibrating causes soundwave intensity to vary.

---

[5] Because this work is being conducted at the same time as the research for RESEARCHER's parser, our knowledge base was built by hand. However, it is faithful to the representation that would be built by RESEARCHER.

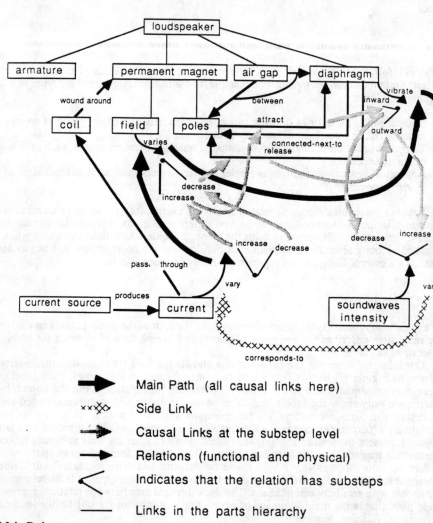

Main Path (all causal links here)
Side Link
Causal Links at the substep level
Relations (functional and physical)
Indicates that the relation has substeps
Links in the parts hierarchy

Main Path:

1. The varying current CAUSES the field of the electromagnet to vary
2. Varying field CAUSES diaphragm to vibrate
3. The diaphragm vibrating CAUSES soundwave intensity to vary

Side Link:
Soundwave intensity varies CORRESPONDS-TO current varies

Figure 3. Main path for the loudspeaker

In this case, all the links on the main path are control links[6]. There is also a side link, the analogical link 'corresponds to'. Finally, the causal links at the substep level are represented with lighter directed arcs between relations. (These represent the sequence of events that occur when a relation is decomposed into its substeps.) Since the program needs to identify the main path before starting generation, our implementation includes an algorithm for obtaining it. This algorithm is essentially a depth first search, with ordered backtracking. It can be summarized as follows:

— Obtain the start and goal states from the object frame.
— Backtrack from the goal state:
   Take all the relations in which the goal event participates as the object. (Since the arcs are directed, there is a beginning point (the subject) and the end point (the object).
   Take the most important (given the importance factors) and repeat this backtracking process from the subject link. When the original start state is reached, the process stops. If the most important link does not lead to the start state, try again with the next most important link.

While backtracking to obtain the main path, the program also keeps track of the side links it encounters.

4.3 Deciding among several links

In general, to produce a coherent text, one should avoid continual side-tracking on different subjects. For the process trace, this means staying roughly on the main path. That is, the focus of the process description will be on the main path. However, including a side link is sometimes useful or necessary as in the following situations:

— The side link introduces an analogy that provides a clearer process explanation. (An example is shown in Figure 4.)
— The side link introduces an important side effect that the user should know about. This can happen in a medical domain, for example, when the side effect of a drug that is prescribed is of vital importance.

Consider the subset of the knowledge base given in Figure 3. Including the *analogical* side link *corresponds to* produces a clearer explanation of the process,[7] as shown in Figure 4.

The variation of the current causes the field of the magnet to vary. This causes the diaphragm to vibrate. The vibration of the diaphragm causes the intensity of the soundwaves to vary. The intensity varies, like the current varies.

Figure 4. An analogical side link can produce a clearer explanation

Furthermore, side links can have various structures with respect to the main path. Based on their structure and type, we classified side links into five cases, each of which requires different treatment:

— the side chain is long but related to the main path
— there is an isolated side link

---

[6] This is the case for most of the objects in our knowledge base.

[7] This text is generated by our system when a short description is asked for (i.e., no substeps are given).

— there are many short links
— there is a long side chain that is not related to the main path
— there are substeps.

These cases and their associated algorithms are presented below.

The side chain is long but related to the main path. In this case, the side link leads to a long chain of events, but that chain is re-attached to the main path. This case is illustrated in Figure 5 and can be characterized by the diagram in (1).

(1)

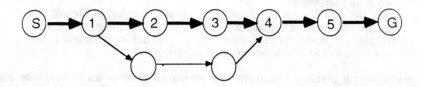

The main path is represented by the thick line ('—>') the side chain by single arrows (—>). The nodes represent the specific events along the chain. The main path going from S (start) to G (goal) is composed of the events (1) through (5). Coming off the main path at (1), there is a side link, resulting in a long side chain that gets re-attached to the main path at event (4).

One case of this structure is when the side link leads to an event which is an enabling condition to an event on the main path, as illustrated in Figure 5. In this figure, the main path is represented with thick directed lines between events. The thick broken line represents the chain. Finally, the dotted lines (---) show the enabling relations that re-attach the side chain to the main path. For example, a precondition for the 'spring decompressing' is the 'spring compressing'. So although this event does not belong on the main path, it is important to mention as it is an enabling condition for an event on the main path. This case is more clearly illustrated in diagram (1) above: while event (3) is the cause of event (4), event (4) is also enabled by another event that results from the side chain leading off event (1). In this case, the side chain is important to mention as, otherwise, the enabling condition for (3) would be missing.

The process strategy dictates tracing through the side chain first, using a focus shift. After the chain is traversed, the program reverts to tracing the main path, returning focus to the main path.

There is an isolated side link. In this case, the diagram is as in (2)

(2)

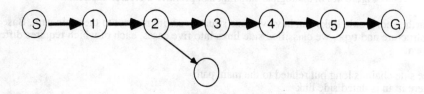

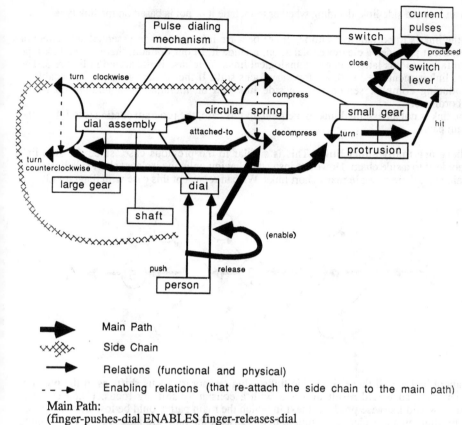

Main Path:
(finger-pushes-dial ENABLES finger-releases-dial
          CAUSES circular-spring decompresses
          CAUSES dial-turns-counter-clockwise
          CAUSES small-gear-turns
          CAUSES protrusion-hits-switch-lever
          CAUSES switch-closes
          CAUSES current-pulse-produced)

Side chain coming off finger-pushes-dial:
(finger-pushes-dial CAUSES dial-turns clockwise
          CAUSES circular-spring compresses)

Figure 5. The side chain is long but related to the main path: as the event *the circular spring compresses* is an enabling condition for the event *circular spring decompresses* in the main path.

Given an isolated side link, deciding whether to include it or not is based on the link type:

— If the link is important to mention, either because it introduces an essential side effect or because it provides a clearer explanation, include it. In our domain, there is one link type that falls into this latter category: analogical links. This case is illustrated in Figure 3. The side link is mentioned with a temporary focus shift. If the surface generator is capable of producing complex sentences, the side link can be included in a relative clause or subordinate.
— The link is not an essential link to mention. In this case, the program continues to follow the main path.

There are many short links. This is similar to the previous case, since the side link does not lead to a side chain. However, instead of having only one isolated short side link along the main path, there now are many short links. We can represent this case with diagram (3).

(3)

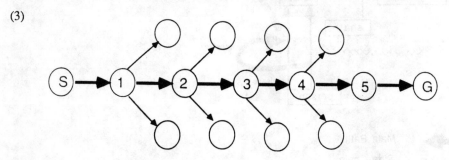

We cannot include all these short side links using temporary focus shifts as in the previous case, as doing so would result in a text with a constantly shifting focus. Using complex sentences would likewise produce a text in which the main path would be lost among the side links, resulting in a less clear description. In this case, if the links are judged to be important to mention, they should be grouped together after the main path is described.

There is a long side chain which is not related to the main path. Here, there is a long side chain that leads to an event unrelated to the main path. This case can be characterized with diagram (4).

(4)

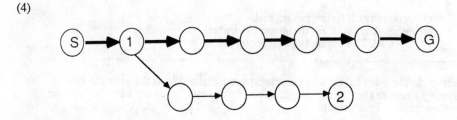

There is a side link coming off the main path at event (1). This link leads to a chain that results in event (2), an event unrelated to the main path. In general, this side link is ignored. An example of this case is shown in Figure 6. (In some rare cases, the side link may be essential. It could then be included after tracing through the main path, using a focus shift[8]. Note that, in order to do so, event (1) has to be re-introduced.)

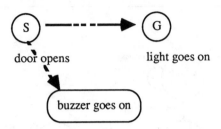

door opens   light goes on

Suppose we want to describe why the light inside a car turns on when the door opens. Our *start* state is the event corresponding to the *opening of the door*. The *goal* state is the *light turning on*.

A side effect of *opening the door* is the *buzzer turning on* after a number of steps not shown here. When explaining why the light turns on, shifting focus to describe why the buzzer turns on is unnecessary and confusing. If this side chain was judged important, it would be possible to include it by mentioning it at the end, after proper re-introduction.

Figure 6. The side chain is long and not related to the main path

Substeps. It is possible that a single event can be decomposed into substeps. For example, consider the representation shown in Figure 3. The event *the diaphragm vibrates* consists of (1) *the diaphragm moving forward* and (2) *the diaphragm moving backward*. The causal link between the event *diaphragm vibrating* and *soundwave intensity vary* can be decomposed into two chains of events: one from the *diaphragm moving forward* and the other from the *diaphragm moving backward*. In this case, substeps are traversed if they are not too lengthy and numerous. (This is controlled by a parameter, which, in our implementation, is set to allow for 3 substeps, each of at most 6 links.) Including longer substep chains is undesirable for two reasons: (1) the generated text becomes too long, and (2) in our domain, the process may be described at too fine a level of detail. Tracing substeps is done by shifting focus until returning to the main path.

Substeps can also arise when a complex object is made of several other complex parts. Tracing through the main path of an object corresponds to describing how the parts achieve the object's function. If a long description is desired, the strategy is repeated for each of the sub-parts. This is similar to schema recursion for the constituency schema presented in McKeown (1985).

Now that we have identified the actions required by the different cases of links, we present an algorithm that traverses links in the knowledge base, taking appropriate actions as it encounters the various cases.

5. STRATEGY REPRESENTATION

We represent both strategies, the constituency schema and the process trace, as augmented transition networks (ATN: Woods, 1973). The constituency schema has been previously

---

[8]   In our knowledge base, this does not happen.

represented using this formalism successfully (McKeown, 1985). Although the process trace is procedural in nature, by using the same formalism for the two strategies (i.e., a declarative form), we obtain the control structure necessary to switch from one strategy to the other, thus gaining the ability to employ both strategies in the same description.

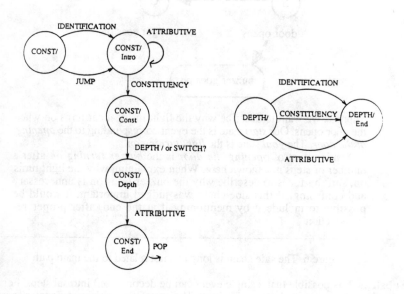

Figure 7. The Constituency Schema

The constituency strategy is shown in Figure 7. The arcs of the ATN dictate what information from the knowledge base to include in the description. For the constituency schema, the arcs correspond to the predicates from the schema, thus defining the type of information to be taken from the database. The predicates are:

— the *identification* predicate, which represents the more general concept of which the present object is an instance
— the *constituency* predicate, which gives the components of an object, if there are any
— the *attributive* predicate, which provides different attributes of an object (such as its shape or material)
— the *cause-effect* predicate, that provides some causal relations between entities or relations.

; Stepping through the Constituency Schema to describe
; a MICROPHONE

Applying the predicates to MICROPHONE:

Identification predicate: DEVICE; (used-for: change soundwaves into current)

Constituency   predicate:DIAPHRAGM (shape disc, material aluminum),
                         DOUBLY-RESONANT-SYSTEM (used-for: broaden
                         response)

Depth-constituency for DOUBLY-RESONANT-SYSTEM:
                        CARBON-CHAMBER, AIR-CHAMBER

Depth-attributive for   DIAPHRAGM: (edges clamped)

English output:
*The microphone changes soundwaves into current. It has a disc-shaped aluminum
diaphragm and a doubly-resonant system to broaden the response. The system has a
carbon chamber, and an air chamber. The diaphragm is clamped at its edges.*

Figure 8. Stepping through the Constituency Schema

The process of filling the ATN for the constituency schema strategy to describe a *microphone* is
shown in Figure 8. The identification predicate is first applied to the microphone. It provides
the superordinate of the object together with the function of the object. The constituency
predicate is then applied, providing the parts of the microphone, together with their properties
and purposes. Finally, the depth-identification predicate is applied to each subpart, the doubly-
resonant system and the diaphragm.

The network for the process trace is shown in Figure 9. In the process trace network, the
arcs dictate how to trace the knowledge base to form a process description, mainly by following
the causal links in the knowledge base. These arcs are not predicates as in the network
corresponding to the constituency schema. The arcs indicate the following actions:

— *Next-main-link.* This arc dictates to follow the next link on the main path.
— *Long-side-chain?* This arc tests for a long side chain that gets re-attached to the main path
  and needs to be followed first. If the test returns True, the subnet long-chain is called. This
  subnet dictates to follow the links of the side chain.
— *Short-Side-link?* A test is made to see whether there is a side link coming off an event at this
  point. The test includes checking the importance of the side link and the length of its
  associated side chain. If this link is important and short, the arc will be taken, i.e., the side
  link will be included. Since the side links were marked while the program was obtaining the
  main path, it is also possible to check for the number of short side links. It there are many
  side links, they will be grouped at the end instead of being mentioned at this point.
— *Attributive.* This arc is similar to the attributive predicate in the constituency schema. We
  noticed that a description is never purely process oriented, but that information about parts is
  presented when parts are mentioned as part of the process. If information about a part just
  introduced is available in the knowledge base, this arc will be taken.
— *Substeps?* If an event at this point can be divided into substeps and the description does not
  have to be short, each substep with its associated chain is followed. To traverse the
  substeps, the subroutine substep is called for each substep. This subroutine is very similar

to the main graph but does not allow for a further decomposition of events. (If a shorter description is desired, we choose not to follow the substeps.)

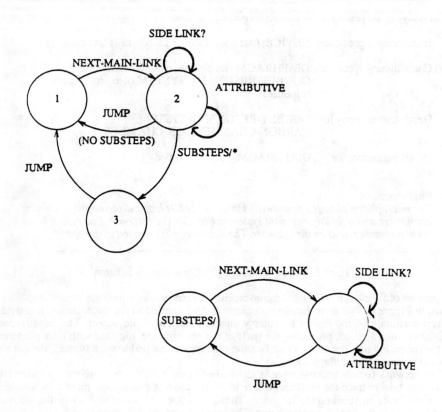

Figure 9. The Process Trace

The process of filling the ATN for the process trace strategy is illustrated by Figure 10[9] which shows the process description for the loudspeaker. This description includes explaining the causal links at the substep level and includes a short side link, an analogical link. This process description is obtained by applying the process strategy to the subset of the knowledge base of Figure 3 above. In Figure 11, we show the process description for the dialing mechanism, which involves following a side chain. (The knowledge base for the dialing mechanism was shown in Figure 5.) In tracing the process description, it is necessary to first mention a side link before mentioning the events on the main path, as the events on the side links are preconditions for the events on the main path.

---

[9] While not all the cases are found in our knowledge base, our algorithm would be able to treat them appropriately.

PROCESS TRACE FOR THE LOUDSPEAKER

MAIN PATH

First Causal Link:

{M-CAUSES} relates the two relations: ; The variation of the current
    [CURRENT] VARIES   ; causes the field of
    [FIELD] VARIES   ; the magnet to vary.

Substeps: first substep: current increases
        second substep: current decreases

Causal link in the **first substep:**
{M-CAUSES} relates the two relations: ; When the current increases
    [CURRENT] INCREASES   ; the field
    [FIELD] INCREASES   ; increases.

Next causal link in the substep chain:
{M-CAUSES} relates the two relations: ; Because the field increases,
    ; the poles
    [FIELD] INCREASES   ; of the magnet
    [POLES] ATTRACT [DIAPHRAGM   ; attract the diaphragm
    ; of the loudspeaker.

Next causal link in the substep chain:
{M-CAUSES} relates the two relations: ; The poles attracting the diaphragm
    ; causes the
    [POLES] ATTRACT [DIAPHRAGM   ; diaphragm to spring
    [DIAPHRAGM] MOVES-FORWARD   ; forward.

Causal link in the **second substep:**

{M-CAUSES} relates the two relations: ; The current decreasing
    [CURRENT] DECREASES   ; causes the field to
    [FIELD] DECREASES   ; decrease.

Next causal link in the substep chain:
{M-CAUSES} relates the two relations: ; This causes the poles
    [FIELD] DECREASES   ; to release the
    [POLES] RELEASES [DIAPHRAGM]   ; diaphragm.

Next causal link in the substep chain:
{M-CAUSES} relates the two relations: ; Because the poles release the
    ; diaphragm, the
    [POLES] RELEASES [DIAPHRAGM]   ; diaphragm springs
    [DIAPHRAGM] MOVES-BACKWARD   ; backward.

Back to the main path

Next causal link in the main path:
{M-CAUSES} relates the two relations: ; The field varying
    [FIELD] VARIES   ; causes the diaphragm
    [DIAPHRAGM] VIBRATES   ; to vibrate.

Figure 10 (first part). Including substeps and an isolated side link (an analogical link)

Substeps: first substep: diaphragm moves forward
second substep: diaphragm moves backward

    Causal link in the first substep:
    {M-CAUSES} relates the two relations: ; Because the diaphragm springs
        [DIAPHRAGM] MOVES-FORWARD   ; forward, the
        [SOUNDWAVE-INTENSITY] DECREASES   ; soundwave intensity
        ; decreases

    Causal link in the second substep:
    {M-CAUSES} relates the two relations: ; The diaphragm springing
        [DIAPHRAGM] MOVES-BACKWARD   ; backward causes the
        [SOUNDWAVE-INTENSITY] INCREASES   ; soundwave intensity to
        ; increase

Back to the main path

Next causal link in the main path:
  {M-CAUSES} relates the two relations: ; The vibration of the diaphragm
      [DIAPHRAGM] VIBRATES   ; causes the soundwave
      [SOUNDWAVE-INTENSITY] VARIES   ; intensity to vary.

Isolated short side-link

Analogical link:
  {M-CORRESPONDS-TO} relates the two relations: ; The soundwave intensity
      [SOUNDWAVE-INTENSITY] VARIES   ; varies, like the current
      [CURRENT] VARIES   ; varies.

English output[10]
*The variation of the current causes the field of the magnet to vary. When the current
increases the field increases. Because the field increases the poles of the magnet attract the
diaphragm of the loudspeaker. The poles attracting the diaphragm causes the diaphragm to
spring forward. The current decreasing causes the field to decrease. This causes the poles
to release the diaphragm. Because the poles release the diaphragm the diaphragm springs
backward. The field varying causes the diaphragm to vibrate. Because the diaphragm
springs forward, the soundwave intensity decreases. The diaphragm springing backward
causes the soundwave intensity to increase. The vibration of the diaphragm causes the
soundwave intensity to vary. The soundwave intensity varies, like the current varies.*

Figure 10 (second part)

---

[10] This is only part of the description that would be generated. The full description includes a statement to
introduce the loudspeaker first and attributive information. This information is omitted here as the emphasis
is on tracing links between events. We are still working on the surface generator to produce smoother texts.
However, as our emphasis in this work is on the content of a description, we are not studying the complexity
and subtleties of surface choice.

PROCESS TRACE FOR DIALING MECHANISM

LONG SIDE CHAIN

First Causal Link of the side-chain:
   {M-CAUSES} relates the two relations: ; That a person pushes
      [ONE] PUSHES [DIAL]   ; the dial of a telephone
      [DIAL-ASSEMBLY] TURNS-CLOCKWISE   ; causes the dialing
                                       ; mechanism to turn clockwise.

Next Causal link of the side chain:
   {M-CAUSES} relates the two relations: ; This causes
      [DIAL-ASSEMBLY] TURNS-CLOCKWISE   ; causes the circular
      [CIRCULAR-SPRING] COMPRESS   ; spring to decompress.

MAIN PATH

First Link:
   {M-ENABLES} relates the two relations: ; A person pushing the
      [ONE] PUSHES [DIAL]   ; dial enables the dial
      [ONE] RELEASES [DIAL]   ; to be released.

Next Causal Link:
   {M-CAUSES} relates the two relations: ; This causes the
      [ONE] RELEASES [DIAL]   ; spring to decompress.
      [CIRCULAR-SPRING] DECOMPRESSES

Next Causal Link:
   {M-CAUSES} relates the two relations: ; This causes the assembly
      [CIRCULAR-SPRING] DECOMPRESSES   ; to turn counterclockwise.
      [DIAL-ASSEMBLY] TURN-COUNTERCLOCKWISE

Next Causal Link:
   {M-CAUSES} relates the two relations: ; This causes the small
      [DIAL-ASSEMBLY] TURN-COUNTERCLOCKWISE ; gear to turn.
      [SMALL-GEAR] TURNS

Next Causal Link:
   {M-CAUSES} relates the two relations: ; This causes the protrusion
      [SMALL-GEAR] TURNS   ; of the small gear to hit
      [PROTRUSION] HITS [SWITCH-LEVER]   ; the lever.

Next Causal Link:
   {M-CAUSES} relates the two relations: ; This causes the lever to
      [PROTRUSION] HITS [SWITCH-LEVER]   ; close.
      [SWITCH-LEVER] CLOSES

Next Causal Link:
   {M-CAUSES} relates the two relations: ; This causes current
      [SWITCH-LEVER] CLOSES   ; pulses.
      [CURRENT-PULSE] PRODUCED

Figure 11. Include a long chain that gets re-attached to the main path

---

Description of a telephone

The telephone changes soundwaves into soundwaves. The telephone has a housing that has various shapes, a transmitter that changes soundwaves into current, a curly-shaped cord, a line, a receiver to change current into soundwaves, and a dialing-mechanism. The transmitter is a microphone. A person speaking into the microphone causes the soundwaves to hit the diaphragm of the microphone. Because the soundwaves hit the diaphragm, the diaphragm vibrates. The vibration of the diaphragm causes the current to vary. The current varies like the intensity varies. The receiver is a loudspeaker with a small aluminium diaphragm. The housing contains the transmitter. The housing contains the receiver. The housing is connected to the dialing-mechanism by the cord. The line connects the dialing-mechanism to the wall.

Figure 12. One possible combination of the two strategies. The telephone is first described using the constituency schema; then the transmitter (an instance of a 'microphone') is described using the process trace, while the other parts are described using the constituency schema.

We have found in previous work that, depending on the user's level of knowledge about the domain, one of the two strategies (declarative or procedural) is more appropriate than the other (Paris, 1985, 1986). In particular, the declarative constituency schema is appropriate for an expert user and the process strategy for a naive user. A system can therefore select a strategy based on the user's assumed domain knowledge level. Users are not necessarily strictly naive or expert, however. For users with intermediate level of domain knowledge, we need to combine the two strategies to obtain the proper mix of structural and process information. In order to do this, we must provide a control strategy that will allow the program to easily switch from one strategy to the other. Using the same formalism (an ATN) for both strategies (instead of of using the ATN for the constituency schema as in McKeown (1985), and an algorithm for the process trace) gives us such a control structure: to switch strategy, the program only needs to jump from a node in one network to a node in the other one. Figure 12 shows an example of a text that combining the strategies allows us to generate.

6. CONCLUSION

We have presented a discourse strategy that can be used to produce descriptions of complex physical objects. Unlike other discourse strategies, this strategy is procedural in nature, in that it consists of directives for tracing the underlying knowledge base. The resulting text thus mirrors the structure of the knowledge base rather than the structure of the strategy as is the case for texts produced using declarative strategies. By representing the procedural strategy in the same formalism as the declarative strategy, we have gained the ability to use the two strategies together to produce a single text. This can be generalized to handle any number of strategies and thus gives a generation system greater flexibility.

ACKNOWLEDGMENTS

Many thanks go to Michael Lebowitz for his help with the research presented in this paper, and to Kwee Tjoe-Liong for his work on the functional grammar. This research was supported in part by the Defense Advanced Research Projects Agency under contract N00039-84-C-0165, and the National Science Foundation grant ISI-84-51438.

REFERENCES

Collier, R. (1962) *Collier's Encyclopedia*. The Crowell-Collier Publishing Company.
Grimes, J. E. (1975) *The Thread of Discourse*. Mouton: The Hague.
Hobbs, J. (1978) *Why is a Discourse Coherent?* Technical Report 176, SRI International.
Hobbs, J. & Evans, D. (1980) Conversation as Planned Behavior. *Cognitive Science, 4*, 349-377.
Kukich, K. (1985) Explanation Structures in XSEL. In: *Proceedings of the 23rd Annual Meeting of the Association for Computational Linguistics*. Chicago, Illinois.
Lebowitz, M. (1983) RESEARCHER: An Overview. In: *Proceedings of the Third National Conference on Artificial Intelligence*. Washington, DC.
Lebowitz, M. (1985) RESEARCHER: An experimental intelligent information system. In: *Proceedings of the Ninth International Joint Conference on Artificial Intelligence*. Los Angeles, California.
Linde, C. & Labov W. (1975) Spatial Networks as a Site for the Study of Language and Thought. *Language, 57*, 924-939.
Mann, W. C. (1984) Discourse Structures for Text Generation. In: *Proceedings of COLING '84*. Stanford, California.
McCoy, K. F. (1986) The ROMPER System: Responding to Object-Related Misconceptions Using Perspective. In: *Proceedings of the 24th Annual Meeting of the Association of Computational Linguistics*. New York.
McKeown, K. R. (1982) *Generating Natural Language Text in Response to Questions About Database Structure*. PhD thesis, University of Pennsylvania.
McKeown, K. R. (1985) *Text Generation: Using Discourse Strategies and Focus Constraints to Generate Natural Language Text*. Cambridge: Cambridge University Press.
Paris, C.L. (1985) Description Strategies for Naive and Expert Users. In: *Proceedings of the 23rd Annual Meeting of the Association for Computational Linguistics*. Chicago.
Paris, C. L. (1986) *Tailoring Object Descriptions to the User's Level of Expertise*. Paper presented at the International Workshop on User Modelling. Maria Laach, West Germany. Will appear in Computational Linguistics (special issue on user modeling).
Shepherd, H. R. (1926) *The Fine Art of Writing*. New York: Macmillan Co.
Weiner, J. (1980) BLAH, a System that Explains its Reasoning. *Artificial Intelligence , 15*, 19-48.
Woods, W. (1973) An Experimental Parsing System for Transition Network Grammars. In: R. Rustin (Ed.) *Natural Language Processing*. New York: Algorithmics Press.

Chapter 9

STRATEGIES FOR GENERATING COHERENT DESCRIPTIONS OF OBJECT MOVEMENTS IN STREET SCENES

Hans-Joachim Novak

ABSTRACT

In this chapter a verbalization strategy for the generation of descriptions is motivated which leads to a specific text structure and to an event selection algorithm that is based on a specialization hierarchy of motion verbs. It is assumed that the hearer is familiar with the static parts of the scene and that the system is to inform him about the motions in such a way that he may image[1] them. This assumption in turn leads to the strategy of anticipated visualization for the selection of optional deep cases of a verb. Both strategies have been operationalized and are implemented in the NAOS system. It is further shown that the generation of restrictive relative clauses and the use of negation arises naturally from the task of generating referring expressions in a dynamic environment.

1. INTRODUCTION

In this chapter we focus on the verbalization component of the NAOS system. (The acronym stands for NAtural language description of Object movements in a traffic Scene.) NAOS is designed to explore the border area between computer vision and natural language processing, especially the realm of recognizing and verbalizing motion concepts in image sequences (*image sequence* and *scene* are used synonymously to denote a temporal sequence of single images as given by a TV-camera or in a film).

In NAOS processing starts with the representation of a scene and ends with a natural language text describing the scene. The representation of a scene basically consists of its geometry (it is therefore called *geometric scene description* or GSD). To give an impression of the representation, a GSD contains for each frame of the image sequence:
— instance of time
— visible objects
— viewpoint
— illumination
and for each object:
— 3D shape
— surface characteristics (color)
— class
— identity

---

[1] The verb *image* is used in the sense of Kosslyn (1980), i.e. to form a visual mental image (here called *imagination*) of motions. In particular, the hearer should be able to draw the trajectories of the objects in a map depicting the static parts of the scene.

— 3D position and orientation in each frame
For a detailed description of the GSD, see Neumann (1984b).

For event recognition we use event models (Neumann & Novak, 1983a, b) which define a reference semantics for motion verbs; i.e., an event model defines the applicability of a motion verb by reference to perceptual situations. An event is understood as a spatio-temporal region of an image sequence that may be described by a motion verb. Thus we adopt the view expressed by Miller & Johnson-Laird (1976) that events '...denote changes of the kind people talk about'. In the current implementation of the NAOS system about 35 motion verbs (events) and the prepositions *behind, beside, by, in front of, near* and *on* can be recognized by matching the event models against the representation of the scene.

In this paper we are concerned neither with the representation of the underlying scene data nor with the question of event recognition, as these issues have been treated in other publications (see Neumann, 1984a, b; Neumann & Novak, 1985, 1986). Instead we focus on the generation of a coherent text describing the image sequence.

In the following section we briefly describe the representation of the recognized events which form the initial data for the verbalization component. Then some basic assumptions are introduced and strategies for composing a coherent description are discussed. The subsequent section first introduces the strategy of anticipated visualization and then discusses selection processes. Next, we show that the use of certain constructions, — e.g., the passive voice, restrictive relative clauses, and negation — is a natural consequence of the task of generating unambiguous referring expressions. In the last section we relate our research to other current work on language generation.

2. INITIAL DATA

In NAOS verbalization starts when event recognition has been achieved. Besides complex events like *overtake* and *turn off*, other predicates like *in front of, besides, move* are also instantiated. Below is a section of the database after event recognition has taken place (the original entries are in German.)

> (MOVE PERSON1 0 40)
> (WALK PERSON1 0 40)
> (RECEDE PERSON1 CS-BUILDING 20 40)
> (OVERTAKE BMW1 VW1 (10 12) (15 32))
> (MOVE BMW1 10 40)
> (IN-FRONT-OF VW1 TRAFFIC-LIGHT1 27 32)

These entries are instantiations of event models containing symbolic identifiers for scene objects (e.g. BMW1). The last two elements of an instantiation denote the start and end time of the event. Note, that for one object, e.g. PERSON1, several events may have been recognized for the same time-interval.

We use the following notation to denote the event time:

> 1. $(....Tb \ Te)$
> 2. $(....(Tb_{min} \ Tb_{max})(Te_{min} \ Te_{max}))$
> 3. $(....(Tb_{min} \ Tb_{max}) \ Te)$
> 4. $(....Tb \ (Te_{min} \ Te_{max}))$

Tb, Te denote start and end time of an event. The first notation is used for *durative* events (e.g. corresponding to the verb *move*). A durative event can also be said to occur in each subinterval of (Tb Te). The second notation is used for *nondurative* events (e.g., corresponding to the verb *overtake*). The start and end times of such an event are both restricted by lower and upper bounds. Note that non durative events cannot be said to occur in each subinterval of the event boundaries. The third notation is used for *resultative* events (e.g. corresponding to *stop*).

The start time of a resultative event lies within an interval whereas the end time is a time point. Finally, the last notation is used for *inchoative* events (e.g. *start moving*, corresponding to the German verb *losfahren*). Inchoative events have a well-defined start time whereas the end time lies within an interval.

In contrast to usual practice in linguistics we distinguish between durative and general nondurative motion verbs and the specializations thereof, inchoative and resultative verbs. These distinctions are necessary for the recognition of the events (for details on the recognition process see Novak, 1985) and correspond to the manner of action of the verbs. The latter is not to be confounded with aspect: One may express an inchoative event like *start moving* in a perfect tense, but this does not change the fact that an inchoative event must have been perceived if one is to use the words *start moving*.

For the task of generating a coherent description of a traffic scene NAOS first instantiates all event models and predicates which may be instantiated using the scene data. This leads to the well-known *selection problem* of natural language generation. In our case, several motion verbs may be applicable to describe the movements of an object in a given time interval, hence the task of the verbalization component is to choose from them.

In the next section we discuss strategies for describing time-varying imagery; in particular, we consider text aim and text constitution. First, however, we present some assumptions about the hearer to establish the communicative situation for the generation process.

2.1 Assumptions

In general, language is not generated per se but is always intended for a hearer. Furthermore, language is used to fulfill certain goals of the speaker, which may sometimes include that of informing the hearer about certain facts.

The overall motivation for the generation of a description of the underlying image sequence is to diminish the discrepancy between the system's knowledge of the scene and the hearer's knowledge. (The same motivation is used in Davey's (1978) program.) We make the following assumptions concerning the hearer:

1. S/he cannot see the scene
2. S/he knows the static background of the scene, i.e. the streets, houses, traffic lights, etc.[2]
3. S/he has not expressed any specific interests, beyond a desire for a description of the scene.

These assumptions put the initiative for generation into the hands of the speaker, and we have to ask: 'What may the goal of the speaker be when he does not know much about the hearer?' For NAOS we define the goal of the speaker (and for reasons of simplicity the aim of the text as well) as follows:

The speaker tries to describe the scene in such a way that the hearer can image it.

We do not aim at explicitly representing the imagination of the hearer; instead, we formulate requirements which the text must fulfill if the hearer is to be able to image the scene. We will show that these requirements lead to algorithms for the selection of events and the selection of optional deep cases of the verbs associated with the events which partially solve the selection problem.

In the next section we motivate the text structure which has been chosen for the NAOS system.

---

[2] *Know* in this context means that we assume the hearer to have the same knowledge about the static background of the scene as the system does. In NAOS this knowledge is given by an extensive street model.

3. TEXT CONSTITUTION

We view a *description* as a kind of text that enables the hearer/reader to construct an image or an imagination of the entity described. Description is in our case restricted to spatial and temporal relations of objects and events. We do not deal with plans or actions. If the text aim lies in the formation of an image, several requirements can be formulated, concerning

1. the completeness of the text with respect to the text aim and the underlying scene data:

   — mention all objects which are necessary to enable the hearer to form a precise imagination, i.e. one resembling the underlying scene[3]
   — verbalize all events of an object, preferably deviations from standard assumptions (e.g. *to speed* instead of *to move* if the object moves faster than at normal speed)
   — mention all relevant spatial relations between the objects
   — if necessary, verbalize the temporal relations between events

2. textual form:

   — coherent text constitution
   — unequivocal object descriptions
   — precise wording
   — omission of inferable and known propositions.

The first point of the above enumeration concerns *verbalization*, i.e., deciding what to say, the second one generation, i.e., deciding how to say it. Viewing the generation of a description in the context of a dialogue, for instance as answer to the question 'What exactly does the film show?', it becomes apparent that the above requirements are an application of the conversational maxims as stated by Grice (1975) to the task of image sequence description given the above text aim.

We now deal with the question 'What is a suitable text constitution for descriptions?'. An answer to this question may be given at different levels. On the one hand, formal text properties like *chapter, paragraph,* and *highlighting* may be relevant, on the other hand categories like *rhetorical schemata* (McKeown, 1985) or *chains of arguments* (Mann, 1984) become relevant. In the following we point out two options for the description of image sequences. First, however, a couple of remarks concerning the segmentation of scenes are in order. We present options for segmentations based on visual data and ignore task- or action-oriented connections. An image sequence, i.e. a film, can be segmented according to different actions or themes. We call this kind of splitting of an image sequence *macroscopic segmentation*. In contrast, the task of the *microscopic segmentation* lies in the identification of spatio-temporal regions of an image sequence which may be described linguistically, e.g., by means of a verb. In NAOS the latter kind of segmentation is realized by the event-recognition process.

In contrast to image description[4], image sequence description has to consider a new dimension, time. On the one hand, this dimension complicates the task, since temporal relations have to be made explicit; on the other hand, time provides a criterion, namely temporal order, along which a description can be constructed. The task is complicated by the fact that in a scene many agents appear whose movements (in general, actions) have to be related to one another.

Consider the following text:

---

[3] Consider the case in which the hearer is asked to draw the trajectories of the objects in a map depicting the streets and houses where the motion occurred.

[4] A strategy for image description based on the notion of *salience* has been proposed in Conklin & McDonald, 1982.

I am standing with my back to the entrance. In front of me is a corridor of about 10m long with a door at the far end. On the right-hand side there are several book shelves and on the left-hand side I can see three doors. Someone comes out of the room at the far end, looks into the adjacent room, goes into the middle room and closes the door.

This text exemplifies a basic verbalization strategy. First, the invariants of the scene (in NAOS called *static background*) are described, then the motions are verbalized with respect to these invariants. The temporal relations between the events need not be made explicit if the events are sequential, as the relations are implied by their linear order (see also Mann et al., 1982). This kind of description relative to a static background is typically used in plays and film scripts. In general, there are two strategies:

1.   The motions of each object are described in temporally consecutive order and are related to each other with adverbs (some adverbs, e.g. *then*, are also conjunctions)
2.   The time axis is segmented by certain events, and for each segment the motions of the each object are described sequentially with the implication that the sequences of events involving the different objects are concurrent.

An example for the second strategy is as follows. (We have left out the initial description of the static background.)

It starts raining. Two pedestrians get their umbrellas out of their bags and open them. A young man jumps backwards as a car drives through the water in front of him. He crosses the road. Suddenly it stops raining.

In this case, the time interval during which it rains segments the time axis. The motion sequences of the different objects that are described during this interval are considered to be simultaneous.

Common to both strategies is the description of the motions relative to a static background, and we do not discuss the more complicated case where the background is also changing. This is usually the case when the observer is moving.

3.1   Descriptions in NAOS

Research within NAOS into the generation of descriptions has aimed at identifying and exploring basic selection processes. Event recognition (see Neumann, 1984b, and Novak, 1985) can be seen as microscopic segmentation of the scene; it yields parts of the image sequence which may be described with verbs. Thus an algorithmic relation between scenes and language is realized. At present we abstract away from higher level concepts such as *actions* and *episodes* and assume a specific text aim and specific a priori knowledge about the hearer. This context, which might be called neutral, yields elementary criteria for the selection of verbs and deep cases and may form the basis for further context-dependent decision processes.

As noted previously, in NAOS the aim of the text is to enable the hearer to build an imagination of the described scene, i.e., to diminish the discrepancy between the system's and the hearer's knowledge about the scene. The textual requirements were discussed in the last section. NAOS only generates the speech act INFORM, i.e. only true and new propositions in conformity with the Gricean maxims are generated. Furthermore, the sentences are all in indicative mode. As we assume the static background to be known, only the trajectories of the objects have to be verbalized. The structure of a text is as follows:

—   The first sentence informs the listener about the number and class membership of the moving objects in the actual scene.
—   For each object there is a paragraph in which the motions of the object are described consecutively; if the verbalized motions are not sequential, this is made explicit by the use of temporal adverbs.

The principles underlying this text structure can easily be recognized by the reader, they thus enhance coherence. Other coherence indicators are anaphora and lexical semantic contiguity, i.e. the use of different lexical items that are semantically close for the same referent (e.g. *vehicle, car, BMW*).

In the next section we present the principle of anticipated visualization which allows the speaker to fulfill the text aim.

4. ANTICIPATED VISUALIZATION

A method for generating texts so that the hearer may construct an imagination implies the anticipation of the way the hearer will interpret each utterance. In our case, we assume the imaginations of the hearer to be spatio-temporal in nature. His task is to integrate a verbally specified trajectory of an object into his internal model of the static background of the scene. The speaker can simplify the task if he does not offer the hearer different ways of integrating an object's trajectory into his internal model. Note that we do not claim that the hearer actually does construct an imagination of the scene but only assume that he can and may do so. Weber (1983) has shown that motion verbs can be represented mentally by images (see also Kosslyn, 1980, for support of this assumption).

The principle is depicted in Figure 1. The figure exemplifies that we are not interested in modeling the hearer but rather in modeling how the speaker anticipates the hearer's interpretation using a *partner model*. At present, the partner model contains information about the static background of the scene and about what has been said so far. This information is represented in the same relational notation as was shown in section 2 for instantiations. The partner model is initialized when the system is started and is updated when an event is verbalized.

On the left-hand side it can be seen that when event models are used, instantiations of the models (called *events* in the figure) can be found by matching them against the geometric scene description. Using the case semantics and the scene description, a case frame of an utterance can be constructed. The case semantics contains information about the prepositions which can be used with a given verb to construct deep cases (e.g., LOCATIVE and SOURCE) and about how they can be computed.

Given that the speaker and the hearer share the same meaning relations (apart from some idiosyncrasies), the speaker can extract the case frame of the utterance and thus anticipate which imagination the hearer might construct. At present we do not represent the imagination explicitly, e.g. with depictions, as proposed by Kosslyn (1980). The process stops at the propositional level, i.e. the instantiated event models plus relations for the computed deep cases — e.g., (LOCATIVE IN-FRONT-OF BMW1 TRAFFIC-LIGHT1 10 20) — are entered into the partner model. Ultimately, an explicit representation of the imagination should be achieved.

The main problem in representing such an imagination stems from the fact that the verbalization of a visual event always leads to a loss of information (see also Olson, 1972). For instance, we cannot assume that the hearer knows the x, y, and z coordinates of an object when he hears the phrase *next to the traffic light*. Such a phrase must be considered as generating a set of coordinates defining the region which corresponds to the preposition *next to*.

Figure 1 also shows that case frames play a central role in our generation component. A case frame specifies all of the deep cases (Fillmore, 1968) that a specific verb may take. Several verbs may share the same case frame. We distinguish further between obligatory and optional deep cases. (See the example of the case semantics for *überholen* below, where we also specify how deep cases are generated.) In NAOS case frames relate scenes to language, as has been proposed by Fillmore (1977).

In the next section we discuss the two main selection processes of NAOS, namely event selection and deep case selection. The first one corresponds to deciding what to say and the second one largely determines how to say it.

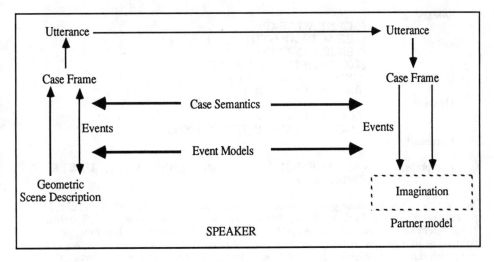

Figure 1. Anticipated Visualization

5. THE SELECTION PROCESSES

The selection processes are based on a specialization hierarchy for motion verbs and on the representation of the case semantics. The hierarchy connects general verbs with more specific ones. It is not a hierarchy of motion concepts like the one proposed by Tsotsos (1980). The general idea is that, e.g., a perceptual situation which may be described using a specific verb like *überholen* (*overtake*) implies the applicability of the more general verbs *vorüberfahren, vorbeifahren* (*drive past*), *passieren* (*pass*), *nähern* (*approach*), *entfernen* (*recede*), *fahren* (*drive*), and *bewegen* (*move*). The reason for the implication is that in order to verify that a situation may be described with the verb *überholen* one must verify all of the features of the more general verbs plus the additional feature of *überholen*, namely that the object being overtaken is also moving. For instance, Levelt, Schreuder & Hoenkamp (1978) showed that people verify specific verbs more easily than general ones (in their terminology: generic ones). Levelt et al. assume that the features of the more specific verbs are also more salient.

The hierarchy is used to select the most specific event for a given time interval from a set of instantiations for this interval. It should be intuitively plausible that such a hierarchy can also be used for event recognition. If, for instance, no *nähern* (*approach*) can be instantiated, the conditions for the more specific events need not be tested, as the features of *nähern* would have to be present in them.

Below is the representation of the case semantics for the event model *überholen* (*overtake*).

```
More general:   (VORBEIFAHREN VORÜBERFAHREN)
More specific:  NIL
Verb type:      LOC
Agent Restr:    VEHICLE
Deep cases:

                (VERB ÜBERHOL)
                (ÜBERHOLEN *OBJ1 *OBJ2 *T1 *T2)
```

Obligatory:

(AGENT AGT-EXP)
(REF AGT-EXP *OBJ1)
(TENSE TNS-EXP)
(TIME-REF TNS-EXP *T1 *T2)
(OBJECTIVE OBJ-EXP)
(REF OBJ-EXP *OBJ2)

Optional:

(LOCATIVE LOC-EXP)
(LOC-REF LOC-EXP *OBJ1 *T1 *T2)

Combinations:

NIL

Loc-preps:

(AN AUF BEI HINTER IN NEBEN ÜBER UNTER VOR ZWISCHEN)

The first slot lists the more general verbs and the second one notes that *overtake* does not specialize further. The third slot shows that *überholen* has the verb type LOC. We distinguish four different verb types: LOC, STAT, DIR, and REO; locomotion verbs like *bewegen* (*move*), static verbs like *stehen* (*stand*), directional verbs like *drehen, abbiegen* (*turn, turn off*), and verbs with reference objects like *erreichen, ankommen* (*reach, arrive at*). This distinction is necessary because the verbs behave differently with regard to the selection of deep cases, as will be shown later. The slot Agent-Restr. specifies the selectional restriction for this verb: Its agent has to belong to the class VEHICLE. The Deep cases slot contains (1) the verb stem of *überholen* which is needed by the generation component, (2) the formal notation for an instantiation, and (3) the case frame of the verb. Obligatory cases must be generated, but they may be omitted in the surface string of an elliptical utterance. Optional cases, on the other hand, need not be generated at all. The Combinations slot specifies which deep cases must be generated together (e.g. it is not permissible to generate only a SOURCE for the verb *fahren* (*drive*); both SOURCE and GOAL must be generated). Finally, the Loc-preps slot specifies the prepositions which may be used with the verb *überholen* in order to generate locative expressions.

The case descriptions in the obligatory and optional slots consist of two parts: a declaration of an identifier for the case expression on the language side, e.g. AGT-EXP for the AGENT, and a predicate (generally a list of predicates) relating the case expression to the scene data, e.g. (REF AGT-EXP *OBJ1). The most important predicates are REF, TIME-REF, and LOC-REF.

REF generates referring phrases for internal object descriptors like BMW1. TIME-REF generates the tense of the verb. As descriptions are usually given in the present tense, TIME-REF only generates this tense.[5] LOC-REF relates the abstract location of the object as given by its coordinates to a natural language expression for a reference object. Note that REF has to be used to generate a referring phrase for the reference object.

In the next section we present the event selection process, which is motivated by the text structure.

5.1 Event selection

In NAOS the overall strategy for generating a descriptive text is as follows:

— Group all moving objects according to their class membership
— For each object in each group describe the motions of the object for the time interval during which it was visible in the scene.

---

[5] The use of tenses other than the present tense would be no problem provided there were appropriate selection mechanisms deciding which tense to use.

Event selection for an object is done according to the following algorithm:

1. Collect all events in the interval during which the object was visible and of which it was the agent
2. Using the specialization hierarchy, determine for each time point during the object's visibility the most specific of the events collected in the previous step
3. If two events have the same degree of specificity, take the one which started earlier and has the same or a longer duration as the other one, or if none started earlier take the one with the longer duration
4. Put the selected events on the verbalization list of the object in temporally consecutive order.

This algorithm may lead to a verbalization list like:

> (((APPROACH VW1 PERSON1 1 20) (1 20))
> ((DRIVE VW1 1 40) (20 40)))

The verbalization list of an object contains the ordered set of events that are to be verbalized for this object. The last entry in parentheses of each selected event denotes the interval for which it is the most specific one.

5.2 Deep case selection

The generation of deep cases aims at allowing the hearer to build an imagination of the described motion which is as close as possible to the data perceived by the speaker. The problem becomes apparent if we ask ourselves: 'What can the hearer image if he hears a sentence like "The BMW overtakes a truck?"'

Even given his knowledge of the static background, he knows neither where the motion occurs nor in which direction the objects move. He can thus image the motion in many different ways. This is at variance with our text aim. We thus have to ask: 'Which spatial deep cases should be verbalized so that the hearer can image the described motions precisely?' Spatial deep cases are, for instance, SOURCE, GOAL, and LOCATIVE, in contrast to AGENT and OBJECTIVE, which do not denote spatial entities.

Our selection algorithm answering the above question is rather straightforward. It is based on the manner of action of the verb, the verb type, and the hearer's knowledge. The algorithm is represented graphically in Figure 2; it is our first implementation of the strategy of anticipated visualization. The abbreviations denote: T_{beg}, T_{end}: start, end time of the event; SB, SE: scene beginning and scene end.

The figure is to be read as follows. If an inchoative event like *losfahren (start moving)* has to be verbalized, which has the verb type loc, then choose direction? and locative? as deep cases. The question mark generally means the following: Look into the partner model to see whether this deep case has already been generated for another event of the object. If so, determine by use of the object's actual location (represented in the scene representation) whether it is still valid; if it is not, generate a natural language expression for this deep case.

Note, that for durative events the decision is based on whether the start and end time of the event coincide with the beginning or ending of the image sequence. Consider the first case for durative events as given in Figure 2. Right from the beginning of the sequence there is a car moving along a street until the sequence ends. In such a case it is not possible to verbalize a source, as the object may have started its motion anywhere. So as to give the hearer a precise imagination, direction and locative cases are verbalized, leading to a sentence like:

> 'The car moves on Schlüter Street towards Haller Square.'

EVENTTYPE	VERBTYPE	CASES
non-durative, inchoative	dir loc reo	locative? direction?, locative? direction?
resultative	dir, loc reo	locative? nil
durative $T_{beg} = SB$, $T_{end} = SE$	reo dir, stat loc	nil locative? direction?, locative?
$T_{beg} = SB$, $T_{end} <> SE$	stat dir, reo loc	locative? nil direction?
$T_{beg} <> SB$, $T_{end} = SE$	stat dir loc reo	locative? locative? source?, direction? nil
$T_{beg} <> SB$, $T_{end} = SE$	reo dir, stat loc	nil locative? source?, goal?

Figure 2. Deep Case Selection

Verbalizing a direction when the static background is known restricts the imagined trajectory to being on one side of the road. Basically, our direction case is a goal or source case for which two prepositional phrases are allowed, the German phrases *in Richtung* and *aus Richtung* (*toward, from the direction of*). These phrases do not imply that the motion ends at the goal location, as do most prepositional phrases in German, which have to be in the accusative surface case to denote a goal.

We have to distinguish different verb types since, e.g., the meaning of a directional phrase changes with the verb type. Consider the sentences 'The car moves toward Haller Square' versus 'The car stands toward Haller Square'. (In German both sentences are well-formed.) The first sentence denotes the direction of the motion, whereas the second one denotes the orientation of the car. We thus distinguish between static (stat) and locomotion (loc) verbs. The third verb type, directional (dir), is used for verbs with a strong directional component like *umkehren* (*return*), *abbiegen* (*turn off*), etc. As they already imply a certain direction, the additional verbalization of a direction using a prepositional phrase does usually not lead to acceptable sentences. The fourth type (reo) is used for verbs like *erreichen* (*reach*) which have an obligatory locative case.

The selection process is based on the event type and on the verb type. Deep cases are chosen according to the information that has to be conveyed in order to allow the hearer a precise imagination. As the decision is based on pragmatic considerations and does not take into account which deep cases may be verbalized with the verb, this procedure may lead to conflicts which have to be resolved.

Consider the case where an 'überholen' (overtake) event has to be verbalized. Since the event type is non durative and the verbtype is loc, direction and locative cases are chosen. The deep case semantics of *überholen* (see above) implies that the verb may only take an optional locative case. The generation algorithm checks whether the cases are allowed; if so, it also checks whether the combination is allowed. If so the cases are generated. When the combinations are not allowed, an appropriate combination is chosen and the cases are generated. If one of the chosen optional cases is not allowed, the specialization hierarchy of the verbs is used to go up to a more general verb that can take the deep case. The verbs *fahren* (*drive, move*) and *gehen* (*walk*) can take any deep case. With the verb *überholen* the direction case is verbalized in a seperate sentence with the verb *fahren* and then the overtake event is generated with the remaining cases.

We now discuss the generation process and the generation of referring phrases.

6. GENERATION

The control structure for the generation process is as follows:

1. Read the scene and verb data
2. Initialize the partner model
3. Build the verbalization lists (event selection)
4. Generate a standardized text beginning (see Section 3.1).

When this has been done, for every event in the verbalization list of each object the following steps are executed:

1. Determine the temporal adverb
2. Verbalize the obligatory cases
   — use referring phrase generation
3. Choose optional cases
4. Resolve conflicts
5. Verbalize the optional cases
   — use referring phrase generation

It has already been mentioned that the temporal relations between events have to be made explicit in the text. At present, our algorithm for generating temporal adverbs is rather simple. When the events of the verbalization list of an object are verbalized sequentially, we proceed as follows:

1. If the current event has a precedent and its event time is included in the precedent's, begin the sentence with *dabei* (roughly: *during this time*).
2. If the current event has a precedent and its event time overlaps with the precedent's, begin the sentence with *unterdessen* (roughly: *in the meantime*).
3. Otherwise, no temporal adverb is generated, as the linear order of the sentences implies consecutivity.

The result of the generation algorithm is a formal representation of the surface sentence which, roughly, contains the verb's stem, genus verbi, modality, and person; all deep cases in random order; and all stems of the lexical entries which are to appear in the surface string. This representation is taken as input by a modified version of the SUTRA system[6] which then generates a correctly inflected German sentence.

Below is an example of the output of NAOS.

DIE SZENE ENTHÄLT VIER BEWEGTE OBJEKTE: DREI PKWS UND EINEN FUSSGÄNGER.
(The scene consists of four moving objects: three vehicles and a pedestrian.)

---

[6] Another version of the SUTRA system is used in the SEMSYN project (see Rösner, this volume). For further details on the formal representation and on the SUTRA system see Busemann, 1984.

EIN GRÜNER VW NÄHERT SICH DEM GROSSEN FUSSGÄNGER AUS
RICHTUNG HALLERPLATZ. ER FÄHRT AUF DER SCHLÜTERSTRASSE.
(A green VW approaches the tall pedestrian from the direction of Haller Square. It
drives on Schlüter Street.)

EIN GELBER VW FÄHRT VON DER ALTEN POST VOR DIE AMPEL.
WÄHRENDDESSEN ENTFERNT ER SICH VON DEM GRÜNEN VW.
(A yellow VW drives from the old post office to the traffic light. During this time it
recedes from the green VW.)

EIN SCHWARZER BMW FÄHRT IN RICHTUNG HALLERPLATZ. DABEI
ÜBERHOLT ER DEN GELBEN VW VOR DEM FACHBEREICH
INFORMATIK. DER SCHWARZE BMW ENTFERNT SICH VON DEM
GRÜNEN VW.
(A black BMW drives toward Haller Square. During this time it overtakes the
yellow VW in front of the Computer Science Building. The black BMW recedes
from the yellow VW.)

DER GROSSE FUSSGÄNGER GEHT IN RICHTUNG DAMMTOR AUF DEM
SÜDLICHEN FUSSWEG WESTLICH DER SCHLÜTERSTRASSE.
WÄHRENDDESSEN ENTFERNT ER SICH VON DEM FACHBEREICH
INFORMATIK.
(The tall pedestrian walks in the direction of Dammtor on the southern sidewalk
west of Schlüter Street. During this time he recedes from the Computer Science
Building.)

6.1 Referring phrases

In this section several aspects of the referring phrase generator are discussed. In contrast to
systems like HAM-ANS (Hoeppner et al., 1983), the underlying data base of our referring
phrase generator is based on an open-, not a closed-world assumption (Reiter, 1978). This
implies that an entry which is not contained in the data base is considered to be false. The
consequences for the description of objects become apparent from the following example.
Assume an object for which there is a data base entry like (COLOR OBJ1 YELLOW) and that
has been characterized as *the yellow OBJ*. If a second object that has no COLOR entry has to be
distinguished from the first one, the closed-world assumption allows us to characterize it as *the
OBJ that is not yellow*.
   The open-world assumption implies that only explicit entries in the data base are considered
to be true and everything else is unknown. In the context of the above example, this implies that
the COLOR-entry for OBJ1 may not be used to distinguish it from the other object, as it is not
known which color the other object has. As a consequence of the open-world assumption we
require that properties that should be used to distinguish objects from each other have to be
perceived and represented in the data base for all objects. In the case of photometric properties,
this can be done through the analysis of color images.
   As can be seen from the example text, objects are characterized by their properties,
introduced with indefinite noun phrases when they are not single representatives of a class.
They may be referred to with pronouns to add to the coherence of the text. Therefore we use
standard techniques as described, e.g., in Goldman (1975) and von Hahn, Hoeppner, Jameson
& Wahlster (1980).
   In the following we will specifically address the question of distinguishing between objects
that have the same properties. In our world of discourse it may easily be the case that a scene
contains two objects with similar properties for which unequivocal referring expressions have
to be generated. It is an interesting fact that we have several options to cope with this problem
each of which has its consequences.

One option is to adopt McDonald's scheme of generation without the system knowing precisely what to say next (McDonald, 1983). According to this scheme, two similar objects are characterized as follows: When the first one is introduced it is characterized by its properties, e.g. *a yellow VW*. When the second one has to be introduced, REF notices that a yellow VW is already known to the partner and generates the phrase *another yellow VW*. The situation starts getting interesting in subsequent references. The objects are then characterized by the events in which they were involved earlier, whether as agent or in another role. This leads to referring phrases like *the yellow VW which receded from the pedestrian* or *the yellow VW which has been overtaken*. Note how passive relative clauses arise naturally from the task of generating referring phrases in this paradigm. The same is true for negation. Consider the case where the first yellow VW, say VW1, has passed an object and the second yellow VW, say VW2, has overtaken another object and both events are already known to the partner. If REF has to generate a second referring phrase for VW1, it notices that *pass* is a more general verb for *overtake* and may thus also be applied to the overtake event. It therefore generates the phrase *the yellow VW which has not been overtaken* to distinguish it unequivocally from VW2.

Below is an example of this strategy in a text for the same scene as above. The only difference to the first scene is that we replaced the green VW by a yellow one.

DIE SZENE ENTHÄLT VIER BEWEGTE OBJEKTE: DREI PKWS UND EINEN FUSSGÄNGER.
(The scene consists of four moving objects: three vehicles and a pedestrian.)

EIN GELBER VW NÄHERT SICH DEM GROSSEN FUSSGÄNGER AUS RICHTUNG HALLERPLATZ. ER FÄHRT AUF DER SCHLÜTERSTRASSE.
(A yellow VW approaches the tall pedestrian from the direction of Haller Square. It drives on Schlüter Street.)

EIN ANDERER GELBER VW FÄHRT VON DER ALTEN POST VOR DIE AMPEL. WÄHRENDDESSEN ENTFERNT ER SICH VON DEM GELBEN VW, DER SICH DEM GROSSEN FUSSGÄNGER GENÄHERT HAT.
(Another yellow VW drives from the old post office to the traffic light. During this time it recedes from the yellow VW which approached the tall pedestrian.)

EIN SCHWARZER BMW FÄHRT IN RICHTUNG HALLERPLATZ. DABEI ÜBERHOLT ER DEN ANDEREN GELBEN VW, DER SICH VON DEM GELBEN VW ENTFERNT HAT, VOR DEM FACHBEREICH INFORMATIK. DER SCHWARZE BMW ENTFERNT SICH VON DEM GELBEN VW, DER NICHT ÜBERHOLT WORDEN IST.
(A black BMW drives toward Haller Square. During this time it overtakes the other yellow VW which receded from the yellow VW in front of the Computer Science Building. The black BMW recedes from the yellow VW which was not overtaken.)

DER GROSSE FUSSGÄNGER GEHT IN RICHTUNG DAMMTOR AUF DEM SÜDLICHEN FUSSWEG WESTLICH DER SCHLÜTERSTRASSE. WÄHRENDDESSEN ENTFERNT ER SICH VON DEM FACHBEREICH INFORMATIK.
(The tall pedestrian walks toward Dammtor on the southern sidewalk west of Schlüter Street. During this time he recedes from the Computer Science Building.)

The consequences of this first strategy for distinguishing similar abjects are rather complex syntactic structures which are not motivated by higher level stylistic choices but arise from the task of generating unambiguous referring expressions.

Let us now look at a second option which has also been implemented. Experience with the above algorithm for different scenes showed that if more than two similar objects are in the scene the restrictive relative clauses become virtually unintelligable. We thus determine how many similar objects there are in the scene before we start the generation process. If there are more than two, REF generates constant definite descriptions for them, e.g., *the first yellow VW, the second yellow VW*, etc., and uses these phrases in subsequent references. An example of this strategy would look like the first example text except that the different vehicles would be described *as the first yellow VW, the second yellow VW*, the rest of the text remaining the same. Taking this option implies leaving McDonald's scheme and approaching a planning paradigm.

It should be noted here that there is a third option which has not received much attention, namely to switch from contextual to cotextual reference, using phrases like *the VW I mentioned last*. Before a system can use this technique we need further research about its application.

7. LIMITATIONS AND RELATED RESEARCH

Currently NAOS is limited with respect to the kind of verbs that can be recognized; only 'observable' verbs have been implemented so far. Verbs like *ausweichen* (*avoid*) imply an intention of the agent and are only identifiable if further world knowledge is encoded in the system. If it is known that a goal of traffic participants is to avoid hitting other participants an *ausweichen* event may be recognized by analyzing the trajectories of the objects.

A second restriction is due to the fact that the conditions of usage of a verb are implicitly represented in the specialization hierarchy of the verbs. In order to distinguish verbs with the same perceptual features according to their pragmatic conditions of usage we need representations similar to those developed by Hovy (this volume) and Jacobs (this volume).

Finally, we did not aim at representing the imaged scene using pictorial or quasi-analogical representations. From the standpoint of cognitive science, this would be an interesting enterprise. The imagery debate (Yuille, 1983) suggests that there is more than one representation for the meaning of a word and it would be worthwhile to use pictorial representations for prototypical scenes as an encoding of a motion verb's meaning (see also Weber, 1983). This would more easily allow us to compare the representation of the imagination with the underlying scene.

Comparing our approach with other ones, the main difference between NAOS and other systems for language generation is that we approach the verbalization problem from the visual side. Other systems like TALESPIN (Meehan, 1981), KDS (Mann & Moore, 1981), TEXT (McKeown, 1985), and HAM-ANS (Hoeppner et al., 1983) start their processing with language, whereas NAOS starts with images and an explicit representation of the temporal validity of recognized concepts. In close connection to our research is the work of Badler (1975), Tsuji, Kuroda & Morizono, (1977), Tsotsos (1980), Okada (1980), and Conklin & McDonald (1982). The first four authors deal with questions of motion recognition and with reference semantics for motion verbs but are not concerned with text generation. They showed that case frames can be used to generate single utterances. Conklin & McDonald use the notion of salience to deal with the selection problem in the task of describing a single image of an outdoor scene.

In contrast to KDS (Mann & Moore, 1981) the strategy in NAOS uses knowledge about what has been said so far and which deep cases have to be verbalized, in order to produce in the hearer an appropriate imagination. We thus avoid generating bad utterances. Presently, NAOS does not employ any rules to combine propositions as is done in KDS. TEXT generates paragraphs as answers to questions about database structure. McKeown has identified discourse strategies for fulfilling three communicative goals: *define, compare*, and *contrast*. These strategies guide the process of deciding what to say next. McKeown uses the question to determine the communicative goal that the text should fulfill. Research of this kind is very important to clarify the relation between the form of a text and its underlying goal. (See also Mann, 1984, this volume.)

One of the domains of HAM-ANS is the kind of traffic scene which is also used in NAOS. In this domain HAM-ANS deals primarily with answering questions about the movements of the objects and with overanswering yes/no questions (Wahlster et al., 1983). The dialogue component of HAM-ANS may be connected to NAOS to also allow the user to ask questions if the generated text was not sufficient for his understanding. An evaluation of the kinds of question asked by users might help in devising better generation strategies.

KAMP (Appelt, 1982) is a system for planning natural language utterances in the domain of task-oriented dialogues. The planning algorithm takes the knowledge and beliefs of the hearer into account. This system shows how a priori beliefs of the hearer may also be integrated in NAOS to generate more appropriate referring phrases.

Directions for further research include using a planning component for NAOS which would first determine all deep cases necessary to maximally restrict the imagination of a trajectory and then try to distribute the cases to the different verbs used in the description according to their case frames.

ACKNOWLEDGEMENT

NAOS was developed while the author was a member of the Department of Computer Science at the University of Hamburg, Germany. My thanks go to Bernd Neumann, who directed this project.

REFERENCES

Appelt, D.E. (1982) *Planning Natural-Language Utterances to Satisfy Multiple Goals*. SRI International, Technical Note 259, Menlo Park, CA.

Badler, N.I. (1975) *Temporal Scene Analysis: Conceptual Description of Object Movements*. Report TR-80, Department of Computer Science, University of Toronto.

Busemann, S. (1984) Surface transformations during the Generation of Written German Sentences. In: Bolc, L. & McDonald, D. (Eds.) *Natural Language Generation Systems*. Berlin: Springer.

Conklin, J.D. & McDonald, D.D. (1982) Salience: The Key to the Selection Problem in Natural Language Generation. In: *Proceedings of COLING-82*.

Davey, A. (1978) *Discourse Production. A Computer Model of Some Aspects of a Speaker*. Edinburgh: Edinburgh University Press.

Fillmore, C.J. (1968) The Case for Case. In: Bach, E. & Harms, R.T. (Eds.) *Universals in Linguistic Theory*. New York: Holt, Rinehart and Winston.

Fillmore, C.J. (1977) Scenes-and-frames Semantics. In: Zampolli, A. (Ed.) *Linguistic Structures Processing*. Amsterdam: North-Holland.

Goldman, N.M. (1975) Conceptual Generation. In: Schank, R.C. (Ed.) *Conceptual Information Processing*. Amsterdam: North-Holland.

Grice, H.P. (1975) Logic and Conversation. In: Cole P. & Morgan, J.L. (Eds.) *Speech Acts*. London: Academic Press.

von Hahn, W., Hoeppner, W., Jameson, A. & Wahlster, W. (1980) The Anatomy of the Natural Language Dialogue System HAM-RPM. In: Bolc, L. (Ed.) *Natural Language Based Computer Systems*. München: Hanser/McMillan.

Hoeppner, W., Christaller, T., Marburger, H., Morik, K., Nebel, B., O'Leary, M. & Wahlster, W. (1983) Beyond Domain-Independence: Experience with the Development of a German Language Access System to Highly Diverse Background Systems. In: *Proceedings of IJCAI-83*.

Kosslyn, S.M. (1980) *Image and Mind*. Cambridge, Mass.: Harvard University Press.

Levelt, W.J.M., Schreuder, R. & Hoenkamp, E. (1978) Structure and Use of Verbs of Motion. In: Campbell, R.N. & Smith, P.T., (Eds.) *Recent Advances in the Psychology of Language*. New York: Plenum Publishing Corporation.

Mann, W.C. & Moore, J. (1981) Computer Generation of Multiparagraph Text. *American Journal of Computational Linguistics, 7*, 17-29.

Mann, W.C. (1984) Discourse Structures for Text Generation. In: *Proceedings of COLING-84*.

Mann, W.C., Bates, M., Grosz, B., McDonald, D.D., McKeown, K.R. & Swartout, W.R. (1982) *Text Generation. American Journal of Computational Linguistics*, *8*, 62-69.

McDonald, D.D. (1983) Natural Language Generation as a Computational Problem: an Introduction. In: Brady, M. & Berwick, R.C. (Eds.) *Computational Models of Discourse*. Cambridge, Mass.: MIT Press.

McKeown, K.R. (1985) Discourse Strategies for Generating Natural-Language Text. *Artificial Intelligence*, *27*, 1-41.

Meehan, J. (1981) TALE-SPIN. In: Schank, R.C. & Riesbeck, C.K. (Eds.) *Inside Computer Understanding: Five Programs plus Miniatures*. Hillsdale, N.J.: Erlbaum.

Miller, G.A. & Johnson-Laird, P.N. (1976) *Language and Perception*. Cambridge, Mass.: Cambridge University Press.

Neumann, B. (1984a) On Natural Language Access to Image Sequences: Event Recognition and Verbalization. In: *Proceedings of the First Conference on Artificial Intelligence Applications (CAIA-84)*, Denver, Colorado.

Neumann, B. (1984b) *Natural Language Description of Time-Varying Scenes*. FBI-HH-B-105/84, Fachbereich Informatik, Universität Hamburg.

Neumann, B. & Novak, H.-J. (1983a) *Natural Language Oriented Event Models for Image Sequence Interpretation: The Issues. CSRG Techn. Note Nr. 34*, University of Toronto.

Neumann, B. & Novak, H.-J.(1983b) Event Models for Recognition and Natural Language Description of Events in Real-World Image Sequences. In: *Proceedings of IJCAI-83*.

Neumann, B. & Novak, H.-J. (1986) NAOS: Ein System zur natürlichsprachlichen Beschreibung zeitveränderlicher Szenen. *Informatik Forschung und Entwicklung*, *1*, 83-92.

Novak, H.-J. (1985) A Relational Matching Strategy for Temporal Event Recognition. In: Laubsch, J. (Ed.) *GWAI-84*. Berlin: Springer.

Olson, D.R. (1972) Language Use for Communicating, Instructing and Thinking. In: Freedle, R.O. & Carroll, J.B. (Eds.) *Language Comprehension and the Acquisition of Knowledge*. Washington, D.C.: Winston.

Okada, N. (1980) Conceptual Taxonomy of Japanese Verbs for Understanding Natural Language and Picture Patterns. In: *Proceedings of COLING-80*.

Reiter, R. (1978) On Closed World Data Bases. In: Gallaire, H. & Minker, J. (Eds.) *Logic and Data Bases*. New York: Plenum.

Tsotsos, J.K. (1980) *A Framework for Visual Motion Understanding*. CSRG TR-114, University of Toronto.

Tsuji, S., Kuroda, S. & Morizono, A. (1977) Understanding a Simple Cartoon Film by a Computer Vision System. In: *Proceedings of IJCAI-77*.

Wahlster, W., Marburger, H., Jameson, A. & Busemann, S. (1983) Overanswering Yes-No-Questions: Extended Responses in a NL Interface to a Vision System. In: *Proceedings of IJCAI-83*.

Weber, G. (1983) *Untersuchungen zur mentalen Repräsentation von Bewegungsverben: Merkmale, Dimensionen und Vorstellungsbilder*. Dissertation, Universität Braunschweig.

Yuille, J.C. (1983) (Ed.) *Imagery, Memory and Cognition*. Hillsdale, N.J.: Erlbaum.

Chapter 10

THE AUTOMATED NEWS AGENCY:
SEMTEX — A TEXT GENERATOR FOR GERMAN

Dietmar Rösner

ABSTRACT

This chapter reports on the development and current status of SEMTEX, an implemented text generator for German. SEMTEX is based on precursory work within the Japanese/German MT project SEMSYN that led to the implementation of a system capable of generating German noun groups and clauses from isolated semantic representations. Starting from this module, SEMTEX was designed to produce German newspaper stories about labor market developments. To be able to generate such texts the SEMSYN generator had to be enriched with:
— mechanisms for maintaining and exploiting contextual information
— techniques for communicating with the domain knowledge base, e.g. for the dynamic determination of grammatical tense from temporal information
— knowledge about abstract rhetorical schemata and the various ways for their realization within simulated political statements.

1. GENERATION OF NEWS STORIES — AN INTRODUCTORY EXAMPLE

The first application of the text generator SEMTEX has been to automatically produce newspaper stories about labor market development. The starting point for this application is data from the monthly labor market statistics (numbers of unemployed, open jobs, etc.). A rudimentary *text planner* takes these data and those of relevant previous months (i.e. the preceding month and the same month of the previous year), checks for changes and significant developments, simulates possible argumentations of various political speakers on these developments, and finally creates a representation of the intended text as an ordered list of frame descriptions. This 'text plan' includes both representations for factual statements (numerical values, changes) and for political comments. SEMTEX then converts this list into a newspaper story in German using an extended version of the generator of the SEMSYN project. (SEMSYN is an acronym for SEMantic SYNthesis.) The current version of SEMTEX generates German news stories such as the example below (see top of next page).

In implementing SEMTEX we combined two research topics that we had been investigating separately before:

— investigation of text structures in German news stories, especially with respect to argumentation and rhetorics (Rösner & Laubsch, 1982; Rösner, 1985)
— development of a generator for German within a Japanese/German MT project (Laubsch, Rösner, Hanakata & Lesniewski, 1984; Rösner, 1986a).

GERINGFÜGIGE REDUZIERUNG DER ARBEITSLOSENZAHL.

NÜRNBERG/BONN (cpa). Die Zahl der Arbeitslosen in der Bundesrepublik Deutschland hat sich während des Oktober nur sehr wenig verringert. Sie ist von 2151600 auf 2148800 zurückgegangen. Die Arbeitslosenquote hatte Ende Oktober einen Wert von 8.6 Prozent. Sie hatte am Ende des Vergleichzeitraumes des Vorjahrs ebenfalls bei 8.6 Prozent gelegen. Regierungssprecher Ost bewertet die Verringerung der Arbeitslosenzahl positiv. Der stellvertretende DGB-Vorsitzende Muhr erklärt, dass der Rückgang der Zahl der Arbeitslosen nicht darüber hinwegtäuschen dürfe, dass sie jetzt unverändert unerträglich hoch sei.

2. SEMSYN — GENERATION WITHIN A JAPANESE/GERMAN MT SYSTEM

The initial implementation of the SEMSYN generator and its first application were carried out within a joint Japanese/German MT project (Rösner, 1986a). The combination of SEMSYN's generator with the ATLAS/II System (Uchida & Sugiyama, 1980) of the Japanese cooperation partner FUJITSU may be seen as the first Japanese-to-German translation system. The analysis of the Japanese input — titles of scientific papers from the field of information technology — and its transformation into the semantic representation has been the task of ATLAS/II. SEMSYN's part has been to produce a correct and understandable German text for these semantic representations. (For some translation results, see Figure 1.)

2.1 The semantic representation

The semantic nets that SEMSYN received from the Japanese partner may be characterized as a variant of a case frame representation. In addition to slots for 'classical' case roles — AGENT, OBJECT, GOAL, INSTRUMENT, etc. — there were various roles providing additional information for concepts: ATTRIBUTES, NAME, SPECIALIZE, etc. Some other arcs were best read as defining relations between parts of the net. In addition to semantic relations like PURPOSE or SCOPE there were 'structural relations' such as the relation between title and subtitle.

2.2 The overall design of the SEMSYN System

SEMSYN's generation from ATLAS/II's nets to German surface structures is organized into three major steps (Rösner, 1986a):

— The first phase — adapting the data delivered by ATLAS/II to SEMSYN's own frame representation formalism — was intended to keep the generation module independent from its first application.
— The second phase — the generator kernel (Rösner, 1986b) — does the main work: Its output is a functional grammatical structure — called Instantiated Realization Schema (IRS) — that fully specifies the intended utterance. IRS-structures determine the syntactic category (e.g. noun group or clause) of the whole utterance and the grammatical functions (e.g. direct object, possessive attribute) and syntactic categories of its subparts. They specify the syntactic features (e.g. number, gender, case) of the head of each syntactic entity. They contain as terminals root forms of the German words to be used or special lexical items for, e.g., proper names (:*PN) or noun compounds (:*NC).

— Finally, the generator front end SUTRA-S[1] gets an IRS-structure and produces the corresponding German surface string that obeys the relevant morphological and syntactical rules for correct German.

Examples of the conceptual and grammatical structures used in the SEMSYN system are given in Figure 2.

```
TIT-1 = 情報技術とその米国教育への影響
Die Informationstechnologie und ihr Einfluß auf die Ausbildung in den USA.

TIT-15 = 目標，概念，重要性
Ziel, Konzept und Bedeutung.

TIT-28 = 帰納的に数えあげ可能な集合の計算の複雑さ
Die Komplexität einer Berechnung für eine rekursiv aufzählbare Menge.

TIT-44 = 画像理解における生成ツールとしてのグラフ文法
Die Graphgrammatik als Generierungs-Werkzeug beim Verstehen von Bildern.

TIT-131 = データセットを消す方法
Ein Verfahren zur Löschung von Datensätzen.

TIT-282 = 高速Walsh変換によるデータ圧縮
Die Komprimierung von Daten mittels schneller Walsh-Transformation.

TIT-360 = 時間間隔に基づくハードウェア意味論
Eine Hardware-Semantik, die auf Zeitintervallen basiert.

TIT-364 = 高速並列アルゴリズムを持つ問題の分類
Die Klassifikation von Problemen mit schnellen parallelen Algorithmen.

TIT-428 = 並行プログラムモジュールの記述
Die Spezifikation von parallelen Programmodulen.
**MORE**
```

Figure 1. Some titles translated via ATLAS/II and SEMSYN

2.3 Generating clauses

From the very beginning of the SEMSYN project we aimed at general solutions. We therefore did not only enable the generator to produce titles — i.e. noun groups of varying complexity —, but provided mechanisms for the generation of various clause forms from appropriate case frames as well. The choice between possible variants is done via global stylistic variables set by the user (e.g. *FORCE-ACTIVE-FLAG* causes the introduction of an anonymous subject — the German pronoun *man* — if there is no :AGENT). These variables are intended as intermediate solutions. In other applications they should be replaced by tests using, e.g., information from the context. As an example, we contrast the results when generating from the following frame structure:

```
(A GENERATE WITH
    (:METHOD = (A METHOD WITH (:ATTRIBUTES = (NEW))))
    (:OBJECT = (A LANGUAGE WITH (:ATTRIBUTES = (GERMAN))))
    (:SOURCE = (A NET WITH (:ATTRIBUTES = (SEMANTIC)))))
```

---

[1] SUTRA stands for SURface TRansformation (Busemann, 1982), the affix 'S' for Stuttgart; for the purposes of the SEMSYN project this morphosyntactic module for German has been reimplemented in ZetaLISP and greatly extended (Emele & Momma, 1985).

---

i) **Frame structure as input to the generator kernel**
    (A GENERATE WITH
        (:AGENT = (A PROJECT (:NAME = (A (:*PN "SEMSYN")))))
        (:OBJECT = (A LANGUAGE WITH (:ATTRIBUTES = (GERMAN)))))

ii) **Functional structure as input to the generator front end**
    (:NG (:HEAD "Generierung")
        (:FEATURES (:DET DEF) (:NUM SG))
        (:CLASSIFIER
            (:PG (:PREP "durch")
                (:POBJ (:NG (:HEAD (:*NC (:*PN "SEMSYN") "-" "Projekt"))
                        (:FEATURES (:NUM SG) (:DET DEF))))))
        (:POSSATTR.
            (:PG (:PREP "von")
                (:POBJ (:NG (:HEAD "Sprache")
                        (:FEATURES (:NUM SG) (:DET ZERO) (:CAS DAT))
                        (:CLASSIFIER "deutsch"))))))

iii) **German surface string**
    "Die Generierung von deutscher Sprache durch das SEMSYN-Projekt."

Figure 2. Main steps of the SEMSYN generator

Generation with title defaults:
'Die Generierung von deutscher Sprache aus einem semantischen Netz
mittels eines neuen Verfahrens'.

Generated as a clause:
'Deutsche Sprache wird mit einem neuen Verfahren aus
einem semantischen Netz generiert'.

Generated as a clause with *FORCE-ACTIVE-FLAG*:
'Man generiert deutsche Sprache mit einem neuen Verfahren aus
einem semantischen Netz'.

2.4 Characteristics of the MT application

Let us summarize some of the characteristics of the MT application:
— Generation was done from isolated structures only. Therefore there was no need for
context. Reference occured only in some rare cases of enumerations (e.g. 'Die
Informationstechnologie und *ihre* Auswirkung ...'; 'The information technology and *its*
effects ...').
— Generation was based on mere textual representations. There was no associated domain
knowledge.
— For the generation of titles, tense was completely irrelevant: No temporal information was
used.

These characteristics are quite ambivalent. They may be seen as advantages since they facilitated
the implementation of the initial system, on the other hand they obviously limit the usefulness of
this system.

3. FROM TITLES TO TEXTS

With a tool like the SEMSYN generator at hand, it was more than natural to use it for experiments with the generation of connected texts. As a first application we decided to generate (or reconstruct) prototypical examples of a class of newspaper stories that are frequently found in the Economics Section of a typical daily newspaper. This class of texts may be labeled as *statistical news*. From an abstract point of view, statistical news reports on
— values of relevant figures or indices,
— changes in those figures,
— prognoses of future developments,
— explanations by official speakers,
— comments by politicians.

3.1 Generating labor market reports

SEMTEX generates labor market reports from raw data:
— The system receives (or fetches) figures like the number of unemployed or the number of open jobs.
— The user may choose from some global options that influence the format and the content (e.g. level of detail) of the report (Headline wanted?, Report on subgroups?, Report on data from previous time-periods?, Include political comments?, ...).
— The system automatically produces a labor market report in typical newspaper style.

Conceptually the system may be divided into two modules which roughly correspond to the 'What to say' and 'How to say it' aspects of generation:
— AMEX (for 'Arbeitsmarktexperte', or labor market expert) simulates a text planner. This module gets the raw labor market figures as input and outputs a list of frame structures (cf. Figure 3.) as a representation of the text's content.
— SEMTEX takes this 'text plan' and converts it, sentence by sentence, into a newspaper story.

```
<frame-descr>      ::== <frame-name>
                        |(<frame-name> . <slot-filler-alist>)
<slot-filler-alist >  ::== ( <slot-name>-1 <frame-descr>-1
                        ...
                        <slot-name>-n <frame-descr>-n)
<frame-name>    LISP symbol
<slot-name>     LISP keyword
```

Figure 3. The format of text plan elements

3.1.1 Representing the labor market situation

AMEX is implemented as a collection of FLAVOR objects (Weinreb & Moon, 1981) incorporating domain-specific knowledge. Its top-level object[2] is a 'snapshot' of the labor

---

[2] An instance of the flavor class AMS; AMS stands for 'Arbeitsmarktsituation' (labor market situation). An AMS object may be viewed as representation of the situation in the sense of McDonald, Vaughan & Pustejovsky (this volume) from which generation starts.

market developments. After initialization it just contains current figures and pointers to previous instances:[3]

```
>(setq ams-dez85 (create-ams (make-month 'dezember 1985.)))
  #<AMS 45775465>
>(describe ams-dez85)
  #<AMS 45775465>, an object of flavor AMS,
  has instance variable values:
  AREA:                         #<GEOPOL-AREA 43226047>
  TIME:                         #<MONTH 45775300>
  NRS-UNEMPLOYED:               ((*GLOBAL* . 10750171)(*MEN . 4746051)
                                  (*WOMEN . 4002120)(*EMPLOYEES . 3004303)
                                  (*WORKERS . 5743666))
  OTHER-NRS:                    ((*OSZ-GLOBAL* . 327067);; open jobs
                                  ... ))
  UNEMPLOYMENT-RATES:           NIL
  AMS-MONTH-BEFORE:             #<AMS 45775402>
  AMS-YEAR-BEFORE:              #<AMS 45775450>
  CHANGES-IN-MONTH:             NIL
  CHANGES-IN-YEAR:              NIL
  SIGNIFICANT-FIGURES:          NIL
  CONCLUSIONS:                  NIL
  REPRESENTATION-FOR-TEXT:      NIL
  #<AMS 45775465>
```

3.1.2 Creating a text plan

In its current shape AMEX is by no means a real text planner, it just simulates one. It is best seen as an implementation of a kind of text grammar which has been abstracted by analyzing authentic examples of the class of texts under investigation. The typical labor market report starts with the most recent changes of the global number of unemployed and the corresponding unemployment rate. As far as other facts are concerned it may vary greatly with respect to the level of detail. It may be confined to the global figures or elaborate on the developments involving various subgroups (e.g., men vs. women), industrial branches, or geographical regions.

In reality a writer may decide to include or leave out facts depending on their relevance or degree of interest (or sometimes simply because of space considerations). Currently AMEX has no such measures; the level of detail is simply determined by the options chosen by the user (cf. Section 3.1) and the availability of the necessary data. AMEX takes the given data, computes changes in the figures, and creates semantic representations from its observations by filling templates.[4] If a certain option has been chosen, the factual statements will be augmented by simulated comments from various speakers (cf. section 3.2). A typical plan produced by AMEX is given in Figure 4; the corresponding generated text is given in Figure 7.

3.1.3 An example: representation of changes

For SEMTEX a text plan is a list of frame descriptions as defined in Figure 3. Changes have as frame name a symbol for the type of change — DECREASE, INCREASE or UNCHANGED — and take some of the following slots:

---

[3] Lines starting with '>' represent input typed in by the user.

[4] Additional variability of AMEX's text plans is guaranteed by including some random choices; for more details cf. Rösner (1986b).

:QUANTITY, :TIME-PERIOD, :MANNER, :FROM, :BY, :TO.

Frequently used are: (a) the 'qualitative description':

```
(INCREASE   :QUANTITY (NR-UNEMPLOYED :GROUP *GLOBAL* :AREA FRG)
            :MANNER NOTICEABLE
            :TIME-PERIOD (DURING :TIME DEZ-85))
```

realized (as in the above text) as:

'Die Zahl der Arbeitslosen in der Bundesrepublik Deutschland ist
im Dezember spürbar angestiegen.'

or (b) the 'quantitative description':

```
(INCREASE   :QUANTITY (NR-UNEMPLOYED :GROUP *GLOBAL*)
            :FROM 10335614
            :TO 10750134
            :TIME-PERIOD (DURING :TIME DEZ-85))
```

realized as:

'Die Arbeitslosenzahl ist im Dezember 1985 von 2210700 auf 2347100
angestiegen.'

```
>(gtl (send ams-dez85 :prepare-sketch))
  ((INCREASE     :QUANTITY (NR-UNEMPLOYED :GROUP *GLOBAL* :AREA FRG)
                 :MANNER NOTICEABLE
                 :TIME-PERIOD (DURING :TIME DEZ-85))
   (INCREASE     :QUANTITY (NR-UNEMPLOYED :GROUP *GLOBAL*)
                 :FROM 10335614
                 :TO 10750134
                 :TIME-PERIOD (DURING :TIME DEZ-85))
   (HAVE-VALUE   :QUANTITY (UNEMPLOYMENT-RATE :GROUP *GLOBAL*)
                 :VALUE (PERCENTAGE :VALUE 9.4)
                 :TIME-POINT (END-OF :TIME-PERIOD DEZ-85))
   (HAVE-VALUE   :QUANTITY (UNEMPLOYMENT-RATE :GROUP *GLOBAL*)
                 :VALUE (PERCENTAGE :VALUE 9.3)
                 :TIME-POINT (END-OF :TIME-PERIOD DEZ-84))
   (*COMMENT*    ;;representation of commentary by speaker of trade union
      :SPEAKER   *DGB
      :COMMENT   (EVALUATE-NEGATIVE
                     :SPEAKER *DGB
                     :FACT (INCREASE.
                              :QUANTITY (NR-UNEMPLOYED :GROUP *GLOBAL*)))))
```

Figure 4. A text plan

3.2 Representing rhetorical structures

AMEX's simulation of political comments on labor market development takes advantage of the observed predictability of those reactions. Speakers of the government or their supporting parties try to see positive aspects in the current situation, whereas speakers of the opposition are expected to underline whatever negative aspects are available.

For the representation of political commentaries in the text plan we use abstract rhetorical schemata (Rösner, 1985):

> Rhetorical schemata have slots for factual statements; one may view them as operating on those facts.[5]
> These schemata are deep structures: They may underlie quite diverse surface constructs (typically involving connectives or phrasal patterns).

For each rhetorical schema, the generator kernel has knowledge about how the conceptual structures from the schema's slots may be realized (e.g. as a noun group or as a clause) and how the corresponding realization results may be combined. Depending on the type of the partial realizations, this combination may call for appropriate connectives or phrasal patterns. In analyzing German news stories (Rösner, 1985), we collected stocks of typical surface structures for the abstract schemata that we now exploit — often as a kind of phrasal lexicon (Becker, 1975) — for the generation task. The following examples will clarify this approach.

3.2.1 EVALUATE-NEGATIVE and EVALUATE-POSITIVE

These schemata are used to express a :SPEAKER's global (positive or negative) evaluation of a :FACT. Among the currently used phrasal patterns for EVALUATE-NEGATIVE are:

> '<:SPEAKER> sieht ein negatives Zeichen in <:FACT>'
> '<:SPEAKER> hält <:FACT> für ein bedenkliches Zeichen'
> '<:SPEAKER> zeigt sich besorgt über <:FACT>'
> '<:SPEAKER> sieht <:FACT> als negativ an'
> ...

Analogous patterns for EVALUATE-POSITIVE are:

> '<:SPEAKER> hält <:FACT> für ein gutes Zeichen'
> '<:SPEAKER> äussert sich erfreut über <:FACT>'
> '<:SPEAKER> bewertet <:FACT> positiv'
> ...

In our example (cf. Figures 4 and 7) the speaker of the German trade union used EVALUATE-NEGATIVE (since embedded in a comment, the EVALUATE-NEGATIVE is generated in indirect speech):

```
(*COMMENT*
    :SPEAKER *DGB
    :COMMENT (EVALUATE-NEGATIVE
          :SPEAKER *DGB
          :FACT (INCREASE
                :QUANTITY (NR-UNEMPLOYED :GROUP *GLOBAL*))))
```

'Der DGB hat erklärt, er sehe in der Vergrösserung der Arbeitslosenzahl ein negatives Zeichen.'

---

[5] For other work on rhetorical structures see Mann & Thompson (this volume).

3.2.2 EMPHASIZE-NEGATIVE and EMPHASIZE-POSITIVE

These schemata are used in rhetorics in order to combine two statements that have different evaluations (:POS-FACT resp. :NEG-FACT). The rhetorical effect is achieved by a kind of noncommutativity of arguments. Given the same two facts one can present them to the hearer with the stress on the negative aspect (EMPHASIZE-NEGATIVE) or such that the positive fact becomes more prominent.

Among the implemented variants for realizing EMPHASIZE-NEGATIVE in German are the following possibilities (cf. Figure 5):

'*Trotz* <:NG :POS-FACT> <:CLAUSE :NEG-FACT>'[6]
'*Zwar* <:CLAUSE :POS-FACT>, *aber* <:CLAUSE :NEG-FACT>'
'<:NG :POS-FACT> *darf nicht darüber hinwegtäuschen,*
    dass <:CLAUSE :NEG-FACT>'

3.2.3 Domain knowledge vs. generation knowledge

Rhetorical schemata are a good example of the division of labor between a text planner and the (tactical) generator: In order to build up an EMPHASIZE-NEGATIVE structure and to decide what statements could be combined, one has to know about the evaluation of facts and their relations within the domain under discussion. The generator, on the other hand, only needs to know in what ways such a structure might be expressed. It does not need to check (at least in our implementation) if a combination of conceptual structures makes sense. In this respect the generator should rely on the text planner's work.

'Der DGB erklärt, ...
... sie habe sich *zwar* vermindert, die Zahl der Arbeitslosen habe jetzt
aber noch immer einen Wert von 2148800.'

... dass die Reduzierung der Zahl der Arbeitslosen *nicht darüber hinweg-*
täuschen dürfte, dass sie jetzt noch immer einen Wert von 2148800 habe.'

... das *trotz* der Verringerung der Arbeitslosenzahl sie jetzt unverändert unerträglich hoch sei.'

Figure 5. Generated examples for EMPHASIZE-NEGATIVE rhetorics

3.3 From text plan to text

The generator developed for the title translation task is able to produce both clauses and nominalized versions from case frame representations. Therefore it is very simple to let this module transform a text plan (i.e. a list of conceptual structures) into a series of isolated sentences. But in general, this will of course not yield a result that would qualify as coherent and acceptable text. For the production of connected text it is crucial to provide the generator with mechanisms for context-sensitive generation.

---

6 Read <:NG :POS-FACT> as: 'realization of the filler of slot :POS-FACT as a noun group'

3.3.1 The effects of context handling

The effects of SEMTEX's mechanisms for context handling are best illustrated by a contrastive example. If we take the text plan from Figure 4 and let it simply be generated as list of isolated structures, the result is as in Figure 6.

Die Arbeitslosenzahl in der Bundesrepublik Deutschland steigt während des Dezember 1985 spürbar an. Die Arbeitslosenzahl steigt im Dezember 1985 von 2210700 auf 2347100 an. Die Arbeitslosenquote beträgt Ende Dezember 1985 9.4 Prozent. Die Arbeitslosenquote beträgt Ende Dezember 1984 9.3 Prozent. Der DGB erklärt, dass der DGB im Anstieg der Arbeitslosenzahl ein negatives Zeichen sehe.

Figure 6. The plan from Figure 4 generated without context handling

SEMTEX, on the other hand, converts the same text plan into the news story in Figure 7.

Die Zahl der Arbeitslosen in der Bundesrepublik Deutschland ist im Dezember spürbar angestiegen. Sie hat von 2210700 auf 2347100 zugenommen. Die Arbeitslosenquote betrug Ende Dezember 9.4 Prozent. Sie hatte sich Ende Dezember des letzten Jahres auf 9.3 Prozent belaufen. Der DGB hat erklärt, er sehe in der Vergrösserung der Arbeitslosenzahl ein negatives Zeichen.

Figure 7. A text generated from the plan in Figure 4

3.3.2 The context handler

During SEMTEX's text generation, an instance of the flavor class *CONTEXT* serves as a context handler, i.e. as an expert for all questions related to the context created so far by previous generation steps and the impact of this context on subsequent generation decisions (cf. Figure 8).

Some of the instance variables of a context handler are used to keep track of various types of information relevant for context-sensitive decisions:

— LEXICAL-CHOICES. Whenever a semantic symbol is lexicalized, the chosen German lexical entry — this may be a single root form or a whole structure — and the syntactic category are stored. For subsequent lexicalizations of the same semantic symbol, this information makes it possible to avoid repetition in wording as long as SLEX — the dictionary that relates semantic symbols to German lexical entries — provides synonyms.[7] In this sense SEMTEX simulates a writer who is careful with respect to word choice.

— EXPRESSED-ROLES. The news stories generated by SEMTEX should be as concise as possible. One way to achieve this is to elide redundant information and to rely on the reader's ability to make use of context defaults set by previous sentences. As long as information — e.g. about the time period concerned — that has been explicitly expressed is still valid in subsequent conceptual structures, it need not be reuttered. The example in

---

[7] A possible extension, which has not yet been implemented, would be the use of hypernyms in order to avoid repetitive wording

Figure 7 is a case in point: When the second sentence is generated, the information about the time period may be elided (although this information has to be present in the conceptual structure to allow for determination of correct tense; cf. Section 3.4.2).

— REFERABLE-ROLES: The information in this list is used both for decisions about pronominalization and their execution. The former involves, e.g., checking for competing possible referents for the intended pronoun in order to avoid the creation of an ambiguity. The latter is simply done by copying the preceding generation result for the current conceptual structure and marking it with the feature (:PRO PRN). This causes the front-end generator to create the appropriate pronoun.

```
>    (DEFFLAVOR *CONTEXT*
>              (CURRENT-TEXT          ;  pointer to text object
>              CURRENT-STRUCT         ;  current element of text plan
>              (LEXICAL-CHOICES ())   ;  lexicalizations made
>              (EXPRESSED-ROLES ())   ;  explicitly realized concepts
>              (REFERABLE-ROLES ())   ;  candidates for reference
>              TIME-OF-SPEECH         ;
>              TIME-OF-INTEREST)      ;
>         ()
>    :SETABLE-INSTANCE-VARIABLES)
```

Figure 8. Defining the context handling expert

```
> (gtl (send *** :referable-roles))
  (((:STRUCT-4
   ...
   ((UNEMPLOYMENT-RATE :GROUP *GLOBAL*)  ;;; conceptual structure
    :AGENT                                ;;; as filler of role
    (:SUBJ                                ;;; syntactic function of
     (:NG (:HEAD "Arbeitslosenquote")    ;;; realized structure
          (:FEATURES (:NUM SG)(:DET DEF)(:PRO PRN))))))
  (:STRUCT-3
   ...
   ((UNEMPLOYMENT-RATE :GROUP *GLOBAL*)
    :AGENT . (:SUBJ
    (:NG (:HEAD "Arbeitslosenquote")
          (:FEATURES (:NUM SG) (:DET DEF))))))
  (:STRUCT-2 ... )
  (:STRUCT-1 ... )
  (:HEAD ((NR-UNEMPLOYED :GROUP *GLOBAL*)
          :AGENT
          (:POSSATTR (:NG (:HEAD "Arbeitslosenzahl")
                     (:FEATURES (:NUM SG)(:DET DEF)))))))
```

3.4 Handling of tense and temporal information

In addition to information from the textual context, SEMTEX takes temporal information into account during generation. Factual statements in text plans should contain information concerning the :TIME-PERIODs or :TIME-POINTs for which they hold. When uttering the corresponding sentences, SEMTEX uses this information in order to determine grammatical tense and to generate appropriate descriptive noun phrases referring to time units.

3.4.1 Representing temporal knowledge

For the domain of labor market developments the primary time periods are months, and relevant time-points are at the beginning or end of the periods.

> (DEFFLAVOR TIME-UNIT () (AM-OBJECT))

> (DEFFLAVOR MONTH
>   ((NAME)   ;;; from (Januar, ... , Dezember)
>   (YEAR)   ;;;
>   (EXTERNAL-NAME))   ;;; as pointer[8]
>   (TIME-UNIT)
>   :SETTABLE-INSTANCE-VARIABLES)

Temporal objects 'know' about their relative position on the time axis:

> (SEND NOV-85 :TIME-RELATION-TO DEZ-85)
>   :BEFORE

3.4.2 Determination of tense

The determination of grammatical tense involves reasoning about temporal relations; it is accomplished in the following way:

— There is a distinct TIME-OF-INTEREST. For the labor market application this is the month for which we want the report.
— The text is uttered at a distinct TIME-OF-SPEEC:. As a default we use here some day at the start of the month following the TIME-OF-INTEREST.
— When semantic structures with temporal information are realized, then the given TIME-PERIOD or TIME-POINT (current time) is related to both TIME-OF-SPEECH and TIME-OF-INTEREST ('double indexing'). This is done by communicating with the time objects concerning in the knowledge base.
— The values of both relations (REL2TIME-OF-SPEECH and REL2TIME-OF- INTEREST) are used to select grammatical tense (cf. Figure 9).

---

[8] Within text plans one may refer to instances of MONTH by symbols made up from the first three characters of the month's (German) name, a '-' and the two digits from year minus 1900.

```
(selectq REL2TIME-OF-SPEECH;; relation of current time to TIME-OF-SPEECH
   (:time-eq 'PRES)
   (:before (selectq REL2TIME-OF-INTEREST;; and to TIME-OF-INTEREST
            (:time-eq 'PERF)
            (:after 'PAST)
            (:before 'PASTPERF)
            (otherwise (wrong-arg REL2TIME-OF-INTEREST ))))
   (:after (selectq REL2TIME-OF-INTEREST
            (:time-eq 'FUT1)
            (:after 'FUT1)
            (:before 'FUT2)
            (otherwise (wrong-arg REL2TIME-OF-INTEREST ))))
   (otherwise (wrong-arg REL2TIME-OF-SPEECH )))
```

Figure 9. Double indexing for determination of tense

3.4.3 Varying the time of speech

The dynamic aspect of SEMTEX's determination of tense is nicely illustrated when the TIME-OF-SPEECH for a text is deliberately varied.

> (send t-10-85 :utter)
Die Arbeitslosenzahl in der Bundesrepublik Deutschland hat sich
im Verlauf des Oktober nur wenig verringert. Sie hat sich von
2151600 auf 2148800 vermindert. Die Arbeitslosenquote betrug
Ende Oktober 8.6 Prozent. Sie hatte sich *am Ende des
Vergleichzeitraumes des letzten Jahres* ebenfalls auf 8.6 Prozent
belaufen.

> (send t-10-85 :time-of-speech?)
(START-OF :TIME-PERIOD *NOV-85*)   ;;;   the default

> (send t-10-85 :set-time-of-speech '(start-of :time-period nov-84))
(START-OF :TIME-PERIOD *NOV-84*)
> (send t-10-85 :utter)
Die Arbeitslosenzahl in West-Deutschland wird sich im Verlauf
des Oktober 1985 nur sehr wenig verkleinern. Sie wird sich von
2151600 auf 2148800 vermindern. Die Arbeitslosenquote wird Ende
Oktober 1985 einen Wert von 8.6 Prozent haben. Sie hatte Ende
Oktober ebenfalls 8.6 Prozent betragen.

> (send t-10-85 :set-time-of-speech '(start-of :time-period jan-86))
(START-OF :TIME-PERIOD *JAN-86*)
> (send t-10-85 :utter)
Die Arbeitslosenzahl in Deutschland hat sich während des Oktober
1985 nur wenig verringert. Sie hat von 2151600 auf 2148800
abgenommen. Die Arbeitslosenquote lag Ende Oktober 1985 bei 8.6
Prozent. Sie hatte sich *Ende Oktober des vorherigen Jahres*
ebenfalls auf 8.6 Prozent belaufen.

These examples exhibit other aspects of the realization of temporal information:

— When referring to months of the current year (i.e. the year of the time of speech) the year's number is left out by convention.

— Temporal units may be referenced not only by name, but also by their function ('Vergleichzeitraum des .. Jahres').

— The selection of referring adjectives in noun group descriptions of months takes the temporal relations into account (*letzt* is used when the referred year is the last one before that of the TIME-OF-SPEECH; *vorherig* on the other hand is used when referring to a year that immediately precedes the last one mentioned in the text).

3.5 Context sensitive descriptions

When the texts report about labor market figures in a more detailed way and, e.g., include unemployment figures for various groups, the generator employs additional techniques of reference. A usual way to talk about a statistical index for a group is to add a possessive or a prepositional adjunct for the group to the noun group for the index (e.g. 'die Arbeitslosenzahl der Frauen'). When we have already talked about an index for a group explicitly and wish to talk about another index for the same group, we can avoid having to repeat the group by using a referring adjective like *entsprechend* or *zugehörig*.

> (send t-12-85 :utter)

VERGRÖSSERUNG DER ZAHL DER ARBEITSLOSEN.

NÜRNBERG/BONN (cpa) 5. 1. 1986
Die Arbeitslosenzahl in Deutschland ist während des Dezember
1985 erkennbar gestiegen. ...
　　　　　...　　　　　　　　　　　　　Der Anstieg der Zahl
der Arbeitslosen bei den Männern fiel deutlicher als die Zunahme
der Arbeitslosenzahl der Frauen aus. *Die Zahl der Arbeitslosen*
bei den Männern hat sich von 1179700 um 117700 auf 1297400
deutlich vergrössert. *Die entsprechende Arbeitslosenquote* lag
Ende Dezember 1985 bei 8.5 Prozent, während sie am Ende des
Vergleichzeitraumes des Vorjahrs 8.7 Prozent betragen hatte. ...

Similarly, when we have mentioned an index for one group, we may elide the noun when a reference to the same index for another group follows. For example, the following partial text plan:

```
(ENUMERATION : ARG-1
        (HAVE-VALUE : QUANTITY (UNEMPLOYMENT-RATE :GROUP *MEN)
                    : VALUE (PERCENTAGE :VALUE 7.4)
                    : TIME-POINT (END-OF :TIME-PERIOD OKT-85))
        : ARG-2
        (HAVE-VALUE : QUANTITY (UNEMPLOYMENT-RATE :GROUP *WOMEN)
                    : VALUE (PERCENTAGE :VALUE 10.4)
                    : TIME-POINT (END-OF :TIME-PERIOD OKT-85)))
```

is realized as:

Die Arbeitslosenquote der Männer belief sich Ende Oktober auf 7.4
Prozent, während *die der Frauen* einen Wert von 10.4 Prozent hatte

4. CURRENT AND FUTURE WORK

The SEMTEX text generator is currently being applied to a second task domain: Generating German text that describes the steps of solving a geometry construction task (GEOTEX). The situation in this application is the sequence of formal commands of a geometry language. An example of GEOTEX's current output is given in Figure 10 (Kehl, 1986). In the GEOTEX application SEMTEX's context handling mechanisms are enriched with:

— more elaborate techniques for elision
— topicalization as a means for constituent ordering
— deliberate choice between various reference techniques (names, pronouns, textual deixis using demonstratives, etc.).

The Japanese/German MT efforts will be continued on a broader basis as well. Main topics of research will be:

— broaden the applicability of the generation system to other input structures (experiments with other semantic structures derived from Japanese; generation from EUROTRA structures)
— development of a declarative specification language for generation rules
— research on linguistic issues related to generation from semantic structures.

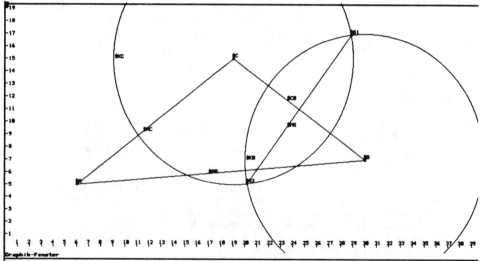

Figure 10. Current status of GEOTEX — a snapshot

5. CONCLUSIONS

Let us summarize the results of the first period of our project:

— We have gained expertise in generating German from semantic structures.
— We have implemented a generator for German noun groups and clauses with broad coverage of the relevant types of syntactic structures.
— The generator front end has full coverage of German morphology.

Based on this work the SEMTEX experiment has enriched our generator for German with

— a variety of context handling techniques needed for the generation of multisentential texts, and
— techniques for the representation and generation of rhetorical structures.

Both topics are further investigated in our ongoing research.

ACKNOWLEDGEMENT

The SEMSYN project is funded by the West German Ministry for Research and Technology (BMFT). In its first phase SEMSYN was carried out in cooperation with FUJITSU Research Laboratories, Japan; the current project is cooperating with partners from Japan (University of Kyoto; NTT Basic Research Laboratories) and USA (International Center for MT at CMU). We thank all of those partners for their support. We are also indebted to Thomas Strothotte and Cecile Paris for helpful comments and very constructive suggestions on a preliminary version of this paper.

REFERENCES

Becker, J. D. (1975) The phrasal lexicon. In: R. Schank & B. Webber (Eds.) *Proceedings of TINLAP, Theoretical Issues in Natural Language Processing*, Cambridge, Mass.

Busemann, S. (1982) *Probleme der automatischen Generierung deutscher Sprache*. HAM-ANS Memo 8, Universität Hamburg.

Emele, M. & S. Momma (1985) *SUTRA-S — Erweiterungen eines Generator- Front-End für das SEMSYN-Projekt*. Studienarbeit, Institut für Informatik, Universität Stuttgart.

Kehl, W. (1986) *GEOTEX - Ein System zur Verbalisierung geometrischer Konstruktionen*. Diplomarbeit, Institut für Informatik, Universität Stuttgart.

Laubsch, J., Rösner, D., Hanakata, K. & Lesniewski, A. (1984) Language Generation from Conceptual Structure: Synthesis of German in a Japanese/German MT Project. In: *Proceedings of COLING 84*, Stanford.

Rösner, D. & Laubsch, J. (1982) Formalisation of argumentation structures in newspaper texts. In: *Proceedings of COLING-82*, Prague.

Rösner, D. (1985) Schemata for Understanding of Argumentation in Newspaper Texts. In: L. Steels & J. Campbell (Eds.) *Progress in Artificial Intelligence*. Chichester: Horwood.

Rösner, D. (1986a) When Mariko talks to Siegfried — Experiences from a Japanese/German Machine Translation Project. In: *Proceedings of COLING-86*, Bonn.

Rösner, D. (1986b) *Ein System zur Generierung von deutschen Texten aus semantischen Repräsentationen*. Doctoral Dissertation, Institut für Informatik, Universität Stuttgart.

Uchida, H. & Sugiyama, K. (1980) A machine translation system from Japanese into English based on conceptual structure. In: *Proceedings of COLING-80*, Tokyo.

Weinreb, D. & Moon, D. (1981) *LISP Machine Manual*, MIT, Artificial Intelligence Laboratory, Cambridge, Mass.

Chapter 11

A CONNECTIONIST APPROACH TO THE GENERATION OF ABSTRACTS

Kôiti Hasida
Shun Ishizaki
Hitoshi Isahara

ABSTRACT

This chapter discusses a method for extracting significant portions out of what we call contextual representation structure (CRS). The method is based on a connectionist paradigm in which information processing in the human brain is accounted for in terms of signal propagation in a network which reflects the topology of neural connections. The key idea is to regard the degree of importance of each node in a CRS network as the activation intensity of that node after a saturation of signal propagation across the relevant part of the network. Both top-down and bottom-up information are naturally accommodated in the abstract by this single principle.

1. INTRODUCTION

Making an abstract concerns some essential problems of human language processing. First, identification of significant parts of contents constitutes a crucial aspect of language understanding, in the sense that understanding should involve detection of importance. Second, generation of an abstract must reflect more cognitive essence than does sentence generation (such as in ordinary machine translation), where the part of semantic structure to be verbalized is predetermined. This is because the former must inevitably be sensitive to what the readers are expected to know in advance. The study of human language processing so far, however, appears to have paid far less attention to these aspects than they deserve.

In this chapter we present a method for making abstracts of texts, keeping in mind a clear perspective on those problems. We shall exploit a connectionist paradigm (cf. Rumelhart & McClelland, 1982; Rumelhart, McClelland et al., 1986; Pearl, 1986) in which information processing in the human brain is accounted for in terms of signal propagation in a network which reflects the topology of neural connections. The key idea is to regard the degree of importance of each part in a network representation of concepts as the activation intensity of that part after a saturation of signal propagation across the relevant domain of the network. We shall discuss how this idea naturally takes relevant information into consideration, and how it may interact with knowledge representation and sentence generation.

1.1 Contextual Representation Structure (CRS)

The abstraction procedure discussed below is part of a natural language processing system called CONTRAST (Ishizaki, Isahara & Handa, 1986), which is currently under development at the Electrotechnical Laboratory. CONTRAST employs a scheme for expressing semantic information. This scheme, called Contextual Representation Structure (CRS), is independent of individual languages, and language-dependent knowledge is described in dictionaries and grammars which refer to CRS. CRS is a network built up out of nodes and links between them. A node is a bundle of slot-value pairs. The value of a slot is again a node. Thus a slot hanging on node A and having node B as its value constitutes a link from A to B. Each such link is accompanied by a backward link from B to A which is not an explicit slot-value pair. Every link belongs to one of these two types.

CRS is designed to represent not only semantic content directly expressed in terms of sentences, but also more contextual or pragmatic content hidden between the lines. The latter sort of content includes, among other things, information about typical ways in which events proceed, i.e., what MOP's (Memory Organization Packets; Schank, 1980) are intended to accommodate. CRS is exploited for representing both longer-term background knowledge and shorter-term information provided directly by sentences or indirectly by inferences. That is, in typical cases the latter sort of information is structured and piled upon the underlying static knowledge.

This completes our brief summary of CRS. Some further details, though not all, will be discussed in connection with relevant issues in the rest of the chapter.

1.2 An overall view of abstraction

In our system, the entire process of abstraction is viewed as comprising three smaller subtasks: *analysis, evaluation*, and *generation*. Roughly speaking, analysis involves establishing the semantic representation of given sentences, evaluation identifying the importance of each part of the content, and generation putting some of these parts into words. Our formalization presented below is a simplification in which these subtasks are separated chronologically from each other and take place successively. We do not claim, of course, that this is the case with actual human language processing, but rather believe that the subtasks are interleaved.

In the analysis stage, input sentences undergo both syntactic and semantic interpretation, giving rise to CRS fragments which semantically subsume these sentences. In an idealized situation, the analysis device should set up all CRS fragments relevant to the understanding of the sentences in question; i.e., not only fragments directly corresponding to the given sentences but also those which are indirectly obtained via inferences. In reality there may well be several oversights here because of processing-related limitations, but the next stage of evaluation has no choice but to assume that the analysis is perfect. Note that these tasks of analysis are the ones that have been granted as ubiquitous in language understanding and thus have received adequate attention in studies in computational linguistics. Hence we shall not go deeper into the analysis stage.

The evaluation stage is the central concern of this chapter. As should be expected from the discussion above, this stage does not carry out any further inference but just attempts to evaluate the importance of each part in the relevant substructure of the allegedly complete CRS network. How this evaluation proceeds will be discussed in the following section.

In the final generation stage, the parts of the CRS network judged to be significant enough are extracted and translated into a natural language. As will be discussed in more detail, the task of generation requires more sophistication than one might suppose, because it must be sensitive to the readers' knowledge if it is to result in an abstract which is both concise and informative. The syntactic aspects of generation are not of serious interest here.

2. EVALUATION OF IMPORTANCE

Before we discuss how to evaluate importance, we must settle two problems: what the measure of importance should be, and what are the minimal substructures of CRS are to which importance should be allocated.

As to the first problem, we consider that the measure of importance must be finer-grained than a simplistic yes/no judgement. The reader may assume that importance of nodes is measured in terms of some dense system such as that of real numbers. The second problem is more delicate. Our answer is that the node is the minimal bearer of importance. Accordingly, the judgment of whether to verbalize or not basically concerns nodes, rather than slots or links. When a node is chosen to be verbalized, some verbal description of the concept represented by that node should be generated. Not all information represented by links (including slots) is necessarily put into words here.

For example, when the expression *Tom kills Mary* appears among the given sentences, a fragment of CRS as shown in Figure 1 will be set up in the analysis stage. Here the node K represents a particular killing event, T a particular individual named Tom, and M the other individual named Mary. (Incidentally, 'KILL' is a node so labeled which represents the concept of the killing relation in general.) Suppose K is evaluated as sufficiently significant to be put into words. Some information represented by the links may be omitted in the expression produced corresponding to K, depending upon the broader context, how long the abstract is allowed to be, and what is assumed to be known in advance. That is, the possible expressions include *Tom kills Mary, Mary is killed, a murder*, etc.

This approach may well appear to lack justification, because one could in principle evaluate the importance of links as well. There is, however, a reason why we do not have to consider the importance of links. It is related to a certain aspect of CRS which we have not mentioned yet. In CRS, a slot name is the name of a binary relation. More precisely, a slot named A with the value B and hanging on node C is regarded as a concise representation of a binary relation holding between B and C, which would otherwise be represented as a node whose ISA-value is A. For instance, the CRS fragment in Figure 1 is logically equivalent to the one shown in Figure 2. However, these representations are different with respect to how they are processed. For instance, the one in Figure 2 can directly give rise to (or be directly obtained from) such expressions as *Tom commits a murder,* but the one in Figure 1 cannot. To put it another way, the relation between Tom and the killing event is highlighted in Figure 2.

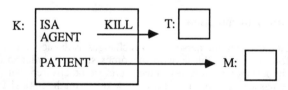

Figure 1. A CRS fragment corresponding to *Tom kills Mary*

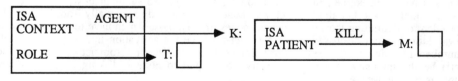

Figure 2. A CRS fragment logically equivalent to the one in Figure 1

Any slot may thus be extracted as a node to indicate that it should be evaluated. We therefore assume that everything to be dynamically evaluated is represented as a node, because the analysis device is sensitive to relations to be highlighted and so sets up a node for each such relation.

2.1 Degree of importance as activation intensity

There are several types of contextual information which should be reflected in the evaluation of importance. Let us consider two of them. First, certain types of nodes should be considered important, and substructures around them should accordingly be evaluated high. These nodes include ones representing typical ways of how events proceed, causal relationships among events, etc. Put more generally, broader views should be more important. For instance, the concept of a case of murder provides a broader view than do the concepts of a killing event, a murderer, a victim, a motive, etc., in the sense that the case of murder involves the latter elements as its typical building blocks. When a node representing a case of murder is created (that is, a viewpoint is introduced in the analysis stage), not only that node but also the nodes representing the associated building blocks should receive high importance assignments.

Second, a node with a greater *degree* (i.e., a greater number of links associated with it) should be evaluated as more important. To put it into more intuitive terms, things which are often referred to (whether explicitly or implicitly) are important.

These two criteria are simultaneously accommodated by a single connectionistic principle: Nodes activate each other via links between them. Here, the intensity of activation of a node is identified with its degree of importance, and the intensity of the activation signal through the link from node A to B is in proportion to the activation intensity of A, the proportion constant being called the *connection coefficient* of that link.

For example, the node representing the concept of a case of murder, which is known to be important in advance, activates through direct connection a node representing a particular case of murder, which in turn activates the nodes representing the murderer, the victim, etc. Note also that nodes associated with greater numbers of links tend to get activated more intensely. That is, minutely described matters are regarded as significant.

The idea that nodes are minimal bearers of importance fits the connectionist paradigm in which short-term processes are regarded as the transition of the activation states of nodes (as in Waltz & Pollack, 1985), and long-term processes like learning are viewed as changes in connection coefficients of links, or maybe as the creation of new nodes and links.

2.2 A mathematical formulation

In the connectionist paradigm, the network states changes as the activation signals propagate. We should therefore wait until the network becomes stable in order to obtain a plausible evaluation of the importance of nodes. It must therefore be ensured that the network states converges as time passes by. So let us now work out a mathematical formulation of the transition of network states on the basis of which the signal propagation stably saturates over the network.

Here we adopt an approximation where time is quantized and the signal propagation along links is synchronized; i.e., all the activation signals are passed simultaneously in accordance with a single clock. Let all of the relevant nodes be numbered sequentially from 1 to n. (The problem of delimiting the set of relevant nodes, that is, those which have to be subjected to evalulation, is not discussed here.) Next let $x(t,i)$ be the activation intensity of the node numbered i at time t, $a(i,j)$ be the connection coefficient of the link from node j to node i, and $c(i)$ be the intensity of a constant activation signal to node i. Taking a simple linear approximation, we would have:

$$x(0) = C$$
$$x(t+1) = A*x(t) + C \quad (t = 0, 1, 2, ...)$$

where '*' represents a multiplication of matrices, and

$$x(t) = \begin{bmatrix} x(t, 1) \\ : \\ x(t, n) \end{bmatrix} \quad A = \begin{bmatrix} a(1, 1) \dots a(1, n) \\ : \qquad : \\ a(n, 1) \dots a(n, n) \end{bmatrix} \quad C = \begin{bmatrix} c(1) \\ : \\ c(n) \end{bmatrix}$$

Vector x(t) converges to some finite value as t approaches infinity, if the absolute value of each eigenvalue of matrix A is smaller than one. In that case the limit value X is obtained by

$$X = (I - A)^{-1} * C.$$

where I is the unit matrix.

A caveat is in order here: This formulation is intended only to ensure that the signal propagation saturates in the long run. It does not imply that we should solve the above linear equation in practical applications. In fact, when the number of links is far smaller than n^2, as is often to be expected in practice, it may be more efficient to obtain x(t) for some sufficiently large t than to figure out X directly by routinely solving the linear equation. Incidentally, the above formulation is nothing more than a (literally!) linear approximation, and currently has little cognitive justification. We do not believe that the network behavior is linear in its nature.

3. AN EXAMPLE

Let us now look at an example of how the above evaluation works. The sample passage shown in Figure 3 is an excerpt from an article in the Asahi Evening News, September 10th, 1986. The passage consists of paragraphs (a) through (d). The fragments of the CRS network corresponding to these paragraphs are depicted in Figure 3. For the sake of expository convenience, these figures are simplified in several aspects. First, the inner structure of each node is omitted, and a node is represented as a name such as b7:RELATIONS. Here RELATIONS indicates which word in the text the node corresponds to. A name uniquely identifies a node. For instance, all occurrences of a8:KOREA refer to one and the same node, while b7:RELATIONS and d9:RELATIONS name different nodes. Second, a link and the accompanying reverse link are represented in Figure 3 as one nondirected link . Third, proper nouns are omitted in the network. For example, a13:JAPAN represents the particular country (or its government), but not its name. Incidentally, a name with a common noun or a verb represents some particular instance, not the generic concept corresponding to that word. For instance, d3:LACK represents a particular state of affairs in which something lacks something else.

There are several substructures in the figure that are not explicitly mentioned in the article but obtained by inference. For example, the original text does not explicitly mention the relation between the contents of Fujio's remarks and the fact that he is a nationalist. This relation is represented as two links in Figure 3(c). As another example, the link between b1:PRIME-MINISTER (representing the state of affairs of Nakasone being prime minister) and a11:DISMISS indicates that the dismissal of Fujio by Nakasone is partly based on the fact that Nakasone is the prime minister. This link is also obtained via some inference using background knowledge.

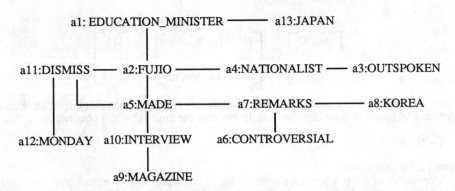

(a) *Education Minister Masayuki Fujio, an outspoken nationalist who made controversial remarks on Korea in a magazine interview, was dismissed from his post Monday.*

Figure 3a. Paragraph (a) and its CRS representation

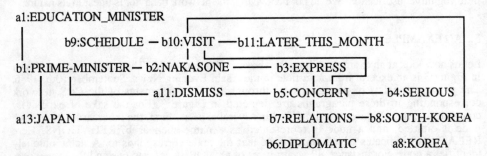

(b) *The action was taken by Prime Minister Yasuhiro Nakasone, who expressed serious concern about diplomatic relations with South Korea, which he is scheduled to visit later this month.*

Figure 3b. Paragraph (b) and its CRS representation

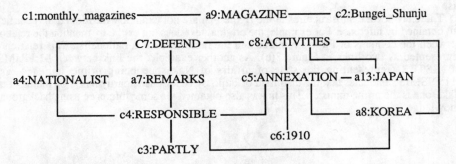

(c) *Fujio said in an interview with the monthly magazine Bungei Shunju that Korea was partly responsible for Japan's annexation of that country in 1910. He also defended some of Japan's past activities in Korea.*

Figure 3c. Paragraph (c) and its CRS representation

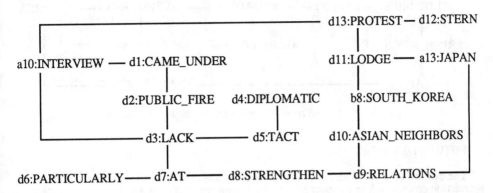

(d) *The interview came under public fire for lacking diplomatic tact, particularly at a time when Japan is trying to strenghten relations with its Asian neighbors. South Korea lodged a stern protest with the government against the interview.*

Figure 3d. Paragraph (d) and its CRS representation

Table 1. The result of an evaluation

a1	3	2.393	a2	4	2.705	a3	1	1.499	a4	4	2.492	a5	4	2.819
a6	1	1.563	a7	5	2.942	a8	5	2.969	a9	3	1.957	a10	5	2.854
a11	6	3.229	a12	1	1.604	a13	5	2.948	b1	5	3.097	b2	3	2.256
b3	1	1.456	b4	1	1.446	b5	3	2.122	b6	1	1.459	b7	4	2.215
b8	1	1.567	b9	1	1.454	b10	4	2.178	b11	1	1.454	c1	1	1.422
c2	1	1.422	c3	1	1.570	c4	5	2.992	c5	5	2.970	c6	1	1.567
c7	3	2.249	c8	3	2.313	d1	2	1.798	d2	2	1.730	d3	4	2.311
d4	1	1.381	d5	2	1.670	d6	1	1.417	d7	3	1.920	d8	2	1.711
d9	3	2.059	d10	2	1.753	d11	3	2.115	d12	1	1.377	d13	2	1.642

Shown in Table 1 is the result of an evaluation. For simplification, each connection coefficient was set to 0.125 (=1/8), every node was linked with itself, and every $c(i)$ was 1.0. Each entry in the table is a triplet consisting of the identifier of a node, its degree, and its activation intensity. Observe that nodes with greater degree tend to be prominent and that the nodes around them are also accordingly evaluated high. It is a good exercise in linear algebra to show that every eigenvalue of the connection matrix A is smaller than 1.0 in absolute value; readers who do not find this trivial are advised to notice that the maximum degree of the nodes is 7. The top ten nodes are extracted in Figure 4, where the links among these nodes are also shown. An abstract based on these top ten nodes might read somewhat like the following hand-generated sentence:

> *The prime minister dismissed Fujio, who in an interview made remarks to the effect hat Korea was responsible for Japan's annexation.*

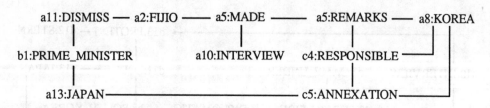

Figure 4. The top ten most important nodes and links among them

4. FUTURE DEVELOPMENTS

The evaluation method just described does not touch upon several important aspects of the abstraction process in human speakers/writers. For example, it does not address the problem of how to delimit the set of 'relevant' nodes which need to be considered during the evaluation stage. Also, various issues concerning old versus new information, typicality, and hierarchies of concepts have not been given the attention they deserve. We are designing an improved evaluation method which we hope can solve some of the deficiencies of the present version.

REFERENCES

Ishizaki, S., Isahara, H. & Handa, K. (1986) *Natural Language Processing System with Deductive Learning Mechanism*, International Symposium on Language and Artificial Intelligence, Kyoto. (To appear in: *Language and Artificial Intelligence*, Amsterdam: North Holland.)

Pearl, J. (1986) Fusion, Propagation, and Structuring in Belief Networks. *Artificial Intelligence, 29*, 241-288.

Rumelhart, D. E. & McClelland, J .L. (1982) An Interactive Activation Model of Context Effects in Letter Perception: Part 2. The Contextual Enhancement Effect and Some Tests and Extensions of the Model. *Psychological Review, 89*, 60-94.

Rumelhart, D. E., McClelland, J. L. & The PDP Research Group (1986) *Parallel Distributed Processing: Explorations in the Microstructure of Cognition*. Cambridge, MA.: MIT Press.

Schank, R. C. (1980) Language and Memory. *Cognitive Science, 4*, 243-284.

Waltz, D. L. & Pollack, J. B. (1985) Massively Parallel Parsing: A Strongly Interactive Model of Natural Language Interpretation. *Cognitive Science, 9*, 51-74.

PART III

Generator Design

Chapter 12

FACTORS CONTRIBUTING TO EFFICIENCY IN NATURAL LANGUAGE GENERATION

David D. McDonald
Marie M. Vaughan
James D. Pustejovsky

ABSTRACT

While differences in starting points, grammatical formalisms, and control structures make it intrinsically difficult to compare alternative designs for natural language generation systems, there are nevertheless many points of correspondence among them. To organize these points, we introduce an abstract reference model for the generation process. We then identify five specific factors with respect to that model that certain designs incorporate to make them more efficient computationally.

1. INTRODUCTION

Our goal in this paper is to provide a way to talk about the consequences of alternative architectures for the generation process. The particular structures that a given generator may have (i.e. its rules, categories, and lexical definitions) and the texts that it can produce will vary as its research team continues to work with it; however the architectural features of the design, including its choice of notations, control structures, and representational levels, will be relatively constant. It is these more fundamental design issues that give each generator its own character, and it is these issues, once the varying skills of the computer programmers have been factored out, which will make one generator design more efficient than another, i.e. able to solve the same problem with fewer steps. In our own research on generation, we have always had the intuition that our architectural choices have deep consequences for our program's runtime efficiency. This paper is an initial attempt to ground that intuition in a proper comparative analysis.

2. DEFINITIONS AND CONCERNS

For the purposes of this paper we take natural language generation to be the process of deliberately producing a natural language utterance in order to meet specified communicative goals in a particular situation. We thus will not consider here systems that produce sentences randomly such as grammar checkers (e.g. Friedman, 1969), systems for language instruction (e.g. Bates, 1980), generation done during mechanical translation (e.g. Luckhardt, 1987), or any other kind of program for text production that does not act in the service of an actual synthetic speaker talking to a human user for a purpose.

'Utterances' are for our purposes fluent sequences of words of any length that would be appropriate as one turn of a conversation, e.g. anything from a single word expletive to a lecture. While we do not care whether the utterance is actually spoken (as opposed to printed), we do assume that the word sequence is accompanied by its phrase structure and other grammatical information necessary to define its intonational structure.

The generation systems that we are concerned with do not operate in isolation. They are ancillary processes in the employ of some other system: a database query system, expert diagnostician, ICAI tutor, etc. This system, which we will refer to uniformly as 'the underlying program', is the source of the communicative goals; it is what is in the situation that defines the context. The conversation is between the underlying program and its human user. We take it for granted that it is sensible to talk about 'the generator' as a faculty independent of this program: The two may interpenetrate each other's processing and liberally influence each other's design, but they dwell in two distinct ontological domains, are arguably distinct physically in the human brain, and are profitably kept separate in computer systems.

We recognize that many of the limitiations on the competence of today's generators — their expressive capacity to aptly use a wide range of syntactic constructions and vocabulary — stem not from the generator designs but from limitations of the underlying programs to conceptually model and represent the range and richness of situations that people can. From this perspective the limitations of particular generators will not for the most part be a concern of this paper: We presume that the authors of the various designs believe that they will be able to extend the linguistic competence of their generators over time in step with extensions to the situational competence of the underlying programs they work with, and that the major architectural features of their designs will not have to change significantly to do so.

2.1 Situations and the amount of effort required to produce an utterance

It is a little appreciated fact that not all utterances take the same effort for humans to produce. Consider, for example, what it feels like to greet a colleague as compared to being interviewed for a job. The greeting is 'automatic' and subjectively effortless; it requires very little of our attention and can be accomplished well enough even when one is mentally impaired due to lack of sleep or inebriation. On the other hand, a job interview, a lecture on a new subject matter, or an important meeting all require our full attention to do well; we often speak more slowly in these situations and sense a greater deliberation in our choice of wording and phrasing.

We believe that the key element governing the difficulty of utterance production is the degree of familiarity of the situation. Completely familiar situations (e.g. answering the phone) require the least amount of effort; highly unfamiliar situations require a great deal more. While we are not yet prepared to present a formalization of this relationship, we do see it already as an important desideratum for generator design: a commonplace situation should require less effort for the generator to handle, i.e. fewer steps in the processing, less scratch memory consumed, less elaborate reasoning required. (See further discussion section 6.2.)

What then is a 'situation' such that it may be more or less familiar? Our use of the term is in the same spirit as Barwise & Perry (1983). A speaker (underlying program) is 'in' a situation, i.e. located in space and time in the presence of a given audience and set of props and as the result of a specific history. These and other contextualizing factors are properties of the real world to which the speaker bears a semantic relationship, in the philosopher's customary sense. Situations are formally only partial descriptions of the world. This design provides a very useful encapsulation of effects, e.g. one is not immediately causally affected by events on the other side of the world.

The speaker maintains his own mental model of the situation he is in — an interpreted description of the actual external situation. This is an identifiable part of his mental state along with, of course, his own goals, perceptions, beliefs, etc. (part of the situation, but not a public part). It is this mental state[1] that controls what the speaker says. Following common practice in AI, we presume that the phrases produced by the generator refer to individuals in the semantic model that the program has of its situation. These individuals, 'objects' denoting people, events, states of affairs, etc., constitute a 'model-level' of representation.

The situation can be distinguished from the generator's 'reference knowledge': its grammar, rules of usage and style, preconstructed phrases, etc. While the situation is a dynamic structure which controls what is said at a particular moment, the reference knowledge is static and is central to the control of what the generator actually does in producing the utterance. All variance in the produced text is thus by definition due to the situation. (See Appendix for examples of reference knowledge in particular generation systems.)

Not all of the objects and parameter values that make up the underlying program's model of its situation will actually be relevant to the actions of the generator; that is, only a few of the individuals in the program's world model will actually be mentioned in any particular utterance. This has led us to posit an abstraction of the full situation, tautologically named 'the relevant portion of the situation' or RPS (see examples in section 5.1). The RPS is defined to be all and only those aspects of the underlying program's model of its situation that the generator refers to in the production of a specific utterance. As an operational definition, imagine that we trace the execution of a generator and put a green mark on every underlying program entity that the generator refers to during its execution. When the process has completed the set of all green entities constitutes the RPS.

3. A REFERENCE MODEL OF THE GENERATION PROCESS

The only effective methodology for comparing different systems is to refer them all to a single model. Picking out one of the systems as the model and translating all of the others into its terms would be presumptuous, and, given the present state of the field, not very fruitful since research projects differ in which parts of the problem they have focused on. Accordingly, we have developed a new, independent model which does not, so far as we know, directly mimic any of the generator designs being persued today. We have kept our model deliberately abstract so that we can apply informatively to any generation system as a rational reconstruction.

We begin by outlining a simplification of the model to set the tone and direction of our explication; we then incrementally elaborate it in the remainder of this section. We identify the following three steps in the generation process:

1. Identifying the speaker's situation.
2. Mapping that situation onto an utterance.
3. Reading out the utterance.

According to this model, the problem that a generator solves is how to navigate from its underlying program's position in situation space to a position in utterance space, i.e. to pick out

---

[1] As for the form in which the underlying program models the situation that it is in, it is most useful in this paper to leave it unspecified. Given today's programming techniques, any number of different means could be used, all equally effective from an engineering point of view: the situation might be explicitly represented as statements in a theory and queried by predicates whenever a situation-dependent decision must be made; it might be given as distributed, active routines that operate directly as the situation changes; it might be completely implicit in the program's structure and execution patterns. As yet we see no basis by which to say that any one of these alternative techniques is psychologically correct and the others wrong.

which utterance in the language is appropriate[2] to use in the particular situation that the underlying program is in. To do this the generator must first identify where in its situation space the program actually is, then apply some mapping function to that point in order to find or calculate a corresponding utterance, which is then read out.

3.1 Canned text

In the simplified form just given, the model is appropriate only for generation in the most familiar of situations, such as greetings or introductions (e.g. 'Pleased to meet you'.). The equivalent of this in a generator is 'canned text'. As an example consider the error statement (ferror) in the following excerpt from the code of the Mumble-86 implementation:

```
(defun Realize (message)
      (typecase message
            (bundle (funcall (driver (bundle-type message)) message)
            (kernel (realize-kernel message))
            (otherwise
                  (ferror  "Unanticipated kind of message - ~A"
                        message)))))
```

This error statement contains a typical canned text. In the Lisp programming language it is an instance of a 'format statement': a string of words enclosed in quotation marks that will be read out onto the user's screen when the statement is executed. As it is being read out, special indicators within the string such as the ~A are interpreted as instructions to substitute into the string at that point the printed form of the value of some indicated Lisp expression, in this case the variable message.

Its limitations aside (see below), the execution of a 'canned' text that has been incorporated directly into an underlying program's code is surely the most efficient generation process possible. In terms of our model, we see that the processor reaching and executing the ferror line of code is identical with initiating and carrying out its generation process. The first step in the sequence, 'identifying the speaker's situation', requires no effort; it is a natural side-effect of the program's regular actions. The mapping step is equally trivial, since an explicit link to the utterance, i.e. supplying the word string as an argument to the generation function, was preconstructed by the programmer at the time he wrote the code. The reading out step is done by a primitive of the programming language, and is, indeed, the only substantive activity that a canned-text generation system does.

As this particular example contains a variable in the string, it is in fact not so much a canned text as a 'template' into which variable information can be inserted, in this case the identity of the unknown type of message. The relevant part of the program's situation is not just being in the state of executing that line of code but also the value of the local variable 'message'. Such a use of variables is an prototypical illustration of a 'distributed state', the norm in all consequential underlying programs and generators. Because of distributed states, we must appreciate that the distinct 'positions' in an underlying program's situation space — the possible situations that it can be in — are not points but highly structured entities, and that the mapping from these situations to utterances can be quite complex.

---

[2] Note that we do not assume that the utterance is the 'most' appropriate one for the situation. People do not seem to need to be optimal in their choice (if they were there would be no need for revision); accordingly we see no need to demand it of our machines.

3.2 The necessity of a compositional analysis of situations

The canned text approach is effective as the generation mechanism for simple programs such as a compiler, because the programmer can easily anticipate which elements are relevant and bring them together into a fixed mapping. But as the relationships between programs and their users become more complex, it becomes progressively more difficult to anticipate at the time the program is written what will be relevant to communicate. When programs must construct the basis from which they are going to generate they then begin to fall under a body of considerations that until recently have only been applied to human use of language. These considerations revolve around whether utterances should be viewed as the result of a fixed mapping or a compositional one.

The classic argument for compositionality of a natural language relies on the so-called 'creativity' of language. The apparent fact that the number of utterances in a natural language is unbounded is one of its more widely remarked upon properties and a core tenet of modern linguistic theory. The classic argument for creativity uses the idea that one can continually add further adjuncts to sentences to establish that there can be no longest sentence and therefore no finite number of sentences (see Chomsky, 1957). Linguists argue from this observation that the total set of utterances cannot possibly be pre-formed in the mind since the mind must be taken to have a finite manifestation. Instead, the generative linguist holds that utterances are assembled dynamically from a finite set of parts (i.e. words and grammatical relations) in accordance with a grammar.

This conventional argument for the creativity of natural language is overly strained: who has actually heard a 500 word sentence? In contrast, anyone who studies generation has available a far more reasonable and commonsense account of creativity, namely that one continually uses new utterances because one is continually faced with new situations — a conclusion that follows directly from our model. The counterbalance to creativity is the 'efficiency' of language (Barwise & Perry, 1983): the fact that many utterances do reoccur countless times (e.g. 'Where did you go for dinner last night?'). This also has a direct account in the fact that many of the situations one finds oneself in are similar.

The assumption of a finite mind applies to situations as well. An interpretation of the world, a situation, must consist of a finite set of relations over a finite vocabulary of elements. The unbounded size of a natural language thus becomes ultimately a consequence of the introduction of new situational terms into the speaker's state set over time as a result of learning or perception.

In a computer program, the finite vocabulary of situation-defining elements is likely to be the values of the reference variables in its code (such as 'message' in the previous example), or the presence or absence of certain structured objects in its database (world model). In addition, an AI program will normally have semantic reference knowledge which supplies the characterizations by which the individuals in the world model are to be understood; this often takes the form of a semantic network which may play an active or a passive role in the program's operation. This is a distributed manifestation of the program's state: There is no single entity, such as the line of code presently being executed, that we could point to as 'the' representation of the state and therefore could associate in any simple way with a set of actions the generator was to take.

3.3 Mapping to intermediate representational levels

Once the situation has been identified, the generator must map it to an utterance. No serious system today moves from its initial situation to an utterance in one leap. This is surely no accident: Program designers do not add structure to a system just to excercise their creativity as linguists or AI researchers. Indeed, as we discuss in section 4.2, the introduction into the generation process of intermediate abstract entities, along with the representational systems and reference knowledge to manage them, is a natural means of increasing efficiency.

Representation in generation is usually not a straightforward case of having data structures (the representation) manipulated by operators (the process) to form new data structures: Structure and operation are often combined in the same formal device, and elements of the structures are often not freely examinable. Even though one talks about a structure being built or selected when some specification is mapped to it, this can often equally well be seen as a process being set in motion. To avoid taking a stand on such questions of algorithmic design in the formulation of our model, we will construe levels not in terms of structures but in terms of theoretical vocabulary. Notions like 'specialization', 'focus', 'subject', and 'consonant doubling before +*ing*' are theoretical concepts identifying linguistic phenomena or structural abstractions. Linguists and AI researchers tend to agree that these concepts can be grouped into families according to the kinds of information they reference and where they occur in theoretical descriptions and rules. We can coordinate the identification of common levels across very different generator designs by attending to what theoretical vocabulary a design's particular level makes use of without factoring in its particular algorithms and data structures.

3.4 The model

We can now give our model in its full form. Examples of its application to actual generators appears in section 5 and the Appendix. We will uniformly refer to the intermediate abstract levels as *specifications*. We will use *mapping* as the general term for moving between levels by applying a function to individual elements at the source level to arrive at elements or specifications for elements at the target level. *Realization* will refer to the usually more elaborate and more composite activity of processing a specification to produce the thing it is a specification of; it may involve mapping. Because of the sequential and incremental nature of the generation process, what were originally given as steps might now be better characterizes as *stages*. Most designs will have some activity at all their stages and representational levels simultaneously.

> IDENTIFY THE RPS The logically first stage in any generation process is to *identify those elements of the underlying program's model of its situation that are relevant to the content of the utterance and the control of the processing (the 'RPS').* This need not happen all at once but may be interleaved with other stages. As we will discuss below, the effort to 'identify' the RPS will include not just the effort of determining what information will be included and what will not, but also that of bringing together the elements of a distributed state and working out the consequences of their context-sensitive combination. This aggregation is necessary since as a field we have no way of thinking about how distributed, independent entities could bring about a single, atomic event.

> MAPPING The logically second, iterated stage is to *map the elements of the RPS, singly or in combination, to a specification of the utterance at some representational level.* A specification at a given level may be a single structure, possibly added to by successive mappings from the previous level, or it may be multiple structures specifying independent aspects of the utterance that will be combined during a mapping to a later level.

> READING OUT The third stage is to *read out the specification* . This final mapping must produce the actual text from the last representational level constructed in stage two.

4. SOURCES OF EFFICIENCY IN GENERATION

Generator designs gain efficiency according to the directness by which they move from situations to utterances. The optimal design with no wasted actions and a direct bridge between situation space and utterance space is unlikely ever to be developed: The conceptual distance between the two spaces is too great. The best we can do is to increase the sophistication of the specifications into which we map the elements of the RPS so that fewer elements will need to be considered simultaneously in determining the mapping, and, from the other end, to look for more versatile abstractions of utterance properties so as to move utterance space closer to the terms in which situations and specifications are couched. Within this framework, we will now give five specific sources of efficiency in the architectural design of natural language generation systems. We will introduce them here, then look at specific examples from actual generation systems in section 5.

4.1 Precomputation

One of the most obvious sources of efficiency in generation is precomputation. Rather than construct a specification or a mapping function from first principles each time it is needed, a system may preconstruct a parametrized structure once, as part of the system's definition, and simply apply it each time it is needed. The greater the extent to which precomputed material can be drawn on as a generator operates, the more efficient it will be.

When preconstructed parts are used, there is always a trade-off between the amount of structure incorporated into each part and the degree to which the parts become specialized to very particular situations. The more parts, the fewer will be required over all and the construction will take fewer steps; however, there is a danger of greatly increasing the effort required to determine which part to use.

Let us consider the consequences of the two extremes of all or no precomputation. Total precomputation gives us the equivalent of canned text: single step, situation specific, executable schemas which anticipate all of the interactions that might occur during identification, mapping, or realization. In effect, the generation process becomes a matter of instantiating and executing exceptionally sophisticated format statements. The most awkward consequence of this extreme is the astronomic number of these statements that would have to be defined and stored: many times larger than the cross product of the elements comprising the space of all possible situations. At the other extreme is a design where every structure and mapping function is assembled anew with the generation of each utterance, with no reusable parts or decision procedures. Such a design would be claiming that there was no redundancy among situations or utterances or that the effort to instantiate a precomputed schema was exorbitantly expensive; both possibilities seem unlikely.

4.2 Size of the steps

A second consideration for efficiency in the generation process is the distance that a mapping must cover in moving between successive levels. The smaller the steps to be covered, the more efficiently each mapping can be designed. Consider a hypothetical design where the derivation for utterances is compositional, yet we move from the situation to the complete utterance in one massive step. In such a design the mapping function would do all of the work: it would require every element of the situation to be an input parameter and would construct the entire utterance as output. This caricature exhibits the poorest imaginable fit between representational levels for the mapping stage since no part of the situation can be considered independently of all the others. (Some designs based on discrimination nets have this flavor (Goldman, 1975) though they do partition utterances sequentially and usually maintain separate sentence-level grammars. See Figure 1.)

Since one goal of an efficient design is to reduce the amount of reference knowledge that must be considered in making each decision, designs that span the distance in smaller steps, each one involving a simpler mapping function with many fewer parameters, will be more efficient. One possible countervailing factor is the additional effort necessary to maintain the 'extra' levels; this may be mitigated by the fact that multi-level designs can make extensive use of precomputed structures to minimize their cost.

Another argument that favors multi-level, heterogeneous designs over single-formalism, homogeneous designs is the engineering principle that *the more narrow and specific the demands on a process, the easier it is to develop highly efficient, special case mechanisms by which to implement it*. There is a countervailing methodological argument, however, since special-purpose mechanisms do take extra time to design; consequently, initial results may be better achieved with a single-formalism design. (See McDonald, 1984, for discussion.)

4.3 Taking advantage of regularities in natural language

Natural languages are very complex, but are systematically organized. Because of this, the properties of any utterance are interdependent, with a redundancy that permits the presence of some properties to predict certain others. This is appreciated in more efficient designs in the reference knowledge that they apply during the process. For example, if the generator is realizing a two-argument transitive verb then it need only determine the surface position of one of its two arguments (e.g. determining the subject on the basis of focus). To independently look for positive criteria for the syntactic positioning of both arguments would mean wasting actions that could have been avoided if the generator had been more aware of linguistic dependencies.

While this efficiency source may seem obvious and automatic, we must point out that Linguistics is not finished: it is still not clear just what the actual regularities of language form and usage are. Consequently, different linguistic theories and approaches to planning can have quite significant impacts on efficiency when they are applied to generation.

4.4 Control sources

Control in a computational system is the determination of the sequence in which a set of actions will be taken. Efficient control means that every action contributes to the goal; inefficiency comes from redundant actions, backtracking, or pursuing tangents. For a given process, its control problem can be construed as the problem of how to select the right sequence of actions from the space of all the possible sequences that the process' notation allows. In general the space will be very highly structured, since most arbitrary action sequences will not lead to sensible results. The question for designers is how this space is to be defined and how the process is to navigate within it.

There are two extremes in the design of a sequence space: implicit or explicit. With completely implicit control, the sequence is supplied from outside, directly as a list of actions, and simply executed. With completely explicit control, the space is implemented as a body of conditional tests that gate and order actions; which sequence to follow is then determined dynamically as the process runs and the tests are evaluated. In the implicit control design, control rests in the externally supplied sequence or the process that was responsible for its construction. In the explicit control design, control rests within the process itself.

Processes based on an implicit sequence space are more efficient: They expend no effort on control decisions because they have all been made by an earlier process. Of course when considering the efficiency of the system as a whole, the effort of the process that choose the sequence must be factored in — a reduction in the effort of one process is not a net gain if it increases the effort of another. Designs with explicit sequence spaces expend an appreciable amount of activity as 'overhead' that does not contribute to their real goals but is rather spent determining which of the possible sequences is appropriate in the situation at hand.

4.5 Lazy evaluation

Another source of efficiency is a processing technique that has been called *lazy evaluation*. By this we mean delaying the evaluation of an expression until the point in the process when it is actually going to be used. Efficiency is gained through a thoughtful ordering of the steps of a process so that information is not requested before it is available. An obvious example is delaying the decision of whether to use a pronoun until the point of the reference has been reached in the linear sequence of the utterance and all of the left context is known (see example in section 5.3.).

In extreme cases, a poor ordering of computations not only can increase the amount of work that is necessary, but cause backtracking as well. Consider the following sequence of actions:

1. compute the number of the verb
2. place the arguments
3. compute the number of the nouns

Ordering step (3) after step (1) creates a redundancy since the number of the subject must be determined before the number of the verb can be computed, then determined again to mark the noun. However, the more serious flaw in this sequence is the ordering of steps (1) and (2). Until the arguments are placed, you cannot be sure which will be the grammatical subject. The wrong choice would necessitate backtracking to recompute the number of the verb.

A complementary aspect of lazy evaluation is employing intermediate representations that retain the results of any computations that might be useful later, so that the calculation will only need to be done once; for example maintaining an explicit surface structure representation to facilitate subject-verb agreement. A possible countervailing factor to explicitly retaining early results is the cost of the representation. Unless the timing between steps is so exact that results can be passed implicitly through the equivalent of functional application, the cost of assembling and maintaining the representation may exceed the cost of recalculation. It will consequently be easier to take advantage of this source of efficiency if a design already uses a series of intermediate representations as part of its normal effort.

5. ILLUSTRATION IN ACTUAL SYSTEMS

In the previous section we enumerated several sources of efficiency, design options that enable a system to take fewer steps to solve the same problem. In this section we use the reference model presented in section three to organize specific examples of these sources. We begin by contrasting how different systems *identify the RPS*, specifically whether it is handed to them by their underlying program or they must identify it through their own effort. We then consider efficiency issues in the *mapping* stage, specifically control, taking advantage of regularies, and precomputation. Finally, we consider how certain control designs in the *reading out* stage can effect a system's intrinsic competence.

5.1. Identifying the Relevant Portion of the Situation (RPS)

According to our reference model, the first stage in generation is to identify the portion of the underlying program's model of its situation that is to be incorporated into the utterance or used for process control. Identification of the RPS may be automatic, where it is done for the generator by the underlying program as part of its input, or it may instead be the generator's active responsibility and the first action that it takes. In the abstract, which of these is preferable is straightforward: It is more efficient to let the underlying program be responsible for identifying what is relevant to the utterance. This is especially true in a process-based underlying program where the identification is just a side effect of the program's execution (see section 4.4).

It may happen that the program does not have a sufficiently rich model of its situation to be capable of providing the information necessary for generation. For example, in order to generate cohesive text, information about the coherence relations among individual propositions may have to be supplied. If the underlying program is simply a database query system, the generator itself may have to supply a model of possible coherence relations.

Two systems that differ in which component is responsible for identifying the RPS are PROTEUS (Davey, 1974) and TEXT (McKeown, 1985). In Proteus, which played tic-tac-toe and produced paragraph length descriptions of the games (see Figure 6), the RPS was the sequence of moves in the game, annotated according to their role, e.g. 'threat' or 'fork'. Since the underlying program was process-based, this information was available as a side effect of its actions, and could be given to the generator without any extra effort. The coherence was provided by virtue of the underlying coherence of the actions themselves.

In McKeown's TEXT program, which produced paragraph length definitions requested by a user (see Figure 7), the underlying program was a conventional data base. It would be difficult (perhaps impossible) for that underlying program to identify the RPS, since it has no basis for coherence. TEXT used the user's request to filter the knowledge base and determine the relevant information, and it used preconstructed schemas to organize the information and provide coherence relations. Preconstructing schemas for definitional paragraphs allows the generator to impose coherence relations more efficiently (see section 4.1).

5.2 Efficiency issues in the Mapping Stage

In our model, a mapping is the constructive relation between two successive representational levels. Comparing mapping techniques across designs can consequently be a complex business, since except for the first and last levels, the RPS and the text, designers are free to choose whatever levels best fit their notions of how generation is done. Furthermore what is a 'level' and what is a 'mapping' can be a matter of judgement: The quite common use of data-directed control in generation systems blurs the lines between static representations and active transition processes.

Our working definition for level and mapping is quite pragmatic. A representational level is a set of expressions *assembled specifically for the utterance being generated*. All the expressions at a given level will have been constructed from a common vocabulary of terms and connectives; the nature of the vocabulary will establish whether the level is semantic, syntactic, logical form, etc. A mapping is a process that draws on information at one representational level (a 'higher' one), plus some fixed body of reference knowledge (e.g. the code of the process, or some set of tables), to construct or add to a second ('lower') level.

The primary efficiency issues that will concern us for the mapping stage involve regularities (Section 4.3), sources of control (Section 4.5), and the possibilities for precomputation (Section 4.1). Mappings will tend to take one of two general forms: Either (1) the mapping will be controlled by its reference knowledge (taking the higher level as a parameter), or (2) it will be controlled by the higher level (drawing on its reference knowledge as needed). The Appendix provides a set of diagrams that show the representational levels and control regimes used in mapping between them for seven different generators from the literature.

Control is given to the higher level when there are comparable structural regularities between the levels and the work that the mapping must do is simply looking up correspondences.

Usually such mappings are implemented as data-directed processes with the expressions at the higher level interpreted literally as mapping actions to be carried out. (In the Appendix diagrams, this type of mapping is given as a downward pointing arrow.) These designs are a case of the action sequence (i.e. the steps of the mapping) being supplied by an earlier process, the one that constructed the higher level. As discussed in Section 4.4, we claim that this makes them the most efficient design for moving between levels because the action sequence has already been tailored specifically to the case at hand and consequently no effort needs to be expended on control decisions.

When there is nothing at the higher level serving as the basis for constructing the lower one, then that basis must be supplied by knowledge embedded in the mapping process. In the cases we have examined, this knowledge takes the form of some general model of the space of the possible structures which the lower level can have. Carrying out the mapping involves using the model to query the higher level, thereby determining what particular lower structures should be built. (In the Appendix diagrams these mappings are given as upward pointing arrows plus braces.) In the terms of Section 4.4, this is a case of control based on an explicit sequence space, since the model must define all of the possible mappings that might occur and then test the higher level to determine which one is appropriate. These tests are control decisions determining the eventual set of actions that will actually construct (i.e. 'map to') the lower level. The additional effort expended on these control decisions makes such designs relatively less efficient.

We will illustrate the alternatives just sketched with the mapping that takes a generator from a level where the information is encoded in a nonlinguistic form, often as propositions expressed in a predicate logic, to a level representing the linguistic relations that define the surface phrase structure and grammatical relations of final text. This mapping is part of nearly every generator we have looked at, and has been approached in quite different and illustrative ways; we will compare the two that have struck us as being the most different: PENMAN (Mann, 1983) and MUMBLE (McDonald, 1984).

In the PENMAN system, a systemic grammar known as NIGEL carries out the mapping between the propositions of the input *demand expression* and the feature-based specification of the linguistic relations that are to realize them. NIGEL represents a text by a set of abstract features that collectively specify the form and grammatical relations of constituents. The dependency relationships between features is encoded by a set of networks which organize them into disjoint sets (*systems*). The networks indicate by the connections between systems when the inclusion of a feature from one system forces the inclusion of some feature from another, linked system. The set of all pathways through NIGEL (connections between systems) defines the set of all possible feature combinations and thereby all possible natural language texts.[3]

For PENMAN, the task of the mapping is to assemble a lower level text specification (i.e. a feature set) that will adequately convey the information in the higher level demand expression. This amounts to selecting a path through the networks of the grammar; in NIGEL this is done system by system following the chain of dependencies indicated by the links between them. In a properly designed systemic grammar such as NIGEL, this means that each system is considered only once since all of the linguistic criteria bearing on it will have already been determined by selections made earlier in the systems leading into it.

Viewed from this perspective it is easy to see that NIGEL's mapping is based on an explicit sequence space; the reference knowledge — the systemic grammar — is in control. The control

---

[3] Being a sentence grammar, Nigel only represents all possible sentences, not all possible texts generally. For texts larger than single sentences the Penman project expects to use a different organizing scheme based on a descriptive formalism called Rhetorical Structure Theory (Mann, 1984; Mann & Thompson, this volume).

N. B. 'paths' through a systemic grammar consist of multiple rather than just single threads because of the presence of conjunctive as well as disjunctive feature systems. This is an opportunity for a multiprocessing implementation since multiple threads can be explored without interfering with each other.

decisions are the feature choices made at each system. In PENMAN these decisions are carried out by *choosers*, specialist procedures that consult the demand expression and the underlying model in order to make their choice.

In contrast, the comparable mapping in MUMBLE is from the elements of a *message* to representations of linguistic phrases rather than features. Messages, technically referred to as *realization specifications*, are broadly comparable to PENMAN demand expressions though they have a more specialized organization and are taken to have been deliberately planned. The mapping is carried out by directly executing the message as though it were a program in a very special programming language (i.e. it is passed through a special interpreter). A table of correspondences is consulted, element by element, and the construction actions indicated by the correspondences are carried out. This makes the design an implicit sequence space where control rests in the message rather than the reference knowledge of the mapping — an intrinsically more efficient design.

MUMBLE's phrases can be viewed as predefined packages of features. By taking the packages as wholes, MUMBLE's mapping is spared the effort of testing (or even representing) whether those particular features can cooccur; the packaging is a given of MUMBLE's reference grammar. NIGEL on the other hand has no representation of possible linguistic form that is independent of function (i.e. the selections made by the choosers) since its phrasal specifications are only implicit in the paths through the systems and these are determined only for specific cases.

MUMBLE's preconstruction of the linguistic form is more efficient only if it does not lead to greater effort in establishing the correspondences from message elements. If a phrase cannot be selected without first making extensive tests on the message, then the net total of tests may turn out to be quite comparable with that required to individually determine each of the features that the phrase consists of. Our intuition (speaking as MUMBLE's developers) is that there is a net savings in tests, because we believe there are regularities at the propositional/message level that closely match the information packaging that linguistic phrases embody.

Systemic grammarians' prime motivation for carrying out their analyses in terms of subphrasal features is that they see the factors that go into text form as being of very different kinds (parallel paths through the grammar), that are reconciled as a group by a 'realization' algorithm once they have all been determined. We would argue that in a design like MUMBLE the same effects can be achieved provided one is careful about how much information phrases are stipulated to contain and how phrases are allowed to combine. This allows us to retain the savings implied by precomputing sets of text properties and deal with them only as units.

Briefly MUMBLE's design is as follows. A propositional unit at message level is not the mapped to a complete surface phrase (e.g. a text string) but to a constraint expression that specifies the phrase's head and the values of the thematic relations that are to accompany it. The constraint expression is then fleshed out: the order of the thematic elements fixed, temporal and other situational anchors inserted, any additional modifiers, adjuncts, or hedging verbs added. Only then will the 'phrase' have its final content and be ready to be read out. MUMBLE does this with a combination of two devices: one maps the constraint expression to a set of alternative thematic orderings (and other transformational variations) from which a selection is then made; the other adds in anchors and modifiers (which originated as independent elements of the message) at points within the phrase as permitted by its grammatical structure, (see McDonald & Pustejovsky, 1985, for discussion). This strategy of breaking down linguistic forms into their smallest units and allowing a versatile set of insertion and adjunction mechanisms for incorporating further minimal units is the key to facilitating a multi-factor mapping using precomputed phrases.

Using minimal units as MUMBLE does imposes a de facto order of importance on the influences on the utterance, since they are effectively considered only one at a time and the indelible selections remove alternatives from later decisions. In contrast, an approach which breaks the mapping down to the selection of individual features, as NIGEL does, and waits to realize them as sequential text only once they all have been chosen, allows an equal consideration of all of the influences on the utterance before committing to any part of its form. This is difficult to achieve in a mapping design that uses direct links to precomputed units. Danlos (1984) discusses this issue. She employs choice sets ('discourse grammars') very much like those in MUMBLE, i.e. selections between entire surface phrases, and argues persuasively that in order to make equitable, balanced decisions one has to have a large number of alternatives in a set and use very large, composite phrases. Ultimately it will be an empirical question whether the texts produced with ordered influences are good enough (e.g. people would not do better in comparable situations) or whether the architecture must be changed.

5.3 The Reading Out Stage: problems due to architecture

The point that we wish to make about the final stage of the generation process — reading out the words from the last abstract representational level and thereby producing the utterance — is not so much one of relative efficiency as of basic competence. A program may generate in a very small number of steps, but if it is incapable of ever producing certain common constructions or communicating certain kinds of information, then we do not want to say that it is more efficient than other programs that can do those things but take longer as a result. We believe that certain designs have a limited competence — specifically a restriction on their ability to properly select pronouns — because of their choice of representation and control structure rather than their particular choice of rules. This makes the problem a matter of architectural decisions in the design of their generator and thus much more serious than just a weakness in an analysis. Potential architectural problems like this may be seen at all stages in different generator designs; the one we will discuss is just easier to describe.

Generators organize their syntactic stages as a recursive descent — top down — through the phrases of their sentences: main clauses are formed and organized before subordinate clauses; the verb and thematic relations of a clause before its noun phrases; head nouns and adjectives before relative clauses. As the work at this stage usually results in fixing the order of the words in the utterance, it is often interleaved with the reading out stage in a very tight coupling: When the recursion reaches a phrasal level with words at its leaves they are collected for reading out.

We can distinguish two architectural alternatives in the design of this recursive descent: One does all of the lower levels in parallel; the other does them sequentially in left to right order. The left to right order is the one taken by ATN designs (e.g. Simmons & Slocum, 1972), and by MUMBLE. The parallel order is taken by Derr & McKeown (1984), who use a Definite Clause Grammar, and also appears to be what the systemic grammar designs of PROTEUS and PENMAN do, though we do not feel absolutely confident of this on the basis of the references we have available.

Recursion in parallel is arguably simpler; certainly it is natural when a DCG is implemented in Prolog. However, it has a cost in what this architecture will allow to be represented: Parallel recursive processes in uncomplicated DCGs deliberately ignore their surrounding context, i.e. they do not carry down with them any record of what phrases were to their left or right. Unfortunately, awareness of this context is essential for the required intrasentential pronominalization that occurs when a reference is c-comanded by its antecedent (e.g. *'Floyd wanted Roscoe to get his fishing pole'* — note that this pronominalization is forced even though it creates an ambiguity). Without the capacity to represent the necessary relationships, the design has no way to do this kind of pronominalization — an intrinsic limitation in its competence. The designs that keep an explicit surface structure have a natural means of recording the information that c-comand needs, and thus have no architectural limitation standing in the way of being competent to do this type of pronominalization.

6. CONCLUDING REMARKS

When we first began this work, it was with the hope of arriving at a proper complexity measure for generation, something analogous to saying that Earley's algorithm has a worst-case complexity of G^2n^3, a formula parametrized by the size of the grammar being used and the length of the sentence being parsed. But the formulation of a complexity metric makes demands which generation, given its present state of the art, does not appear to be able to meet.

6.1 Difficulties in defining a complexity metric

To investigate the complexity of an algorithm, one must have a clear definition of what problem is to be solved, stated in terms of a relevant set of variables, and one must have a statement of the properties of an adequate solution. We know of course that the solution in generation must be some grammatical text, but that is about as useful as knowing that the solution to some arithmetic problem is the number 3 — an infinite number of problems could have that solution. At the other end we are in a still worse position, since as we all know there is no clear model in the field of what the generation process actually starts from: The neighborhood gossip who tells us that 'John loves Mary' surely has more on his mind that just the proposition *loves(John, Mary)*.

We cannot declare arbitrarily that the generation process begins at some well defined point, for example, the semantic 'message' that many projects have pragmatically chosen as the earliest level they will work from in their research. But while the message level might be precise enough for the definition of a metric, it lacks other essential qualities. First, no two projects' message levels contain really comparable information (Contrast for example McDonald & Pustejovsky, 1985, and Sondheimer & Nebel, 1986). Second, such a metric would beg the question since it makes no allowance for the effort required to construct the message expression, which will vary widely depending on the assumptions of the design.

In this respect, understanding systems have no adequate complexity metric either, since while the subproblem of parsing a stream of words into a grammar-defined structural description is precise enough for metrics to be defined, the question of what happens after that, of how this structural description comes to have any impact on the hearer's future behavior, is as illdefined as the early stages of generation.

We also have no empirical or even consensus notion of the full problem that speakers are solving when they produce an utterance. It is clear that the problem is not just to convey 'an idea' from the speaker's mind to the hearer's; that does not even begin to cover the reasons why people talk (e.g. for amusement, to convey sympathy, for group identification, etc.) It is also unlikely that the more recent view of generation, i.e. as another of the speaker's mechanisms for achieving his goals, is going to yield an interesting metric; talking about 'goals' and 'speech acts' is just putting a more interesting name to the problem, not identifying it.

6.2 An initial proposal

While we are not yet prepared to propose an entire complexity metric, we do believe we have identified one of its primary parameters, namely the familiarity of the situation. We also believe we can characterize the architectures that will turn out to rate most highly on this metric, namely those that draw on the efficiency sources that we have identified, particulary precomputation. We summarize our reasoning below.

Introspection and Gedankenexperiments suggest that the simplest utterances to generate are those that are overlearned: conventional greetings, rehearsed speeches, idioms and highly stylized phrases. The only work that must go on to produce them is (1) assessment of the situation to identify it as one where the memorized utterance is appropriate, (2) retrieval of the utterance (presumably by table look up from the identity of the situation), and (3) uttering (reading out) the words.

We assume that any complexity metric will factor out the length of the recalled word string: if the memorization or overlearning is effective then it will be just as simple (i.e. minimally complex) to produce a long memorized text as a short one. Similarly at higher levels in the generation process we would expect that the length of any precomputed specification or mapping function would also be discounted as trivial in cost when compared with the effort to assemble the structure from primitives by reference to non-specific reference knowledge. It is no doubt true that the physical details of the actual human generation process must put some limit on the size and character of what can be precomputed, stored, and instantiated, but we presume that these limits are liberal enough to have no practical impact on our claims.

A more significant parameter of the metric is the familiarity of the situation (see section 2.1). Increased familiarity makes for more certain and probably easier identification, and the recognition of regularity — the reification of a situation type — makes it possible to directly associate it with memorized phrases or specifications, i.e. to precompute elements of the generation process that situation type will initiate.

The vast human capacity for categorized recognition and recall suggests to us that the space-time trade-offs for mental computation weigh heavily in favor of using space to save time[4]. Consequently, we claim that it is always more efficient to implement the mapping stage of generation as the selection and instantiation of a preconstructed schema or specification rather than assemble such structures dynamically from primitive elements each time they are used.

The greater the familiarity a speaker has with a situation, the more likely he is to have modeled it in terms of a relatively small number of situational elements which can have been already associated with linguistic counterparts, making possible the highly efficient 'select and execute' style of generation.

When a situation is relatively unfamiliar, its pattern of elements will tend not to have any direct mapping to natural, preconstructed structures. When this occurs, the mapping will have to be done at a finer grain, i.e. using the more abstract text properties from which preconstructed schema are built, and the process will necessarily require more effort.

In summary, we see the total effort required to produce an utterance varying in proportion with the degree to which the speaker is able to identify the situation as a familiar one and can thereby model the RPS in terms of known situational types. Since the generation process is more efficient to the extent that it can be done using preconstructed elements, greater familiarity will result in quicker generation.

ACKNOWLEDGEMENT

Support for the preparation of this paper was provided in part by the Defense Advanced Research Projects Agency under contract number N00014-85-K-0017 monitored by the Office of Naval Research.

REFERENCES

Appelt, D. (1985) *Planning English Sentences.* Cambridge: Cambridge University Press.
Barwise, J. & Perry, J. (1983) *Situations and Attitudes.* Massachusetts: MIT Press, Cambridge.

---

4   This may of course not be the case for present day computers if we want them to have a high degree of competence and still function in real time. But we still suggest that machine designs at least emulate a space-intensive design, since in the engineering of artificial counterparts of natural phenomena like language, cognitive theories are our best guidelines for achieving an extendible and robust system.

Bates, M. & Ingria, R. (1981) Controlled transformational sentence generation. In: *Proceedings of the 19th Annual Meeting of the Association for Computational Linguistics.* Stanford.

Chomsky, N. (1957) *Syntactic Structures.* The Hague: Mouton & Co.

Conklin, E. (1983) *Data-driven Indelible Planning of Discouse Generation Using Salience,* Ph.D. Thesis, University of Massachusetts.

Danlos, L. (1984) Conceptual and Linguistic Decisions in Generation. In: *Proceedings of COLING-84.* Stanford University.

Davey, A. (1974) *Discourse Production,* Ph.D. Thesis, University of Edinburgh. Published in 1978 by Edinburgh University Press.

Derr, M. & McKeown, K. (1984) Using Focus to Generate Complex and Simple Sentences. In: *Proceedings of COLING-84.* Stanford University.

Friedman, J. (1969) Directed random generation of sentences, *Communications of the ACN,* 12, 40-46.

Goldman, N. (1975) Conceptual Generation. In: R. Schank (Ed.) *Conceptual Information Processing.* Amsterdam: North-Holland.

Luckhardt, H.D. (1987) Generation of Sentences from a Syntactic Deep Structure with a Semantic Component. In: D. McDonald & L. Bolc (Eds.) *Papers in Language Generation.* New York: Springer-Verlag.

Mann, W. (1983) *An Overview of the Penman Text Generation System,* USC/ISI Technical Report RR-83-114.

Mann, W. (1984) *Discourse Structures for Text Generation,* USC/ISI Technical Report RR-84-127.

Mann, W. & Matthiessen, C. (1985) Nigel: a Systemic Grammar for Text Generation. In: R. Freedle (Ed.) *Systemic Perspectives on Discourse: Selected Theoretical Papers of the 9th International Systemic Workshop.* Norwood, N.J.: Ablex.

Mann, W. & Moore, J. (1981) Computer generation of multi-paragraph English text. *American Journal of Computational Linguistics 7,* 17-29.

McDonald, D. (1984) Description Directed Control: Its implications for natural language generation. In: N. Cercone (Ed.) *Computational Linguistics.* New York: Plenum Press. Reprinted in B. Grosz, K. Spark Jones, & B. Webber (Eds.) *Readings in Natural Language Processing,* Morgan Kaufman, California, 1986.

McDonald, D. & Pustejovsky, J.D. (1985) TAGs as a Grammatical Formalism for Generation. In: *Proceedings of ACL-85.* Chicago.

McKeown, K. (1985) *Text Generation.* Cambridge: Cambridge University Press.

Sondheimer, N. & Nebel, B. (1986) A Logical-form and Knowledge-base Design for Natural Language Generation. *Proceedings of AAAI-86,* Philadelphia.

Simmons, R. & Slocum, J. (1972) Generating English discourse from semantic networks. In: *Communication of the ACM,* 15, 891-905.

APPENDIX

One of our major goals in this paper has been to find a way to compare different approaches to generation. In the following diagrams we attempt to capture in a uniform way how different systems compare along the dimensions we have raised in this paper: how they relate to our three stage model, what the various representational levels are, what controls the mapping between representational levels, and what the reference knowledge is. We also give a short biographical sketch of each system. Appearances to the contrary, the diagrams should not be taken to imply a sequential processing. In all these systems multiple levels are typically active simultaneously and processes may operate recursively.

We have discussed generation abstractly in terms of a series of mappings between representational levels. Our model divides those mappings into three stages: The first is characterized by considerations of what is relevant in the situation the underlying program is in (what we generate must meet the goals of the underlying program) and the third is constrained to be English (or some other natural language). The second stage spans the distance between the situation space and the utterance space. (Stages are indicated on the left of each diagram.)

The representational levels are shown in bold. The mappings between them are indicated by the arrows, with descriptions of the processes on their right. We distinguish between two types of mappings based on whether the representational level is in control or the reference knowledge is in control. The down arrow indicates a mapping in which the higher representation is controlling in the mapping to the lower representation. (In some cases it is actually an executable representation, for example Mumble's surface structure.) These processes access the reference knowledge, but control decisions are not based on it. The bracket and up arrow indicate a mapping process governed by the reference knowledge. Such a process accesses the higher representation in the production of the lower representation, but control decisions are based on the reference knowledge.

Our choice of which systems to include was based on our familiarity with them and the availability of reference materials. We present them in alphabetical order by system name, to avoid any unintended implications.

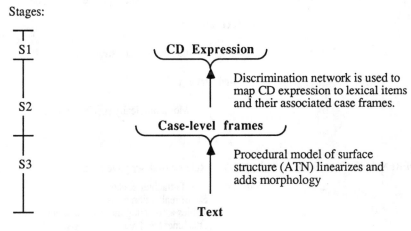

Stages:

S1

S2

S3

CD Expression

Discrimination network is used to map CD expression to lexical items and their associated case frames.

Case-level frames

Procedural model of surface structure (ATN) linearizes and adds morphology

Text

REFERENCE KNOWLEDGE: Discrimination networks
                        ATN grammar

Babel (Goldman, 1975) produced sentence length text exemplifying various paraphrases of isolated Conceptual Dependency expressions. The focus of the project was on using a discrimination network for lexical choice. It has one of the fewest number of representational levels of any system in the literature, with the bulk of the linguistic work done by its ATN generator, which was developed by Simmons &.Slocum (1972).

Figure 1. Babel

Stages:

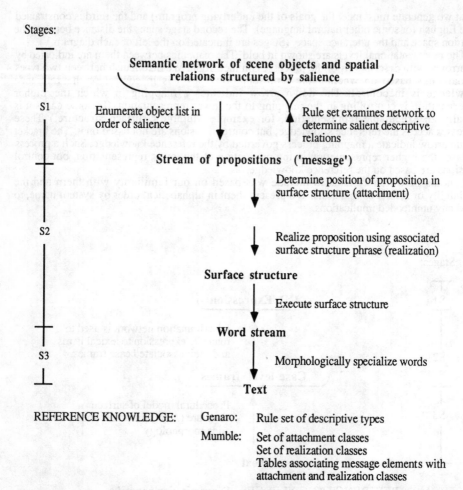

Semantic network of scene objects and spatial
relations structured by salience

S1   Enumerate object list in   Rule set examines network to
     order of salience   determine salient descriptive
                                          relations

Stream of propositions   ('message')

                    Determine position of proposition in
                    surface structure (attachment)

S2   Realize proposition using associated
                    surface structure phrase (realization)

Surface structure

                    Execute surface structure

Word stream

S3   Morphologically specialize words

Text

REFERENCE KNOWLEDGE: Genaro: Rule set of descriptive types
                        Mumble: Set of attachment classes
                                  Set of realization classes
                                  Tables associating message elements with
                                  attachment and realization classes

This diagram represents two systems: the text planner Genaro (Conklin, 1983) and the linguistic component Mumble (McDonald, 1984). Genaro was the first substantitive text planner used with Mumble, which has been evolving since 1976. Genaro planned paragraph length descriptions of pictures of houses, using visual salience for organization. Mumble is one of the few systems that doesn't assume an intermediate representation aggregated into sentence sized chunks before phrase structure decisions are made. Mumble's attachment process allows a unit to be incorrorated into an already realized phrase structure or to become a separate sentence depending on its relation to previous text and stylistic considerations.

Figure 2. Genaro/Mumble

Stages:

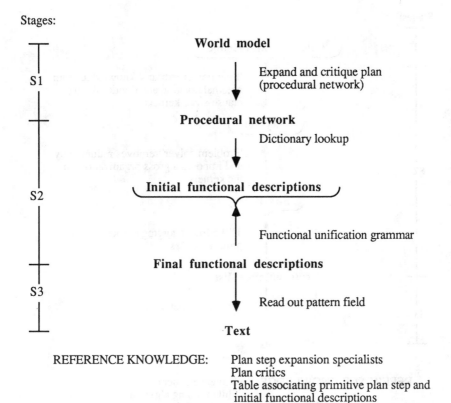

S1

S2

S3

REFERENCE KNOWLEDGE: Plan step expansion specialists
                         Plan critics
                         Table associating primitive plan step and
                            initial functional descriptions
                         Functional unification grammar

Kamp (described in Appelt, 1985) did first principles planning of an utterance in a cooperative dialog. Appelt's major concern was that the axiomatization of the text planning process be on a firm foundation. This careful reasoning about what should be included in the utterance and how the information was related allowed the system to produce complex sentences.

Figure 3. Kamp

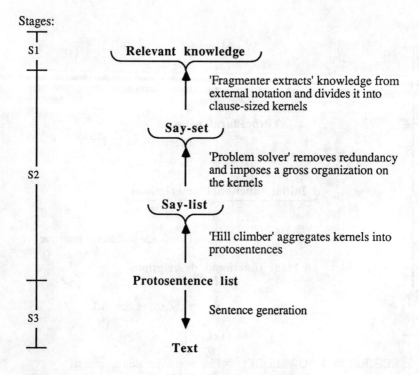

Stages:

S1   **Relevant knowledge**

'Fragmenter extracts' knowledge from external notation and divides it into clause-sized kernels

Say-set

S2   'Problem solver' removes redundancy and imposes a gross organization on the kernels

Say-list

'Hill climber' aggregates kernels into protosentences

Protosentence list

Sentence generation

S3

Text

REFERENCE KNOWLEDGE: Sentence generator
                         Hill climbing algorithm
                         Problem Solver
                         Fragmenter

KDS (Mann & Moore, 1981) produced multiparagraph text describing procedures (such as emergency fire procedures). They took as assumptions (1) a lack of isomorphism between the size and organization of objects in the underlying program and the phrases in the surface structure text and (2) a restriction that the input to the generation component must be in sentence sized chunks (contrast MUMBLE, figure 2); they then looked at how the system could produce complex sentences which were cohesive with the surrounding text.

Figure 4. KDS

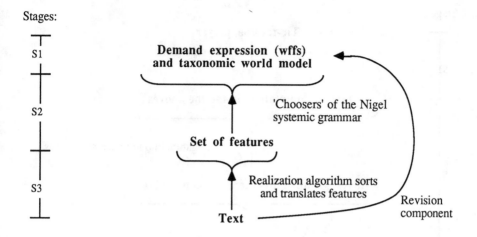

Figure 5. Penman

Penman (Mann, 1983) focuses on the use of systemic grammar in generation. Nigel, Penman's grammar (Mann & Matthiessen, 1985) is the largest systemic grammar and possibly the largest machine grammar of any kind. It produces isolated sentences using a complex system of choosers which query the demand expression for the utterance and the hierarchical world model. The other components of Penman, the planner which determines the demand expression and the revision component, are still in the design stages.

Stages:

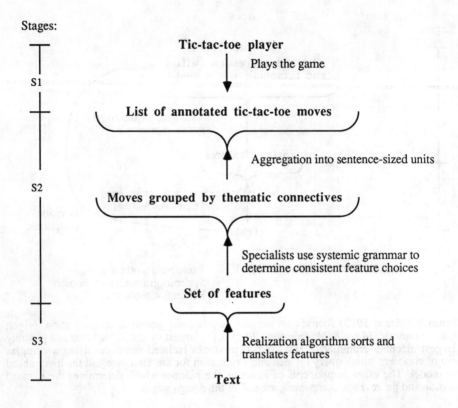

REFERENCE KNOWLEDGE: Procedural encoding of all possible aggregations
                         Procedural encoding of system grammar
                         Realization algorithm

Proteus (Davey, 1974) is one of the earliest serious generation systems, yet the text it produced is still among the best machines have generated. Proteus both played tic-tac-toe and generated paragraph length commentaries on the games, using a systemic grammar. Since the system was both the underlying program and the generator, it was able to take advantage of the structure of its model of tic-tac-toe to organize the structure of the text.

Figure 6. Proteus

Stages:

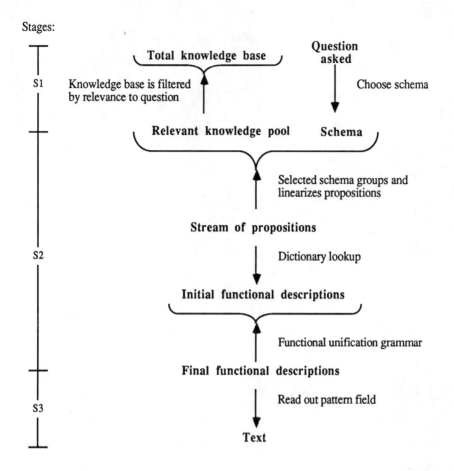

S1

S2

S3

REFERENCE KNOWLEDGE: Predefined schemas
                            Association table of propositions to initial
                                 functional descriptions
                            Functional unification grammar

Text (McKeown, 1985) focuses on the rhetorical structure of text. It used predefined schemas and focus information to organize definitional paragraphs in response to questions about the meaning of terms in a conventional data base. In the version of TEXT presently used at the University of Pennsylvania, the functional unification grammar has been replaced with the generator Mumble.

Figure 7. Text

Chapter 13

REVIEWING AS A COMPONENT OF THE TEXT GENERATION PROCESS

Masoud Yazdani

ABSTRACT

Most computer-based text generation systems produce their output in a one-stage operation. We argue that following the human cognitive processes involved in writing as a model, computational generators would be able to produce better text if they were composed of independent but interacting processes dealing with the text at different levels of abstraction and performing various transformations on it. Four levels of *purpose, situation, specification* and *utterance* are identified. It is further argued that there are three process of *planning, generation* and *reviewing. Reviewing* is singled out as a process which not only produces segments of a lower level from a higher one, but also generates higher level segments from lower level ones. Some heuristics are presented for sentence, paragraph and text revision.

1. INTRODUCTION

My basic interest has been in creative writing (cf. Yazdani, 1982) — an act which differs from other language generation tasks such as explanation (Swartout, 1983), or spontaneous speech production (De Smedt & Kempen, this volume). However, some of what follows might be of interest to builders of computer-based generation systems who would like to improve the quality of the text produced. The model of story writing which I have proposed (Yazdani, forthcoming) is concerned with what an ideal story generation system should be able to do.

The model proposed is composed of five distinct processes of plot making, world making, simulation, narration and text generation. These processes interact in a variety of ways as indicated in Figure 1. However, psychological and educational research in the study of competent human writers (Gregg & Steinberg, 1980; Frederiksen & Dominic, 1981) sheds doubt on the possibility of always producing texts by a straight (one-pass) translation from knowledge structures produced by the simulator. This outcome could have implications for other workers in the field. McDonald, Vaughan & Pustejovsky (this volume) indicate how the simple view of generation (Figure 2a) has been replaced by a more sophisticated one: a situation (a set of relations) is translated into various levels of specifications of linguistic output before an utterance is made (Figure 2b). Two clear tasks of planning and generation are therefore identified.

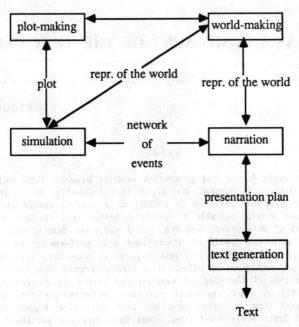

Figure 1

Comparing this view with the model of story generation presented in figure 1, we can see a one-to-one correspondence between 'situation' and 'network of events', between 'presentation plan' and 'specification' and between 'utterance' and 'text'. However our model indicates at least one further level above the 'situation'. McDonald et al. refer to this as the goals of 'the underlying program'. In our model therefore it is the combination of plot-making, world-making and simulation which would constitute the underlying program in their terminology. The goals of these processes (figure 2c) are similar to those discussed by Hovy (this volume) and Appelt (1985).

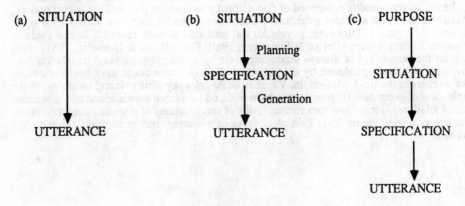

Figure 2

This extended view of generation begins to approximate the human writing process. Flower & Hayes (1980), by using protocol analysis techniques (cf. Newell & Simon, 1972), have extracted basic strategies used by human writers. Through these 'thinking aloud' protocols, they have discovered that the major difficulty of human writers is coping with the complexity of the task at hand:

> 'A writer caught in the act looks much more like a very busy switchboard operator trying to juggle a number of demands on her attention and constraints on what she can do.'

They expose three separate kinds of problem which human writers have to deal with:

— *Rhetorical problems*. Whatever the writer chooses to say, it must conform to her purpose, to the audience, and to the projected personality of the writer. Hovy (this volume) refers to these issues as pragmatic decision-making criteria.
— *Knowledge*. Moving from a rich array of unorganized, and perhaps contradictory propositions, to relatively organized, conceptually integrated knowledge structures is a demanding task. This seems to agree with McDonald et al.'s point that if the knowledge is structured appropriately in the first place, the generation task is greatly simplified.
— *Written speech*. The experienced and inexperienced writer alike (in their own way) suffer from the unenviable constraints imposed by language itself, which seems to resist attempts to form a set of continuous sentences. The rules of grammar and conventions of usage of syntax may make an enormous demand on time and attention.

These three tasks are denoted by Collins & Gentner (1980) as purpose, content and structure levels. The purpose level deals with the goals of the writer, the content level with the ideas to be expressed and how they are relate;. the structure level, with good sentence forms, good paragraph forms, text forms, etc. The tasks match McDonald et al.'s (figure 2b) levels of situation, specification and utterance respectively.

The extensive study by Hayes & Flower (1980) indicates that writing consists of three major cognitive processes: *planning, generation* and *reviewing*. The language generation work (cf. Kempen, 1987) has addressed the first two of these issues rather well, for example in the work by Appelt (1985) and Jacobs (1985) for planning and generation respectively. However, there seems to be very little concern with the reviewing process.

It could be argued that the objective of Hayes & Flowers' reviewing process, which is concerned with evaluating of the reader's view of the text, is adequately covered at the planning stage by such detailed axiomatizations as those by Cohen & Perrault (1979) and Appelt (1985). However, when the reviewing process is embedded in the planning, the computations necessary to generate reasonable length sentences can become so extensive as to make it impossible to be performed by a device such as the human brain (cf. the efficiency argument advanced by McDonald et al.).

If one accepts that efficiency of the generation process is a desirable issue, one could relax some of the constraints imposed by planning systems similar to Appelt's, and use the assumption that in spoken language the hearer would ask for details missing from the utterance. However, in written language, which is the concern of the present article, this cannot be assumed, and the writer needs to produce text as close to perfect as is possible. The producers of written text can afford to be sloppy as long as they re-evaluate text through a reviewing process at a later stage. Text generation is therefore an underconstrained task, unlike systems such as MOLGEN (Stefik, 1981) where the constraints play a major role in the planning process.

The basic thesis is therefore that reviewing is an independent process from planning and generation, applied during and after other stages of the writing process. The reviewing process not only produces segments of a lower level from a higher one, but also generates higher level segments from lower level ones. This, in turn, leads to further work by other processes, making the overall system nondeterministic.

2. A MODEL OF HUMAN WRITING COMPETENCE

Hayes & Flower's (1980) work on the analysis of human writing behaviour has led to a competence model which, although not fully utilized by all writers, perhaps to their disadvantage, is a 'target to shoot at' when faced with a person on the doorstep saying 'I have never written anything before, teach me how to write'. Their model argues that such a person must plan and generate knowledge structures, translate them into speech and edit what has been written. This operation is carried out in a task environment which includes both the relevant task and the growing text produced. Further, it benefits from general information stored in the writer's memory (figure 3). As mentioned before, the planning and generation processes in this model already have strong counterparts in computational approaches (cf. Kempen, 1987) and therefore are not considered further in this chapter.

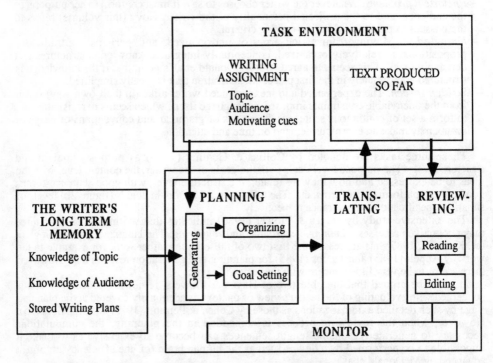

Figure 3. The organization of writing processes (Hayes & Flower, 1980).

Hayes & Flower explain the notion of *reviewing* as improving the quality of the text produced by the translation process. They note two subprocesses for *reading* and *editing* which detect and correct weaknesses in the text with respect to language conventions and accuracy of meaning. Obviously the reviewing process interacts with other processes. For example, some goals set by the planning process may have to be satisfied by the editing process ('Better keep it simple'). The editing process would also have goals of its own such as 'Will this argument be convincing?' and 'Have I covered all parts of the plan?'

Hayes & Flower stipulate that the whole of the writing operations could be called as a subroutine of the editing process recursively. Take, for example, a writer who recognizes that the reader will not have sufficient context to understand the relation between two consecutive sentences. To correct this fault, he may construct a small explanatory essay to insert between these sentences.

There appears to be a great deal of agreement on the role of editing/reviewing in the writing processes. Collins & Gentner (1980) report that 'most writers feel that editing is as crucial an aspect of good writing as is initial text production'. Wason (1980) reports one of his subjects as saying 'I write a complete first draft in longhand. As I go along I tend to revise a bit, but when I've finished I revise a great deal'.

If it is true that competent human writers spend some effort reviewing and editing their text as a separate task from the planning and generation of the utterances, then there must be some good reasons behind this behaviour. Here I mention three important ones:

— Collins & Gentner (1980) argue that without reviewing as an independent process, the quality of the writing could suffer by 'downsliding'.They define downsliding as 'the phenomenon of getting pulled into lower and more local levels of task processing'. Scardamalia (1981) observed a version of this in one subject who says: 'I have all my thoughts in my mind but, when I come to a word I can't spell, it throws me off my writing'.
— McDonald et al.'s efficiency arguments can be taken to indicate that an architecture with an independent reviewing process would be more efficient. Intermediate structures could be thrown away and reconstructed later when needed. Such decisions parallel compiler design for programming languages where the task is distributed over various passes.
— A further benefit from reviewing is that it could be a creative process in its own right. Wason (1980), studying human writers, observes that 'it is not that the subjects had clear thought but failed to find the right words to express it but that the thought had not at the time been discovered.'

3. THE STRUCTURE OF THE REVIEWING PROCESS

So far I have argued for the need of an independent *reviewing* process. I have implied that this process has to satisfy a number of tasks. In this section I shall present a structure for the process which further divides it into three subprocesses of *reading, evaluation* and *revising*. A system which cannot rebuild a mental model of its own creation is bound to be inadequate. However, most text generation systems do not attempt to understand what they have generated. Humans, however, do and they are bound to make use of it when they want to evaluate their creation from the point of view of the intended readers.

The evaluation process would compare the intentions inferred from the text from those intended by the generation process. It is obvious that the text should then be revised if there are elements which exist in the old structure which are not found in the new one. However, it is possible that intentions are found in the text which did not exist in the older structure. As Nold (1981) observes, writers communication problems are often ill-defined; therefore the act of producing a draft implies clarifying intentions at higher levels. She argues that 'feedback from the text generated thus far plays a major role in revising higher level structures'. She also points out that when writers read their text fresh they can sometimes come to the 'decision that their text is even better than intended'. We therefore believe that the *revising* process is a two-way activity. It includes the possibility of *editing* the text produced as well as *restructuring* the higher levels of the generation process. This view is consistant with Hayes & Flower's (1980) model where the text produced so far plays the role of a resource for the writing process.

We have so far argued that *editing* serves the role of changing the text when the text produced is in conflict with the intended purpose. However, the observations of Collins & Gentner (1980) also point to a number of self-contained heuristics which are applied at this stage in order to improve the text at various surface levels:

Text level

— delete extraneous materials
— add explicit structure (such as headings)
— move important ideas to the front of the text
— factorize qualifications into one general section at the beginning

Paragraph level

— shorten long paragraphs
— make lists or tables ('There are 3 things I want to say: 1)... 2)... and 3)...')
— add topic and concluding sentences
— put connective phrases ('therefore', 'nevertheless')

Sentence level

— delete empty phrases ('as a matter of fact...')
— create similar syntactic structures for similar sentences
— break long sentences into shorter ones
— turn passive sentences into active ones

The existence of such heuristics is another indication of independence of the editing and other reviewing processes from the planning and generation processes. This point is also argued by Vaughan & McDonald (1986). However, their model seems to take into account only a limited type of revisions: 'The decisions that revision affect are at the stylistic level; only stylistic decisions are free of fixed constraints and may therefore be changed'.

While the stylistic role of revision is important, what I have argued for in this chapter is a rather more radical view. I have attempted to break down the reviewing process into various components within a creative writing framework. Empirical observations of story writers indicate that some writers start with a small piece of text and then build a whole story around it. Here the revision process is, in fact, the driving force in the decision making at higher levels. A proposal which falls somewhere between that of Vaughan & McDonald (1986) and the one presented in this chapter is that of Mann (1983) for an 'improvement' module in the Penman system. Here the system 'evaluates the text applying measures of quality and comparing the text with the plan to attempt to improve the text'. Humes (1983), in her comprehensive study of the research on human composing processes, reports that 'revising is a process that is acquired as writers develop competence. In early stages of development, they concentrate on correcting errors and changing surface features in this text. As they mature, writers progressively concentrate on restructuring and shaping their discourse, redefining their ideas as they compose, and adjusting their writing to meet their audiences' need'.

At this point one might like to challenge the broad notion of revision adopted here. Would such acts not better be called regeneration and not revision (i.e., throw away the old sentences or paragraphs and write completely new ones)? What kinds of information would come from the old text that would help to formulate the new? Yazdani (1982) adopts the position that any model of creative writing should also address closely related abilitiy of people to use *some*, but not all, of the processes used in story writing:

— create imaginary events that you claim happened to you (creating events, using the representation of your actual environments)
— say what happened to you yesterday (using real-life events rather than simulated ones), or report an event in a newspaper
— retell an old story in a new way (using the same story network, creating a new representation plan)
— translate a story into a different language (the same presentation plan, creating a new text).

At some level of abstraction, a new generation of an old story can indeed be considered as a revision, while at another level it could be viewed as a new story altogether. We are not really bothered with this issue here, nor do we think it a fruitful issue to consider further. However, there is a related question which is vitally important to consider: When would we stop revising? Mann (1983) has put forward the most straightforward proposal to date: if further revision is not to lead to improvement on a preset 'measure of quality' then it should not take place. Obviously measures of quality in computers and people will differ on the richness of consideration of content for a long while. Vaughan & McDonald (1986) have therefore rightly chosen the non-content/ non-purposive decisions for their revision system.

4. CONCLUDING REMARK

This paper poses more questions than it answers. Most of the remarks made are not something the reader will accept to be correct or even plausible at face value. When searching for an answer he will be disappointed not to find it in this or any of the other papers in this volume. The intention behind this paper has been to put these questions higher on the agenda of research workers in the field of language generation. For too long the methodological context of the work in language generation has been influenced by what is possible *today*. The theoretical work has been deliberately restricted to that part of the total context where a particular system can actually be built given today's state of the art. However, I feel justified in my attempt to point out that a human-like generation system will involve a more complex architecture. The proposal presented in this paper will only serve as a first approximation to that end.

5. ACKNOWLEDGEMENT

I am grateful to Gerard Kempen, Marie Vaughan, David McDonald, Claire O'Malley and Mike Sharples for their support and advice.

6. REFERENCES

Appelt, D. (1985) *Planning English Sentences*. Cambridge, UK: Cambridge University Press.
Cohen, P. R. & Perrault, C. R. (1979) Elements of a Plan-based Theory of Speech Acts. *Cognitive Science, 3*, 177-212.
Collins, A. & Gentner, D. (1980) A Framework for a Cognitive Theory of Writing. In: Gregg & Steinberg.
Flower, L. S. & Hayes J. R. (1980) The Dynamics of Composing: Making Plans and Juggling Constraints. In: Gregg & Steinberg.
Frederiksen, C. H. & Dominic, J. F. (Eds.) (1981) *Writing (Vol. 2): Processes, Development and Communication*. Hillsdale, NJ: Erlbaum.
Gregg, L. W. & Steinberg, E. R. (Eds.) (1980) *Cognitive Processes in Writing* . Hillsdale, NJ: Erlbaum.
Hayes, J. R. & Flower L. S. (1980) Identifying the Organization of Writing Processes. In: Gregg & Steinberg.
Humes, A. (1983) *The composing process: A summary of the Research*. ERIC Report No ED-222-925.
Jacobs, P. (1985) *A Knowledge-based approach to Language Production*. Ph. D. Thesis, University of California, Berkeley.
Kempen, G. (1987) Language Generation Systems. In: Batori, I., Lenders, W. & Putschke, W. (Eds.) *Computational Linguistics. An International Handbook of Computer Oriented Language Research and Applications*. Berlin: de Gruyter.
Mann, W. C. (1983) *An Overview of the Penman Text Generation System* . USC/ISI Technical Report RR-83-114.

Newell, A. & Simon, H. (1972) *Human Problem Solving*. Englewood Cliffs, N.J.: Prentice-Hall.

Nold, E. W. (1981) Revising. In: Frederiksen & Dominic.

Stefik, M. (1981) Planning with constraints. *Artificial Intelligence*, *16*, 111-140.

Swartout, W. (1983) XPLAIN: A system for creating and explaining expert consulting systems. *Artificial Intelligence*, *21*, 285-325

Vaughan, M. M. & McDonald, D. D. (1986) A Model of Revision in Natural Language Generation . *Proceedings of the 24th annual meeting of the Association for Computational Linguistics*. New York.

Wason, P. C. (1980) Specific Thoughts on the Writing Process. In: Gregg & Steinberg.

Yazdani, M. (1982) How to Write a story. In: *Proceedings of the First European Conference on Artificial Intelligence*. Orsay, France.

Yazdani, M. (forthcoming) *A computational perspective on creative writing*. D. Phil. Thesis, University of Sussex.

Chapter 14

A FRENCH AND ENGLISH SYNTACTIC COMPONENT FOR GENERATION

Laurence Danlos

TABLE OF CONTENTS

1.	Introduction
2.	Preliminaries
3.	Synthesis of clauses
3.1	Syntactic information in a clause template
3.2	Agreement rules
3.3	Synthesis of complements
3.4	Reflexive pronouns
3.5	Personal pronouns
3.6	Nominal clauses
3.7	Noun groups
4.	Synthesis of sentences
4.1	Coordination and modifiers
4.2	Subordinate sentences
4.2.1	Conditions of reduction
4.2.2	Synthesis of a subordinate made up of a clause
4.2.3	Synthesis of a subordinate made up of a coordination of clauses
4.3	Deletion of repeated elements in a coordination of sentences
4.3.1	Cases treated
4.3.2	Deletion of repeated subject in a coordination of clauses
4.3.3	Deletion of repeated subjects in a coordination of sentences
5.	Conclusion

1. INTRODUCTION

The application of syntactic rules (e.g. agreement rules, deletion of repeated elements in a coordination, reduction of nominal or subordinate clauses) is domain-independent. Thus, it is of the utmost interest that a syntactic component applying such rules be developed 'once and for all'. A syntactic component will be described for both French and English.

The same recursive phenomena are observed in these two languages, as in all Romance and Germanic languages. In particular, coordination and embeddings (i.e. relative, nominal and subordinate clauses) are observed in all of these languages. A grammar will be presented that allows these recursive phenomena to be generated. This grammar takes into account the fact that semantics is given in a text generation system whose task is to go from meaning to form. Given this grammar, the application of syntactic rules that involve recursive phenomena (e.g. deletion of repeated subjects in a coordination of clauses) will be described in Section 4.

The main difference between French and English is that syntactic rules are often more complex in French than in English; an illustration of this claim is the large number of French agreement rules. As a consequence, a French syntactic component has to appeal to sophisticated processes, for example, to conjugate a passive verb in the infinitive in agreement with its (erased) subject in a reduced nominal clause:

Jean veut être aimé (John wants to be loved)
Marie veut être aimée (Mary wants to be loved)

Another difference between French and English is that some French reflexive pronouns must appear before the verb, thus changing its conjugation, as shown in the pair:

Marie a détesté Jean (Mary hated John)
Marie s'est détestée (Mary hated herself)

As far as I know, all Romance and Germanic languages require processes similar to those developed for French. Therefore, the emphasis will be put on these processes in Section 3.

A French syntactic component was implemented in COMMON LISP. However, my concern here is not programming but designing an algorithm, especially determining which linguistic data are necessary and how to access these data at the appropriate time. The only technical notion that will be used is that of a list.

This syntactic component is intended to be the last module of any generation system. However, its input needs to be specified. As a consequence, some suppositions are going to be made concerning a complete generation system.

2. PRELIMINARIES

The input to the generator is a semantic representation that provides the information to be generated. The semantic representation is in a 'frame' style. For a given domain, there are a number of generic classes that are organized into a hierarchy. The instances of a class are created during the execution of the program. They are identified by means of 'tokens' which are names so constructed that there is only one individual per name. Each class is characterized by a set of 'slots'. Here is an example of a semantic representation:

EVENT1 =: BARGAIN	HUM1 =: PERSON	HUM2 =: PERSON	TOK1 =: VEHICLE
SELLER = HUM1	NAME: John	NAME: Mary	TYPE: bicycle
BUYER = HUM2	SEX: masc	SEX: fem	NUMBER: 1
MERCHANDISE = TOK1			

EVENT1 is an instance of the class BARGAIN. This class is characterized by three slots: SELLER, BUYER and MERCHANDISE. These slots are filled respectively by the tokens HUM1, HUM2 and TOK1. HUM1 and HUM2 are instances of the class PERSON, which is characterized by the slots NAME and SEX. The slot NAME of HUM1 has John as value, etc.

We will suppose that the generic class hierarchy is of the following form:

Every class (except THING, ENTITY and PREDICATE) is either a sub-class of ENTITY or a sub-class of PREDICATE. The class ENTITY groups together the persons (e.g. HUM1, HUM2), the animals and the objects of a concrete type (e.g. TOK1). The class PREDICATE groups together the elements that are predicates (in the logical sense of this term) connecting entities (or predicates). BARGAIN is a predicate that connects three entities called SELLER, BUYER and MERCHANDISE. Instances of the class ENTITY are always synthesized as a noun group or a pronoun (e.g. *John, her, a bicycle*). Instances of the class PREDICATE are synthesized by means of 'clause patterns' such as the following for an instance of BARGAIN:

(1)   ?BUYER *buy* ?MERCHANDISE *from* ?SELLER

The notation ?BUYER stands for a variable to which the value of the slot BUYER in the instance of BARGAIN is assigned. The binding of the variables of a clause pattern results in a 'clause template'. For example, the clause pattern (1) results in the clause template: HUM2 *buy* TOK1 *from* HUM1. In a clause pattern, the lexical item expressing the predicate (often a verb) is explicitly indicated together with its complementation. For example, the clause pattern (1) states that the verb *buy* has a subject which designates the ?BUYER, a direct object which designates the ?MERCHANDISE and an indirect object introduced by the preposition *from* which designates the ?SELLER. This information must be supplied to a generator because it cannot 'guess' the complementation of a verb. As a consequence, any generator includes associations between predicates and clause patterns in one way or another. For example, these associations are made by means of 'pattern-concept pairs' in the generator developed by Jacobs (1985, this volume).

A clause pattern is a basic form which corresponds to the active construction of a verb. It can undergo transformations that modify the order and/or number of its complements (e.g. passive transformation with or without agent, ergative transformation). Nominalization transformations allow an instance of the class PREDICATE to be synthesized as a noun group:

> *I confirm that Mary purchased a bicycle*
> = *I confirm the purchase of a bicycle by Mary*

The synthesis of a token of the class PREDICATE requires the following operations to be carried out:

(1) Determine the clause pattern expressing the predicate involved (e.g. choose between '?BUYER *buy* ?MERCHANDISE *from* ?SELLER' and '?SELLER *sell* ?MERCHANDISE *to* ?BUYER'). This operation results in a clause template after binding of variables.
(2) Determine whether the clause template should undergo transformations (e.g. choose between active, passive with agent and passive without agent).
(3) Synthesize the tokens appearing in the clause template (e.g. determine if HUM1 should be synthesized as a reflexive pronoun, a relative pronoun, a personal pronoun or a noun group).
(4) Apply the syntactic rules that take effect within a clause (e.g. subject-verb agreement).

A text is a sequence of the following form: S_1 $Punct_1$ S_2 $Punct_2 \ldots S_n$ $Punct_n$ where $Punct_i$ is a punctuation mark and S_i a sentence. A sentence consists of a single clause or a sequence of clauses. The synthesis of a text translating the semantic representation requires, on the one hand, the operations (1)-(4) to be carried out for each predicate, and on the other hand, the clauses so obtained to be linearized into sentences. The linearization into sentences requires the following operations to be carried out:

(5) Determine the order in which the clauses have to appear in the text.
(6) Determine the linearization mode (e.g. choose between juxtaposition, coordination or subordination). The operations (5) and (6) result in sentence templates.
(7) Apply the syntactic rules that take effect within a sentence (e.g. deletion of the repeated elements in a coordination of clauses).

The fact that a generation system has to go through the operations (1)-(7) should not be debatable. On the other hand, there is much debate about the order in which these operations should be performed (Kempen, 1987). For example, some authors (e.g. McKeown, 1985) hold the view that operation (5) should be performed before operation (1), while I consider that these two operations should be performed simultaneously (Danlos, 1985, 1987a). In any case, it is clear that the purely syntactic operations, namely (4) and (7) must be performed last. This paper deals only with these syntactic operations and also with operation (3), namely the synthesis of the tokens in a clause template. Performing this operation at a late stage raises some problems which will be discussed in Section 3.5. From now on, we assume that certain modules perform operations (1), (2), (5) and (6), in whatever order, and provide clause or sentence templates.

3. SYNTHESIS OF CLAUSES

3.1 Syntactic information in a clause template

Let us first consider what syntactic information must be indicated in a clause template such as:

> HUM2 *buy* TOK1 *from* HUM1
> HUM2 *acheter* TOK1 *à* HUM1

— HUM2 is the subject. This information is needed for subject-verb agreement and for the computation of the form of a relative or personal pronoun if HUM2 is to be synthesized as such a pronoun.
— *Buy* is a verb. This information is needed for the conjugation of this term.
— TOK1 is a direct object. This information is needed for the computation of the form of a reflexive, relative or personal pronoun, if TOK1 is to be synthesized as such a pronoun, and for the determination of its placement.
— HUM1 is an indirect object introduced in English by *from*, in French by *à*. This information is needed if HUM1 is to be synthesized as a pronoun.
— 'HUM2 *buy* TOK1 *from* HUM1' or 'HUM2 *acheter* TOK1 *à* HUM1' is a syntactic unit, called a 'clause', within which syntactic rules such as subject-verb agreement take effect.

This information can be represented in the list

> (:Cl   (:subject HUM2) (:verb *buy*) (:dir-object TOK1)
>   (:prep-object (:prep *from*) (:object HUM1)][1]

which is equivalent to the tree:

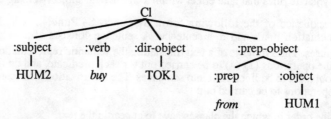

More generally, a clause template has the following structure:

---

[1]   The symbol ']' stands for the closing parentheses required to complete the representation of a list.

[Cl] = (:Cl [subject] [verb] elt^n $(0 \leq n \leq 2)$)
[subject] = (:subject token)
[verb] = (:verb *verb*)
elt = object / [attribute]
object = [dir-object] / [prep-object]
[dir-object] = (:dir-object token)
[prep-object] = (:prep-object [prep] (:object token))
[prep] = (:prep *preposition*)
[attribute] = (:attribute *adjective*)

The sign '/' means 'or' . The elements preceded by ':' are functional categories (e.g. :subject) or morphological categories (e.g. :preposition). The elements written in italics are words of the morphological category indicated. The notation [X] stands for a list whose first element is :X. It is also the name I give to such a list. The value of [X] is its second element, except for [prep-object] whose value is the value of its [object]. A clause template or [Cl] may be noted Cl*i* so as to permit cross-references. The term 'complement' designates the [subject] or one of the objects of a clause template.

My formalism is close to that of functional or systemic grammars. In particular, it is close to the formalism presented by Winograd (1983, Appendix B). The main difference between Winograd's formalism and mine is that he uses the single term 'clause' where I use two terms: 'clause' and 'sentence'. The distinction between these two terms is clearly needed in automatic generation (see Section 4).

Modifiers (i.e. adverbial groups and subordinate clauses) will be set aside for the moment, along with all coordination phenomena. Modifiers and coordination will be discussed simultaneously in Section 4.1.

3.2 Agreement rules

Agreement rules in English are limited to subject-verb agreement. A [verb] agrees in number and person with its [subject]. The number and person of the [subject], which is a list (:subject token), are semantic information that is computable from the token. In the clause template

(:Cl (:subject HUM1) (:verb *love*) (:dir-object HUM2))

with   HUM1 =: PERSON
              NAME: John
              SEX: masc

the semantic representation of HUM1 is the only parameter needed to determine that the [verb] must be conjugated in the third person singular.

Agreement rules are more numerous in French than in English. First, epithet or attribute adjectives and articles agree with the noun they modify; second, the agreement rules for a verb are complex. As an illustration of this complexity, let us present some conjugation rules in the active voice:

— In any simple tense, any verb agrees in person and number with its subject:

j'aimais, tu aimais, il aimait, nous aimions, vous aimiez, ils aimaient
I loved, you loved, he loved, we loved, you loved, they loved

— In a compound tense, the auxiliary is generally *avoir* (*to have*) but it must be *être* (*to be*) with some intransitive verbs:

Jean avait aimé Marie (John had loved Mary)

Jean était allé à Paris (John had gone to Paris)

A past participle used with the auxiliary *avoir* does not agree with the subject

Jean avait aimé Marie (John had loved Mary)
Marie avait aimé Jean (Mary had loved John)

A past participle used with the auxiliary *être,* by contrast, agrees in gender and number with the subject

Jean était allé à Paris (John had gone to Paris)
Marie était allée à Paris (Mary had gone to Paris)

However, a past participle used with the auxiliary *avoir* agrees in gender and number with a direct object when the latter is placed before the verb because it has been pronominalized:

Jean avait aimé Marie -> Jean l'avait aimée
(John had loved Mary -> John had loved her)

Jean avait aimé ces femmes -> Jean les avait aimées
(John had loved these women -> John had loved them)

More generally, a verb of any tense, voice, and mood agrees in gender, number and person with its subject and with a direct object placed before the verb.

Person and number are semantic information in French as in English. On the other hand, gender in French is not semantic but lexical information. For example, the token HUM1 can be synthesized as the masculine noun group *Jean* or as the feminine noun group *cette personne* (*this person*). Moreover, there is no neuter gender in French. An entity which is not a person (or an animal) is synthesized as a masculine or feminine noun group in a way that is not predictable on semantic grounds. For example, the token TOK1 can be synthesized as a masculine noun group *un vélo* (*a bike*) or as a feminine noun group *une bicyclette* (*a bicycle*). Gender in English is needed only for computing the form of a reflexive, personal or possessive pronoun (as also the case in French). But gender in English is semantic:

— An English pronoun refering to a person has a gender corresponding to his/her sex, which is not the case in French:

John is weird. This person is always talking about <u>himself</u>.
Jean est bizarre. Cette personne parle toujours d'<u>elle même</u>.

Mary is weird. This person is always talking about <u>herself</u>.
Marie est bizarre. Cette personne parle toujours d'<u>elle même</u>.

In English, the reflexive pronoun is either masculine or feminine depending on whether *this person* refers to *John* or to *Mary*. In French, the reflexive pronoun is feminine in either case because *personne* is a feminine noun.

— An English pronoun referring to a nonhuman entity is always neuter (with a few exceptions), unlike in French:

My bicycle is broken. <u>It</u> is at the garage.
Ma bicyclette est cassée. <u>Elle</u> est au garage.

My bike is broken. It is at the garage.
Mon vélo est cassé. Il est au garage.

Subject-verb agreement is a nonlocal operation in the sense that the synthesis of the [verb] depends upon factors that are external to this element (e.g. the value and gender for French of the [subject]). Suppose for the moment that the synthesis of a clause template proceeds from left to right: first, synthesis of the [subject] followed by synthesis of the [verb] followed by synthesis of the first object, etc. Two methods can be considered for carrying out nonlocal operations such as subject-verb agreement. The first one, which can be caracterized as 'forward', consists of preparing the subject-verb agreement when synthesizing the [subject]. The forward method can be implemented by storing the value (and gender for French) of the [subject] in a variable when synthesizing it. Then, the synthesis of the [verb] requires only the value of this variable to be retrieved. The second method, which can be caracterized as 'backward', involves not storing information that may be needed later but rather retrieving it when needed. The synthesis of the [verb] requires then that the value (and gender) of the [subject] be retrieved. However, many other categories than [verb] require information about the [subject]. It is also the case for a [dir-object] or a [prep-object] (in order to determine if a reflexive pronoun should be synthesized; see Section 3.4) and for an [attribute] in French (for subject-attribute agreement). The synthesis of the following clause template:

(:Cl (:subject HUM2) (:verb *être*) (:attribute *fier*) (:prep-object (:prep *de*) (:object HUM2]

which should result in *Marie est fière d'elle-même* (Mary is proud of herself), requires that information about the [subject] be retrieved three times if the backward method is used, which is inefficient. As a consequence, the forward method must be selected.

There exist at least two ways of implementing the forward method. The first one, mentioned previously, involves the use of variables. The second one involves marking directly into an element [X] the information that is relevant to its synthesis and that comes from another element [Y]. This can be done by modifying [X], for example by modifying '(:verb *love*)' into '(:verb *love* (:subject-number sing) (:subject-person third))'. These two ways will be used in this paper. Without going further into programming details, let us point out that both the use of variables and direct marking must take into account embeddings (i.e. relative, subordinate and nominal clauses). Consider the following clause template for *John is washing the dishes so that Mary will be happy* whose structure will be explained in Section 4.1:

(:Cl (:subject HUM1) (:verb *wash*) (:dir-object TOK2)
    (:sub (:sub-conj *so that*)
        (:Cl (:subject HUM2) (:verb *be*) (:attribute *happy*)]

The verb *wash* must agree with HUM1 and *be* with HUM2. If a variable *subject-cl* is used to store information about the [subject] of a clause template — as we will assume from now on — this variable must have the right value for each of the two clauses.

3.3 Synthesis of complements

Recall that a complement is the [subject] or an object (i.e. a [dir-object] or a [prep-object]) of a clause template. The value of a complement is a token that is synthesized as a reflexive, relative or personal pronoun or as a nominal clause or noun group. The synthesis of a pronoun requires (1) determining that a pronoun must be synthesized and determining its nature, gender, number and person, (2) computing its form and placing it, if necessary, according to its syntactic position in the clause (see Winograd, 1983, p. 290). The first operation is executed by a function SAY-TOKEN, the second by the functions SAY-SUBJECT, SAY-DIR-OBJECT and SAY-PREP-OBJECT. Let us outline these functions, which will be described in more detail in the following Sections. The function SAY-TOKEN takes a token as its argument. It returns a list of four elements: the second, third and fourth ones are respectively the gender, number and person. To determine the first element, SAY-TOKEN goes through the following steps:

(1) Determine if the token must be synthesized as a reflexive pronoun, in which case the first element of the list returned by SAY-TOKEN is ':reflexive-pro'. Otherwise:
(2) Determine if the token must be synthesized as a relative pronoun, in which case the first element is ':relative-pro'. Otherwise:
(3) Determine if the token must be synthesized as a personal pronoun, in which case the first element is ':personal-pro'. Otherwise:
(4) Synthesize a nominal clause or a noun group, in which case the first element is a word sequence.

The function SAY-SUBJECT, which is called to synthesize the [subject] of a clause template, i.e. a list (:subject token), goes through the following steps:

(1) Call the function SAY-TOKEN, which returns a list of four elements, for example (:personal-pro masc sing third) or (*John* masc sing third).
(2) If the first element of this list is not a word sequence, compute the pronoun. For example, the list (:personal-pro masc sing third) results in *he* .
(3) Replace in the clause template the list (:subject token) by a list such as (:subject *John*) or (:subject *he*) if the first element of the list returned by SAY-TOKEN is not ':relative-pro'; otherwise see Section 3.7.
(4) Assign to the variable *subject-cl* the value (token gender number person) where the last three elements are the last three values returned by SAY-TOKEN.

The functions SAY-DIR-OBJECT and SAY-PREP-OBJECT go through the steps (1), (2) and (3) of SAY-SUBJECT. However, the step (3) may be different in French (see Sections 3.4 and 3.5).

We are going to start with the synthesis of reflexive pronouns. Next, we will study the synthesis of personal pronouns. However, we will not study step (3) of SAY-TOKEN, namely the conditions governing the decision to synthesize a personal pronoun. Next, we will study the synthesis of nominal clauses, which will lead us to present the notion of a 'lexicon grammar'. We will finish with the synthesis of noun groups, which includes the synthesis of relative clauses. As we advance, the function SAY-CL, which is called to synthesize a [Cl], will be specified. Let us stipulate that SAY-CL calls two functions, SAY-VERB and SAY-ATTRIBUTE, in addition to SAY-SUBJECT, SAY-DIR-OBJECT and SAY-PREP-OBJECT. SAY-VERB conjugates the value of [verb] given its syntactic features (mood, tense, person, etc.). SAY-ATTRIBUTE computes the inflectional form of the value of [attribute] for French, given the gender and number of the complement the attribute modifies.

3.4 Reflexive pronouns

In English and French, a token must be synthesized as a reflexive pronoun if two conditions are fulfilled: (1) the token is the value of an object in a clause template, and (2) it is equal to the value of the [subject] of this clause template:

> (:Cl (:subject HUM2) (:verb *hate*) (:dir-object HUM2))
> *Mary hated herself*

> (:Cl (:subject HUM1) (:verb *dream*) (:prep-object (:prep *of*) (:object HUM1]
> *John dreamt of himself*

The function SAY-TOKEN, when called by SAY-DIR-OBJECT or SAY-PREP-OBJECT, determines if a token must be synthesized as a reflexive pronoun by testing the equality between the token and the first value of *subject-cl*. If the result is positive, the gender, number and person of the reflexive pronoun are given by the last three values of *subject-cl*.

The form of a reflexive pronoun in English depends only on the gender, number and person of the entity to which it refers. The synthesis of reflexive pronouns is thus straightforward. When SAY-TOKEN returns (:reflexive-pro gender number person), SAY-DIR-OBJECT or SAY-PREP-OBJECT computes the reflexive pronoun and replaces the value of [dir-object] or [prep-object] with it.

In French the form and position of a reflexive pronoun depends upon the type of object where it functions as, in addition to the gender, number and person of the subject:

(a) If the object is a [prep-object] whose preposition is not *à* , the synthesis of a reflexive pronoun proceeds much as in English:

(:Cl (:subject HUM1) (:verb *rêver*) (:prep-object (:prep *de*) (:object HUM1]
Jean a rêvé de lui-même (John dreamt about himself)

(b) If the object is a [dir-object] or a [prep-object] whose preposition is *à,* the reflexive pronoun, which I denote as *SE*, appears before the verb. Moreover, if the verb is in a compound tense, it is conjugated with the auxiliary *être* instead of *avoir* and it agrees with the reflexive pronoun when the latter synthesizes a [dir-object]:

Cl1 = (:Cl (:subject HUM2) (:verb *détester*) (:dir-object HUM1))
Marie a détesté Jean (Mary hated John)

Cl2 = (:Cl (:subject HUM2) (:verb *détester*) (:dir-object HUM2))
Marie s'est détestée (Mary hated herself)
(*s'est* is a contraction of *se est*)

The fact that the conjugation of the verb changes when there is a reflexive pronoun *SE* implies the following rule: The [verb] must not be synthesized before it is known whether a reflexive pronoun has to be synthesized[2]. The solution I adopted to implement this rule consists of synthesizing the [verb] *after* a [dir-object] or [prep-object]. More precisely, the synthesis of Cl1 or Cl2 goes through the following steps:

(1) Synthesis of the [subject], i.e. (:subject HUM2), by SAY-SUBJECT. This function calls SAY-TOKEN which returns, for example, the list (*Marie* fem sing third). SAY-SUBJECT replaces HUM2 by *Marie*

Cl1-1 = (:Cl (:subject *Marie*) (:verb *détester*) (:dir-object HUM1))
Cl2-1 = (:Cl (:subject *Marie*) (:verb *détester*) (:dir-object HUM2))

and assigns the list (HUM2 fem sing third) to *subject-cl*.

(2) Synthesis of the [dir-object], i.e. (:dir-object HUM1) in Cl1-1 and (:dir-object HUM2) in Cl2-1, by SAY-DIR-OBJECT. This function calls SAY-TOKEN which first tests the equality between the token and the first value of *subject-cl*.

(a) The test is negative for HUM1. SAY-TOKEN returns, for example, the list (*Jean* masc sing third). SAY-DIR-OBJECT replaces HUM1 by *Jean*:

Cl1-2 = (:Cl (:subject *Marie*) (:verb *détester*) (:dir-object *Jean*))

---

2   This rule is valid only if backtracking is ruled out, which I assume.

(b) The test is postive for HUM2. SAY-TOKEN returns the list (:reflexive-pro fem sing third) where the last three values are identical to those of *subject-cl*. SAY-DIR-OBJECT computes the reflexive pronoun, here *se*. This pronoun is pushed onto a list *ppv* that is used to store all of the pronouns that must appear in preverbal position. (Some French personal pronouns also appear before the verb, see Section 3.5.) The [dir-object] is erased from Cl2-1, the [verb] is marked as having to be conjugated with the auxiliary *être*, the gender and number of the pronoun are marked in the verb:

Cl2-2 = (:Cl   (:subject *Marie*)
                (:verb *détester*   (:auxiliary *être*)
                                    (:gender-object fem)
                                    (:number-object sing]

(3) Synthesis of the [verb] by SAY-VERB. This function accesses the variable *subject-cl* = (HUM2 fem sing third) to conjugate the verb in agreement with its subject. It returns *a détesté* for CL1-2 and *est détestée* for CL2-2. These word sequences replace the value of the [verb]:

Cl1-3 = (:Cl (:subject *Marie*) (:verb *a détesté*) (:dir-object *Jean*))
Cl2-3 = (:Cl (:subject *Marie*) (:verb *est détestée*))

(4) If the list *ppv* is not empty, its elements are arranged (see Section 3.5) and placed in front of the value of the [verb], with contraction if necessary. This step is not executed for Cl1-3 and gives the following result for Cl2-3:

Cl2-4 = (:Cl (:subject *Marie*) (:verb *s'est détestée*))

(5) Erasing of the auxiliary vocabulary and bracketing:

Cl1-4 = *Marie a détesté Jean*
Cl2-5 = *Marie s'est détestée*

The placement of the elements of *ppv* in front of the verb requires the syntactic categories to be kept to the very end. If Cl2-3 were (:Cl *Marie est détestée*), it would be impossible to place *se*. That is the reason why the functions SAY-X do not replace [X], but rather the value of [X] with their result. In this way, the category :X is kept. (At the end of Section 3.5 I will return to this approach to the synthesis of French reflexive pronouns.)

3.5 Personal pronouns

Recall that the conditions governing the decision to synthesize a token as a personal pronoun (i.e. the conditions under which SAY-TOKEN returns (:personal-pro gender number person)) are not under consideration here. In English, the gender, number and person of a personal pronoun are semantic information that SAY-TOKEN computes from the token. On the other hand, recall that gender is not semantic but lexical in French. The gender of a personal pronoun synthesizing a token is generally identical to the gender of the last occurrence of the token. It is thus necessary to store the gender of each occurrence of every token so as to enable the computation of the gender of a personal pronoun by SAY-TOKEN (Danlos, 1987b).

The form of a personal pronoun in English depends upon the gender, number and person of the entity to which the pronoun refers and upon the type of complement in which it appears ([subject] versus object). When SAY-TOKEN returns (:personal-pro gender number person), the functions SAY-SUBJECT, SAY-DIR-OBJECT and SAY-PREP-OBJECT compute the personal pronouns and replace the value of their argument with it.

As for reflexive pronouns, the form and the position of a French personal pronoun depends upon the type of complement in which it appears.

(a) If the complement is the [subject] or a [prep-object] whose preposition is *sur*, for example, a personal pronoun is synthesized much as in English:

(:Cl   (:subject HUM1) (:verb *compter*)
          (:prep-object (:prep *sur*) (:object HUM2]
Jean compte sur elle (John relies on her)

(b) If the complement is a [dir-object] or a [prep-object] whose preposition is *à*, for example, the personal pronoun must appear before the verb. Moreover, the verb agrees in gender and number with the personal pronoun when the latter synthesizes a [dir-object]:

(:Cl (:subject HUM1) (:verb *détester*) (:dir-object HUM2))
Jean l'a détestée (John hated her)

(:Cl (:subject HUM1) (:verb *obéir*) (:prep-object (:prep *à*) (:object HUM2)))
Jean lui a obéi (John obeyed her)

The form of such personal pronouns depends on the type of complement ([dir-object] versus [prep-object]), on the preposition for a [prep-object], on the gender, number and person of the last occurrence of the token involved, and in some cases on whether this token represents a person. In fact, the situation is even more complex than this. The form of a personal pronoun may also depend on lexical data, namely the verb. It is thus necessary in French to appeal to a 'lexicon grammar' in order to determine the form of a personal pronoun. (The notion of lexicon grammar will be discussed in Section 3.6.)

Suppose that the tokens HUM1 and HUM2 are to be synthesized as personal pronouns, and consider the synthesis of

Cl3 = (:Cl (:subject HUM1) (:verb *détester*) (:dir-object HUM2))

The synthesis of this clause template goes through the steps described in Section 3.4, namely:

(1) Synthesis of the [subject] by SAY-SUBJECT which calls SAY-TOKEN which returns (:personal-pro masc sing third). SAY-SUBJECT modifies Cl3 into

Cl3-1 = (:Cl (:subject *il*) (:verb *détester*) (:dir-object HUM2))

and assigns the value (HUM1 masc sing third) to *subject-cl* .

(2) Synthesis of the [dir-object] by SAY-DIR-OBJECT which calls SAY-TOKEN which returns (:personal-pro fem sing third). SAY-DIR-OBJECT computes the form of the pronoun, namely *la* . This pronoun is pushed on the list *ppv*. The gender and number of this pronoun are marked in the [verb]. The [dir-object] is erased from Cl3-1:

Cl3-2= (:Cl (:subject *il*)
                  (:verb *détester* (:dir-object-gender fem) (:dir-object-number sing]

(3) Synthesis of the [verb] by SAY-VERB. This function takes into account the fact that :dir-object-gender and :dir-object-number have non-nul values and returns *a détestée*:

Cl3-3 = (:Cl (:subject *il*) (:verb *a détestée*))

(4) If the list *ppv* is not empty, its elements are arranged and placed in front of the value of the [verb], with contraction if necessary. Given that *ppv* is (*la*), this step results in:

Cl3-4 = (:Cl (:subject *il*) (:verb *l'a détestée*))

(5) Erasing of the auxiliary vocabulary and bracketing:

Cl3-5 = *Il l'a détestée*

Let us now examine the arrangement of *ppv* when its value is a list of several elements. The pronouns that appear in a preverbal position must appear in the following order: subject < SE < LE < LUI < *y* < *en* < verb, with SE = *me / nous / te / vous / se,* LE = *le / la / les* , LUI = *lui / leur*. This order does not always correspond to the order of the objects in the clause template. Suppose that the token TOK1 is to be synthesized as a personal pronoun and consider the following clause template:

(:Cl   (:subject HUM1) (:verb *offrir*) (:dir-object TOK1)
        (:prep-object (:prep *à*) (:object HUM1]

This clause template must not be synthesized as **Jean la s'est offerte* but as *Jean se l'est offerte* (John offered it to himself) where the pronoun *se* synthesizing the [prep-object] appears on the left of the pronoun *la* synthesizing the [dir-object], although the [prep-object] is on the right of the [dir-object] in the clause template. The discrepancy between the order of the objects in the clause template and the order of the preverbal pronouns implies that the elements of *ppv* must be arranged and placed after synthesizing all the objects.

With the solution presented for synthesizing French reflexive or personal pronouns, the synthesis of the elements in a clause template is not made in the left-to-right order which corresponds to the order of the elements in the clause template.[3] The [verb] is always synthesized last, even if it is followed by objects. This does not mean that the verb will be the last element of the synthesized clause, as the synthesis of Cl1 shows. In other words, the order in which the elements of a clause template are synthesized may differ both from the order in

---

[3]   Although there seems to be no way to generate French personal pronouns without violating the left-to-right order, there might be one for reflexive pronouns. This solution consists of synthesizing a clause such as *Marie s'est détestée* (Mary hated herself) not from Cl2 but from a clause template such as
                        (:Cl (:subject HUM2) (:verb *détester* (:voice pronominal]
This is possible if the module that determines a clause pattern to express a predicate takes into account the identity of two slots. For example, this module can determine that an instance of the class HATE which is characterized by two slots, HATER and HATED, is to be expressed by means of '?HATER *détester* ?HATED' if the values of the slots HATER and HATED are different, and by '?HATER *se détester*' otherwise. So, there is a way to synthesize French reflexive pronouns without violating left-to-right order. However, this method does not work for French personal pronouns, because the decision to form a personal pronoun is not based on semantic grounds only. The decision to form a personal pronoun, which must be made at the text level and not at the clause or sentence level, depends upon many complex considerations of a pragmatic as well as a semantic, syntactic, lexical or stylistic nature (Hirst, 1981). One of the syntactic considerations involved in pronominalization is 'structure parallelism' (Harris, 1982). In *Mary dressed Sue and Ann made her up* the pronoun *her*, which synthesizes a direct object, is interpreted as being coreferential with *Sue* , the direct object of the first clause. Similarly, in *Mary dressed Sue and she was made up by Ann* the pronoun *she*, which synthesizes the subject, is interpreted as being coreferential with *Mary*, the subject of the first clause. The structure parallelism issue implies that the decision to form a personal pronoun must be made late, more precisely, after determination of the syntactic structures of the sentence (i.e. the clause or sentence template). As a consequence, there is no way to synthesize French personal pronouns without violating left-to-right order. Hence, it seems more economical to synthesize French reflexive pronouns the way described in Section 3.4, which violates left-to-right order, than to design a complex module for the determination of a clause pattern expressing a predicate, which takes the identity of two slots into account.
        Decisions to form personal pronouns must be postponed until clause or sentence templates have been determined, since pronominalization involves syntactic considerations. However, this proposal does not solve all problems. It implies that deciding to choose a clause or sentence template does not involve an pronominalization issues, which is incorrect. For example, the decision to apply the dative transformation to a clause pattern should not be made without taking pronominalization issues into account, so that the synthesis of sentences such as: **John gave Mary it* can be avoided (Danlos, 1987b).

which they appear in the clause template and from the order in which they appear in the synthesized clause. This situation is unusual, at least for English. Most English generators operate in a left-to-right order: The elements of a clause template (or what corresponds to a clause template) are synthesized from left to right and appear in the synthesized clause in the same order as in the clause template. This issue is even considered as theoretical by some researchers (see Section 3.6). However, other researchers (e.g. Jacobs, 1985) are aware that a left-to-right generator cannot produce texts in more richly inflected languages than English.

3.6 Nominal clauses

A token is synthesized as a nominal clause if it is an instance of the class PREDICATE. Consider the following semantic representation:

EVENT2 =: PROMISE   TRAVEL1 =: TRAVEL
AGENT = HUM1   AGENT = HUM3
THEME = TRAVEL1   TO = LOC1
BENEFICIARY = HUM2

HUM1 =: PERSON   HUM2 =: PERSON   HUM3 =: PERSON   LOC1=: CITY
NAME: John   NAME: Mary   NAME: Bill   NAME: Paris

The clause template that expresses EVENT2 may be:

Cl1 = (:Cl (:subject HUM1) (:verb *promise*) (:dir-object HUM2) (:dir-object TRAVEL1))

In the course of synthesizing Cl1, the function SAY-DIR-OBJECT calls SAY-TOKEN to synthesize TRAVEL1. Suppose that SAY-TOKEN rules out the possibility of synthesizing TRAVEL1 as a pronoun. Then it determines that TRAVEL1 is an instance of the class PREDICATE and therefore calls the module that determines a clause pattern to express a predicate. This module may return the following clause template:

Cl2 = (:Cl (:subject HUM3) (:verb *go*) (:prep-object (:prep *to*) (:object LOC1]

This clause template may be synthesized by SAY-CL as *Bill would go to Paris*. This clause is embedded in the main clause CL1 by SAY-DIR-OBJECT, which gives:

John promised Mary that Bill would go to Paris

The main problem arising in connection with nominal clauses is their reduction. Consider a token EVENT3 whose definition is identical to that of EVENT2 except that the value of the slot THEME is TRAVEL2 with

TRAVEL2 =: TRAVEL
AGENT = HUM1
TO = LOC1

The clause template that expresses EVENT3 is

Cl1' = (:Cl (:subject HUM1) (:verb *promise*) (:dir-object HUM2) (:dir-object TRAVEL2))

and the one expressing TRAVEL2 is:

Cl2' = (:Cl (:subject HUM1) (:verb *go*) (:prep-object (:prep *to*) (:object LOC1]

These clause templates must result in

John promised Mary to go to Paris

where the nominal clause is reduced: Its subject is erased and its verb is in the infinitive. The reduction of a nominal clause depends upon the verb of the main clause. When this verb is *promise*, the nominal clause is reduced if its subject is equal to the subject of *promise* When this verb is *persuade,* the nominal clause is reduced if its subject is equal to the first object of *persuade:*

> *John persuaded Mary that Bill should go to Paris*
> *John persuaded Mary to go to Paris*

A generator must have in its data this lexical information, as well as any other lexical information governing the application of syntactic transformations. Hence, a generator must include a 'lexicon grammar' (Gross, 1979, 1984, 1986). A lexicon grammar is a linguistic data base that records the syntactic properties of each 'elementary sentence' of a language. An elementary sentence is an abstract unit such as

> *N0 eat N1*
> *N0 dream of N1*
> *N0 believe N1*
> *N0 buy N1 from N2*
> *N0 promise N1 to N2*

where the verb and its object(s) are explicitly indicated. The notation *N0* stands for the subject, *N1* for the first object, *N2* for the second object. A sample of the syntactic properties recorded for each elementary sentence is the following:

— whether each *Ni* of an elementary sentence can be a nominal clause
— whether each *Ni* which may be a nominal clause can be reduced, and if so, the conditions and form of the reduction
— whether each elementary sentence can undergo the passive transformation
— whether each elementary sentence can undergo the ergative transformation
— whether each *Ni (i>0)* of a simple sentence can be omitted
— the distributional properties for each *Ni* of a simple sentence.

A lexicon grammar takes the form of a binary matrix: Each line corresponds to an elementary sentence and each column to a syntactic property. At the intersection of a line and a column, the sign '+' appears if the simple sentence possesses the property, the sign '-' otherwise. A French lexicon grammar aiming at exhaustiveness has been developed at the Laboratoire d'Automatique Documentaire et Linguistique (LADL). It includes 56,000 elementary sentences for which more than 600 syntactic properties have been described. Since a 56,000 * 600 matrix would be cumbersome, the lexicon grammar is divided up into 'tables'. Each table groups together elementary sentences that share a set of syntactic properties. Lexicon grammars are in an advanced state of development for Romance languages. Fragments of lexicon grammar have also been developed for English, German, Korean, Arabic and Malagasy.

A clause template can be viewed as an instantiation of an elementary sentence. However, a clause template can include modifiers (see Section 4.1.), which is not the case for an elementary sentence. From now on, we will suppose that a generator has access to the subset of the lexicon grammar that concerns the elementary sentences of the domain involved. Each elementary sentence of the lexicon grammar is indexed with an identification number. For the generator to access the information of the lexicon grammar, a clause template must indicate the identification number of the elementary sentence underlying it. For the sake of readability, I indicate the identification number of an elementary sentence such as *N0 love N1* in the following way:

(:Cl (:id-number 44) (:subject HUM1) (:verb *love*) (:dir-object HUM2))

Let us return to the synthesis of a clause template embedding a nominal clause such as

Cl1 = (:Cl (:id-number 132) (:subject HUM1) (:verb *promise*)
        (:dir-object HUM2) (:dir-object TRAVEL2))

and suppose that the synthesis of TRAVEL2 calls the function SAY-CL to develop the following clause template:

Cl2 = (:Cl (:id-number 418) (:subject HUM1) (:verb *go*)
        (:prep-object (:prep *to*) (:object LOC1]

The synthesis of CL1 must result in *John promised Mary to go to Paris*. The synthesis of *to go to Paris* from Cl2, or more generally the reduction of nominal clauses, involves the following steps:

(1) Retrieve the id-number of the main clause; for Cl1, it is 132.
(2) Consult the lexicon grammar to determine whether it is possible to reduce the nominal clause occurring in the elementary sentence indexed under this id-number. For the id-number 132, the lexicon grammar indicates that the nominal clause is reduced to an infinitive form when the value of its [subject] (i.e. a token) is equal to the value of the [subject] of the main clause.
(3) Check whether the conditions indicated by the lexicon grammar are fulfilled. This is the case in our example.
(4) If the previous result is positive, modify the clause template so that SAY-CL synthesizes it in the form indicated by the lexicon grammar. The following operations have to be carried out to reduce a nominal clause to an infinitive form:
    (4-1) Mark the [verb] as having to be conjugated in the infinitive.
    (4-2) Mark the [subject] as having to be erased
    (4-3) Indicate in the [subject] the gender, number and person of the complement of the main clause that governs the reduction of the nominal clause.

Steps (4-2) and (4-3) are necessary since one cannot simply erase the [subject] from the clause template. If this were done, it would be impossible to test for the synthesis of reflexive pronouns (as in, *John promised Mary to take care of himself* ; cf. Section 3.4) and to respect, in French, the subject-verb and subject-attribute agreement rules. (A past participle used with *être* agrees in gender and number with the subject even if *être* is in the infinitive and the subject is erased.) Step (4-3) will be discussed in more detail below. Steps (4-1), (4-2) and (4-3) modify Cl2 into:

Cl2-1 = (:Cl (:id-number 418)
         (:subject HUM1 (:erase +) (:gender masc) (:number sing) (:person third))
         (:verb *go* (:mood infinitive))
         (:prep-object (:prep *to*) (:object LOC1]

(5) Synthesize the modified clause template by calling SAY-CL. In Cl2-1, SAY-SUBJECT erases the [subject] because of the mark (:erase +), but assigns the value (HUM1 masc sing third) to *subject-cl*. This variable is accessed in connection with reflexive pronouns and agreement rules, as usual. The synthesis of Cl2-1 results in *to go to Paris*.

Let us now discuss step (4-3). This step is necessary in French because of the agreement rules and because gender is not semantic but lexical information (see Section 3.2). It requires the complement of the main clause that governs the reduction of the nominal clause to be synthesized before the nominal clause. This is not a problem for Cl1: The complement of the main clause of Cl1 that governs the reduction is the [subject], and this complement is synthesized before the [dir-object] where the nominal clause Cl2 appears. On the other hand, consider the following clause template:

Cl3 = (:Cl   (:subject (:Cl (:subject HUM2) (:verb *être*) (:attribute *cruel*)))
             (:verb *amuser*) (:dir-object HUM2))

in which the id-numbers are omitted and the nominal clause is presented as the value of the [subject] of the main clause for the sake of clarity. Cl3 must be synthesized as *Etre cruelle amuse Marie* (Being cruel amuses Mary) where the nominal clause subject is reduced since its [subject] is equal to the [dir-object] of the main clause. Step (4-3) cannot be achieved if this [dir-object] has not yet been synthesized. Thus, step (4-3) in fact develops the following way:

(4-3-1) If the complement of the main clause that governs the reduction of the nominal clause has not yet been synthesized, then synthesize it.

(4-3-2) Indicate in the [subject] of the nominal clause the gender, number and person of this complement.

Step (4-3-1) leads to synthesizing the [dir-object] of Cl3 before its [subject], thereby violating the left-to-right order. Cl1 involves a left-to-right dependency (the [subject] of the nominal clause has to be erased since it is equal to an element placed on its left), whereas Cl3 involves a right-to-left dependency (the [subject] of the nominal clause has to be erased since it is equal to an element placed on its right). McDonald (1983) presents an English generator that takes only left-to-right dependencies into consideration. McDonald justifies this position by the hypothesis that only the sequential dependencies can be assessed in oral discourse. His generator therefore operates from left-to-right. Thus, it cannot produce *Being cruel amuses Mary* and it could certainly not produce the French clause *Etre cruelle amuse Marie*, which not only involves a right-to-left dependency, but also requires the left-to-right order to be violated. We have already seen in Sections 3.4 and 3.5 that, in French, reflexive and personal pronouns require the left-to-right order to be violated. We will see in Section 4.2 that this is also the case for the reduction of subordinate clauses (*Before leaving, John washed the dishes*) which raises in English the same problems as the reduction of nominal clauses in French. All in all, it is out of the question that a French generator should operate from left to right. It is likely that generators for other Romance or for Germanic languages cannot operate from left to right either. In these languages, either reflexive or personal pronouns function like the French ones or there are other movement phenomena that cannot be handled with a left-to-right generator. Let us add that violating the left-to-right order allows us to deal correctly with some pronominalization phenomena (Danlos, 1987b).

3.7   Noun groups

A token of the class ENTITY is synthesized as a noun group when it is not pronominalized. A French or English noun group has the following structure (taken from Winograd, 1983, Appendix B):

Determiner—Sequence—Modifiers—Head—Qualifiers

However, the synthesis of noun groups will not be discussed thoroughly since it cannot be done independently of the study of pronominalization, which does not fall within the scope of this paper. The choice of the Determiner and Head and the presence of Modifiers and Qualifiers are decisions that all depend on whether the token has already been mentioned, and they therefore have to do with the pronominalization issue. On the other hand, we will look at the synthesis of relative clauses, which are Qualifiers in Winograd's terminology.

The clause template underlying the sentence

The student who was drunk kissed Mary

may be

Cl1 = (:Cl (:subject HUM4 (:rest-relative
                                (:Cl (:subject HUM4) (:verb *be*) (:attribute *drunk*))))
           (:verb *kiss*) (:dir-object HUM2))

where a relative clause of the restrictive type, denoted as rest-relative, is attached to the [subject]. Similarly, the clause template underlying the sentence

Bob, who was drunk, kissed Mary

may be

Cl2 = (:Cl (:subject HUM5 (:non-rest-relative
                                (:Cl (:subject HUM5) (:verb *be*) (:attribute *drunk*))))
           (:verb *kiss*) (:dir-object HUM2))

where a non restrictive relative clause is attached to the [subject]. Finally, the clause template underlying

Mary was wounded by John who shot her

is

Cl3 = (:Cl (:subject HUM2) (:verb *wound* (:voice passive))
           (:prep-object (:prep *by*) (:object HUM1
                (:sub-relative (:Cl (:subject HUM1)(:verb *shoot*)(:dir-object HUM2]

where a relative clause of a third type, called: sub-relative, is attached to the [prep-object]. The three types of relative clauses determine the article introducing the antecedent of the relative clause and the presence of commas surrounding it (Danlos, 1987a), but all of them are synthesized in the same way.

When the function SAY-TOKEN is applied to a token to which a relative clause is attached, this token and its gender, number and person are stored in a variable called *relative* in the form of a list. For example, when SAY-TOKEN is called by SAY-PREP-OBJECT in Cl3, the list (HUM1 masc sing third) is stored in *relative*. Next, the synthesis of the relative clause is executed by SAY-CL which goes through the steps described in Sections 3.4 and 3.5. These steps are going to be specified as far as relative clauses are concerned and illustrated with the synthesis of the relative clause of Cl3, namely:

Cl4 = (:Cl (:subject HUM1) (:verb *shoot*) (:dir-object HUM2))

(1) Synthesis of the [subject] by SAY-SUBJECT, which calls SAY-TOKEN. This function first determines that HUM1 cannot be synthesized as a reflexive pronoun. Next, it checks whether a relative pronoun must be synthesized by comparing the token with the first value of *relative*. This gives a positive result and SAY-TOKEN returns (:relative-pro masc sing third) where the last three values come from *relative*. SAY-SUBJECT computes the relative pronoun, here *who*, and stores it in a variable *relative-pro*. The subject of CL4 is erased:

Cl4-1 = (:Cl (:verb *shoot*) (:dir-object HUM2))

and the list (HUM1 masc sing third) is assigned to *subject-cl*.

.(2) Synthesis of the [dir-object]. Let us admit that HUM2 is to be synthesized as a personal pronoun, which yields:

CL4-2 = (:Cl (:verb *shoot*) (:dir-object *her*))

(3) Synthesis of the [verb]:

Cl4-3 = (:Cl (:verb *shot*) (:dir-object *her*))

(4) If *relative-pro* is not empty, its value is placed in front of the clause and the auxiliary vocabulary and bracketing are erased:

 Cl4-4 = *who shot her*

In French, unlike in English, a relative pronoun must to be present in all relative clauses.

*la chose (que / *E) Jean veut le plus* [4]
the thing (that / E) John wants most

and 'dangling prepositions' are prohibited:

*le yoyo (que / E) Jean a voté pour
the yoyo John voted for

le yoyo pour lequel Jean a voté
the yoyo for whom John voted

In the approach just described, a French or English relative clause always starts with a relative pronoun which stems from a completement of the relative clause template and is always positioned to the front of this clause template. Thus nested relative clauses can be generated:

```
(:Cl   I like
        (:dir-object TOK3
            (:rest-relative (:Cl (:subject HUM6
                                    (:rest-relative  (:Cl we told the story to HUM6)))
                (:verb buy ) (:dir-object TOK3]
        I like the book that the man to whom we told the story bought
```

However, this approach does not allow us to handle cases where the relative pronoun comes from a completement of a nominal clause embedded in the relative clause. The following clause template

```
(:Cl   I   like
        (:dir-object TOK4
            (:rest-relative (:Cl  (:subject HUM1) (:verb want )
                                    (:dir-object (:Cl (:subject HUM1) (:verb read ) (:dir-object TOK4]
```

does not come out as *I like the book that John wants to read.*

---

4   The symbol *E* stands for an empty sequence.

4. SYNTHESIS OF SENTENCES

Recall that a text is a sequence of the following form: S_1 Punct$_1$ S_2 Punct$_2$ ... S_n Punct$_n$, where Punct$_i$ is a punctuation mark and S_i a sentence. A sentence consists of a single clause or a combination of clauses. Let us examine combinations of clauses.

4.1 Coordination and Modifiers

All coordinations of clauses can be obtained with the following definition of a sentence template:

    S = [Cl] / [coord-S]
    [coord-S] = (:coord-S [coord-conj] S1 S2 ... Sn)
    [coord-conj] = (:coord-conj *coordinating-conjunction*)

For example, the sentence

John washed the dishes and Mary cleaned the house, but Bill did not do anything

can be generated from the following sentence template:

    (:coord-S (:coord-conj *but*)
            (:coord-S (:coord-conj *and*)
                    (:Cl *John washed the dishes*)
                    (:Cl *Mary cleaned the house*))
            (:Cl *Bill did not do anything*))

in which the clause templates are replaced with the English clauses for the sake of readability.

The category Modifier includes the adverbs (e.g. *yesterday, inevitably, first*), the preposition groups that are not prep-objects (e.g. *in one hour, at ten, with enthusiasm*), some noun groups (e.g. *last year, next week*) and the subordinate sentences. The definition of a subordinate sentence template is

    [sub] = (:sub [sub-conj] S)
    [sub-conj] = (:sub-conj *subordinating-conjunction*)

All of the Modifiers can be obtained if the definition of a clause template proposed in Section 3.1, namely

$$[\text{Cl}] = (\text{:Cl [subject] [verb] elt}^n \ (0 \le n \le 2))$$

is modified to

    [Cl] = (:Cl Modifier* [subject] Modifier* [verb] Modifier*
          elt! Modifier* elt! Modifier*)

with the asterisk (*) indicating that an element appears zero or more times, and the exclamation mark (!), that an element appears at most once.

However, these definitions of [coord-S] and [Cl] do not account for the scope of Modifiers when coordinated clauses are involved. In the sentence

Yesterday, John washed the dishes and Mary cleaned the house

the two coordinated clauses are within the scope of the adverb *yesterday*, while in

Yesterday, John washed the dishes and today, Mary cleaned the house

only the first clause is within the scope of *yesterday*. From a linguistic viewpoint, it could be said that the former of these two sentences derives from

Yesterday, John washed the dishes and yesterday, Mary cleaned the house

with deletion of the repeated element, i.e. *yesterday*. In automatic generation, this approach amounts to generating it from the following sentence template:

(:coord-S (coord-conj *and*)
                (:Cl (:adv DATE1) *John washed the dishes*)
                (:Cl (:adv DATE1) *Mary cleaned the house*)))

However, it is well known (Quirk et al., 1985) that not all cases of coordination can be explained in terms of the deletion of repeated elements. For example, the following two sentences are not synonymous:

In one hour, John washed the dishes and cleaned the house
In one hour, John washed the dishes and in one hour, John (he) cleaned the house

The semantic representation underlying these sentences must specify the scope of the temporal modifier 'in one hour': both events, or one event only ('John washed the dishes' or 'John cleaned the house'). The following principle can be formulated: Clause or sentence templates must mirror accurately the information of the semantic representation. This principle derives from the fact that it would be 'weird' to go through the following steps: (1) right semantics in the input to the generator, (2) wrong semantics in the templates, (3) right semantics in the output of the generator. It leads us to generate the two sentences, respectively, from clause templates:

(:coord-S (:coord-conj *and*)
                (:adv DURATION1)
                (:Cl *John washed the dishes*)
                (:Cl *John cleaned the house*))

and

(:coord-S (:coord-conj *and*)
                (:Cl (:adv DURATION1) *John washed the dishes*)
                (:Cl (:adv DURATION1) *John cleaned the house*))

In a more general way, the definition of [coord-S] is the following:

[coord-S] = (:coord-S [coord-conj] Modifier* S1 S2 . . . Sn Modifier*)

where the Modifiers that bear on all of the coordinated clauses are factorized. This definition, along with the definition of [Cl] that we recall

[Cl] = (:Cl Modifier* [subject] Modifier* [verb] Modifier*
        elt! Modifier* elt! Modifier*)

allows the scope of Modifiers to be handled correctly . For example:

```
(:coord-S (:coord-conj and )
          (:adv DATE1)
          (:Cl John washed the dishes (:adv HOUR1))
          (:Cl Mary cleaned the house (:adv HOUR2]
```
Yesterday, John washed the dishes at ten and Mary cleaned the house at eleven

The same kind of reasoning applies to coordinated complements and coordinated modifiers within a clause. I cannot go into these constructions here. I only remark that the clause template underlying *Mary loves John and Bill* is

```
(:Cl (:subject (HUM2)) (:verb love) (:dir-object (HUM1 HUM3]
```

where the value of the [dir-object] is a list of tokens, i.e. (HUM1 HUM3). For the sake of homogeneity, the values of all complements are written in the form of a list, e.g. (:subject (HUM2)) instead of (:subject HUM2).

In Section 3, the syntactic operations that take effect within a clause were studied. The remaining Sections concern operations that take effect within a sentence, namely reduction of subordinate sentences and deletion of repeated elements in sentence coordination.

4.2 Subordinate sentences

4.2.1 Conditions of reduction

A subordinate sentence is reduced to an infinitive or a present participle when the subordinating conjunction allows such a reduction and the subject of the subordinate sentence is identical to the subject of the main clause. With conjunctions such as *because* or *now that,* the reduction is never allowed. In the sentence *John is cruel because he is sick, he* can be interpreted as referring to *John* . With conjunctions such as *before* or *after,* the subject of the subordinate sentence is erased when it is identical to the subject of the main sentence, and the verb of the subordinate sentence is in the present participle form:

John washed the dishes before Mary left
John washed the dishes before leaving

With other conjunctions, a subordinate sentence is reduced to an infinitive form:

John washed the dishes in order that Mary would be pleased
John washed the dishes in order to please Mary

We consider the *by V-ing* form (*John killed Mary by blowing up her car*) and the *V-ing* form (*John blew up Mary's car, killing her*) as subordinate sentences which are introduced respectively by *by* and *E* (empty sequence). These cases imply the reduction of the subordinate sentence to present participle form.

The synthesis of subordinate sentences requires a lexicon grammar that records for each subordinating conjunction whether it allows or implies the reduction, and if it is the case, the form of the reduced subordinate (infinitive or present participle) and the form of the reduced conjunction (e.g. *in order that* —> *in order to*). Such a lexicon grammar has been developed for French subordinating conjunctions by Piot (1978).

Recall that a subordinate sentence is a Modifier and that a Modifier appears in a [Cl] or [coord-S] under the following conditions:

```
[Cl] = (:Cl Modifier* [subject] Modifier* [verb] Modifier* elt!
            Modifier* elt!  Modifier*)
[coord-S] = (:coord-S [coord-conj] Modifier* S1 S2 . . . Sn Modifier*)
```

The main clause of a sentence (S = [Cl] / [coord-S]) is the sentence without its Modifiers. The subject of the main clause of a [Cl] is the value of the unique element [subject], i.e. a list of tokens. The subject of the main clause of a [coord-S] is the union of the subjects of the main clauses of S1, S2 . . . Sn, a list of tokens being treated as a set. Recall that the subject of the main clause of a [Cl] is stored in a variable *subject-cl* which records also its gender, number and person. Similarly, the subject of the main clause of a [coord-S] is stored in a variable *subject-coord-S* along with its gender, number and person.

4.2.2 Synthesis of a subordinate made up of a clause

Consider first a subordinate sentence of the following form:

[sub] = (:sub [sub-conj] [Cl])

If the subordinating conjunction allows reduction (this information is provided by the lexicon grammar of conjunctions), the reduction takes place when the subject of [Cl] is equal (in the set-theoretical sense of the term) to the subject of the main clause. The reduction of a [sub] requires the following operations to be carried out: (1) replace the subordinating conjunction with its reduced form if necessary; (2) conjugate the verb as an infinitive or present participle; (3) erase the [subject] from [Cl]. The erasing of the [subject] raises the same problems as those raised by the reduction of nominal clauses (see Section 3.6). It cannot be done before the value of this [subject] with its gender, number and person are stored, so as to make the test for the reflexive pronouns (e.g. *After taking care of himself, John washed the dishes*) and French agreement rules possible. Thus, it requires the [subject] of the main clause to be synthesized beforehand. As a consequence, the order of the synthesis of the elements of a sentence template is as follows:

A. If the sentence template is a clause template:

[Cl] = (:Cl   Modifier* [subject] Modifier* [verb] Modifier* elt!
        Modifier* elt! Modifier*)

(1) The [subject] is synthesized first[5], even if there are Modifiers on its left. The function SAY-SUBJECT stores the value of the [subject] with its gender, number and person in *subject-cl*.
(2) All of the elements of the [Cl], except the [subject] and the [verb], are synthesized from left to right. The synthesis of a [sub] made up of a clause goes through a test on the equality of the subject of the [sub] and the first value of *subject-cl* (when the subordinating conjunction allows the reduction). If the subject of the [sub] is to be erased, its gender, number and person are given by the last three values of *subject-cl*.
(3) Synthesis of the [verb], see Sections 3.4 and 3.5.

Example:

(:Cl (:sub (:sub-conj *pour que*)
            (:Cl (:subject (HUM2 HUM7)) (:verb *être*) (:attribute *beau*)))
        (:subject (HUM2 HUM7)) *sont allées chez le coiffeur*]
Pour être belles, Marie et Sue sont allées chez le coiffeur
(To be beautiful, Mary and Sue went to the hairdresser)

---

5   This is not true if the [subject] is a nominal clause, for which case see section 3.6.

B. If the sentence template is a template of coordinated sentences:

[coord-S] = (:coord-S [coord-conj] Modifier* S1 S2 . . . Sn Modifier*)

(1) The sentences S1 S2 . . . Sn are synthesized from left to right. This allows the value of
   the subject of the main clause of [coord-S] with its gender, number and person to be
   stored in the variable *subject-coord-s*.
(2) All of the Modifiers are synthesized from left to right. The synthesis of a [sub] made up
   of a clause proceeds as in the previous case except that the variable *subject-coord-s* is
   used instead of *subject-cl*.

Example:

(:coord-S   (:coord-conj *et*)
            (:sub   (:sub-conj *pour que*)
                    (:Cl (:subject (HUM2 HUM7)) (:verb *être*) (:attribute *beau*)))
            (:Cl (:subject (HUM2)) *est allée chez le coiffeur*)
            (:Cl (:subject (HUM7)) *a acheté une robe*]
Pour être belles, Marie est allée chez le coiffeur et Sue a acheté une robe
(To be beautiful, Mary went to the hairdresser and Sue bought a dress)

4.2.3 Synthesis of a subordinate made up of a coordination of clauses

Consider a subordinate sentence of the form:

(:sub [sub-conj] (:coord-S [coord-conj] Modifier* Cl1 Cl2 ... Cln Modifier*))[6]

When the subordinating conjunction allows reduction, a clause Cli ($1 \le i \le n$) is reduced to an
infinitive or present participle form if its subject is equal to the subject of the main clause. The
reduction of a clause Cli proceeds as in the previous case. The main problem is that of repeated
conjunctions. Consider the template:

(:Cl   (:subject HUM1) *washed the dishes*
       (:sub (:sub-conj *in order that*)
             (:coord-S (:coord-conj *and*)
                       (:Cl (:subject HUM1)(:verb *please*) (:dir-object HUM2))
                       (:Cl (:subject HUM1) (:verb *make*) (:dir-object HUM7)
                             (:attribute *jealous*]

in which the two clauses of the subordinate sentence must be reduced to an infinitive form. This
template should not be generated as

John washed the dishes in order to please Mary and in order to make Sue jealous

where each Cli is introduced by *in order to* , but as

John washed the dishes in order to please Mary and to make Sue jealous

To obtain such a text, the lexicon grammar of the conjunctions includes the nonreduced
coordinated form and the reduced coordinated form of each conjunction. For example, the

---

6   The general case, namely
        (:sub [sub-conj] (:coord-S [coord-conj] Modifier* S1 S2 . . . Sn Modifier*))
     has been implemented but will not be presented here.

conjunction *in order that* has *in order to* as its reduced form, *that* as its nonreduced coordinated form and *to* as its reduced coordinated form. These linguistic data allow the form of the conjunction that is to introduce Cli to be computed.

4.3 Deletion of repeated elements in a coordination of sentences

4.3.1. Cases treated

Our treatment of the deletion of repeated elements is guided by the fact that not deleting deletable elements does not produce a catastrophic result (*John took a book and Mary (took / E) an umbrella*) whereas deleting nondeletable elements does (*John took a book and Mary (took / *E) a walk*). I therefore implemented, for the time being, only the deletion of repeated subjects (*John washed the dishes and (he / E) cleaned the house*)[7]. However, let us make some remarks about the deletion of repeated verbs, for example, in cases such as (:coord-S (:coord-conj *and*) Cl1 Cl2). The deletion of the verb of Cl2 does not depend on the fact that this verb is identical to the verb of Cl1, as shown by *John took an umbrella and Mary (took / *E) a walk*. It depends on the fact that the two 'elementary sentences' (see Section 3.6) underlying Cl1 and Cl2 are identical, which is not the case for *John took an umbrella* and *Mary took a walk:* The latter, but not the former, is constructed with a 'support verb' (Gross, 1981). It also depends on the identity of the syntactic features of the verbs (mood, tense, voice, etc): *John loved Mary and (loves / *E) Sue*. If the two elementary sentences underlying Cl1 and Cl2 are not identical but the syntactic features of their verbs are, any auxiliaries can be deleted: *John was loved by Mary and (was / E) hated by Sue*. However, in French, the deletion of auxiliaries depends not only on the syntactic features of the verbs but also on lexical data, namely the verbs involved. More accurately, it depends on the elementary sentences underlying CL1 and Cl2, since some elementary sentences conjugate in the active voice with the auxiliary *avoir*, others with the auxiliary *être*.

Let us now examine the deletion of repeated subjects. Only coordinations of sentences whose coordinating conjunction is *and* will be treated.

4.3.2 Deletion of repeated subjects in a coordination of clauses

Consider first coordinations in which all of the sentences are clauses:

(:coord-S (:coord-conj *and*) Modifier* Cl1 Cl2 . . . Cln Modifier*)

The [subject] of Cli (i>1) is deleted when it is identical to the [subject] of Cli-1, as illustrated by the following example:

(:coord-S (:coord-conj *and*)
        (:Cl (:subject (HUM1)) *washed the dishes*)   Cl1
        (:Cl (:subject (HUM1)) *cleaned the house*]   Cl2
John washed the dishes and cleaned the house.

in which the subject of Cl2 is deleted. However, this rule does not apply

— if Cli begins with a Modifier:

---

[7]   Other cases of deletion of repeated elements are treated by Pijls & Kempen (1986).

```
(:coord-S  (:coord-conj and)
              (:Cl (:sub to please Mary)                              Cl1
                   (:subject (HUM1)) washed the dishes))
              (:Cl (:sub to please Sue)                               Cl2
                   (:subject (HUM1)) cleaned the house]
```

The [subject] of Cli (when equal to the subject of Cli-1) is then synthesized as a personal pronoun (Danlos, 1987b):

To please Mary, John washed the dishes and to please Sue, (he / *E) cleaned the house

— if Cli-1 ends with a Modifier:

John washed the dishes to please Mary and (he / ?E) cleaned the house to please Sue

— if the [coord-S] is an embedding, i.e. a relative, nominal or subordinate clause.

The following three sentences illustrate, these cases:

```
(:Cl I hate
     (:dir-object (HUM8)
        (:rest-relative
           (:coord-S  (:coord-conj and )
                         (:Cl (:subject (HUM1)) like HUM8)            Cl1
                         (:Cl (:subject (HUM1)) vote for HUM8]        Cl2
I hate the yoyo whom John likes and for whom (he + *E) voted
```

John washed the dishes in order that Mary will be pleased and that (she / *E) will love him

John believes that Mary works and that (she / *E) is happy

In all three examples, the [subject] of the second embedded clause cannot be deleted since it is preceded by a complementizer. It could be deleted if the complementizer were absent, as in:

I like the yoyo for whom John voted and wrote this song

The synthesis of this sentence requires erasing the second complementizer because it is equal to the first one.

As in the other cases where a [subject] is deleted (cf. Sections 3.6 and 4.2.3), the deletion of the [subject] of Cli requires its value and its gender, number and person to be stored beforehand, so as to permit the formation of reflexive pronouns and the correct application of agreement rules. This information about the [subject] of Cli comes from the [subject] of Cli-1.

4.3.3 Deletion of repeated subjects in a coordination of sentences

Consider coordinations of the following form:

(:coord-S (:coord-conj and) Modifier* S1 S2 . . . Sn Modifier*)

The 'first-clause' of a [coord-S] is defined as S1 if S1 is a clause and the first-clause of S1 otherwise. The [subject] of the first-clause of a [coord-S] is never deleted. Let us examine the deletion of the other subjects.

(1) Si is a [Cl], i>1

When the [subject] of Si is equal to the [subject] of Si-1, it is deleted under conditions equivalent to those described in the previous Section, namely if Si does not start with a Modifier, if Si-1 does not end with a Modifier and if the [coord-S] is not an embedding. For example, in the template

```
(:coord-S  (:coord-conj and )
           (:coord-S  (:coord-conj and )                                  S1
                      (:adv TIME1)
                      (:Cl (:subject (HUM0)) washed the dishes )
                      (:Cl (:subject (HUM0)) cleaned the house ))
           (:Cl (:adv TIM2) (:subject (HUM0)) mowed the lawn ]          S2
```

the subject of S2 is equal to the subject of S1, but it is not deleted, because S2 starts with a Modifier:

*Yesterday, John washed the dishes and cleaned the house, and today (he / *E) mowed the lawn*

On the other hand, the subject of the second clause of S1 is deleted, which falls within the next case.

(2) Si is a [coord-S], i≥0

Si = (:coord-S (:coord-conj *and*) Modifier* Si1 Si2 . . . Sin Modifier*)

The subject of the first-clause of Si1 is never deleted. If Si1 is a [coord-S], the deletion of the subjects in this [coord-S] is performed by the recursive process we are describing. The subject of Sij, j>1, is deleted if it is equal to the subject of Si(j-1) with the same constraints as before. For example, in the template

```
(:coord-S  (:coord-conj and )
           (:Cl (:subject (HUM1)) washed the dishes )                   S1
           (:coord-S  (:coord-conj and )                                S2
                      (:Cl (:subject (HUM1)) drank )                     S2-1
                      (:Cl (:subject (HUM1)) slept )                     S2-2
                      (:sub when he had finished ]
```

the subject of the first-clause of S2, i.e. S2-1, is not deleted although it is equal to the subject of S1; the subject of S2-2 is deleted because it is equal to the subject of S2-1:

*John washed the dishes and (he / ?*E) drank and slept when he had finished*

5. CONCLUSION

I implemented a French syntactic component in COMMON LISP[8]. This program is the last module of a generator that produces reports of terrorist crimes in a journalistic style[9]. The CPU time needed to generate a terrorist crime report (30-50 words) from its semantic representation is less than a second. This syntactic component was modified to be used in a Semantic-Representation-to-Speech system, i.e., a system that communicates orally the information given

---

8   This program is running on the VAX-780 of the Centre Mondial de l'Informatique under the VMS operating system. I thank Jean-Daniel Fekete for his invaluable programming advice.

9   An earlier version of this program produces reports in both French and English (Danlos, 1985, 1987). However, this program does not use the more sophisticated syntactic component described here.

in a semantic representation (Danlos, Emerard & Laporte, 1986).[10] This system uses the syntactic information of the templates for both phonetic conversion and prosody.

The syntactic component described in this paper does not handle all the forms of French or English; for example, it does not yet handle imperative, negative or interrogative forms. However, it covers a significant portion of these languages. In particular, it covers the recursive phenomena which are quite similar in French, English and other Romance or Germanic languages. The grammar which has been presented allows (affirmative) sentences with any number of embeddings (i.e. relative, subordinate and nominal clauses) to be generated and takes advantage of the fact that meaning is known in a generation system. French and English differ mainly with respect to the the synthesis of a clause (e.g. agreement rules and reflexive, personal or relative pronouns). An English generator can more or less operate from left to right, which is out of the question for a French generator. French (and other Romance or Germanic languages) involves three orders: (1) the order of the elements in a clause template, (2) the order in which these elements are synthesized, and (3) and the left-to-right order of the synthesized elements in a clause. This difference between English and other languages must be kept in mind to separate rules that apply only to English from rules that apply to all languages.

ACKNOWLEDGMENT

I thank Paul Jacobs, Eric Laporte and Maurice Gross for the fruitful comments they made on this paper.

REFERENCES

Danlos, L. (1985) *Génération automatique de textes en langues naturelles*. Paris: Masson.
Danlos, L. (1987a) *The linguistic basis of text generation*. Cambridge: Cambridge University Press.
Danlos, L. (1987b) *On the use of syntax for pronominalization*. Paper, LADL, Université de Paris 7.
Danlos, L., Emerard, F. & Laporte, E. (1986) Synthesis of Spoken Messages from Semantic Representations (Semantic-Representation-to-Speech-system). In: *Proceedings of COLING86*, Bonn.
Gross, M. (1979) On the failure of generative grammars. *Language, 55*, 859-885.
Gross, M. (1981) Les bases empiriques de la notion de prédicat sémantique. *Language, 63*, 7-52.
Gross, M. (1984) Lexicon grammar and the syntactic analysis of French. In: *Proceedings of COLING84*, Stanford.
Gross, M. (1986) Lexicon Grammar. In: *Proceedings of COLING86*, Bonn.
Harris, Z. (1982) *A grammar of English on Mathematical Principles*. New York: Wiley.
Hirst, G. (1981) Discourse oriented anaphora resolution: A review. *American Journal of Computational Linguistics, 7*, 85-98.
Jacobs, P. (1985) PHRED: a Generator for Natural Language Interfaces. *American Journal of Computational Linguistics, 11*, 219-242.
Kempen, G. (1987) Language Generation Systems. In: Batori, W. Lenders & W. Putschke (Eds.) *Computational Linguistics. An International Handbook on Computer Oriented Language Research and Applications*. Berlin/New York: de Gruyter.
McDonald, D. (1983) Natural Language Generation as a Computational Problem: An Introduction. In: Brady & R. Berwick, (Eds.) *Computational Models of Discourse*. Cambridge, Mass.: MIT Press.
McKeown, K. (1985) *Text Generation*. Cambridge: Cambridge University Press.

---

[10] This work was supported by the Centre National d'Etudes des Télécommunications under contract no. 857B068 with LADL.

Pijls, F. & Kempen, G. (1986) Een psycholinguistisch model van grammatische samentrekking. *Nieuwe Taalgids, 79* , 217-234. (English translation available as a report of the Department of Experimental Psychology, University of Nijmegen, The Netherlands.)

Piot, M. (1978) *Une classification des conjonctions de subordination*. Thèse de 3ème cycle, Université de Paris 7.

Quirk, R., Greenbaum, S., Leech, G. & Svartvik, J. (1985) *A Comprehensive Grammar of the English Language*. London/New York: Longman.

Winograd, T. (1983) *Language as a Cognitive Process: Syntax*. Reading, Mass.: Addison-Wesley.

Chapter 15

KING: A KNOWLEDGE-INTENSIVE NATURAL LANGUAGE GENERATOR

Paul S. Jacobs

ABSTRACT

The principal impediment to the success of most natural language systems is the problem of extending and adapting their capabilities. Language generation programs thus often evidence certain successes but succumb when they are applied to new tasks and domains. The *Ace* knowledge representation is a hierarchical linguistic framework designed to facilitate the interaction between abstract and specialized linguistic knowledge that seems essential in order to achieve this versatility.

A natural language generator called *KING* (Knowledge INtensive Generator) has been designed and implemented to apply the Ace framework to the generation task. The generation process in KING consists of mapping from conceptual relations to linguistic structures, selecting linguistic patterns that realize these structures, and applying constraints to the selected patterns. This model compares favorably with other methods both in the power of the generation mechanism and the ease with which new constructs may be handled by the system.

1. INTRODUCTION

Much of the recent work on language generation (Appelt, 1985; McKeown, 1985; Danlos, 1984; Mann, 1984 and McDonald, 1985) has served to highlight the complexity of the linguistic and conceptual choices involved in the generation process. The traditional what-to-say/how-to-say-it distinction becomes blurred, and the knowledge structures used in each aspect of the process grow more complex. The production of language has emerged as a knowledge-intensive process, an interaction between knowledge about the world and knowledge about language at various levels of abstraction.

Particularly in systems that operate in limited domains, one means of addressing the complexity of the generation task has been through the increased schematization of linguistic knowledge structures. In other words, these pieces of linguistic knowledge incorporate a great deal of syntactic and lexical information in order to simplify the encoding of knowledge and reduce the computation involved in the generation task. For example, the PHRED generator (Jacobs, 1985) used pattern-concept pairs, associating linguistic patterns with conceptual templates, in producing responses for the UNIX Consultant system (Wilensky, Arens & Chin, 1984). A generator called Ana (Kukich, 1983) used schematic knowledge to generate reports on stock market activity. And the TEXT system (McKeown, 1985) used rhetorical schemas at a high level and a functional unification grammar similar to that of PHRED at the tactical level in answering questions about database structures.

A major problem with these knowledge-based approaches has been that the specialized knowledge structures used in generation are really *too* specialized; that is, they fail to embody a general linguistic capability. Thus the systems are difficult to extend within their domains, and fail to adapt well to new domains. As an example of extending the linguistic component of PHRED, for example, the generator had to be able to produce responses such as the following:

— 'Chmod' *gives* you write permission.
— The 'mv' command *takes* two arguments.

PHRED seemed well-equipped to handle phrases like 'write permission', and even the special uses of 'give' and 'take' in the above sentences. The problem was that it was difficult for the expression 'write permission' to have anything to do with the expressions 'read permission' and 'write protection'. Even worse, it was nearly impossible to have the template used to generate the 'give' and 'take' constructs above interact in any way with any more general sense of 'give' or 'take'. Thus if PHRED were to generate the sentence 'You must *give* the "mv" command two arguments', this would be done using an entirely different linguistic template. It was apparent that the linguistic knowledge base and generation mechanism were not flexible enough.

The system designed as an extensible, adaptable replacement for PHRED embodies two elements: a framework for representing knowledge about language, called *Ace* (Jacobs & Rau, 1984; Jacobs, 1986), and a knowledge-intensive generation mechanism called *KING* (*Knowledge INtensive Generator*; Jacobs, 1985). The work suggests that certain features of a knowledge representation, integrated with a knowledge-intensive generator, promote the versatility of the system.

2. SOME FEATURES OF ACE

The Ace framework applies knowledge representation principles from a variety of systems (Wilensky, 1986; Brachman & Schmolze, 1985; Bobrow & Winograd, 1977; Moore & Newell, 1974) to the representation of knowledge about language. Ace is an extension of the KODIAK representation language (Wilensky, 1984, 1986). The main characteristics of Ace are a hierarchical, uniform encoding of both linguistic and conceptual knowledge, and the explicit representation of the relationships that may be used in analyzing or constructing utterances.

2.1. Structured associations

Knowledge structures in the Ace framework are linked together by *structured associations*, explicit relationships between concepts that include correspondences between other related concepts. As an example, the association between the *selling* concept and the action concept is shown in Figure 1. The 'D' link, for *DOMINATE*, roughly analogous to 'a-k-o' or 'isa', indicates that selling is a subcategory of *action*. The 'm' relation, for *MANIFEST*, indicates a role of a concept, for example, that seller is a role of selling. The relation marked 'R-P' designates a *ROLE-PLAY* relation; here, the *seller* of a *selling* action plays the role of *actor*. In the abbreviated notation in the right part of the diagram, the ROLE-PLAY is implicit.

This type of structured association is important for generation because it allows knowledge about expressing *actor* roles to be applied to *seller* roles. On the other hand, there may also be more specific knowledge associated with *selling* and *seller*. The ROLE-PLAY relation is a simple solution to a problem with many feature-based generation systems (Bossie, 1982; Appelt, 1983; Jacobs, 1985): The problem was that linguistic and conceptual attributes, such as *actor* or *protagonist*, *destination*, *subject*, and the like, were treated purely as labels, without regard to the relationships among them. To create a specific role, for example, to correspond to both *recipient* and *destination*, was generally difficult, and relied upon syntactic unification of the various features. In short, structured associations make explicit the relationships among features that are otherwise awkward in such systems.

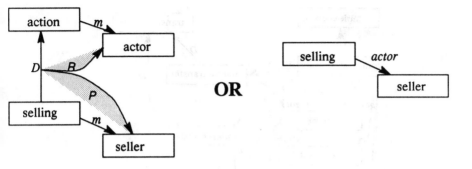

Figure 1. The *selling* action

A more complex but well-motivated example of the use of structured associations is in the representation of the *commercial-transaction* concept, expressed using verbs such as 'buy' and 'sell'. The problem here is to capture both the semantics of the event and the knowledge required to express the event. This knowledge is shown in Figure 2.

The details of the representation in Figure 2 are complex, but the main point is to represent the *commercial-transaction* through two *transfer-events*, *merchandise-transfer* and *tender-transfer*, corresponding to the exchange of merchandise and money. In these events, the *customer*, for example, plays the role of *source* in the *tender-transfer* and the role of *recipient* in the *merchandise-transfer*. The *merchant*, or whoever plays the *merchant* role, plays the role of *source* in the *merchandise-transfer* and *recipient* in the *tender-transfer*. Among the points here are the following:

— *It is no coincidence that the direct object of 'buy' or 'sell' expresses the* merchandise *role, while the direct object of 'pay' expresses the* tender *role.* While both 'sell' and 'pay' may be used indirectly to describe the same event, the choice of direct object is dictated by the fact that 'sell' refers to the transfer of merchandise, while 'pay' refers to the transfer of money. The direct object expresses the role of conceptual *object* of the expressed event.
— *The indirect object of 'sell' or 'pay' is determined by the role of* recipient *in the expressed* transfer-event. Since 'pay' expresses the transfer of money, the *recipient* of this transfer is the *merchant*, while the *recipient* of the *merchandise-transfer* expressed by 'sell' is the *customer*.
— *No special knowledge about 'buy', 'sell', or 'pay' is necessary* . In other words, the above information is not particular to the verbs used, but rather derives from the conceptual roles played in the event expressed.

The use of structured associations to represent a hierarchy of roles is important for generation, because it allows knowledge about expressing general roles, such as *actor* and *recipient*, to be applied in expressing more specific roles, such as *merchant* and *customer*. The next step is to describe how linguistic knowledge is encoded, and then to show how this 'knowledge about expressing' is represented in Ace.

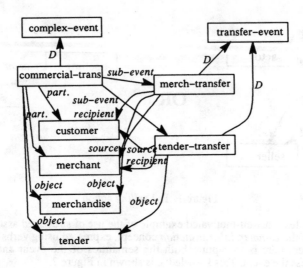

Figure 2. The *commercial-transaction* event

2.2. The Ace linguistic hierarchy

The main characteristics of the linguistic representation of Ace are that linguistic knowledge is encoded using structured associations in much the same way that conceptual knowledge is organized, and that a great deal of the linguistic knowledge of the system is embodied by linguistic relations rather than by patterns or ordering relations.

A piece of the verb phrase hierarchy of Ace is shown in Figure 3. This snapshot of linguistic knowledge about the dative (or ditransitive or double transitive) verb phrase shows how the *verb-indir* relationship between the verb part and indirect object, as well as the *verb-object* relationship between the verb part and the direct object, are distinct from the *dative-vp* pattern; that is, these relationships might be expressed by other patterns as well. Like immediate dominance rules in the ID/LP framework of Generalized Phrase Structure Grammar (Gazdar, Klein, Pullum & Sag, 1985; Gawron, King, Lamping, Loebner, Paulson, Pullum, Sag & Wasow, 1982), linguistic relations in Ace provide a means for expressing linguistic relationships distinctly from constituent order.

The two main advantages of this representation over, for example, the unification-based feature systems mentioned earlier, are that the hierarchy of linguistic knowledge allows these features to be represented at the appropriate level, and that the linguistic relations allow much of the knowledge to be separated from the syntactic or ordering information. Important knowledge about verb phrases, such as the correspondence between the person and number attributes of the verb phrase and those of the verb part, can be encoded at the level of the verb phrase node in the hierarchy. Knowledge about the case of the direct object and the conceptual role that the direct object expresses can be attached to the *verb-object-relation*, rather than to the *dative-vp* and other verb phrase patterns.

Like the use of structured associations for conceptual knowledge, the encoding of linguistic knowledge in this hierarchical form seems to make the representation more parsimonious, as well as suggesting that extension will be easier. The next section shows how relationships between conceptual and linguistic knowledge are represented in Ace.

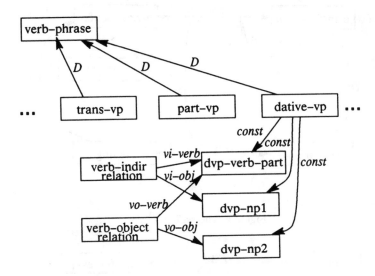

Figure 3. The verb phrase hierarchy of Ace

A piece of the verb phrase hierarchy of Ace is shown in Figure 3.

2.3. Expressive and metaphorical relationships

The discussion of events such as *merchandise-transfer* and *tender-transfer* in section 2.1 neglected the fact that these events have more than one potential *actor*; that is, in order to express any *transfer-event* concept, either the *source* or *recipient* must play an *actor* role. For example, in 'Mary was sold the book by John', John plays the role of *seller* or *actor*, while in 'Mary bought the book from John', Mary plays the *buyer* or *actor* role. In other words, the conceptual role of actor is not entirely determined by the event described, but also by *how* the event is being described. This is an example of what in Ace is known as a *VIEW*.

Buying and selling are two concepts that are VIEWs of the *merchandise-transfer* event. When the event is VIEWed as a *selling*, the role of *seller* corresponds to the *source* of the transfer, or the *merchant* in the *commercial-transaction*. When it is VIEWed as buying, the role of *buyer* corresponds to the *recipient*, or the *customer* of the transaction.

But these VIEWs are simply special cases of the way *transfer-events* in general are expressed. Figure 4 shows the representation of the VIEW relationship between *merchandise-transfer* and *selling*, explicitly shown as a subcategory of the VIEW between *transfer-event* and *giving*. This means that when the *selling* VIEW is used in expressing the event, the role of *source* is played by whatever plays the role of *actor*, or the *seller*. Concepts such as *telling*, *sending*, and *selling* thus all share the same ROLE-PLAYs with the concept *giving*.

Like the structured associations presented in section 2.1, the VIEW association is used to encode important correspondences among conceptual roles that may be used in expressing events. The difference between VIEW and DOMINATE is that a VIEW may be used in describing a concept without asserting that the concept is really an instance of both categories related by the VIEW. This is especially apparent in metaphorical descriptions. For example, when one says 'The command takes three arguments', or 'Andy gave Fergie a kiss', we need not assert that the event being described is a *taking* or a *giving* in order to apply any linguistic knowledge about *taking* or *giving* to the expression. In the latter case, what we have is an example of the VIEW in Figure 5; that is, a *kissing* action is being VIEWed as a *transfer-event*.

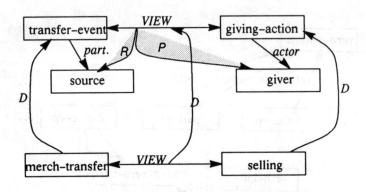

Figure 4. The *selling* VIEW

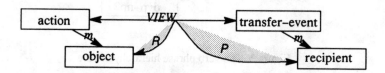

Figure 5. The metaphorical action-as-transfer VIEW

Figure 5 is an example on one type of metaphorical VIEW that may be used in a range of constructs. An obvious problem is how to control the application of such VIEWs, which if used indiscriminantly in generation would result in strange expressions such as 'Fergie took a kiss from Andy' and 'Ali gave Frazier a sock'. This issue is covered in detail (Jacobs, 1985); the two most useful techniques are stringing together sequences of VIEWs in what are called *macro-associations*, and applying certain heuristic constraints to the application of VIEWs.

The VIEW association joins concepts to other concepts that may be used in indirect descriptions. Ace also provides an explicit relationship used to relate linguistic structures, especially linguistic relations, to conceptual structures. This relationship is called *REF*, for 'refer', and is structurally identical to VIEW. An example is given in Figure 6.

The REF association in Figure 6 joins the linguistic relation *verb-indir* to the *transfer-event* concept, incorporating the relationship between the conceptual role of *recipient* and the linguistic role of *indirect-object*. The important point of having such a relation is that it may be applied to expressing specific types of *transfer-events*, as in 'John sold Mary a book', or in expressing other concepts that may be VIEWed as *transfer-events*, as in 'Andy gave Fergie a kiss'.

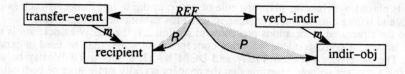

Figure 6. A REF association

Figure 7 shows a segment of an Ace knowledge base including knowledge about several types of *transfer-events*, expressed using verbs such as 'tell', 'send', and 'give'. The node *g-*

transfer-event, for 'generalized transfer event', represents a concept that includes transfers of possession as well as physical transfer. The linguistic *to-pmod* relation designates the relation between a verb or nominalization and an adverbial or postnominal prepositional phrase with the preposition 'to'. This relation may be expressed in a range of constructs from 'sent the book to John' and 'giving a kiss to Fergie' to 'the sale of the book to Bill'. Notice that the role of *destination* expressed by this relation is more general than the role of recipient expressed by the indirect object: A *recipient* must at least be a participant in the event. This helps to explain examples such as Langacker's (1986), which show that 'Reagan sent a Walrus to Antarctica' is a valid construct while 'Reagan sent Antarctica a Walrus' is not: Presumably, Antarctica does not make a good *recipient* but does make a good *destination*.

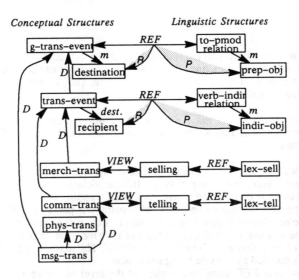

Figure 7. Putting it all together

The result of the Ace framework described here is to distribute knowledge about language across a hierarchy of linguistic and conceptual information. This has a good flavor from the standpoint of parsimony and extensibility, but casts doubt about the control of the mechanism that must apply this knowledge to the generation task. The important features of one such mechanism are described in the next section.

3. THE KING GENERATOR

The KING generator is designed to accomplish the grammatical realization of utterances using a knowledge-intensive, incremental mechanism; that is, building a complete linguistic structure by combining bits and pieces of appropriate structure. Since the overall effect of Ace is to distribute the essential knowledge, the generation mechanism must do a great deal of knowledge manipulation and combination. The main idea for KING's design was to use the structure of the knowledge as much as possible, and to make the most of simple heuristics for control.

The process of constructing an utterance in KING may be broken down into three basic phases: *Mapping* is the process of retrieving and applying structured associations that relate the concept to be expressed to other conceptual structures and ultimately to linguistic structures. *Pattern selection* is the task of accessing templates specifying linguistic patterns from the knowledge base of the system, and of selecting the pattern that best fits the input constraints and the structures derived from mapping. *Restriction* consists of applying a set of constraints to a selected pattern, thereby producing a pattern whose constituents are further specified using the constraints that have led to the selection of the pattern.

As an example, consider the generation of the sentence, 'Andy gave Fergie a kiss'. Mapping consists of applying VIEW associations to produce the *transfer-event* and *giving* concepts with the appropriate roles, then REF associations to instantiate linguistic relations such as *subject-predicate*, *verb-indir*, and *verb-object*. Pattern selection includes the choice of the basic sentence and *dative-vp* pattern. Restriction fills out the constituents of the selected patterns, including constraints such as the person, number, and voice of the verb.

The details of the generation process and the principles used to select structured associations are described in Jacobs (1985). The discussion here will present a sketch of each aspect of the process and a synopsis of the heuristics that guide the generator.

3.1. Mapping

A conceptual structure to be expressed may be directly or indirectly associated with a range of other conceptual or linguistic structures. The mapping process must choose a path that results in a linguistic structure and fill out the roles of that structure. The guiding rules of this mechanism may be summarized as follows:

> *Synopsis: Apply the most specific associations that result in valid structures, and instantiate the most specific valid roles of those structures.*

Figure 8 shows the sequence of mappings that are applied at the top level in the expression 'Andy gave Fergie a kiss', consisting of two VIEW associations and a REF association. The generation mechanism is constrained to use 'give' once it applies the first VIEW, but the choice of active versus passive is arbitrary unless some constraint is passed to KING.

The node labeled *giver* in Figure 8 indicates that it is the *role* of *giver* itself that plays the role of *predicate* in the relation, rather than the player of the *giver* role. In other words, a verb phrase expresses a role of an action as well as the action itself. The reason for this is that the voice of the verb phrase is dictated by the role being expressed.

Figure 9 shows the REF mappings applied at the level of the verb phrase 'gave Fergie a kiss'. The *giver* role, because it is an actor role, maps into the voice active constraint, while REF associations applied to the giving action produce the instantiated *verb-indir* and *verb-object* relations.

The important feature of the mapping process in KING is how little of the knowledge used is particular to the concept being expressed. Except for lexical constraints such as those that guide the selection of 'give' and 'kiss', the knowledge structures that guide the mapping mechanism all derive from fairly abstract levels in the hierarchy. This contrasts with the application of a functional unification grammar template, in which a set of features in the grammar are unified with the specific features of the input. Also in contrast with FUG is the knowledge-driven aspect of the KING mapping mechanism, which works essentially independently of the grammar. The patterns of the grammar are applied only after mapping, in the pattern selection phase, described in the next section.

3.2. Pattern Selection

Since a great many linguistic choices are essentially predetermined by the mapping process, the principal job of pattern selection is to find a pattern that realizes the linguistic structures produced by mapping. This may be stated as follows:

> *Synopsis: find a pattern that subsumes as many relations as possible without violating any constraints.*

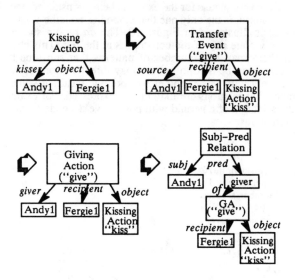

Figure 8. Mapping across VIEWs and REFs

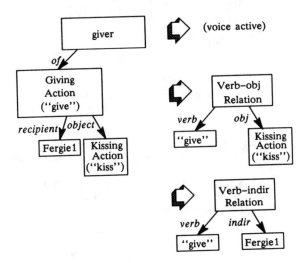

Figure 9. Mapping across REF associations

In the selection of the verb phrase for the example being considered, the choice of the dative verb phrase is easy because it is the only one that embodies both the *verb-indir* and *verb-object* relations. This choice is illustrated in Figure 10. The *dative-vp* shown expresses the two relations and does not violate any of the constraints at the left. This choice is not always so straightforward, as there may be a number of patterns that subsume the same number of relations, and in fact, it may be that no pattern may directly expresses any relations. KING seems to deal effectively with this problem by 'looking ahead' at some constituents of the patterns to determine what relations are likely to be expressed. For example, in 'John's being kissed by Mary', the selection of a gerund with possessive depends on the realization that this pattern includes a verb phrase.

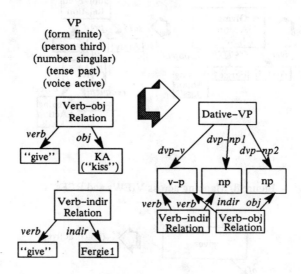

Figure 10. Pattern Selection

The pattern selection process in KING introduces a certain degree of complexity into the system, but, because a great deal of information is contained in relations rather than patterns, the consideration of large numbers of worthless patterns is rare. Furthermore, the design of the knowledge base keeps the grammar small, which keeps the pattern selection process under control.

The selection of a pattern is followed by the process of restriction, which simply instantiates the pattern and customizes it according to the constraints and relations derived from mapping. This process is described in the next section.

3.3. Restriction

Restriction is the process of applying constraints to a selected pattern, matching it with the relations it is to subsume and preparing the constituents of the pattern for completion. This role is often played by unification in systems such as those of Appelt (1983) and McKeown (1985). This may be summarized as follows:

> *Synopsis: Check each relation and constraint, and assign each constraint to the appropriate constituent of the pattern.*

In PHRED the restriction process was divided into three components: unification, which matched the attributes of the input to the features of a pattern template, *elaboration*, which added constraints to individual constituents of the pattern, and *combination*, used to combine ordering patterns with flexible-order patterns. Restriction in KING uses a simpler mechanism. Unification is avoided by applying simpler checks to perform constraint matching. As in PHRED, the system depends on the pattern selection mechanism to ensure that constraints are satisfied. Elaboration makes use of ROLE-PLAY relationships rather than variable binding. For example, attributes such as person, number, tense, and form are used to specify constraints on verbs, and they may be grouped into a common category, *verb-constraint*. Associated with verb-phrase constructs, then, is a ROLE-PLAY which indicates that all *verb-constraints* are constraints on the *verb-part* constituent of the verb phrase construct. This knowledge is then inherited by all verb phrase constructs. Figure 11 illustrates the input and result of the restriction process in the generation of the verb phrase 'gave Fergie a kiss'.

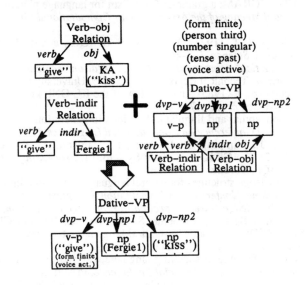

Figure 11. Restriction

This section has presented an overview of the process by which KING constructs an utterance. Because structured associations are applied repeatedly to a concept to derive linguistic structures, a variety of loosely related concepts may be described using the same linguistic knowledge. In this way 'gave Mary a hug' and 'sold John the book' may be realized using the same knowledge about dative verb phrases.

4. CONCLUSION

A major problem in knowledge-based generation systems is the design of a knowledge base and generation mechanism that facilitate extensibility. The Ace representation promotes extensibility by organizing knowledge about linguistic expression into a hierarchy of structured associations. This representation supports the interaction of general and specialized knowledge about language and thereby broadens the applicability of the generation mechanism.

ACKNOWLEDGEMENTS

This paper is based on the thesis research conducted while the author was at the University of California, Berkeley. The research was supported in part by the Office of Naval Research under contract N00014-80-C-0732, the National Science Foundation under grants IST-8007045 and IST-8208602, and the Defense Advanced Research Projects Agency (DOD), ARPA Order No. 3041, Monitored by the Naval Electronic Systems Command under contract N00039-82-C-0235.

REFERENCES

Appelt, D. (1985) *Planning English Sentences*. Cambridge: Cambridge University Press.

Appelt, D. (1983) TELEGRAM: a grammar formalism for language planning. In: *Proceedings of the 21st Annual Meeting of the Association for Computational Linguistics* . Cambridge, Massachusetts.

Bobrow, D. & Winograd, T. (1977) An overview of KRL, a knowledge representation language. *Cognitive Science, 1*, 3-46.

Bossie, S. (1981) *A tactical component for text generation: sentence generation using a functional grammar*. Technical Report MS-CIS-81-5, University of Pennsylvania.

Brachman, R. & Schmolze, J. (1985) An overwiew of the KL-ONE knowledge representation system. *Cognitive Science, 9*, 171-216.

Danlos, L. (1984) Conceptual and linguistic decisions in generation. In: *Proceedings of the Tenth International Conference on Computational Linguistics*. (COLING'84), Stanford.

Gawron, J.M., King, J., Lamping, J., Loebner, E., Paulson, A., Pullum, G., Sag, I. & Wasow, T. (1982) The GPSG Linguistic System. In: *Proceedings of the 20th Annual Meeting of the ACL*. Toronto.

Jacobs, P. (1986) Knowledge structures for natural language generation. In: *Proceedings of the Eleventh International Conference on Computational Linguistics*. Bonn, Germany.

Jacobs, P. (1985) *A Knowledge-Based Approach to Language Production*. PhD thesis, University of California, Berkeley. Computer Science Division Report UCB/CSD86/254.

Jacobs, P. (1985) PHRED: a generator for natural language interfaces. *American Journal of Computational Linguistics, 11*, 219-242.

Jacobs, P. & Rau, L. (1984) Ace: associating language with meaning. In: *Proceedings of the Sixth European Conference on Artificial Intelligence*. Pisa, Italy.

Kukich, K. (1983) *Knowledge-Based Report Generation: A Knowledge-Engineering Approach to Natural Language Report Generation*. PhD thesis, University of Pittsburgh.

Langacker, R. (1986) An introduction to cognitive grammar. *Cognitive Science, 10*, 1-40.

Mann, W. (1984) *Discourse Structures for Text Generation*. Technical Report ISI/RR-84-127. University of Southern California, ISI.

McDonald, D. & Pustejovsky, J. (1985) Description-directed natural language generation. In: *Proceedings of the Ninth International Joint Conference on Artificial Intelligence*. Los Angeles, California.

McKeown, K. (1985) *Text Generation: Using Discourse Strategies and Focus Constraints to Generate Natural Language Text*. Cambridge: Cambridge University Press.

Moore, J. & Newell, A. (1974) How can MERLIN understand? In: L. Gregg, (Ed.) *Knowledge and Cognition*. Erlbaum: Halsted, New Jersey.

Wilensky, R. (1984) KODIAK — a knowledge representation language. In: *Proceedings of the Sixth Annual Conference of the Cognitive Science Society*. Boulder, Colorado.

Wilensky, R., Arens, Y. & Chin, D. (1984) Talking to UNIX in English: an overview of UC. *Communications of the ACM, 27*, 574-593.

PART IV

Grammars and Grammatical Formalisms

THE RELEVANCE OF TREE ADJOINING GRAMMAR TO GENERATION

Aravind K. Joshi

ABSTRACT

Grammatical formalisms can be viewed as neutral with respect to comprehension or generation, or they can be investigated from the point of view of their suitability for comprehension or generation. Tree Adjoining Grammars (TAG) is a formalism that factors recursion and dependencies in a special way, leading to a kind of locality and the possibility of incremental generation. We will examine the relevance of these properties from the point of view of sentence generation.

1. INTRODUCTION

Grammatical formalisms can be viewed as neutral with respect to comprehension or generation, or they can be investigated from the point of view of their suitability for comprehension and generation. Tree Adjoining Grammars (TAG) is a formalism that factors recursion and dependencies in a special way, leading to a locality that is different from the CFG based grammatical systems. We will first briefly describe the TAG formalism and then give several linguistic examples to show how the formalism works. McDonald & Pustejovsky (1985) have discussed TAG as a grammatical formalism for generation. In this paper, we will examine several properties of TAG from the point of view of generation. In particular, we will discuss the locality of dependencies, the structure of elementary trees, the representations provided by TAG, and the elementary structures (a generalization of the elementary trees) for dealing with the phenomenon of word order variation. We will show how TAG can serve as a flexible interface between the planner and the grammatical component of the generation system.

2. A SHORT DESCRIPTION OF TREE ADJOINING GRAMMARS

The main characteristics of TAG's are as follows.
1. TAG is a tree generating system. It consists of a finite set of elementary trees (elaborated up to preterminal (terminal) symbols) and a composition operation (adjoining) which builds trees out of elementary trees and trees derived from elementary trees by adjoining. The terminal strings of a TAG constitute a string language. However, a TAG should be viewed primarily as a tree generating system in contrast to a string generating system such as a context-free grammar or some of its extensions.
2. TAG's factor recursion and dependencies in a novel way. The elementary trees are the domain of dependencies which are statable as co-occurence relations among the elements of the elementary trees and also relations between elementary trees. Recursion enters via the operation of adjoining. Adjoining preserves the dependencies. Localization of dependencies

in this manner has both mathematical and linguistic significance. Such localization cannot be achieved directly in a string generating system.

3. TAG's are more powerful than context-free grammars, but only 'mildly' so. This extra power of TAG is a direct corollary of the way TAG factors recursion and dependencies.

2.1 Tree adjoining grammar formalism

A *tree adjoining grammar* G = (I, A) where I and A are finite sets of *elementary trees*. The trees in I will be called the *initial trees* and the trees in A, the *auxiliary trees*. A tree α is an initial tree if it is of the form in (1).

(1) $\alpha = S$

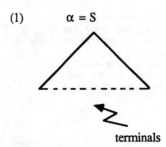

terminals

That is, the root node of α is labelled S and the frontier nodes are all terminals. A tree β is an auxiliary tree if it is of the form in (2).

(2) $\beta = X$

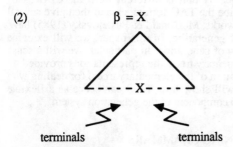

terminals   terminals

The root node of β is labelled X where X is a non-terminal and the frontier nodes are all terminals except one which is labelled X, the same label as that of the root. The node labelled X on the frontier will be called the 'foot node' of β. The internal nodes are non-terminals. The initial and the auxiliary trees are not constrained in any manner other than as indicated above. The idea, however, is that both the initial and auxiliary trees will be *minimal* in some sense. An initial tree will correspond to a *minimal* sentential tree (i.e., without recursing on any non-terminal) and an auxiliary tree, with root and foot node labelled X, will correspond to a *minimal* recursive structure that must be brought into the derivation, if one recurses on X.

We will now define a composition operation called *adjoining* (or *adjunction*), which composes an auxiliary tree β with a tree γ. Let γ be a tree containing a node n bearing the label X and let β be an auxiliary tree whose root node is also labelled X. (Note that β must have, by definition, a node (and only one such) labelled X on the frontier.) Then the adjunction of β to γ at node n will be the tree γ' that results when the following complex operation is carried out:

1) The sub-tree of γ dominated by n, call it t, is excised, leaving a copy of n behind;

2) The auxiliary tree β is attached at n and its root node is identified with n;

3) The sub-tree t is attached to the foot node of β and the root node n of t is identified with the foot node of β.

Figure 1 illustrates this operation.

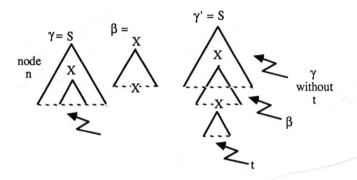

Figure 1

The intuition underlying the adjoining operation is a simple one, but the operation is distinct from other operations on trees that have been discussed in the literature. In particular, we want to emphasize that adjoining is not a substitution operation[1]. Strictly speaking adjoining is an operation defined between an elementary tree γ and an auxiliary tree (β) which is adjoined to γ at an address n in γ. See section 2.4 for a discussion of a derivation structure.

Let us now define two auxiliary notions: the tree set of a TAG grammar and the string language of a TAG. Suppose G=(I, A) is a TAG with a finite set of initial trees, a finite set of auxiliary trees, and the *adjoining* operation, as above. Then we define the *tree set* of a TAG G, T(G), to be the set of all trees derived in G starting from initial trees in I. We further define the *string language* (or *language*) of G to be the set of all terminal strings of the trees in T(G). TAG's are strictly more powerful than CFG's, but this extra power is limited: it appears to be just adequate to provide appropriate structural descriptions and capture certain non context-free aspects of language structure. For further details see Joshi (1983, 1985).

EXAMPLE 2.1: LET G = (I, A) where

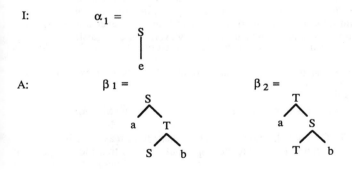

---

[1] Adjoining reduces to substitution only in the special case where an auxiliary tree adjoins to the root node of another tree so that it 'sits on top of' the tree to which it is adjoined. In this special case the adjoining operation has the same effect as would the substitution of a tree at its root node for the foot node of the auxiliary tree.

The language generated by G is context-free; but there is no CFG that is strongly equivalent to G. We can see this if we examine some derivations in G. Thus, consider the following trees:

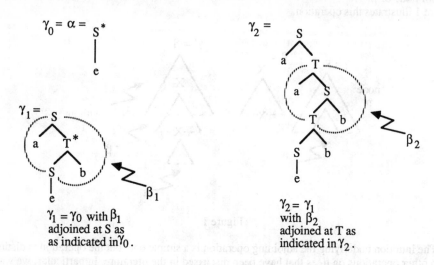

$\gamma_0 = \alpha =$

$\gamma_1 =$

$\gamma_1 = \gamma_0$ with β_1
adjoined at S as
as indicated in γ_0.

$\gamma_2 =$

$\gamma_2 = \gamma_1$
with β_2
adjoined at T as
indicated in γ_2.

Clearly, L(G) is $\{a^n e\, b^n\, /\, n \geq 0\}$, which is a context-free language. Thus, there must exist a context-free grammar, G', which is at least weakly equivalent to G. It can be shown however, that there is no context-free grammar G' which is strongly equivalent to G; i.e., for which T(G) = T(G'). *Thus a TAG may generate a context-free language, yet assign structural descriptions to the strings that cannot be assigned by any context-free grammar*. It can be shown also that TAG's can generate strictly context-sensitive languages (Joshi, 1985).

Although TAG's are more powerful than CFG's, this extra power is highly constrained and apparently it is just the right kind for characterizing certain structural descriptions (see Joshi, 1985, for further details).

2.2 TAG's with 'links'

In principle, any two nodes in an elementary tree are 'related' simply by virtue of the fact that they belong to the same elementary tree and this relationship will be symmetrical. 'Linking' is an asymmetrical relation introduced primarily to characterize filler-gap dependencies. Linking can be defined for any two nodes in an elementary tree. However, in the linguistic context we will require the following conditions to hold for a link in an elementary tree. If a node n_1 is linked to a node n_2 then

(1) n_2 c-commands n_1, (i.e., n_2 does not dominate n_1 and there exists a node m which immediately dominates n_2 and also dominates n_1);
(2) n_1 and n_2 have the same label;
(3) n_1 dominates a null string (or a terminal symbol in the non-linguistic formal grammar examples).

A TAG with links is a TAG in which some of the elementary trees may have links. Links are defined on the elementary trees. However, the important point is that the composition operation of adjoining will *preserve* the links. Links defined on the elementary trees may become *stretched* as the derivation proceeds (see Section 2.5 below).

2.3 TAG's with local constraints on adjoining

The adjoining operation as defined in Section 2.1 is 'context-free'. An auxiliary tree β is adjoinable to a tree t at a node n if the label of node n is X, independently of the (tree) context around n. In this sense, adjoining is context-free.

A *TAG with local constraints* is defined as follows. G = (I, A) is a TAG with local constraints if for each node n, in each tree t, one (and only one) of the following constraints is specified:

(1) *Selective Adjoining (SA)*: Only a specified subset of the set of all auxiliary trees are adjoinable at n. SA is written as (β), where β is a subset of the set of all auxiliary trees structurally adjoinable at n. If β equals the set of all auxiliary trees adjoinable at n, then we do not explicitly state this at the node n.

(2) *Null Adjoining (NA)*: No auxiliary tree is adjoinable at the node N. NA will be written as (ø). This is a special case of SA.

(3) *Obligatory Adjoining (OA)*: At least one (out of all the auxiliary trees adjoinable at n) must be adjoined at n. OA is written as O(β) where β is a subset of the set of all auxiliary trees adjoinable at n.

It is necessary to modify our definition of adjoining to take care of the local constraints. We will not give the details here. Basically, what we require is that the constraints on the auxiliary tree at the root and the foot nodes supersede the constraints at the node where adjunction is made.

2.4 Derivation in a TAG

Although we shall not describe formally the notion of derivation in a TAG, we want to give the reader a more precise understanding of the concept than (s)he might form from our illustrative example. Adjoining is an operation defined on an elementary tree, say γ, an auxiliary tree, say β, and a node (i.e., an address) in γ, say n. Thus, every instance of adjunction is of the form 'β is adjoined to γ at n', and this adjunction is always and only subject to the local constraints associated with n. Although we very often speak of adjoining a tree to a node in a complex structure, we do so only for convenience. Strictly speaking, adjoining is always at a node in an elementary tree; and, therefore, it is more precise to talk about adjoining at an address in an elementary tree. More than one auxiliary tree can be adjoined to an elementary tree as long as each tree is adjoined at a distinct node. After all these auxiliary trees are adjoined to the elementary tree, only nodes in the auxiliary trees are available for further adjunction.

Now suppose that α is an initial tree and that $β_1$, $β_2$,... are auxiliary trees in a TAG, G. Then the derivation structure corresponding to the generation of a particular tree and the correspondence string in L(G) will look as follows:

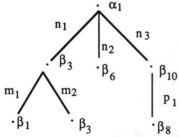

$α_1$ is an initial tree. $β_3$, $β_6$ and $β_{10}$ are adjoined at nodes n_1, n_2, and n_3 respectively in $α_1$, where n_1, n_2, and n_3 are all distinct nodes. $β_1$ and $β_3$ are adjoined to $β_3$ at nodes m_1 and m_2 respectively. Again, m_1 and m_2 are distinct. $β_6$ has no further adjunctions but $β_8$ is adjoined to $β_{10}$ at node p_1. This is a top-down derivation; a bottom-up derivation can be defined also and it is more appropriate for the multicomponent adjunction discussed in Kroch & Joshi (in press, b). Note that the derivation structure D implicitly characterizes the 'surface' tree that is generated by it. D also serves as the basis for defining a compositional semantic interpretation (Vijay-Shanker, 1986). In this way the derivation structure can be seen as the basic formal object constructed in the course of sentence generation. Associated with it will be two mappings, one to a surface syntactic tree and the other to a semantic interpretation, as below:

surface tree <---- derivation structure ----> semantic interpretation

2.5 Some linguistic examples

We will give some simple linguistic examples that illustrate the applicability of the TAG formalism to the description of natural language phenomena. Many details which do not serve the purpose of illustration have been ignored or simplified.

Let G = (I, A) be a TAG where I is the set of initial trees and A is the set of auxiliary trees. We will list only some of the trees in I and A, those relevant to the derivation of our illustrative sentences. Rather than introduce all these trees at once, we shall introduce them as necessary.

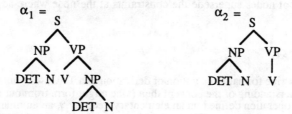

Tree α_1 corresponds to a 'minimal sentence' with a transitive verb, as in (1); and α_2 corresponds to a minimal sentence with an intransitive verb, as in (2):

    (1) The man met the woman.
    (2) The man fell.

Initial trees as we have defined them require terminal symbols on the frontier. In the linguistic context, the nodes on the frontier will be preterminal lexical category symbols such as N, V, A, P, DET, etc. The lexical items are inserted for each of the preterminal symbols as each elementary tree enters the derivation. Thus, we generate the sentence in (1) by performing lexical insertion on α_1, yielding:

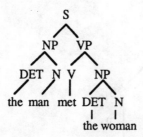

As we continue the derivation by selecting auxiliary trees and adjoining them appropriately, we follow the same convention, i.e., as each elementary tree is chosen, we make the lexical insertions. Thus in a derivation in a TAG, lexical insertion goes hand in hand with the derivation. Each step in the derivation selects an elementary tree together with a set of appropriate lexical items. Note that as we select the lexical items for each elementary tree we can check a variety of constraints, e.g., agreement and subcategorization constraints on the set of lexical items. Thus, for example, (1) and (2) will not be permitted:

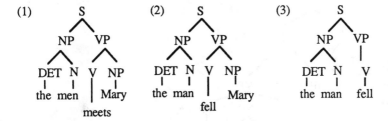

In (1) number agreement has been violated and in (2) the intransitive verb *fell* has been inserted into a transitive verb phrase. These constraints can be checked easily because the entire elementary tree that is the domain of the constraints is available as a single unit at each step in the derivation. If we had started with the initial tree α_2 then the choice of the intransitive verb would be permitted, yielding the well-formed tree in (3). When an auxiliary tree enters the derivation, similar considerations hold. In addition, further constraints, both contextual and lexical, can be checked by means of local constraints, which will be illustrated later.

As the reader will have noted, we require different initial trees for the sentences *John fell* and *the man fell* because the expansion of NP is different in the two cases. Since the structure of these two sentences is otherwise identical, we cannot be content with a linguistic theory that treats the two sentences as unrelated. In a fully articulated theory of grammar employing the TAG formalism, the relationships among initial trees is expressed in an independent module of the grammar that specified the constraints on possible elementary (initial or auxiliary) trees. These constraints might be expressed in a number of alternative ways; for example as a set of rules for the projection of syntactic structure from lexical heads, perhaps incorporating features of categorial grammar. We might even provide schemata or rules for obtaining some elementary structures from others. In any case, the rules will be abbreviatory, in the sense that they will generate only a finite set of trees and so will not affect the formal power of the TAG. The most important point regarding the source of elementary trees is that using the TAG formalism allows us to treat as orthogonal the principles governing the construction of minimal syntactic units and those governing the composition of these units into complex structures.

Linked trees can be used to represent so-called 'unbounded' dependencies like topicalization and *wh*-constructions. In (4) we give a possible topicalized structure, and in (5)-(6) we give two *wh*-questions (In this paper we use coindexing to indicate a linking relation between nodes. Since in the linguistic case the link mother node is always an empty category, the coindexing notation is adequate.) In (4) we have shown a link from the lower PP node to a higher PP node. When the lexical items below the tree are inserted for the preterminal nodes in α_3, we can check not only that a verb requiring an NP and a PP has been inserted, but also that the preposition P is *to* as required by the verb *give*.

Thus far, all of the initial trees that we have defined correspond to 'minimal' root sentences. We now introduce, in (7) below, some initial trees which are minimal but do not give root sentences. The motivation for introducing these trees will be clear from the examples and the subsequent use of these trees in derivations. Since these trees are not possible root sentences, it is necessary that they undergo at least one adjunction (of a specific type) and the resulting tree becomes a possible independent sentence. This requirement can be very easily stated as a local constraint.

(4) $\alpha_3 =$

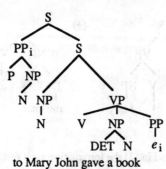

to Mary John gave a book

(5) $\alpha_4 =$ (6) $\alpha_5 =$

who met Mary   who did John meet

(7) $\alpha_6 =$ $\alpha_7 =$

PRO to invite Mary   who PRO to invite

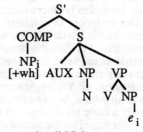

Tree α_6 will be used in the derivation of sentences like (3) and (4).

(3) John persuaded Bill PRO to invite Mary.

(4) John tried PRO to invite Mary.

α_7 will be used in deriving sentences like (5).

(5) Who did John try to invite?

In (8) we introduce auxiliary trees that will adjoin to the above infinitival initial trees to produce complete independent sentences. The reader can easily check that the sentences of (3) - (5) will be derived if the appropriate auxiliary trees listed as satisfying the obligatory adjoining constraint are adjoined at the starred nodes of the initial trees in (7).

Now let us introduce some auxiliary trees that will allow us to generate sentences with relative clauses: see (9).

(8)

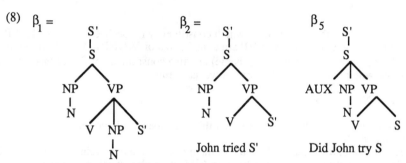

(9)

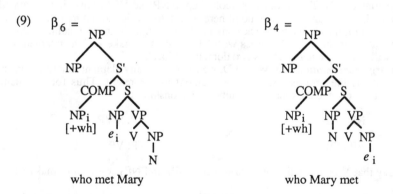

Tree β_4 can be used to build sentences with subject relatives, as in (6); and β_5 can be used to build sentences with object relatives, as in (7).

(6) The boy who met Mary left.

(7) The boy who Mary met left.

As in the case of initial trees, we see here explicitly that some auxiliary trees will have to be related to simpler structures by a theory that constrains the form of elementary trees.

3.   PROPERTIES RELEVANT TO GENERATION

3.1 Domains of locality

Each grammatical formalism can be characterized by a domain of locality. Different grammatical formalisms can be compared from the point of view of generation by examining how certain specific aspects of grammar (to be discussed below) are expressible with respect to the corresponding domain of locality. Let us first consider CFG. Let G be a CFG with the rules

(1) S —> NP VP (2) VP —> V NP (3) NP —> N

Each rule in a CFG is a domain of locality (D) in the following sense. Consider

(1) S —> NP VP

1. *Constituency*: D is the domain over which constituency is specified. Thus in (1), NP and VP are constituents of S. In (2) V and VP are constituents of VP. NP_1, V, NP_2 (indexing of NP's is for the purpose of distinguishing theme) are also constituents of S, but this statement cannot be made with respect to D. Of course, if we had a rule

S —> NP V NP

then such a statement could be made, but then this rule does not have the same information which is in (1) and (2).

2. *Constraints (e.g. agreement)*: D is the domain over which constraints can be specified. For example, the constraint that VP agrees with NP (say, with respect to *Number*) is statable (and has to be stated) at D. The appropriate *Number* information has to percolate up to a level such that it is available in D. Thus it has to percolate up to NP and VP because in (1) both NP and VP are sisters, i.e., they are in D. The point here is that the particular nature of D specifies the flow of information necessary to check constraints. Constraints are checkable within D. Note that if we wanted to state that V agrees with NP, we cannot make such a statement with respect to D, it will have to be made across two domains of locality.

3. *Function-argument relationship*: Within D, we can choose any element as a function and the other elements as the arguments, and one element as the result. Thus for (1), using categorial notation, we encode the function-argument relationship as

NP : NP		NP: S/VP
	or	
VP : S\NP		VP: VP

If we want to say that V is a function with arguments NP_1 and NP_2, we cannot make such a statement in D.

4. *Word-order*: D is the domain over which word order variations can be specified. In (1), we have implicitly specified an order, namely, NP precedes VP. We could specify word-order variations (following the ID/LP format; Gazdar, Klein, Pullum, and Sag, 1985; Pullum, 1983) by specifying only the ID (immediate domination) in D and then a set of LP (linear precedence) statements. Although the LP statements appear separately, the domain of applicability of the LP statements is D. Thus the only order variations that can be specified are those which are definable over D. Hence, given

(1') S —> NP, VP
(2') V —> V, NP

we can get the following sequence

(4) NP_1 V NP_2 (5) NP_1 NP_2 V
(6) V NP_2 NP_1 (7) NP_2 V NP_1

but not

(8) V NP_1 NP_2 (9) NP_2 NP_1 V

5. *Unifications*: D is the domain for specifying 'unifications', i.e., a set of constraints that hold across a set of feature structures (Shieber, 1986). Thus a rule schema in D of the form

(10) $X_0 \longrightarrow X_1 X_2$

serves as the domain for specifying unifications across a set of feature structures, F_0, F_1, F_2, associated with X_0, X_1, X_2, respectively. Thus, for example, we may specify the unification as follows

(11) F_0 <CAT> = S   (12) F_1 <CAT> = NP
(13) F_2 <CAT> = VP   (14) F_0 <HEAD> = F_2 <HEAD>, etc.

These unifications correspond to

(1) S $\longrightarrow$ NP VP

which serves as the domain over which the unifications are specified.
We will briefly examine different grammatical formalisms with respect to the above five aspects (constituency, constraints, function-argument relationship, word-order and unifications) in terms of the corresponding domains of locality.
Instead of (1)

(1) S $\longrightarrow$ NP VP

we can describe the domain of locality for CFG in terms of a local tree (2)

(2)

and the grammatical formalism can be described in terms such local trees (e.g., GPSG). The discussion we have provided for the domain of locality holds equally well for domain specified in terms of local trees.
In a Unification Grammar (UG), as we have stated before, the domain of locality is exactly the same as in a CFG, as the unifications are defined over this domain. So the discussion about the five aspects considered for CFG carries over to UG. By UG we mean the grammatical formalism defined by Shieber (1986) which has a context-free skeleton. Functional Unification Grammar (FUG) has a larger domain of locality, more like TAG. The generation systems described by Appelt (1983, 1985) and McKeown (1985) incorporate FUG.
The domain of locality in a Head Driven-Phrase Structure Grammar (HPSG) or Categorial Grammar (CG) are more structured than the domain of locality for CFG. For example, in a CG, although 'function application' can be regarded as a rewriting rule, the category symbols can encode more structure than the nonterminals in a CFG. Thus, the category assigned to a transitive verb can be

(5) (S\NP)/NP

which encodes the entire argument structure. Such structured domains of locality have important consequences for the five aspects we have considered before. Some of these consequences are similar to those for TAG, which we will now discuss. In a TAG the elementary trees, initial and auxiliary, are the domains of locality. Thus, for example, the initial tree

$$\alpha =$$

is one element in the domain of locality, D. (For convenience, we will treat NP as preterminals. Strictly speaking, each elementary tree is elaborated up to preterminals (terminals).) The auxiliary trees β_1 and β_2 below are also elements of D.

$$\beta_1 =$$

$$\beta_2 =$$

Let us consider α.

$$\alpha =$$

(indexing is for convenience only)

1. *Constituency*: α defines an elementary constituency domain (elementary domination domain). NP, VP are constituents of S, V, NP are constituents of VP, and NP_1, V, NP_2, are constituents of S.

2. *Constraints*: Any complex predicate P can be defined over any set of nodes in an elementary tree. The domain of P is localized to α. For example, number agreement can be defined between NP_1 and V, if we wanted to do so.

3. *Function-argument relationshiop*: We can regard V as the function with NP_1 and NP_2 as arguments, i.e., the entire argument structure is in D.

4. *Word-order*: α is an element of D and it defines the domination domain. If α is a tree, then the conventional tree ordering is implied. But we can regard α as defining only the

constituency domain and then linear precedences can be defined over this domain. We will pursue this point in considerable detail in Section 4.

5. *Unifications*: Unifications can be defined over an element of D, say α, for example. That is, unifications are defined across feature structures associated with the nodes of α. This permits constrained flow of information for feature checking. We will not pursue this point in this paper.

3.2 Structure of elementary trees

Besides the formal characterization of elementary trees given in Section 2, the elementary trees obey the following linguistic constraints. Each elementary tree consists of a predicate plus the heads of all its arguments. The initial trees roughly correspond to simple sentences (simple propositions) and the auxiliary trees correspond to minimal recursive or iterative constructions. Auxiliary trees have the structure of *modifers* and *complements*.

The composition operation of *adjoining* preserves all the dependencies defined in the elementary trees. The dependencies may become long distance, but this is only a corollary of the adjoining operation. The adjoining operation also preserves the argument structure, i.e., the predicate argument structure is not disturbed by adjoining. This preservation of argument structure is to be understood as preserving the structure at the level of the predicate and the heads of the arguments. Thus in an initial tree corresponding to (1)

(1) The man fell

the man is an argument (subject argument) of *fell* and both appear in the same elementary tree. Now if we adjoin an auxiliary tree (2) corresponding to an adjective to the tree for (1) at the subject NP node, we will obtain (3).

(2)

(3)   The big man fell

Now in (3) *the big man* is the subject argument of *fell*, but the argument structure is preserved in the sense that the head of *the big man* continues to be the subject argument of *fell*.

To summarize, TAG has the following four properties (not necessarily independent), which are relevant to generation:
   (1) local definability of all dependencies,
   (2) locality of feature checking,
   (3) locality of the argument structure, and
   (4) preservation of the argument structure.
These four properties make the elementary trees appropriate (minimal) structures to serve as sentence planning units. The larger structures are built out of the elementary structures which have the four properties stated above. McDonald & Pustejovsky (1985) have discussed similar issues in their discussion of TAG as a grammatical formalism for generation. This incremental building of a sentential structures in TAG can be well matched to incremental building of conceptual structures. Thus the TAG system can be interfaced to the planning system not in a sequential manner, but in an interlaced fashion without destroying the modularity of the two components. This kind of interface is very difficult (impossible?) to achieve for a CFG based system, the primary reason for this difficulty, to repeat once more, is the difference in the domains of locality between the CFG based system and TAG.

3.3 Representations provided by TAG

A TAG, G, consists of a finite set of trees, I, and a finite set of auxiliary trees, A. The derivation starts with an initial tree, say α. Then an auxiliary tree, say β, can be adjoined to α, say, at a node n, subject, of course, to the local constraints specified at n. Adjoining is always at a node in an elementary tree at some address. More than one auxiliary tree can be adjoined to an elementary tree as long as each tree is adjoined at a distinct node. After these auxiliary trees are adjoined to the elementary tree, only nodes in the auxiliary trees are available for further adjoining. Thus associated with a tree, t, derived in a TAG, there is a derivation structure indicating how the elementary trees are composed. Note that the derivation structure shows only the elementary trees used in the derivation. *Thus, in a sense, the derivation structure of a tree t has all the information about t, including what is needed for semantic interpretation.* If one wants to build a tree explicitly, then all these adjoinings have to be carried out, but otherwise they can be left as they are, i.e., only the points of adjoining need be indicated. *This has the advantage that the sentence can be incrementally built or a sentence can be only partially built with some adjoinings actually carried out* . In that case the planner can decide whether to carry out all these adjoinings or to detach some of these auxiliary trees and use them appropriately during the construction of the next sentence, without disturbing the current sentence (ignoring some problems about obligatory adjoinings for the time being). The representations provided by TAG thus appear to provide considerable flexibility in the generation of a sentence and also for the interface between planning and the grammatical component of the generation system.

We will now show some derivation structures and then illustrate some of the points discussed above.

EXAMPLE 1:

Derivation Structure

The derivation structure below corresponds to a derivation where β_6 is adjoined to α_1 at * and β_7 at **. Now consider the following sentences:

(1) The girl saw a man.
(2) The girl who met Bill saw a man.
(3) The girl saw a man with a telescope
(4) The girl who met Bill saw a man with a telescope

(1) corresponds to a conceptual unit, say,

i1 saw i2

where i1 and i2 are referents of *the girl* and *the man* respectively. β_6 and β_7 can be used by the speaker for elaborating the descriptions of i1 and i2 respectively, for a variety of reasons such as making sure that the hearer picks up the referents i1 and i2 successfully, providing some additional information to the hearer, etc. Such decisions are under the control of the planner, thus the planner and the grammatical component can work in an interlaced fashion and not just sequentially.

EXAMPLE 2:

Derivation Structure

Consider the following sentences:

(5) The box is on the table.
(6) The box with a lock is on the table.
(7) The box is on the table, the one with a lock.

(5) and (6) illustrate the same points as in Example 1. (Note that β_8 is the same auxiliary tree as β_7 in Example 1, except that β_8 has different lexical items. We have used different indices on the two auxiliary trees only for convenience.) In (7) the description for the referent of *the box* has been realized by just the definite noun phrase *the box*, without the modifier represented by the auxiliary tree β_8, i.e., β_8 has not been adjoined to α_2 at *. However β_8 can stay in the derivation structure and then get detached later and realized as an additional clause or used in the planning of the next sentence. This gives flexibility in the interface between the planner and the grammatical component by providing a way of passing information from the planning process of one sentence to the planning process of the next sentence.

3.4 Word-order variation

It is well known that all languages allow for word-order variation, but some allow for considerably more than others, the extreme case being the so-called 'free' word-order. The linguistic relevance of word-order variation for generation is as follows. First of all, the different word orders (if not all) carry some pragmatic information (topic/focus, for example). The question is at what point the grammatical component should decide on the word order and what point it should reorder the words (or phrases) to reflect this order. The planner can certainly give the pragmatic information to the grammatical component long before all the descriptions are built or even planned. It is difficult to see how a CFG based grammatical system can take advantage of this information at the early stages of planning. In a TAG, if we work with elementary structures, the grammatical component can use this information immediately and select the appropriate elementary structure. The correct word-order will then be preserved as the sentence is incrementally built. The ability of TAG to specify a given word order at the elementary structure level appears to provide a better interface between the planner and the grammatical component.

We will now describe how word-order variation can be handled in a TAG. This feature of TAG is a direct consequence of the extended domain of locality (as compared to CFG) of TAG and the operation of adjoining. FUG shares the first aspect with TAG. It will be interesting to compare the word-order variation permitted in TAG with that in FUG.

We will now take the elementary trees of a TAG as *elementary domination structures (initial structures and auxiliary structures)* over which linear precedences can be defined. In fact, from now on we will define an *elementary structure* (ES) as consisting of the *domination structure* and *linear precedences*.[2] Thus, α below is the domination structure of an ES.

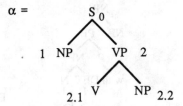

The addresses for nodes serve to identify the nodes. They are not to be taken as defining the tree ordering. They are just labels for the nodes.

Let $LP_1{}^\alpha$ be a set of linear precedence statements associated with α

$$LP_1^\alpha = \begin{bmatrix} 1 & < & 2 \\ 2.1 & < & 2.2 \end{bmatrix}$$

where $x < y$ (x precedes y). Precedence is defined only if x and y are nondominating nodes (i.e., x does not dominate y and y does not dominates x). Of course, precedence need not be defined for every pair of nondominating nodes. However, if precedence is defined then it must satisfy the consistency condition: if x dominates z_1 and y dominates z_2, then $z_1 < z_2$.

---

2 The idea of factoring constituency (domination) relationships and linear order is basically similar to the ID/LP format of GPSG (Gazdar, Klein, Pullum & Sag, 1985). However, there are important differences. First, the domain of locality is the elementary structures (and not the rewrite rules or local trees). Second, we have defined the LP for each elementary structure. Of course, a compact description of LP over a set of elementary structures can be easily defined, but when it is compiled out, it will be in the form we have stated here. The ID/LP format of GPSG cannot capture the range of word-order variation permitted by the TAG framework.

Note that $LP_1{}^\alpha$ correspondents exactly to the standard tree ordering. Given $LP_1{}^\alpha$ the only terminal string that is possible with the ES $(\alpha, LP_1{}^\alpha)$, where α is the domination structure and $LP_1{}^\alpha$, is the linear precedence statement (1).

(1) NP_1 V NP_2

Now suppose that, instead of $LP_1{}^\alpha$, we have $LP_2{}^\alpha$.

$$LP_2^\alpha = \begin{bmatrix} 1 & < & 2.1 \\ 2.1 & < & 2.2 \end{bmatrix}$$

Note that in $[1 < 2.1]$, 2.1 is not a sister of 1. We can define precedences between nonsisters because the precedences are defined over α, the domain of locality. Once again the only terminal string that is possible with the ES $(\alpha, LP_2{}^\alpha)$ is

(2) NP_1 V NP_2

but there is an important difference between $(\alpha, LP_1{}^\alpha)$ and $(\alpha, LP_2{}^\alpha)$ which will become clear when we examine what happens when an auxiliary tree is adjoined to α. Before we discuss this point, let us consider

$(\alpha, LP_3{}^\alpha) = \emptyset$,

i.e., there are no precedence constraints. In this case, we will get all six possible orderings

NP_1 V NP_2, NP_1 NP_2 V, V NP_2 NP_1, NP_2 V NP_1, V NP_1 NP_2, and NP_2 NP_1 V

Let us return to $(\alpha, LP_1{}^\alpha)$ and $(\alpha, LP_2{}^\alpha)$. As we have seen before, both ES's give the same terminal string. Now let us consider an ES which is an auxiliary structure (analogous to an auxiliary tree) with an associated LP, LP^β.

$$\beta = \quad \begin{array}{c} VP\ 0 \\ \diagup \diagdown \\ 1\ \ V \quad VP\ \ 2 \end{array} \qquad LP^\beta = [\,1 < 2\,]$$

When β is adjoined to α at the VP node in α. We have

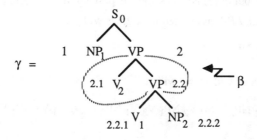

We have put indices on NP and V for easy identification. NP_1, V_1, NP_2 belong to α and V_2 belongs to β. If we have $LP_1{}^\alpha$ associated with α and LP^β with β, after adjoining the LP's are updated in the obvious manner.

$$LP_1{}^\alpha = \begin{bmatrix} 1 & < & 2 \\ 2.2.1 & < & 2.2.2 \end{bmatrix} \qquad LP^\beta = [\, 2.1 < 2.2 \,]$$

The resulting LP for γ is

$$LP^\gamma = LP^\alpha \cup LP^\beta$$
$$= \begin{bmatrix} 1 & < & 2 \\ 2.1 & < & 2.2 \\ 2.2.1 & < & 2.2.2 \end{bmatrix}$$

Thus γ with LP^γ gives the terminal string

(3) $NP_1\ V_2\ V_1\ NP_2$

If, instead of $LP_1{}^\alpha$, we associate $LP_2{}^\alpha$ with α, then after adjoining β to α as before, the updated LP's are

$$LP_2{}^\alpha = \begin{bmatrix} 1 & < & 2.2.1 \\ 2.2.1 & < & 2.2.2 \end{bmatrix} \qquad LP^\beta = [\, 2.1 < 2.2 \,]$$

The resulting LP for γ is

$$LP^\gamma = LP_2{}^\alpha \cup LP^\beta$$
$$= \begin{bmatrix} 1 & < & 2.2.1 \\ 2.1 & < & 2.2 \\ 2.2.1 & < & 2.2.2 \end{bmatrix}$$

Thus γ with LP^γ gives the terminal strings

(4) $NP_1\ V_2\ V_1\ NP_2$ (5) $V_2\ NP_1\ V_1\ NP_2$

(4) is the same as (3), but in (5) NP_1 has 'moved' past V_2. If we adjoin β once more to γ at the node VP at 2, then with $LP_1{}^\alpha$ associated with α, we will get

(6) $NP_1\ V_3\ V_2\ V_1\ NP_2$

and with $LP_2{}^\alpha$ associated with α, we will get

(7) $NP_1\ V_3\ V_2\ V_1\ NP_2$ (8) $V_2\ NP_1\ V_3\ V_1\ NP_2$ (9) $V_3\ V_2\ NP_1\ V_1\ NP_2$

Let us consider another LP for α, say LP_3^{α}.

$$LP_3^{\alpha} = [1 < 2.1]$$

Then we have the following terminal strings for α (among others):

(10) $NP_1 \, V_1 \, NP_2$ (11) $NP_1 \, NP_2 \, V$

It can be easily seen that given LP_3^{α} associated with α and LP^{β} associated β with $LP^{\beta} = \emptyset$, after two adjoining with β, we will get (among other strings)

(12) $NP_1 \, V_3 \, V_2 \, V_1 \, NP_2$ (13) $NP_1 \, V_3 \, V_2 \, NP_2 \, V_1$
(14) $NP_1 \, V_3 \, NP_2 \, V_2 \, V_1$ (15) $NP_1 \, NP_2 \, V_3 \, V_2 \, V_1$

and, of course, several others. In (13), (14), and (15), NP_2, the complement of V_1 in α has 'moved' past V_1, V_2, and V_3 respectively.

Karttunen (in press) discusses several problems centering around word-order variations in Finnish in the context of a categorial unification grammar. In particular, he deals with auxiliaries and verbs taking infinitival complements. The word order variations lead to dependent elements arbitrarily apart from each other (i.e., long distance dependencies). These long distance dependencies are reminiscent of those which are due to topicalization or *wh*-movement (which we have seen before). There is a difference however. In topicalization or *wh*-movement, the 'moved' element occupies a grammatically defined position in the structure. The 'moved' element in a long distance dependency of the type Karttunen is concerned about does not move into any structurally defined slot, it 'moves' freely in the host clause. It can be seen from (13), (14), and (15) that NP_2 (the complement of V_1) can be arbitrarily to the left of V_1 and does not occupy any grammatically defined position. The following examples by Karttunen can all be worked into the framework described above.

(16) mina en   ele   aikonut ruveta pelaamaan   tennista
     I   not   have   intend   start   play   tennis
     (I have not intended to start to play tennis)
(17) en mina ele tennista aikout ruveta pelaamaan
(18) en mina ele aikout tennista ruveta pelaamaan
(19) en mina ele ikout ruveta tennista pelaamaan

Karttunen also has an adverbial phrase (*in these shoes*) in these sentences, which can be 'moved' also. We have omitted it for simplicity. There is no problem in incorporating it and realizing the corresponding patterns in the present framework. Karttunen uses the devices of type raising (in categorial grammars) or floating types as proposed by Kaplan (unpublished work) to achieve these long distance dependencies.

The elementary structures (ES) with their domination structure and the LP statements factor the constituency (domination) relationships from the linear order. The complex patterns arise due to the nature of the LP and the operation of adjoining. The main point here is that both the constituency relationships (including the filler-gap relationship) and the linear precedence relationship are defined on the elementary structures. *Adjoining preserves these relationships.* We have already seen in Section 2 how the constituency relationships are preserved by adjoining. Now we have seen how the linear precedence relationships are preserved by adjoining. Thus we have a uniform treatment of these two kinds of dependencies; however, the crucial difference between these two kinds (as pointed by Karttunen) clearly shows up in our framework.

The elementary trees of TAG have four properties (as stated in Section 3.2) that can be well matched to incremental building of conceptual structures. These properties are: local definability of all dependencies, locality of feature checking, locality of the argument structure, and preservation of argument structure. All these properties have to do with the constituency structure and 'movement' of consituents to grammatically defined positions. Our discussion in this section shows that the word-order variation (although distinct from constituent movement as described above) can be localized to elementary trees. Thus by working with elementary structures as described in this section it appears that we can maintain the incremental generation, including word-order variation. This feature of TAG has not been implemented in any generation system as yet.

AKNOWLEDGEMENTS

I want to thank Vijay Shanker, David Weir, and Tony Kroch for valuable discussions. I am grateful to Graeme Ritchie who reviewed an earlier draft of this paper. His technical and editorial comments have helped me immensely in preparing this revised draft.

This work is partially supported by NSF grant IRI-10413 A02, US Army grant DAA6-29-84K-0061, DARPA grant N0014-85-K0018, and Advanced Technology Center (PA) grant #309.

REFERENCES

Appelt, D.E. (1983) Telegram. *Proceedings IJCAI 1983*. Karlsruhe.

Appelt, D.E. (1985) *Planning English Sentences*. Cambridge: Cambridge University Press.

Gazdar, G., Klein, J.M.E., Pullum, G.K. & Sag, I.A. (1985) *Generalized Phrase Structure Grammar*. Oxford: Blackwell.

Joshi, A.K. (1985) How much context-sensitivity is required to provide reasonable structural descriptions: tree adjoining grammars. In: D. Dowty, L. Karttunen, & A. Zwicky, (Eds.) *Natural Language Processing: Psycholinguistic, Computational And Theoretical Perspectives*. Cambridge: Cambridge University Press.

Karttunen, L. (in press) Radical lexicalism. In: M. Baltin & A. Kroch (Eds.) *Proceedings of Workshop on New Conceptions of Phrase Structure*. New York University.

Kroch, A. & Joshi, A.K. (in press, a) Linguistic significance of tree adjoining grammars. To appear in *Linguistics and Philosophy*.

Kroch, A. & Joshi, A.K. (in press, b) Analyzing extraposition in a tree adjoining grammar. In: G. Huck & A. Ojeda, (Eds.) *Syntax and Semantics (Discontinuous Constituents)*. New York: Academic Press.

McDonald, D.D. (1980) Natural language generation. Ph.D. Dissertation, MIT.

McDonald, D.D. & Pustejovsky, J (1985) TAG'S as a grammatical formalism for generation. In: *Proceedings of the 23rd Annual Meeting of the Association for Computational Linguistics*..

McKeown, K.R. (1985) *Text Generation*. Cambridge: Cambridge University Press.

Pullum, G.K. (1982) Free word order and phrase structure rules. In: J. Pustejovsky & P. Sells (Ed.) *Proceedings of NELS (North Eastern Linguistic Society)*. Amherst, MA.

Shieber, S. (1986) *Unification Based Approaches to Grammar*. Chicago: University of Chicago Press.

Vijay-Shanker, K. (1986) *A study of tree adjoining grammars* . Ph.D. Dissertation. Department of Computer and Information Science, University of Pennsylvania.

Vijay-Shanker, K. & Joshi, A.K. (1985) Some computationally significant properties of tree adjoining grammars. In: *Proceedings of the 23rd Annual Meeting of the Association for Computational Linguistics*.

Chapter 17

NOTES ON THE ORGANIZATION OF THE ENVIRONMENT OF A TEXT GENERATION GRAMMAR

Christian Matthiessen

TABLE OF CONTENTS

1.   Supporting a text generation grammar
1.1   Lexicogrammar in generation
1.2   Using lexicogrammar to infer other organization
2.   Method: the inquiry interface between grammar and environment
2.1   The environment
2.2   The organization of the grammar
2.3   The inquiry interface between the grammar and its environment
3.   Functional decomposition of grammar and invironment
3.1   Metafunctions in the grammar
3.2   Functional decomposition of the environment
4.   The knowledge base
4.1   The composition of a phenomenon
4.2   Types of ideational organization
4.2.1 Logical metafunction: the sequential organization of supercomplex
      phenomena
4.2.2 Experiental metafunction: the comfigurational kind of organization
4.2.3 Type of knowledge and knowledge representation
4.3   Correlations between taxanomies in the knowledge base
4.3.1 Configuration types
4.3.2 Participant types
4.4   Metaphor
5.   The discourse model
5.1   Controlling context and THEMATIZATION
5.2   Rhetorical relations and CONJUNCTION
5.3   Identifiability and DETERMINATION
6.   Conclusion

1. SUPPORTING A TEXT GENERATION GRAMMAR

One of the many tasks in building a text generation system is to design the environment in which the lexicogrammar (i.e. lexis and grammar) works. In this chapter, I will use English lexicogrammar to infer aspects of the organization of other parts of a text generation system.[1] The basic question is how the environment should be organized to support the lexicogrammar.

---

[1] *Lexicogrammar* is Halliday's term; see e.g. Halliday (1978). The term grammar is used in the traditional way, not in the recent more inclusive way it has been used in the transformational literature; it refers to syntax and morphology. Lexis is vocabulary. Lexicogrammar is the unified combination of the two; the resources of grammar and vocabulary.

1.1 Lexicogrammar in generation

In the generation of text, there are a number of varied communicative demands on lexicogrammar, representing different kinds of considerations. We can think of these demands as being embodied in 'messages' given to lexicogrammar for expression. Consider just the 'messages' in a text that will be expressed as clauses. For any given 'message', three general tasks have to be accomplished. (1) An action or relation has to be represented together with one or more of the entities participating in it. (2) The reader/listener has to be told what to do with the representation (e.g. agree with it as say a description of past shared experience, supply some information requested by the speaker, treat the representation as an instruction to perform the action represented). (3) The current 'message' has to be presented in such a way that the reader can relate it to its context, e.g. the entities participating in the action/relation have to be identified to the reader. These varied demands are integrated and represented as one wording, i.e. one (linear) combination of structure and lexical items. This integration and representation is the process of *lexicogrammatical* expression in text generation, and the resource used is the lexicogrammar of the system.[2]

1.2 Using lexicogrammar to infer other organization

Now, what I want to do is this: I will take the lexicogrammatical resources of English as a starting point, and explore what demands the resources put on the design of the part of a text generation system that supports the process of lexico-grammatical expression. In a sense, this exploration means putting the generation process on its head. After all, in generation, communicative demands are made on the lexicogrammar; it is the servant that integrates and represents the varied communicative demands I mentioned earlier. However, I will be talking about the *design considerations* we have to take into account when we construct a text generation system, not the flow of control during generation. The exploration is a partial solution to the problem of designing and specifying the parts of a text generation system.

One reason for using the lexicogrammar to infer the organization of other parts of the system is that we know a good deal more about lexicogrammar than we know about the organization of other parts. In particular, we have functional accounts such as those by Halliday, other systemic functional linguists, and other functional linguists that interpret lexicogrammar as a resource in a communicating system.

It is in fact quite common to reflect English *lexical* organization in the knowledge base of a text generation system when the domain model for a particular generation task is built. The semantic net is often a lexicosemantic net. The approach can be generalized; we can take the grammar part of lexicogrammar as well as the lexis part into consideration when we build a knowledge base, so that it reflects not only lexical semantics but also *grammatical* semantics.

The strategy of considering what the lexico-grammatical demands for support are is somewhat analogous to what happens when we take our demands to an expert who provides services. If I wanted to build a house, I would take my wishlist to a builder, but since I'm not an expert at all myself, it is very likely that he or she would take the lead and make demands on me for information — information I would never have thought to supply since my view of the house would be as a place to live, not as a thing to build.

In this chapter, I will look at the lexicogrammatical resources statically and will consider the static distinctions needed to support lexicogrammar. I will leave the consideration of the *processes* involved in generation for another time. Furthermore, I will focus on the content of

---

[2] In what follows I shall treat lexicogrammatical expression as a unified process and lexicogrammar as a unified resource rather than as distributed process and distributed resources. In this respect, my treatment follows to a large extent the design of text generation systems such as Davey's Proteus (Davey, 1978) and Penman (Mann, 1982). However, what I want to present is not really affected by the difference between a *unified* design and a *distributed* design. In fact, Halliday's functional decomposition of lexicogrammar (Halliday, 1967/8, etc.) suggests why distributed designs are sometimes used.

these distinctions rather than the formalisms needed to encode them; for the latter, see Nebel & Sondheimer (1986) and, for a discussion of a linguistically based functional logic, Dik (this volume). In Section 2, I will sketch a particular interface between the grammar and its environment, the inquiry interface, which can be used to project organization from the grammar to its environment. In Section 3, I will note the most general aspect of the interaction between grammar and environment, viz. the metafunctional decomposition. I will then discuss two functional components of the environment, the knowledge base (Section 4) and the discourse model (Section 5).

2. METHOD: THE INQUIRY INTERFACE BETWEEN GRAMMAR AND ENVIRONMENT

In our work on the design of one particular text generation system, Penman, we have made use of the strategy of asking what demands the grammar makes on the rest of the system. I will present some of the results of our work. We have been using a large systemic functional grammar of English, the so-called Nigel grammar (Matthiessen, 1981, 1983a, 1985; Mann, 1982, 1983b; Mann & Matthiessen, 1985). It is based on Halliday's work on English grammar, and I will rely heavily on his work in this chapter (e.g. Halliday, 1985).

2.1 The environment

I will not discuss the organization of Penman here (an early architecture is given in Mann, 1983a); for our purposes, we can simply think of the Nigel part of the generator as embedded in the rest of the system, which constitutes Nigel's environment; see Fig. 1.[3] This environment includes the knowledge base of the system (both general knowledge of taxonomies of conceptual classes and instantial knowledge of particular states of affairs), plans for particular generation tasks, a dynamic discourse model, and so on. For discussions of the environment in systemic terms, see Halliday (1978) and Fawcett (1980).

Communicative demands on Nigel come from the environment and, as we will see in the next section, Nigel demands information from the environment to achieve its task of lexicogrammatical expression. We will see how the grammar makes demands on different aspects of the environment (Section 3).

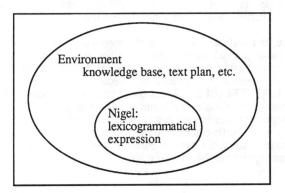

Figure 1. Nigel and its environment

2.2 The organization of the grammar

The Nigel grammar is a systemic functional one. Systemic grammar is presented as a computational grammar in Davey (1978), Winograd (1983), Matthiessen (1983a), Mann & Matthiessen (1985), and Patten (1986) and I will only mention a few general characteristics that will indicate how the grammar can be used to infer facts about its environment. The organizing principle of systemic grammars in general is that of *choice;* the grammar is one large *network* of inter-related choice points, called *systems* (see Figure 2 to be discussed below). A system consists of an entry condition or input condition and a disjunction of terms or output features. The options that constitute the alternative choices are represented by *features*, the so-called terms or output features of the system. A system can be reached when its *entry condition* has been satisfied; the entry condition is the output feature from another system or a complex of output features from various other systems. It is the system network organization of the grammar in particular that has made it possible to use the grammar to explore the organization of its environment: the systems are the focal points of the interface between the grammar and its environment.

2.3 The inquiry interface between the grammar and its environment

In order for the generation process to make grammatical choices in a purposeful way, we have equipped each system (choice point) with a *chooser* or choice expert. The chooser of a system asks a number of questions, called *inquiries*, of Nigel's environment, i.e. of the knowledge sources outside the grammar, to obtain the information relevant to the choice it has to make.

To generate the structure of a grammatical unit (a clause, a nominal group, a prepositional phrase, etc.), the generation procedure traverses the grammatical system network. As the network is traversed, the environment is asked one inquiry after another. Whenever a response or a set of responses satisfy the condition for choosing a grammatical feature, it is chosen . It may have a specification of a fragment of grammatical structure (a realization statement) associated with it, in which case the specification is activated. The generation of a unit finishes when the system network has been traversed. Assume the task is to generate a short biographical note and that the first part of it comes out as a clause combination: *J.G. Farrell was born in Liverpool in 1935 but spent much of his childhood in Ireland.* To produce this wording, the grammar is re-entered several times so that the system network is traversed several times. On one re-entry the task is to refer to Farrell's childhood, and the nominal group part of the system network is traversed. Nigel asks a number of inquiries of the reference plan for the nominal group.

For instance, the first system of a number of systems dealing with DETERMINATION in the nominal group (noun phrase) has two choice options, the features 'definite' and 'indefinite'. The chooser of the system asks the environment whether the referent of the nominal group can be identified by the listener(s), i.e. whether it is recoverable, or not. If the response to the inquiry is '(YES:) IDENTIFIABLE', the chooser chooses the grammatical feature definite, which leads to further distinctions in the grammar. The interaction is represented graphically below. The circle represents the embedding of Nigel in its environment (cf. Figure 1 above). The figure shows a network fragment of three systems. If the option 'instantiable class' is chosen in the leftmost system, the system with the options 'definite' and 'indefinite' can be entered. Choosers are represented by small circles.

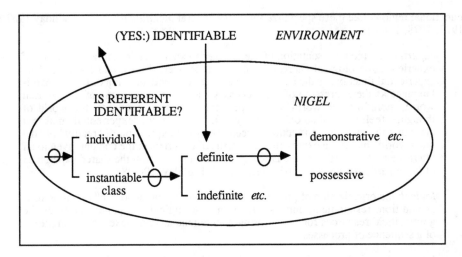

Figure 2. The chooser of the DEFINITENESS system

The inquiry concerning identifiability is one instance of a demand on Nigel's environment. It points to the need for a dynamic discourse model in the system which can keep track of referents identifiable to the addressee and distinguish them from referents that are not identifiable. In the example of Farrell's childhood, this referent is identifiable because Farrell has already been introduced earlier in the text as a referent and his childhood can be identified by reference to him: *his childhood*.

Thanks to the chooser and inquiry framework, we now have a lot of very detailed information concerning what kind of support is needed for the grammar; there are about 250 systems in the Nigel grammar currently and the chooser of each system contains one or more inquiries, each one of which makes a very specific demand. As I have already said, I will draw on the results of examining the inquiries, but I do not intend this chapter to be a detailed account of Nigel. The distinctions are needed in any large and versatile system that generates English; they are not artifacts of the chooser and inquiry framework.[4] As I proceed, I will make reference to the grammatical system network, but I will not attempt to show how every single distinction in the environment can be justified by reference to a particular inquiry.

3. FUNCTIONAL DECOMPOSITION OF GRAMMAR AND ENVIRONMENT

The most general observation about the interaction between the grammar and its environment is probably that it is functionally differentiated. We can learn something about this functional differentiation by looking at the metafunctional decomposition of the grammar.

3.1 Metafunctions in the grammar

The lexicogrammar of a language is a *functionally* organized resource. We can identify *functional regions* such as mood, transitivity, theme, modality, tense, and determination.

---

[4] To be more precise, the distinctions obviously depend on a particular analysis of English, but different analyses could clearly be accomodated by the chooser and inquiry framework. For some discussion, see Matthiessen (in press).

Functional regions like these specialize four very general *metafunctions* (see Halliday 1967/8, 1973, 1978, 1985):

> *experiential*: the representation of the speaker's experience, organized in terms of experiential/ontological categories such as processes, things, and qualities. 'The experiential function, as the name implies, is the "content" function of language: it is language as the expression of the processes and other phenomena of the external world, including the world of the speaker's own consciousness, the world of thoughts, feelings, and so on' (Halliday, 1974). 'The term "experiential" makes it clear that the underlying function is seen not as the expression of "reality" or "the outer world" but as the expression of patterns of experience; the content given to an utterance by this portion of the language system derives from the shared experience of those participating in the speech situation.' (Halliday, 1967/8)

> *logical*: the organization of processes, etc., into very general 'logical' relations such as addition, restatement, and modification. The logical component gives us the grammatical resources for representing phenomena as complexes, e.g. complexes of a sequence of processes.

> *interpersonal*: the speaker's interaction with the listener, indicating how the experiential representation is intended to be taken. 'Here, the speaker is using language as a means of his own intrusion into the speech event: the expression of his comments, his attitudes and evaluations, and also of the relationship that he sets up between himself and the listener — in particular the communication role that he adopts, of informing, questioning, greeting, persuading and the like.' (Halliday, 1973)

> *textual*: the creation and presentation of the text as a text in context, fluent and cohesive for the listener, i.e., enabling the creation of text. 'The textual component is concerned with the creation of text; it expresses the structure of information, and the relation of each part of the discourse to the whole and to the setting.' (Halliday, 1973)

The two first metafunctions, the experiential one and the logical one, can be grouped together as the ideational metafunction, the function concerned with ideation. The first mode of ideating is experience specific, while the second is highly generalized.[5]

3.2 Functional decomposition of the environment

Each metafunction places different kinds of demands for support on a text generation system. The experiential one is supported by the knowledge base, the interpersonal one by a model of the speaker-listener interaction which includes, e.g., speech act planning and epistemic and attitudinal assesments, and the textual one by a discourse model that keeps track of referents introduced, controls topic (focus) continuity and shift, and so on. The grammar brings these different demands together, although they may come from distinct sources of reasoning. (This is what I had in mind when I said in the introduction that the lexicogrammar serves as an integrator in a text generation system.)

---

[5] Halliday's metafunctional proposal can be compared with e.g. Dik's (1978). Halliday's ideational metafunction corresponds roughly to Dik's semantic component, his interpersonal partly to Dik's syntactic, and his textual to Dik's pragmatic. One difference is Halliday's differentiation of ideational into logical and experiential. Another difference is that Halliday proposes an interpersonal metafunction and interprets Subject as an interpersonal contribution to the structure of the clause, while Dik takes Subject to be a syntactic function.

The observation that the environment is decomposed into various knowledge sources is no news, of course; what is of interest is the correspondence between the decomposition of the environment and the functional organization of the grammar. Systemic linguists have studied the differentiation depicted in the figure in terms of correlations between the metafunctional organization of the linguistic system and the organization of the context; see, e.g., Halliday (1978) and Halliday & Hasan (1985); cf. also Fawcett (1980).

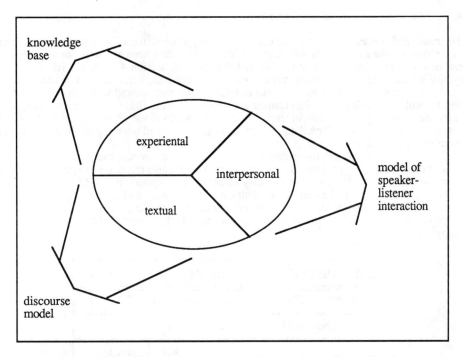

Figure 3. The differentiation in sources of support according to function

In text generation systems, it is common to find *distributed lexicogrammars*, where different functional regions are handled in different ways. For example, TRANSITIVITY may be handled by associating case frames with concepts in the knowledge base hierarchy (cf. Jacobs' (1985) PHRED, for instance). These associations are often thought of as lexical entries for verbs. MOOD and THEME are then seen as later specifications of the basic case frame information. I will now explore two of the three components in Figure 3, the knowledge base (Section 4) and the discourse model (Section 5). For a longer discussion, see Matthiessen (1986), on which the present chapter is based. For a discussion of speaker-listener interaction, see Hovy (1986) and Hovy & Schank (1984).

4. THE KNOWLEDGE BASE

The knowledge base of a text generator contains knowledge about phenomena such as episodes, procedures, events, actions, relations, circumstances, things, qualities, quantities, and so on. These can be organized in a variety of different ways, of course, but there are certain guiding principles of organization derivable from the lexicogrammar of English that will facilitate the process of generation and I will focus on these principles. When the knowledge base is viewed from this perspective, concepts can be thought of as semantic types and the knowledge base itself as a *meaning base*, to put it in Halliday's terms. I will start with the most general categories of phenomena recognized in the knowledge base, and then move to a brief consideration of the different modes of organization that characterize the most general types. Finally, I will note correlations between different taxonomies in the knowledge base. My aim is not to be exhaustive but to bring out some aspects of the nature of what lexicogrammar can tell us about the organization of the knowledge base.

4.1 The composition of a phenomenon

The ranks and classes of the grammar constitute a very general 'theory' or interpretation of our experience of phenomena. The nature of this 'theory' has often been obscured for a number of reasons. Grammatical metaphor is often not factored; cf. section 4.4 below. Scholars have typically tried to state correspondences in terms of word classes, which is simply a continuation of the orientation towards words we find in traditional grammar, and word classes are much less helpful as a starting point than clauses and groups/phrases. Thus we find attempts to make semantic sense of the 'universe' in terms of nouns and verbs alone. Further, interpretations of grammar have often been formal and oriented towards logic and not designed to bring out the functional nature of grammar.

If we take the grammar's distinction of clause complexes, clauses, and groups/phrases and look at the kinds of inquiries that have to be asked to distinguish these, we can project upwards from the grammar and posit corresponding semantic (conceptual) types. Clause complexes represent sequences, clauses represent composite phenomena, and groups represent simple phenomena. Further, nominal groups represent participants, verbal groups represent processes, prepositional phrases represent circumstances, and adverbial groups represent circumstances or qualities[6] (see Figure 4).

SEMANTIC TYPES		GRAMMATICAL CLASSES	
supercomplex phen.		clause complexes	
complex phenomena		clauses	
simple phenomena	circumstances	prepositional	phrases
		adverbial	
	participants	nominal	groups
	processes	verbal	

Figure 4. Grammar and the basic semantic (conceptual) phenomena

These are the default ways of expressing the different kinds of phenomena. There are marked ways of coding phenomena in addition to the default strategies given in the table above. These are usually metaphorical. For example, a composite phenomenon may be coded by a nominal group, which is a metaphor of a complex phenomenon treated as if it was a simple one (e.g., *The terrorist assaults were followed by more U.S. reprisals*). I will return briefly to

---

[6]   Adverbial groups may code qualities, for example, the quality of the performance of a process; its speed, skill, etc.; or circumstances, for example, times and places. The distinctions on both sides of the table are best thought of in terms of prototypes; see Hopper & Thompson (1984) for a discussion of nouns and verbs in terms of prototypes.

metaphors after the main discussion, but will not focus on them; they are discussed in some detail in Halliday (1985).

The most general consideration in the taxonomy of phenomena introduced above is composition. Phenomena are simple ('simple phenomena': participants vs. processes vs. circumstances), composites of more than one phenomenon ('composite or configurational phenomena' or 'macro-phenomena'), or composites of composite phenomena ('supercomplex phenomena' or 'sequences'). The three ranks of phenomena are organized according to different principles:

— Supercomplex phenomena are organized as sequences of interdependent composite phenomena related causally, temporally, spatially, or by some other type of a small set of highly generalized relations.

— Composite phenomena are organized as configurations of unique parts: a process, participants involved in it, and attendant circumstances.

— Simple phenomena are non-composite, elemental: participants, processes, and circumstances.

As a rank-based taxonomy, this can be compared to oragnizations such as crystal-molecule-atom (except that sequences are not organized like crystals!).The three general semantic (conceptual) types and their subtypes are displayed in Figure 5. The subtypes are discussed in, e.g., Matthiessen (1986) and Moore & Arens (1985).

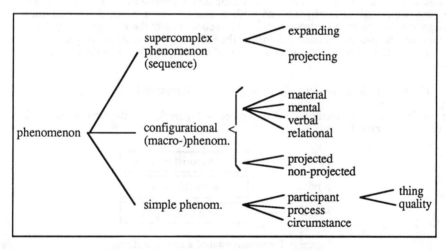

Figure 5. Most general semantic (conceptual) types

The concepts are organized into an inheritance hierarchy. For example, 'thing' is classified under 'phenomenon' as a subtype; it inherits whatever attributes 'phenomenon' has.

The most general distinction is, as just mentioned, based on considerations of composition or complexity. To simplify, the basic question is 'how big is the phenomenon?'. And the answer is in terms of a scale from micro to macro: phenomena are simple ones, macro-phenomena, or supermacro-phenomena. We might have based the taxonomy on another very fundamental distinction based not on size but on order of existence: 'does the phenomenon exist in reality or does it exist symbolically?'. And the answer would have been in terms of a distinction between phenomenon and meta-phenomenon. This distinction is, in fact, incorporated into the taxonomy of semantic types above as the distinction between projected (ideas, facts, sayings) and non-projected (acts): projected configurations are metaphenomena and all other phenomena are ordinary and 'non-meta'.

4.2 Types of ideational organization

The distinction between sequences and configurational phenomena in Figure 5 was characterized in terms of 'size': configurations are complex and sequences are supercomplex. At the same time, they differ in their modes of organization and the difference correlates with the differentiation between the two subtypes of the ideational metafunction, the logical subtype and the experiential subtype (see Halliday 1979):

    logical - sequential
    experiential - configurational

4.2.1 Logical metafunction: the sequential organization of supercomplex phenomena

Supercomplex phenomena are sequences or chains whose links are composite phenomena. Sometimes these sequences are episodes with only two links. For example, a causal chain may have cause and effect as links or condition and consequence. But, more generally, a sequence may extend indefinitely, because it is organized as a chain of interdependent links and not as a configuration of a unique set of parts. To anticipate the presentation of complex phenomena, they are organized as configurations with a unique set of parts. A certain subtype of configurations organize an episode temporally as consisting of three unique parts: the temporal relation, and the two events related. Consider the following representation of a temporal episode as a configuration of two events with a coding of the temporal between them as *follow* in one clause[7]:

The terrorist assaults were *followed* by more U.S. reprisals.

The configurational organization is diagrammed in Figure 6, with the three parts 'relation' and the two events related simply labelled '1' and '2'.

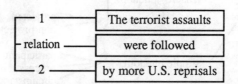

Figure 6. Representation of a configuration

Now contrast it with the representation of a supercomplex phenomenon as a sequence by means of a clause complex rather than as a configuration. The following examples are both substeps in procedures:

If the rotor is not pointing to the mark, pull the distributor part way out, turn the rotor some, and reinsert the destributor until the rotor point to within a half inch of the mark.

---

[7]   The result is a metaphor where a sequence of two processes is represented as if it were a configuration and the two processes are represented as if they were things, see Halliday (1985: chapter 10) and cf. Hopper & Thompson (1984) on nominalizations.

Add the remaining ingredients, stir to coat the chicken well and continue until a
   thick sauce has formed and the chicken is tender.
The organization of the second sequence can be diagrammed as in Figure 7. The
interdependency relations linking the units in the chain are marked by arrows between pairs of
links.

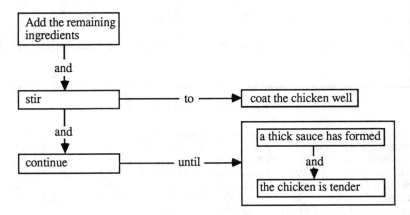

Figure 7. Representation of a supercomplex phenomenon

The phenomenon diagrammed in the Figure 7 is organized as a temporal sequence (*and*
[*then*]) of three process configurations *add*, *stir*, and *continue to stir*, two of which are further
expanded purposively ([*in order*] *to* and temporally (*until*). The temporally related unit is itself
an additive sequence (*and* [*also*]). The sequence might have been expanded further, since it is
organized as a chain of interdependent units; and in this respect it contrasts with the
configuration in Figure 6. (Although sequences are dynamically expandable, they may be
'institutionalized' as scripts applicable in specific situations.)

4.2.2 Experiential metafunctional: the configurational kind of organization

As already mentioned, a complex phenomenon is a composite configuration of a limited set of
parts with unique values in relation to the whole configuration. The parts of a given
configuration are a nuclear process, one to three different kinds of participants taking part in the
process, and up to around seven different kinds of circumstances associated with it. (Both
participants and circumstances have been discussed extensively in terms of (deep) cases in
linguistics and computational linguistics, but usually without a distinction between the two. The
process is typically not given a deep case.) Participants are inherent in the process; they bring
about its occurrence or mediate it. There are a number of specific ways in which a participant
may take part in a process; it may act out the process, it may sense it, it may receive it, it may be
affected by it, it may say it, and so on. The different configurations of participants are the bases
for a typology of process types, to be sketched below in section 4.3.1. The distinction between
participants and circumstances is a cline rather than a sharp division, but is semantically quite
significant. Circumstances are typically less closely associated with the process and are usually
not inherent in it. They specify the spatial or temporal location of the process, its extent in space
or time (distance or duration), its cause, the manner of its occurrence, and so on.

Grammatically, the nuclear process, its participants, and its circumstances are typically
represented as constituents in the transitivity structure of a clause. For instance, a particular
process of awarding may be represented as having a Time (*in 1966*) , an awardee or, in more

general terms, a Recipient (*he*), and a commodity awarded or, more generally, a Goal (*a two-year Harkness Scholarship*). See Figure 8.

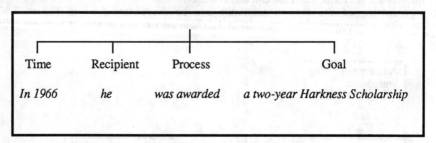

Figure 8. The transitivity structure of a clause

In logic, configurations are reflected in the predicate-argument structure of predicate logic. The process typically comes out a predicate and the participants as its arguments. However, there are significant differences between the way a configuration is represented in predicate logic and the way it is represented grammatically in English. In knowledge representation, a configuration is typically represented as a concept frame with a number of roles (slots; as in Brachman's KL-ONE; e.g. Brachman, 1978; Brachman & Schmolze, 1985). Configurations can be represented in two ways by means of such a frame.

(i) The configuration itself may be taken to constitue the frame (cf., for example, the treatment in Anderson, 1983), much as in the grammatical constituency diagram in Figure 8. The process is represented as a role (slot) in the frame in the same way as participants and circumstances (Figure 9).

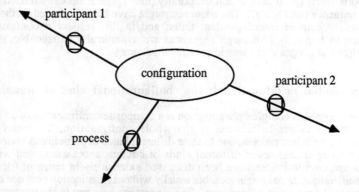

Figure 9. Configuration as frame

(ii) Alternatively, the process part of the configuration can be treated as the frame rather than one of the roles of the frame (Figure 10).

In either case, the roles have restrictions on what concepts they can be, so-called value restrictions. They are themselves concepts from other parts of the conceptual taxonomy not included in the figure. The two representations make different claims about a configuration, of course. In particular, the first approach allows the process to be a role that is filled by another concept frame that may have its own internal organization. The process part of a configuration may in fact have an internal organization. At the same time, the second approach is simpler and it may be sufficient for many generation purposes.

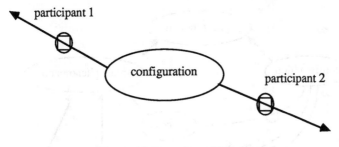

Figure 10. Process as frame

4.2.3 Type of knowledge and knowledge representation

The frame-based representation exemplified by the KL-ONE family of knowledge representation is reasonably good at (static) experiential knowledge since the experiential principle of organization is configurational and a configuration can be represented by means of a concept frame. However, it is much less well suited to the logical subtype of the ideational metafunction (Section 4.2.1) and to the other two metafunctions. For example, the following kinds of knowledge are problematic and require additional devices such as partitioning and spreading activation:

— logical: sequences and collections of configurations.
— interpersonal: modality (possibility, probability, permission, etc.), cognitive assessment (belief, doubt, etc.), affective assessment, key (contradiction, reservation, assertion, etc.), and so on.
— textual: identifiability, thematicity, newsworthiness, etc.

4.3 Correlations between taxonomies in the knowledge base

The taxonomies of sequences, configurations, and simple phenomena are not independent of one another, of course. The roles of a configuration are restricted to be filled by particular types of simple phenomena. If we use the first approach to representing a configuration (Figure 9), we can see that the three kinds of roles a configurational frame is made up of (i) the process role, (ii) participant roles, and (iii) circumstance roles, each has a default filler from the hierarchy of simple phenomena, processes, participants, and circumstances respectively (see Figure 11).

The taxonomy of configurations is based largely on the nature of the particular types of the general process, participant, and circumstance roles. Configurations, just as concepts in general, are thus organized into an inheritance hierarchy and the subtypes of the configuration frame classified under it inherit its role configuration.[8] Each new step in the taxonomy of configurations is likely to correlate with a step in the taxonomy of simple phenomena. I will give some examples below.

---

[8] The conceptual inheritance hierarchy correlates with the system network in the grammar; moving downwards in the hierarchy corresponds to moving to the right in the system network.

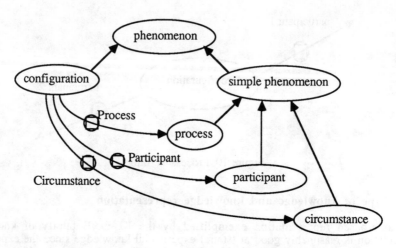

Figure 11. Configuration with role types and role fillers

4.3.1 Configuration types

There is a small number of configuration types that can be recognized on various grounds: material, verbal, mental, and relational.[9] Since they are always reflected in the nature of the process part of a configuration, they are called process types. These and their most immediate subtypes are given in Figure 12. (Although we are likely to find reflections of these general types in many languages, perhaps all, it is important to emphasize again that the taxonomy is based on English. It would look different if we tried to accommodate Tagalog transitivity , for example; see Martin, 1986.)

The four major types can be glossed as follows.

— *material*: doings or happenings; some input of energy is needed for the process to take place
— *mental*: sensing by a conscious being of a phenomenon; the sensing is inert on the part of the conscious being rather than active
— *verbal*: saying by some kind of signal source; the saying may or may not be actively performed by the signal source depending on its nature
— *relational*: being or having; in the limiting case it is is the existence of one participant, but it is almost always a relation between two participants.

Each process type has its own set of roles with particular value restrictions and number restrictions (Figure 13). For example, material configurations have an Actor which is a thing (rather than any kind of phenomenon). Meteorological configurations have no Actor, which is allowed by a number restriction associated with Actor, (0,1), where the first number is the minimum number of Actors and the second is the maximum one. In contrast, mental configurations do not have an Actor but a Senser, which is value restricted to 'conscious being', and a Phenomenon, which can be almost any kind of phenomenon.

---

[9] The distinction into four types comes from Halliday. It is intermediate in delicacy between three types (cf. Halliday, 1968) and six types (cf. Halliday, 1985). Alternative taxonomies can be found in, e.g., Chafe (1970; elaborated in Cook, 1977), Longacre (1976), and Dik (1978).

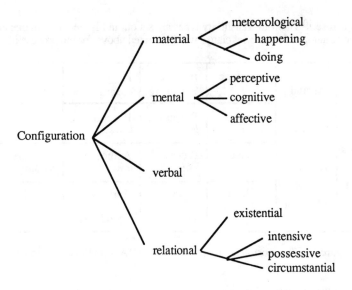

Figure 12. Organizational types of configurations

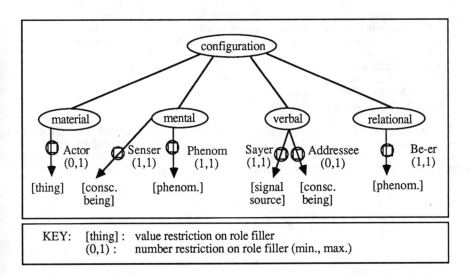

Figure 13. Subtypes of processes in the concept hierarchy

The process types are reflected in the grammar of transitivity. The most general TRANSITIVITY distinctions are grammatical rather than lexical. That is, they have general structural consequences; they determine the number and the nature of participants that are present in the clause.[10] The four transitivity types are set out in Figure 14, with one example for each type. The structure of a material clause was illustrated above for the process of awarding.

	Actor I	Process *'m making*	Goal *lasagna*	*for dinner*
material				
mental	Senser I	Process *like*	Phenom. *lasagna*	
verbal	Sayer I	Process *told*	Addressee *him*	Verbiage *the story*
relational	Be-er Attribuend I	Process *'m*	Attribute *a good cook*	

Figure 14. The most general options in the TRANSITIVITY grammar

4.3.2 Participant types

The value restrictions in Figure 13 indicate some of the correlations between the two hierarchies of configurations and participants. There are two kinds of participants, things and qualities. Things can fill any participant roles in a configuration, but qualities are much more restricted. In effect, they can only occur as Attributes, either in ascriptive relational configurations or in material configurations denoting the result or condition of the performance of the Process. Examples:

> This is [Attribute:] delightful (relational)
> until the mixture becomes [Attribute:] thick (relational)
> Serve [Attribute:] hot (material)
> It can be eaten [Attribute:] raw (material)

Moving down the participant taxonomy to further subtypes, we can establish another correlation with the taxonomy of configurations. The Senser of a mental configuration is value restricted to be a a conscious being. Based on this value restrictionsand other considerations, we can posit a fundamental distinction between conscious beings and non-conscious beings:

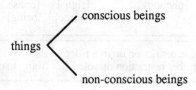

Figure 15. Some types of things

---

[10] Halliday (1985) shows how these general categories of process, material, mental, verbal, and relational, are reflected in the grammar of transitivity in English and I will not repeat his discussion here. Briefly, the categories influence the number and nature of participants. For example, only verbal processes have an Addressee participant. A factive clause cannot participate in a material process, but does so quite naturally in a mental one. And so on. The use of marked tense combinations depends on the process type. Further, the possibilities of using a 'pro-verb' vary depending on the process type, and so does the unmarked tense selection.

Once we have posited the distinction between conscious beings and non-conscious beings, we find that it supports demands made in the area of reference. It is also reflected in the pronominal resources of the nominal group, in the choice between *he/she* and *it; who* and *which,* and so on.

This kind of interaction between the taxonomy of participants and the taxonomy configurations is an illustration of the very general principle mentioned above: There are groupings of kinds of processes and kinds of things. As Halliday has observed, the tightest restrictions tend to occur between the process and a particular participant, the medium. (The Medium (or 'Affected') is general across the four process types. It is explained in, e.g., Halliday, 1967, 1967/8, 1985.) For example, we find this in the area of processes of 'sounding' by animals: *bark + dog, neigh + horse, moo + cow,* and so on. Hasan (to appear) unravels correspondencies between e.g. processes of collecting and things.

4.4 Metaphor

The taxonomy as discussed up to this point represents the basic outline of semantic (conceptual) types. It can and should be elaborated by adding further detail. It could be extended by adding further subtypes at particular nodes. However, there is another more radical way of expanding the taxonomy by recombining semantic types that are taxonomically distinct. This happens through the strategy of metaphor. One type is semanticized (conceptualized) as if it was another type. For example, in the final analysis, anything can be conceptualized (semanticized, and hence grammaticalized) as if it was a thing. We find qualities as things and processes as things (i.e., nominalizations grammatically speaking): *creation, destruction, protection, grammaticalization,* etc. But we do not find things as processes; a verbalization does not entail a metaphor as a nominalization does (see Hopper & Thompson, 1984). Nouns turned into verbs typically denote a general process plus a specification of the class of one of its circumstances, e.g. *bottle* 'put ... into a bottle', *ship* 'send by ship', *finger* 'to touch etc. ... with fingers', and so on. One of the most common kinds of metaphor was illustrated in Section 4.2.1: a sequence is treated as if it were a configuration.

5. THE DISCOURSE MODEL

We now move from the experiential world view embodied in the knowledge base to the textual world view embodied in the discourse model. The textual 'world view' is ever-changing; it changes as the text and its context evolve: what was new becomes old, what was rhematic becomes thematic, what was non-identifiable becomes identifiable, and so on. By nature, the textual metafunction is dynamic rather than static like the experiential one: it is concerned with the ongoing presentation of the text. (A 'rose' is a 'rose', but 'it' is not necessarily 'it'!) For example, from a textual point of view, things are instantiated referents, not classes in an experiential taxonomy.

The textual component in the grammar demands information about a number of distinctions, in particular thematic vs. non-thematic (THEMATIZATION), given vs. new (INFORMATION), and identifiable vs. non-identifiable (DETERMINATION), but these are not part of elaborate taxonomies of textual distinctions. Thus, the textual function contrasts with the experiential one, which organizes the elaborate taxonomies. Although CONJUNCTION draws on an elaborate taxonomy of rhetorical relations, these relations are not unique to the textual metafunction but can be coded experientially as well. What the textual metafunction requires is procedures for managing the presentation of information as identifiable or non-identifiable, and so on. In section 3.2, I simply referred to these procedures as a discourse model.

One important aspect of this dynamic model is a plan for the organization of the discourse (text) itself in terms of Rhetorical Structure Theory (Mann, 1984; Mann & Thompson, this volume, to appear) or a comparable rhetorical strategy. The textual resources in the grammar do a lot of the work involved in realizing this plan:

THEME selection is guided by the method of organization that is operative at any given point in the unfolding text. For example, if the text is being organized temporally, temporal themes are typically selected.

The resources of CONJUNCTION are used to mark the rhetorical relations being used to organize the text, relations such as elaboration, temporal sequence, and contrast.

The resources of DETERMINATION are employed partly to indicate shifts in stages in the organization of the text. For example, paragraph initial references to a particular referent tend to be different from subsequent references.

I will now explore these three resources in some more detail, noting what they require of our discourse model.

5.1 Controlling context and THEMATIZATION

Before characterizing Theme, I will indicate what the thematic options are in the clause. Part of the grammar of THEMATIZATION (or THEME, for short; the selection of the Theme(s) of a clause) is set out in Figure 16, with examples in the column to the right. It includes only experiential themes. The default Theme is the Subject in a *declarative* clause. (The VOICE options in the grammar determine which participant is the Subject.) The non-default Theme is a circumstance or participant other than the one in the Subject role. There may be more than one non-default Theme: *In 1966, in Oxford, he was honoured by his peers*.

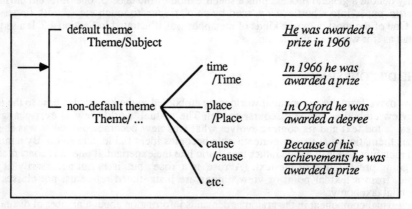

Figure 16. Part of the grammar of THEME

The selection of the Theme of a clause determines its local context. Theme has been glossed as 'starting point of the clause as message', 'context', 'frame', 'setting', or 'orientation'. (These glosses are not formal definitions, but are only intended as ways of thinking about the category of Theme.) In English, it is expressed by initial position in the clause, as in the following example (taken from The Desert Sun, April 5, 1986; Theme in Italics):

On March 27, as President Reagan departed for a working vacation at his secluded mountain-top ranch, he applauded the Senate's approval of a bill for $100 million to aid Contra forces in their struggle against the Managua government.

A week previously, the House voted down the proposal for new aid to the Contras. Congressional opponents of the anti-Sandinista force contend the group is ineffective.

In this extract, the Themes are non-default. They are times and they have been chosen to show the temporal organization of this span of text. The first orienting context is a date, *on March 27,* and the second relates to it and changes the temporal context to one week earlier. There is an important generalization to be made here: Fries (1983) has shown that Theme is selected to bring out the method of development of a span of text. Methods of development include organizations that are temporal (as in the example above), spatial, lists, general-to-specific, object-to-attributes, object-to-parts, and compare&contrast (cf. Danes, 1974).

What is needed to support the selection of Theme is an account of text organization in the generator. More specifically the discourse model must

— keep track of the changing context of each new message; and
— identify which aspect of the context relates to the method of development.

Fairly few generation systems have addressed these needs, either because they are single-sentence generators or because the domain (field of knowledge) gives the text its organization. In texts that define or describe an object, e.g. in entries in dictionaries and encyclopaedias, the the organization is often centered around the object being defined or described. After it has been introduced, the class it is a subtype of is mentioned, its attributes are identified, and subparts are specified. The Theme is likely to be the object itself throughout the text; in descriptive texts, the Theme is often also the 'topic' or 'subject matter' of the description. Further, the Themes are likely to be default ones, i.e. they are likely to be Subjects. McKeown's (1982) TEXT system generates texts that define objects and compare and contrast objects; the Themes are also the Subjects of the clauses, the default choice. TEXT keeps track of the topic (called focus by McKeown) and can change the topic. The method might be extended to, e.g., spatial and temporal contexts.

For Penman, the general theory of text organization mentioned above, Rhetorical Structure Theory, can be used to support reasoning about the local context. The rhetorical plan for a text specifies how a particular message or cluster of messages is related rhetorically to the rest of the text and this relationship can be thematized. For example, if one segment contrasts with another segment, the point of contrast can be thematized.

Before I leave the area of THEME, I would like to point out that the notion of Theme (opposed to Rheme) is distinct from the notion of New (opposed to Given); see Halliday (1967/8, 1985) and Fries (1983). New belongs to the functional region of INFORMATION. It is realized by intonational prominence; it is thus a category of spoken English. However, in the default case, the intonational prominence comes at the end of the clause, so there is a default association between final position in the clause and New. The meaning of New is discussed in e.g. Halliday (1985: chapter 8); it can be glossed as 'attend to this; this is news'. It is a strategy for directing the listener's attention to the news of the current message. Again, this is a textual strategy that requires a dynamic model of the addressee.

5.2 Rhetorical relations and CONJUNCTION

Theme sets up the local context of a clause; the context may be specified interpersonally, experientially, or textually. The textual context of a clause is its rhetorical relation to preceding text as specified by CONJUNCTION; the resources of CONJUNCTION are used to mark rhetorical relations in a text (elaboration, addition, alternation, contrast, temporal sequence, simultaneity, reason, and so on: see Halliday & Hasan, 1976 and Martin, 1983.) For example, alternation is often marked in recipes:

Fry some onions, mushrooms and sweet peppers in butter. Stir in some cooked macaroni and a chopped hard-boiled egg for each person. Moisten well with cheese, tomato or herb sauce and finish as for macaroni cheese. *Alternatively,* the macaroni may be served without the sauce, sprinkled with cheese only.

Like THEMATIZATION, CONJUNCTION needs the support of an account of the rhetorical organization of the text. There have been accounts of specific relations in past generation systems. For example, Davey's Proteus system looked for and expressed contrast between actual and possible moves in the game commentaries generated (Davey, 1978). But no general account that will support CONJUNCTION in generation has been put forward yet. Such support should be provided by Rhetorical Structure Theory. In addition, there has to be an account of when to make a rhetorical relation explicit by using a conjunction and when to leave them implicit.

By looking at the resources of CONJUNCTION, we can determine a number of characteristics the discourse model must have:

(i)   it must control the full range of conjunctive relations
(ii) it must support the external as well as the internal organization of a text, and
(iii) it must handle pairs of *clusters* of messages to be related conjunctively in addition to pairs of single messages.

(i) The conjunctive resources include not only simple additive, disjunctive, temporal, and causal relations, but also more complex relations such as addition with reinforcement (*again, furthermore, moreover*) dismissive relations (*anyhow*), resumptive relations (*to resume, to return*), verificative relations (*actually, in fact*), distractive relations (*incidentally, by the way*), and interpretive relations (*that is, I mean*). These relations indicate among other things that the discourse model must be able to leave one context, work within a new context, and then return to the old one.

(ii) CONJUNCTION also points to a very general principle of text organization. Conjunctions are external or internal, which reflects the fact that text can be organized according to a sequence of events external to the text itself or it can be organized according to the sequence of the rhetorical acts of speaking that constitute the text and thus are internal to it. External and internal development may used one by one or together. The distinction is discussed and exemplified in Halliday & Hasan (1976).

(iii) A conjunction may relate two simple messages, as in

Leave to set, *then* fry in deep fat or oil until a golden brown.

but it may also relate a sequence of messages to another sequence:

Pour on to the hot butter and cook gently until the bottom is set and light brown. *Then* either place in a warm oven at 300-350° F., M2-4, until the omelette is set, or place under medium grill and cook until the top is nicely browned.

In fact, this observation takes us back to section 4.2.1 and the organization of supercomplex phenomena as sequences: texts are typically supercomplex phenomena and the discourse model has to be able to handle the kind of internal nesting we often find in sequences.

5.3 Identifiability and DETERMINATION

In the clause, THEMATIZATION determines the thematic status of participants and circumstances (thematic vs. rhematic). In the information unit in spoken English, INFORMATION determines their information status (given vs. new). These textual statuses are independent of but clearly related to a third textual status, the identifiability status of referents, which is controlled by DETERMINATION in the nominal group.

In the experiential perspective, a thing is a general class, possibly with subcategorizations and descriptive attributes. The textual perspective on a thing is concerned with the instantiation of the class; with the thing as a referent. Both perspectives are integrated in the nominal group. DETERMINATION is the grammatical resource for indicating how the class is instantiated as a referent or a set of referents; whether the instantiations are identifiable or not, and so on. The most general DETERMINATION choices are given in the network fragment in Figure 17.

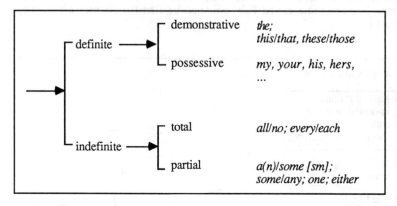

Figure 17. The most general DETERMINATION systems

Determiners are used with lexical nouns, as in *the terminal*. But we find the same kind of distinctions among pronouns as among determiners.

Like THEMATIZATION, DETERMINATION depends on a dynamic model of the context, in particular of the addressee/reader. In this dynamic reader model, it has to be possible to determine whether a given referent is identifiable to the reader or not (cf. Figure 2). Non-identifiable determiners in particular overlap in coverage with the quantifiers of formal logic, but the distinctions are not the same.

I will concentrate the *identifiable* case. A simple case is the following: The referent has just been introduced in the text and has thus been established by the text itself as identifiable (anaphoric reference: e.g. *Farrell ... he*). However, a referent can be identifiable by virtue of standing in one of a small set of relations (e.g. part-whole) to a previously mentioned referent without having been mentioned previously itself (so-called bridging: *Leeks have one fault. Because they are blanched the stem seems to accumulate ...*), by virtue of being part of the setting of the speech event (exophoric reference: *Rock Cakes. Heat the oven to 425° F.*), by virtue of being part of shared cultural knowledge (homophoric reference: *the sun, the boss, the queen*), by virtue of an anticipated future mention in the text (cataphoric reference) and so on (cf. Halliday & Hasan, 1976; Rochester & Martin, 1977). The different sources of identifiability are diagrammed in Figure 18.

A general account of identifiability has not been incorporated into any text generation system yet. In addition to a dynamic reader model, the account will have to rely on the text organization for some kind of notion of paragraph, since different *strategies* are often used for referring to an identifiable referent depending on whether it is paragraph-initial or not (cf. Hinds, 1977; Fox, to appear; see also Givon, 1983, on referring strategies and topic continuity). Here is an example from a news item (The Desert Sun, April 5, 1986). Two strategies are used, pronouns (underlined) and individual (proper) names (italicized), to refer to Marcos:

Former Philippines President Ferdinand Marcos says the United States aided rebel military forces against <u>him</u> in the final hours of <u>his</u> regime, with Americans refueling and rearming helicopters that attacked <u>his</u> presidential palace.

In an interview on Friday night's broadcast of ABC's 'Nightline', *Marcos* also denied stealing or misappropriating money from <u>his</u> country, said <u>he</u> still considered himself president of the Philippines, and defended his wife's collection of 3,000 pairs of shoes.

A partial transcript of the interview was released by ABC News Friday night and portions were broadcast on 'World News Tonight'.
Marcos' 20-year rule ended Feb. 26 when he fled the country after a popular uprising ...

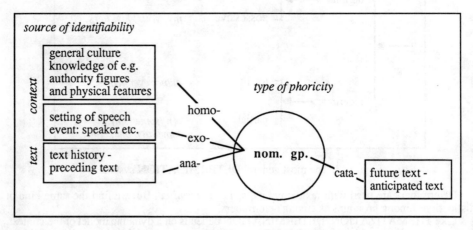

Figure 18. Sources of identifiability

Furthermore, the knowledge base has to be organized in such a way that the relations that are used in bridging are supported.

The types of phenomena in Figure 4 define possible types of referents. Among them, definite pronouns can be used to refer to participants, of course. But the referents of *this, that,* and *it* (cf. also relative *which*) can be extended in two ways, which correspond exactly to the two perspectives we can put on phenomena: 'size' (from micro to macro-phenomena) and 'order of reality' (from phenomena to meta-phenomen; cf. the end of section 4.1). (i) They can be extended literally from micro to macro, from simple phenomena to complex phenomena, which is called extended reference. (ii) They can also be extended metaphorically from phenomena to metaphenomena; they can be used to refer to facts, called text reference. Halliday & Hasan (1976) give an account of extended and text reference and offer the following example to bring out the difference:

> It rained day and night for two weeks. The basement flooded and everything was under water. *It* spoilt all our calculations.

The example is ambiguous and the ambiguity resides with the pronoun *it,* which refers either to the macrophenomenon of raining and flooding, in which case the calculations are physical records, or to the metaphenomenon, the fact that it rained, in which case the calculations are forecasts of the weather. The resolution of this ambiguity has brought us full circle to Section 4.1 where I began the discussion of the knowledge base and the discourse model.

6. CONCLUSION

In this chapter, I have given a selective overview of what kinds of support the lexicogrammar of a text generation system needs. I have focused on static distinctions that have to be made in the system, rather than on the processes involved in generating text, and have presented them in terms of Halliday's metafunctions. An account of the processes involved would have to include the selection of relevant information in the knowledge base, the planning of the speech acts to be performed, and the planning of the rhetorical organization of the text. Furthermore, I have focused on the content of the distinctions rather than on the notations or formalisms needed to deal with them.

What is needed as this point is really a more detailed treatment, not a summary; this chapter is a very sketchy summary itself. However, I will put the discussion in a summary perspective by way of one example, in which I consider what is needed to support the generation of (5) in the excerpt below, just in terms of clause structure. It is taken from the short biographical note in one of the novelist Farrell's books, parts of which have already been used for illustration.

(1) J. G. Farrell was born in Liverpool in 1935 but (2) spent much of his childhood in Ireland. (3) After leaving Oxford (4) he taught English in France for several years. (5) In 1966 he was awarded a two-year Harkness Scholarship. [...]

So let us assume we want to generate a 'message' (cf. section 1.1) according to the following specifications:

(i) *Discourse model*: The message should be temporally contextualized so that it orients the reader to a particular time in Farrell's biography. Furthermore, it should present Farrell as a topical referent that has already been introduced at this point in the text.

(ii) *Knowledge base*: The message should represent the particular event in Farrell's life in which he benefits as the recipient of the Harkness Scholarship, suggesting but not mentioning those who awarded him the scholarship.

These specifications concern textual and experiential considerations in the use of the lexicogrammatical resources.

Textual considerations. At the point when (5) is generated, the text is organized according to the chronology of Farrell's life, information which leads to the selection of *in 1966* as Theme. The message thus starts out by orienting the reader temporally and this orienting temporal context has to be specified in the plan for the message. Nigel will then discover this specification and generate Time: *in 1966* as Theme of the clause. There is no conflict in the selection of *in 1966* as Theme with other textual considerations. If the year had been the news or the new point of the message, there would have been a good reason to put it towards the end of the clause, but it is not the news of the message. Assuming that the generator keeps track of what the news is, Farrell's achievement, the scholarship, is given that status and *a two-year Harkness Scholarship* appears as the last constituent. Consider the textual variants just in terms of the clause structure:

(a) Farrell was awarded a two-year Harkness Scholarship in 1966
(b) A two-year Harkness Scholarship was awarded (to) him in 1966
(c) They awarded him a two-year Harkness Scholarship in 1966
(d) A two-year Harkness Scholarship he was awarded in 1966
(e) It was Farrell who was awarded a two-year Harkness Scholarship in 1966

The variant (a) presents Farrell rather than the year as Theme. It would be motivated if the plan for the organization of the text had specified Farrell to be introduced or re-introduced as 'topic'. In fact, the little biographic text starts out with this pattern: *J. G. Farrell was born in Liverpool in 1935*. In this first message, the news is Farrell's place and year of birth. Variant (b) does not present the scholarship as (unmarked) news, but makes it thematic rather than the year, which appears last. Thus, this variant gets the textual organization of the message wrong in two ways. Variant (e) would be appropriate if there were several candidates being discussed and Farrell had to be singled out, but it is not appropriate in this short biography where we are only concerned with Farrell.

Experiential considerations. The event in Farrell's life is represented as a benefactive material process, in which Farrell participates as Beneficiary (more specifically: Recipient) and the scholarship as Goal. There is an inherent Agent (Actor) in a process of this kind, but the writer has chosen not to represent it, since the particular identity of the Agent is not important. Experiential variants include

     (f) In 1966 he received a two-year Harkness Scholarship
     (g) From 1967 to 1968 he had a two-year Harkness Scholarship

Variant (f) represents the event as a material action, but leaves out the indication of an Agent whose action benefits Farrell: Grammatically, Farrell is not the Beneficiary, and there is no inherent Agent as in *was awarded.* The version in the text represents the event from the perspective of the world honouring Farrell by acting to benefit him. Variant (g) is not a material action, but a relation; it represents the states of affairs resulting from the action of awarding, leaving the reader to infer the awarding action which honoured Farrell.

There is also a specification of the Time, *in 1966,* motivated by the fact that the text represents the biography of Farrell's life, something that proceeds through and is fixed in time.

The two metafunctional considerations are integrated and achieved simultaneously by the clause (cf. Figure 4 and the notion of the grammar as integrator). The diagram in Figure 19 below brings this out and summarizes my remarks.

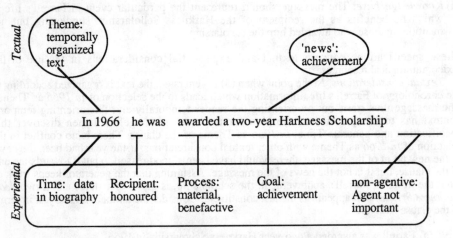

Figure 19. One (integrated) wording, multiple functions

The diagram leaves out the interpersonal metafunction, since I have not discussed it in this chapter. It is the metafunction we need to control variants such as *was he, he may have, he was ... wasn't he, he was not surprisingly,* etc.

ACKNOWLEDGEMENTS

I am greatly indebted to Michael Halliday. I have drawn heavily on his work and several ideas have been developed or clarified in discussions with him. I am also grateful to Bill Mann and Norm Sondheimer. They have lead the work on modeling within the Penman project, which has provided the context for this chapter. I have benefited from comments by Bill Mann, Lynn Poulton, and Susanna Cumming on earlier versions of the paper. I am, of course, solely repsonsible for the use or misuse I have made of the various ideas and comments that have shaped the chapter.

The research reported on was supported by the Air Force Office of Scientific Research under contract no. FQ 8671-84-01007. Views and conclusions in this paper are the author's and should not be interpreted as representing the official opinion or policy of AFOSR or the U.S. Government.

REFERENCES

Allerton, D.J., Carney, E. & Holdcroft, D. (Eds.) (1979) *Function and Context in Linguistic Analysis*. Cambridge: Cambridge University Press.

Anderson, J.R. (1983) *The Architecture of Cognition*. Cambridge: Harvard University Press.

Bara, B.G. & Guida, G. (Eds.) (1984) *Computational Models of Natural Language Processing*. Amsterdam: North-Holland.

Benson, J. & Greaves, W. (1985) *Systemic Perspectives on Discourse. (Volume 1)*. Norwood, NJ: Ablex.

Benson, J., Cummings, M. & Greaves, W. (in press) *Systemic Perspectives on Discourse*. Amsterdam: Benjamins.

Brachman, R.J. (1978) *A Structural Paradigm for Representing Knowledge* . BBN Report No. 3605.

Brachman, R.J. & Schmolze, J. (1985) An Overview of the KL-ONE Knowledge Representation System. *Cognitive Science, 9*, 171-216.

Chafe, W. (1970) *Meaning and the Structure of Language*. Chicago: Chicago University Press.

Cook, W. (1977) *Case Grammar: Development of the Matrix Model (1970-1978)*. Washington, D.C.: Georgetown University Press.

Danes, F. (1974) *Functional sentence perspective and the organization of the text*. In: Danes (Ed.).

Danes, F. (Ed.) (1974) *Chapters on Functional Sentence Perspective*. The Hague: Mouton.

Davey, A. (1978) *Discourse Production*. Edinburgh: Edinburgh University Press.

Derr, M.A. & McKeown, K.R. (1984) Using Focus to Generate Complex and Simple Sentences. In: *Proceedings of COLING 84*.

Dik, S. (1978) *Functional Grammar*. Amsterdam: North-Holland.

Fawcett, R.P. (1980) *Cognitive Linguistics and Social Interaction*. Heidelberg: Julius Groos Verlag.

Fawcett, R.P. & Halliday, M.A.K. (Eds.) (to appear) *New Developments in Systemic Linguistics*. London: Frances Pinter.

Fox, B. (to appear) *Discourse structure in written and conversational English*. Cambridge: Cambridge University Press.

Freedle, R.O. (Ed.) (1977) *Discourse Production and Comprehension*. Norwood, N.J.: Ablex.

Fries, P.H. (1983) On the Status of Theme in English: Arguments from Discourse. In: Petöfi & Sozer (Eds.).

Givon, T. (Ed.) (1983) *Topic Continuity in Discourse*. Amsterdam: Benjamins.

Haiman, J. & Thompson, S.A. (Eds.) (in press) *Clause Combining in Discourse and Grammar*. Amsterdam: Benjamins.

Halliday, M.A.K. (1967) *Grammar, society, and the noun*. Inaugural lecture, reprinted in Halliday 1977.

Halliday, M.A.K. (1967/8) Notes on Transitivity and Theme. *Journal of Linguistics, vol. 3*, 37-81; 199-244; *vol. 4*, 179-215.

Halliday, M.A.K. (1973) *Explorations in the Functions of Language*. London: Arnold.

Halliday, M.A.K. (1974) Michael Halliday. In: Parret, (Ed.) *Discussing Language*. The Hague: Mouton.

Halliday, M.A.K. (1978) *Language as social semiotic*. London: Edward Arnold.

Halliday, M.A.K. (1979) *Modes of Meaning and Modes of Saying*. In: Allerton, Carney, & Holdcroft (Eds.).

Halliday, M.A.K. (1985) *An Introduction to Functional Grammar*. London: Edward Arnold.

Halliday, M.A.K. & Hasan, R. (1976) *Cohesion in English*. London: Longman.
Halliday, M.A.K. & Hasan, R. (1985) *Language, context, and text*. Victoria: Deakin University Press.
Hasan, R. (to appear) The Grammarian's Dream: Lexis as Most Delicate Grammar. In: Fawcett & Halliday (Eds.).
Hinds, J. (1977) Paragraph Structure and Pronominalization. *Chapters in Linguistics, 10*, 77-99.
Hopper, P. & Thompson, S. (1984) The Discourse Basis for Lexical Categories in Universal Grammar. *Language, 60*, 703-52.
Hovy, E. (1986) Putting Affect into Text. In: *Proceedings of the Eighth Conference of the Cognitive Science Society*.
Hovy, E. & Schank, R. (1984) *Language Generation by Computer*. In: Bara & Guida (Eds.).
Jacobs, P. (1985) PHRED: A Generator for Natural Language Interfaces. *Computational Linguistics, 11*, 219-243.
Longacre, R.L. (1976) *An Anatomy of Speech Notions*. The Hague: Peter de Ridder Press.
McKeown, K.R. (1982) *Generating Natural Language Text in Response to Questions about Database Structure*. Ph.D. Dissertation, University of Pennsylvania.
Mann, W.C. (1982) *The Anatomy of a Systemic Choice*. Paper ISI/RR-82-104.
Mann, W.C. (1983a) *An Overview of the Penman Text Generation System*. Paper ISI/RR-83-114.
Mann, W.C. (1983b) *An Overview of the Nigel Text Generation Grammar*. Paper ISI/RR-83-113.
Mann, W.C. (1984) Discourse Structures for Text Generation. In: *Proceedings of COLING84*.
Mann, W.C. & Matthiessen, C. (1985) *A demonstration of the Nigel text generation computer program*. In: Benson & Greaves (Eds.).
Mann, W.C. & S.A. Thompson (to appear) Rhetorical Structure Theory: A Theory of Text Organization. In: Polany (Ed.).
Martin, J.R. (1983) *Conjunction: the Logic of English Text*. In: Petöfi and Sozer (Eds.).
Martin, J.R. (1986) *Transitivity in Tagalog: a functional interpretation of case*. Mimeo. Department of Linguistics, University of Sydney.
Matthiessen, C. (1981) A Grammar and a Lexicon for a Text-Production System. In: *Proceedings of the 19th Annual Meeting of the ACL*.
Matthiessen, C. (1983a) Systemic Grammar in Computational Linguistics: The Nigel Case. In: *Proceedings of the 1st Meeting of the European chapter of the ACL*.
Matthiessen, C. (1983b) How to Make Grammatical Choices in Text Generation. In: *Tenth LACUS Forum*. Columbia: Hornbeam Press.
Matthiessen, C. (1985) *The Systemic Framework in Text generation: Nigel*. In: Benson & Greaves (Eds.).
Matthiessen, C. (1986) *The organization of the environment of a text generation grammar*. MS at ISI/USC, to appear as ISI research report.
Matthiessen, C. (in press) A systemic semantics: The chooser and inquiry framework. In: Benson, Cummings & Greaves.
Matthiessen, C. & Thompson, S.A. (in press) The Structure of Discourse and Hypotaxis. In: Haiman & Thompson (Eds.).
Moore, J. & Arens, Y. (1985) *A Hierarchy for Entities*. MS, ISI/USC.
Nebel, B. & Sondheimer, N.K. (1986) A Logical-Form and Knowledge-Based Design for Natural Language Generation. In: *Proceedings of AAAI-86*.
Patten, T. (1986) *Interpreting Systemic Grammar as a Computational Representations: A Problem Solving Approach to Text Generation*. Ph.D. Dissertation, Edinburgh University.
Petöfi, J. & Sozer, E. (1983) *Micro and Macro Connexity of Texts*. Hamburg: Helmut Buske Verlag.
Polanyi, L. (Ed.) (to appear) *Discourse Structure*. Norwood, N.J.: Ablex.
Rochester, S. & Martin, J.R. (1977) *The Art of Referring: The Speaker's Use of Noun Phrases to Instruct the Listener*. In: Freedle (Ed.).
Winograd, T. (1983) *Language as a cognitive process*. Reading: Addison-Wesley.

Chapter 18

A FORMAL MODEL OF SYSTEMIC GRAMMAR

Terry Patten
Graeme Ritchie

TABLE OF CONTENTS

1.   Introduction
2.   Systemic syntactic structures
3.   A formalisation of systemic grammar
4.   Generation
5.   Soundness and completeness
6.   Some realisation rules
7.   Generating structures
8.   Formulating realisation rules in logic
9.   Comparison with Penman
10.   Comparison with functional unification grammar
11.   Conclusion

1. INTRODUCTION

Despite the fact that systemic grammar (see Halliday, 1973, 1978; Winograd, 1983, chapter 6) has a relatively long history, and has been adopted in several computer implementations (Davey, 1978; Mann & Matthiessen, 1983), it has never been rigorously formalised in the way that traditional grammars have. The reason for this appears to be that the formal tools applied to traditional structural grammars are not so easily applied to a functional theory. In addition, it seems that the 'rigorous rules' used to formalise traditional grammars are viewed by systemic linguists as inherently structural (e.g. Halliday, 1978, pp. 191-192). The formal model of systemic grammar presented here will involve 'rigorous rules' but will not compromise the functional perspective of language as a 'resource'. This formalisation will allow us to define such notions as the language generated by a grammar, and to demonstrate results relating to properties of two algorithms for producing text from a grammar. The central issues discussed include the correctness and efficiency of these generation processes.

Three warnings should be given concerning this work. First, the the generation algorithm presented (Sections 4 and 5) is based on Halliday (1978). As a result of certain assumptions (especially concerning the input to the generation), it may not be compatible with models based on other versions of the theory. Second, this formalisation is largely exploratory, in that it is meant to investigate and illustrate the possibility of providing a rigorous formalisation of systemic grammar suitable for defining a generation mechanism — it is not meant to be the definitive formalisation of systemic grammar. Third, we assume a general familiarity with systemic grammar as normally outlined (the uninitiated reader should consult Winograd, 1983), so no attempt is made to justify the constructs or provide linguistic examples.

The first section of the formal model (Section 2) will describe the syntactic structures specified by systemic grammars. This will require a more complex treatment than for many other grammars because of the need to interrelate constituency and the sophisticated functional treatment of structure. Section 3 defines a systemic grammar and gives a declarative definition of the language generated by the grammar. The grammar is defined using familiar terms such as 'feature', 'system', 'grammatical function' and 'terminal symbols'; but the notion of a system network will be defined in terms of a set of production rules which embody the same information.

Sections 2 and 3 deal only with abstract systemic ideas and should therefore be applicable to any systemic model. In contrast, Section 4 describes a generation algorithm for searching through the system network. In keeping with the representation of the system network as production rules, the generation algorithm has been designed as a forward- and backward-chaining process that implements an efficient goal-directed search. Section 5 proves some results about the behaviour of this generation algorithm given certain kinds of inputs.

Regardless of the method used to search the system network, the systemic syntactic structures will be specified by realisation rules attached to the features found during that search. Section 6 presents a typical set of realisation relationships, and an algorithm for constructing structures from these is outlined in Section 7. Realisation rules in systemic grammar can be interpreted both as a declaration of some characteristics a structure must have and as a procedure for modifying partial descriptions of a structure during generation. Both of these interpretations are usefully captured in Section 8 where realisation rules are formulated as rules in logic.

Section 9 contrasts the formal generation algorithm presented here with Penman, another systemic generation system (Mann & Matthiessen, 1983). This comparison is made by recasting both of the generation methods in a general AI problem-solving formalism. Section 10 provides a brief informal comparison with functional unification grammar, another grammar formalism often used for text generation.

2. SYSTEMIC SYNTACTIC STRUCTURES

Before defining a systemic grammar, we shall define the kind of grammatical structures which systemic grammars characterise. (As in many formal definitions, there is a problem concerning the order of presentation, as many definitions are mutually dependent.) One traditional notion which we need is that of a 'tree':

A *tree* is a finite set of *nodes* connected by directed *edges*, which satisfy the following three conditions (if an edge is directed from node 1 to node 2, we say the edge *leaves* node 1 and *enters* node 2):
1) There is exactly one node which no edge enters. This node is called the *root*.
2) For each node in the tree there exists a sequence of directed edges from the root to the node. Thus the tree is connected.
3) Exactly one edge enters every node except the root. As a consequence there are no loops in the tree. (Hopcroft & Ullman, 1969, pp. 18-20.)

An important relationship between nodes in a tree is descendancy:

The set of all nodes n, such that there is an edge leaving a given node m and entering n, is called the *direct descendants* of m. A node n is called a descendant of node m if there is a sequence of nodes n_1, n_2, ..., n_k such that $n_k = n$, $n_1 = m$, and for each i, n_{i+1} is a direct descendant of n_i. We shall, by convention, say a node is a direct descendant of itself. (ibid.)

A *leaf node* or *terminal node* of a tree is a node that has no descendants. We shall represent a tree by a pair (A,p) where A is a finite set — the 'nodes' of the tree — and p is the partial function from A to A which maps every node (except the root node) to its parent node. Further, we need to impose an ordering on certain trees, to reflect the idea of left-right order in syntactic structure. An *ordered tree* is one in which a binary irreflexive asymmetric transitive relation is defined upon nodes such that:

if $n_1 < n_2$, m_1 a descendant of n_1, m_2 a descendant of n_2, then $m_1 < m_2$;

if m_1 is a descendant of n_1 then neither $n_1 < m_1$ nor $m_1 < n_1$;
if m_1 and m_2 are direct descendants of n_1, with $n_1 \neq m_1$, $n_1 \neq m_2$, $m_1 \neq m_2$, then
either $m_1 < m_2$ or $m_2 < m_1$.

We shall write an ordered tree as a triple (N, p, <) where N is the set of nodes, p is the parent function (see above), and < is the 'left-right' ordering relation.

Within systemic grammar, each constituent in a sentence has one or more 'functional analyses', each of which is a simultaneous hierarchical decomposition of the constituent. We can represent such a decomposition as a labelled tree, where each node apart from the root is labelled with some grammatical function:

2.1 Defn.

Let V be some finite set. A *functional analysis over V* is a pair ((A,p), h) where (A,p) is a tree and h is an injective mapping from the non-root nodes of (A,p) to V.

2.2 Defn.

Let $V_1, ... V_m$ be a family of finite sets. A *constituent analysed with respect to $V_1, ... V_m$* consists of a triple $c = ((A_1, ... A_m), B, g)$ where:

(a) each A_i is a functional analysis over V_i
(b) B is a finite set (the *daughter nodes* of c).
(c) g is a mapping from B to the powerset of the set of terminal nodes in the trees in $A_1, ...$ A_m (i.e. for every daughter node n, g(n) is a set of leaf nodes from the trees in the m functional analyses $A_1, ... A_m$).

The above definition allows us to link the structural parts of a constituent (which will be a set of daughter nodes) to the various functional analyses of that constituent. Each daughter node is linked to one or more of the leaves of the functional analyses.

2.3 Defn.

A *grammatical function scheme* is an ordered sequence $(R_1, ... R_k)$ of families of finite sets. (That is, each R_i is of the form $\{V_1, ... V_m\}$ (for some m), each V_j being a finite set.) In such a scheme, R_i is said to be 'at rank i'.

Informally, R_i represents the set of functions available at rank i, which are grouped into sets to reflect the fact that, at a given rank, the grammatical functions are grouped according to availability for functional analyses of a constituent at that rank. Lower rank numbers correspond, loosely speaking, to larger constituent sizes — clause has a lower rank number than group, etc.

We now need to define the nature of a syntactic structure within our model. Informally, this consists of a conventional ordered tree (i.e. a set of constituents, hierarchically connected), where each constituent has one or more functional analyses, in the sense of the definitions 2.1 and 2.2 above, and where the leaf nodes of the tree are associated with terminal symbols.

2.4 Defn.

Let $S = (R_1, ... R_k)$ be a grammatical function scheme, and Vt some finite set. A *systemic syntactic structure within S and Vt* consists of a tuple $T = (C, r, M, <, L)$ such that:

(a) C is a finite set $\{c_1, \ldots c_t\}$, where each c_i is a constituent analysed with respect to some R_i in S. (The set consisting of all the nodes of the various trees in the functional analyses of the constituents in C is called the set of *function-nodes* of the structure T.)

(b) r is an item (the 'root node') distinct from all daughter nodes in constituents in C.

(c) Let N denote the set of all daughter nodes in constituents in C. M is a total function from N to N $\cup$ {r} and < is an ordering relation on N such that:

   (i) (N $\cup$ {r}, M, <) is an ordered tree,

   (ii) within each constituent c $\in$ C, M(n) is the same for each daughter node n in c,

   (iii) there is exactly one constituent c_j such that M(n) = r for each daughter node n in c_j,

   (iv) if $M(n_1) = n_2$ then n_1 and n_2 are in distinct constituents in C.

(d) L is a mapping from the leaf nodes of the tree (N $\cup$ {r}, M, <) to Vt.

In a structure as above, N $\cup$ {r} is called the set of *unit nodes* of the structure, and (N $\cup$ {r}, M, <) is called the *constituent tree* of the structure.

2.5 Defn.

In a systemic syntactic structure as above, if c is a constituent in C analysed with respect to R_j (where $1 \leq j \leq k$), then c is said to be *at rank j*, and if $M(n_1) = n_2$, n_1 is in a constituent c_1 at rank j_1, n_2 is in a constituent c_2 at rank j_2, and $j_2 \geq j_1$, then c_1 is said to be *rank-shifted*.

2.6 Defn.

Let $S = (R_1, \ldots R_k)$ be a grammatical function scheme, and Vt some finite set. Let T = (C, r, M, <, L) be a systemic syntactic structure within S and Vt. Then the *terminal string of T* is the sequence s of elements of Vt defined by a traversal of the leaves of the tree (N $\cup$ {r}, M, <) in ascending ('left-right') order. That is, $s = (L(n_1), \ldots L(n_t))$ where $\{n_1, \ldots n_t\}$ is the set of leaf nodes of (N $\cup$ {r}, M, <) and where $n_i < n_{i+1}$ for every i from 1 to t-1.

3. A FORMALISATION OF SYSTEMIC GRAMMAR

First, we need some basic definitions of some constructs which are used in the definition of a systemic grammar. Each constituent has to be associated with a feature-set from the systemic grammar, which will contribute to characterising its grammatical well-formedness.

3.1 Defn.

Let $S = (R_1, \ldots R_k)$ be a grammatical function scheme, and Vt some finite set. Let T = (C, r, M, <, L) be a systemic syntactic structure within S and Vt. Let $F = (F_1, \ldots F_k)$ be a family of disjoint finite sets. A *feature-assignment from T to F* is a mapping h from C to the powerset of $F_1 \cup F_2 \ldots \cup F_k$ such that, for any node c $\in$ C at rank j ($1 \leq j \leq k$), h(c) is a subset of some F_j (i.e. for any constituent c in C, h(c) is a subset of exactly one of the sets in F.)

3.2 Defn.

Suppose S is a grammatical function scheme, F is a family of disjoint finite sets and Vt is a finite set. Let SS(S, Vt) denote the set of systemic syntactic structures within S and Vt. Let FA(S,Vt,F) denote the set of feature-assignments from SS(S,Vt) to F. Let CON(T) be the set of constituents in a systemic syntactic structure T (where T is in SS(S,Vt)). A *realisation*

rule based on S, F and Vt is a mapping from triples of the form (T, h, c) (where T ∈ SS(S,Vt), h ∈ FA(S,Vt,F) and c ∈ CON(T)) to the set {0,1}.
That is, a realisation rule is a mapping which given a syntactic structure, a feature labelling, and a particular constituent in the structure, yields either 0 or 1 (intuitively, 'false' or 'true' respectively). These rules can be viewed as predicates over feature-labelled syntactic structures, in which one constituent is taken as a point of reference. A triple (T, h, c) where T is a syntactic structure, h is a feature-assignment, and c is a constituent in C, is said to *satisfy* a realisation rule J if J(T,h,c) = 1, and is said to *satisfy* a set of realisation rules if it satisfies each rule in the set.

System networks will be defined below as rules which stipulate permissible combinations of features, using conjunction and disjunction (both ordinary and exclusive) to combine them. We thus need various basic definitions concerning feature sets.

3.3 Defn.

Let A be some finite set such that Ø (the empty set) is not an element of A. *A logical expression over A* is either:

(a) an element of A
(b) a tuple $(0, a_1, ... a_n)$ where the a_i are logical expressions over A. (Conventionally, such a triple will be written '$a_1 \vee a_2 ... \vee a_n$', or '$a_1$ OR a_2 ... OR a_n', and will be called a 'disjunctive logical expression'.)
(c) a tuple $(1, a_1, ... a_n)$ where the a_i are logical expressions over A. (Conventionally, such a triple will be written '$a_1 \wedge a_2 ... \wedge a_n$', or '$a_1$ AND a_2 ... AND a_n', and will be called a 'conjunctive logical expression'.)

3.4 Defn.

Let Q be a logical expression over some set A, and B be some subset of A. Then B is said to *satisfy* Q if either

(a) $Q = a$ for some element a of B
(b) $Q = (0, Q_1, ... Q_n)$ and B satisfies at least one of $Q_1, ... Q_n$
(c) $Q = (1, Q_1, ... Q_n)$ and B satisfies all of $Q_1, ... Q_n$.

3.5 Defn.

Let Q be a logical expression over some set A, and c be some element of A. Then c is *mentioned in Q* if either:

(a) $c = Q$
(b) $Q = (N, a_1, ... a_n)$ (for some N in {0,1}) and c is mentioned in at least one of $a_1, ... a_n$.

3.6 Defn.

Let $Q = (N, a_1, ... a_n)$ (for some N in {0,1}) be a logical expression over some set A, and c be some element of A. Then c is *a term in Q* if $c = a_i$, for some i.

3.7 Defn.

Let Q be a logical expression over some set A, and c be some element of A. Then c *occurs purely conjunctively in Q* if either

(i) $c = Q$,
(ii) $Q = (1, a_1, \dots a_n)$ and c occurs purely conjunctively in some a_i.

Notice that if a set B satisfies a logical expression Q, and c occurs purely conjunctively in Q, then it must be the case that $c \in B$. Also, since there is no logical negation in these definitions, if all the features mentioned in an expression Q are in a set B, then B must satisfy Q.

3.8 Defn.

Let A be a finite set. Then a *production over A* is a pair (Q, b) where Q is either the empty set (written '$\emptyset$') or a logical expression over A, and b is an element of A.

Now we can present a definition of a systemic grammar. A system network will be defined as a set of productions, in the above sense, which impose constraints on feature-combinations, and each of which has a set of structural constraints associated with it ('realisation rules' in the sense of 3.2 above).

3.9 Defn.

A *systemic grammar* is a pair (VT, NETWORKS) where NETWORKS is a finite sequence $(N_1, \dots N_k)$ such that each N_i is a tuple (F_i, Ψ_i, VN_i, P_i) where:

(a) F_i is a finite set (the *features*), such that F_i and F_j are disjoint if $i \neq j$;
(b) Ψ_i is a set of proper subsets of the set F_i (the *systems*);
(c) VN_i is a finite set $\{A_1, \dots A_m\}$ of finite sets — the elements of each A_i are *functions* which act as grammatical labels within the functional analyses of a constituent;
(d) P_i is a finite set of pairs (p, R) where p is a production (ξ, α) over F_i and R is a set of realisation rules based on $(VN_1, \dots VN_k)$, $(F_1, \dots, F_k)$ and VT. (These will normally be written '$\xi \longrightarrow \alpha$, R', and any rule r in R will be said to be 'associated with' α.) Each feature α in F_i appears exactly once in a production of the form $\xi \longrightarrow \alpha$, R, and for any system S in Ψ, there is a single ξ such that every feature α in Ψ appears in a production $\xi \longrightarrow \alpha$, R for some R ('all the features in a system have the same entry conditions').

VT is a finite set (the *terminal symbols*), disjoint from all the sets F_i and from all the sets in the VN_i.

It is often convenient to consider the separate portions of a systemic grammar individually, so a tuple $(F_i, \Psi_i, VN_i, VT, P_i)$ (for some i) will be called a *system network*.

3.10 Defn.

Suppose (F, Ψ, VN, VT, P) is a system network as above. A subset ω of F is said to be *consistent* if there are no features $\alpha, \beta \in \omega$ and system $\Sigma \in \Psi$ such that $\alpha \in \Sigma$ & $\beta \in \Sigma$ & $\alpha \neq \beta$.

3.11 Defn.

Suppose (F, Ψ, VN, VT, P) is a system network as above. A subset ω of F is said to be *valid* if it is a consistent feature set such that:

(a) There is no production $\xi \longrightarrow \alpha$, R in P such that ξ is satisfied by ω, but there is no β in ω such that $\xi \longrightarrow \beta$, R' is in P (i.e. if an entry condition is satisfied, there must be at least one feature with that entry condition present in ω).
(b) There are no productions $\xi \longrightarrow \alpha$, R such that $\alpha \in \omega$, but ξ is not satisfied by ω.

3.12 Defn.

Suppose (F, Ψ, VN, VT, P) is a system network as above. A subset ω of F is said to be *conflicting* if there is no valid subset φ of F such that $\omega \subseteq \varphi$. (Similarly, a subset ω is said to be *non-conflicting* if there exists a valid subset of F which is a superset of ω.)

The distinction between 'consistent' and 'non-conflicting' (or between 'inconsistent' and 'conflicting') may not be obvious at once. An analogy with sets of logical formulae may be useful in clarifying this point. 'Inconsistency' here is similar to the explicit presence of a contradiction in a set of formula (P and not-P), whereas 'conflicting' is comparable to a contradiction being derivable from the set of formulae. 'Consistent' is local to a system, and can be checked directly; 'non-conflicting' is more global and can be checked only by a computation equivalent to carrying out a complete derivation. Notice that a non-conflicting set is necessarily consistent — this follows from the definition of 'valid'.

Often, when discussing a systemic grammar, it is convenient to allude to all the features, functions, and terminal symbols in the grammar, without distinguishing different networks. We shall therefore, given a grammar $G = (VT, (N_1, ... N_k))$, where each $N_i = (F_i, \Psi_i, VN_i, P_i)$, adopt the notation of referring to G as a quintuple $[F, \Psi, Vn, Vt, P]$ where $F = (F_1, F_2, ..., F_k)$, $\Psi = \Psi_1 \cup \Psi_2 ... \cup \Psi_k$, and $Vn = (VN_1, ..., VN_k)$. That is, F is an ordered family of feature-sets, Vn is a grammatical function scheme in the sense of Defn 2.3, and VT is simply the complete set of terminal symbols. For further convenience, we may also refer to a feature α as being 'in F' when what we mean is that α is an element of some set F_i.

The grammar has been presented but the language it generates has not yet been defined. First we need to define how a syntactic structure is characterised by the grammar. The essential idea is that a pair consisting of a syntactic structure and a feature-assignment is well-formed if each constituent is assigned a valid feature set, and all the realisation rules which are linked to constituents by the feature-assignment and the grammar are satisfied by the structure.

3.13 Defn.

Let G be a systemic grammar $[F, \Psi, Vn, Vt, P]$. Let $T = (C, r, M, <, L)$ be a systemic syntactic structure within Vn and Vt. Let h be a feature-assignment from T to F. Then (T,h) is said to be *well-formed with respect to G* if, for every constituent $c \in C$:

(a) $h(c)$ is a valid feature set
(b) (T, h, c) satisfies every realisation rule associated with (see Defn 3.9(d)) every feature in $h(c)$.

3.14 Defn.

Let G be a systemic grammar as in the above definition. A string s of elements of Vt is said to be *generated* by G if there exists a systemic syntactic structure T within Vn and Vt, and a feature-assignment h from T to F, such that (T,h) is well-formed with respect to G and s is the terminal string of the constituent tree of T.

The set of strings generated by a grammar G is called 'the language generated by G' and is written 'L(G)'.

4. GENERATION

The definition of L(G) above was independent of any notion of generating a syntactic structure from some initial set of features — it simply stated what constituted a well-formed structure (and hence string). To relate these notions to some notion of generation or computation, it is useful to consider the notion of a process which starts from some initial specification (e.g. some partial structure) and computes a well-formed structure according to that description. Patten (1986) defines a method for doing exactly this, by operating on a *feature heap* which is, roughly, a set of syntactic constituents labelled with clusters of features. The generation process consists of expanding the labelling of each constituent until it is a valid feature set (in the sense defined in Section 3 above), with each selected feature's realisation rules being used to build up a fuller picture of what the eventual structure will be. The partial structure maintained during this process consists of the feature heap (i.e. the labelled constituents so far constructed) and a record of all the stipulations imposed by the realisation rules — adjacency, expansion, conflation, lexification, etc. Section 7 below outlines a formalisation of the structure-building process, but first we will concentrate on another aspect of the generation mechanism, namely the generation of valid feature sets from initial feature sets. This is a computation which proceeds locally, within a system network, and so we shall present here a simplified version in which other aspects of the generation are ignored, and we concentrate on the issue of using the information in a single system network to generate a valid set of features. Informally, this should be acceptable since entry condition features should apply to the same unit as the features for which they are entry conditions (e.g. if *indicative* is generated from *declarative* these two features should both refer to a particular clause). In fact the constituent remains constant during a generation within any particular system network. (Any features in the clause network that are generated — however indirectly — from *declarative* will still refer to the same clause as *declarative*.)

4.1 Defn.

Given a systemic grammar G = [F, Ψ, Vn, Vt, P], where F = (F_{i_1} ... F_k), a *generation relationship* is a binary relation '=>' between subsets of the sets F_{i_1} such that

(a) if A => B then there is exactly one F_i such that A $\subseteq$ F_i, and B $\subseteq$ F_i.
(b) if A => B then A $\subseteq$ B.

Suppose that ω_1, ω_2, ω_3, ..., ω_m are feature sets such that ω_1 => ω_2, ω_2 => ω_3, ..., ω_m-1 => ω_m. Then it is said that ω_1 =>* ω_m, and that ω_1 *generates* ω_m. By convention ω =>* ω.

Alternative generation processes will embody different generation relationships — the following definitions correspond to the generator in Patten(1986).

4.2 Defn.

(a) In a system network (F, Ψ, VN, VT, P) as defined above, an *S-feature* is a feature α such that either $\alpha \in \cup (\Psi)^1$ or there is a production $\xi \longrightarrow \beta$, R in P where β is an S-feature and α is mentioned in ξ. (Informally, α is in a system or is in the entry conditions for an S-feature.)

(b) Any member of F that is not an S-feature is defined to be a *G-feature*.

4.3 Defn.

A production $\xi \longrightarrow \beta$, R is said to be a *gate* if β is a G-feature.

Informally, the initial feature set for the generation consists of those features preselected by higher ranks or by the semantic stratum. These initial features act as goals or constraints that guide the search through the grammar — the generation is that search. The initial features will typically be scattered through the middle of the system network, and the generation proceeds from these in two opposite directions — toward the left of the network through progressively less delicate systems (generating S-features), and toward the right through the gates (generating G-features).

4.4 Defn.

Suppose ω is a feature set from a system network N = (F, Ψ, VN, VT, P). If $\xi \longrightarrow \delta$,R is a production in P, then

a) $\omega \Rightarrow \omega \cup \{\delta\}$ when ω satisfies ξ and δ is a G-feature.

b) $\omega \Rightarrow \omega \cup \{\alpha\}$ when
   (i) α occurs purely conjunctively in ξ
   (ii) $\delta \in \omega$
   (iii) δ is an S-feature
   (iv) there is no system S $\in \Psi$ such that $\alpha \in$ S and there is a $\beta \in$ S, $\beta \neq \alpha$, $\beta \in \omega$.

In each case the production $\xi \longrightarrow \delta$, R is *applied* to feature set ω. (a) and (b) are *forward-* and *backward-applications* respectively. Thus $\Rightarrow$ relates two feature sets exactly when the second is obtained from the first by the application of a single production, and for two feature sets φ and ω, $\omega \Rightarrow^* \varphi$ if φ can be obtained from ω by application of some number of productions of P.[2]

5. SOUNDNESS AND COMPLETENESS

To show that a generation relationship is an appropriate generation mechanism, we have to demonstrate that it generates only valid feature sets, and that any valid feature set can be generated in this way. This is analogous to proving the correctness of an inference mechanism in formal logic — the first condition is analogous to soundness, and the second to completeness. It might be thought that 'soundness' would be defined in terms of preserving validity of feature sets. In fact, since many generation processes (including the one defined in Section 4 above) will be driven by invalidity (features are added to the feature set to try to

---

[1] $\cup(\Psi)$ denotes the union of the sets in Ψ. For example, if Ψ is a set of sets {A, B, C, ..., M} then $\cup(\Psi)$ = A $\cup$ B $\cup$ C ... $\cup$ M.

[2] If all the steps are forward applications, say ω generates φ by *forward-chaining*. *Mutatis mutandis*, ω may also generate φ by *backward-chaining*, or by a combination of the two.

achieve a valid feature set), it will not be the case that '=>' preserves validity at all stages. What matters is the validity of the final feature set produced by '=>'; i.e. the set of features when no further productions can be applied.

It is not very useful to discuss soundness of a generation relationship in isolation from assumptions about initial feature sets, since generation relations tend to be devised to work appropriately with particular kinds of initial feature sets. The appropriate soundness result for the relationship defined in 4.4 above is the following:

Soundness Theorem: If ω_0 is a non-conflicting feature set, and $\omega_0 => \omega'$, then ω' is non-conflicting.

Proof: Since ω_0 is non-conflicting, there is some superset φ of ω_0 which is valid.
  (a) Suppose $\omega_0 => \omega_0 \cup \{\alpha\}$ by Defn. 4.4(a); that is, using a production $\xi \longrightarrow \alpha$, R where α is a G-feature. Since ω_0 satisfies ξ, φ must contain α (by Defn. 3.11(a) for 'valid'). Hence φ is a valid superset of $\omega_0 \cup \{\alpha\}$. Hence $\omega_0 \cup \{\alpha\}$ is non-conflicting.
  (b) Suppose $\omega_0 => \omega_0 \cup \{\alpha\}$ by Defn. 4.4(b); that is, using a production $\xi \longrightarrow \delta$, R where δ is a S-feature and α occurs purely conjunctively in ξ. Since ω_0 contains δ, φ must satisfy ξ (by Defn. 3.11(b) for 'valid'). Hence, since α occurs purely conjunctively in ξ, it must be the case that $\alpha \in \varphi$ (see remark following Defn. 3.7). Hence φ is a valid superset of $\omega0 \cup \{\alpha\}$, which is therefore a non-conflicting feature set.

Corollary: If ω_0 is a non-conflicting feature set, and $\omega_0 =>^* \omega'$, then ω' is non-conflicting.

It is interesting to note that this proof does not make explicit use of part (b)(iv) of definition 4.4. An implementation of the => generation algorithm which omitted checks on the consistency of its feature choices would therefore still be sound *providing the original feature set was non-conflicting*.

Lemma 1: If $\omega => \omega \cup \{\delta\}$, and δ is not in ω, then ω is not valid.

Proof: If $\omega => \omega \cup \{\delta\}$, then there are two cases:
  (i) There is a production $\xi \longrightarrow \delta$, R where δ is a G-feature and ω satisfies ξ. Since δ is not in ω, this would mean that ω is not valid (by Defn. 3.11(a)).
  (ii) There is a production $\xi \longrightarrow \alpha$, R where α is a S-feature, δ occurs purely conjunctively in ξ, and $\alpha \in \omega$ Since δ is not in ω, ω does not satisfy ξ, despite containing α. This would mean that ω is not valid (by Defn. 3.11(b)).

Corollary: If ω is valid, then there is no feature set ω' such that $\omega \subset \omega'$ and $\omega =>^* \omega'$.

The above results also suggest that if we have a sequence of feature-sets $\omega_1 => \omega_2 =>...$, where ω_1 is non-conflicting, then this sequence is bound to lead to a valid feature set (since size of the feature-set increases at each step, and only finite feature sets are involved).

Defining completeness is similarly complicated by the issue of initial feature sets. Clearly, since $\omega =>^* \omega$ for any feature set ω, it will trivially be the case that any valid feature set can be generated via any reasonable generation relationship (i.e. from itself). We shall prove a particular variant of 'completeness' for the generation relationship given in 4.4 above, but we do not regard it as appropriate to attempt a fully general definition of completeness. Also, in Section 9, we indicate what the corresponding result might be for another generation relationship.

As mentioned in Section 4 above, the generation relationship of Defn. 4.4 is devised to operate on an initial set of preselected features spread throughout the network. In order to discuss completeness of the relationship, it is first necessary to give a precise definition of how those initial features should be distributed; the next few definitions provide that characterisation.

5.1 Defn.

For any feature set ω, a feature $\alpha \in \omega$ is a *seed feature with respect to* ω if (a) it is an S-feature and (b) there is no production $\xi \longrightarrow \beta$, R such that β is an S-feature in ω and α occurs purely conjunctively in ξ.

Informally, a seed feature is an S-feature which cannot be generated by backward-chaining (Defn. 4.4(b)) from other features in the set.

5.2 Defn.

A feature α is *immediately less delicate than* a feature δ if and only if P contains a production $\xi \longrightarrow \delta$, R and α is mentioned in ξ.

5.3 Defn.

A feature α is *less delicate than* a feature δ if and only if either (a) α is immediately less delicate than δ; or (b) there is a feature β such that α is less delicate than β and β is immediately less delicate than δ.

Traditionally, features at the right hand side of a system network are more 'delicate' in the sense of representing a finer classification of linguistic entities.

5.4 Defn.

A feature α is a *root feature* if $\varnothing \longrightarrow \alpha$, R $\in$ P (i.e. if it has no entry conditions — a least delicate feature: e.g. *clause, nominal-group*, etc.).

5.5 Defn.

A system network is *acyclic* if the less delicate than relation over P is a strict partial order.

The notion of an acyclic network will be used to restrict the discussion to those grammars that do not contain recursive systems. Notice that this does not rule out recursive syntactic structures, since a recursive system affects only the feature configurations for a particular constituent.

5.6 Defn.

An S-feature α is said to be a *most delicate S-feature* if there is no S-feature β such that α is less delicate than β.

5.7 Defn.

A system network is *expressive* if all root features are S-features. (Informally, this means that the system network must have at least one system.)

Completeness Theorem: Let $N = (F, \Psi, VN, VT, P)$ be an acyclic expressive system network. Let ω be a valid subset of F. Then there exists a non-conflicting set of features ω_0 such that each element of ω_0 is a seed with respect to ω, and $\omega_0 =>* \omega$.

Proof: Let ω_0 be the set of all features in ω which are seeds with respect to ω. ω_0 must be non-conflicting, since ω is valid. Let ω_1 be a feature set such that $\omega_0 =>* \omega_1$, and such that there is no $\omega_2 \neq \omega_1$ with $\omega_1 => \omega_2$ (i.e. ω_1 is a maximal set generated from ω_0). We show that every feature in ω lies in ω_1. Since ω is valid, it follows by lemma 1 that this set ω_1 must equal ω, and the result follows. The proof proceeds separately for S-features and G-features.

(a) *S-features*. Suppose $\alpha \in \omega$ is an S-feature.
  (i) If α is a seed feature with respect to ω, then it follows that $\alpha \in \omega_1$ since $\alpha \in \omega_0$, and $\omega_0 \subseteq \omega_1$.
  (ii) Suppose α is not a seed feature with respect to ω. Then α must occur purely conjunctively in the left side of a production which has an S-feature β on the right, and where $\beta \in \omega$. If β is in ω_0 (i.e. is a seed w.r.t. ω), then β is in ω_1, so by Defn. 4.4(b) α is in ω_1 (since ω_1 is maximal). On the other hand, if β is not in ω_0 (i.e. is not a seed with respect to ω), then a similar argument can be applied to β, using the fact that there must be some rule in which β occurs purely conjunctively, with an S-feature γ that is in ω on the right hand side. This sequence of features $\alpha, \beta, \gamma, ...$ must eventually terminate at a seed feature with respect to ω, since the network is acyclic and most delicate S-features are seeds with respect to any feature set which contains them. Hence, all the features in the sequence, including α, are in ω_1.

(b) *G-features*. We prove this by induction on the *depth* of a G-feature, where we define the 'depth' of a G-feature γ to be the length of the longest sequence of features $\{\alpha_1, ... \alpha_M\}$ such that α_1 is a root feature, $\alpha_M = \gamma$, and for each i, α_i is immediately less delicate than α_{i+1}. (Informally, the depth of a feature is the length of the longest path from the left side of the network to the feature.) Suppose we have proven that the theorem holds for all G-features of depth less than or equal to N (i.e. every such G-feature lies in ω_1), where N > 1. Let β be a G-feature of depth N+1, appearing in a production $\xi \longrightarrow \beta$, R. (Each feature appears on the right hand side of exactly one production — see Defn.3.9.) Each feature mentioned in ξ must either be an S-feature or a G-feature of depth less than N+1. Hence each feature mentioned in ξ is in ω_1 (assuming part (a) of the proof, above). Hence ω_1 must satisfy ξ (see remark following Defn. 3.7). Therefore, by Defn. 4.4(a) and the fact that ω_1 is the maximal set generated from ω_0, β must be in ω_1.

Since the network is expressive, there are no G-features of depth 1, and G-features of depth 2 have entry conditions which are entirely made up of S-features. By part (a) of the proof, it follows that all the features mentioned in the entry conditions of G-features of depth 2 are in ω_1, and hence all depth 2 G-features are in ω_1. This establishes the induction.[3]

6. SOME REALISATION RULES

So far, all that has been said is that the realisation rules are mappings from triples (T, h, c) to {0,1}. It is expected that some basic set of these mappings will be provided by systemic theory,

---

[3] This proof is simplified by assuming that there is an 'initial feature set' that contains not only those seeds which are given initially (as described in the discussion on generation), but also seeds which would be preselected during the generation. This does not affect the relevance of the proof because the origin of the seeds and the order in which they are added to the feature set are irrelevant.

to be used as needed in writing systemic grammars. That is, there will not be arbitrary mappings defined for each new grammar, but a small repertoire of realisation rules will serve for a wide range of grammars. The sample realisation rules used by different systemic writers vary slightly, but the following are typical (and are the ones used in Patten, 1986). Assume a systemic grammar $G = [F, \Psi, Vn, Vt, P]$, a syntactic structure $T = (C, r, M, <, L)$, and a feature-assignment h; A and B are any grammatical functions from the sets in Vn, α is in F, a is in Vt.

Adjacency. The notation 'A^B', where A and B are functions from the same set of functions at
some rank, is taken to mean the mapping R-adjacent[A,B] which is 1 for (T, h, c) iff there
exist two daughter nodes m_1 and m_2 in c, such that $m_1 < m_2$, there is no m_3 with $m_1 < m_3 <$
m_2, m_1 is associated with a node in the functional analysis which has the grammatical
function A, and m_2 is similarly associated with the grammatical function B.

Expansion. The notation 'A(B)', where A and B are functions from the same set of functions at
some rank, denotes the mapping R-expands[A,B] which is 1 for (T,h,c) iff the functional
analyses of c include one in which there is a node n which is associated with the function A
and a node m, a direct descendant of n, which is associated with B.

Conflation. The notation 'A/B' denotes the mapping R-conflated[A,B] which is 1 for (T, h, c)
iff there is a daughter node n in c such that n is associated with both grammatical functions
A and B (via its links to nodes in the functional analyses).

Lexify. The notation 'A = a' indicates the mapping R-lexify[A,a] which is 1 for (T, h, c) if
there is a terminal node m which is a daughter of c, such that L(m) = a, and m is associated
with grammatical function A.

Preselection. The notation '$A_1<A_2< ... <A_i:\alpha$' denotes the mapping R-preselects[$A_1,A_2, ... A_i$,
α] which is 1 for (T, h, c) iff there is a sequence of daughter nodes ($n_1, ... n_i$) such that n_1
is in c, $M(n_{j+1}) = n_j$ (for j = 1 to i-1), n_j is associated with A_j (j = 1 to i), and $\alpha \in h(n_j)$.

As an informal example of a preselection path, consider the clause *'The book's cover was judged'*. The Subject of this clause (*'the book's cover'*) has a Deictic element (*'the book's'*) which itself has a Deictic element (*'the'*). During the course of generating this clause, the preselection 'Subject<Deictic<Deictic:non-selective' may be made.[4]

Aside from the fact that different realisation relations and notation may be used, a similar treatment of realisation will appear in any systemic model.

7. GENERATING STRUCTURES

As described in Sections 4 and 5, the design of a generation algorithm for this systemic model consists largely of devising an algorithm which, given a set of initial features for a set of constituents, produces a derivation of a valid feature set for each constituent using the productions of the grammar (equivalent to traversing the system networks, collecting features). Such an algorithm should have, as a side-effect, the development of a syntactic structure (as defined in Section 2 above) using the information in the realisation rules attached to the selected features. Each realisation rule makes some very local, limited statement about the final structure (in terms of adjacency, conflation, etc.). The generator must accumulate these statements or constraints as contributions to the description of the final structure.

We can regard a systemic syntactic structure as being characterised by various relationships, which embody the information required in the definitions in Section 2. Assuming a systemic grammar $G = [F, \Psi, Vn, V_t, P]$, the approach will be to build up sets of nodes, constituents, functional analyses, and feature-assignments which will eventually form a syntactic structure T = (C, r, M, <, L). We require various dynamically altering sets of entities — DN (a set of daughter-nodes), C (a set of constituents), FN (a set of function-nodes) — and various

---

4   This notation was introduced in Patten(1986); previously there did not seem to be any standard notation for
    preselecting features for nested constituents.

relations defined on these sets and on the sets from the grammar — F (a set of features), Vn' (the set of grammatical functions in the scheme Vn), Vt (a set of lexical items).

The relationships needed are:

NEXT, subset of DN x DN : (dn_1, dn_2) are in NEXT iff dn_1 and dn_2 are in the same constituent and immediately adjacent according to the left-right order, $dn_1 < dn_2$.

DAUGHTER, subset of DN x C : (dn_1, c) are in DAUGHTER iff dn_1 is in the constituent c.

MOTHER, subset of DN x DN : (dn_1, dn_2) are in MOTHER if $M(dn_1) = dn_2$, where M is the mapping described in Defn. 2.4.

HAS-FUNCTION, subset of DN x FN : (dn_1, fn_1) are in HAS-FUNCTION iff fn_1 is in the set $g(dn_1)$, where g is the mapping described in Defn. 2.2 (i.e. the node dn_1 is associated with fn_1 in the functional analysis).

HAS-FEATURE, subset of C x F : (c, y) are in HAS-FEATURE iff y is in the set f(C) where f is the feature-assignment.

HAS-LABEL, subset of FN x Vn' : (fn_1, y) in HAS-LABEL iff $h(fn_1)=y$, where h is the mapping in Defn. 2.1 (i.e. the attachment of labels to the nodes of the tree in a functional analysis).

IN-ANALYSIS, subset of FN x C : (fn_1, c) are in IN-ANALYSIS iff fn_1 is a node in a functional-analysis in c.

LEX, subset of DN x Vt : (dn_1, w) are in LEX iff dn_1 is a terminal node in the constituent-tree and $L(dn_1)=w$ (see Defn. 2.4(d)).

We also need a relationship to define the hierarchy of functions represented, for each constituent, by its set of functional analyses. The tree-defining relation in Defn 2.1 is purely local to a single constituent, but for various purposes (in particular, the 'preselection' realisation rule), it is convenient to consider paths of function-labels which reach through several constituents. This can be done via the association of function-nodes with unit-nodes, and the tree-structure of the unit-nodes. We associate a function-node with a unit-node (as in HAS-FUNCTION above), that unit-node itself has a daughter (defined by DAUGHTER), and that daughter will be associated with one or more function-nodes. The resulting relation will not define a strict tree, but rather an acyclic graph, as the linking of unit-nodes to multiple function-nodes does not give a 'single-parent' arrangement:

SUPER, subset of FN x FN : (fn_1, fn_2) are in SUPER if fn_1 is the parent of fn_2 in a functional analysis, or if the parent of fn_2 is the root of a functional analysis in a constituent c, and the parent node dn_1 of c is such that (dn_1, c') is in DAUGHTER, (fn_1, c') is in IN-ANALYSIS, and (dn_1, fn_1) are in HAS-FUNCTION.

The generation process should, on encountering a realisation rule, alter the contents of the sets DN, FN, C, and the nine relations described above to reflect the updated syntactic structure. (We assume that the whole of F, Vn and Vt are available throughout). Notice that the nine relations above have been chosen not on the basis of some particular set of realisation rules, but because they characterise the essential structural relationships involved in a syntactic structure as defined in Section 2 — they form an atomic vocabulary of ways of connecting items, which should suffice to state most reasonable systemic realisation rules.

For example, the algorithm for responding to the realisation rules given in Section 6 above could be phrased thus, where CC is a variable denoting the constituent currently being built (i.e. the grammatical unit whose features are being accumulated):

A^B: if there are no fn_1, fn_2 in FN, and dn_1, dn_2 in DN such that (fn_1, A) and (fn_2, B) are in HAS-LABEL and (fn_1, CC), (fn_2, CC) are in IN-ANALYSIS, and (dn_1, fn_1), (dn_2, fn_2) are in HAS-FUNCTION, then create such nodes and entries; ensure that (dn_1, dn_2) are in NEXT.

A(B): if there are no fn_1, fn_2 in FN such that (fn_1, A) and (fn_2, B) are in HAS-LABEL, (fn_1, CC) and (fn_2, CC) are in IN-ANALYSIS, then create such nodes and entries; ensure that (fn_1, fn_2) is in SUPER.

A/B: if there are no fn_1, fn_2 in FN such that (fn_1, A) and (fn_2, B) are in HAS-LABEL and (fn_1, CC), (fn_2, CC) are in IN-ANALYSIS, then create such nodes and entries; ensure that there is a unique node dn_1 in DN such that both (dn_1, fn_1) and (dn_1, fn_2) are in HAS-FUNCTION.

A=a: if there is no fn_1 in FN such that (fn_1, CC) are in IN-ANALYSIS, and dn_1 in DN such that (dn_1, fn_1) are in HAS-FUNCTION, then create such nodes and entries; ensure that (dn_1, a) is in LEX.

$A_1 < A_2 < ... A_m : \alpha$:

   ensure, by creating new nodes and entries if necessary, that there is a sequence of nodes $fn_1, ... f_m$ in FN and a sequence of nodes $dn_1, ... dn_m$ in DN such that:
  (a) dn_1 is in CC
  (b) for all i (2 to m), (dn_i, dn_{i-1}) is in MOTHER
  (c) for all i (1 to m), (dn_i, fn_i) is in HAS-FUNCTION
  (d) (c', α) is in HAS-FEATURE, where c' is the constituent such that $(dn_m, c') \in$ DAUGHTER
  (e) for all i (1 to m), (fn_i, A_i) is in HAS-LABEL.

Notice that it is virtually impossible to guarantee that the node-sets and relations formed from the realisation rules attached to the various collected features will characterise a completely well-formed structure as defined in Section 2. The grammar-writer has complete freedom to define any realisation rules at all, and so could write a grammar which was itself well-formed, but whose derivations produced bizarre or partial syntactic structures.

8. FORMULATING REALISATION RULES IN LOGIC

In characterising the notion of a well-formed syntactic structure, a realisation rule was said merely to be a mapping from constituents within feature-labelled structures to the set $\{0,1\}$; that is, a predicate over structures. A generation algorithm must have a way of using the information in realisation rules to define a final structure, building up the information as it proceeds. The approach in Section 7 above (which is based on the implementation in Patten, 1986) essentially associates with each variety of realisation rule a mapping from partial syntactic structures to partial syntactic structures. Hence we are regarding a realisation rule as denoting *two* mappings — the declarative predicate which defines well-formedness of the final structure, and the algorithmic mapping which transforms a partial structure into another partial structure. It would be more elegant to have a formulation of realisation rules which conflates these two uses, allowing a single statement both to act as a predicate over structures and as a recipe for building a structure which conformed to the predicate. This appears to be possible by formalising the content of realisation rules using a first-order logic, so that the generation algorithm manipulates a gradually-increasing set of statements defining the content of the eventual structure.

This approach would involve associating with each realisation rule (in a systematic way) a formula of this first-order theory, free in one variable which denotes a constituent. Such a formula can be used to define the mapping from complete syntactic structures to truth-values in a fairly straightforward way (i.e. $Q(x)$ is true of (T, f, c) if $Q(c)$ is true). The same open formulae can be used to build up a structure description gradually, by having the generation procedure transform the formula for each realisation rule it encounters into a closed formula, by instantiating the free variable to the name of the constituent being built. The final structure is then a well-formed syntactic structure (as in Section 2) which is an interpretation (in the logical sense) of the final set of statements, with the symbolic constants mapped to nodes within the structure and using certain interpretations of predicate symbols (cf. Marcus, Hindle & Fleck, 1983).

For added clarity, we will outline this proposal using a sorted logic. There are the following basic sorts: daughter-nodes, function-nodes, constituents, function-labels, grammatical features, and lexical items. There are nine predicate-names, corresponding to the nine relations defined in Section 7 above, with the obvious interpretations; for example:

next(X:daughter-node, Y:daughter-node) — true iff X and Y are in the same constituent and immediately adjacent according to the left-right order.
daughter(X:daughter-node, C:constituent) — true iff X is in the constituent C.

For example, the realisation rules given in Section 6 above could be phrased thus, where X is in each case a free variable of type constituent:

$A \wedge B$: (Exist n_1, n_2: daughter-node; fn_1, fn_2: function-node) daughter(n_1,X) $\wedge$ daughter (n_2,X) $\wedge$ has-function(n_1, fn_1) $\wedge$ has-function(n_2, fn_2) $\wedge$ has-label (fn_1,A) $\wedge$ has-label(fn_2,B) $\wedge$ next (n_1, n_2).

A(B): (Exist fn_1, fn_2: function-node) super(fn_1, fn_2) $\wedge$ has-label(fn_1, A) $\wedge$ has-label(fn_2,B) $\wedge$ in-analysis(fn_1, X) $\wedge$ in-analysis(fn_2,X)

A/B: (Exist n: daughter-node; fn_1, fn_2: function-node) daughter(n,X) $\wedge$ has-function(n,fn_1) $\wedge$ has-function(n, fn_2) $\wedge$ has-label(fn_1, A) $\wedge$ has-label(fn_2, B)

A=a (Exist n: daughter-node; fn_1: function-node) daughter(n, X) $\wedge$ has-function(n, fn_1) $\wedge$ has-label(fn_1, A) $\wedge$ lex(n, a)

$A_1 < A_2 < ... A_m : \alpha$:
(Forall i: 1 to m) (Exist fn_i: function-node; dn_i: daughter-node; c_i: constituent) daughter(dn_i, c_i) $\wedge$ mother(dn_i, dn_{i-1}) $\wedge$ has-function(dn_i, fn_i) $\wedge$ daughter(dn_1, X) $\wedge$ has-feature(c_m, α) $\wedge$ has-label (fn_i, A_i)

As commented in Section 7, there is no guarantee that the structure-description produced by the generator will be coherent; in the formulation in logic, this would show up as a set of realisation statements which were inconsistent, or for which there was more than one interpretation.

9. COMPARISON WITH PENMAN

Certainly the best-known of the current systemic text-generation systems is Penman (Mann & Matthiessen, 1983). Linguistically, the formulation of the grammatical stratum given in Sections 2 and 3 above is compatible with the Penman model. Indeed, some of the realisation relationships described above, and the notion of a 'gate', originated in the work on Penman. However, there are some important differences between Penman's processing framework and the the generation mechanism outlined in Sections 4 and 5 above. These differences will be discussed briefly in this section.

The major difference between Penman and the approach outlined in Sections 4 and 5 above is the control structure used for exploring the productions (i.e. traversing the networks), and the interface through which this control structure interacts with the higher-level linguistic components (which manifests itself in the nature of the initial feature sets used for generation). As commented in Section 4, the notion of 'generation' given there is better viewed as an abstract statement of a control structure, rather than a declarative notion of derivation, and we can characterise the control structure of Penman by providing amended definitions of the generation relationship '=>' as follows:

9.1 Defn.

(a) *G-features*: Suppose ω is a feature set from a system network N = (F, Ψ, VN, VT, P), $\xi \longrightarrow \delta$, R is a production in P, and δ is a G-feature. Then $\omega => \omega \cup \{\delta\}$ iff ω satisfies ξ.[5]

(b) *S-features*: Suppose S $\in$ Ψ, S = $\{\alpha_1, ... \alpha_n\}$, so that for each i $(1 \leq i \leq n)$, $\xi \longrightarrow \alpha_i$, R is a production in P. Then, for each i $(1 \leq i \leq n)$, $\omega => \omega \cup \{\alpha_i\}$ iff:

---

5   Note this is the same as in Defn. 4.4(a) above.

(i) ω satisfies ξ
(ii) $\omega \cap (S - \{\alpha_i\}) = \emptyset$

However, to capture the spirit of the control structure used in the implemented system, we need to take account of the choice mechanism used for selecting features within systems. Mann and Matthiessen associate with each system a 'chooser' which interrogates the environment (text plan, etc.) to decide which feature to select for the system.

9.2 Defn.

Let N = (F, Ψ, VN, VT, P) be a system network. A *choice function* for N is a mapping ch from Ψ to F such that, for any system S $\in$ Ψ, ch(S) $\in$ S.

Informally, a choice function selects exactly one feature from each system — that is, it plays the role of the 'choosers' together with the environment. We can now give a more accurate statement of the Penman generation process.

9.3 Defn.

Let N be a system network, => be a generation relationship defined on N as in 9.1 above, and let ch be a choice function defined for N. The *guided generation relationship based on ch and* => is the generation relationship '==>' defined as the follows.

ω_1 ==> $\omega_1 \cup \{\alpha\}$ iff
(a) ω_1 => $\omega_1 \cup \{\alpha\}$, AND
(b) if α is in a system S, then ch(S) = α.

The relationship '==>*' can then be defined as the transitive closure of '==>' in the obvious way. These definitions, together with the normal assumptions about initial feature sets used by Mann & Matthiessen, leads to the following two conjectures, which we believe to be provable.

Soundness Theorem: For any choice function ch, if α is a root feature, ω is a feature-set, and $\{\alpha\}$ ==>* ω, then ω is consistent.

Completeness Theorem: If ω is a valid feature set, then there is a choice function ch, and a set $\omega_0 = \{\alpha_1, ... \alpha_m\}$ of root features such that ω_0 ==>* ω.

The completeness of the generation algorithm depends on the behaviour of the 'chooser' mechanism, which must be 'fair' in the sense of allowing all possible choices, under appropriate environments; that is, for each possibility there must exist some choice function which allows it.

The important aspects of the two approaches to processing a systemic grammar (i.e. definitions 4.4 and 9.3) can be brought to the surface by expressing each of them in terms of the problem-solving algorithm of 'problem reduction' (see Nilsson, 1971). Only a very informal discussion will be presented here — for a more rigorous treatment see Patten (1986).

The problem reduction algorithm involves transforming 'problem descriptions' into 'reduced' problem descriptions (descriptions of subproblems) through the use of problem-reduction operators. The objective is to reduce an original problem to a set of primitive problems whose solutions are either trivial or known. A problem may be reduced to a disjunctive set of subproblems, only one of which must be solved; or a conjunctive set of subproblems, all of which must be solved.

Problem reduction can be illustrated by drawing AND/OR graphs. Following Nilsson, suppose problem A can be solved if either problems B and C are solved, or problems D and E are solved, or problem F is solved. This situation can be illustrated with the graph in Figure 1.

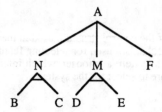

Figure 1. An AND/OR graph (from Nilsson, 1971).

The nodes labelled N and M are introduced as exclusive parents for the sets of subproblems {B,C} and {D,E} respectively. It is conventional to draw the graph such that each conjunction of subproblems is under its own graph node. If M and N are thought of acting as problem descriptions, the diagram shows problem A as having been reduced to the alternative subproblems N, M or F. The graph nodes N, M and F are thus called OR nodes. Problem N is reduced to the set of subproblems B and C and these subproblems are represented by AND nodes. AND nodes are represented by bars between their incoming arcs.

The processing of a systemic grammar can be characterised as problem reduction in both Penman (Defn. 9.3) and our model (Defn. 4.4). In neither case do the gates involve search, so they will be omitted from the following discussion.

(a)   (b)

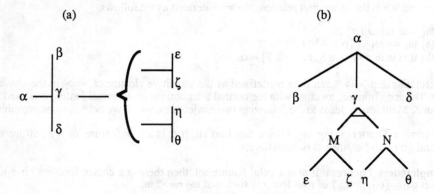

Figure 2. Problem reduction in Penman.

Figure 2(a) above shows a fragment of a system network. One way of interpreting this network as an AND/OR graph is to simply treat terms in systems as OR nodes and treat the curly bracket as specifying AND nodes. The corresponding AND/OR graph is shown in Figure 2(b). This is the approach taken by Penman. Penman would begin with the original problem α, and reduce it to solving exactly one of β, γ or δ (this is really an AND/EXCLUSIVE-OR graph). The 'chooser' for this system (see above) may select γ after interacting with higher-level components such as the text planner. The problem is now reduced to solving problems N and M. Two different choosers are invoked to choose between ε and ζ, and between η and θ. Note that the initial problem description corresponds to the least delicate feature in the system network, and the problem reduction corresponds to traversing the system network from left to right.

The processing of a system network in the model of Defn. 4.4 can also be expressed as problem reduction, but here the initial problem descriptions correspond to seed features and the problem reduction corresponds to traversing the network from right to left, as sketched in Figure 3, where 3(a) shows a network fragment and 3(b) the corresponding AND/OR graph.

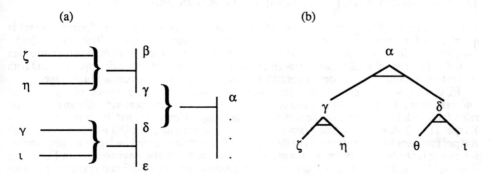

Figure 3. Problem reduction in our model.

The initial problem description in this case is a seed feature α. The problem is reduced (by a backward-chaining production $\gamma \wedge \delta \longrightarrow \alpha$) to solving γ and δ. The problem γ is then reduced to solving ζ and η, and the problem δ is reduced to solving θ and ι. It is no coincidence that there are no OR nodes in the AND/OR graph — for this generation relationship problems *always* reduce to AND nodes. This is because the two sources of disjunction — systems and disjunctive entry conditions — are resolved implicitly or explicitly by the preselected seed features. Each of the seed features in the initial feature set is treated as an initial problem description and reduced in this way. The result is that the grammar is traversed from right to left, by a number of small AND trees. These AND trees gradually converge as they stretch left. If one of the subproblems in a particular tree is already part of another tree, it is treated as a primitive problem (see above) and not reduced. The seed features thus constrain the search so heavily that it is deterministic, meaning that the grammar can be traversed very efficiently without needing to seek further guidance from other components.

Thus, problem reduction for Defn. 4.4 is best understood in terms of AI search strategy. The semantic stratum of a systemic grammar sets up grammatical goals (i.e. the initial data for the generation) in the form of the seed features. In other words, the exploration of the grammatical search space is guided by the knowledge contained in the semantic stratum through the mechanism of goal-directed backward-chaining. In contrast, the goal given to Penman is the least-specific feature possible (a root feature such as *clause, nominal-group,* etc.) which provides almost no guidance at all — the guidance comes from the choice function. That is, if we consider both Penman and the model in Section 4 as doing goal-directed search, the goals (initial problem descriptions) provided in the former are very general, providing little constraint, whereas in the latter case the goals are very specific and greatly constrain the outcome of the generation, which should lead to greater efficiency. (This is, of course, subject to the assumption that a suitable set of seed features can be supplied as the initial set. Patten (1986) argues that this is a linguistically plausible assumption, since the semantic stratum acts as a highly-compiled interface between the grammar and the higher-level components.)

It is worth noting that the use of preselected features is closely based on the linguistic mechanism described by Halliday (1973, 1978).

10. COMPARISON WITH FUNCTIONAL UNIFICATION GRAMMAR

This section will offer some brief and informal comparisons with another formalism that is often used for generation: functional unification grammar (see Kay, 1979; 1984; 1985). Functional unification grammar (FUG) and systemic grammar share many of the characteristics desirable for generation. Both are intended to facilitate a functional linguistic approach, and both are feature grammars that to some extent allow a paradigmatic representation of language.

FUG is a wholly general notation with an associated all-purpose computational interpretation (cf. Ritchie, 1984), and as such can be used to represent virtually any symbolic rules (although the elegance of the statements may vary). Hence it is hardly surprising that, as Kasper (1987) shows, systemic grammars could be represented in FUG notation. (Although Kasper proposes further extensions to the basic FUG notation to avoid inelegance; there seems, for example, to be a problem with representing the paradigmatic environment in FUG. See Kasper, (1987); Section 4.3.2.) Some important contrasts between FUG and systemic grammar notation are made by Kasper, but the purely linguistic differences are for the most part superficial, and will not be dwelt upon here.

There are, however, some important processing issues that merit discussion. Generation from unification grammars is described (e.g. Kay, 1979, 1985) as starting with a 'functional description', and simply unifying it with the grammar using the unification algorithm recursively on all constituents. The trouble is that this approach amounts to an unguided search through the generation search-space, and is very inefficient (Appelt, 1983 pp. 599; see also Ritchie, 1986). This is related to a difference between FUG and our model of systemic grammar in their way of specifying choices between disjunctive options. In systemic grammar, each significant point in the grammar is labelled with a feature-name, and hence a feature-name can be used to specify which option within a system is to be taken. We have assumed that such specifications of choices can be 'preselected' between grammatical levels (different networks) using 'paths' to indicate where a feature has been chosen. The form of preselection statements is '$A_1 < A_2 \ldots < A_m : \alpha$', where the sequence A_i ($1 \leq i \leq m$) forms a 'path' to a particular constituent identified by the function A_m. This is a specialisation of the idea of a 'path' in FUG which can be used to assign feature values, or any other values, to nested constituents. However, in FUG a feature-name (or a path) does not uniquely indicate a particular disjunct; all that is stipulated is that the correct choice of disjunct must be able to unify with the given path. If we assume that the input to a systemic generator is a set of preselection statements (i.e. a set of paths with features attached), then these can indicate the choices to be made, either by selecting single features from systems (i.e. giving the effect of a 'choice function' as in Section 9 above), or by selecting suitable 'seed' features (see Section 5 above). In contrast, an FUG functional description does not give this guidance, and to achieve the same effect would need an enhanced form of input structure which indicated which disjuncts were to be chosen in the description of each constituent. It might appear that some higher-level mechanism (perhaps an equivalent to Halliday's semantic stratum) could include seed features in the initial functional description, and these could be used to guide the search. Unfortunately, there is a problem with this. Embedding is used to represent delicacy in FUG (Kasper, 1986). Since the vast majority of seed features are (excluding gates) the most delicate features in the grammar, they will, *ipso facto*, be the *last* features to which the unification algorithm will have access in its recursion. Hence detailed paths in the initial functional description do not obviate the search to find a valid unification, as there is no direct relationship between these paths and the choices facing the generator.

One attempt to deal with the question of choice in FUG generation was Appelt's (1983) TELEGRAM system that resulted in an approach to choice-making very similar to Penman (ibid., p. 599), in that at each choice-point the unification would stop and seek guidance from the higher-level components of the system.

Another way out of this problem might be to compile the FUG into some other representation amenable to efficient guidance. Kay (1985) has already suggested that FUGs be compiled for the purposes of analysis, and it is possible that generation would also benefit from a similar intermediate step.

11. CONCLUSION

Systemic grammar is a linguistic theory of grammar that has played, and is likely to continue to play, an important role in text-generation research. We have provided a formalisation of systemic grammar in an attempt to make the existing ideas more precise. This includes formal definitions of a systemic grammar, of systemic syntactic structures, and of the language generated by a systemic grammar. We have also defined two generation methods for this model. One algorithm from the current literature, based on Mann & Matthiessen (1983, see Section 9), starts from feature sets consisting of root features and assumes a choice function that will select a unique feature from each system. Another algorithm (see Sections 4 and 5) is shown to compute a valid feature set from a non-conflicting set of seed features. The latter algorithm can be informally described as receiving guidance from the semantic stratum and higher ranks in the form of preselected features (Halliday, 1978), resulting in a highly-constrained goal-directed search. In Section 10 we compare and contrast this generation algorithm with generation from functional unification grammars.

Although the formalisation given here is largely exploratory, we hope we have paved the way for a more substantial treatment along these lines.

REFERENCES

Appelt, D. (1983) TELEGRAM: a Grammar Formalism for Language Planning. In: *Proceedings of the Eighth International Joint Conference on Artificial Intelligence.* Karlsruhe.

Davey, A.C. (1978) *Discourse Production.* Edinburgh: Edinburgh University Press.

Halliday, M.A.K. (1973) *Explorations in the Functions of Language.* London: Arnold.

Halliday, M.A.K. (1978) *Language as a Social Semiotic.* London: Arnold.

Hopcroft, J. & Ullman, J. (1969) *Formal Languages and their Relation to Automata* . Reading, Mass.: Addison-Wesley.

Kasper, R. (1987) Systemic Grammar and Functional Unification Grammar. In: J. Benson & W. Greaves (Eds.) *Proceedings of 12th International Systemic Workshop.* Norwood, N.J.: Ablex.

Kay, M. (1979) Functional Grammar. In: *Proceedings of the Fifth Annual Meeting of the Berkeley Linguistics Society.* Berkeley.

Kay, M. (1984) Functional Unification Grammar: a Formalism for Machine Translation. In: *Proceedings of COLING-84.* Stanford.

Kay, M. (1985) Parsing in Functional Unification Grammar. In: D. Dowty, L. Karttunen & A. Zwicky (Eds.) *Natural Language Parsing.* Cambridge: Cambridge University Press.

Mann W. & Matthiessen C. (1983) *Nigel: A Systemic Grammar for Text Generation.* RR-83-105, Information Sciences Institute, University of Southern California, Marina Del Rey.

Marcus, M.P, Hindle, D. & Fleck, M.M. (1983) D-Theory: Talking about Talking about Trees. In: *Proceedings of the 21st Annual ACL Conference.* Cambridge, Mass.

McKeown, K. (1982) *Generating Natural Language Text in Response to Questions about Database Structure.* Ph.D. Dissertation, University of Pennsylvania.

Nilsson, N. (1971) *Problem-solving Methods in Artificial Intelligence.* London: McGraw-Hill.

Patten, T. (1985) A Problem Solving Approach to Generating Text from Systemic Grammars. In: *Proceedings of the Second Conference of the European Chapter of the Association for Computational Linguistics.* Geneva.

Patten, T. (1986) *Interpreting Systemic Grammar as a Computational Representation: A Problem Solving Approach to Text Generation.* Ph.D. Thesis, University of Edinburgh.

Ritchie, G. (1984) Simulating a Turing Machine Using Functional Unification Grammar. In: *Proceedings of ECAI-84,* Pisa.

Ritchie, G. (1986) The Computational Complexity of Sentence Derivation in Functional Unification Grammar. In: *Proceedings of COLING-86.* Bonn.

Winograd, T. (1983) *Language as a Cognitive Process.* London: Addison-Wesley.

Chapter 19

GENERATING ANSWERS FROM A LINGUISTICALLY CODED KNOWLEDGE BASE

Simon C. Dik

TABLE OF CONTENTS

1. Introduction
2. How to answer a question
3. Application to question-answer sequences
4. Knowledge representation
5. More complicated cases
6. Conclusion and discussion

1. INTRODUCTION

The computational processing of natural language data is sometimes approached as a purely practical problem, for which 'anything goes' as long as the results are reasonably acceptable. Given sufficient ingenuity of the analyst, this approach may yield short-term successes, which will, however, be of limited theoretical interest. As a theoretical linguist, I am more interested in attempts at finding more principled, linguistically and psychologically motivated solutions to the problems involved. I also believe that such more principled solutions will yield better long-term practical results in any attempt to attack anything more complicated than the simplest natural language processing puzzles.

For this reason I believe it is essential for computer specialists, psychologists , and linguists to cooperate in this area of research. One aim of such cooperation would be to arrive at 'converging models' of natural language processing, models which are linguistically adequate, psychologically realistic, and computationally feasible. What is brought in from each of these disciplines may teach us a lot about the potentialities and constraints to be respected in the other fields. Where linguistic, psychological, and computational requirements converge, we may be certain to have hit upon some essential feature of natural language processing.

The attempt at arriving at converging models of natural language behavior is especially important for a linguist who, as I do, takes a functional view of natural language; a view, that is, in which 'form', 'meaning', and 'use' are seen as three components which interactively define the nature of language. This interaction is taken into account in the particular linguistic theory I have been involved in for the last ten years: Functional Grammar (FG) in the sense of Dik (1978) and later publications. Research on FG aspires to develop a model of grammar which is typologically, pragmatically, and psychologically adequate. By *typological adequacy* we mean that the model should be applicable to natural languages of any type. *Pragmatic adequacy* means that the model should help us understand how linguistic expressions can be used for communicative purposes. And *psychological adequacy* requires the model to be compatible with what is known about the ways in which language users process these expressions. An interesting working hypothesis is, I believe, that what is good for typological adequacy is also good for pragmatic and psychological adequacy, and conversely. For example, if we can develop a theory of constituent ordering which can, with suitable parametrization, be applied to any natural language, then this theory may be assumed to also tell us something about how speakers and hearers work in processing and exploiting constituent ordering patterns.

From a functional point of view on language, the most basic question to be asked is: How does the natural language user work? A constructivist version of this question, very useful as a mental exercise for clarifying the many intricate problems involved, is: How could we build a model of a natural language user? And an operational version of the latter question can be formulated as: How could we build a *computational* model of (part of) a natural language user? Looked at in this way, the computational implementation of language processing capacities provides one entry point into the underlying theoretical questions that a functionally oriented linguist is interested in.

Against this general background, this paper argues that the automatic generation of answers to natural language questions were simplified if the knowledge required to answer a question would be coded and stored in the same format as the abstract structures underlying the linguistic form of both question and answer. *Underlying structure* is interpreted in terms of the notion *underlying predication* of Functional Grammar. If this course is taken, however, it must also be granted that what might seem to be the 'same' knowledge may be coded in a number of different, though cognitively equivalent forms. In order to account for this nonuniqueness of knowledge representation, the question-answering device must be provided with an inference mechanism through which predications (pieces of knowledge) can be inferred from other predications under conditions of logical or probabilistic validity. Some aspects of this inference mechanism will be discussed and illustrated below.

2. HOW TO ANSWER A QUESTION

Answering a question in an appropriate way is a rather complex business. A question can get many different response types, only some of which can be considered to provide a real 'answer' to the question. Some of the complex decision structure underlying question answering is outlined in the following display.

(1)**INPUT: utterance U**   **OUTPUT: response types R**

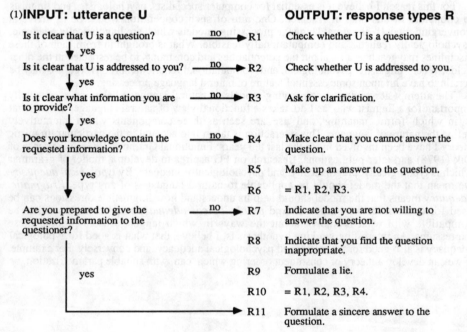

Is it clear that U is a question? —no→ R1		Check whether U is a question.
↓ yes		
Is it clear that U is addressed to you? —no→ R2		Check whether U is addressed to you.
↓ yes		
Is it clear what information you are to provide? —no→ R3		Ask for clarification.
↓ yes		
Does your knowledge contain the requested information? —no→ R4		Make clear that you cannot answer the question.
	R5	Make up an answer to the question.
yes	R6	= R1, R2, R3.
Are you prepared to give the requested information to the questioner? —no→ R7		Indicate that you are not willing to answer the question.
	R8	Indicate that you find the question inappropriate.
yes	R9	Formulate a lie.
	R10	= R1, R2, R3, R4.
→R11		Formulate a sincere answer to the question.

By R6 and R10 I mean that in the relevant conditions one may revert to earlier response types, e.g., in order to conceal one's ignorance or one's unwillingness to answer. Note that each of the response types may be formulated in different ways, depending on such factors as the social relationship between speaker and addressee. Among all the response types, only R5, R9, and R11 can be called *answers* in the sense that they provide the requested type of information; these three answer types differ in their relation to the knowledge/belief structure of the answerer:

(2) | Types of answer: | Answerer replies | Answerer knows/believes |
|---|---|---|
| a. Made-up answer | X | Ø |
| b. Insincere answer (lie) | X | Y ($\neq$ X) |
| c. Sincere answer | X | X |

Note that a sincere answer to a question may well be false in a wider, objective sense. Thus, if I have been taught that Acapulco is the capital of Mexico, then (4) is a sincere answer on my part to question (3), even though in fact my statement is false:

(3)   What is the capital of Mexico?
(4)   Acapulco is the capital of Mexico.

Sincerity is a matter of the relation between an answer and the knowledge possessed by the answerer; truth is a matter of the relation between that knowledge and what is (in some sense) 'really the case'. If we feed a system with incorrect knowledge, then that system's sincere answers may in fact be false. In the same way, an insincere or a made-up answer may in fact be true.

In approaching the problem of how to devise an automated question-answering system, we shall not try to tackle the full complexity of (1) in one go. Let us simplify the decision structure somewhat in the following ways:
(a) We assume that the system understands the question, i.e. understands that it is a question to be answered, and understands what information is to be provided.
(b) We assume that the system is sincere in that it either provides a sincere answer to our question or tells us that it cannot do so.
(c) We assume that the system is prepared to answer our questions if it possesses the relevant knowledge.
On these assumptions, we can discern in the question-answering process the steps depicted in (5).

I shall now propose a specific articulation of this minimal and rather trivial system in terms of the principles of the theory of FG.

A model of the natural language user should, to the extent that this is possible at all, be independent of any one particular language. Only in that way do we account for the fact that the human faculty of language is such that any human being can in principle learn to use any natural language. If we conceive of a model of the natural language user as consisting of language-independent and language-dependent modules, we will want to maximize the former as long as possible without blocking the operation of the latter. Ideally, and in the long run, we will have to be able to change our model of a speaker of Dutch into a model of a speaker of Japanese simply by replacing the Dutch-specific module with the Japanese-specific one.

One way in which FG tries to achieve such typological adequacy is through the assumption that the linguistic expressions of any one language can be analyzed in terms of more abstract underlying *predications*, i.e. structures which contain all of the information required both for the semantic interpretation and the formal constitution relevant to the linguistic expression. The idea is that these underlying predications, while not identical across languages, at least have identical structural properties no matter what type of language is involved. The underlying predications of two semantically equivalent sentences in two different languages are taken to be much more alike than the sentences themselves.

(5)

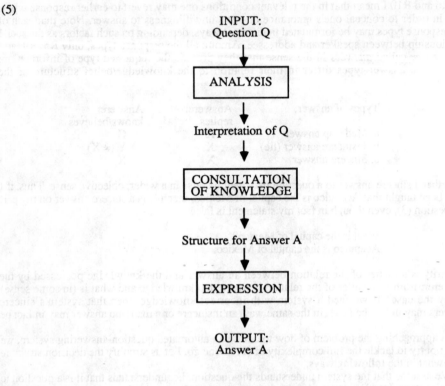

INPUT:
Question Q

↓

ANALYSIS

↓

Interpretation of Q

↓

CONSULTATION
OF KNOWLEDGE

↓

Structure for Answer A

↓

EXPRESSION

↓

OUTPUT:
Answer A

(6)

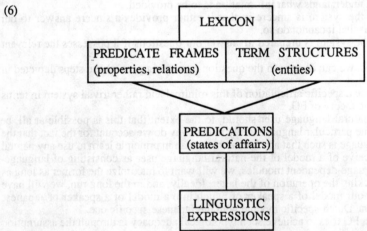

LEXICON

PREDICATE FRAMES
(properties, relations)

TERM STRUCTURES
(entities)

PREDICATIONS
(states of affairs)

LINGUISTIC
EXPRESSIONS

The global structure of FG can be represented as in (6).The predications underlying linguistic expressions are taken to designate various types of States of Affairs (Actions, Processes, States, Positions); each predication consists of a *predicate* (designating a property or relation) and an appropriate number of *terms* (designating entities). All predicates are contained in *predicate frames,* which define their essential semantic and combinatorial properties. All lexical items of a given language are treated as either basic predicates or basic terms. The lexicon consists of those predicates and terms which cannot be formed by rule. Derived predicates and terms can be formed using rules of predicate and term formation.

In actual fact, obviously, the organization of FG is rather more complex than this sketch of the bare outlines would suggest. There is not enough space here, however, to go into all the details. Rather, I will give one simple example to illustrate what a predication looks like and how it is built up. Consider the following expressions of English:

(7)   Q. What was the boy doing?
        A. The boy was kissing a beautiful girl.

The predication underlying (7A) would have the following form:

(8)   DECL (PastProg $kiss$ $_{VFoc}$($d1x_i$: boy $_N$ (x_i) $_\emptyset$) AgSubjTop
                    ($i1x_j$: $girl$ $_N$ (x_j) $_\emptyset$: $beautiful$ $_A$ (x_j) $_\emptyset$) GoObjFoc)

This predication has been constructed from the following basic predicate frames:

(9)   a. $kiss$ $_V$ $(x_1 :< $human$ >(x_1))$ $_{Ag}$ (x_2) $_{Go}$
        b. boy $_N$ $(x_1 : < $human$ > (x_1))$ $_\emptyset$
        c. $girl$ $_N$ $(x_1 : < $human$ > (x_1))$ $_\emptyset$
        d. $beautiful$ $_A$ (x_1) $_\emptyset$

Predicate frame (9a) says that $kiss$ is a verbal (V) predicate with two argument positions x_1 and x_2, in the semantic functions Agent (Ag) and Goal (Go = Patient), where the first argument position is reserved for terms indicating human entities by the selection restriction <human>. $Kiss$ thus indicates a two-place relation which can be used to construct Action predications. The same goes for the other predicate frames, where N = nominal, A = adjectival, and $\emptyset$ = zero semantic function, indicating that the predicates in question can be used to form State predications.

The rules of term formation allow for the construction of terms such as:

(10)   ($i1x_j$: $girl$ $_N$ (x_j) $_\emptyset$: $beautiful$ $_A$ (x_j) $_\emptyset$)
        'indefinite (i) single (1) entity x_j such that (:) x_j has the property "girl" such
        that (:) x_j has the property "beautiful" '

In (8), two such terms have been inserted into the argument slots of the predicate frame of $kiss$. The resulting structure has been further developed by means of the following elements:

(11) DECL   Predication operator indicating that the predication has declarative illocution.
     Past, Prog Predicate operators specifying the tense as Past and the aspect as Progressive.
                 These predicate operators will be interpreted in terms of relations between
                 states of affairs and reference points on the time axis (cf. Ehrich's paper in
                 this volume).
     Subj, Obj   Syntactic functions leading to an active realization of the predication,
                 interpreted as signaling that the Action in question is presented from the
                 perspective of the Agent.
     Top, Foc   Pragmatic functions specifying the informational status of the constituents in
                 question in the given context. Topic: the entity about which the predication
                 says something; Focus: the most essential information contained in the
                 predication, given the context.

It is important to note here that the particular string-like notation in which the predication is presented in (8) is not essential to its nature. Any other notation is just as good, as long as it preserves the essential components and their hierarchical relations within the predication. For example, the predication of (8) could just as well be represented in a list format such as in (12).

Similarly, the same predication could be represented in a tree-like format, expressing either the constituency or the dependency relations. The structure of the predication is that network of elements and relations which is preserved through all these notational variants. The relational network of the predication is supposed to be universally applicable to all natural languages. The functions and operators may be different for different languages, but they are considered to be drawn from restricted universal subsystems of the relevant type. For example, the Tense operator Past is drawn from a restricted subsystem of possible Tense operators valid across languages. The actual predicates figuring in predications (such as *kiss*, *boy*, *girl*, *beautiful* in (8) and (12)) are language-specific elements of lexical organization. However, even these items are monitored by language-independent principles defining the possible articulations of the lexicon across languages.

The theory of FG specifies how underlying predications may be mapped onto actual linguistic expressions by expression rules. These rules specify the form and the order of realization of the constituents, given their structural and functional properties in the predication. A reversed application of these expression rules would be used to parse linguistic expressions, i.e. to reconstruct the predications underlying these expressions.

(12)   Ill: DECL
          Tense: Past
          Aspect: Progr
          Pred: *kiss*
          PredCat: V
          PragFn: Foc
          Arg1: Def: d
          Num: 1
          Var: x_i
                    Restr1: Pred: *boy*
                            PredCat: N
                            SemFn: Ø
          SemFn: Ag
          SyntFn: Subj
          PragFn: Top
          Arg2: Def: i
          Num: 1
          Var: x_j
                    Restr1: Pred: *girl*
                            PredCat: N
                            SemFn: Ø
                    Restr2: Pred: *beautiful*
                            PredCat: A
                            SemFn: Ø
          SemFn: Go
          SyntFn: Obj
          PragFn: Foc

3. APPLICATION TO QUESTION-ANSWER SEQUENCES

Returning to schema (5) we shall now assume that the Analysis comprises at least the reconstruction of the predication underlying the question Q; and that what the Expression does is map the predication underlying the answer onto the linguistic expression constituting the answer. Let us apply this to the following sequence:

(13)   Q. Where does Peter Brown live?
       A. Peter Brown lives in London.

(14) Q. INT (Pres *live* $_V$ (d1x$_i$: *PB* (x$_i$))$_{PosTop}$ (Qx$_j$ LocFoc))
    A. DECL (Pres *live* $_V$ (d1x$_i$: *PB* (x$_i$))$_{PosSubjTop}$ (d1x$_j$: *London* (x$_j$))$_{LocFoc}$)

Live is analyzed as a predicate designating a State of Affairs of the semantic type Position; its first argument bears the semantic function Positioner (Pos). The predication operator INT indicates that the predication has interrogative illocution. This operator is common to both Yes-No questions and to specific or question-word questions. Question-word questions such as (13Q) are interpreted as 'open' predications in the sense that one (or more) term positions are left unspecified. The unspecified term position is marked by the term operator Q. In (13Q) it is the Location argument position which is left unspecified in the predication. The configuration (Qx) $_{Loc}$ is expressed by *where*. The assumption is that any position marked by Q has Focus function, since the question word marks the informationally most essential component of the predication. This is strengthened by the fact that languages which have special Focus-marking particles typically add such particles to both questioned constituents and constituents providing the answers to these.
    The whole structure of the question will be interpreted along the lines of:

(15)   I request you to give me the information which is missing in the following
      predication: 'Peter Brown lives in ...'

In the structure underlying the answer (14A), the term *London* has been inserted into the position marked by Q in the question. That term again receives Focus function because of its salient informational status in the answer; the term *Peter Brown,* on the other hand, receives Topic function because both question and answer are 'about' the entity referred to by *Peter Brown.* For the assignment of Subject, see Dik (1978, chapter 5).
Different, but equivalent answer forms may be defined with the following two rules:

(16)   (i) the Topic may be expressed in pronominal form.
      (ii) the answer may consist of only the Focus constituent.

These rules define the following answers as equivalent to (13A):

(17)   a. He lives in London.
      b. In London.

Our assumption is that a person (or system) that is to answer (13Q) works in the following way:

(18)   1. Reconstruct predication underlying Q.
      2. Recognize instruction contained in Q.
      3. Check knowledge to see whether instruction can be carried out.
      4. If so, construct predication underlying A.
      5. Express A.

It is clear that, if this type of procedure is to be automated, we need at least a Parser which can map linguistic expressions onto underlying predications and a Generator which can map underlying predications onto linguistic expressions. Kwee (1979, this volume) has written a program in Algol68 which can be taken as indicating that a Generator of this type is feasible. Work on the relevant type of Parser is in progress. It will be assumed here that such a Parser is feasible as well.
    Step 2 in (18) can be automated by interpreting INT and Q as abbreviations for instructions to the system:

(19)   INT =
             a. Go to knowledge base.
             b. Check whether requested knowledge is available there.
             c. If so, formulate structure for answer containing that knowledge.

             Q = Requested knowledge is knowledge to fill this position.

It will be clear that the way in which these instructions are to be carried out depends on (i) what knowledge is contained in the answerer's system, and (ii) how that knowledge is represented. This brings us to the question of knowledge representation.

4. KNOWLEDGE REPRESENTATION

In discussing the problem of knowledge representation we shall start from the very simple example (13), suggest a solution for this example, generalize that solution into a general hypothesis, and finally discuss the implications of that hypothesis.

If a person is to be able to answer question (13Q), then, apart from a number of general conditions such as knowledge of the language and knowledge of the decision structure given in (1), two more specific conditions must be fulfilled:

(i)   he must know a certain person called Peter Brown, to whom he can relate the term *Peter Brown* in the question;
(ii)   he must have knowledge equivalent to 'Peter Brown lives in L', where L is some specified location; for example, he must have knowledge equivalent to 'Peter Brown lives in London'.

If it is correct, as assumed above, that that knowledge is to be used to construct the underlying predication (14A), starting from the underlying predication (14Q), then it follows rather immediately that the most convenient form of knowledge representation would result from the following assumption:

(20)   Knowledge is represented in the form of predications.

On that assumption, the knowledge required to bridge the gap between question and answer in (13) would take the following form:

(21)   Pres *live* $_V$ (d1x$_{33}$: *PB* (x$_{33}$))$_{Pos}$ (d1x$_{98}$: *London* (x$_{98}$))$_{Loc}$

in which x$_{33}$ is that specific entity known by the subject under the name *Peter Brown*, and x$_{98}$ is that specific entity known by him as *London*. Note that this piece of knowledge is 'dated' via the predicate operator Pres, indicating that the state of affairs holds at the moment of speaking. The default assumption for a piece of knowledge such as (21) is that the predication is believed to be true at the interval defined by the predicate operator.

The whole sequence of structures from question to answer can now be represented as follows:

(22)   QUESTION Q   Where does Peter Brown live?
         PREDICATION-Q   INT (Pres *live* $_V$ (d1x$_i$: *PB* (x$_i$))$_{PosSubj}$ (Qx$_j$)$_{LocFoc}$)
         KNOWLEDGE   Pres *live* $_V$ (d1x$_{33}$: *PB*$_{33}$))$_{Pos}$ (d1x$_{98}$: *London* (x$_{98}$))$_{Loc}$
         PREDICATION-A   DECL (Pres *live* $_V$ (d1x$_i$: *PB* (x$_i$))$_{PosSubjTop}$ (d1x$_j$: *London* (x$_j$))$_{LocFoc}$)

         ANSWER   Peter Brown lives in London.

It is then also clear that, in this simple case, the predication underlying the answer can be formed by pressing the specified Location term from the knowledge into the position marked by Q in the predication underlying the question. This can obviously be generalized along the following lines:

(23)   When you are to answer a question of the general form:
    (a)   INT (...(Qx)...)
    check your knowledge for a predication of the form
    (b)   (...(α)...)
    which matches the predication of (a) except for containing the specified
        constituent (α) in the place of (Qx);
    then construct a predication of the form:
    (c)   DECL (...(α)...)
    and express this as an answer to the question.

I think it can be taken for granted that, as far as this simple example goes, a system provided with facilities for analyzing and producing predications, and provided with knowledge also stored in the form of predications, could be made to provide sincere answers to questions of this type automatically. In other words, it is worthwhile to investigate the implications of the assumption (20) that knowledge is stored in the form of predications. Let us consider some of these implications.

(A) It is generally acknowledged that knowledge can be divided into perceptual and conceptual knowledge. Perceptual knowledge will consist of percepts: images of things perceived by any of the senses. It is clear that percepts do not take the form of predications. My visual image of my house, for example, cannot be thought of as being stored in the form of predications. We must therefore restrict assumption (20) to the conceptual part of knowledge and assume that knowledge consists of perceptual images, predications, and combinations of these.

(B) Since predications are language-specific in that they contain lexical items of the language concerned, our assumption leads to the further assumption that conceptual knowledge representation is language-specific in the same sense. In other words, our assumption rejects the idea that knowledge should be represented in some language-independent cognitive code or alphabet, distinct from the language we speak. But is this a disadvantage? I do not believe so. Note that if there were a language-independent cognitive code, then any operation involving language and knowledge would require linguistic structures to be translated into cognitive ones, and these back into linguistic ones. Our assumption does not require such translation.

(C) On the other hand, since predications are largely identical across languages as far as their structure is concerned, thanks to the typological adequacy of the notion of *predication*, our assumption does not lead to the untenable position that what a speaker of L_1 knows is completely different from the otherwise equivalent knowledge of a speaker of L_2. In fact, the predications underlying L_1 are rather easily translatable into the equivalent predications of L_2; on a limited but non-trivial scale, such a translation procedure has been implemented by Van der Korst (1986). Therefore, the knowledge embodied in L_1 predications is just as easily translatable into knowledge embodied in L_2 predications. Our hypothesis requires us to accept, therefore, that a piece-of-knowledge-in-L_1 is different from a piece-of-knowledge-in-L_2, even if the two pieces of knowledge concern 'the same fact'. On the other hand, we assume that knowledge is represented in structures of such a level of abstraction that it is, at that level, easy to bridge the gap between two languages.

For more extensive discussions of the approach to knowledge representation presented here, see Dik (1986). That paper develops a much more detailed typology of distinct kinds of knowledge. For example, it distinguishes *general knowledge* (e.g., of general rules and principles) from *episodic knowledge* (concerning specific facts and events), etc. The general assumption is, however, that all nonperceptual knowledge can be coded in the form of predications.

5. MORE COMPLICATED CASES

Let us now consider some more complicated cases of question-answer sequences:

(24)   Knowledge: Sally is the daughter of Peter.
                Question: Who is the father of Sally?
                Answer: Peter.

Everybody will accept the answer as correct, given the knowledge available; nobody will accept a response such as 'I don't know' from a person who possesses this knowledge. Nevertheless, the answer cannot be construed on the basis of a simple matching operation like the one described in (23), since the predication contained in the question does not match the predication representing the knowledge. It is clear that, for this gap to be bridged, some inferencing mechanism is required which defines the following as valid:

(25)   a. Sally is the daughter of Peter.
                b. Therefore, Peter is the father of Sally.

On the basis of the conclusion of (25), the question of (24) can be answered via the matching operation of (23).

An inference mechanism which defines certain inferences as valid and others as non-valid, may be called a *logic*. In the present case we need a logic which takes predications as input and delivers predications as output. Such a logic we shall call *Functional Logic* (FL). Note that we can say that a certain inference is valid *by virtue of* a logic. We are thus interested in the inferences which can be drawn from (sets of) predications by virtue of FL.

There are now various ways of widening the scope of our system so that sequences like (24) can be taken into account. I prefer doing this through an extension of the notion of *conceptual knowledge* in the following way:

(26)   To know X conceptually is to possess either a predication φ whose content is X or a set of predications ψ and an inference mechanism FL such that φ is validly inferrable from ψ by virtue of FL.

This definition of conceptual knowledge allows me to say that if I know that Sally is the daughter of Peter, then I also know that Peter is the father of Sally, provided I possess the logic which allows me to infer the latter from the former.

To give some more content to the notion of Functional Logic, let us add the following. A logic can be defined as consisting of a syntax and a semantics. The syntax specifies which formulae are well-formed *logical forms*. In the case of FL we assume that the syntax is defined by those rules which specify which FG-predications are well-formed. In other words, the logical form of a linguistic expression is equated to the underlying predication of that expression according to FG. Note that, according to this conception of FL, logical form coincides with grammatical form, if the latter is taken in the intended sense. The semantics of a logic may be divided into rules of semantic interpretation and rules of inference. In the case of FL the assumption is that the domain of interpretation consists of mental models, consisting of perceptual and conceptual information. The conceptual information is itself again coded in FG predications, i.e., in well-formed logical forms of FL. The inference rules define which predications can be validly inferred from given sets of predications. Some examples of such inference rules will be given below.

A logic can also be characterized in terms of the types of elements whose logical properties it defines. In that sense we speak of *propositional, predicate, class,* and *relation logic* . In the case of FL we need at least the following levels of logical analysis:

(27)   Components of Functional Logic:
              a. Illocutionary Logic
              b. Predication Logic
              c. Predicate Logic
              d. Term Logic
              e. Lexical Logic

Let us consider how the desired result could be obtained in the case of example (24) . It is clear that inference (25), which is essential to a proper understanding of (24), depends on a certain relationship between the meanings of the lexical items *father* and *daughter*. We shall say that this inference pertains to Lexical Logic.

In our framework the relevant relationship can be established by associating, with each predicate frame, one or more meaning postulates of the following general form:

(28) $\alpha\,(x)\;\rightarrow\;\beta\,(x)$

which says that when α is predicated of x, then it follows that we can also predicate β of x. It will be clear that if a meaning postulate works both ways, the relation between two predicates (or combinations of predicates) can be written:

(29) $\alpha\,(x)\;\leftrightarrow\;\beta\,(x)$

in which case we can say that α and β are semantically equivalent, i.e., designate the same set of states of affairs. In the particular case in which α is a simplex predicate and β is a combination of predicates, we can say that β provides a definition or paraphrase of α.

Let us now consider the predicate frames of *father* and *daughter*:

(30)   a. *father* $_N$ $(x_1 : \text{<male>}\ (x_1))_\emptyset$ $(x_2 : \text{<anim>}\ (x_2))_{Ref}$

            $\leftrightarrow$

      parent $_N$ $(x_1)_\emptyset$ $(x_2)_{Ref}$ *male* $_A$ $(x_1)_\emptyset$

      b. *daughter* $_N$ $(x_1 : \text{<female>}\ (x_2))_\emptyset$ $(x_2 : \text{<anim>}\ (x_2))_{Ref}$

            $\leftrightarrow$

      child $_N$ $(x_1)_\emptyset$ $(x_2)_{Ref}$ *female* $_A$ $(x_1)_\emptyset$

Both predicates are analyzed here as two-place nominal predicates. These structures can be interpreted as follows: 'saying of a male entity that he is father with reference to an animate entity is equivalent to saying that he is a parent of that entity and that he is male'. Likewise for (23b). As a next step, we must establish the relationship between *parent* and *child*. This can be done through the following meaning postulate:

(31)   *parent* $_N$ $(x_1 : \text{<anim>}\ (x_1))_\emptyset$ $(x_2 : \text{<anim>}\ (x_2))_{Ref}$

            $\leftrightarrow$

      child $_N$ $(x_2)_\emptyset$ $(x_1)_{Ref}$

This rule says that *parent* and *child* are each other's converses. Obviously, the rule defining converse predicates must be generalized into a general definition such that a statement to the effect that:

(32)   converse (*parent, child*)

is sufficient to establish the desired relationship.

Finally, we must be able to infer, from the proper name *Peter*, that this proper name indicates a male entity. This will be coded in the entry for *Peter*, in some such way as the following:

(33)   Peter $_{Np}$ (x_1 : <male> (x_1))$_\emptyset$

             $\leftrightarrow$

             'Peter' (d1x_i : *name* $_N$ (x_i) : {(x_1)$_{Poss}$ } (x_i))

That is, to apply the predicate *Peter* to some entity x_1 is to say of that entity, who is male, that the name that he possesses is 'Peter'. Np indicates that *Peter* is a proper noun.

With these various meaning postulates we have the information required to construct, starting from the predication underlying (25a), the predication underlying (25b); that predication can then be used to derive the answer of (24) via the matching operation described in (23).

In the example discussed above, the properties relevant to valid inferencing reside in the lexical elements used and will thus be coded in the lexicon. Obviously, there are many other bits and pieces of linguistic structure relevant to logical inferencing. Let us consider two more examples:

(34)   Knowledge: John bought an expensive book.
             Question: What did John buy?
             Answer: a. An expensive book.
                             b. A book.
                             c. Something expensive.

Answer (34a) can be derived straightforwardly by matching the predications underlying Question and Knowledge. (34b) and (34c) need some inferencing along the lines of:

(35)   If somebody bought an expensive book, then it may be inferred that he bought a book and that he bought something expensive.

In this case the inference is not determined by the lexical meanings of the predicates involved. Rather, it concerns the internal structure of terms, as illllustrated in:

(36)   a. Past *buy* $_V$ (d1x_i : *John* $_{Np}$ (x_i)) $_A$ (i1x_j : *book* $_N$ (x_j): *expensive* $_A$ (x_j))Go
       b. .... (i1x_j : book$_N$ (x_j))Go
       c. .... (i1x_j : expensive$_A$ (x_j))Go

This type of inferencing will therefore pertain to Term Logic.

The general structure of terms according to FG may be represented as:

(37)   (ωx: φ_1 (x) : φ_2 (x) : ... : φ_n (x))

where ω represents the term operators, x the term variable, and each φ (x) an 'open predication' acting as a restrictor on the possible values of x. The relevant rule of Term Logic says that from any predication containing a term of the general form (37), we may infer any predication which is otherwise identical, but where the term is specified by any proper subsequence of the restrictors of the original term. This general formulation allows us to draw such inferences as:

(38)   a. John bought an expensive book that he had always wanted to have.
                 Therefore:
             b. John bought an expensive book.
             c. John bought a book that he had always wanted to have.

    d. John bought something expensive that he had always wanted to have.
    e. John bought a book.
    f. John bought something expensive.
    g. John bought something that he had always wanted to have.

Therefore, if the Knowledge is as in (38a), an answer to the question *What did John buy?* may sincerely come up with any of (38b) - (38g).
    As a last example, consider:

(39)   a. There are six cookies.
               b. John ate two of the cookies.
               c. Bill ate the rest of the cookies.
               Question: How many cookies did Bill eat?
               Answer: Bill ate four cookies.

For the Answer in (39) to be accepted as sincere and correct, we need quite a complicated machinery involving term quantification, elementary arithmetic, and a system for 'anchoring' the referents of terms in the information built up in the context. Much of the machinery required has been sketched in Brown (1985). Informally explained, this machinery works as follows. (39a), which contains the indefinite term:

(40) $(i6x_i : cookie_N (x_i))$ 'six cookies'

thereby introduces a domain set D whose cardinality is 6. (39b) contains a term with a complex proportional quantifier:

(41) $(i2/dn \; x_i : cookie_N (x_i))$ 'two of the cookies'

This term indicates an indefinite subset of cardinality 2 out of a definite set of cardinality n. The definiteness of the superset allows us to identify this set with the domain set D, and to conclude that n = 6. (39c) now introduces the term:

(42) $(d \; rest/dn \; x_i : cookie_N (x_i))$ 'the rest of the cookies'

where the domain set will again be contextually anchored in D (n = 6), and the term operator *rest* will be defined as the complement of R in D, where R is some other subset of D already specified in the context. This must be the subset introduced in (39b). Therefore, the cardinality of 'rest' must be card(D) minus card(R) = 6-2 = 4. Therefore, the answer in (39) is correct.
    It is to be noted that, given the analysis of term structures in FG, matters of quantification again pertain to Term Logic in FL, rather than to Predicate Logic as is the case in Standard Logic.

6. CONCLUSION AND DISCUSSION

Question-answering can be mediated through simple matching and substitution operations if the following conditions hold:
(i)   Questions are analyzed in terms of underlying FG predications.
(ii)   Answers are constructed from underlying FG predications.
(iii)   Conceptual knowledge is coded in FG predications, plus a Functional Logic which authorizes the derivation of predications which constitute valid inferences from given (sets of) predications.

(iv)   'Knowing X' is defined as either possessing a predication φ with content X or possessing a set of predications ψ and a logic FL such that φ can be derived from ψ by virtue of FL.

Note the following corollaries to this theory:

1. When I know that Sally is the daughter of Peter, and you know that Peter is the father of Sally, we may, according to (iv), still both be said to know that Peter is Sally's father; however, you know this according to the first alternative of (iv), I know it according to the second one.

2. The *predication* is the central concept in this theory. The predication is (i) the output of the Parser, (ii) the vehicle for knowledge representation, (iii) the input and the output of the inferencing mechanism, and (iv) the input to the Generator. We may add to this that, because of the typological adequacy of the predication, the predication would also constitute the most appropriate level for translating both linguistic expressions and knowledge representations into other languages (cf. Van der Korst, 1986).

3. If a system is provided with a Parser which can map linguistic expressions onto underlying predications, and if the system's knowledge is coded in predications, then we can 'teach' the system (i.e. change or extend its knowledge) by means of linguistic expressions.

For a further elaboration of the theory sketched in this paper, from the point of view of the interpretation of linguistic expressions, see Dik (1986).

ACKNOWLEDGEMENT

I am grateful to Christian Matthiessen for critical notes which led to improvements in this paper.

REFERENCES

Brown, D. Richard (1985) Term operators. In: A.M. Bolkestein, C. de Groot & J.L. Mackenzie (Eds.) *Predicates and terms in Functional Grammar*. Dordrecht: Foris.

Dik, S. C. (1978) *Functional Grammar*. Dordrecht: Foris. (Third edition, 1981.)

Dik, S. C. (1986) *Linguistically motivated knowledge representation*. Working papers on Functional Grammar 9. Amsterdam.

Korst, B. van der (1986) *Twelve sentences; a translation procedure in terms of Functional Grammar*. MA Thesis, Institute for General Linguistics, University of Amsterdam.

Kwee Tjoe-Liong (1979) A68-FG(3): *Simon Dik's funktionele grammatica geschreven in Algol68*. Publikaties van het Instituut voor Algemene Taalwetenschap 23. Amsterdam.

Chapter 20

A COMPUTER MODEL OF FUNCTIONAL GRAMMAR

Kwee Tjoe-Liong

TABLE OF CONTENTS

1. Overview
2. Linguistic theory and computational model
2.1 Outline of grammar and program
3. Embedded predications and raising
3.1 Correspondence between grammar and program
3.2 Raising and expression rules
4. Open predications: relative clauses and term questions
5. Anaphoric terms: personal pronouns
6. Non-verbal predicates and cleft constructions
6.1 Non-verbal predicates and copula support
6.2 Identifying constructions and pragmatic functions
6.3 Focus constructions and the generation program
6.4 Focus constructions and another view on questions
6.5 Focus constructions and generation, again
7. Tense and aspect
8. Linguistics and programming
9. Conclusion

1. OVERVIEW

How can we, in using a computer, serve best the advancement of general linguistics? In my view, by modeling as faithfully as possible the rules of an existing grammatical theory. Since vagueness, gaps, and inconsistencies in the theory will be brought to light during the design and execution of the program, the linguist will be stimulated to formulate even more precise and explicit rules. In our case the linguistic theory to be tested is the Functional Grammar paradigm of S.C. Dik (1978, 1983). After a short overview of the theory's basic tenets, a program (written in Algol68) is described that simulates a Sample Grammar (Dik, 1980a) for a substantial fragment of English, by way of random sentence generation. Some specific results involving proposed rules for Raising, Restrictive Relative Clause Formation, and Anaphoric Personal Pronoun Insertion are presented, as well as extensions concerning Interrogatives and Cleft Constructions. The paper is organized as follows. In the next Section the process of generating a simple Predication is briefly sketched. After that, a number of particular phenomena that necessitate special adaptations of the simple cycle, is treated, each along this line of exposition: theoretical description — puzzles for the programmer — solution found.

2. LINGUISTIC THEORY AND COMPUTATIONAL MODEL

This paper describes an attempt to model a given, existing linguistic theory on the computer. Pioneering work in this field has been done by Friedman (1971) on Transformational Generative Grammar and Janssen (1976) on Montague Grammar. The linguistic theory in question is the Functional Grammar paradigm developed by Simon C. Dik (see also Dik's chapter in this volume).

The simulation is meant to be a contribution to theoretical linguistics, insofar as it aims at testing grammatical rules as regards their effectiveness, completeness, and consistency. In short, it is an assessment of claims. For that reason, I initially felt obliged to mimic in my program as faithfully as possible every single structure and every single rule of the theory. The theory, however, I must emphasize, was not originally designed with the special view of building a natural language processing system. It has its own independent roots and motivations in general linguistics. Its goals and means were defined by the linguists who worked on it and with it. As a consequence, the grammatical structures and rules could not be translated easily and straightforwardly into well-known computational counterparts, such as linear lists or context-free rewrite rules. For a programmer this certainly is a handicap. But at the same time it is a challenge to design structures that noncomputational linguists can recognize as akin to the objects they are familiar with, and to write algorithms that they can understand and recognize as being a fair translation of their ideas.

The theory of Functional Grammar (henceforth abbreviated as FG) views language as an instrument for social communication and verbal interaction. Its aim is adequacy at three different levels: descriptive-typological, pragmatic, and psychological. The linguistic units are called Expressions. The theory postulates a small number of metalinguistic entities — structures, functions, and operators — but no conceptual entities. It is assumed that knowledge is basically linguistic knowledge. In this point of view I find a very attractive Whorfian flavor, combined with a methodological constraint as mighty as Ockam's razor: You have here at your disposal all lexical items of a language; you can't have any other tools, but you don't need any other tools.

The aspect that I am concerned with is the formal description of the way in which an Underlying Predication (the ultimate structure which is assumed to find its expression in the Linguistic Expression) is thought to be built up from smaller elements, and how it eventually is realized at what other linguists would call the level of Surface Structure. The theory chosen is still in full development, and it is anything but complete. The program only covers that part that has been formalized enough to be testable by computer simulation. It is mainly concerned with what elsewhere would have been called the syntactic component. It is not specifically claimed to have psychological reality as a production model. In writing this program — a random sentence generator— the primary goal has not been to construct an efficient, fast running text generation system. It might be interesting, though, to try to implement an adapted version as the tactical component of a much larger text or discourse generator.

2.1 Outline of grammar and program

The organization of FG is displayed in Figure 1. We distinguish, as is usual in formal grammar, between Structures and Rules. There are four fundamental structures. The Predication is clearly the most central one because, on the one hand, a Fully Specified Predication is assumed to underlie every (spoken or written) Linguistic Expression and, on the other hand, a Predication is built up out of a Predicate Frame together with a number of Terms, the whole being enriched with Functions, Operators, and the like. Predicate Frames (typically: a verb with a certain number of argument positions) and Terms (typically: an expression that can be used to refer to an entity) either are Basic and contained in the Lexicon (which contains all and only content words), or have been derived from Basic ones by appropriate rules. A Basic Predicate Frame of Category VERB, for instance, looks like this:

$$\text{read}_{\text{Verb}} \quad (x1:<\text{human}>(x1))_{\text{Agent}} \quad (x2)_{\text{Goal}}$$

In this example we see a Term Position with a Selectional Restriction. The idea of Selectional Restrictions is very common in linguistics, but unlike many other theories FG posits that Selectional Restrictions are Predicate Frames, that is, they are (other) lexical items themselves, not abstract features.

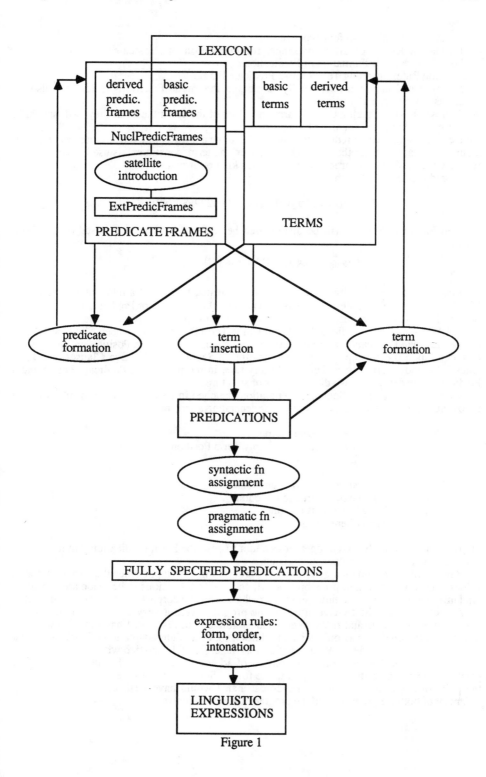

Figure 1

There are, roughly, also four types of rules:
— Formation Rules, of different kinds: for Derivation of Predicate Frames, for Term Formation, and for Formation of Predications
— Insertion Rules, inserting Terms into a Predicate Frame
— Assignment Rules, not only for Syntactic and Pragmatic Functions (roles) but also for various Operators; and
— Expression Rules, taking care of form and order of the constituents as they will appear in the final product, the Linguistic Expression.
Notice, in passing, that a Predication is not meant to be a linearly ordered structure (neither is it a binary or n-ary tree, for that matter). Moreover, the term 'constituent' is used in an informal way; it does not denote a particular, well-defined kind of Structure.

A Predication looks like this:

$$\text{read}_{\text{Verb}} \quad (x1 : \text{Mary}(x1))_{\text{Agent}} \quad (a\ x2 : \text{book}(x2))_{\text{Goal}}$$

Derived Predicate Frames will be disregarded here. Term Formation is based on the Term Scheme:

$$(\ \omega\ x : \varphi_{\text{Noun}}(x) : \varphi_{\text{Adj}}(x) : \varphi_{\text{Verb}}(x))$$

with positions to be filled by Term Operators (indicated by ω) and a number of Restrictors: Nominal, Adjectival and Verbal. Restrictors are just Predications, or Predicate Frames — this point is a bit unclear. The theory does not draw a sharp distinction between these two. In fact, it defines Predications as Predicate Frames in which Term Positions have been filled. But it also defines an Open Predication as a Predication having exactly one Term Position unfilled. I shall comment upon the concept of Open Predication in Sections 4 (Relative Clauses and Term Questions) and 5 (Anaphoric Terms). At any rate, in the program a Predicate Frame and a Predication are defined as two distinct types of structure.

The overall process of Sentence Generation sketched in Figure 1 can be mirrored by the following algorithm, the *Main Procedure* for generating a sentence:

> 1) Choose Predicate Frame
> 2) WHILE There Is An Empty Term Position
>   DO 2.1) Form Term
>   2.2) Insert Term
> 3.1) Assign Syntactic Functions
> 3.2) Assign Pragmatic Functions
> 4) Apply Expression Rules
> 5) Print Sentence.

Steps 1) and 2) could be taken together as a unit to describe Form Predication, but in the next Section I shall argue for another subdivision.

Being a random sentence generator, the program has no input other than some numeric values needed to set certain probabilities. All choices and decisions to be made are subject to random chance only. For the time being, a small Lexicon is incorporated in the program itself.

As noted above, the first versions of the program were a very close simulation of the grammatical structures and rules. When undesirable output resulted, I had to find a way out. Sometimes the change was only a small addition to, or a slight adaptation of, or a particular interpretation of Dik's ideas. Whenever this was the case, I felt satisfied with the compromise. Of course, part of the compromising consists of ad hoc tricks. These, I hope, are temporary patches and should be straightened out in the future. Sometimes, however, my deviation from the point of departure is rather more radical than I would have wished; in such cases, my judgment of both the grammar and the program are rather ambivalent.

3. EMBEDDED PREDICATIONS AND RAISING

After having designed the Main Procedure for the production of a (simple) sentence, I had to extend it in various directions. To start with, let us have a look at embedded and subordinate clauses. In FG it is assumed that a Predication can be inserted either in an Argument Term Position, in which case we roughly expect to have a THAT-clause, or in a Satellite Position, usually resulting in a corresponding adverbial clause (temporal, causal, etc.). Obviously, not every Term Position would admit of one. Actually, at this stage, not any Term Position would admit of one. The first rough draft needs more details. First, the attractive idea of having other lexical Predicate Frames function as Selectional Restrictions for Term Positions is going to be diluted. The theory posits, in fact, an abstract Selectional Restriction <SUB> in order to be able to mark the intended kind of Term Position. This holds for Argument Positions as well as for Satellite Positions. Here, we shall concentrate on the first case: an Embedded Predication as Argument. Satellite subordinate clauses do not cause extra problems. Second, the theory subcategorizes the Verbal Predicate class for exactly those verbs that have an embedded clause as one of their arguments, as VSUB.

Insertion of a Predication at a Term Position is done at the very same moment, and within the same Procedure, as insertion of any other term of the usual noun phrase kind. The theory leaves it as an open question, or rather does not mention, whether the Embedded Predication is to be completely filled with its own Terms before or after being inserted into the higher, 'matrix' Predication. I was forced to find an answer to this question when I tried to program the rules for producing what is called in classical Latin grammar AcI (Accusativus cum Infinitivo) Constructions, more commonly known as Raising Constructions. FG has no ready-made label for them. The theory describes these constructions as a special case of Syntactic Function Assignment. In an English Predication, as in a Latin one, the Syntactic Functions Subject and Object need not always be assigned to Terms inserted at their own Argument Positions. When a Predication contains an Embedded Predication, Syntactic Function Assignment is allowed to 'dip down' into this Embedded Predication and to select the 'lower' Subject as its own Subject, or Object. In the first case we have the classical Latin NcI (Nominativus cum Infinitivo), which is the Passive version of the AcI.

This particular type of Syntactic Function Assignment, which I shall continue to refer to by the abbreviatory name of Raising, has its own particular consequences in the morphological part of the Expression Rules. First, the Embedded Verb Predicate takes a nonfinite form, in English TO + Infinitive. Second, if the Subject of the 'lower' Predication has the function of Object in the 'higher' Predication, it also takes the form of an Object, that is, it receives Accusative case.

3.1 Correspondence between grammar and program

Algorithm. I dissected a maximally large part of the Main Procedure and made it into an autonomous unit that will be applicable to any Predication; we will use it for Embedded Predications now and for Relative Clauses later on. The reason is the following. Before Raising can be applied in the 'matrix', the Embedded Predication must itself have already undergone Syntactic Function Assignment. The simplest way to guarantee this is to insert it at its Term Position in the form of a Completely Filled Predication in which at least Syntactic Functions have been assigned. So the autonomous unit also needs to include step 3.1. Because it is to be expected that Pragmatic Function Assignment, too, can be incorporated, we may even include step 3.2. I refer to this autonomous unit as the general procedure *Form Fully Specified Predication*, to distinguish it from the Main Procedure proper. This distinction is well-motivated, for Expression Rules (step 4) cannot be part of the intended general unit. When an Embedded Predication is inserted, it is not yet known whether its Subject will be expressed in Nominative or in Accusative case. (As for the demarcation of Form Fully Specified Predication with respect to another kind of Assignment Rules — Introduction of Tense — see Section 7.)

Data structures. We have seen that FG displays a Predication in the form of a string of subscripted items in a fixed order: Predicate, Argument Terms. The Predicate is subscripted with its Lexical Category; the Terms with a Semantic, a Syntactic and a Pragmatic Function, in this order (if any of the latter two are applicable). Functions are of course binary, noncommutative relations between a Term and a Predication, although the string notation could suggest that they are properties of Terms, or of Term Positions. Some Terms may have more functions than other Terms. Moreover, in the case of Raising, the Raised Term is assumed to carry two Syntactic Functions, each at a different level. See for instance:

$$\text{believe}_{\text{VSub}} \quad \text{(John)}_{\text{AgentSubject}}$$
$$\text{([read}_{\text{Verb}} \quad \text{(Mary)}_{\text{AgentSubjectObject}}$$
$$\text{(the book)}_{\text{GoalObject}}]) \, _{\text{Goal}}$$

Contrary to this notation, I decided to attach Functions as attributes to a Predication. The value then is a Term, or rather a pointer to a Term. This representation has certain advantages over the one used in the grammar, since all Predications have roughly the same Functions or at least the same number of Functions, while Terms do not. That is, every Predication has exactly one Subject and at most one Object, but a Term can be Subject at one level and Object at another, or it can be Subject at more than one level, or it can have no Syntactic role at all, etc. Access from a Predication to its Argument Terms as well as to those of a lower, Embedded, Predication, is easier to handle than in the inverse direction. See Figure 2 for a graphic representation of the data structure corresponding to the above complex Predication.

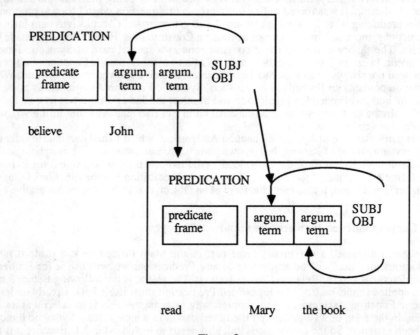

Figure 2

Expression Rules. With regard to Constituent Order, the theory assumes just two basic patterns for English sentences. The most important one is presented as:

P1 S Vfin Vinf O X

Here, P1 denotes a special sentence-initial position reserved for particular constituents. Vfin and Vinf stand for the finite and infinite part of the Verb constituent. S and O indicate the position of the Subject and Object Term, and X stands for all constituents (Argument and Satellite Terms) other than Subject and Object. This pattern is valid for almost all English sentence types and has one variant for Main Clause Questions (with Subject-Finite Verb Inversion). It is obvious that we can program this as a recursive procedure (call it Linearize) at the very end of the generation process Main Procedure.

3.2 Raising and expression rules

We meet a slightly puzzling aspect of Raising when indiscriminately applying the recursive procedure Linearize to the above complex Predication. How are we to avoid printing (outputting) 'Mary' twice, once as Object of the matrix and once as Subject of the Embedded Predication? Grammarians seem to take it for granted that, when a constituent is expressed once and only once, this would imply that that constituent has one and only one position in the structure. Transformationalists spend a lot of energy moving things around from one position to another, leaving traces behind. FG sees Predications as structures that are unordered but contain elements that have various relations to each other. These functions and relations compete with each other in getting certain elements into certain positions in the final linear ordering. Once an element has found a place on the base of one of these competing forces, however, the 'human linearizer' seems to forget all of its other roles and relations, since 'the constituent has already been dealt with', or 'a constituent can not occupy more than one position'.

For a time I considered introducing into my program a fourth kind of Function, alongside the Semantic, Syntactic, and Pragmatic level. Positional Functions A[1], A[2], A[3], etc., would be assigned to elements (Terms, Relators, Operators), and then the complete array A[1] through A[n] would be output, expressing the whole of the complex Predication. The radical departure from the given grammar and the lack of linguistic motivation for overall Positional Functions deterred me from coding this rather deviant view. Instead, I found a minimal deviation from the informal process. To introduce it, I will first indicate step by step how the output of Raising is constructed intuitively, 'by hand', following the left-to-right order of the basic pattern:

no Focus, so P1 remains empty;
Subject (of main Predication): John --> position S;
finite form of Verbal Predicate: believes --> position Vfin;
no infinite verbal form;
Object (of main Predication): Mary --> position O;
other arguments (of main Predication): Goal Term --> position X;
now, the Goal Term of the main Predication is itself an Embedded Predication, so we have recursion at a lower level:

no Focus, so P1 remains empty;
Subject (of embedded Predication): ALREADY PROCESSED ... ;
no finite form of Verbal Predicate;
infinite form of Verbal Predicate: to read --> position Vinf;
Object (of embedded Predication): the book --> position O;
other arguments (of embedded Predication): none.

The informal remark 'ALREADY PROCESSED' inspired me to embellish the Term Scheme with a Boolean marker 'Imprimatur' (=Fit to Print), with True as initial value. Expressing a Term, then, consists not only of outputting (printing) each of its internal elements, but also of switching its Boolean marker Imprimatur to False. In this way, the recursiveness in applying Linearize to every Predication, at all levels, is saved. (As a welcome side-effect, this device made it possible to leave out a rather cumbersome trick previously needed to get the right order of constituents in Passive sentences.)

4. OPEN PREDICATIONS: RELATIVE CLAUSES AND TERM QUESTIONS

The theory mentions a special kind of not-yet-completely-filled Predications which it calls Open Predications. They are defined as having exactly one Term Position unfilled. This intermediate stage is given a privileged role. Several different phenomena are thought to originate at this point: Relativization, Question Formation, and Anaphora. In these cases, a particular action takes place at the single Position left open. The actions are, respectively, insertion of a special Term (marked R for Relative or Q for Question; the second is more commonly known as WH-Term) or application of the Anaphora operator A. Relativization is the process of finding a Verbal Restrictor during Term Formation and realizing it as a restrictive Relative Clause for the head.

The problems I met in trying to program this process, as well as the changes I had to make, have been described extensively elsewhere (Kwee, 1981). Here I shall summarize the results. The theory defines a Verbal Restrictor as an Open Predication in which the last unfilled Position is compatible with the given Nominal Restrictor in the Term Scheme. Formation of such an Open Predication cannot be realized in an effective way along the lines of the Main Procedure. Therefore, I devised a special procedure that, given the selectional predicates of the Nominal Restrictor, looks for an appropriate Verbal Predicate Frame. 'Appropriate' here means 'having at least one position among its Argument Positions that is compatible with the given head noun and that is also accessible to Relativization.' Then, at the first step of Term Insertion, this position is immediately occupied with an R-Term. Thus, the order of things is reversed: the R-Term is not the last Term to be put into its place, but rather the very first one. The concept of Open Predication has no role in Relative Clause Formation.

A second problem came up in combining Relativization with Raising, that is, the generation of a Relative Clause in which the Relativized Term is raised from a deeper, embedded, Predication. For example:

> (the : student : believe (John) ([read (R) (the book)]))
> the student that John believes to read the book

Notice that here the last unfilled position of the Verbal Restrictor is not one of its own Term Positions but is to be found in an Embedded Predication. To save recursiveness, I again reversed the order of things. Remember the 'top down' method in 'normal' circumstances: the Main Procedure is started for the matrix Predication, and later on, if necessary, part of it (the autonomous unit called Form Fully Specified Predication) is invoked again for any Embedded Predication. After all Term Positions at one level have been filled, Syntactic Function Assignment is applied at that level, and Raising is one of the possible choices. To generate Relative Clauses of the above type, however, the program works 'bottom up': it starts with a 'simple' Predication-with-R-Term and makes it into a Fully Specified Predication. After that, and on condition that the R-Term has been assigned Subject Function, the possibility arises of inserting this Predication-with-R-Term as an Embedded Predication into an arbitrary matrix, with obligatory raising of the lower Subject.

This 'upgrading' of the Relative Clause can be repeated as long as the R-Term has Subject Function:

> the student that reads the book
> the student that is believed by Mark to read the book
> the student that is expected by John to be believed by Mark to read the book
> the student that is known by Frank to be expected by John to be believed by Mark to read the book

This special procedure does not yet account for all possible types of Raising in Relative Clauses. That, however, is a consequence of the fact that Raising has not yet been completely accounted for in full generality by the theory.

I will now briefly outline the generation of Questions. Although not all types of questions are yet handled by the theory, a couple of simple types can be produced with relatively little effort. Echo Questions cause no problems at all and are actually generated in the same way as declarative sentences. Yes/No Questions require an additional step: somewhere late in the process, the postulated Expression Rule of DO-support is realized. Subject-Aux Inversion for the correct order of constituents is provided for, both in Yes/No Questions and in Non-Echo (that is, Focus Q-Term) Questions. I expect that Questions with Raised Q-Terms can easily be generated by a special bottom-up procedure similar to the one described for Relative Clauses with Raised R-term. I have not worked this out, however.

There are two reasons for mentioning Questions. One is that, as already mentioned, Q-Term Questions in the Sample Grammar are based on Predications with one Term Position left open. I assume that the Q-Term will be assigned Focus Function, which makes it eligible for sentence-initial position. It was easy to program this for Questions at Main Clause level. Since almost every Term Position can be questioned, that is, filled with a Q, we need not invoke a special procedure as I did for Relative Clauses, where the order of Term Insertion had to be reversed. Nor do I need to wait until all positions but the last one are filled, for Focus Q-Term Questions are distinguished from Echo Q-Term Questions only by the Focus Function that is assigned to Q. But in the case of Echo Q-Term Questions there is no need for an Open Predication, since they can be generated in the same way as declarative sentences. So, with Focus Q-Term Questions there is no need for an Open Predication either. The other reason for mentioning Questions is that here Q-Terms are treated as Argument Terms. (I shall come back to this point in Section 6.4.)

5. ANAPHORIC TERMS: PERSONAL PRONOUNS

The problem of anaphora is one of the hardest in Parsing. (Hirst 1981, presents a concise and thorough survey.) But is is not an easy problem in Generation either, not even in random generation. Dik (1980a) describes a very simple case of Personal Pronoun Insertion and states that there are a lot of conditions to be fulfilled, one of which is that the Antecedent Term — which can occupy a Term Position in quite a different Predication — can be retrieved in some way or another, and that the Position where the Anaphoric Pronoun is about to be inserted in the Open Predication is accessible for that Antecedent. The notions Retrievable and Accessible are not any detailed further. I suppose that something like the 'precede and command' conditions known from the transformational approach can be utilized here as well.

Again, as in the previous case of Relative Pronoun Insertion, the essential point is the order of things. The theory describes a complex sentence as built up out of several subordinate clauses, but it does not give a hint as to the order in which the Term Positions at the various levels are to be filled. The program has been written with a modular design in mind. This results in a procedure that uniformly fills the Term Positions at one level and is invoked recursively for Embedded Predications in Term Positions as well as for Relative Clauses, that is, Verbal Restrictors in a Term Scheme.

In the case of Anaphora Insertion, at Antecedent Retrieval it is problematic for the procedure to reach levels other than the Predication at which it is invoked. In fact, in the actual program this is impossible, and an attempt to rewrite the program would involve blurring considerably the desired modularity.

The Sample Grammar briefly treats three points:
— When is Anaphoric Term Insertion to be applied? At the last step of Term Insertion, in an Open Predication, but only under favorable conditions.
— How is the Antecedent to be retrieved? From the previously inserted and duly indexed Terms ('for each new Term to be inserted, a new index i, j, k, ... is chosen, in order to symbolize nonidentity of referents').
— How is the Anaphoric Term eventually to be expressed? Depending on the selectional predicates of its antecedent, and depending on its syntactic function, as: *it/he/she/him/her*; furthermore, depending on the Subject of the Predication, as + SELF.
However, this creates a serious problem. Consider the following Open Predication:

believe (-) ([like (Ann) (Bill)])

where (-) denotes the position where the Anaphoric Pronoun is to be inserted, on the assumption that the Antecedent Term (*Bill*) is retrievable, and that this position is accessible to that Antecedent Term. Now, after Term Insertion has been completed, Assignment of Function SUBJECT should preferable be applied as freely as possible. Likewise, order of constituents should be decided upon by general rules, not by accidental facts such as whether a certain Term is Anaphoric, whether its Antecedent precedes it or not, etc. We are bound to generate, however, not only the correct sentences

> That Ann likes Bill is believed by him
> That Bill is liked by Ann is believed by himself
> Bill is believed by himself to be liked by Ann

but also the incorrect ones (incorrect if *he/him* and *Bill* are coreferential)

> He believes that Ann likes Bill
> He believes that Bill is liked by Ann
> He believes Bill to be liked by Ann
> It is believed by him that Ann likes Bill
> It is believed by him that Bill is liked by Ann

Likewise, in addition to

> Mary mailed the book to herself

we would also get, incorrectly if *her* and *Mary* are coreferential,

> The book was mailed to her by Mary

This needs repair. If we don't like filtering out bad results, then we have to grow a list of constraints, such as:
— do not retrieve Antecedent from a lower Predication, or
— do not assign Subject to Anaphoric Term if Antecedent is in lower Predication or in same Predication.
Basically, I guess, it is possible to prohibit the production of undesired output in this way maybe even, in the long run, exhaustively. The cost would only be an ever-growing list of constraints. Therefore I would like to present a tentative solution that is less cumbersome and maybe more elegant. As a preliminary remark, let me remind the reader of the tiny ornament I added in the Term Scheme Structure, the Boolean marker Imprimatur introduced in Section 3.2. My tentative solution aims at maximum generality. It enables random Anaphoric Term Insertion to take place at any moment where 'normal' Term Insertion is possible — it does not need the concept of Open Predication — provided an appropriate Antecedent Term can be found. The two of them are co-indexed as $ANTECEDENT_i$ and $ANAPHOR_i$. Function Assignment and Constituent Order impose no supplementary constraints. When it comes to printing the sentence, the principle of 'First come first serve' applies: Whichever of the two ($ANTECEDENT_i$ or $ANAPHOR_i$) is going to be expressed first will get full Term realization; the other one will be realized as a Personal Pronoun.

All Term Positions are equal, but not all Terms are. I will disregard for a while Embedded Predications, Relative Terms, and Question Terms and concentrate on the Terms created by Term Formation. A newly formed Term will no longer be inserted in the Predication, but will be added to a sequential list — or put on a stack if you prefer — where it gets the current index as its Index. The Argument Position in the Predication is filled instead with a Shadow Term, which is provided with that very same Index.

As just said, an attempt at Anaphora can now be realized if Antecedent Retrieval succeeds for the Position at hand. Antecedent Retrieval simply consists of searching the list or stack for an appropriate Antecedent Term anywhere in the overall complex Predication. If it succeeds, a second Shadow Term, which must be properly co-indexed, is inserted in the Argument Position. But if it fails, nothing of the sort happens, and Term Formation is called to create a new Term.

We can now have a look at a revised version of the structure for the above Predication:

$$\text{believe } (A_i) \ ([\text{like } (A_j) \ (A_i)])$$

and its Stack of Term Scheme Terms:

$$j = \text{Ann}$$
$$i = \text{Bill}$$

Notice that, as a consequence of this approach, our former ANTECEDENT$_i$ and ANAPHOR$_i$ have become indistinguishable.

Now for Expression Rules and the role of the Boolean marker Imprimatur. Both the Shadow-Term-in-Argument-Position and the Term-on-Stack have their own marker. When it is the turn of a Term-in-Argument-Position to be output, its marker tells whether this can be done; if it can, the marker of the co-indexed Term-on-Stack tells whether it can be realized in full Term form or must be realized as a Pronoun.

One final remark on a little detail that I passed over deliberately in order not to distract attention from the main points. Adding the current stack index to the Term can take place at several points in time. It is not necessary to do it, as suggested above, after or just before completion of Term Formation. Actually, there is a better moment: at the first possible occasion, right after the Nominal Restrictor (the 'head noun') has been picked. For from that moment on its Selectional Predicates are available for possible further procedures. The advantage of this is clear: we now can have anaphoric reference to a Term from within its own Term Scheme, as for instance in the following (where I use the abbreviated notation, and where (A) stands for Anaphoric Term):

$$(\text{the : man : believe } (R) \ ([\text{like } (Ann) \ (A)]))$$
the man who believes that Ann likes him

The device appears to work fine. The intended sentences have again been generated, but now without undesired results. As an extra bonus, reference from inside a complex term to the head noun comes out naturally. It is up to the grammarians to decide whether or not this idea would fit into their theory.

This solution is just a partial one, of course. It only aims at repairing an inconsistency in the FG approach to Personal Pronouns in Term Positions. I do not claim to have described the generation of all possible instances of Personal Pronouns. FG has not yet treated Possessive Pronouns, for instance. Neither has it studied Cataphoric or Backward Reference in all its subtleties. I suppose, however, that it is possible to produce Cataphoric Terms by disobeying — or, rather overruling — under proper conditions to be established by the theory, the 'First come first serve' principle. Another difficulty that remains to be solved concerns Reflexive Pronouns. While these seem to be unproblematic at Main Clause level, they are hard to get correct at Relative Clause level.

6. NON-VERBAL PREDICATES AND CLEFT CONSTRUCTIONS

6.1 Non-verbal predicates and copula support

In this section I consider Terms which fulfill the role of Predicate in a Predicate Frame. The generation of sentences with adjectival predicates is a simple matter. The Predicate Frame contains an Adjectival Predicate and has exactly one Term Position. In English, and also in some other languages, a copular verb is called for in case of non-verbal predicates. FG provides for a rule of Copula Support. With that, everything runs smoothly:

$$\text{expensive }_{Adj}\text{ (the book) }_{Zero}$$

Generation of sentences with a nominal predicate is much more complicated. It will not suffice to proceed just in the same way, taking a Predicate of category Noun instead of one of category Adjective, and invoking Copula Support again. In English, an article is obligatory, although this is not the case in Dutch. For example:

> Mary is a linguist and Olga is a mathematician
> Marie is taalkundige en Olga is wiskundige

Moreover, a noun can be modified in many more ways than an adjective. Therefore, FG posits a rule of Term Predicate Formation, thus creating the possibility of deriving Predicate Frames from any Term whatsoever. In the program, I now have to revise my original definition of Predicate Frame into: ' ... consists of (1) either a Lexical Predicate or a Term, (2) a number of Term Positions, ... '

The rule of Copula Support leads into the domain of the manifold meanings of the verb *to be*. Here opinions among theoretical linguists differ widely. At this moment, I would not dare to tread the thorny path of existential or locative constructions, which are subject to hot debate. I prefer to start with the more simple-looking and more basic Identifying Constructions.

6.2 Identifying constructions and pragmatic functions

Dik (1980b, chapters 4 and 10, which are the source for my entire Section 6) defines Identifying Constructions as 'describing the relation of identification between the intended referents of two Terms'. Basically this can be realized by having either of the two Terms as the Predicate Term and the other one in Term Position. Clearly enough, the latter one will get assigned Subject Function. So far, no problems:

$$\{ \text{(term}_j) \} \text{ (term}_i) \text{ }_{ZeroSubject}$$

My motivation for handling Identifying Constructions resides in FG's treatment of sentences of the type commonly known as Cleft and Pseudo-Cleft (or IT-cleft and WH-cleft) such as

> It is the book Mark wrote that Mary reads
> What Mary reads is the book Mark wrote

Formulated more generally:

> It is X + [headless relative clause]
> [relative clause with included antecedent] is X

FG concentrates, for the time being, on a certain subclass of Identifying Constructions for which it proposes (for reasons that will become clear in a moment) the name 'Focus Constructions'. These 'define a specific distribution of Topic and Focus over the structure of the clause.' We conclude that this class must lie in the intersection of Identifying Constructions and Cleft and Pseudo-Cleft sentences, but it is not clear from the text whether they are meant to fill the entire intersection or to form a proper part of it. Let us simply accept the following statements (Dik, 1980b, Section 10.5):

— Focus is a pragmatic function that can be assigned to different constituents of a given underlying predication;

— the general schema underlying the Focus construction can thus be represented as follows, where braces indicate that the term is used as a predicate:

$$\{ (\text{term}_j) \}_{\text{Focus}} (\text{term}_i)_{\text{ZeroTopic}}$$

— the Focus term, being part of the predicate, cannot receive Subject function; we will thus get structures of the following form:

$$\{ (\text{term}_j) \}_{\text{Focus}} (\text{term}_i)_{\text{ZeroSubjectTopic}}$$

6.3 Focus constructions and the generation program

It is here that a substantial problem arises for the programmer. Assignment of Pragmatic functions has not been dealt with in the Sample Grammar (Dik, 1980a), but on the basis of informal discussions, it seems justified to assume a formal status for Pragmatic Functions that is not entirely different from that of Syntactic Functions. The pair of formulae in Section 6.2, however, rather seriously disturbs the neat picture sketched in the Main Procedure designed in Section 2 (see also Figure 1). Syntactic Functions are assigned prior to Pragmatic Functions. Furthermore, they are assigned to Terms in Argument Positions, not to Predicates, and certainly not to just 'constituents' (which, after all, were not well-defined). Moreover, from these cited formulae we get the impression that the designated Term-as-Predicate already should have Focus function before the Rule of Predicate Formation is invoked. Focus Constructions seem to be a special case in which the General Main Procedure is twisted upside down: First there is a Focus Term, then a Predicate Frame is derived from it, and finally the one and only Argument Position is filled by a Term which must contain a Relative Clause, and this term receives Subject and Topic function. We managed to write a Special Procedure along these lines, which, added to the program, indeed impeccably generates sentences of the intended form.

After deciding to have a Term-as-Predicate, and to have Focus Constructions (which make Relative Clause Formation obligatory in the formation of the designated Subject Term), the choice between IT-cleft and WH-cleft dictates whether the Relative Clause receives no antecedent at all (at least, no overt one) or a kind of 'general filler word' antecedent like *the one*, *the person*, or *the thing*, *the object*. If no overt Antecedent has been generated, the Expression Rules have to invoke IT-Preposing.

In our Special Procedure, the choice between IT-cleft and WH-cleft was made early, during formation of the designated Subject Term. Another approach would have been to leave open the Antecedent position in the Subject Term scheme and to postpone the choice between IT-cleft and WH-cleft until the very last moment, that is, until just before entering the stage of the Expression Rules. At that point, the 'filler word' Antecedent could be added if such a constituent were decided upon.

An orthodox transformational treatment would start with a 'neutral' assertion at Deep Structure level, comparable with the Predication

$$\text{read (Mary)}_{\text{Agent}} \text{(the book Mark wrote)}_{\text{Goal}}$$

and apply Left Dislocation, Topicalization, or Extraposition to shuffle the constituents around until they landed at the intended position. As said before, FG does not have linearly ordered structures to start with, so it need not account for any movement at all. That is why the difference between IT-cleft and WH-cleft is so minimal in FG and in contrast to some orthodox transformational approaches, not at all problematic.

6.4 Focus constructions and another view on questions

The real idea behind Focus Constructions, however, is revealed in a wider context: questions and answers. (Dik, 1980b, Section 10.3.) It turns out that a question as to the identity of 'the thing that Mary reads' can be formed according to different strategies. One involves forming an Open Predication and then inserting a Q-Term into its last open position. (The computer simulation of this strategy has been described in Section 4.) This Q-Term would be assigned Focus function later on. In the answer, a definite Term would replace the Q-Term and also get Focus function. Notice that both the Q-Term and the substituted 'answer term' occupy an Argument Position, and therefore may have Subject or Object as Syntactic Function, in addition to Focus as Pragmatic Function. For example:

> read (Mary) $_{\text{AgentSubject}}$ (Q) $_{\text{GoalObjectFocus}}$
> What does Mary read?
> read (Mary) $_{\text{AgentSubject}}$(the book Mark wrote) $_{\text{GoalObjectFocus}}$
> THE BOOK MARK WROTE [stress] Mary reads.

A second strategy depends more on pragmatic conditions of discourse. As argued by FG, one would like to know the identity of a hitherto unknown object for which one can only provide a definite description — preferably in the form of a Relative Clause construction (e.g.: 'the thing that Mary reads'). This definite description would be used as the Topical Subject Term, and its identity (that is, the Term Predicate that applies to this Argument Term) would be questioned. It is this Term Predicate that would receive Focus, both in the question version and in the derived answer version:

> {(Q)}$_{\text{Focus}}$ (thing:[read (Mary)$_{\text{AgentSubject}}$ (R)$_{\text{GoalObject}}$])$_{\text{Zero,Topic}}$
> What is what (=the thing that) Mary reads?
> { (the book Mark wrote) } $_{\text{Focus}}$ ...
> The book Mark wrote is what Mary reads

Notice that, unlike in the first case, here the Q-Term and the substituted answer cannot have a Syntactic Function, since they do not occupy an Argument Position.

6.5 Focus constructions and generation, again

This context makes it better understandable why Focus Constructions require some special preparations in a random generation system. There is something missing, something that plays the role of the Given Topic in discourse. In a sentence generator, the order as depicted in Figure 1, — Predicate Formation, Term Formation, Term Insertion — apparently is reversed. In a discourse generator, it is completely different. We save the Topical Subject Term from the preceding part of the discourse. It need not come out of Term Formation any more; it is already there, ready to be inserted. We only have to generate the identifying Term Predicate Frame that it will fit into, and everything will run smoothly. And indeed, if we look carefully at the general schema that FG assumes to underly Focus Constructions (Section 6.2) we see that the Argument Term has index i and the Term Predicate index j. What would be the deeper meaning of this? It is a common implicit convention that i<j. It is also a common convention to index from left to right, in case the order is not relevant. Consequently, this must mean that indeed the Argument Term was there before the Term-as-Predicate.

I doubt, though, whether this is enough of an explanation. To generate the question that leads to the Focus Construction answer (the preceding discourse) we would have to proceed in the same way, since that would be a Focus Construction Question itself again. So the puzzle has not been solved yet. Note that the puzzle is not a computational one any more. We added a Special Procedure to the program, and it runs fine. The intended output is generated and no undesired results have shown up. But a completely different approach would have been feasible as well, and most probably it would have come up with exactly the same results. However, it would radically depart from the order of the General Procedure Form Specified Predication, and not just twist it slightly.

Now, here is a theoretical dilemma. Should different types of sentences be generated by disparate procedures? Of course this method could be called 'modular' too, if one wished. But then the Grammar would be an aggregate of modules, of partial grammars each of which generates a different type of sentences like Questions, Focus Constructions, and so on. This method would practically make void the general applicability of the unit Form Specified Predication. Or should we rather aim at a uniform treatment of a maximally wide variety of sentence types, i.e., at modularity in the 'right' sense?

7. TENSE AND ASPECT

In the preceding sections I treated generation of various sentence types one by one. The special procedures were built on the Main Procedure as a general base. I have argued that there were strong reasons for having a large part of the Main Procedure as an autonomous unit, called Form Fully Specified Predication, recursively applicable in Term Formation when it is necessary to produce an Embedded Predication or a Relative Clause. Recursion in the case of Form Fully Specified Predication means that specification of any Predication only comes to an end after all lower level elements have been specified. Thus, Syntactic Functions are assigned at the lower level, before it can be done at the immediately higher level. We could say, to put it briefly, that Syntactic Function Assignment works bottom-up.

There is another process quite similar to Function Assignment, namely introduction of Tense and Aspect. These are proposed by FG to be formalized by means of Predicate Operators, since Tense and Aspect are expressed in English in the different forms of the (Verbal) Predicate. In the Sample Grammar, the introduction of these two Operators is ordered, tentatively, as late as possible, i.e. after Function Assignment, just before Expression Rules. The question arises as to the possibility of incorporating the introduction of Tense/Aspect into the autonomous unit Form Fully Specified Predication. The answer is negative.

FG describes Introduction of Tense by way of an ordered pair of context-sensitive expansion rules:

$$\text{Tense} \longrightarrow \text{Present, Past [blocked in the context (SUB \_\_\_)]}$$

$$\text{Tense} \longrightarrow \left\{ \begin{array}{l} \text{Past / Past ... (SUB \_\_\_)} \\ \text{Present, Past} \end{array} \right\}$$

This allows, for example, both:

> John believes that Mary writes a paper
> John believes that Mary wrote a paper

but only:

> John believed that Mary wrote a paper

In other words, these two ordered rules describe the well-known phenomenon of *consecutio temporum*: 'Dependent clause gets Past Tense if main clause has Past Tense'. But this implies that Introduction of Tense must work top-down.

In conclusion: between steps (3) and (4) of the overall Main Procedure there is an extra step, say Assign Predicate Operators, containing at least Introduction of Tense. It is recursive as well, but goes in a top-to-bottom direction opposite to that taken by steps (1) through (3), which were put together to become Form Fully Specified Predication. Now, the question remains whether FG intends 'Fully Specified Predication' to include Tense. If so, then we should simply rename the autonomous unit, and leave out the 'Fully'.

8. LINGUISTICS AND PROGRAMMING

The algorithms and data structures described in this paper have been coded in the language Algol68, and I would like to justify this choice here in a few words.

Linguists of all schools and directions traditionally express their thoughts and theories verbally, in natural language — even if they use symbols and formulae as shorthand. I think that the most convenient translation of a linguistic theory into a computer program, without too much distortion, is one written in an Algol-like language. Of this family, Algol68 so far has the best facilities from a design as well as from a technical point of view, as regards abstract data types, string handling, garbage collecting, and availability. On the CDC Cyber mainframe of our university's computer center, with one of the world's best Algol68 compilers under maximal support, an average execution run, randomly generating one hundred sentences, takes about thirty system seconds, of which one third is needed for I/O. (Actually, there is no input but only output.) Even more important is the inverse translation: I wish linguists to be able to read without too much effort computer algorithms that are meant to model the grammatical rules they espouse. Algorithms, as written for human readers, are most easily coded in a procedural style. Moreover, the freedom to define in Algol68 a data structure type of any desired complexity in a most natural way, fits — in my opinion — far better a theoretical linguist's practice than does the rigid list structure, however flexible the latter may be in an experienced programmer's hands. As for the practical matter of exchanging program modules however, the situation of an Algol68 Natural Language Processing programmer is, unfortunately enough, an isolated one. An attempt to overcome this isolation might very well involve giving up the aforementioned advantages.

Shieber (1985) enumerates three aspects of computer use in linguistics. I fully agree with the 'touchstone' and the 'mirror' aspect, but only hesitantly with the 'straitjacket' aspect. I completely agree with everything he says about rigorous consistency and explicitness, but I would not like to accept a possible consequence — not mentioned by Shieber but perhaps plausible to others — regarding the *notation* of linguistic formalizations. I think linguists should not feel obliged to using Augmented Transition Networks, Context-Free Rewrite Rules, and the like. A straitjacket in that sense would be very unfortunate.

There is another remark I would like to make about metatheoretical matters such as well-formedness of rules and generative power. Here I have two intuitive feelings. The first is that any form of grammatical rule is acceptable (cf. my remark on the straitjacket problem) provided one can translate it without too much distortion or trickery into a computer algorithm. The second is that the set of grammatical linguistic expressions could very well be recursively enumerable without necessarily being recursive, that is, decidable. But this last point is more of a worry for our sisters and brothers in Parsing.

9. CONCLUSION

Van Bakel (1979) claims that there is no difference between theoretical linguistics as such and computational linguistics. The addition of 'computational', he argues, actually should be redundant, because the use of an electronic device is not only self-evident but even a *sine qua non* for theoretical linguistics if it will ever really become a formal science.

This paper is a report on a particular attempt to serve the advancement of theoretical general linguistics by modeling part of a given, existing, fully grown and well-established linguistic grammatical theory in the form of a computer program. The fragments of the grammar handle a variety of linguistic phenomena and sentence types. The program generates sentence tokens in a random manner. The random decisions concern the choice of lexical predicates of different categories, the order in which the term positions are filled, the expansion of terms based upon the term scheme, the assignment of syntactic functions, the introduction of predicate operators, and so on. These last two choices determine the shape of the linguistic expression. Abstraction is made from the informational content. The program is not about *what* to say, but about *how* to say it.

In this computer simulation of the formal grammatical rules and theoretical constructs, care has been taken to deviate as little as possible from their original FG representation. Some grammatical rules appeared ineffective, in the sense that a computer program strictly following these rules could end in an infinite loop. Some other rules, it turned out, were able to produce undesired, that is, ungrammatical, output. Examples were Relativization and Anaphora. In those cases, an alternative approach has been proposed.

The goal has been to assess the explicitness, completeness, and consistency of the theory, in short, its effectiveness. The goal has not been to build an efficient text generator, but the program might be useful as a module in a larger system of that sort. However, since nearly all systems in Natural Language Generation have been or are being written in some dialect of Lisp, it will be rather difficult to find a system that could incorporate my Algol68 program. Therefore I would be inclined, if and when I would undertake a second attempt at modeling FG, to do so in a Lisp environment. Furthermore, if I considered another attempt to model Dik's Functional Grammar, I might try the machinery of (Functional) Unification Grammar as promoted by Kay (1979, 1983, 1984) and as used in the grammar module of McKeown's TEXT system (1985).

ACKNOWLEDGEMENTS

I would like to thank Bengt Sigurd and Gerard Kempen for their extensive and thorough comments on draft versions of this paper. Responsibility for anything stated in or missing from this final version is of course completely mine.

REFERENCES

Bakel, J. van (1979) *Linguistic Engineering*. Nijmegen: Afdeling Computerlinguistiek, Faculteit der Letteren, Katholieke Universiteit Nijmegen.

Dik, S.C. (1978) *Functional Grammar*. Amsterdam: North-Holland.

Dik, S.C. (1980a) Seventeen Sentences: basic principles and application of Functional Grammar. In: E. Moravcsik & J. R. Wirth (Eds.) *Syntax and Semantics 13: Current Approaches to Syntax*. New York: Academic Press.

Dik, S.C. (1980b) *Studies in Functional Grammar*. New York: Academic Press.

Dik, S.C. (1983) Basic principles of Functional Grammar. In: S. C. Dik (Ed.) *Advances in Functional Grammar*. Dordrecht: Foris.

Dik, S.C. (1987) Generating answers from a linguistically coded knowledge base. (This volume.)

Friedman, J. (1971) *A Computer Model of Transformational Grammar*. New York: Elsevier.

Hirst, G. (1981) *Anaphora in natural language understanding: a survey*. Berlin: Springer.

Janssen, T. M.V. (1976) A computer program for Montague Grammar: theoretical aspects and proofs for the reduction rules. In: J. Groenendijk & M. Stokhof (Eds.) *Proceedings of the Amsterdam Colloquium on Montague Grammar and Related Topics*. Amsterdam: Centrale Interfaculteit, Universiteit van Amsterdam.

Kay, M. (1979) Functional Grammar. In: *Proceedings of the Fifth Annual Meeting of the Berkeley Linguistic Society*. Berkeley.

Kay, M. (1983) *Unification Grammar*. Unpublished memo. Palo Alto: Xerox PARC.

Kay, M. (1984) Functional Unification Grammar: A Formalism for Machine Translation. In: *Proceedings of the Tenth International Conference on Computational Linguistics (Coling'84)*. Stanford.

Kwee Tjoe-Liong (1981) In search of an appropriate relative clause. In: T. Hoekstra, H. van der Hulst & M. Moortgat (Eds.) *Perspectives on Functional Grammar*. Dordrecht: Foris.

McKeown, K.R. (1985) *Text Generation. Using Discourse Strategies and Focus Constraints to Generate Natural Language Text*. Cambridge: Cambridge University Press.

Shieber, S.M. (1985) Criteria for designing computer facilities for linguistic analysis. *Linguistics, 23*, 189-211.

Chapter 21

UTTERANCE GENERATION FROM SEMANTIC REPRESENTATIONS AUGMENTED WITH PRAGMATIC INFORMATION

Harry Bunt

TABLE OF CONTENTS

1. Introduction
2. Two-level model-theoretic semantics
3. The pragmatic framework
4. The TENDUM dialogue system
5. EL/R-EL/F translation
6. (Augmented) Discontinuous Phrase-Structure Grammar
7. From EL/F to natural language
7.1 Types, categories and features
7.2 The generation of syntactic trees
7.3 The percolation of feature constraints
7.4 The generation of discontinuous constituents
8. More semantic control

1. INTRODUCTION

This chapter reports on an exploration of the problems and possibilities of the automatic generation of natural language utterances from formal semantic/pragmatic representations, using the syntactic, semantic and pragmatic formalisms developed for natural language interpretation in the context of the TENDUM dialogue system (Bunt et al., 1985). The three formalisms have explicitly been designed to support one another, and present a highly formalized approach to each of the areas concerned: syntax, semantics, and pragmatics. The syntactic formalism is a kind of (generalized) phrase-structure grammar that allows discontinuous constituents: it is motivated by the aim of obtaining semantic and pragmatic interpretations in a systematic way. The semantic formalism applies the methods of model-theoretic semantics while keeping general and specific world knowledge in separate models. The pragmatic formalism can be viewed as a formalization, in model-theoretic terms, of a variant of speech act theory based on context-changing functions. The combination of these formalisms has proved successful for the interpretation of natural language expressions in the context of an information dialogue and has been implemented in the TENDUM dialogue system.

Generating and interpreting natural language with the same formalisms, in particular with the same grammar, is presumably an ideal of every computational linguist involved in language generation. For one thing, it is intuitively implausible that humans should use separate grammars for speaking and for listening. And even if psychological considerations are not taken into consideration, it is simply a matter of economy in the development of language processing systems to avoid duplication of grammars for generation and interpretation. But most important, presumably, is the consideration that an adequate grammar is a representation of the possible syntactic structures in a language, paired with their meanings. It therefore ought to be possible to use the same grammar both for generation and for interpretation. In fact, this may provide us with a criterion for evaluating grammars. For instance, versions of Transformational Grammar that were popular until fairly recently would fail on on this criterion, since they included deletion transformations that make these grammars unsuitable for interpretation (see Winograd, 1983). Quite a number of linguists, notably linguists with the explicit aim of modeling the human language faculty, seem not to have recognized this immediately. Similar problems turn up when we try to generate language using an analysis grammar, in which certain lexical items and phrases are ignored in the semantic components of rules, such as phrases expressing politeness. The danger of 'semantic negligence' is that, if the syntactic part of the rule is recursive, the grammar used in generative mode may allow infinite repetitions of the neglected phrases and cause the generation process not to terminate: Because of the recursion, there is no syntactic reason why the rule should not be applicable again and again, and because of the semantic emptiness there is no semantic reason either.

When language generation is conceived in the context of communication with an information-processing system, the grammar is just one of the components involved — that is, if we understand 'grammar' in the usual sense of a description of syntactic structures with associated formal semantics. Other components are:

(A)   a world-knowledge representation system, including both general, 'common-sense' knowledge and knowledge of specific facts concerning the domain of discourse
(B)   a lexical semantic component, relating content words to the elements of the world-knowledge representation system
(C)   a dynamic representation of the communication situation, including such things as the information available to each participant and their communicative intentions
(D)   a pragmatic component, relating aspects of utterances to elements of the representation of the commmunication situation.

Each of these components is equally indispensable for language interpretation and language generation, and our intuition that an adequate grammar should be equally usable for generation and interpretation extends to these components as well. The TENDUM dialogue system brings specific proposals for these components together with a syntactic-semantic-pragmatic grammar.

A proposal for the representation of world knowledge (component A) and its incorporation in a lexical semantic component (B) has been worked out in the framework called 'Two-level model- theoretic semantics'. An approach to the representation of the communication situation (component C) has been developed for so-called 'information dialogues', i.e. dialogues with no other purpose than the exchange of factual information. Finally, a grammar formalism has been designed which incorporates mechanisms for identifying pragmatic features of utterances and interpreting these in terms of the aspects of the dialogue context (component D). This chapter explores the possibility of using each of these components in a language generation process which is roughly the reverse of the interpretation process for which they were originally designed.

The chapter is organized as follows. Section 2 briefly describes the components A and B. Section 3 describes the approach to user modeling and communicative action that forms the basis of components C and D. Section 4 sketches the combination of these components for language interpretation in the currently implemented version of the TENDUM system, and discusses language interpretation within that context. Section 5 discusses the first step in a language generation process which results from attempting to reverse the TENDUM interpretation process, involving in particular the components A and B. Section 6 sketches the grammar formalism. Section 7 deals with the use of the grammar and the lexicon to generate natural language expressions from the intermediate representations considered in section 5. Section 8 describes the possible exploitation of the tight coupling of syntax and semantics in the grammar to control a language generation process.

2. TWO-LEVEL MODEL-THEORETIC SEMANTICS

The framework of two-level model-theoretic semantics has been described in detail elsewhere (Bunt, 1985), so we only give a brief summary here. It derives from the interpretation method developed for the PHLIQA1 question answering system (Bronnenberg et al., 1979). Its most conspicuous property is that natural language expressions are interpreted in two steps, each resulting in a semantic representation in a formal language. The formal languages used for this purpose are two members of the same family, that of Ensemble Languages (the EL family). These languages are based in their semantics on Ensemble Theory, an extension of classical Set Theory designed for the purpose of natural language interpretation. The languages of this family all have the same syntactic constructions, but they differ in their constants. The constants of the language used in the first stage, called EL/F ('Ensemble Language, Formal'), have a one-to-one correspondence with content words (lexemes) in the natural language. One might say that the semantic representations constructed at this level are *in terms of the content words*; what the formal language does is to make the formal, or 'logical' semantic aspects of a sentence explicit — hence the name 'Ensemble Language, Formal'. The language used in the second stage has constants standing in a one-to-one relation to the elements in a model of the discourse domain. The semantic representations constructed at this level are elaborations of those constructed in EL/F, the elaborations consisting in the replacement of the content words by expressions made up of terms that refer to elements in the discourse domain; this language is therefore called 'Ensemble Language, Referential', or EL/R.

The following example illustrates this. Consider the question:

(1)   Does the KL402 come from the U.S.?

At the first level of analysis, a formal semantic structure is assigned to the sentence, expressed in EL/F:

(2)   COMEFROM(<kl402, usa>)

Here, 'COMEFROM' is a two-place predicate corresponding to the verb 'come from'; 'kl402' and 'usa' are individual constants corresponding to the proper names 'KL402' and 'U.S.', respectively. The second stage of analysis is extremely simple in this case, since the flight 'KL402' and the country 'USA' are simple concepts in the domain of discourse; only 'come from' is not such a concept. Therefore, all that needs to be done is to express the latter relation in terms of EL/R concepts, and to replace the EL/F constants 'kl402' and 'usa' by their EL/R counterparts (which are written in capital letters). The result is:

(3)   Country(Departureplace(KL402)) = USA

Here, 'Country' and 'Departureplace' are function constants relating a city to its country and a flight to its city of departure, respectively. It is important to note that the second stage of analysis, that of EL/F — EL/R translation, consists simply of looking up the EL/F constants in the EL/F — EL/R lexicon, making appropriate replacements, and simplifying the resulting expression if possible. For the present example, the following part of the lexicon would be relevant:

(4)   EL/F   EL/R

kl402	KL402
usa	USA
COMEFROM	1. $(\lambda x: \text{Departureplace}(\text{elem}_1(x)) = \text{elem}_2(x))$
	2. $(\lambda x: \text{Country}(\text{Departureplace}(\text{elem}_1(x))) = \text{elem}_2(x))$

The variable x in the translations of COMEFROM ranges over pairs of individuals, $\text{elem}_1(x)$ denoting the first element of such a pair, $\text{elem}_2(x)$ the second.

Since the EL/F constants are in fact simply lexical items of the natural language, they are in general ambiguous, and not all combinations of their EL/R interpretations are meaningful. The combinations which are not meaningful are filtered out by means of an articulate type system, which forms part of the EL/R definition. In the example, the first possible translation of COMEFROM would violate the EL/R type restrictions since the type of Departureplace requires the right-hand side of the equality to be an expression of type *city*, whereas USA is of type *country*. Formula (3) is obtained by replacing the EL/F constants in (2) by their translations (for COMEFROM: the second), and simplifying the result by applying lambda conversion.

3. THE PRAGMATIC FRAMEWORK

In a dialogue system which is more than a question-answering system, the inputs do not always have the function of a question but may have other functions such as confirmation, correction, or verification; consequently, their interpretation is not 'just' a matter of truth-conditional semantic interpretation but also involves the recognition of the input qua function in the communication. In other words, we need a framework for dealing with utterances as communicative actions. The pragmatic framework developed for this purpose, as it underlies the TENDUM dialogue system, was designed for information dialogues. The framework rests on the assumption that participating in an information dialogue is a form of goal-directed, rational cooperative action (see Allwood, 1976), where a participant chooses his communicative actions on the basis of his current model of the situation. Based on an analysis of the dimensions of partner modeling in information dialogues, a set of communicative action types has been defined with rules specifying, on the one hand, how the recognition of the communicative function of an input guides the construction of a user model and, on the other hand, under what conditions certain actions are chosen to continue a dialogue. The reader is referred to Bunt (1986) for details.

4. THE TENDUM DIALOGUE SYSTEM

In this section we indicate very briefly how the approaches to semantics and pragmatics mentioned above are combined in the TENDUM dialogue system, and what the input for a language generation component is (see Bunt et al., 1985, for a general overview of the system).

The implementation of the semantic and pragmatic frameworks outlined in the preceding sections has resulted in a system design which includes the following main functions (see Figure 1):

1. Analysis of the input for syntactic and formal semantic structure and for features that contribute to the determination of its communicative function.
2. Expression of the semantic content of nouns, verbs, adjectives, and other content words in terms of the concepts of the model of the discourse domain.
3. Interpretation of bundles of syntactic-pragmatic features as communicative functions.
4. Updating of the user model according to the communicative function and semantic content of the input.
5. Evaluation of the information which the input may intend to convey about the discourse domain and updating of the domain model if appropriate.
6. Construction of a plan for continuing the dialogue on the basis of the current user model, the pending goals, and the results of:
7. Consultation of the data base, containing a model of the state of the discourse domain.
8. Determination of indirect interpretations of the input, if appropriate.
9. Creation of the expected effects of the communicative actions in the plan, set up in steps 6 through 8.
10. Execution of the plan by expressing its actions in natural language.

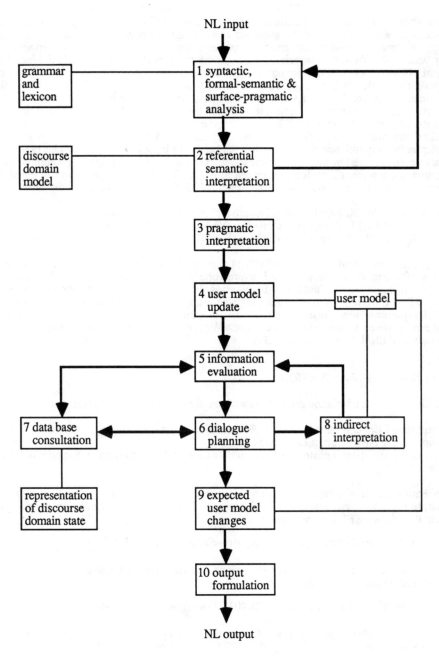

Figure 1. Main components of TENDUM dialogue system.

One part of the pragmatic framework underlying the TENDUM design has not yet been mentioned. It is the distinction between two categories of communicative action: those that serve to accomplish (some of) the intended information transfer, called *factually-informative acts* , and those serving to monitor the dialogue. The latter are called *dialogue control acts;* they play an often underestimated role in natural dialogues (Bunt, 1979; Van Katwijk, 1981). In our framework, we view a dialogue control act as a signal from one of the modules in a natural language communication and information processing system by which the module reports on its own processing. Two subcategories of dialogue control acts can be distinguished. First, there are the obligatory ones, which are produced by a module running into problems in carrying out its task. (Examples: 'Did you say Tuesday?'; 'What do you mean by that?'; 'I don't have this information.') Second, there are the optional ones, occurring, for instance, when a module reports success; examples of this class are: 'I see', 'Aha', 'O.K.', 'Yes'. The TENDUM system at present only performs obligatory dialogue control acts.

The module, whose task it is to produce natural language output has so far been implemented only rudimentarily, as we will see below. Its input consists of elements of the plan structure, constructed by module 6; these are pairs consisting of the name of a communicative function and a semantic content, expressed in EL/R. For example, in response to the above example question 'Does the KL402 come from the U.S.?', the plan will contain the pairs:

(5)   <YNANSWER, NOT[Country(Departureplace(KL402)) = USA]>
       <WHANSWER, Country(Departureplace(KL402)) = CANADA>
       <WHANSWER, Departureplace(KL402) = MONTREAL>

This paper is concerned with the feasibility of expressing such structures in natural language by means of a kind of inversion of the interpretation process, namely by translating the EL/R expressions involved first 'back' into EL/F, using the domain-specific semantic knowledge of module 2, and from there into natural language, using the pragmatic knowledge of module 3 and the grammar used in module 1. So far, this has only been explored for single pairs <Communicative function, Semantic content>. We now turn to the first part of this process, the translation of EL/R expressions into EL/F.

5. EL/R — EL/F TRANSLATION

The EL/F — EL/R translation consists, as we have seen above, of three operations:

1. replacing EL/F constants by their EL/R translations, by means of dictionary lookup;
2. simplifying the resulting EL/R expression;
3. checking the meaningfulness of the combination of EL/F-constant interpretations (i.e., translations).

Concerning the simplification operations involved, let us consider the example of section 2 again. In the case where the correct combination of EL/F constant interpretations is taken, we obtain the following EL/R translation of (2):

(6) $(\lambda x: \text{Country}(\text{Departureplace}(\text{elem}_1(x))) = \text{elem}_2(x))(<\text{KL402}, \text{USA}>)$

This expression can be simplified in two respects. The lambda abstraction can be eliminated by lambda conversion, with the result:

(7) $\text{Country}(\text{Departureplace}(\text{elem}_1(<\text{KL402}, \text{USA}>))) = \text{elem}_2(<\text{KL402}>, \text{USA}>)$

Second, the simplest representation of the first element of a pair is the element itself, and similarly for the second; thus the constructions 'elem$_1$' and 'elem$_2$' can be eliminated, with the result:

(8) $\text{Country}(\text{Departureplace}(\text{KL402})) = \text{USA}$

This illustrates the two most important ways of simplifying expressions in the EL/F — EL/R translation: lambda conversion and 'tuple elimination'.

Let us now consider what would happen if we tried to reverse the EL/F — EL/R translation. This means that we should use the EL/F — EL/R dictionary in the opposite direction and 'undo' any simplification operation.

We can begin by looking in the EL/F — EL/R dictionary and check whether there happens to be an EL/F constant whose translation is precisely our EL/R expression. If this is not the case, we can do two things. One is to try the same for subexpressions of the EL/R expression; the other is to perform some inverse simplification operations and try again. An algorithm for EL/R — EL/F translation will be a combination of these two actions. Performing inverse simplification operations is very unattractive, however. The inverse of lambda conversion, lambda abstraction, can be applied in 2^n-1 different ways on an expression with n constants. And the inverse of tuple elimination is still worse, since every constant c can be replaced by $elem_i(<..., c, ...>)$, where $<..., c, ...>$ indicates any tuple of at least i elements, with c as its i-th member. This can be repeated *ad infinitum*.

Therefore, an algorithm was designed which is based not on inverse simplification operations but on the unification of EL/R (sub)expressions and EL/F — EL/R dictionary entries. To illustrate this, we consider the above example of the EL/F — EL/R translation in the opposite direction; now we would like to 'match' (8) with the pattern of the dictionary entry (9):

(9)   COMEFROM ==> $(\lambda x: Country(Departureplace(elem_1(x))) = elem_2(x))$

This can be achieved by considering only the 'body' of the abstraction expression, removing the '$elem_i$' constructions, and unifying the resulting expression (10) with (9) after renaming the variables:

(10) $Country(Departureplace(y)) = z$

In fact, this comes down to considering only those inverse simplifications suggested by the EL/F — EL/R dictionary.

The next step in the generation process involves the translation of EL/F expressions into natural language. To discuss this step, we must first consider the formalism of Discontinuous Phrase-Structure Grammar.

6. (AUGMENTED) DISCONTINUOUS PHRASE-STRUCTURE GRAMMAR

The grammar for linguistic interpretation in the TENDUM system has developed from an augmented (generalized) phrase-structure grammar, generalized in the sense that syntactic features are used in the same style as in GPSG (Gazdar, Klein, Pullum & Sag, 1985), and augmented by semantic rules and the use of pragmatic features. Since the first and foremost requirement for the grammar is that the syntactic analysis should play into the hands of semantic interpretation, only semantically well-motivated constituent structures should be used, i.e., the syntactic rules should avoid the use of constituents that have no clear semantic significance.

On this view, one of the most problematic phenomena is formed by discontinuous constituents, such as the noun phrase 'a car which has five doors' in the sentence 'John bought a car for Mary which has five doors'. Moreover, in order to allow efficient parsing, it is desirable that the grammar remain close to context-free.

This has led to the design of a grammar formalism which is not a pure phrase-structure grammar, though it bears a close resemblance to one. To indicate both the similarity and the fact that there is a difference, this formalism has been called '(Augmented) Phrase-Construction Grammar', or 'APC Grammar'. But since the significant difference with a phrase-structure grammar is that discontinuous constituents are allowed (which has rather intricate consequences, as we shall see), it is perhaps more appropriate simply to call the formalism 'Discontinuous Phrase-Structure Grammar', or DPSG. We will use this term to refer in particular to the syntactic side of the grammar, and speak of 'Augmented DPSG' (ADPSG) when we take the semantic and pragmatic augmentations into account.

A DPSG rule has the following form:

(11) a:A + [b:B] + c:C + ... + n:N ==> r:R {..}
        — conditions on features of a, b, c, ... n.
        — specification of features of r.

The top line should be read as follows. If we neglect both the square and the curly brackets for a moment, we simply have a context-free rewriting rule R ==> A B C ... N, written from right to left. A constituent enclosed in square brackets has the status of so-called 'internal context', which means, in the example, that the constituent of category B is not a subconstituent of the R-constituent; it just happens to separate the subconstituents A and C. In other words, R is a discontinuous constituent. The part in curly brackets may contain certain conditions on the linear order of the immediate subconstituents of the elements on the left of the arrow; we will leave this aspect out of consideration here (but see Bunt 1985, Section 8.8.2).

The crucial reason why rules like (11) are not ordinary phrase-structure rules is that discontinuous constituents destroy the left-right order in a tree representation. For example, the rules (12) would generate the tree-like structure (13):

(12) a:A + [b:B] + c:C + d:N ==> r:R
        a:B + [b:C] + [c:N] + d:Q ==> r:P
        a:R + b:P ==> r:S

(13)

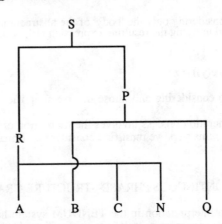

The crossing branches in this diagram reflect that R and P are not adjacent constituents in the usual sense, in spite of what the third rule in (12) suggests. The '+' sign in these rules denotes a more complex concept of adjacency, which is defined as follows. The definition consists of two parts. First, the notion of *adjacency pair* is defined:

(14) Two constituents C1 and C2 form an adjacency pair iff:
        (i)   The leftmost immediate constituent of C1 is further to the left than that of C2
        (ii)   C1 and C2 do not share any constituent (either as immediate constituent or as indirect constituent)
        (iii) There is no constituent with the same properties as C2 whose leftmost immediate constituent is further to the left than that of C2.

For example, in (13) R and P form an adjacency pair, and so do R and B, and P and C. The members of an adjacency pair are also called *neighbours*.

The second part of the definition extends the notion of adjacency pair to that of *adjacency sequence*:

(15) A sequence of constituents <a, ..., n> is an (n-place) adjacency sequence iff:
    (i)   every pair <i, j> in the sequence is either an adjacency pair or is connected by a chain of adjacency pairs of which all members are constituents of elements in the subsequence <a, ..., i>;
    (ii) the constituents in the sequence do not share any constituents.

For example, in diagram (13) the triple <R, B, Q> is a three-place adjacency sequence since R and B form an adjacency pair, and B and Q are connected by the chain B-C-N-Q, with C and N constituents of R. Thus, a rule a:R + b:B + c:Q ==> r:S could be applied here, to produce an alternative parse.

In general, the sequence of constituents to the left of the arrow in a DPSG rule forms an adjacency sequence; the '+' sign is used as an infix notation for this relation. For more about DPSG and its formal properties, the reader is referred to Bunt (1987) and Bunt, Thesingh & van der Sloot (1987).

In augmented DPSG, features are used not only for syntactic but also for *pragmatic* purposes. When an expression has been parsed, the top node of the syntactic tree has acquired a feature list, because of the feature percolation mechanisms. This feature list contains a few elements that serve a pragmatic purpose. Two such features are *mood* and *concord*; the latter is used for expressions indicating a speaker's assumption that his partner does (concord = 'positive') or does not (concord = 'negative') agree with him on the propositional content concerned. This feature is used to recognize an utterance as, for example, a confirmation, a disconfirmation, or a correction. TENDUM module 3 in figure 1 has the task of interpreting these features and computing a communicative function from them.

This must be reversed in the language generation process. Given a communicative function computed by the dialogue planning module, the corresponding possible feature values are determined and used as restrictions on the class of target expressions.

7. FROM EL/F TO NATURAL LANGUAGE

We now turn to the translation into natural language of structures of type (16):

(16) <Semantic content expressed in EL/F, List of feature restrictions>

To permit exploration of the possibilities and problems involved, the following rather crude algorithm was designed and implemented. At the end of this paper we shall briefly consider a more sophisticated design.

1. Compute the logical type of the EL/F-expression.
2. Determine the set of pairs <C, L> of syntactic category C and feature restriction list L which correspond to that type.
3. Select from this set those pairs where L is compatible with the feature restriction list of the input.
4. Using the grammar in generative mode, produce in a top-down manner all syntactic structures whose associated semantic representation matches the input EL/F-expression. Take the sequences of natural language words at the leaves of those trees.
5. Choose one of the resulting strings.

Let us look at a simple example to see how this algorithm works. As input we take the pair:

(17) <COMEFROM(<kl402, montreal>), [mood: declar; concord: neg]>

1. The type of the EL/F-expression is t (truth value).
2. The set {<S, L>| S is the category 'sentence', L is empty} corresponds to this type.
3. We select those pairs <S, L> where L includes the sublist [mood: declar; concord: neg].

4. We generate all syntactic tree structures of category S allowed by the grammar, where the root has a feature list including [mood: declar; concord: neg]. With the small grammar and lexicon used for testing the algorithm, this produces the following sentences:
   a. De KL402 komt niet uit Montreal. (= The KL402 comes not from Montreal.)
   b. Uit Montreal komt niet de KL402. (= From Montreal comes not the KL402.)
   c. De KL402 komt uit Montreal niet. (= The KL402 comes from Montreal not.)
   d. Uit Montreal komt de KL402 niet. (= From Montreal comes the KL402 not.)
5. In absence of criteria for preferring one of these sentences over the others, one of them is picked at random. (Criteria to be used here should relate, for instance, to what is currently in focus in an ongoing dialogue.)

Let us now consider some of each of these steps in more detail.

7.1 Types, categories and features

The types of EL/F-expressions and the syntactic categories of natural language expressions are related through the coupling of syntactic and semantic rules in the grammar, since all rules which construct an expression of a certain category R build, in their semantic components, an EL/F-expression of the same logical type. We should bear in mind, however, that the syntactic components in the grammar rules construct not just expressions with a certain syntactic category but rather expressions with a certain category and a certain feature list; moreover, the possible ways of using an expression as a building block in other expressions are not determined solely by the syntactic category but rather by the combination of category and features. Therefore, combinations of category and feature list are associated with a unique type through the grammar. (Note that, if categories are conceived as complex feature bundles, there is simply one type associated with every category.) The reverse is not always true; expressions of different syntactic categories may have the same type. The relation between syntactic categories and semantic types is more complicated then, for instance, in Montague Grammar (see, e.g., Montague, 1971), but the important thing is that for every EL/F type there is a corresponding set of zero, one, or more category/feature combinations. For example[1], type t corresponds to <S, [mood:declar]>; type $((e \longrightarrow t) \longrightarrow t)$ to <NP, []>; type $(<e,e> \longrightarrow t)$ to <V, [argnr:2]>. From the type of an EL/F-expression we thus know the syntactic categories of the possible translations and maybe some constraints on features.

It may be observed that the EL/F definition allows very complex types, which do not always correspond to any syntactic category. This means that, with the present approach, we can only hope to translate into natural language those EL/F expressions that can occur as semantic representations of natural language expressions. For a natural language dialogue system, this seems quite reasonable.

So much for steps 1 and 2 of the alogrithm. Step 2 may produce feature constraints which are only partly compatible with the constraints derived from the communicative function in step 1. Step 3 detects and discards the incompatible cases.

7.2 The generation of syntactic trees

Step 4 in the algorithm concerns the generation of all syntactic structures sanctioned by the grammar, with the right category and features, and with a semantic representation that matches the input EL/F-expression. A question of central importance is how this process can be

---

[1] The names e and t stand for 'entity' and 'truth value', as in Montague's type system. Unlike Montague's system, the type system underlying EL/F has several ways of forming complex types (Bunt, 1985). A type of the form $(a \rightarrow b)$ corresponds to functions from arguments of type a to values of type b. A type of the form $<a_1, a_2, ..., a_n>$ corresponds to n-tuples consisting of objects of the types $a_1, a_2, ..., a_n$.

controlled by syntactic and semantic information. The algorithm we are describing is especially crude in this respect; so far, the following control strategy has been implemented.

a. *Syntactic control*: Delete from the grammar all those rules which construct expressions that cannot occur as constituents of an expression with the given syntactic category and features. (For instance, if a declarative sentence is to be built, delete all rules that construct WH-noun phrases.)
b. *Semantic control*: Delete all lexical insertion rules introducing EL/F constants that do not occur in the given EL/F expression.

Here, the importance of the one-to-one correspondence between content words and EL/F-constants becomes apparent. Moreover, this control strategy rests on the important assumption that the semantic components of grammar rules never delete EL/F constants.

This control strategy leads to the generation of a large number of syntactic trees (with their EL/F semantics) of which the semantic irrelevance is only detected afterwards. For instance, for the EL/F expression

(18) LOVES(<john, mary>)

not only the syntactic trees for the sentences

(19) John loves Mary
Mary is loved by John
Mary loves John

with Mary as direct object are generated, but also those for the corresponding sentences with Mary as subject, which are discarded afterwards. This can be avoided with a more sophisticated semantic control of the process; in the algorithm sketched here, the semantics is only used at the beginning, in restricting the lexicon, and as a check at the end. However, our first concern has not been the optimization of the process but rather the specific complications that relate to the use of ADPSG: the use of feature constraints and especially the treatment of internal context elements in the generation of discontinuous constituents. We briefly deal with each of these now.

7.3 The percolation of feature constraints

In the generation of a syntactic tree, restrictions on features of the top node come from two sources, as we have seen: the communicative function and the type of the semantic content to be expressed. As grammar rules contain conditions on features of the subconstituents and specifications of the percolation of these features to the newly constructed phrase, the use of the rules in reverse order implies that the feature restrictions of the top node not only restrict the applicable rules to those where the feature conditions are satisfied but also induce feature restrictions on the subconstituents.

Conditions on features come, as usual, in two kinds: local ones, which impose a restriction on the values of a feature for a single constituent, and global ones, which require a certain combination of feature values for two or more constituents. In a top-down tree generation process, local feature conditions imply restrictions on individual daughter nodes. Global feature conditions give rise to a complex process of feature restriction percolation, due to the interactions among conditions on different nodes, and the need to take feature values into account as they become available when parts of the tree are expanded. For instance, a global feature condition may require two sister nodes X and Y to have the same value for a certain feature F. In addition, a local condition on some higher node in the tree may already have restricted the possible values of F to the set {val1, val2}. Now suppose node X is expanded, and it turns out that, due to restrictions on other features of X, only expansions are possible that correspond to F having the value val2 for X. This information should then percolate upwards to node X, and from there as a restricion to the sister node Y. We thus see that feature restrictions must continually be computed and passed on to dominating, dominated and sister nodes in the tree.

7.4 The generation of discontinuous constituents

The generation of discontinuous constituents represents a notorious problem in language generation (e.g., see Block, 1986; Horacek, 1987) — one for which DPSG might be expected to offer a solution. Indeed, this turns out to be the case. A simple, though inefficient algorithm that generates all correct expressions, including those with discontinuities, consists of first applying the DPSG rules in a top-down fashion, generating internal context nodes as if they were ordinary constituents (though without expanding them) and subsequently unifying the context nodes in the tree with 'real' nodes. The following example illustrates this.

Suppose the generation algorithm is to construct a tree with a top node of category C, and let the grammar contain rules with the following components:

(20)   a:P + [b:Q] + c:R ==> r:A
        a:Q + [b:R] + c:S ==> r:B
        a:A + b:B ==> c:C

Application of these rules will give us the following structure:

(21)

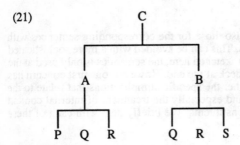

This is not, of course, an acceptable structure, since two of the nodes have not been attached. What needs to be done is to match each internal context node (Q and R) with a node that has the same category, features and neighbourhood relations, and make the appropriate identifying connections. In the present example, this would lead to constituency diagram (22).

(22)

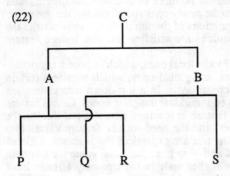

Things can be much more complicated than in this example, since the same node may occur more than once as internal context; moreover, the question whether the unification of two nodes succeeds, may depend on the success of unifying other nodes. This is the case in structure (23).

(23)

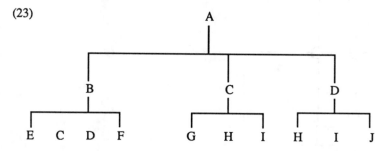

Here the unification of the two C nodes depends on that of the two D nodes, because the contextual C node has a D node as right neighbour, whereas the C node dominated by A does not. (The latter C node has the contextual H node as its right neighbour.) So the two C nodes unify only if the D nodes also unify. Unification of both the two C nodes and the two D nodes gives the result (24):

(24)

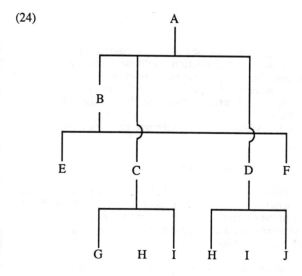

In the structure (24), two contextual nodes remain to be connected. Again, the unifications of these nodes are interdependent; unifying the two H nodes, for instance, implies unifying the two I nodes, in view of their adjacency relations. The result of these unifications is the constituency structure (25). For reasons of efficiency, the algorithm that has been implemented does not postpone node unifications to the end but alternates between node expansion and unification.

(25)

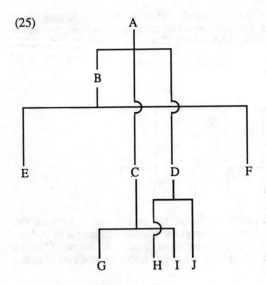

8. MORE SEMANTIC CONTROL

We already noted that the generation algorithm outlined above is controlled by semantic information in a very crude way only, namely through restrictions on the lexicon at the start of the process and through a check at the end whether the semantic representation of the generated tree matches the input EL/F expression. However, it is possible to use the semantic information during the generation process as well, thereby greatly reducing the number of syntactic possibilities that are taken into consideration.

To see this, let us take again the example where the input to the tree generation process is the pair

(17)   <COMEFROM(<kl402, montreal>), [mood:declar; concord:neg]>.

The EL/F-expression has type t (truth value), so we should build trees where the top node has syntactic category S and a feature list including [mood:declar; concord:neg]. Rather than blindly generating all these trees, we can look at the semantic components of the rules in the grammar for category S, and see how semantic representations of type t can be formed. In the current grammar there are three ways in which this is possible:

(1)   An EL/F-expression of type t is formed from two other expressions of type t (sentences) plus one of type $(t \longrightarrow t)$, i.e. a conjunction; this is the case of conjoined sentences.
(2)   An EL/F-expression of type t is formed from one of type t (a sentence) and one of type $(t \longrightarrow t)$, i.e. a sentential modifier; this is the case of sentence modification.
(3)   An EL/F-expression of type t is formed from one of type $(<e,e, ... e>_k \longrightarrow t)$, i.e. a k-place verb) and one of type $((<e,e, ... e>_k \longrightarrow t) \longrightarrow t)$, i.e. asequence of k argument phrases; this is the case of combining a k-place verb with k arguments to form a simple sentence.

As in the algorithm outlined above, we can use the feature list of the input to constrain the applicability of grammar rules; in the present case this means that possibility (1) can be ruled out, since conjoined sentences cannot have a negative 'concord' feature in the current grammar. We now consider the possibilities (2) or (3) to see whether they could lead to the input EL/F expression. However, we should take into account that the simplifications performed during the

EL/F — EL/R translation remove lambda abstractions and tuple constructions wherever possible, regardless of whether these have been introduced by the EL/F — EL/R dictionary or by the semantic parts of grammar rules. We should therefore check whether the grammar rules for the possibilities (2) and (3) give rise to a semantic representation that matches the given EL/F expression after simplification. It is readily seen that possibility (2) applies in this case, as the input EL/F expression may result from an application of lambda-conversion to the expression:

(26) $(\lambda x\colon x)(\text{COMEFROM}(<kl402, montreal>))$

where x is a variable of type t. Clearly, the identity function $(\lambda x\colon x)$ may always be added in this way, which could bring the process in danger of getting into a loop. However, the grammar rules implementing case (2) are recursive only in their phrase-construction parts; the feature conditions make sure that the application of a sentential modifier with empty semantic content is only allowed if there is some pragmatic content, represented in the features of the modified sentence. In the example, this means that the top S node has the associated feature list [mood:declar; concord:neg], but the embedded S node has the feature list [mood:declar; concord:unspec]. To generate such a node, only possibilities (1) and (3) are open.

We can continue along this course, using category and feature information to select candidate rules from the grammar, and comparing the semantic representations built up by these rules with the input EL/F expression to find those rules which deserve further consideration. This shows clearly that the tight coupling of syntax and semantics in ADPSG, on a rule-to-rule basis, permits the systematic generation of well-formed natural language expressions from semantic/pragmatic representations in a highly controlled fashion.

ACKNOWLEDGEMENTS

This paper draws heavily on the work done by two of my students for their master's theses; Ron Doesborg developed and implemented the algorithm for EL/F — EL/R translation mentioned in section 5 and did much of the work on the percolation of feature restrictions mentioned in section 7.3; Guido Minnen designed and implemented the algorithm for generating discontinuous constituents mentioned in section 7.4. I would like to thank both of them, as well as Jan Thesingh, Ko van der Sloot, Joop van Gent, Yvette Cramer, Hilde van der Togt and Miriam Mulders for discussions about phrase-structure grammar which helped to develop DPSG to what it is at the moment.

REFERENCES

Allwood, J. (1976) *Linguistic communication as action and cooperation.* Gothenburg Monographs in Linguistics, no. 1.

Block, R. (1986) *Lexical Functional Grammar and Natural Language Generation.* Report, WISBER Project Group, Saarbrücken.

Bronnenberg, W.J., Bunt, H.C., Landsbergen, S.P.J., Scha, R.J.H. & Utteren, E.P.C. van (1979) The question-answering system PHLIQA1. In: L. Bolc (Ed.) *Natural Language communication with computers.* München: Hanser.

Bunt, H.C. (1979) Conversational principles in question-answer dialogues. In: D. Krallmann & G.H. Stickel (Eds.) *Zur Theorie der Frage.* Tübingen: Narr.

Bunt, H.C. (1985) *Mass terms and model-theoretic semantics.* Cambridge: Cambridge University Press.

Bunt, H.C. (1986) Information dialogues as communicative action in relation to partner modeling. In: *Proceedings of conference on the structure of multimodal dialogues including voice.* Venaco, Corsica.

Bunt, H.C. (1987) *Discontinuous Phrase-Structure Grammar: a formalism for language generation?* Paper presented at the First European Workshop on Language Generation. Royaumont, France.

Bunt, H.C., Beun, R.J., Dols, F.J.H., Linden, J.A. & Schwartzenberg, G.O. thoe (1985) The TENDUM dialogue system and its theoretical basis. *IPO Annual Progress Report* , *19*, 105-113.

Bunt, H.C., Thesingh, J.C. & Sloot, K. van der (1987) Discontinuous constituents in trees, rules and parsing. In: *Proceedings of the Third ACL/Europe Conference.* Copenhagen.

Gazdar, G., Klein, E., Pullum, G.K. & Sag, I.A. (1985) *Generalized Phrase Structure Grammar.* Cambridge, MA.: Harvard University Press.

Horacek, H. (1987) *The application of unification grammar to syntactic generation in German* . Paper presented at the First European Workshop on Language Generation. Royaumont, France.

Katwijk, A.F.V. van (1981) Explorations in the experimental study of information dialogues. *IPO Annual Progress Report*, *16*, 108-113.

Montague, R. (1971) The proper treatment of quantification in ordinary language. Reprinted in: R. Montague (1974) *Formal Philosophy.* New Haven, Conn.: Yale University Press.

Winograd, T. (1983) *Language as a cognitive process.* Reading, MA.: Addison-Wesley.

PART V

Stages of Human Sentence Production

EXPLORING LEVELS OF PROCESSING IN SENTENCE PRODUCTION

Kathryn Bock

TABLE OF CONTENTS

1. The levels-of-processing approach to sentence production
2. Interactions between levels of processing
3. Lexical interaction and conceptual accessibility
4. Conclusion

Typically, the production of speech involves the conversion of ideas into sounds. The ideas seem to precede the sounds. These truisms form the rudiments of two less self-evident claims to be examined in this chapter. The first is that different types of linguistic information, or different representational vocabularies, are called on at different points in the creation of a sentence's syntactic structure. This is the levels-of-processing hypothesis. The second claim is that these levels of processing are hierarchically organized, with no interaction between lower and higher levels. This is the non-interaction hypothesis.

To anticipate the arguments to be presented, there is both observational and experimental support for the levels-of-processing hypothesis, but little in favor of the non-interaction hypothesis. A fragment of a production theory will be outlined that accounts for these patterns of evidence with the assumptions that there is feedback from phonological to semantic representations within the lexicon (Dell & Reich, 1981) and that this feedback can influence the assignment of semantic representations to syntactic functions (Bock & Warren, 1985). Because different levels of syntactic processing call on the lexicon, although for different types of information, this feedback mediates the interaction between levels.

1. THE LEVELS-OF-PROCESSING APPROACH TO SENTENCE PRODUCTION

The levels-of-processing and non-interaction assumptions are embodied in an influential model of sentence production that was originally proposed by Fromkin (1971) and elaborated by Garrett (1975, 1980, 1982). Although the model is based on errors observed in spontaneous speech, it is intended to be a model of normal production processes, on the plausible view that the constraints that are obeyed even by errors must represent fundamental features of the production system.

As it has been detailed by Garrett, this speech-error-based model (the speech-error model[1], for short) posits two major linguistic levels in the creation of an utterance's syntactic form. These two levels and their characteristics are outlined in the two bottom rows in Table 1. The top row

---

[1] There are a number of other speech-error-based models of production, including those of Dell (1986), Harley (1984), Motley, Baars, & Camden (1983), and Stemberger (1985), which reject some of the assumptions of the Fromkin-Garrett model. Referring to the latter as 'the speech-error model' is thus somewhat misleading.

Table 1.   The Levels of Processing of the Speech Error Model of Sentence Production

PROCESSING LEVEL	REPRESENTATIONAL CHARACTERISTICS	ROLE IN SENTENCE GENERATION
MESSAGE	———————	NONLINGUISTIC REPRESENTATION OF IDEA TO BE EXPRESSED
FUNCTIONAL	MEANING-BASED REPRESENTATIONS OF LEXICAL ITEMS ASSIGNED TO FUNCTIONAL SYNTACTIC ROLES	CONTROL ELABORATION OF SYNTACTIC STRUCTURE
POSITIONAL	PHONOLOGICALLY SPECIFIED REPRESENTATIONS OF LEXICAL ITEMS ASSIGNED TO POSITIONS IN PLANNING FRAME	CONTROL ELABORATION OF PHONETIC FORM

shows the input to these levels, called the message; this is the non-linguistic representation of the speaker's communicative intention.

The first linguistic level is the functional level. Briefly, this is an abstract representation of the utterance that includes semantically specified lexical items assigned to syntactic roles (these roles are not specified in the model, but can for convenience be thought of as basic grammatical relations such as subject, direct object, main verb, and so on.) The representation incorporates information from a unit roughly comparable to a clause, although it is not arrayed in any particular order. Most critically for the evidence to be presented, only the syntactic and semantic features of words are represented here. The functional level is deaf to the phonological features of words.

The second linguistic level is the positional. Information at this level, unlike that in the functional representation, is ordered. The order is represented in terms of a planning frame that specifies the locations of words within a string. The planning frame is essentially a phrase-structure representation of the sentence that also includes closed-class morphemes and a representation of the intended intonation, something along the lines depicted in Figure 1. This representation develops in a phrase-by-phrase fashion, with phonologically specified words being inserted into the slots of the frame. So, in contrast to the functional level, information at the positional level is both ordered and phonologically elaborated.

The levels-of-processing assumptions of the model follow from these characteristics of the functional and positional representations. There is one level, the functional, at which semantically and syntactically specified words are assigned to grammatical functions. At a second level, the positional, phonologically specified words are assigned to locations in a phrasal frame. This further implies two steps in the lexical retrieval process, one to locate a lexical item with an appropriate meaning, and another to retrieve its sound (Garrett, 1980). There is evidence consistent with the levels-of-processing hypothesis for syntactic assembly as well as with the double-retrieval hypothesis for lexical access. These will be summarized in turn.

Levels of processing in syntactic assembly. One piece of evidence for distinct levels of processing in the creation of sentences comes from errors in which one word substitutes for an intended word (as in *hot under the belt,* when *collar* was intended; Fromkin, 1973). Stemberger (1983) noted the existence of errors of this sort, but with a strong semantic relationship between the substituted word and a word *elsewhere* in the utterance (e.g., *a fork wrapped up in a spoon?,* when *napkin* was intended), rather than between the substituted word and the intended word. Very much rarer are errors in which there is only a phonological relationship between the substituted word and another word in the sentence (Stemberger, personal communication). The semantic characteristics of words thus seem to exert a greater influence than their phonological features on the selection of other words in the same sentence, implying that it is primarily semantic information that is active during the early stages of syntactic assembly.

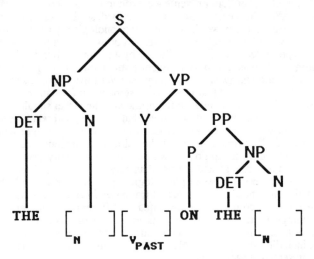

Figure 1. An example of a planning frame for a sentence such as *The company relied on the senator*, before the insertion of phonologically specified word forms.

The features of two other types of errors, sound and word exchanges, constitute one of the central arguments for differences between levels of processing (Garrett, 1975, 1980). Sound exchanges (e.g., *mell wade*, when *well made* was intended; Fromkin, 1973) occur predominantly within phrases and show strong effects of such phonological characteristics as within-syllable position and vowel or consonant status (Boomer & Laver, 1968; MacKay, 1970), but negligible effects of the syntactic categories of the words in which the exchanging sounds originate. On the other hand, word exchanges (e.g., *a wife for his job* ; Fromkin, 1973) typically cross phrase boundaries, are less obviously influenced by phonological characteristics (though see below), and are strongly constrained by their syntactic category. Such divergences suggest that sound and word exchanges may occur at different points in the development of an utterance.

One of the most powerful speech-error-based arguments for levels of processing comes from exchanges between stem morphemes, such as *I went to get a cash checked* (when *check cashed* was intended; Garrett, 1980). Such errors leave inflectional affixes (*-ed* in the error cited) in their intended positions. Since these affixes are hypothesized to be a part of the syntactic planning frame (Garrett, 1975, 1980), their stranding is consistent with the claim that the frame is assembled before lexical elements are inserted. Moreover, according to Garrett (1980), the constraints on stem morpheme exchanges resemble those on sound exchanges. Specifically, they are more likely than word exchanges to occur between words of different form classes (though see Stemberger, 1985), and to occur within rather than across phrases. This associates them with sound exchanges as positional-level errors, as they should be if they occur when lexical elements are inserted into phrasal frames.

There are nonetheless several gaps in the speech error evidence for levels of processing. One of these has to do with the absence of semantic relations between the misplaced words in word exchanges. If the semantic privileges of words, like their syntactic categories, are specified at the functional level, one would expect strong semantic similarities between the exchanging words. These do not occur. Garrett (1980) speculated that this may be attributable to the rarity of semantic relationships between words in the same clause, but this hypothesis has not been carefully evaluated.

There is, however, experimental evidence consistent with the proposed differences in the representational vocabularies at the functional and positional levels. This evidence points to differences in the structural effects on sentence production of semantic and phonological information (Bock, 1986). Subjects in two experiments described pictured events that were preceded by priming words. These words were either phonologically or semantically related to target words commonly used in describing the events. For example, a prime such as *frightening* or *thunder* would be presented to subjects, followed by a picture of lightning striking a church. Each of the priming words was linked to the agent or the patient (so *lightning* was primed by *frightening* or *thunder*, and *church* was primed by *search* or *worship*). If sentence structure is determined at a level of processing that taps lexical-semantic information, as the speech-error model assumes, semantic relations between the prime and the target should have a substantial impact on the syntactic form of picture descriptions, but phonological relations should not.

The predicted result was found in both experiments: There was a significant tendency for speakers to use semantically primed targets as the subjects of sentences (alternating between active and passive forms in order to do so), whereas phonologically primed targets were no more likely to appear in different syntactic roles than matched controls. There was no syntactic effect for either of two different types of phonological primes, those which rhymed with the targets, or those which had the same consonantal frames and syllabic structure. Other findings indicated that these results could not be attributed to differences in the effectiveness of the semantic and phonological primes, nor to subjects' awareness of relations between the priming words and the pictures. This evidence lends support to the proposed division between processing levels, including the syntactic roles of those levels and the assumed characteristics of the information represented at each of them.

Double retrieval in lexical access. If semantically specified words can be retrieved without their phonological features, it should be possible to discover or create dissociations between meaning and form. A number of these dissociations have been documented.

From observational investigations, there are findings about tip-of-the-tongue states and errors of lexical selection that point to the possibility of having the meaning of a word in mind without its sound becoming available. In tip-of-the-tongue states, it is evident from common experience that the meaning of a desired word can be quite clear without its form making an appearance (though vestiges of the form sometimes *do* appear; Brown & McNeill, 1966). The evidence from lexical selection errors comes from the properties of two different categories of word substitutions. These two categories consist of substitutions of similar-meaning words, as in *blond eyes,* when *hair* was intended (Fromkin, 1973) versus similar-sounding words, as in *He's the kind of soldier a man looks up to and wants to emanate* , when *emulate* was intended. Phonological substitutions have been found to be significantly more likely than semantic substitutions to match the intended words in such characteristics as number of syllables, stress patterns, and phonological features (Fay & Cutler, 1977), suggesting that semantic substitutions occur at a point at which the sound of a word is less important to its processing than its meaning.

Experimental studies, particularly studies of object naming, provide evidence for two different stages in the retrieval of a word (Balota & Chumbley, 1985; Clark & Clark, 1977; Huttenlocher & Kubicek, 1983; McCauley, Parmelee, Sperber, & Carr, 1980; Oldfield & Wingfield, 1964, 1965; Wingfield, 1968). These stages consist of object categorization and name retrieval. The object categorization stage is influenced by such semantic characteristics as category membership and category relationships across successive pictures in a list, while the name retrieval stage is most strongly affected by variables such as word frequency, age of acquisition, and intersubjective name agreement. The information accessed in these two stages corresponds at least roughly to the types of information hypothesized to be retrieved from the lexicon at different levels in the formulation of an utterance, and research reported by Kempen & Huijbers (1983) suggests that this correspondence is more than an incidental similarity (also see Levelt & Schriefers, this volume).

In summary, there is evidence consistent with the levels-of-processing assumption of the speech error model. Since different processing levels make use of different types of lexical information, it is particularly significant that the evidence pertinent to the creation of structural features is complemented by evidence that the meanings and forms of words can be accessed somewhat independently. The question that remains to be considered has to do with the *degree* of independence between levels of sentential and lexical representation. That issue is taken up in the next section.

2. INTERACTIONS BETWEEN LEVELS OF PROCESSING

The speech-error model assumes that the levels of syntactic processing involved in the creation of sentences are hierarchically organized, so that lower levels elaborate the information constructed at higher levels but do not change it in any way. The positional level therefore spells out the phonological shapes of words and their locations in the serial string, but has no impact on the assignment of more abstract lexical representations to such grammatical functions as subject and direct object. Garrett makes this assumption explicit in his statement that 'we have not provided for possible feedback connections from lower to higher levels, nor, indeed, for any direct connection between non-adjacent levels' (1982, p. 68).

There are two possible reasons for maintaining this position. The first is simply that it makes for a stronger theory. The second is more complex, and has to do with the feasibility of interactions between levels that are related to one another by processes that are formally comparable to grammatical transformations. Because transformations are not reversible (Peters & Ritchie, 1973), and because of the complex feeding relations among them (Bresnan & Kaplan, 1982), it is difficult to relate elements of a lower-level syntactic representation (roughly comparable to a surface structure) to their precursors at a higher level. Although the speech-error model has never been firmly linked to transformational grammars or their psycholinguistic counterparts, Garrett's discussions of the model have occasionally implied this association (1975, 1980). If the association is taken seriously (even though Garrett's cautions on this point make it doubtful that it should be; see Garrett, 1980), the properties of the processes that relate the levels severely restrict the possible interactions between them.

Although considerations such as these provide a rationale for the non-interaction assumption, there is mounting evidence against it. The evidence comes once again from studies of syntactic formulation and lexical retrieval processes.

Interaction in syntactic formulation. Just as studies of speech errors provide support for levels of processing in production, they also provide support for interactions between levels. The first piece of evidence has to do with the phonological features of word exchanges. Recall that an important characteristic of such exchanges, one hypothesized to distinguish them from sound exchanges in the syntactic level at which they occur, is the absence of phonological relations between exchanging words. However, Dell & Reich (1981; also see Harley, 1984; Stemberger, 1985) found that the degree of phonological similarity between such words exceeded chance expectations. The strength of this similarity can be compared only subjectively to the strengths of the form-class constraint on word exchanges or the syllable-position and sound-class constraints on sound exchanges (which approach inviolability). It nonetheless appears that the phonological relationship between exchanging words may be of a different, more probabilistic and less categorical sort. This leaves the levels-of-processing argument intact, but suggests that the levels 'leak' (Dell & Reich, 1981).

There is also a case to be made for interactions between levels from two sets of experimental studies. In both of these, the evidence indicates that problems in integrating words with phrasal frames at the positional level may sometimes prompt reformulation of the sentence at the functional level. Levelt & Maassen (1981) examined how variations in the ease of naming figures affected sentence construction processes, using a task in which subjects described the movements of geometric forms on a screen. The major result of this manipulation was that it took longer to initiate utterances in which the difficult name appeared early, but there were no differences in the syntactic forms of the sentences. Since a preliminary experiment made it possible to factor out the effects of perceptual recognition and categorization processes on lexical difficulty, the implication is that problems encountered in the retrieval of the phonological forms of words rarely cause the structure of sentences to be modified. However, in their third experiment, a detailed analysis of sentence durations indicated that speakers sometimes switched from a construction such as *A and B go up* to one such as *A goes up and B goes up* when the name of the *B* figure was a difficult one. Thus, although problems connected with the assembly of phonological forms do not appear to have a general or direct effect on syntactic form (again consistent with the levels of processing view), they can lead to revisions of a sentence's structure.

A comparable finding has been reported by Bock (in press a) using an experimental task with a different manipulation of phonological accessibility. This investigation used the primed picture description paradigm described earlier (Bock, 1986), but the experiments differed in two ways. First, they did not attempt to compare semantic with phonological priming, a comparison that required equating the strength of the semantic and phonological primes. The semantic priming conditions were therefore omitted. Second, the priming words were selected so that, across the full set of priming words, there were stronger phonological relationships between the primes and the words denoting the target objects in the pictures. Within limits imposed by the English lexicon, the primes were maximally similar to the targets without being identical to them. So, for example, a picture of a horse kicking a cow was primed by the words *horn* and *cowl*. The question was whether, with these strong phonological similarities, changes in the accessibility of the phonological representations of words would influence the syntactic structures of the sentences that subjects produced.

The results revealed a clear effect of phonological priming: There was a significant tendency toward the production of sentences in which phonologically accessible words served as subjects, rather than as objects, of active and passive sentences[2]. But this was accompanied by a marked increase in sentence-initial dysfluencies (filled pauses, long hesitations before speaking, and false starts). A second experiment showed the same results, both for sentence form and dysfluencies, when prime presentation was varied between the auditory and articulatory modalities. Thus, the effect seems to originate in a source (presumably the lexicon) that is shared by perception and production. A third study revealed nearly identical word ordering patterns when speakers simply produced two-word lists of objects. In all likelihood, then, the ordering effects found in sentences are attributable to the impact of lexical retrieval processes on syntactic construction, and not the other way around. So the suggestion, once again, is that disruptions in the integration of the phonological forms of words into sentence frames instigates a reformulation of the sentence's syntax.

In each of these experiments, post-experimental debriefings revealed that the participants generally did not notice the phonological relationships between the words and pictures (in part because the priming trials were embedded in a large number of fillers trials, and in part because they were administered in the context of a recognition memory task). This reduces the probability that the effects were due to strategic modifications of the descriptions. Rather, they appear to be manifestations of normal, relatively unconscious adjustments in production processes. Such processes, it seems, permit changes in the syntactic forms of sentences to accommodate variations in the retrievability of the phonological forms of words.

Interaction in lexical retrieval. Interactions have also been documented between the phonological and semantic stages of lexical retrieval in production. This evidence comes in part from phonological contamination of semantic substitution errors and semantic contamination of phonological substitution errors.

Semantic substitution errors, as noted earlier, involve a word that is semantically related to the intended one intruding into an utterance. Phonological substitutions, conversely, involve a word that is phonologically but not semantically related to the intended one. In the study cited above, Fay & Cutler (1977) found significantly greater phonological relationships between the target and the intruding word in errors that they had classified as phonological substitutions than

---

[2] This appears to contrast with Levelt & Maassen's finding of no differences in the order of words. However, in their major experiments (Experiments 2 and 3), the trends were in fact toward ordering words in terms of phonological accessibility, although these trends did not achieve significance. The results of these studies are thus not at odds with those of the priming experiments.

in those they had classified as semantic substitutions, a finding that is consistent with the view that there can be dissociations between the meanings and forms of words. However, Dell & Reich (1981) found that the degree of *phonological* similarity between intended and target words in *semantic* substitutions nonetheless exceeded chance expectations[3] (see also Harley, 1984). Apparently, relationships between words in the way they sound influence whether one will substitute for another. Thus, even though words are presumably selected for utterances on the basis of their meanings, their sounds seem to have an impact on the process.

The same phenomenon crops up in a small class of children's jokes. Tell someone to say the word *cloak* ten times, and then ask *What do you call the white of an egg?* The answer is invariably *yolk* (and, of course, wrong). What seems to be going on here (since people do not give the incorrect answer if they have not repeated or been exposed to the rhyming word) is that the phonological relationship between the repeated word and the incorrect answer prompts a semantic substitution.

There is corresponding evidence for a quasi-semantic effect on phonological substitutions. Kelly (1986) contrasted the phonological substitutions from the Fay and Cutler corpus with the intended words on the dimension of imageability. The reasoning behind this comparison was that high-imagery words tend to be more accessible in memory than low-imagery words (e.g., Paivio, 1971; Rubin & Friendly, 1986), and so might be more likely to intrude to produce an error. The hypothesis was strongly supported: The proportion of substitutions in which low-imagery targets were replaced by high-imagery intrusions was significantly larger than the proportion of substitutions with the opposite replacement pattern. Moreover, the average frequency for the high-imagery intrusions was lower than that for the low-imagery intrusions, making it difficult to account for the pattern in terms of frequency. Apparently, even when there are no obvious semantic commonalities between targets and intrusions that would lead to accessing one rather than the other from the intended message (for example, it is hard to imagine *apartment* being confused with *appointment* on the basis of their semantic privileges), the relative imageability of the two words contributes to the likelihood of an error.

This result is interesting in the present context because it suggests that the probability of a phonological intrusion can be raised if the phonological representation of the intruding word is bound to a semantic or message-level representation that is itself high in strength. One way in which this could work is that activation patterns set up by phonological relationships between the target word and other words feed back to their semantic representations, which then return activation to the phonological representation. The strength of this resonance may be proportional to the strength of the semantic representation, thereby increasing the probability of a high-imagery phonological substitution.

Levelt & Schriefers (this volume) have carried out experiments designed to directly investigate semantic and phonological effects on lexical processing in production. The subjects in their studies saw pictures of objects that they were instructed to name. On some trials, at varying intervals after the picture was exposed, they received auditory words or non-words to which they had to make auditory lexical decisions. Sometimes these probes were semantically related to the object name (which the subjects were presumably in the process of retrieving), and sometimes phonologically related. At the shortest interval both semantic and phonological relationships had an effect on lexical decision times, but at longer intervals only the phonological relationship was effective. These data suggest that the retrieval of words proceeds through a stage at which semantic information is active to another stage at which it is not, one where phonological processing dominates. Interestingly, however, they also indicate that there may be no point at which lexical representations are fully divorced from their phonological features.

In short, there are good reasons to suspect that the processes that retrieve the semantic representations of words are influenced by the characteristics or states of their phonological representations. Likewise, there are good reasons to suspect that processes at the positional level interact with those at the functional level in the creation of a sentence, contrary to the non-

---

[3] Because semantic substitutions constitute a different type of error than word exchanges, the results of this analysis are independent of those reported earlier from Dell & Reich's work.

interaction assumption of the speech-error model. But at the same time, there are good reasons — some reviewed in the preceding section, and some noted in conjunction with the evidence for interaction — for maintaining distinctions among the levels of processing and stages of lexical retrieval that are involved in sentence production. The next section proposes a reconciliation of these somewhat dissonant arguments within a fragment of a production model.

3. LEXICAL INTERACTION AND CONCEPTUAL ACCESSIBILITY

An adequate theory of the formulation process must account both for the errors and dysfluencies observed in spontaneous speech and for the syntactic variations that appear to arise as a result of disruptions in the assembly of sentence structures. It must explain how semantically represented lexical information is linked to syntactic functions, and how phonologically represented lexical information is linked to positions in constituent structures. Elsewhere (Bock, in press b), I have sketched a model of these processes that combines the levels-of-processing approach of the Fromkin-Garrett framework with arguments about the dynamics of lexical retrieval developed in an earlier paper (Bock, 1982). Here I want to consider the mechanism of interaction between the levels of syntactic formulation.

The research reviewed in the two preceding sections suggested that events that occur during the assignment of the phonological representations of words to constituent frames may have an impact on the way in which the *semantic* representations of words are assigned to syntactic roles such as subject and direct object. It also suggested that activation of the phonological representations of words may influence choices among their semantic representations. There is an obvious shared feature here, in the involvement of phonologically and semantically specified words. In the first case they constitute the lexical representations hypothesized to be tapped for different syntactic processing levels, and in the second, the two forms of lexical representation hypothesized to be involved in word selection. In view of this common characteristic, it may be possible to explain both types of interaction in terms of a common mechanism.

The lexical interaction hypothesis. Gary Dell (Dell, 1985, 1986; Dell & Reich, 1981) has proposed an elegant theory of interactions within the lexicon that goes a long way toward such an explanation. In Dell's theory, the lexicon consists of a hierarchy of concepts, words, phonemes, and phonological features. All of the connections within this hierarchy are bidirectional. As a result, activation at a lower level in the hierarchy (e.g., the phoneme level) feeds back to the information at higher levels (e.g., the word level). The higher level in turn sends activation back to the representations below. The resonance created in this way helps to explain a number of important error production phenomena, including lexical bias (the tendency for sound exchanges to create actual words; Baars, Motley & MacKay, 1975; Dell & Reich, 1981; Stemberger, 1985), and the repeated phoneme effect (the increased probability of exchanges between sounds that occur in the vicinity of a repeated phoneme, as in *heft lemisphere*; Dell, 1984; MacKay, 1970).

Dell (1986) has fully developed and tested this model only for phonological processes, though he assumes that the same principles apply at higher levels. In fact, Dell & Reich (1981) argued persuasively that interactions of this sort, but between semantic representations and word forms, could account for the phonological effects that they observed on word exchange errors in their corpus. In essence, their proposal was that changes in activation created by the existence of phonological relationships between word forms could in turn change the activation of the words' semantic representations. Since relative degree of activation is the basis for the selection of elements at each level of processing, these changes in semantic activation might cause a word to be assigned to the wrong syntactic role when semantic representations are tapped for integration into a functional syntactic representation, thereby precipitating an error.

It is worth examining how far such a mechanism can go toward explaining variations in syntactic form. There are two essential requirements. First, it must account for word order variations — in general, for the tendency for accessible words to precede those that are less accessible. This is clearly within the scope of the model. Since selection among elements at every level is made on the basis of relative activation, it follows that more highly activated — and thus more accessible — words will be selected before less activated words. Furthermore, this is consistent with the evidence that such ordering patterns are due to lexical retrieval and not syntactic assembly processes (Bock, 1985, 1986).

The second requirement for an explanation of syntactic variation is an account of the syntactic adjustments that commonly accompany changes in word order. Typically, speakers do not simply produce words in the order in which they come to mind, whether or not that creates an error. Rather, the syntactic forms of sentences seem to be changed so as to accommodate word order variations without altering the intended meaning. So a speaker who might otherwise have said *Lightning struck the church* instead says *The church was struck by lightning* when the word *church* is momentarily more accessible.

This second requirement is more difficult to meet. Dell (1986) discusses the possibility that rule application processes might be made sensitive to spreading activation via linkages between lexical networks and networks of syntactic rules. In such a scheme, activation of a word's representations would spread to rules capable of applying to that word or to syntactic structures containing it (see also Stemberger, 1985). However, as Dell also notes, it may be hard to cast generative systems in the form of a network, given such stumbling blocks as the need for recursion in grammatical rules. A different approach appears to be warranted.

The conceptual accessibility hypothesis. There is an alternative solution to the syntactic adjustment problem that still incorporates the lexical interaction feature of Dell's model. This solution includes an account proposed elsewhere (Bock, in press b) about the coordination of lexical-semantic representations with syntactic functions. The coordination occurs at a level, termed the functional integration level, that is in some ways comparable to the functional level of the speech-error model. This proposal assumes that (a) variations in *conceptual accessibility* influence the assignment of semantically specified words to grammatical functions, and (b) the grammatical functions correspond to surface rather than deep structure roles.

The conceptual accessibility assumption itself has two parts. First, it makes the claim that assignments to grammatical functions such as subject and direct object will be affected by the ease of finding a lexical representation consistent with the intended meaning. Second, it assumes that, other things equal, the subject is assigned first, with other functions following according to a hierarchy of grammatical relations (Bock & Warren, 1985; Keenan & Comrie, 1977; Perlmutter & Postal, 1977; Pullum, 1977; note that the interpretation of the term *accessibility* here is different from, and orthogonal to, its interpretation in the relevant linguistic literature). In this hierarchy, the subject dominates the direct object, which dominates the indirect object, which dominates yet other objects, including oblique objects and objects of comparison.

There is obviously much more than conceptual accessibility to be taken account of in the functional integration process. Other factors include the thematic roles (agent, patient, beneficiary, etc.) of message elements, the compatibility of these roles with the types of arguments allowed by the verb or predicate to which words are linked (i.e., the verb's specification of functional relations), and the strength of alternative verb forms (e.g., the passive versus the active form of a transitive verb). Thematic roles in conjunction with the functional specifications of predicates determine a set of grammatical functions that a word can serve. For example, in an utterance describing an event in which a dog (the agent) chases a mailman (the patient), *dog* may be either the subject of an active verb (*The dog chased the mailman*) or the object of a passive verb (*The mailman was chased by the dog*). However, because the active verb form has greater base strength than the passive, it has a higher probability of selection, overall.

According to the conceptual accessibility hypothesis, there are processes operating within this complex set of constraints that predispose the assignment of lexical items to grammatical functions according to the ease of retrieving or activating them via their semantic specifications. So, whenever alternative assignments are possible (as they are for *dog* and *mailman* in the example just cited), the highest-level role assignment that is consistent with the constraints in force should be made. If *mailman* is more accessible than *dog*, it should be linked to the subject role of the passive verb.[4] Similarly, whenever there is a conflict between alternative objects in immediate postverbal position, as there is for *dream* and *mother* in *The little girl told her dream to her mother* versus *The little girl told her mother her dream*, the tendency should be to assign the more accessible candidate to the postverbal object role.

Some evidence for an integration process with these characteristics can be found in an experiment by Bock & Warren (1985). They examined grammatical function assignments in sentences containing concepts that differed in imageability. If functional integration proceeds by assigning the first available and appropriate noun to the subject role of one of the activated verb forms, as the accessibility hypothesis predicts, the subjects of sentences should tend to be more imageable than the direct objects. Likewise, concepts assigned as direct objects should tend to be more imageable than those assigned as indirect or oblique objects.

This was the result that Bock & Warren obtained. There was a reliable tendency for more concrete concepts to appear as the subjects rather than direct objects in active and passive sentences (see also James, Thompson, & Baldwin, 1973), and for direct objects to be more concrete than indirect objects in prepositional and double object dative sentences. In addition, concreteness did *not* predict the order of words in conjunctive noun phrases (e.g., *time and winter*), suggesting that the effects were indeed attributable to the assignment of grammatical functions and not to simple serial ordering mechanisms. Because the grammatical functions of words in conjoined phrases are the same, there is no reason to predict any difference in order resulting from variables that influence function assignment (although variables that influence other aspects of the formulation process may and do affect order within conjunctions; Bock, in press b; Bock & Warren, 1985; Kelly, Bock, & Keil, 1986; Kelly, 1986).

The conceptual accessibility hypothesis also predicts that the integration process will be influenced by semantic activation. Thus, a highly activated word should be integrated into a functional representation faster than a less activated word. As a result, highly activated words will tend to occur more often as the subjects of sentences than as the objects. These are the results that were obtained in the experiment reported above (Bock, 1986): Nouns were more likely to be used as the heads of subject phrases when they were semantically primed than when they were not.

The conceptual accessibility hypothesis also makes predictions about errors. One way in which the assignment process can go wrong is that words may be linked to the wrong syntactic functions. When this happens, a word exchange error can occur. If conceptual accessibility is an important factor in functional integration, such errors should typically have the more accessible word earlier. Examination of exchange errors in the corpus published by Fromkin (1973), in a subset of the exchanges from the Toronto corpus (Dell & Reich, 1981), and in a set collected by the author supported this hypothesis. The errors that were included in this analysis had to have exchanging words of the same form class, but assigned to different syntactic functions, and the words had to differ either in concreteness or animacy (both of which affect accessibility; see, for example, Dukes & Bastian, 1966, and Rohrman, 1970). There were fourteen errors that met these criteria. Thirteen of these contained words that differed in concreteness, and one contained words that differed in animacy. In ten of the thirteen with differences in concreteness, the more concrete word had a higher-level syntactic role than the less concrete. In the one error in which the exchanging words differed in animacy, the animate word appeared in the higher-level function. Eleven of fourteen errors therefore showed the predicted pattern (p<.05 by a sign test). This difference does not appear to be attributable to word frequency (a variable related to phonological rather than conceptual accessibility; cf. Bock, in press b), since in five of the eleven errors supporting the hypothesis (and in one of the three that did not support it), the less frequent word was assigned to the higher-level role.

These kinds of findings lend credence to the conceptual accessibility hypothesis. Words whose semantic representations are more accessible because their representations are in some

---

4   This may be insufficient to yield a passive utterance because of the weakness of passive forms, but it should increase the probability of a passive. The assumption is that verb forms compete with one another as function assignments proceed. Successfully linking a subject may increase the chances of the passive form winning the competition, but the greater base strength of the active gives it the edge even when it acquires an appropriate subject later than the passive does.

sense stronger, more tightly connected to other elements of knowledge, or more highly activated tend to be assigned to higher-level syntactic roles than those whose representations are less accessible. Because there is a very strong correlation between syntactic roles and surface positions, it will generally be the case that more accessible words in sentences precede those that are less accessible, but the claim here is that this is an indirect effect of the role assignment process. While there are other factors — factors related to the accessibility of the phonological forms of words — that may directly influence word order, these are not at issue here (see Bock, in press b).

Given the proposed role of conceptual accessibility in the functional integration process, it is clear how to combine it with the lexical interaction feature of Dell's (1986) model to account for effects of phonological activation on syntactic form. Phonological activation spreads to the semantic representation of a word, raising its accessibility to function assignment processes and increasing the probability of a higher-level assignment than it might otherwise have had. Because these feedback processes take time to work, they will generally have a weaker effect than factors operating directly at the functional level, such as semantic activation. In addition, because they can interrupt an assignment process that is already in progress, they may produce speech disruptions (Bock, 1985, 1986; Levelt & Maassen, 1981) or mid-course changes in syntactic plans (Levelt & Maassen, 1981).

4. CONCLUSION

The suggested solution to the feedback problem has several attractive features. First, it preserves the relative independence of the level of syntactic formulation that deals with meaning from the level that deals with sound, consistent with the evidence for such a division from studies of speech errors and syntactic variations. Second, following Dell & Reich (1981), it accords an important role to the lexicon in mediating interactions between the levels. If the same lexicon is used in both production and in comprehension, it presumably must contain bidirectional connections between semantic and phonological representations anyway. The existence of feedback from lower to higher levels is obviously consistent with such architecture. Finally, it couples this feedback mechanism with an independently motivated account of the grammatical role assignment process to explain phonological effects on syntactic processes.

The proposals advanced in this paper have little directly to say about the impact of the pragmatics of communication on syntactic form. There is a clear inlet for pragmatic factors in the hypothesized role of conceptual accessibility on function assignment, though it is an open question whether this is how they exert their effects. But whether they make their contribution during functional integration or elsewhere in the formulation process, the approach taken in this paper assumes that natural rhetorical principles are by themselves insufficient to explain all of the features of language production. Many of these features seem designed not to facilitate communication, but to serve a system whose major purpose is the creation of articulate speech in time.

ACKNOWLEDGEMENT

Preparation of this paper was aided by a Biomedical Research Support Grant from Michigan State University. Gerard Kempen provided helpful comments on an earlier version of the manuscript.

REFERENCES

Baars, B.J., Motley, M.T. & MacKay, D.G. (1975) Output editing for lexical status in artificially elicited slips of the tongue. *Journal of Verbal Learning and Verbal Behavior, 14,* 382-391.

Balota, D.A. & Chumbley, J.I. (1985) The locus of word-frequency effects in the pronunciation task: Lexical access and/or production? *Journal of Memory and Language,* *24,* 89-106.

Bock, J.K. (1982) Toward a cognitive psychology of syntax: Information processing contributions to sentence formulation. *Psychological Review, 89,* 1-47.

Bock, J.K. (1986) Meaning, sound, and syntax: Lexical priming in sentence production. *Journal of Experimental Psychology: Learning, Memory, and Cognition, 12,* 575-586.

Bock, J.K. (in press a) An effect of the accessibility of word forms on sentence structures. *Journal of Memory and Language.*

Bock, J.K. (in press b) Coordinating words and syntax in speech plans. In: A. Ellis (Ed.), *Progress in the psychology of language* (Vol. 3). London: Erlbaum.

Bock, J.K. & Warren, R.K. (1985) Conceptual accessibility and syntactic structure in sentence formulation. *Cognition, 21,* 47-67.

Boomer, D.S. & Laver, J.D.M. (1968) Slips of the tongue. *British Journal of Disorders of Communication, 3,* 2-12.

Bresnan, J. & Kaplan, R.M. (1982) Introduction: Grammars as mental representations of language. In: J. Bresnan (Ed.) *The mental representation of grammatical relations.* Cambridge, MA: MIT Press.

Brown, R. & McNeill, D. (1966) The 'tip of the tongue' phenomenon. *Journal of Verbal Learning and Verbal Behavior, 5,* 325-337.

Clark, H.H. & Clark, E.V. (1977) *Psychology and language.* New York: Harcourt Brace Jovanovich.

Dell, G.S. (1984) Representation of serial order in speech: Evidence from the repeated phoneme effect in speech errors. *Journal of Experimental Psychology: Learning, Memory, and Cognition, 10,* 222-233.

Dell, G.S. (1985) Positive feedback in hierarchical connectionist models. *Cognitive Science, 9,* 3-23.

Dell, G.S. (1986) A spreading-activation theory of retrieval in sentence production. *Psychological Review, 93,* 283-321.

Dell, G.S. & Reich, P.A. (1981) Stages in sentence production: An analysis of speech error data. *Journal of Verbal Learning and Verbal Behavior, 20,* 611-629.

Dukes, W.F. & Bastian, J. (1966) Recall of abstract and concrete words equated for meaningfulness. *Journal of Verbal Learning and Verbal Behavior, 5,* 455-458.

Fay, D. & Cutler, A. (1977) Malapropisms and the structure of the mental lexicon. *Linguistic Inquiry, 8,* 505-520.

Fromkin, V.A. (1971) The non-anomalous nature of anomalous utterances. *Language, 47,* 27-52.

Fromkin, V.A. (Ed.) (1973) *Speech errors as linguistic evidence.* The Hague: Mouton.

Garrett, M.F. (1975) The analysis of sentence production. In G.H. Bower (Ed.) *The psychology of learning and motivation* (Vol. 9). New York: Academic Press.

Garrett, M.F. (1980) Levels of processing in sentence production. In B. Butterworth (Ed.), *Language production* (Vol. 1). London: Academic Press.

Garrett, M.F. (1982) Production of speech: Observations from normal and pathological language use. In: A. Ellis (Ed.) *Normality and pathology in cognitive functions.* London: Academic Press.

Harley, T.A. (1984) A critique of top-down independent levels models of speech production: Evidence from non-plan-internal speech errors. *Cognitive Science, 8,* 191-219.

Huttenlocher, J. & Kubicek, L.F. (1983) The source of relatedness effects on naming latency. *Journal of Experimental Psychology: Learning, Memory, and Cognition, 9,* 486-496.

James, C.T., Thompson, J.G. & Baldwin, J.M. (1973) The reconstructive process in sentence memory. *Journal of Verbal Learning and Verbal Behavior, 12,* 51-63.

Keenan, E.L. & Comrie, B. (1977) Noun phrase accessibility and universal grammar. *Linguistic Inquiry, 8,* 63-99.

Kelly, M.H. (1986) *On the selection of linguistic options.* Unpublished doctoral dissertation, Cornell University.

Kelly, M.H., Bock, J.K. & Keil, F.C. (1986) Prototypicality in a linguistic context: Effects on sentence structure. *Journal of Memory and Language, 25,* 59-74.
Kempen, G. & Huijbers, P. (1983) The lexicalization process in sentence production and naming: Indirect election of words. *Cognition, 14,* 185-209.
Levelt, W. & Maassen, B. (1981) Lexical search and order of mention in sentence production. In: W. Klein & W. Levelt (Eds.) *Crossing the boundaries in linguistics.* Dordrecht: Reidel.
MacKay, D.G. (1970) Spoonerisms: The structure of errors in the serial order of speech. *Neuropsychologia, 8,* 323-350.
McCauley, C., Parmelee, C.M., Sperber, R.D. & Carr, T.H. (1980) Early extraction of meaning from pictures and its relation to conscious identification. *Journal of Experimental Psychology: Human Perception and Performance, 6,* 265-276.
Motley, M.T., Baars, B.J. & Camden, C.T. (1983) Experimental verbal slip studies: A review and an editing model of language encoding. *Communication Monographs, 50,* 79-101.
Oldfield, R.C. & Wingfield, A. (1964) The time it takes to name an object. *Nature, 202,* 1031-1032.
Oldfield, R.C. & Wingfield, A. (1965) Response latencies in naming objects. *Quarterly Journal of Experimental Psychology, 17,* 273-281.
Perlmutter, D.M. & Postal, P.M. (1977) Toward a universal characterization of passivization. In: K. Whistler, R.D. van Valin, Jr., C. Chiarello, J.J. Jaeger, M. Petruck, H. Thompson, R. Javkin & A. Woodbury (Eds.) *Proceedings of the 3rd Annual Meeting of the Berkeley Linguistics Society.* Berkeley: Berkeley Linguistics Society.
Paivio, A. (1971) *Imagery and verbal processes.* New York: Holt, Rinehart, & Winston.
Peters, P.S. & Ritchie, R.W. (1973) On the generative power of transformational grammars. *Information Sciences, 6,* 49-83.
Pullum, G.K. (1977) Word order universals and grammatical relations. In: P. Cole & J.M. Sadock (Eds.), *Syntax and semantics: Vol. 8. Grammatical relations.* New York: Academic Press.
Rohrman, N. (1970) More on the recall of nominalizations. *Journal of Verbal Learning and Verbal Behavior, 9,* 534-536.
Rubin, D.C. & Friendly, M. (1986) Predicting which words get recalled: Measures of free recall, availability, goodness, emotionality, and pronunciability for 925 nouns. *Memory & Cognition, 14,* 79-94.
Stemberger, J.P. (1983) Inflectional malapropisms: Form-based errors in English morphology. *Linguistics, 21,* 573-602.
Stemberger, J.P. (1985) An interactive activation model of language production. In: A. Ellis (Ed.) *Progress in the psychology of language* (Vol. 1). London: Erlbaum.
Wingfield, A. (1968) Effects of frequency on identification and naming of objects. *American Journal of Psychology, 81,* 226-234.

INCREMENTAL SENTENCE PRODUCTION, SELF-CORRECTION AND COORDINATION

Koenraad De Smedt
Gerard Kempen

TABLE OF CONTENTS

1. Introduction
1.1 Stages of processing
1.2 Incremental production
2. Causes of incrementation and correction
2.1 Conceptual modifications
2.2 Monitoring
2.3 Overview
3. Syntactic mechanisms
3.1 Expansion
3.2 Coordination
3.3 Self-correction
3.4 Control structure
4. Related research
5. Summary

1. INTRODUCTION

1.1 Stages of processing

Since Garrett's (1975, 1980) seminal work on speech error phenomena, it has become customary to distinguish four levels of representation within the sentence production process: a message level, a functional level, a positional level, and a phonetic level (see also Bock, this volume). Garrett's model has been further elaborated and modified by Kempen (Kempen & Hoenkamp, in press; Van Wijk & Kempen, in press) who proposes the global sentence production model depicted in Figure 1. The four modules listed have the following functions:

1. The *conceptual* module forms a conceptual (semantic) representation of the message which the speaker wishes to communicate. The nature of the semantic structures output by this component need not concern us here.
2. The *lexico-syntactic* module constructs an ordered tree structure consisting of constituents and their functional relations. The terminal nodes of syntactic trees (both content and function words) are instances of abstract (not phonologically specified) lexical items called *lemmas* which are retrieved from the lexicon. While Garrett assigns the tasks of inserting function words and computing word order to a later module (the positional stage), Kempen assigns them to this one.

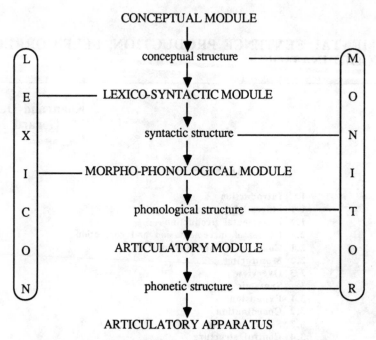

Figure 1. A global model of the sentence production process

3. The *morpho-phonological* module computes the word form of all lemmas by retrieving their phonological specifications (*lexemes*) from the lexicon and making various morphological and phonological adjustments.
4. The *articulatory* module produces a phonetic specification which is used to control the articulatory apparatus.

The intermediate results, which are passed from one module to another, are inspected by a monitor. If the monitor notices that the output of one of the modules is inappropriate or detects a violation of some prevailing constraint, any ongoing activity may be interrupted and backtracking to an earlier point in the production process may be forced. This course of events may give rise to self-corrections.

1.2 Incremental production

The four sequential modules of Figure 1 need not necessarily operate on input structures which correspond to whole sentences. If the modules did operate in this fashion, hesitations *during* the pronunciation of a sentence could not have a nonarticulatory (i.e. a conceptual, syntactic, or lexical) origin. Since this is both counterintuitive and counterfactual, we favor the view that the modules can work on different parts of the final utterance simultaneously, as depicted in Figure 2. We call this piecemeal mode of production *incremental production* (Kempen, 1978).

Although the modules involved in sentence production may work in parallel, each fragment of an utterance still goes through the different stages sequentially. The communication channel between the modules operating in this incremental fashion can be modeled in terms of *streams* (cf. Hoenkamp, 1983, pp. 114-117). For instance, we hypothesize that conceptual fragments are entered at one end of a stream and 'consumed' by the lexico-syntactic module at the other end, as shown in Figure 3.

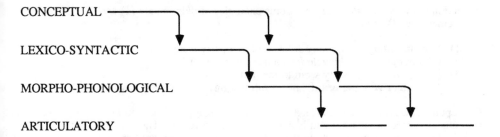

Figure 2. Incremental processing of two fragments

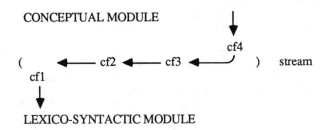

Figure 3. Stream of conceptual fragments

While the lexico-syntactic module is processing elements from the stream, the conceptual module can run simultaneously and add more elements to the end of the stream. We assume that the flow of information between modules is downward; in other words, each module passes intermediate structures to the next module but receives no information back from that module. All upward information, we assume, is a result of monitoring. The conceptual fragments contain markers which indicate their relationship to fragments earlier in the stream.

Such a framework can easily accommodate the fact that hesitations may occur within the sentence as well as between sentences. Also, it can account for *syntactic deadlock* , i.e., the fact that people sometimes 'talk themselves into a corner' when they have produced a partial sentence which they cannot continue in any way they consider appropriate or meaningful, because of lexico-syntactic restrictions. In such circumstances, self-corrections may be triggered. Moreover, the framework allows for 'changes of mind', i.e., decisions by the speaker to revise the conceptual content which has already been expressed. This is represented in the stream as a conceptual fragment marked as a substitute for an earlier fragment.

We will now discuss incremental sentence production and self-correction from the point of view of their origins: conceptual modifications and monitoring. Then some lexico-syntactic mechanisms for dealing with these events will be proposed. We conclude with some comparisons with related research.

2. CAUSES OF INCREMENTATION AND CORRECTION

2.1 Conceptual modifications

We distinguish three basic kinds of modification to a conceptual structure which will affect the shape of an utterance: *deletion, replacement* and *addition* of conceptual elements. Deletion and replacement will both give rise to a self-correction, which is often signaled by a pause or a correction term such as *uh*, *no*, *sorry*. Some examples of deletion are (1) and (2). Examples of replacement are (3) and (4).

(1) John and Mary ...uh... only John went to a party last week.
(2) John bought a new bicycle for ...uh... a bicycle for his son.
(3) John ...uh sorry... Mary went to the party.
(4) The runner with the beard ...no... with the glasses is leading now.

Conceptual replacement may also lead to a non-retracing repair. The result is ungrammatical but contains no correction marker and is uttered without hesitation. The examples for English (5) and for Dutch (6) show how a constituent can be replaced without retracing. One or more constituents which have already been uttered are used as a hook to attach a new sentence pattern with a different word order.

(5) That's the only thing he does is fight.
(6) Willemse heeft gisteren heeft de dokter nog gezegd dat het mag.
     (Willemse has yesterday has the doctor said it is allowed.)

While conceptual deletion and replacement seem to be relatively infrequent as causes of incrementation or correction, addition is frequent. We assume that conceptual processing, just like syntactic processing, takes place in a piecemeal way, so that the continual addition of conceptual fragments to existing ones will be quite normal. Addition can be of two kinds. The first kind is an addition of a conceptual fragment which is to be in *conjunction* or *disjunction* with an existing fragment and thus leads to a syntactic coordination, as in (7) and (8).

(7) John ... and Mary went to a party.
(8) John ... or Mary went to a party.

The second kind is the addition of a new conceptual fragment in any other relationship than conjunction or disjunction. This may give rise to an *expansion*, i.e., the current utterance is continued with a syntactic fragment which is not a member of a coordination but has some syntactic relation (such as subject, direct object, modifier, etc.) to the current utterance or part of it. Simple examples are (9) and (10).

(9)   John and Mary ... went to a party.
(10) John and Mary went ... to a party.

2.2 Monitoring

After a conceptual addition, it may not always be syntactically possible to continue a partially uttered sentence. The lexico-syntactic restrictions imposed by what has already been uttered may severely limit the possible ways of expanding the syntactic structure or finding an appropriate word order. In English, for example, it seems impossible to expand (11) to express a conceptual increment corresponding to *likes to*, as in (12).

(11) John comes ...
(12) John likes to come.

By contrast, an equivalent downward expansion is possible in Dutch, where the meaning underlying *likes to* can be expressed by means of an adverbial phrase as in (13).

(13) Jan komt ... graag.

The difference between the English and the Dutch example shows that the restrictions are lexico-syntactic in nature. In circumstances where expansion is impossible, the monitor will receive no output from the lexico-syntactic component. A syntactic deadlock will thus be detected and a self-correction will be triggered by causing the conceptual structure to re-enter the lexico-syntactic module and thus to be reformulated, as in (14).

(14) John comes ...uh... likes to come to the party.

Another example of an impossible expansion in English is the expansion of (15) to (16). However, the apposition in (17) or the relative clause in (18) offer alternatives. There may be a covert self-correction during the formulation of these sentences, marked by a pause.

(15) The man ...
(16) The bald man ...
(17) The man ... the bald one that is, ...
(18) The man ... who is bald, ...

Syntactic deadlock is of course but one possible cause of self-correction. Other types of error which are detected by the monitor and which may thus result in a self-correction include the choice of wrong lexical material, fusion errors, and articulation errors. It is often unclear whether in a particular utterance, e.g. (3), the cause of the correction is a conceptual modification or the detection of a lexical error. A discussion of these phenomena is beyond the scope of this chapter. The question of how much conceptual material re-enters the stream to produce a self-correction is an interesting one, but it will likewise not be discussed here (see Van Wijk & Kempen, in press, for some relevant findings and ideas). Our present aim is to show the global picture of the relations between incremental conceptualization and self-correction.

2.3 Overview

Figure 4 gives a schematic overview of the conceptual and monitoring processes discussed in this section. The process flow is downward. Non-retracing repairs and normal incrementation are grouped together in this overview.
   In the following section, the three types of lexico-syntactic mechanisms involved (expansion, coordination and correction) will be discussed in more detail.

3. SYNTACTIC MECHANISMS

3.1 Expansion

We distinguish three kinds of expansion, depending on the location in the tree where a new syntactic fragment is added. *Upward* expansion causes the tree to grow upward, i.e., the original root node is no longer the root node of the expanded tree. Other cases we term *downward* expansion, when new branches are added below an existing node. Finally there is a special case called *insertion*, when syntactic material is inserted between existing nodes. Figure 5 shows roughly how the various kinds of expansions affect a syntactic tree. The utterance depicted is (19).

(19) John and Mary are at the party ... seem to be at the party.

Insertion does not necessarily lead to a self-correction, as was the case in (19). An example where insertion leads to the continuation of a fragment which has already been uttered is the Dutch sentence (20). The English translation contains a correction, but the Dutch original does not. The insertion is depicted in Figure 6.

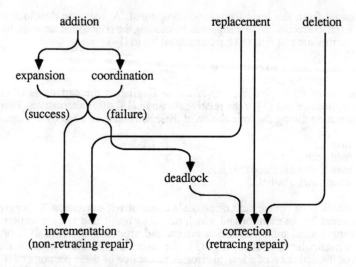

Figure 4. Conceptual modifications, monitoring and lexico-syntactic consequences

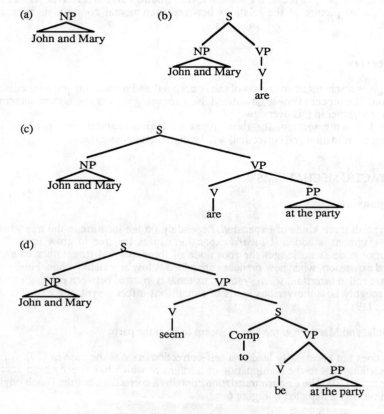

Figure 5. Upward (b) and downward (c) expansion, insertion (d)

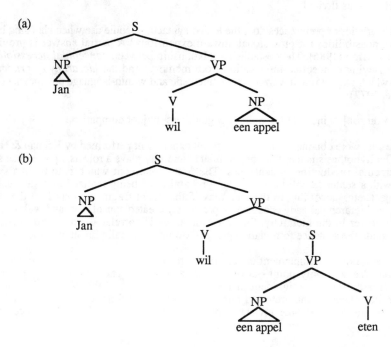

Figure 6. Insertion in utterance (20)

(20) Jan wil een appel ... eten.
(John wants an apple ... wants to eat an apple.)

If upward expansion is allowed, then one must also allow situations where an initial conceptual fragment does not lead to the construction of a main clause. Instead, an isolated noun phrase may be uttered, as in (21).

(21) He ...

Such an initial constituent is 'unattached' in the sense that it does not have a syntactic relation to a mother node. Although a subsequent conceptual fragment may cause the construction of a mother node, it would be a handicap if uttering the initial constituent had to be postponed until the constituent was assigned a relation to it. However, how should the lexico-syntactic module make decisions which depend on such a syntactic relation, for example choosing the surface case marking (*he, him, his*) while that relation has not yet been specified? One possible solution consists in carrying out one or more *provisional* upward expansions until a sentence node has been created. Subsequent conceptual fragments may lead to syntactic fragments which are *actual* upward expansions. The system then attempts to combine the actual syntactic nodes with the provisional ones. If this *unification* (Kay, 1979) is successful, the nodes are merged. This leads to a successful expansion, as in (22). The unification will fail when the syntactic functions in the provisional and the actual expansions of nodes are different. In that case, either a *restart* using a different syntactic structure (an *anacoluthon*) may take place (23), or lexico-syntactic alternatives may be explored which might lead to a successful expansion, for example, by means of passivization (24).

(22) He ... left.
(23) He ... They invited him.

(24) He ... was invited.

What heuristics or preferences does the lexico-syntactic module use when choosing between alternative possibilities for provisional upward expansions? A partial answer is provided by Bock and Warren (1985). They establish a relationship between *conceptual accessibility* (the ease of retrieving conceptual information from memory) and the *hierarchy of grammatical relations* which plays a role in various cross-linguistic and within-language phenomena (Keenan & Comrie, 1977):

subj. > dir. obj. > indir. obj. > oblique > genitive > obj. of comparison

Similar results were obtained in a sentence recall experiment performed by Keenan & Hawkins (1987). Our hypothesis is that this (or a similar) hierarchy plays a role as a preference scale in the incremental production of sentences. The first constituent which is to be in a syntactic relation with a sentence will have a higher probability of being realized as a subject than as direct object, etc., according to the hierarchy. Subsequent fragments may find the relations higher in the hierarchy already occupied by previously created constituents and will be assigned a function lower in the hierarchy. Since the hierarchy is correlated with word order, it thus serves to guide the sentence formulation process toward maximally fluent incremental sentence production.

Other factors may complement the use of the relational hierarchy in incremental sentence production. We will only point out one other factor here. There is probably some direct interaction between the assignment of a syntactic function and the type of the conceptual fragment. For example, the preferred function assigned to a time-indicating NP such as (25) may not be subject but some lower member of the hierarchy such as sentence modifier (oblique).

(25) Monday morning, ...

3.2   Coordination

Coordination is viewed as an iteration of the lexico-syntactic process on several conceptual fragments which are linked to each other as members of a conjunction or disjunction. The result of lexicalizing and formulating these is a special phrase called a *coordination* which has a number of conjuncts as its immediate constituents.

Often coordinations come about during an incremental process because the speaker may keep adding conjuncts, even after some have been uttered. Therefore, the list of conceptual fragments to be coordinated is viewed as a stream (cf. Figure 3). The stream is buffered to allow detection of the end of the stream. Conjuncts are often realized with 'comma intonation' as long as there is at least one further element in the stream. If it is the final element, it is added after insertion of a conjunction like *and*. This treatment of coordination as an incremental process accounts for sentences in which 'afterthoughts' may give rise to multiple occurrences of the conjunction word (26) or even *dislocations* (27).

(26) John, Peter and Mary ... and Anne came home.
(27) John, Peter and Mary came home ... and Anne.

Utterances like these are not unusual in spoken language. We account for them by assuming that new descriptions have entered the stream after it had been emptied.

3.3   Self-correction

Self-corrections are governed by rules which determine how much of the original utterance needs to be repeated. For example, (28) is not well-formed because in the self-correction all constituents to the right of the replaced main verb should be reformulated, as in (29). Likewise, (30) is not grammatical because the entire NP should be reformulated (31).

(28) * You should have sent that letter ...uh... handed over.
(29) You should have sent that letter ...uh... handed it over.
(30) * Tony is baking a cake ... sugar-free.
(31) Tony is baking a cake ... a sugar-free cake.

Levelt (1983, p. 78) has observed that the rule which speakers obey when deciding how far they should retrace is similar to the retracing rule for coordinations. He then stated a *well-formedness rule* for repairs in terms of the grammaticality of coordinations, linking the ill/well-formedness of (28) and (29) to that of (32) and (33) respectively.

(32) * You should have sent that letter or handed over.
(33) You should have sent that letter or handed it over.

Following Levelt's rule, we propose a mechanism for generating self-corrections which has the same underlying principles as the mechanism for coordination. If an error has been detected by means of monitoring and its cause has been diagnosed (deadlock, conceptual replacement, lexicalization error, etc.), a conceptual fragment marked as the correction of some earlier fragment is inserted at the end of the stream. This correction fragment may include 'old' concepts that have already been linguistically realized. The correction marker is treated by the lexico-syntactic module in much the same way as the conjunction marker, the only difference being that it is realized as a pause or as a correction term (such as *uh*), rather than as comma intonation or a conjunction (*and, or*). Thus Levelt's observation is fully accounted for.

However, Van Wijk & Kempen (in press), who have verified Levelt's well-formedness rule, found that it covers only one type of self-corrections, which they call *reformulation*. Self-corrections of another type, which they call *lemma substitution*, e.g. (34), do not need computing a new syntactic structure, because simply replacing a lemma in the existing structure suffices.

(34) Dou you really want to buy that record ...uh... compact disc?

Other self-corrections are really restarts, i.e., instead of carrying out a repair, a whole utterance is rejected and the speaker starts all over (cf. (35)).

(35) Did the student ...uh... Did you ask the student anything?

Although restarts could be seen as a special case of reformulation, perhaps they should be handled by a mechanism which is different from that for repairs because the relationship between reparation and reparandum is a different one.

The choice between correction strategies made by the lexico-syntactic module seems to be partially dependent on the origin of the correction. Van Wijk & Kempen found that conceptual addition often leads to reformulation while replacement and deletion often trigger lemma substitution. In addition, we would like to suggest a causal relation between syntactic deadlock and restart.

Example (36) shows that self-correction and coordination can occur in one and the same constituent. In addition, examples (36) and (37) illustrate that the ambiguity of certain self-corrections is similar to that of corresponding coordinations, which again suggests that they should be treated in a similar way.

(36) Peter and Mary ...uh... John left the house.
(37) Peter and Mary or John left the house.

3.4 Control structure

Because the process of deleting, replacing and adding conceptual material may occur repeatedly and independently of each other, the various lexico-syntactic mechanisms involved, namely self-correction, coordination and expansion, may occur in one utterance and even embedded in one another. For example, a conceptual addition may cause a coordination; within one of the conjuncts, a conceptual addition may lead to an attempt at expansion, which, if unsuccessful, will cause a correction to occur, etc. An annotated example of such a sequence is (38).

(38) Peter ...
    and a woman ... (conjunction)
    who sleeps ... (downward expansion)
    who never sleeps more than five hours a night ... (downward expansion with retracing)
    or even less ... (disjunction)
    came early to my party. (upward expansion)

Consequently, the lexico-syntactic module will need a control structure where the processes can complement each other. We propose a control structure with *nested* iteration loops on the output of the conceptual module. One loop is expansion, which may cause the addition of mother or daughter nodes in the syntactic tree. The other loop combines correction and coordination. It may iterate within each constituent, where it causes the addition of coordinates or corrections. Each of the two loops may be nested within the other one.

4. RELATED RESEARCH

Most natural language generation systems in the literature have not been designed for the simulation of spontaneous speech but for the construction of carefully planned sentences and texts. Hence it will not be surprising that in most systems the conceptual and lexico-syntactic stages are ordered strictly serially for a complete sentence. However, some attention has been given to incremental production in at least two other systems: MUMBLE and KAMP.

In MUMBLE (McDonald & Pustejovsky, 1985a), a conceptual 'planner' and a linguistic module call each other recursively. A surface structure of the sentence is extended in the process. Predefined 'attachment points' in that surface structure determine where and how it can be extended. These extensions seem to be limited to downward expansions and possibly conjuncts: 'another adjective added to a certain noun phrase, a temporal adjunct added to a clause...'(p. 189).

McDonald & Pustejovsky (1985a, 1985b) point out that there is a similarity between their 'attachment' and the grammar formalism in Tree Adjoining Grammars (TAGs; Vijay-Shankar & Joshi, 1985; see also Joshi, this volume). This suggests that TAGs are formalisms which may be especially suitable for incremental generation. They seem capable of simulating a variety of expansions, although the integration with other modules involved in sentence production remains to be worked out. McDonald & Pustejovsky's (1985b) discussion of TAGs is limited to insertions. The example they work out concerns the expansion of (39) to (40). In our treatment, (40) would be realized as a self-correction (41), once the initial sequence (39) has been uttered. However, McDonald & Pustejovsky's system does not seem to start uttering a sentence until it is complete, thereby obviating the need for self-correction.

(39) The ships were hit.
(40) The ships were reported to be hit.
(41) The ships were hit ...uh... were reported to be hit.

In the KAMP system (Appelt, 1983), there is a component called TELEGRAM which couples the processes of conceptualization and formulation in an incremental architecture. In Functional Unification Grammar (Kay, 1979), a sentence can be produced by the *unification* of two *functional descriptions* (FDs). One of these represents a partially specified utterance and possibly includes some conceptual information. The other one is the grammar of the language. Instead of doing a single unification between a completely specified FD for the sentence as a whole (the 'text' FD) and the grammar (the 'grammar' FD), the TELEGRAM planner works by gradual refinement. Initially, a high-level, incomplete text FD is produced by the planner and unified with the grammar FD. Subsequent planning produces more FDs, which are unified with the grammar FD and incorporated into the text FD. However, the system plans hierarchically, and the resulting enrichments of the text FD seem to be limited to downward expansion and possibly coordination.

There seem to be no natural language generation systems which produce incrementally in such a way that every now and then the system 'talks itself into a corner' and has to backtrack for a self-correction. Existing systems are only partially incremental: Even if they allow the conceptual input to be modified while syntactic sentence construction is already on its way, the uttering of the sentence is delayed until its surface structure is complete. Thus the need for self-corrections is avoided.

One could argue that there is no practical need for artificial language generation systems which can generate truly incrementally and that the risk of an occasional self-correction is only a nuisance. Als long as the systems generate printed output, we agree. But in the case of spoken output, the situation is different. Human listeners hardly have any trouble with corrections and retracings in speech. Therefore, in order to prevent unnaturally long pauses between successive sentences, the system could profitably resort to an incremental production strategy.

In theoretical linguistics, formal grammars seem to be biased toward one or the other kind of expansion, upward or downward. While phrase structure grammars present rules in a manner which is suitable only for downward expansion, categorial grammars specify rules for upward expansion. TAGs seem to suffer less from this bias because they use insertion as a basic mechanism. However, it is not clear whether they could handle cases such as Figure 5a-b, where an isolated NP is attached to an S as a daughter node.

We conclude that a new type of grammar is needed which can generate not only complete grammatical sentences and their structural trees but also sequences of incomplete trees which may arise during the planning of a full sentence. (For an initial proposal concerning such a grammar, see Kempen, 1987).

5. SUMMARY

We have seen how incremental production and self-corrections can be accounted for by allowing increments and other modifications to the conceptual input after the syntactic formulation process has already started. We assume that different modules which are involved in sentence production (i.e. conceptualization, formulation and articulation) can run in parallel. Three types of conceptual modifications may occur while the formulation is already on the way: deletion, replacement and addition. Deletion and replacement of a conceptual fragment which is already being formulated typically give rise to a self-correction. Addition may give rise to a coordination or an expansion. Of the latter there are three types: upward and downward expansion and a mixed case called insertion.

A monitor inspects the results of the production process, which allows the detection of errors. One such error, deadlock, occurs when it is impossible to continue a syntactic fragment with the desired increment. Upon the detection of errors, self-corrections may be triggered. To our knowledge, there is at present no formalism which can generate truly incrementally.

ACKNOWLEDGEMENTS

We would like to thank all people who provided helpful comments on earlier versions of this chapter, in particular Willem Levelt, Carel van Wijk and Anthony Jameson.

REFERENCES

Appelt, D. (1983) TELEGRAM: a grammar formalism for language planning. In: *Proceedings of the Eighth IJCAI*, Karlsruhe.
Bock, J. & Warren, R. (1985) Conceptual accessibility and syntactic structure in sentence formulation. *Cognition, 21*, 47-67.
Garrett, M. (1975) The analysis of sentence production. In: G. Bower (Ed.) *The psychology of learning and motivation (Vol. 9)*. New York: Academic Press.
Garrett, M. (1980) Levels of processing in sentence production. In: B. Butterworth (Ed.) *Language production (Vol. 1: Speech and Talk)*. New York: Academic Press.
Hoenkamp, E. (1983) *Een computermodel van de spreker: psychologische en linguistische aspecten.* Ph.D. Dissertation, University of Nijmegen, The Netherlands.
Kay, M. (1979) Functional grammar. In: *Proceedings of the fifth annual meeting of the Berkeley Linguistic Society.*
Keenan, E. & Comrie, B. (1977) Noun phrase accessibility and universal grammar. *Linguistic Inquiry, 8*, 63-99.
Keenan, E. & Hawkins, S. (1987) The psychological validity of the accessibility hierarchy. In: E. Keenan, *Universal Grammar*: 15 Essays. London: Croom Helm.
Kempen, G. (1978) Sentence construction by a psychologically plausible formulator. In: R. Campbell & P. Smith (Eds.) *Recent advances in the psychology of language (Vol. 2: formal and experimental approaches)*. New York: Plenum Press.
Kempen, G. (1987) A framework for incremental syntactic tree formation. In: *Proceedings of the Tenth International Joint Conference on Artificial Intelligence (IJCAI-87)*, Milan.
Kempen, G. & Hoenkamp, E. (in press) An incremental procedural grammar for sentence formulation. To appear in *Cognitive Science.*
Levelt, W. (1983) Monitoring and self-repair in speech. *Cognition, 14*, 41-104.
McDonald, D. & Pustejovsky, J. (1985a) A computational theory of prose style for natural language generation. In: *Proceedings of the second conference of the European Chapter of the Association for Computational Linguistics*, Geneva.
McDonald, D. & Pustejovsky, J. (1985b) TAG's as a grammatical formalism for generation. In: *Proceedings of the 23rd annual meeting of the Association for Computational Linguistics*, Chicago.
Vijay-Shankar, K. & Joshi, A. (1985) Some computational properties of Tree Adjoining Grammars. In: *Proceedings of the 23rd annual meeting of the Association for Computational Linguistics*, Chicago.
Van Wijk, C. & Kempen, G. (in press) A dual system for producing self-repairs in spontaneous speech: evidence from experimentally elicited corrections. To appear in *Cognitive Psychology.*

Chapter 24

A THEORY OF GRAMMATICAL IMPAIRMENT IN APHASIA

Herman Kolk

TABLE OF CONTENTS

1. Introduction
2. Positive and negative symptoms
3. Agrammatism and paragrammatism
4. Telegraphic speech is grammatical
5. Telegraphic speech is optional
6. The nature of the impairment
7. PROZIN, a simulation model of agrammatism
8. What makes the choice of elliptical forms adaptive?
9. How does one 'shift'?
10. Is there an alternative to shifting?
11. Patterns of language behavior in Broca's aphasia
12. Concluding remarks

1. INTRODUCTION

In this paper we will present an overview of a new theory of grammatical impairment in aphasia called *adaptation theory*. We begin by introducing a basic distinction between two kinds of deviant behavior: *negative* symptoms, which result when the patient tries to behave the same way as he did premorbidly, and *positive* symptoms, which are the consequence of a process of adaptation by which behavioral goals are changed. This analysis is then applied to grammatical impairment in aphasia and to the traditional distinction between agrammatism and paragrammatism. It is argued that whereas paragrammatic speakers are the ones who keep trying to produce fully elaborated sentences as they used to before their illness, agrammatics make a strategic choice in favor of abbreviated forms, which leads to telegraphic speech. It is maintained that for this purpose they employ the normal capacity to produce elliptical sentences. We discuss the most direct evidence for this latter claim: that telegraphic speech as produced by agrammatic speakers is grammatical, if analyzed as a sequence of elliptical strings. A second prediction derives from the assumption that the shift to telegraphic speech is due to a strategic choice rather than being a mandatory way of speaking, given the impairment. Evidence is presented suggesting that this choice can be affected by pay-off manipulations, which result in a completely different behavior: Paragrammatic rather than agrammatic output is observed.

After this discussion of adaptation, we deal with the impairment itself to which the patient may adapt. We argue that the existence of various forms of variability in aphasic behavior constitutes strong evidence against current approaches in which some kind of loss of grammatical competence is postulated. The alternative solution is that agrammatism and paragrammatism are due to a specific resource limitation. We argue that temporal restrictions are primarily responsible in this case. A computer simulation study of this hypothesis is described. We then specify the adaptive process further: why the choice of elliptical forms is adaptive, given an impairment as postulated; how these forms are selected both in the normal and the aphasic case; and in what other ways an aphasic could adapt to the impairment. Finally we indicate how this theory explains patterns of deviant language behavior within Broca's aphasia.

2. POSITIVE AND NEGATIVE SYMPTOMS

Figure 1 shows a sample of deviant writing. It is a postcard text, obtained from a person who tells us he has burned his hand. Understandably, his writing is disturbed. Though legible, it contains some clear distortions. Now suppose you were the addressee of this postcard. You would certainly be interested to know how badly your friend was hurt. Since he doesn't tell you, you may want to infer the degree of burning from the quality of the writing. Although not foolproof, this method might give you at least a crude impression. You would then probably argue that, since the writing is only moderately distorted, the degree of burning will be relatively mild.

The situation we have put you in, as a reader, appears to be quite typical for the student of language pathology. In studying abnormal language behavior one almost always makes a judgment of this type, not only with respect to the severity but also with respect to the nature of the underlying disorder. As in the writing example, when making such judgments one tends to assume a direct relationship between overt behavior and underlying impairment. However, this bias can be seriously misleading. In the writing example it leads to a conclusion which is simply wrong. There is no such relation in this case since the writer of the postcard wrote it with his left hand. There was a shift of control by which the use of the burned hand was avoided. It is this shift that is responsible for the abnormal behavior that is observed. Needless to say, the actual degree of burning can vary from rather mild — using the burned hand must of course bring about some minimal amount of trouble if the shift is to be motivated — to extremely severe.

In Kolk & Van Grunsven (1985), a terminology is introduced that reflects these distinctions. It was adopted from Jackson (1884). The distortions in the sample in Figure 1 are called *positive symptoms*. Positive symptoms are defined as aspects of behavior that (1) are abnormal in the statistical sense that they occur only infrequently in the behavior of undamaged individuals, but (2) are normal in a functional sense, since they are produced by an undisturbed mechanism. In contrast, *negative symptoms* are not only statistically abnormal but functionally abnormal as well: They result from the use of an impaired system.

As stated, the distinction between positive and negative symptoms was originally invented by the neurologist Jackson. Our definitions, however, differ from Jackson's in a number of ways. We share with him the basic view that behavior can be normal and abnormal at the same time, that it can be statistically deviant and yet be 'the outcome of activity of nervous elements untouched by any pathological process'. We believe that this view has more general relevance than Jackson gives it in his theory. Also, the term *positive symptom* to refer to this behavior seems particularly felicitous, and for this reason we want to retain it. In other respects, however, we deviate from Jackson's use of the terminology. Since his definition has become quite popular, it seems necessary to elaborate a bit on his views, in order to avoid confusion.

Jackson's background is the theory that behavior is governed by a hierarchy of behavioral systems, higher ones having control over lower ones. The lower systems were supposed to produce simple and 'automatic' behavior and were thought to be low on the evolutionary scale. The addition of higher systems later in evolution made behavior complex and purposive ('voluntary') because the higher systems were now in control of the lower systems; the latter were no longer exclusively controlled by environmental conditions. Thermoregulation may serve as an example. A lower system on its own would only exhibit thermoregulation in immediate response to the temperature, for instance by shivering. Addition of higher-level systems leads to voluntary thermoregulation, for instance searching for a warm place to hide. In brain damage, according to Jackson, we see the reverse of evolution: 'dissolution'. We see higher systems losing rather than gaining control. The result in twofold. First, there is a loss of voluntary, purposive behavior. The fact that particular behaviors no longer occur is called a 'negative symptom' (e.g., the organism no longer tries to find a warm spot). However, the lower system still produces behavior on its own. That behavior may change because of the loss of the higher systems. In our example we may expect an increase in the frequency of shivering behavior (because the animal can no longer prevent exposure to low temperatures). This behavior is normal in the sense that it is a product of an undamaged system. However, it is statistically abnormal. In this case Jackson applies the term 'positive' symptom. So, if we compare our terminology with Jackson's, we see that the two have the damaged-undamaged contrast in common. Unlike Jackson however, we do not assume that undamaged systems producing positive symptoms are necessarily low-level systems; they are just 'alternative' systems. Furthermore, the undamaged systems produce statistically abnormal behavior not because they are no longer controlled by higher sytems, as Jackson assumes, but because they are in some way less good with respect to the task at hand (e.g., writing with the left hand). Finally, for us, both positive and negative symptoms refer to real instances of behavior. For Jackson, only positive symptoms have this property. Negative symptoms consist of the absence of particular behaviors (e.g., 'The patient can't speak properly'). So for Jackson, it is always clear what in a given case should be called positive or negative. Positive behaviors are ones that are new, that is, were absent or infrequent before onset of the disease. Negative behaviors are ones that were present premorbidly but disappeared at the onset of the disease. For us, *any* behavior can be called positive or negative, depending upon the particular hypothesis one has in mind.

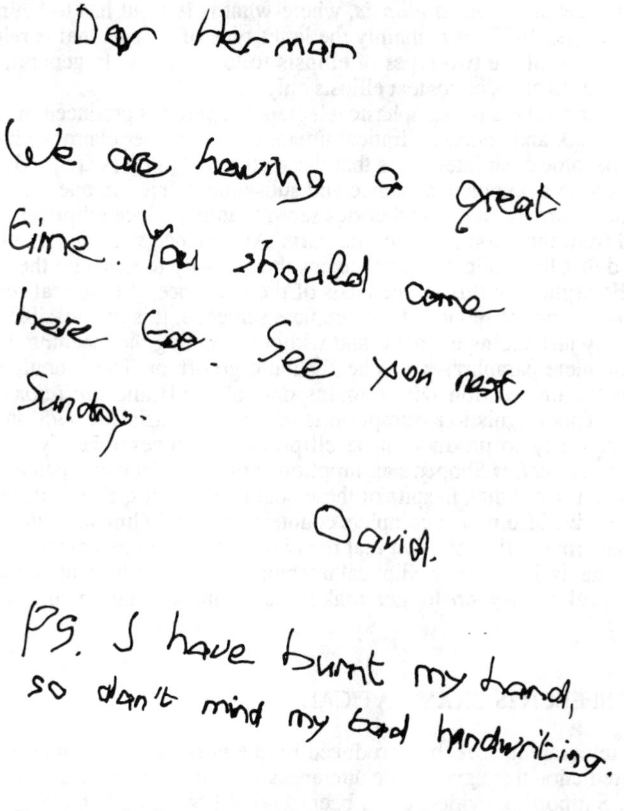

> Dear Herman
>
> We are having a great time. You should come here too. See you next Sunday.
>
> David.
>
> PS. I have burnt my hand, so don't mind my bad handwriting.

Figure 1. Can you infer from the quality of the writing how badly burnt David's hand is?

3. AGRAMMATISM AND PARAGRAMMATISM

We will now apply this analysis to sentence production in aphasia. Since Kleist (1916), a distinction has been made between agrammatism and paragrammatism. Agrammatism is a type of speech output that differs from normal output only as far as particular elements are lacking: function words and inflectional endings. Paragrammatic speech, on the other hand, may contain omissions, but in addition there are also many substitutions of grammatical morphemes as well as errors in word order. Agrammatism is considered to be an aspect of the syndrome of Broca's aphasia, whereas paragrammatism is associated with Wernicke's aphasia (cf. Goodglass & Kaplan, 1972).

The hypothesis we put forward is that in aphasia, there is a tendency to avoid the use of an impaired system, in this case the syntactic system (cf. Heeschen, 1980). In particular, we propose that agrammatism in speech production (telegraphic speech) is a positive symptom. That is, we assume that aphasics who show this type of speech produce it on purpose. This hypothesis of course implicates that it is a capacity of normal speakers to do this, just as it is a normal capacity to do something with the nonpreferred hand. This assumption is supported by the existence of special *registers* of language output that have the character of telegram style: baby talk (language directed to small children) and foreigner talk (language to foreigners) (Ferguson, 1982). Furthermore, the 'normal' language register does not consist only of complete utterances but also contains many elliptical phrases, such as *not for me* and *two beers*. When one distinguishes between *sentential ellipsis*, where the omitted elements occurred previously in the sentence, and *context ellipsis*, where what is left out has to be inferred from the context (Clark & Clark, 1977), it is mainly the latter type of ellipsis that is relevant to our purposes. More discussion of the two types of ellipsis follows below. In general, we will use the term *elliptical* to refer to cases of context ellipsis only.

The claim to be defended here is that aphasic telegraphic speech is produced in the same way as baby talk, foreigner talk and context-elliptical utterances. A further claim we have to make, for reasons that will become clear later on, is that these elliptical phrases are produced as such, rather than by a detour via a complete sentence and subsequent deletion operations. The latter possibility is what most current linguistic theories seem to imply, since elliptical sentences are described as derived from their complete counterparts. At variance with this tradition, Shopen (1972) has postulated that linguistic competence has the capacity to generate these incomplete sentences directly. He argues for this on the basis of the existence of elliptical sentence types that are productive but cannot be reduced to a complete sentence; it is not possible to think of a complete counterpart by just adding elements and without changing the meaning. Examples are *off with his head* (complete paraphrase: 'His head should go off' or 'They should cut his head off' — in both cases the preposition *with* remains unexplained) and *the idiot* (paraphrase: 'He(she) is *an* idiot'). This linguistic assumption is of course consistent with our hypothesis that it is a normal capacity to produce these elliptical sentences directly. Whether this psychological hypothesis *implies* Shopen's assumption about linguistic competence remains to be seen. Perhaps it will turn out that, in spite of these counterexamples, elliptical sentences must be analyzed as being derived from their complete counterparts within linguistic theory. But even then this state of affairs may reflect the fact that the two types are related diachronically rather than synchronically. That is, historically elliptical utterances may have been abbreviations of full sentences, but the speaker may no longer make use of these relationships in his actual computation.

4. TELEGRAPHIC SPEECH IS GRAMMATICAL

The hypothesis that telegraphic speech is produced by the normal and unimpaired system for ellipsis leads to the prediction that agrammatic utterances must be grammatical when analyzed as elliptical utterances. Supporting evidence has been reported by Heeschen (1985), by Kolk & Van Grunsven (1985) and by Kolk, Van Grunsve & Keijser (1985). Additional data to be described briefly here will be presented in more detail elsewhere (Heeschen & Kolk, in preparation). They were obtained from both Dutch (n=8) and German (n=9) Broca's aphasics. All of these patients fullfilled Kleist's criterion for agrammatism, in that in their spontaneous speech is primarily characterized by omissions of grammatical morphemes, with very few substitutions (less than 2%). If substitutions were more frequent, the grammaticality prediction would already have been rejected because grammatical ellipsis cannot, of course, contain substitutions.

Specific predictions referred to two critical cases. The first case concerns the position of the verb with respect to three types of sentence elements: (a) separable prefixes (b) object (pro)nouns and (c) many — though not all — adverbs. Both in Dutch and German, the rule is that in main clauses where the main verb takes a finite form, all three types of elements appear *after* that verb. On the other hand, if the verb has a nonfinite form (infinitive, present participle, past participle), these elements are positioned in front of the verb. This holds both when the nonfinite form is accompanied by a finite auxiliary — either in main or in subordinate clauses — and when it stand on its own in an elliptical construction. For example, one would say '*Hij schrijft mooi*' (*He writes beautifully*) but '*Mooi schrijven*' (*Beautifully write*; infinitive verb.). Thus, the prediction is that whenever a verb is used in combination with any of these elements, their relative ordering will be the one described by this rule. Both the Dutch and the German speech samples showed the predicted pattern; on the average there were about 6% counterexamples.

A second type of confirmatory evidence was found with the German patients. In German, articles carry case marking. This is also true if the noun is preceded by an adjective (e.g. *der blaue Engel* — *the blue angel*). However, when the article is omitted, the adjective carries the case marker (e.g. *blauer Engel*). So if agrammatic speech is grammatical one should either find *der blaue Engel* or *blauer Engel* but not *der blauer Engel* or *blaue Engel*. This pattern was indeed observed (about 8% counterexamples).

5. TELEGRAPHIC SPEECH IS OPTIONAL

The idea that telegraphic speech as produced by aphasics is actually the result of a particular form of normal language stems from Isserlin (1922; English translation in 1985). There is one aspect, however, in which Isserlin's approach appears to be different from the one taken here. He writes: 'The telegram speaker does not, however, "elect" this form of speech as the one that is most convenient to him. His attitude to it derives from *necessity;* if the agrammatic wants to express himself clearly this is the only way that he can do it' (1985, p. 339; italics ours). Marshall (1978), commenting upon Isserlin, puts it even more explicitly: 'What we are seeing in agrammatism is the *obligatory* (and exaggerated) use of a perfectly normal, albeit optional, stragegy' (p. 141; italics ours). Both authors (in particular Marshall) seem to have in mind the hypothesis that the *un*impaired system is accessed mandatorily. That is, if the patient tries to speak, he automatically employs the normal system rather than the damaged one.

In contrast to Marshall and Isserlin, it is our hypothesis that telegraphic style is optional: Using it depends upon a strategic choice. If the impaired system is totally disrupted, accessing it, does not of course, result in behavioral output. One could compare this situation to that of a person whose right arm is completely paralyzed: he can still, though in vain, try to use it.[1] With decreasing degrees of severity, however, a point is reached where the impaired system is able to produce some output. Here the two hypotheses make different predictions. We predict the possibility for the patient to shift from the unimpaired back to the impaired system. Suppose we can make telegram style less useful to the patient by somehow changing the pay off conditions. The patient will then try to use the unimpaired system. Negative symptoms must appear. Marshall and Isserlin, however, would not predict any effects of varying pay off conditions.

What will be negative symptoms in this context? Following suggestions by Heeschen (1985) and by Kolk & Van Grunsven (1985), we assume that the use of a language system

---

[1] In the case of the most severely disturbed patient, our position may seem paradoxical. This patient appears to have no choice but to use telegraphic speech. How can we still maintain that he makes a choice? The paradox seems to derive from the fact that the word 'choice' is ambiguous. The first meaning in this context is volitional selection. This meaning is employed when we say, for instance, that we cannot choose our own emotional state, that we cannot become afraid by decision. A second meaning refers to the number of alternatives, given volitional selection. Saying of a person that he has little choice, is equivalent to saying that there are few alternatives to choose from. This is the sense in which there is 'necessity' — in Isserlin terms — for the severe aphasic to use telegraphic speech: It is the only alternative left. We can still maintain, however, that the patient must make a choice to actually do so. Similarly, a brain-damaged patient who has both legs paralyzed, so that he is unable to walk, has no choice but to use the wheelchair. And yet, he has to choose. Having his paralysis does not automatically put him into this wheelchair.

which has a grammatical impairment will lead to the other type of grammatically deviant aphasic speech that is described in the literature: paragrammatism. In particular, we predict that *substitutions* of grammatical morphemes will now be observed.

There are three ways in which we have manipulated the pay off conditions for telegram style in order to study the appearance of paragrammatic phenomena in aphasics with agrammatic spontaneous speech. The first two procedures were applied to the group of Dutch Broca's aphasics only: sentence reading, and a Cloze procedure (filling in missing words in sentences). The third procedure,developed by Heeschen (1985), was employed with the group of German Broca's aphasics. It consists of a constrained picture description task (more details will be found in Heeschen & Kolk, in preparation). In the reading task, the patients were presented with a series of 28 sentences printed on separate cards and were asked to read them aloud. There were fourteen different types of construction (e.g. indirect object, passive), with two sentences per type. Reading aloud implies putting effort into every word of the sentence. Adopting a telegram style implies failure to follow the instructions and is therefore not a useful strategy in this particular situation. So we predict an appearance of paragrammatic substitution errors. This was in fact what happened. For the function words, for instance, the percentage of substitutions rose from about 1% in spontaneous speech to 18% in the reading aloud task. [2]

A second test we used was the Cloze procedure. A sentence was read twice to the patients, with one element missing which they had to supply. All major subcategories of function words were sampled this way: articles, pronouns, prepositions and auxiliaries. Compared with the findings in spontaneous speech for this subgroup of function words, the percentage of substitutions rose from 1% to 26%, whereas the percentage of omissions dropped from about 40% to 9%. Of all substitutions, 87% were within the same subcategory of function words. So these errors were not wild guesses: They seem to reflect true grammatical confusion.

In the third task, a group of German-speaking patients was asked to describe pictures of reversible actions like '*The black boxer hits the white boxer*'. They were explicitly instructed to do this in such a way that a third person could identify the picture described from within a set of two: one describing the critical action and the other one its reversal. The critical distinction between the two possible sentences relates to case marking (nominative or accusative) on the article. In this task, a shift to paragrammatic speech output was again evident: Instead of a pattern of just omissions, a mixture of omissions and substitutions was observed, percentages ranging from 15% to 20% for both error types. This result was obtained both for the group of grammatical morphemes as a whole and for the subgroup of the critical obligatory case markings. It appears that these aphasics did not selectively shift control just for the case marker, but did so globally, for the whole sentence.

An example observed by Heeschen with a German patient may clarify the nature of the behavioral difference in the two situations. Utterance (1) is a typical example of telegraphic speech. Although no verb is present, grammatical morphology is correct. The second utterance was observed with the same patient when he tried to describe a picture. The correct sentence in this case should have been 'The boy gives an apple to the girl'. As we see, this sentence does have a verb but case marking is wrong on two occasions.

(1) *Spontaneous speech*:

ein	Unfall	auf	der	rechten	Seite	aufwärts
an	accident	on	the	right	side	upward
			(correct case)	(correct inflection)		

---

[2] A problem with the reading test is that substitution errors may result from visual rather than grammatical confusion. However, 34% of the substitutions were clear cases of the latter, since they had no orthographic relationship with the target and, at the same time, represented a confusion within a particular subcategory of function words (determiners, pronouns, conjunctives, auxiliaries).

(2) *Elicited speech:*

der	Apfel	schenkt	dem	Jungen	dem	Mädchen
the	apple	gives	the	boy	the	girl
(incorrect		(incorrect			(correct	
nominative case)		dative case)			dative case)	

The paragrammatic pattern of speech output, characterized by substitutions and errors of word order, has traditionally been viewed as a symptom of Wernicke's aphasia. We now have evidence that this pattern can also occur in Broca's aphasics, when they are forced to use their impaired system. This raises the question whether, as Heeschen (1985) puts it, agrammatism (in Broca's aphasia) and paragrammatism (in Wernicke's aphasia) form a 'fictitious opposition'. By this he means that the two types of output may not stem from different impairments but from different reactions to the same impairment. In terms of the present analysis we would say: Agrammatic Broca's use their unimpaired system, whereas paragrammatic Wernicke's keep using their impaired sytem.

This of course raises the question why there should be no adaptation in Wernicke's. Heeschen (1985) makes two suggestions. First, there may be less awareness of errors because of the impairment in auditory comprehension that Wernicke's have. Secondly, Wernicke's may be less concerned about their errors. If this analysis is right, the prediction is that the 'anti-shift' procedures described above would have no effect on the Wernickes: their output would remain similar to their spontaneous speech. Furthermore, the output produced would be similar to the paragrammatic output elicited from the agrammatic Broca's. Both predictions were confirmed for German patients (cf. Heeschen, 1985; Heeschen & Kolk, in preparation). First, no change in language output under experimental conditons was observed for the Wernicke's. Second, in terms of percentages of omissions and substitutions, there was no significant difference between the paragrammatic output produced by the Broca's and the Wernicke's.

This promising result notwithstanding, there remain a number of problems. First of all, how can we explain the fact that the elicited paragrammatic utterances in Broca's aphasics were produced at a slow rate of speech, while Wernicke's aphasics generated them with normal fluency? Second, although the overall percentages of errors were the same for the two groups, were the types of error also the same? Third, what about comprehension? The older claim that Wernicke's do not have a grammatical impairment (Berndt & Caramazza, 1980; Von Stockert & Bader, 1976), is not supported by recent studies (cf. Heeschen, 1980; Kolk & Friederici, 1985). On the other hand, work by Friederici (1985) in on-line sentence comprehension shows specific differences between the two groups that may point to different grammatical impairments in the two cases. It is conceivable, then, that such differences are responsible for the fact that Broca's avoid use of the impaired system while Wernicke's don't.

6. THE NATURE OF THE IMPAIRMENT

So far, we have talked about patients shifting to unimpaired systems and back to impaired ones, without saying anything about what the impairment is. In Kolk & Van Grunsven (1985) we have discussed the relevant proposals in the literature. Most of these try to explain primarily how agrammatics behave on various receptive tasks (sentence-picture matching, lexical decision, grammaticality judgments), the assumption being that one single impairment causes difficulties with sentences on both the productive and the receptive side. We concluded that all varieties of the 'loss' hypothesis (i.e., loss of grammatical knowledge) had to be rejected because they were unable to account for one basic phenomenon: the existence of *variability*. Two types of variability were demonstrated experimentally: variation between subjects in degree of severity and variation between sentences (longer and syntactically more complex sentences inducing more errors than short and simple ones). On the other hand, if one assumes a resource limitation to be responsible, both types of variability are accounted for in a natural way. To explain the difficulty Broca's aphasics have with sentences, we proposed that the impairment should be a (variable) reduction of the capacity to keep sentence elements in computational simultaneity. Such an underlying impairment would have as its immediate effect *premature disintegration of sentence representations.*

There appear to be two possible causes for this reduction: a reduction in 'memory space' or in 'memory time'. An explanation of the first kind could be phrased in terms of the size of a special short-term memory buffer dedicated to retaining sentence representations.[3] The reduction in 'memory time' could take two forms. There could be either faster decay or slower activation of elements of this representation.

In addition to variation due to sentence length and complexity and to degree of severity, there is a third type of variability not explicitly discussed by Kolk & Van Grunsven (1985) but derivable from their data and, besides, well-known from clinical observations: *within subject-variation.* By this we mean that a difficulty with a particular type of sentence (e.g. passives) *may not be present all the time* in a particular patient. To explain this phenomenon, it is not sufficient to postulate a specific degree of limitation (either spatial or temporal) for a particular patient. For instance, if the buffer is too small for a particular construction, it should be too small for all tokens of this sentence type. So we should assume in addition that there is variation over time in the normal speaker with respect to these capacities. For the temporal hypothesis, this means that activation rate is not always identical for a particular element or, alternatively, that the exact decay rate varies from time to time. Such variation could be due to autonomous biochemical changes in the brain.[4]

We have chosen to further study the possibilities of the *temporal* hypothesis since the idea of temporal restrictions fits into an old — though not widespread — tradition in aphasiology. In this tradition, sometimes labeled 'chronogenetic', the real-time nature of normal language representation is emphasized; brain damage is thought to affect the real-time genesis of this representation (Grashey, 1885; Von Monakow, 1914; Luria, 1970; Lenneberg, 1967; Tallal & Newcombe, 1978; Gigley, 1983; Tzeng & Wang, 1984). Gigley has developed a computer model for sentence *understanding.* Her model operates in (simulated) real time; 'lesions' are defined as changes in specific temporal parameters, such as propagation rate. In the following section, we will report on a preliminary attempt to construct a real-time computer model of sentence *production* with time-defined 'lesions' (Van de Kerkhof, 1986).

7. PROZIN, A SIMULATION MODEL OF AGRAMMATISM

PROZIN employs Kempen & Hoenkamp's (in press) model of sentence formulation (Incremental Procedural Grammar or IPG) as its grammatical model. IPG rules were rewritten as condition-action rules for a production system. The system was implemented in PRISM (Langley, 1983), a production system interpreter which is especially well suited for the simulation of cognitive processes. In PROZIN a particular value is assigned to each node of the syntactic tree that is built as a result of applying the production rules. This value reflects the activation level of that node. It decreases as a function of computation time. (Computation time is defined as the number of 'process cycles'; on each cycle, the set of production rules whose conditions are satisfied is determined and the actions of these rules are executed.) By changing this function, one can manipulate decay rate. It is also possible to vary computation time by delaying the execution of actions. This corresponds to variation in activation rate.

In order for a sentence representation to be completed, different units must be synchronically active. That is, over a certain range of elements, there must be computational simultaneity. When this is not the case, basic syntactic operations cannot be performed, in particular interconnecting smaller units (syntactic constituents) to form larger ones. Figures 2

---

[3] This dedicated memory cannot be identical to the general short-term memory which subserves, among other things, the repetition of digit series. This is because there are patients with a severely reduced memory span but without abnormal sentence formulation (Shallice & Butterworth, 1977).

[4] Perhaps it could also be maintained that buffer size varies from moment to moment, although such an assumption seems somewhat less plausible as the number of slots appears to be a property of the hardware rather than an aspect of process.

and 3 illustrate what is happening in PROZIN in a condition in which the normal activation rate is halved (Figure 2) and with a rate which is still further reduced (one fourth of the normal rate; see Figure 3).

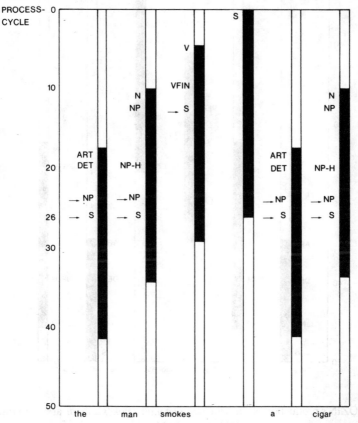

Figure 2. PROZIN's production of the sentence *The man smokes a cigar* at half the normal activation rate.

Figure 2 depicts, in a simplified form, the process underlying the production of *The man smokes a cigar* when the delay is relatively mild. The labels refer to nodes becoming active at a particular point in time. Order and labelling of nodes are as specified within the IPG frame - work. The production of this five-word sentence can be described as consisting of six sets of operations, five of which are dealing with a lexical node (ART, M, V) and one with the S-node. Each set begins with the activation of an initial node which triggers subsequent operations within this set. Although all nodes start decaying immediately after activation and reach subthreshold values after 26 cycles, this process is only depicted for initial nodes within each set, since it is the life span of these initial nodes which is critical. The S-node is the one all other nodes have to be connected to. The other initial nodes have to remain active for later operations within the set, including the connection of activated nodes with the S-node. All initial nodes (except S) are actually terminal nodes of the syntactic tree which is to be built. Their early availability in Figures 2 and 3 follows from the lexically-driven approach of IPG, in which lexical items with their attached syntactic information initiate syntactic tree formation.

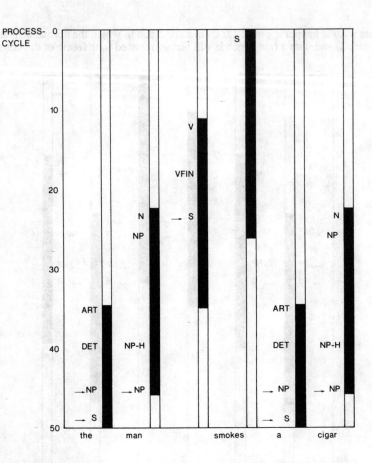

Figure 3. PROZIN's production of the sentence *The man smokes a cigar* at one fourth of the normal activation rate.

At a final step within each set of operations, the initial node (except S) is attached to some node higher in the syntactic tree. ART and N are connected to NP (-> NP), NP and V are connected to S (-> S). For these attachment operations to be possible, two conditions must be fulfilled. First, the nodes to be connected must be above threshold. Second, the destination nodes must also be active. In Figure 2, all attachment operations are still possible, though the S-node is about to 'die'. In Figure 3, however, when activation rate is still further decreased, this is no longer possible, since S dies at a very early stage and, furthermore, both N nodes drop below threshold before they can be further connected.

We have also simulated the effect of increased decay rates. The results are identical to the previous simulation. When comparing Figures 2 and 3 we see that the effect of reducing activation rate is that, for a given pair of initial nodes, the number of cycles that both are active is reduced. By increasing decay rate, one gets exactly the same effect. This does not imply, however, that the difference between the two temporal parameters is vacuous. We have assumed that activation and decay are the same function of processing time. But perhaps it is possible to argue for different functions, linear or nonlinear. In that case 'equivalent' changes in temporal parameters might well have different effects.

The other limitation of PROZIN is that only syntactic information was considered. This is perhaps the most plausible, but certainly not the only possible type of information to suffer from delayed activation or accelerated decay. A major alternative would be morpho-phonological information. Since actual words must also be integrated into the syntactic structure, asynchrony in this area would also lead to premature disintegration. This holds for 'abstract' word specification ('lemmas') as well as for phonological specifications ('lexemes'). Thus it might be possible for a 'syntactic' disorder to be caused by a nonsyntactic impairment.

8. WHAT MAKES THE CHOICE OF ELLIPTICAL FORMS ADAPTIVE?

We hypothesized that agrammatics suffer from delayed activation and/or accelerated decay of sentence elements and as a consequence have to deal with a reduced size of a 'temporal window'. Whether a particular construction fits into that window will depend on the total amount of computation time. This amount will in particular be determined by sentence length and sentence complexity. Why is the use of elliptical forms adaptive? Because some of these present the lowest values for length and complexity. That is, it is not their 'elliptical status' per se, whatever that may be. First of all, not every elliptical utterance will fit into this window. A form like 'my father in his twenty-year-old car with the daughter of his former colleague next to him on his way home', might well be classified as elliptical, since it contains no verb. However, the length of such an utterance will certainly surpass the size of most agrammatics' temporal window and will therefore rarely be observed. For the same reason, we have not included sentential ellipsis in our discussions. In sentential ellipsis there is omission, but what can be omitted is narrowly constrained by parts of the sentence that have already been produced. For sentential ellipsis to be grammatical, the whole sentence must fit into the window, not only the fragment containing the omissions. This means that constructions with sentential ellipsis are no good candidates for selection. They will typically exceed the size of the window. So it appears that what is critical is not whether a construction is elliptical or not but how much time is saved by choosing that construction rather than a different one.

Related to the above is the question of whether there is an exclusive shift to elliptical speech. This appears rarely to be the case. Kolk & Van Grunsven (1985) found the highest percentage of agrammatic utterances in a group of 11 aphasics to be 86%; the lowest percentage was 32%. An agrammatic utterance was defined as one from which at least one grammatical morpheme was missing. This means that all these aphasic patients produced substantial numbers of complete sentences. Most frequently, these sentences were syntactically simple: Passive sentences and subordinate clauses were rare, for instance. This state of affairs is reflected in the Goodglass & Kaplan (1972) definition of Broca's aphasia which includes 'reduced variety of grammatical form' as a symptom, apart from telegraphic speech. It is a symptom one would expect, given the assumption of a narrow temporal window. To adapt to this reduction, the patient can selectively access simple and short sentence types. A subset of these would be the short elliptical forms, with the one-word utterance being the extreme. It is the simplicity of a particular form rather than its elliptical status which is crucial.

9. HOW DOES ONE 'SHIFT'?

We have assumed that in agrammatism there is a shift of behavioral control, just as in the case of the burned hand. A shift from complex to simple forms is predicted, causing the symptom of 'reduced variety of grammatical form' and a shift from complete to elliptical forms, leading to telegraphic speech. In Kolk et al. (1985) we have suggested that one and the same mechanism would be responsible for both types of shift: *message simplification*. Following Garrett (1975), we use the term *message* to refer to the conceptual conditions for a particular sentence. We have proposed that a message is a necessary and sufficient condition for a particular form to be selected: it 'causes' a sentence to be produced by the sentence generator. By formulating simpler messages than the average speaker does (and than the aphasic speaker does premorbidly), one gets both simpler sentence forms and, in the extreme case, telegraphic speech. For instance, we proposed that for the sentence *The old man lit the awful cigar* the following set of basic propositions was responsible:

Man(-)	Cigar(-)	Light(Man, Cigar)
Known(Man)	Known(Cigar)	Past(Light)
Old(Man)	Awful(Cigar)	

The two types of shift could both be accomplished by eliminating elements from this message. For instance, just dropping Old(Man) and Awful(Cigar) would lead to the simpler but still complete sentence *The man lit the cigar*. On the other hand, reducing the message to Man(-), Cigar(-) and Light(Man, Cigar) would cause a telegraphic sentence to be produced: *Man lighting cigar*.

With PROZIN, it is possible to study the effects not only of delayed activation or accelerated decay but also of message simplification. Remember that for sentence production to be successful, all elements of the syntactic representation must be active simultaneously, at least during one process-cycle. Now, as soon as the generation process starts, an S-node is created and its activity level starts decaying. The point in time at which this level reaches subthreshold values serves as a deadline. In Figures 2 and 3, this deadline is reached after 26 cycles. A sentence representation can only succeed if it is finished before this deadline. By message simplification, one gets the system to produce relatively simpler forms that will be finished earlier. For instance, the sentence *The man smokes a cigar in a chair* is finished at 50 cycles, far beyond the deadline. By simplifying the message, one gets *The man smokes a cigar*, which is finished just in time, after 26 cycles.

How do elliptical forms fare? The theory holds that these sentences will be finished even earlier than the short but complete ones. The simulation showed that this was the case for article reduction: *Man smokes cigar* is finished two cycles earlier than *The man smokes a cigar*. However, it did not apply to inflection reduction. Producing the above sentence with the verb in the nonfinite form rather than the finite one is not faster. To be sure, the computations within the branch starting with V are completed earlier, but because computations on both subject and object NP's continue far beyond this point, this has no effect on the point at which the final operation gets finished. It is not easy to see how this problem can be solved within the IPG architecture. The crucial factor seems to be that IPG does not work strictly from left to right but starts working on V, and somewhat later continues to work on V and both NP's in parallel. Given this, V will always be finished earlier than the first NP. What the consequences of this finding are for our characterization of the impairment remains to be seen.

10. IS THERE AN ALTERNATIVE TO SHIFTING?

As a result of temporal restrictions, the patient faces the possibility of premature desintegration of planned utterances. By shifting to simple structures the patient can avoid disintegration. But what can the patient do if he has shifted control insufficiently or not at all? In that case, disintegration is unavoidable. The patient may decide to use this degraded representation as the basis for speaking; this will lead to the selection of incorrect morphology and thus to paragrammatic output. On the other hand he may try to *repair* the representation by generating it anew. For this, he can employ the same capacity as normal speakers do when they correct themselves. Kolk & Van Grunsven (1985) refer to this possibility as *corrective* adaptation to contrast it with *preventive* adaptation (shifting).

There is a difficulty, however. If a patient with a restricted temporal window regenerates a particular representation that did not fit the first time, how can it fit a second time? We see two possible ways in which repeating the process might lead to improvement — if not immediately than at least eventually, after a number of attempts. The first is related to the assumption of natural random variation of temporal parameters. Remember that we used this assumption to explain within-subject variability, that is, the phenomenon that a patient is successful with a particular construction on one trial but fails on another trial. A second possibility is that from one trial to the next one something is saved. For instance, part of the representation may be retained and need to be reactivated; or perhaps reactivation is neeeded but can proceed faster because a particular unit, though below threshold, still has some remaining activity.

It will be clear that although both factors may help to get a representation established which originally did not fit into the temporal window, there is a limit to this effect. A representation that is much oversized in terms of time will never fit into the window, no matter how much corrective adaptation there is. This means that, given an average degree of severity, some preventive adaptation must precede corrective adaptation in order for the latter to be helpful.

Is there evidence for corrective adaptation? We have been assuming that corrective adaptation is analogous to the phenomenon of (overt or covert) self-repair. The occurrence of a self-repair has two effects. If it is overt it has a surface effect: The current sentence is interrupted and a retracing or restart takes place. Whether it is overt or covert, it leads to a pause. We assume the frequency of these phenomena to be greatly enchanced in aphasia.In our terminology, two *positive symptoms* are to be expected, both resulting from the occurrence of multiple attempts: *effortfulness* and a *reduced rate of speech*. So the question is: Are these phenomena part of the syndrome of Broca's aphasia? With respect to rate of speech, it seems clear that this is a characteristic symptom (cf. Goodglass & Kaplan, 1972). Effortfulness is also mentioned by these authors, but as a feature of articulation only. The present analysis implies that this is too limited a view. We predict that effortfulness will also be observable in Broca's aphasics with little or no articulatory impairment.

11. PATTERNS OF LANGUAGE BEHAVIOR IN BROCA'S APHASIA

In adaptation theory, corrective adaptation and preventive adaptation are optional. Therefore, since both can be either present or absent, it appears that there can be only four patterns of behavioral output. However, there is one complicating factor: severity. We have already made it clear that if severity is high, one cannot do with just corrective adaptation; one needs some degree of preventive adaptation in addition. So severity is an important factor. Secondly, severity determines the *effect* of a particular type of adaptation. In particular, if a patient with a relatively mild impairment who could speak in complete sentences with corrective adaptation decides to shift to telegraphic speech, he will become more fluent, because there is no longer a need for the time-consuming correction process. However, for a patient with a severe impairment, telegraphic speech might still be difficult and corrective adaptation might be neccessary, leading to slow telegraphic speech. The latter fact would not be so troublesome if there existed some independent measure of severity of grammatical impairment. Since this is not yet the case, the only possible predictions relate to the behavior of individual patients under different task conditions (for instance, free versus constrained speech).Comparisons between patients presuppose a particular degree of severity for each patient and are therefore necessarily post hoc. However, it still seems instructive to specify on a theoretical basis what speech output is to be expected.

In Table 1, we have summarized the predicted patterns. We have dichotomized the continuum of severity: 'severe' means: unable to produce simple subject-verb-object sentences; 'mild' means: able to produce these sentences as well as more complex ones, though sometimes only after corrective adaptation. Three levels of preventive adaptation have been defined, depending on the type of sentence primarily selected: elliptical, simple (SVO) and complex (the rest). Again, this subdivision is artificial: like normal language, aphasic language is a mixture of the three, the relative proportions varying from patient to patient. For instance, in our own studies the proportion of elliptical utterances within a group of aphasics varied from 10% to 90%. With respect to corrective adaptation we have made similar simplifying assumptions.

The first pattern given in Table 1, nonfluent telegraphic speech, is the classical textbook case. Case I reported by Miceli, Mazzucchi, Menn & Goodglass (1983) may serve as an example. Fluent telegraphic speech is a pattern which deviates from the classical description but which is reported in the literature (cf. Miceli et al. 1983, case II; Kolk & Van Grunsven, 1985, patient *La*). The pattern 'non-fluent simple speech' is applicable to the nonfluent Broca without agrammatism (cf. cases J.R. and P.D. described by Berndt, 1987).

Table 1. Patterns of language behavior in Broca's aphasia as predicted by adaptation theory.

Degree of Severity	Preventive Adaptation (= selected sentence forms)	Corrective Adaptation	Speech Output
severe	elliptical	yes	nonfluent telegraphic speech
mild	elliptical	no	fluent telegraphic speech
	simple	yes	nonfluent simple speech
	complex	yes	nonfluent complex speech with paragrammatism

Finally, 'non-fluent complex speech with paragrammatism' is obtained when the patient employs corrective adaptation but no preventive adaptation: He tries too much. This will lead to the occurrence of paragrammatic errors. We are unaware of a published case that fits this description.

We have not included the possibility of patients who would select complex sentence forms without corrective adaptation. Our assumption is that a Broca's aphasic will always adapt spontaneously, one way or the other. Complete lack of adaptation, which would lead to fluent paragrammatic output, we consider to be typical of Wernicke's aphasics.

12. CONCLUDING REMARKS

The history of the recent study of agrammatic aphasia shows a remarkable shift around 1980. In the seventies, the dominant picture was one of uniformity; all patients were implicitly or explicitly considered to be 'without syntactic competence'. Primarily as the result of the discovery of patients with agrammatic speech but good syntactic comprehension (cf. Miceli, Mazzucchi, Menn & Goodglass, 1983; Kolk, Van Grunsven & Keyser, 1985), the existence of variation between patients had to be acknowledged. As a reaction, it is now being claimed that all agrammatic patients are different, that there is no underlying unity in the behavior we use to call 'agrammatic' (Badecker & Caramazza, 1986). Adaptation theory tries to account for agrammatism as a variable phenomenon. Differences between patients are attributed not to the nature of the impairment itself but to differences in severity of and adaptive reactions to the impairment. It seems that with the help of these concepts, the various agrammatic behaviors can still be related to one and the same underlying impairment.

REFERENCES

Badecker, W. & Caramazza, A. (1986) On considerations of method and theory governing the use of clinical categories in neurolinguistics and cognitive neuropsychology: The case against agrammatism. *Cognition, 20*, 97-125.

Berndt, R. (1987) Symptom co-occurrence and dissociation in the interpretation of agrammatism. In: M. Coltheart, R. Job & G. Sartori. *The cognitive neuropsychology of language*. London: Erlbaum.

Berndt, R.S. & Caramazza, A. (1980) A redefinition of the syndrome of Broca's aphasia: Implications for a neuropsychological model of language. *Applied Psycholinguistics, 1*, 225-278.

Clark, H.H. & Clark, E.V. (1977) *Psychology and Language*. New York: Harcourt Brace Jovanovich.

Ferguson, C.A. (1982) Simplified registers and linguistic theory. In: L. Menn & L. Obler (Eds.) *Exceptional language and linguistics*. New York: Academic Press.

Friederici, A.D. (1985) Levels of processing and vocabulary types: Evidence from on-line comprehension in normals and agrammatics. *Cognition, 19*, 133-166.

Garrett, M.F. (1975) The analysis of sentence production. In: G. Bower (Ed.) *The psychology of learning and motivation: Advances in research and theory, Vol. 9*. New York: Academic Press.

Gigley, H.M. (1983) HOPE—AI and the dynamic process of language behavior. *Cognition and Brain Theory, 6*, 39-87.

Grashey, P. (1885) Über Aphasia und ihre Beziehungen zur Wahrnemung. *Archiv für Psychiatrie und Nervenkrankheiten, 16*, 654-688.

Heeschen, C. (1980) Strategies of decoding actor-object-relations by aphasic patients. *Cortex, 16*, 5-19.

Heeschen, C. (1985) Agrammatism versus paragrammatism: A fictitious opposition. In: M.-L. Kean (Ed.) *Agrammatism*. New York: Academic Press.

Isserlin, H. (1922) Ueber Agrammatismus. *Zeitschrift für die Gesamte Neurologie und Psychiatrie, 75*, 332-416. English translation in *Cognitive Neuropsychology*, 1985, 2, 303-345.

Jackson, J.H. (1884) The Croonian Lectures on the evolution and dissolution of the nervous system. Reprinted in: R.J. Herrnstein & E.G. Boring (Eds.) *A source book in the history of psychology*. Cambridge, MA.: Harvard University Press, 1965.

Kempen, G. & Hoenkamp, E. (in press) An incremental procedural grammar for sentence formulation. *Cognitive Science*.

Kleist, K. (1916) Über Leitungsaphasie und grammatische Störungen. *Monatschrift für Psychiatrie und Neurologie, 40*, 118-199.

Kolk, H.H.J. & Van Grunsven, M.F. (1985) Agrammatism as a variable phenomenon. *Cognitive Neuropsychology, 2*, 347-384.

Kolk, H.H.J., Van Grunsven, M.F. & Keijser, A. (1985) On parallelism between production and comprehension in agrammatism. In: M.-L. Kean (Ed.) *Agrammatism*. New York: Academic Press.

Langley, P.W. (1983) Exploring the space of cognitive architectures. *Behavior Research Methods & Instrumentation, 15*, 289-299.

Lenneberg, E.H. (1967) *Biological foundations of language*. New York: Wiley.

Levere, T.E. (1980) Recovery of function after brain damage and a theory of the behavioral deficit. *Physiological Psychology, 8*, 297-308.

Luria, A.R. (1970) *Traumatic aphasia*. The Hague: Mouton.

Marshall, J.C. (1977) Disorders in the expression of language. In: J. Morton & J.C. Marshall (Ed.) *Psycholinguistics Series, Vol. 1*. London: Elek Science.

Miceli, G., Mazzucchi, A., Menn, L. & Goodglass, H. (1983) Contrasting cases of Italian agrammatic aphasia without comprehension disorder. *Brain and Language, 19*, 65-97.

Shallice, T. & Butterworth, B. (1977) Short-term memory impairment and spontaneous speech. *Neuropsychologia, 15*, 729-735.

Shopen, T. (1972) *A generative theory of ellipsis: a consideration of the linguistic use of silence*. Indiana University Linguistics Club.

Tallal, P. & Newcombe, F.C. (1978) Impairment of auditory perception and language comprehension in dysphasia. *Brain and Language, 5*, 13-24.

Tzeng, O.J.L. & Wang, W.S.Y. (1984) Search for a common neurocognitive mechanism for language and movement. *American Journal of Physiology, 246*, 904-911.

Van de Kerkhof, M.M. (1986) *PROZIN, een computermodel van Agrammatisme*. Master's Thesis, Department of Psychology, University of Nijmegen.

Von Monakow, C. (1914) *Die Lokalisation im Grosshirn*. Wiesbaden: Bergmann.

Von Stockert, T.R. & Bader, L. (1976) Some relations of grammar and lexicon in aphasia. *Cortex, 22*, 183-186.

PART VI

Aspects of Lexicalization

STAGES OF LEXICAL ACCESS

Willem J.M. Levelt
Herbert Schriefers

TABLE OF CONTENTS

1. A Saussurian introduction
2. Stages, modules, and parallel processing
3. Localizing access effects: the case of semantic markedness
4. Are lemma and sound form access two successive stages?
5. How does a lexical item check the satisfaction of its conceptual conditions?

1. A SAUSSURIAN INTRODUCTION

One of the most impressive capabilities of the human language user is the ability to access the right word at the right moment. In fluent speech words are produced at a rate of about two or three per second. That means that, on the average, every 400 milliseconds an item (a word, a root) is selected from the speaker's sizable lexicon (which can easily contain 30,000 words, dependent on the speaker's language and education). What is a lexical item? What kind of internal structure does it have? Let us recall Saussure's analysis of the linguistic sign.

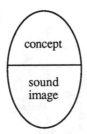

Figure 1. Saussure's egg: the linguistic sign

According to him, it is a two-sided psychological entity, representable as in Figure 1. The two elements, concept and sound image, are intimately linked, he says; each recalls the other. When we consider lexical access in speech, we might rephrase this as follows: A sound image can be recalled through the meeting of its conceptual conditions. This raises some important psycholinguistic questions: What is the nature of the conceptual conditions to be fulfilled, and by what kind of process is the appropriate lexical item singled out from among its many thousands of competitors? That process should meet the real-time requirements mentioned above, as well as others that we will return to in the course of this paper. Though these questions are crucial ones for a theory of the speaker, it should immediately be added that Saussure's picture of the linguistic sign is incomplete. It ignores (at least) a third kind of information, the item's syntactic properties, or to stay closer to De Saussure, its syntagmatic properties, the ways in which the item can enter into phrasal combinations with other linguistic signs. The obvious expansion of the above picture would be Figure 2.

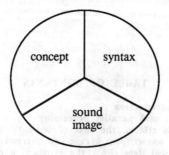

Figure 2. From egg to pie: including the sign's syntagmatic properties

In speaking, certain sound images are retrieved not so much on the basis of conceptual conditions as by prevailing syntactic conditions. The accessing of auxiliaries is conditioned in this way; it is also the case for idiomatic prepositions, certain articles, and items of minor syntactic categories.

An item's syntactic properties always play a crucial role in the sentence generation process. They determine the syntactic environments that must be realized if that item is to be used, and these in turn impose constraints on the syntactic properties of further items to be retrieved. Or to put it differently: where concepts clearly serve as input for lexical access in speech production, yielding sound images as output, syntax plays both input and output roles. These input/output relations can be depicted as in Figure 3.

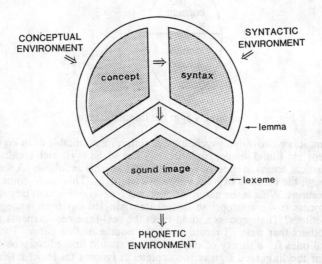

Figure 3. The activation of a linguistic sign in language production

It can be read as follows: The lexical item 'resonates' to the current conceptual environment, the speaker's speech act intention, message, or whatever it is called. When the item's conceptual conditions are sufficiently present in that environment, its syntactic properties become available for the procedures of sentence generation. The retrieval of other items is directly conditioned by the current syntactic environment. Whatever the cause is for an item's activation, it eventually leads to the recall of its sound image, to use Saussure's terms. In fact, this 'recall' is a highly complex process, involving several steps (see Levelt & Schriefers, forthcoming). Before we leave this Saussurian introduction, it should be noticed that the generation of syntactic surface form may exclusively hinge on the conceptual/syntactic properties of lexical items. There is, indeed, psychological evidence for the assumption that a speaker's construction of surface form is relatively independent of the accessibility of the sound images of the words involved. (That there can be *some* dependence has been argued by Levelt & Maassen, 1981, Dell, 1986 and Bock, forthcoming.) This has led various authors (Garrett, 1980; Kempen & Huijbers, 1983; Levelt & Maassen, 1981; Levelt, 1983) to suppose that lexical access in fluent speech is a two-stage process: In a first stage the conceptual/syntactic properties of a lexical item are activated and used for the generation of syntactic surface form; in a second phase the item's sound form properties are retrieved and made available for the generation of a phonetic plan. Kempen & Huijbers proposed calling the lexical information which is active in the first phase, i.e. the conceptual and syntactic pieces of the Saussurian pie, *lemma*, and the sound form information retrieved in the second phase *lexeme*. These terms have been inserted in Figure 3. It should, however, immediately be added that this two-stage notion of lexical access is an *assumption* in need of empirical verification. It is not entailed by the observation that the generation of syntax is highly independent of the sound form properties of its constituent lexical items.

2. STAGES, MODULES, AND PARALLEL PROCESSING

The potential stages of lemma and lexeme access are necessarily preceded and followed by additional processing stages. A preliminary step to lexical access is, of course, to create the conceptual environment which includes the conceptual conditions for the activation of the lexical item.

This stage is followed by lexical access proper: the activation of lemma and lexeme, either in two successive stages or simultaneously. This leaves us with the 'sound image', the basis for the construction of a phonetic or articulatory program. To execute this articulatory program, i.e. to utter the lexical item, the articulatory machinery must unpack and execute the program. This is the articulatory stage.

These four stages in the generation of a lexical item relate to four processing modules involved in the generation of speech: The first one, the *conceptualizer,* maps a communicative intention onto a preverbal message. The second, the *grammatical encoder*, takes a message as input and produces a surface structure as output. The third module, the *sound form encoder*, maps the surface structure onto a phonetic or articulatory plan. The fourth one, finally, the *articulator*, interprets and executes the phonetic plan for an utterance as an articulatory motor program. This is depicted in Table 1.

Before turning to lexical access proper, we should say a few words about these processing modules. The *conceptualizer* is the rather open set of mental procedures involved in the planning of speech acts, in message encoding. This planning is an intentional non-automatic activity, which relies heavily on the speaker's attentional resources. Message encoding begins with the speaker's conception of some communicative intention, some goal to be achieved by speech. It may, for instance, be the speaker's goal to let the interlocutor know his intention to have her believe that P.[1] The speaker will then find a speech act which will have the intended effect. In the example case, a good choice will be: Declare P (see Appelt, 1985 for a detailed analysis of these issues).

But P can be declared in different ways. If P is that X has a dog, where X is a particular friend of the speaker, he may refer to X by using his name (*Harry*), by mentioning their mutual relation (*my friend*), by anaphoric reference (*he*), or otherwise. These choices depend on the

---

[1] In the present paper the current speaker and addressee are taken to be male and female, respectively.

discourse situation, the mutual knowledge of the interlocutors, and so forth. Also, the possession relation may take different shades, which will eventually surface as, for instance, *have* or *own* or *possess*. This, again, depends on subtle features of the discourse context, the formality of the interaction, etc. The final result of specifying the speech act in all this precious conceptual detail we call the *preverbal message*; it includes the conceptual conditions for the activation of one or more lexical items.

Table 1. Processing modules in speech generation and their relation to phases of lexical access.

PROCESSOR	INPUT	OUTPUT	RELATION TO LEXICAL ACCESS
1. Conceptualizer	communicative intention	preverbal message	creating a lexical item's conceptual conditions
2. Grammatical encoder	preverbal message	surface structure	retrieval of the lemma, i.e. making the item's syntactic properties available, given appropriate conceptual or syntactic conditions.
3. Sound form encoder	surface structure	phonetic or articulatory plan for the utterance	retrieval of the lexeme, i.e. the item's stored sound form specifications, and its phonological integration in the articulatory plan.
4. Articulator	phonetic plan	overt speech	executing the item's context-dependent articulatory program

This preverbal message is the input to the *grammatical encoder*. Grammatical encoding is lexically driven in that the conceptually activated items specify how conceptual relations are to be mapped onto grammatical relations. The lemmas for verbs, in particular, require the realization of specific grammatical relations for their conceptual arguments (or theta-roles). The syntactic categories of the lemmas trigger the grammatical encoder to build phrases that can be headed by that category: VPs for verbs, NPs for nouns, and so forth. This phrase-building involves the assignment of order over the constituents involved, and the attachment of phrases to higher level nodes. Kempen & Hoenkamp (in press) have proposed an artificial encoding system which involves these features and which has the additional psychological attraction of being able to generate surface structures incrementally from left to right. The grammatical encoder also assigns focus to particular elements in surface structure. This originates in conceptual focussing, but is further shaped by phrase-constructional processes.

The *sound form encoder* takes successive fragments of surface structure, as they become available, as input and produces a phonetic representation which the articulator will have to interpret as a speech motor program. Sound form encoding is, again, lexically driven. The metrical and segmental form specifications stored with each lexical item (i.e. its lexeme) are made available; they impose rhythmic and coarticulatory restrictions on the item's environment. The sound form encoder builds phonological phrases around focussed elements, which are given pitch accent. An element's free sound form parameters, such as metrical stress, syllable length, vowel quality (reduced/ non-reduced), and pitch movement are adapted to conditions prevailing in the phonological phrase. Still, the resulting phonetic representation for an utterance is probably quite context-free as far as the articulatory motor context is concerned; the representation is probably not different for situations where the speaker has or does not have a pipe in his mouth, has or does not have a cold, etc.

It is precisely the task of the articulatory system to translate the phonetic plan in a sequence of context-sensitive articulatory gestures. The articulatory goals laid down in the phonetic plan can, within limits, be reached in a variety of ways. Groups of muscles form so-called *synergisms* or *coordinative structures* which function as units to reach a certain goal, compensating for prevailing contextual conditions. This involves no effort or attention on the part of the speaker; it is rather the wisdom of the body.

Since, after message encoding, each module operates on the output of the previous one, it is reasonable to ask how the previously mentioned speed of lexical processing, some two or three words per second, can be attained when so many stages have to be chained. Can one run through all these processing steps in less than some 400 milliseconds? The answer is 'no'. Still, a high speed in speaking can be attained by what Kempen & Hoenkamp (in press) call *incremental production* . The modules operate in parallel and deliver their characteristic output in small chunks 'from left to right'. Once a module has delivered an element, it is immediately picked up and processed by the next module, for which it is characteristic input, and so forth. This puts substantial constraints on the modules' processing. If there were a lot of backtracking, such a system could not function; speech would be dysfluent, with frequent restarts and long lapses. Incremental processing is both serial and parallel processing. The parallelness of the modules' functioning is essential for the maintenance of a high speaking rate and fluency. Seriality does imply relatively long 'front-to-end' processing durations. The latter is especially apparent in tasks, such as object naming, which involve single-word responses. These consist almost entirely of lexical processing. From the presentation of a familiar object, such as a table, to the end of the naming response involves, on the average, one and a half seconds. Of this, only about 300 to 400 milliseconds are used to recognize the object, i.e. for visual processing; all of the rest of the time is spent on lexical access and articulation.

We will now turn to a discussion of some recent experimental results which, we believe, support and further qualify the framework just sketched. The first set of experiments was designed, among other things, to localize in this processing framework some peculiar accessing effects which were observed in the use of semantically marked versus unmarked comparatives. The second set addresses the issue, raised above, of whether lemma and sound form (lexeme) information are successively or simultaneously retrieved during lexical access. The final section of this chapter will return to the important theoretical issue of how a lexical item 'recognizes' its conditions of use in the conceptual environment.

3. LOCALIZING ACCESS EFFECTS: THE CASE OF SEMANTIC MARKEDNESS

In a recent series of experiments (Schriefers, 1985) it was discovered that, in making comparative judgments, speakers take more time to generate a semantically marked adjective than a semantically unmarked one. The effect arises, for instance, in an experimental task where the subject is presented with a pair of objects which differ only in size (cf. Figure 4).

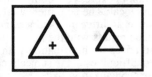

Figure 4. Example of stimuli used in a relation-naming experiment

After 1.5 seconds a corss appears near one of the two objects, and the subject is to say whether that object is the bigger or the smaller one of the two. We measured the time from the appearance of the cross to the speaker's speech onset. It took about 40 milliseconds longer to initiate the response 'smaller' than the response 'bigger'. The same markedness effect was found for situations where the judgment was 'longer' versus 'shorter'. These effects were statistically highly significant.

Which accessing stage is responsible for this difference? A first possibility is that the effect is due to conceptual decisions, i.e.decisions made in the message-encoding stage. One might well argue that it is easier to judge that an object is bigger or longer than to judge that it is smaller or shorter; people may have judgmental biases of this sort. If this is so, the markedness effect should also arise in a nonverbal judgment task, i.e. in a task where the subject does not give a verbal response but rather pushes one button when the indicated object is bigger and another button when the object is smaller. This experiment was done, and the results were unequivocal: The markedness effect disappeared completely. This shows that the effect is not due to conceptual decision making. The effect can only be obtained if the response is verbal. In other words, the effect must reside in either the lexical-access phases or in the final articulatory phase.

Is the effect articulatory? Is it harder to initiate the speech motor program for a semantically marked item than for an unmarked one? To test this possibility, an experiment was done where the speaker was presented with the printed words *bigger* or *smaller* (or with the words *longer* or *shorter*). In half of the trials the word was, after 1 second, followed by a cross. This was the signal for the subject to pronounce the word. Again, speech onset latencies were measured. In this task, the subject could prepare the verbal response and release it as soon as the cross appeared. Would response initiation take more time for *smaller* and *shorter* than for *bigger* and *longer*? It did not. There was no statistical difference between speech onset latencies for marked and unmarked items. That means that the markedness effect cannot be located in the final articulatory stage.

By exclusion, the markedness effect must be due to lexical access proper, the retrieval of the lexical item from the mental lexicon. We do not know what is so hard to retrieve for a marked element, the lemma information or the lexeme information or both. Is it the case that a semantically marked lexical item requires more time for the recognition of the satisfaction of its conceptual conditions than does a semantically unmarked item? Or is the effect rather due to sound form access? The more general issue is whether these are indeed distinguishable successive phases. We will return to this in the next section.

The present series of experiments also showed the existence of a so-called *congruency effect*. The effect is the following: When the two figures to be compared in the comparative judgment task were both relatively large (or relatively long), this facilitated the *bigger (longer)* response, and interfered with the *smaller (shorter)* response. If, however, both figures were relatively small (or short), the *smaller (shorter)* response was facilitated at the expense of the *bigger (longer)* response. In other words, naming a relation which was congruent with the absolute size of the two figures in the picture involved shorter speech onset latencies (by about 70 milliseconds) than did incongruent reactions. Congruency and markedness effects were, moreover, fully additive.

This congruency effect could also be located with respect to processing stage. In order to test whether it is preverbal in nature, i.e. originates in the conceptual decision making which precedes lexical access, the experiment was repeated with nonverbal responses; the subject had to push a 'longer' or a 'shorter' button to express the comparative judgment. The results of this nonverbal task were, again, unequivocal: The congruency effect reappeared in undiminished fashion. What disappeared was the additive markedness component, and this was to be expected given the above-mentioned results with the pushbutton task. Unlike the markedness effect, the congruency effect also arises in the situation with the nonverbal response mode, which shows that it must be due to difficulties in the subjects' comparative decision making. In other words, it arises during the conceptualization stage.

What are the difficulties? Apparently, the subject in this task not only generates a *comparative* judgment, involving the concept BIGGER or SMALLER , but he cannot fully suppress the generation of another judgment, an *absolute* judgment, as well: It is a pair of BIG figures, or a pair of SMALL figures. It is easier to generate the BIGGER judgment in the presence of the concept BIG than it is in the presence of the concept SMALL, and inversely for the SMALLER judgment. This interference is very much like the one obtained in so-called 'Stroop tasks', such as reading the word *green* when it is printed in red letters. The source of interference is also apparent from the occasional speech errors subjects make: The inappropriate response (i.e. *smaller* for *bigger* or inversely) is made almost exclusively when the comparative size relation is incongruent with absolute size. Many real-life speech errors, in particular the Freudian ones, are no doubt due to a similar competition between concepts.

4. ARE LEMMA AND SOUND FORM ACCESS TWO SUCCESSIVE STAGES?

Though there is independent empirical evidence (especially from the analysis of speech errors) for the assumption that the grammatical encoding module and the sound form encoding module function in relative independence and are serially ordered, this does not imply that lexical access also proceeds in two phases, one for lemma retrieval and one for lexeme or sound form retrieval. An alternative view could be that an item's lemma and sound form information are always simultaneously retrieved when the conceptual and/or syntactic conditions are fulfilled; the two kinds of information are only *employed* by different modules, and therefore in different stages of the speech generating process.

We have tried to test these alternative views in a series of experiments. These studies will be reported elsewhere, but the basic idea is this: If the lemma and sound form are retrieved in subsequent phases, one should be able to find a moment in time during lexical access at which there is measurable semantic activation but no phonological activation. In addition, a strong version of this view would imply that there is a later phase where there is only phonological activation, but no semantic activation. In the experiments, the subjects performed an object naming task. They saw a series of slides, each depicting an object, and were asked to name each object. When they saw a table, they had to say *table*; we will call this the 'target word'. In one-third of the cases the subjects also performed a secondary task. Shortly after presentation of the slide, but before the naming response, the subject heard an acoustic stimulus. This was either a word or a nonword. The subject's task was, apart from naming the displayed object as always, to push a 'yes' button when the stimulus was a word, and a 'no' button when it was a nonword. The subject was instructed to give priority to the lexical decision response over the naming response. A little training was enough for most subjects to learn to do this. Only the 'yes' responses were relevant for the experimental purposes; the corresponding stimulus word we will call the *test word*.

The test word could stand in various relations to the target word. It could, first, be semantically related to it; for example, when the target word was *table*, the test word would be *chair*. It could also be phonologically related to the target word, as would be the case with *tailor* as the test word. As a control, there were also unrelated test words; *chicken* would be such a case. Finally, the identical word (i.e. *table* when the target word was *table*) could appear as test word. If there are two successive phases in accessing the target word, a semantic and a phonological one, one would expect to find an early moment in time, i.e. very soon after presentation of the slide, where lexical decision times for the semantically related test word would be affected, but where there would be no effect for the phonologically related test word. Also, it would be pleasant to find a late moment, i.e. just before the naming response, where the response to the phonologically related test word would show an effect, but the response to the semantically related one would not.

We did obtain the latter result: There is clearly a moment in time in the preparation of a naming response where the item's sound form representation is in an active state but where its semantic representation is inactive. However, we were not able to obtain the inverse effect. When we presented our test words right after the slide (70 milliseconds after the onset of the slide, on the average), we did find the expected effect of semantic activation, but there was always also evidence for phonological activation: The lexical decision times for both the semantically and phonologically related test word were significantly delayed in this early phase of lexical access.

The tentative conclusion from these experiments is that lemma and lexeme information are *simultaneously* accessed, i.e. not in two successive phases. An item's conceptual information, however, may be subject to faster decay than its sound form information. The longer availability of the sound form information is functional, given its role in the later processing stages.

5. HOW DOES A LEXICAL ITEM CHECK THE SATISFACTION OF ITS CONCEPTUAL CONDITIONS?

Psycholinguists have devoted surprisingly little attention to a fundamental problem of lexical access in production, namely, how the lexical item is retrieved, or becomes activated, when its conceptual conditions are satisfied. In Artificial Intelligence, Goldman (1975) was the first to propose a solution to this problem in the framework of a Schankian Conceptual Dependency system. Goldman introduced discrimination nets to mediate between a conceptualization (message) and a lexical response. In essence, his discrimination nets are binary tree structures. Each nonterminal node in the tree represents some predicate which is either true or false for the conceptualization at hand. Terminal nodes correspond to lexical items. The access procedure starts by running the test for the tree's root predicate. If it yields the value *true* for the conceptualization at hand, control moves to the node's right-hand daughter; if it is *false*, it goes to the left-hand daughter node. The next test concerns the daughter node's predicate. The procedure is self-terminating; it iterates until a terminal node is reached. The lexical item at that terminal node is the system's lexical response to the concept. With these means, which were enriched and qualified in several ways, Goldman could build a working model for generating paraphrases in a limited conceptual domain. No claims were made with respect to linguistic or psychological adequacy of the model.

But using the discrimination net approach as a psycholinguistic model probably leads to insurmountable problems. In order to find a lexical item in, say, a 30,000 word lexicon, between 15 and 15001 binary tests are necessary to reach a lexical item, on the average. The serial arrangement of these tests leads to unrealistic real-time properties. This argument is strengthened by another unrealistic consequence. Conceptually more complex items will take longer to retrieve than less complex ones, because they involve a larger number of successive tests. There is, however, no evidence that access to semantically more complex words systematically takes longer than access to less complex ones. Though the above results on semantic markedness seem to be in support of such a view, there is as much evidence for the opposite position: Levelt, Schreuder & Hoenkamp (1978) and Schreuder (1978) found that more complex verbs take systematically less time to access than less complex ones do. They related this finding to the greater *specificity* of the complex verbs. We will return to this notion shortly.

An additional problem with discrimination nets is that there are large parts of the lexicon which do not seem to be hierarchically organized; there are cross-classifications, circular arrangements, and so forth (cf. Miller & Johnson-Laird, 1976). Finally, hypernymy creates serious problems. When the conditions for *dog* are met, those for *animal* are also met, because the *dog* predicates imply the *animal* predicates. But then, how can a discrimination net have a terminal node for *dog* when it has one for *animal*? When the concept is that of a dog, testing will necessarily be terminated at *animal*; its hyponyms cannot be represented on the same tree. This would predict that we speak in hypernyms only, or alternatively that there are no hypernym relations in a lexicon.

Alternative accessing mechanisms have been proposed by Miller & Johnson-Laird (1976). They arranged conceptual components (predicates, semantic tests) and lexical items in so-called *decision tables*. Allowing for parallel execution of all tests, high-speed access can be achieved: The (first) lexical item whose characteristic column pattern of *true*, *false*, and *not applicable* evaluations is matched will be the one accessed. Elsewhere (Levelt & Schriefers, forthcoming) we have discussed some of the problems with this approach. One major obstacle resides again in the case of hypernymy. If an item's column is matched by the test outcomes, the columns for all of its hypernyms will also be matched. Matching the hypernym will, moreover, never be slower than matching the target item, but potentially faster. (The slowest test sets the pace in a parallel system.) Hence, though hyponyms are representable in this model, hypernym reactions will be preferred.

Though we are not able to present an alternative model at this point, we wish to sketch one step towards solving the hypernym problem. For each (open class) lexical item, we propose that it contains a *unique* conceptual condition. We have termed this the item's *core sense*. There are reasonably reliable empirical procedures for determining this semantic core. One is Miller's (1969) negation test (for various applications see Noordman, 1979; Levelt, Schreuder & Hoenkamp, 1978; Schreuder, 1978). Negating the item affects its core sense only. When asked to complete the sentence 'They do not walk, but they...', most subjects react with 'run'. This leaves the sense of locomotion, which is shared between *walk* and *run*, unaffected. But the specific manner of locomotion which is uniquely characteristic of walking is given up. Given this notion of core sense, one may conjecture that the following access principle holds:

> *A lexical item is retrieved if and only if its core conditions are fulfilled by the concept to be expressed.*

Since these core conditions are unique to the lexical item, their satisfaction in the concept to be expressed guarantees the item's retrieval. This is a first step towards solving the problems with hypernyms discussed above. But what about the hypernym's core conditions? Let us compare *eat* and *devour*, where the former is a hypernym of the latter. According to the accessing principle, a speaker will retrieve *devour* if its core condition, something like the voracious manner of eating, is satisfied. But, since devouring implies eating, isn't the core condition for *eat* always simultaneously satisfied when the conceptual conditions for *devour* are satisfied? If so, *eat* should also be retrieved. There is a way out of this dilemma. It is to invoke an additional principle of specificity. Accessing would then be governed by the following dual principle:

> (a) *A lexical item is retrieved only if its core conditions are fulfilled by the concept to be expressed.*
>
> (b) *Of all items whose core conditions are satisfied by the concept, the most specific one is retrieved.*

The addition of the latter principle prevents *eat* from becoming activated when the core condition for *devour* is satisfied. It is reminiscent of Grice's maxim of quantity. It is not immediately obvious what kind of processing mechanism would realize this specificity principle, but this does not appear to be an insoluble problem.

REFERENCES

Appelt, D.E.(1985) *Planning English sentences*. Cambridge: Cambridge University Press.

Bock, K. (in press). An effect of the accessibility of word forms on sentence production. *Journal of Memory and Language*.

Dell, G.S. (1986) A spreading activation theory of retrieval in sentence production. *Psychological Review, 93*, 283-321.

Garrett, M.F.(1980) Levels of processing in sentence production. In: B.Butterworth (Ed.) *Language production. Vol.1*. London: Academic Press.

Goldman, N. (1975) Conceptual generation. In: R. Schank, *Conceptual information processing*. Amsterdam: North-Holland.

Kempen, G & E. Hoenkamp (in press). An incremental procedural grammar for sentence formulation. *Cognitive Science*.

Kempen, G. & P. Huijbers (1983) The lexicalization process in sentence production and naming: indirect election of words. *Cognition, 14*, 185-209.

Levelt, W.J.M. (1983) Monitoring and self-repair in speech. *Cognition, 14*, 41-104.

Levelt, W.J.M. & B. Maassen (1981) Lexical search and order of mention in sentence production. In: W. Klein and W.J.M. Levelt (Eds.) *Crossing the boundaries in linguistics. Studies presented to Manfred Bierwisch*. Dordrecht: Reidel.

Levelt, W.J.M., R. Schreuder & E. Hoenkamp (1978) Structure and use of verbs of motion. In: R.N. Campbell & P.T. Smith (Eds.) *Recent advances in the psychology of language* New York: Plenum.

Levelt, W.J.M. & H. Schriefers (forthcoming) Issues of lexical access in language production. In: H. Clark (Ed.) *Proceedings of Workshop on Language Processing,* Stanford.

Miller, G.A. (1969) A psychological method to investigate verbal concepts. *Journal of Mathematical Psychology*, 6, 169-191.
Miller, G.A. & P.N. Johnson-Laird (1976) *Language and perception* . Cambridge: Harvard University Press.
Noordman, L.G.M. (1979) *Inferring from language*. Heidelberg: Springer.
Schreuder, R. (1978) *Studies in psycholexicology*. Doctoral dissertation, Nijmegen.
Schriefers, H.J. (1985) *On semantic markedness in language production and verification*. Doctoral dissertation, Nijmegen.

Chapter 26

WHERE DO PHRASES COME FROM: SOME PRELIMINARY EXPERIMENTS IN CONNECTIONIST PHRASE GENERATION

Karen Kukich

ABSTRACT

Some of the assumptions that were inherent in many of our early models of language generation (assumptions such as the unidirectional flow of information from conceptualization to verbalization, the serial processing of semantic, lexical, syntactic and phonetic information, and the importance of the word as the lexical unit) are coming under closer scrutiny within the symbolic modeling paradigm. At the same time, interest in another paradigm of cognitive modeling, one that has been variously referred to as neural network modeling, parallel distributed processing, and connectionism, has been growing. Certain characteristics of connectionist models, in particular their broad bandwidth information channels which permit parallel, multidirectional information flow, seem especially relevant to current language generation problems. Other useful properties of these models, such as their content addressable memory capacity, their ability to respond to novelty, their capacity to degrade gracefully and the existence of automatic learning procedures, would contribute to the solutions of other language generation problems. This paper gives an overview of the connectionist paradigm and a brief summary of some of the language processing research being done under it. It then describes the results of some experiments aimed at training connectionist networks to perform two language generation tasks. In one study a network was trained to produce appropriate words given a set of semantic attributes, and in another study a network was trained to produce syntactically well-formed phrases given the unordered words. The networks finally did achieve their intended behaviors, and in doing so they exhibited evidence of having acquired linguistic knowledge of synonymy relations and collocation relations in addition to proper semantic associations. Many of the errors made by the networks suggested revisions to network configurations and encoding schemes, and the effects of those revisions are also briefly described.

1. SOME PROBLEMS IN TEXT GENERATION

Intuition has it that an utterance arises from some underlying representation of its intended meaning which is then transformed by linguistic processes into a phrase or sentence. Under the conventional Artificial Intelligence paradigm of symbolic information processing, this intuition is explored by building computational models in which meaning is represented in some knowledge representation formalism and the semantic and linguistic processes that operate on meaning are executed in some symbolic processing language. Some of the well-known knowledge representation formalisms include conceptual dependency notation, KL-ONE, OPS5 production rules, and a variety of other hand-crafted, LISP-based formalisms. Most of these formalisms include symbolic processing operators; if they do not, LISP operators are used for executing semantic and linguistic operations. Some examples of text generation systems that have been implemented under this paradigm include those of Mann (1983), McDonald (1983), Appelt (1983), McKeown (1982), Kukich (1983), Danlos (1984), Jacobs (1985) and Bienkowski (1986).

Some of the fundamental questions concerning text generation that are addressed by these models are: (1) what are the elements of meaning that must be represented, (2) what are the semantic and linguistic processes that operate on meaning, (3) how might both meaning and the processes that operate on it best be represented. There are as yet no definitive answers to these questions. Different text generation systems have found it necessary to incorporate different elements of semantic and linguistic information to achieve their individual goals. Similarly, different symbolic representation languages have proven useful in different applications.

Despite this lack of consensus the symbolic processing paradigm is valuable, precisely because it provides a means for scrutinizing and revising the tenets of the models we build. For example, some of the assumptions that were implicit in many early text generation models (often for the sake of computational manageability) are now being carefully re-examined. These include (1) the assumption that the flow of information from conceptualization to verbalization is unidirectional, (2) the assumption that linguistic processes such as lexical choice, syntactic formation and phonetic articulation proceed in series, and (3) the assumption that the unit of linguistic processing is the word, among others.

Some compelling arguments against the assumption of unidirectional flow of information have been articulated by Kempen (1977). He points out that (1) semantic content revision often occurs when a writer or speaker encounters a syntactic dead-end while planning or speaking a sentence; (2) because languages differ with respect to the expression of tense, number, and addressing conventions, it is more efficient to make such decisions at the linguistic stage, yet that information must be passed back to the semantic processor to complete a semantic representation; and (3) at the time a lexical choice is made, if a single word or phrase cannot be found to express exactly those semantic attributes in the concept, then the speaker must decide between revising the concept to conform to the lexical unit or constructing a larger lexical unit to cover the concept (in which case the problem is recursive because the lexical units used in the larger unit may not be exact matches for the target concept). In his KAMP system, Appelt (1983) attempts to accommodate some of these difficulties by providing for an intelligent planner with some knowledge of grammar to guide the semantic formulation process. Danlos (1984) has argued that because linguistic and conceptual decisions are strongly interdependent, it follows that these components must not be modularized in a generation grammar. Most recently, Hovy (1985) has pinpointed five key decision points in the generation process at which two-way information flow is essential. They are: topic choice, sentence content, sentence organization, clause organization, and word choice.

The assumption of serial processing is also under question. One psychological model of sentence production proposed by Bock (1982) relies on the parallel access of lexical and syntactic units. Activation from a semantic module simultaneously reaches lexical units (words) and syntactic units (syntactic structures). As candidate words become activated they feed activation to candidate syntactic structures with which they are consistent, and similarly, as candidate syntactic structures are activated they simultaneously feed activation to words with which they are consistent. For example, transitive verbs feed activation to syntactic structures that take direct objects, and those structures feed activation back to words that can fill the slots of transitive verbs and direct objects. Such feedback loops quickly select out the best structure and words to go with it. A different level of parallelism is exploited in a computational model of sentence formulation devised by Kempen & Hoenkamp (1986) which takes advantage of parallel operation of modules while maintaining serial processing within modules.

It is interesting to note (as observed by Cumming, 1986) that the default assumption that the unit of linguistic processing is the word has been overridden in most text generation implementations. Text generation system developers have frequently found it necessary to deal with language in chunks larger than single word units. This is due to the fact that not only is natural language full of non-compositional idioms, but it is also very restrictive in its allowance of fluent-sounding phrases. That is, many otherwise well-formed phrases are unconventional. To borrow an example from Cumming, the phrases 'dozens and dozens' and 'hundreds and hundreds' are fine, but 'twelves and twelves' and 'fifties and fifties' sound strange. Such observations led Becker (1975) to propose that generation frequently accesses a phrasal lexicon, and that linguistic processing frequently consists of tailoring these chunks to fit semantic concepts. This technique was exploited in the ANA (Kukich, in press) stock report generation system in which macro-sized semantic and linguistic information units were used. But a more realistic view of the generation process must accommodate both the compositional power and the conventional limitations of natural language. A truly intelligent generator would have the ability to handle both larger chunks and their constituent parts, and it would have the wisdom to decide when to use which.

All these problems suggest that text generation research is alive and healthy under the symbolic processing paradigm. At the same time, however, they invite investigation under an alternative paradigm, one that has been variously referred to as neural network modeling, parallel distributed processing, and connectionism. One relevant attribute of the connectionist paradigm is the broad bandwidth of the information channel that interconnects the units of connectionist models. Such broad bandwidth channels permit the parallel interaction of hundreds or thousands of information elements, so they are highly suited to exploring the consequences of multi-directional and non-serial information flow. Furthermore, the algorithms that exist for automatically setting the weights in connectionist networks require that the network be 'trained' on a representative sample of the patterns that the system must be able to recognize or produce. A representative sample of the naturally occurring phrases of a domain would embody both the compositional abilities and the conventional restrictions of the language of that domain. A network trained on such a sample would capture the same abilities and constraints, and in doing so might shed some light on the problem of the size of semantic and linguistic units. In particular, words that are collocated in frequently occurring phrases would tend to create mutually reinforcing groups of nodes in a connectionist network. Feldman and Ballard (1982) refer to such groups of nodes as 'stable coalitions'. Stable coalitions of words would explain the tendency for phrases to be treated as whole units while at the same time maintaining their compositionality.

In addition to their relevance to the questions of knowledge interaction and information unit size, connectionist networks also exhibit some other properties that make them attractive for natural language processing models. First, they embody content addressable memory devices capable of recovering a complete pattern from partial input. This physical property was first derived by Hopfield (1982). Second, they are capable of learning internal representations automatically, as demonstrated by Rumelhart, Hinton & Williams (1986). Third, they have the capacity to generalize and respond to novel situations. Fourth, they have the capacity to degrade gracefully under minor damage. And finally, they have the capacity to relearn rapidly after major damage. These last three properties have been demonstrated by Hinton & Sejnowski (1986). Given the virtues of connectionism, it is worth exploring its applicability to the problems of text generation. The remainder of this paper is divided into two main parts. In the first part an overview of the connectionist paradigm is given, some language-related connectionist models are described, and some connectionist learning algorithms are sketched. The second part presents some preliminary experiments on the topic of connectionist phrase generation.

2. WHAT IS CONNECTIONISM

A connectionist model consists of a network of hundreds or thousands of simple nodes (even more if computational facilities permit). Concepts or objects in the domain to be modeled are represented as patterns of activity over one or more nodes in the network. The nodes are highly interconnected by a set of weighted links. Mode of processing is by spreading activation. Each node performs some simple computation — a linear threshold function in some models, a differentiable sigmoid function in others — to sum the activity impinging on it and pass it on to other nodes. Because activation is modulated by the weights of the connections between nodes, knowledge is implicitly represented in connections, hence the name connectionism. This is in contrast to symbolic information processing in which knowledge is explicitly represented by symbols and processed by a symbol manipulation language.

Most connectionist models fall into one of two broad categories. These can be referred to as pre-configured networks and learning networks. Pre-configured networks usually make use of a local representation scheme in which each node represents a single concept, object, or primitive. These networks are usually small, on the order of tens of nodes, and the weights on the links connecting nodes are manually set. In contrast, learning networks frequently (though not always) make use of a distributed representation scheme in which a concept or feature is represented by a pattern of activity over a number of nodes. Learning networks are usually larger, on the order of hundreds of nodes, and the weights on the connections are set by an automatic procedure that is often referred to as a learning algorithm.

Pre-configured networks are usually implemented for the purpose of demonstrating how properties inherent in network representations can account for certain natural phenomena. The following are some examples of pre-configured network models of natural language processing.

One well-known connectionist psychological model is McClelland & Rumelhart's interactive model of letter perception (1981, 1982). In this model, input nodes act as detectors for visual features of a display. These excite additional nodes (detectors) for letters, which in turn excite detectors for words. At each level active nodes send inhibition to competing nodes and send positive feedback to consistent lower-level nodes. Computer simulation of the model reproduced many of the psychological characteristics of letter-perception, in particular the word-superiority effect, in which letters appearing within words are more easily recognized than letters appearing within random strings.

Cottrell & Small have devised a connectionist word sense disambiguation model based on similar principles (1983). Their model posits three levels of nodes, a lexical level, a word sense level, and a case level. Each node at the lexical level represents a single word; each node at the word sense level represents a single sense; and each node at the case level represents a single case. Input sentences are processed/parsed by having each word activate the corresponding node in the lexical level, which in turn causes the activation of connected nodes in the word sense level and the case level. The sense of an ambiguous word is easily resolved by mutual inhibition and positive feedback among nodes; the sense that is most consistent with its context quickly accrues the most activation. A connectionist model of anaphora resolution devised by Reilly (1984) extends the Cottrell & Small model to incorporate a focus level and a schema level both of which contribute to anaphora resolution. It demonstrates how some larger aspects of discourse may be represented in a connectionist model.

Waltz & Pollack (1985) have proposed a connectionist model of natural language interpretation that has four levels of nodes: a contextual level, a lexical level, a syntactic level, and an input level. In their model, an 'active coalition of phrase-markers' represents a well-formed parse. Furthermore, the model demonstrates how spreading activation would account for garden-path behavior and cognitive doubletakes, as in the sentence 'The astronomer married a star'. Gigley's (1983) model of natural language comprehension, HOPE, was designed to explore aphasic behavior. Its nodes represent phonetic, semantic, grammatical, and pragmatic knowledge. Simulated lesions are then introduced and their effects on processing are observed to parallel certain aphasic symptoms. In Dell's connectionist model of phoneme production (1985) the recognition process of the McClelland and Rumelhart model is reversed. Activation flows from a morpheme layer to a phoneme layer to a phonetic feature layer, and, as in the letter recognition model, feedback between layers plays a crucial role. Computer simulation of this model has duplicated many aspects of naturally occurring slip-of-the-tongue behavior, in particular the tendency for errors to create morphemes.

The pre-configured network models mentioned here were designed to demonstrate the fact that connectionist networks are well-suited to the task of modeling many natural phenomena. But pre-configured network models start from the assumption that the weights interconnecting the nodes of the network have been set to suitable values a priori. They do not address the issue of how the weights were determined in the first place. This is no small problem considering the fact that even a network containing only tens of nodes might have thousands of interconnecting and interacting links. The problem of how the weights might be derived is one main focus of research on learning networks.

A number of algorithms have been derived for automatically setting the weights of a network to achieve certain effects. One of the earliest was the perceptron convergence procedure described by Minsky & Papert (1969). This algorithm guaranteed convergence on a set of useful weights, but only if the behavior to be learned fell within a small class of problems such that the input patterns were sufficiently similar to the output patterns. Minsky & Papert's demonstration of the limitations of the algorithm put a damper on connectionist research for almost a decade. However, interest was rekindled when automatic learning procedures were developed for a broader class of problems. Two algorithms that have received much attention recently are the Boltzmann algorithm (Ackley, Hinton & Sejnowski, 1985) and the the back-propagation algorithm (Rumelhart, Hinton & Williams, 1986).

The Boltzmann algorithm is a probabilistic algorithm. Paired input-output associations to be learned by the network are represented as binary vectors. Certain nodes in the network are designated as input nodes; others are designated as output nodes; the remainder are referred to as hidden nodes. All nodes are fully interconnected. The training procedure for setting the weights consists of repeatedly 'clamping' the input and output nodes of the network with a pair of input-output patterns, allowing the activation to spread throughout the network until it reaches a state of equilibrium, observing the probability of activity at each of the hidden nodes, and adjusting the weights slightly in accordance with the observed probability. This process is repeated many times for each pair of input-output patterns in the corpus to be learned. By analogy to thermodynamics, the activation function incorporates a temperature variable which is used to simulate an annealing process. During the training procedure the temperature variable is initially set at a high value and then gradually reduced. Higher temperatures result in greater variability of activation, thus helping network to escape from local minima in the early phase of training. The Boltzmann algorithm has been used to train networks to perform a variety of tasks. Its only flaw is its extreme computational intensity. Training a network of hundreds of nodes and thousands of links can take many days of processor time.

The back-propagation algorithm, which is deterministic, is a somewhat less computationally intensive learning algorithm. This algorithm is a generalization of the perceptron convergence procedure for multilayered networks. The ability to make use of intermediate layers of 'hidden' nodes expands the class of problems that a learning network can model beyond the limited set that can be solved by perceptrons. The back-propagation algorithm is described here in more detail than other learning algorithms because it is the algorithm used in the experiments that follow. But for a complete analysis of the back-propagation algorithm the article by Rumelhart, Hinton and Williams (1986) is recommended.

The architecture of a back-propagation network is usually depicted visually as three horizontal layers of nodes, with the lowest layer representing input nodes, the middle layer representing hidden nodes, and the highest layer representing output nodes. The nodes are fully connected between layers. That is, each node in the input layer is connected to each node in the hidden layer, and each node in the hidden layer is connected to each node in the output layer. There are no direct connections from input to output nodes nor are there any lateral connections within layers. When an input pattern is presented to the network, activity is propagated forward from input nodes to hidden nodes and from hidden nodes to output nodes where it may be read off. The same function is used to compute the activity at each node in the network. The activity at a node is computed by first taking the sum of the weights times the activities of each lower node leading to it and then inserting that sum into a squashing function to obtain a value between zero and one. The suggested squashing function is

$$\frac{1}{1 + e^{-\Sigma}},$$

so the actual function for computing the activation at node i is:

$$activation_i = \frac{1}{1 + e^{-\Sigma \; activation_j \; * \; weight_{ji} \; + \; \theta_i}}$$

A threshold is simulated by positing an additional weight for each hidden and output node which is connected to a permanently 'on' unit. Treating the threshold as an ordinary weight simplifies computation and allows the threshold to be 'learned' like all other weights.

The goal of the training procedure, or learning algorithm, is to find a set of weights for the connections such that the network will produce the desired output pattern given a specific input pattern for all of the input-output patterns in a corpus. To achieve this goal the weights in the network are initially set to small random values (usually between +.1 and -.1) and are then adjusted in accordance with the learning algorithm. This consists of presenting the network with an input pattern, propagating the activation forward through the hidden nodes to the output nodes, and then comparing the activation on the output nodes to the target output pattern for that input. If the actual output pattern is sufficiently close to the the target output pattern (usually within .01 for the sum of squares of the differences on each node), no adjustment of the weights is required. But if the difference is not negligible, a correction is propagated back through the network (hence the name back-propagation) by adjusting each weight by a small amount.

The amount of adjustment for each weight is determined by first computing an error signal for a node and then adjusting each weight leading to that node by an amount proportional to the product of the error signal for the node and the activation of the lower level node connected to it by the weight. That is, the formula for computing the adjustment to weight$_{ji}$ is:

$$delta\_weight_{ji} = \eta \; * \; error\_signal_j \; * \; activation_i$$

where η is a proportional constant, e.g. .1. The error signal for an output node is simply the difference between the actual and the target output value for that node times the first derivative of the activation function. Since the first derivative of the activation function taken at node i is simply activation$_i$ * (1.0 - activation$_i$), it follows that the error signal for an output node is the following:

$$output\_error_i = (target_i - activation_i) * (activation_i * (1.0 - activation_i))$$

In the case of a hidden node where a target value is not known, the error signal is determined by first computing the sum of the error signals of the output nodes to which the hidden node connects times their weights, and again multiplying by the first derivative of the activation function. So the formula for computing the error signal at a hidden node is:

$$hidden\_error_i = \Sigma output\_error_j * weight_{ji} * (activation_i * (1.0 - activation_i))$$

All error signals should be computed before adjusting any weights. The adjustment on any weight is computed by multiplying the product of the activation from the lower node and the error signal of the higher node by a proportional constant. The smaller the constant the slower the learning will be, hence the constant, designated η, is referred to as the learning rate. It is typically assigned a value of .1, but higher values may be used provided they do not lead to oscillation during learning. In addition to the learning rate, weight adjustment may also be mediated by a momentum term, which is simply some fraction (typically .9, designated α) of the weight adjustment for the same node on the previous presentation. Adding a momentum term diminishes the risk of oscillation at higher learning rates. Thus, the complete formula for adjusting weight$_{ji}$ on presentation n+1 is given by:

$$\text{delta\_weight}_{ji}\,(n+1) = \eta * \text{activation}_i * \text{error\_signal}_j + \alpha * \text{delta\_weight}_{ji}(n)$$

The two-phased learning process (forward-propagation, backward-propagation) is repeated for each input-output pair in the corpus to be learned, and the whole cycle is reiterated until the weights converge.

Although the back-propagation algorithm is significantly more efficient than the Boltzmann algorithm, the computational requirements of both algorithms impose fairly severe constraints on the size of networks. However, these constraints are beginning to be eased as hardware and software advances such as vector-processing machines, parallel processing machines, and special purpose chips become available.

All three of the learning algorithms mentioned here have been used to train networks to perform language-related tasks. In one early experiment Hinton, (1981) used the perceptron convergence procedure to train a network to make semantic associations. More recently, Rumelhart & McClelland, (1986) used it to train a network to produce the past tense of a verb given its base form. In this network, the phonetic features of the base form of a verb were represented by a binary pattern over the input nodes, and the phonetic features of the past tense of the verb were represented by a binary pattern over the output nodes. The network was trained first on the ten most frequent English verbs, of which eight were irregular. After it learned those ten verbs it was trained on an additional set of 410 medium frequency verbs. Finally, the network was tested on 86 low frequency verbs which it had never seen. During training the network passed through the same three stages of past-tense acquisition that children go through. That is, in stage one they correctly produce the past tenses of both regular and irregular verbs. During stage two they overgeneralize, applying regular past tense endings to both regular and irregular verbs, producing such words as 'comed' and 'wented'. This behavior is usually cited as evidence that a past-tense-formation rule has been learned, yet, as McClelland & Rumelhart stress, no rules have been explicitly represented in the network. Rather, the network seems to embody rules implicitly. Finally, in stage three both the children and the network regain the correct use of irregular forms.

The Boltzmann algorithm has been used to create a connectionist parser. Selman (1985) created a network whose nodes represented the syntactic categories of a context-free grammar and trained it so that its equilibrium states at low temperatures represented valid syntactic parses. In addition to the parsing layer, the network also contained an input layer whose nodes represented the terminal symbols of the grammar. An input sentence would activate these units, and they would in turn activate the parsing layer which would settle on a valid parse.

The connectionist model that has received the most attention recently is Rosenberg & Sejnowski's NetTalk (1986). NetTalk is a back propagation network consisting of 203 input nodes, 80 hidden nodes, 23 output nodes, and some 20,000 weighted connections. The input nodes are divided into seven 29-unit groups which represent a window of seven letters of running text. The 23 output units represent the phonetic features of a single letter. As running text is passed through the input window, the task of the network is to produce as output the phonetic translation of the letter that appears in the center window of the input stream. Thus, the three letters on each side of the center window provide some context. The network was trained using the back-propagation algorithm on a corpus of text for which a machine-readable phonetic transcription was available. The text consisted of 1024 words of informal, continuous children's speech. After initial training, the network was tested on a 439 word continuation of the text. It achieved a performance of 78 percent correct output given the novel text as input.

Two other connectionist models that do not fit neatly into the categories of pre-configured and learning networks are Anderson's brain-state-in-a-box model (1983), and Jones & Driscoll's (1985) active production network model of grammatical movement. Anderson's model demonstrates the capacity of connectionist networks for automatic categorization, and Jones & Driscoll's model demonstrates their application to higher order syntactic processes such as subject-auxiliary inversion, WH-movement, and NP holes in relative clauses.

3. SOME PRELIMINARY EXPERIMENTS IN CONNECTIONIST PHRASE GENERATION

This section describes some preliminary experiments aimed at exploring the potential for the acquisition of semantic and syntactic knowledge in a connectionist phrase generation system. The experiments described here are connectionist versions of portions of the ANA report generation system (1983) which was previously implemented in the OPS5 production system language. That system takes half-hourly stock market data as input and produces natural language summaries of the day's activities as output. During processing, production rules create and instantiate intermediate knowledge structures, called messages, which represent semantic content prior to linguistic expression. So for example, if the input data indicated that the market was broadly down at the close of the day, a message with the semantic attribute-value pairs (topic:market-status, time:close, direction:down, degree:nil, and scope:broad) would be created. Further along in processing, other production rules are used to match the semantic attributes of messages to those in a pre-stored phrasal lexicon, thus retrieving the components of a partially formed phrase, such as (topic:market-status, time:close, direction:down, degree:nil, scope:broad, verb-past:'closed', verb-participle:'closing', verb-infinitive:'to close', predicate-remainder:'out the day with a broad decline'). Still later, additional rules decide upon an appropriate syntactic form for the current message, such as simple-sentence or participial clause, depending on the structure of the incomplete complex sentence in focus. The final output of the system is a highly accurate and fluent natural language summary report.

The main shortcoming of the system is the problem inherent in all knowledge-based systems, that of knowledge acquisition. None of ANA's knowledge was acquired automatically; all of the production rules and the phrasal lexicon had to be hand encoded. Samples of human-written stock reports were used as the corpus both for creating the phrasal lexicon and for targeting the message classes that the system must be able to generate. However, given the ability of connectionist networks to automatically learn internal representations, it is worth investigating what portions of the process of report writing a network might be automatically trained to perform. Ideally, we would like to train a network by simply presenting it with the data and the corresponding human-generated natural language reports for a period of a year or so. Once trained, the network could be presented with fresh data and would produce an accurate and fluent original report. Given the scope of the problems involved in text generation, it seems obvious that the number of nodes required to accommodate all of the semantic and linguistic knowledge in a single network would certainly place such a network outside the realm of computational feasibility. As usual, the real problem is one of segmenting the larger task into workable subparts. One possibility would be to limit the task to that of generating phrases for just one of the message classes known to ANA, and that approach was adopted for these experiments.

Included in ANA's phrasal lexicon is a set of 113 phrases for expressing potential semantic messages in the closing market status class. Examples include the phrases 'finished on the minus side', 'posted a sharp loss', 'closed out the day with a broad advance', 'staged a modest rally', 'was swept into a broad and steep decline', 'was catapulted sharply and broadly higher', 'trembled', 'was down', 'wound up settling for a modest gain', etc. Each of these phrases is marked for its semantic attributes. So for example, the phrase 'was catapulted sharply and broadly higher' is marked with the following attribute-value pairs: (verb-type:process, time:nil, direction:up, degree:great, scope:broad, and duration:nil). Similarly, the phrase 'trembled' is marked: (verb-type:process, time:nil, direction:down, degree:great, scope:broad, and duration:nil), and the phrase 'closed down' is marked: (verb-type:process, time:close, direction:down, degree:nil, scope:nil, and duration:nil). In a series of connectionist experiments, the task of recognizing the semantic attributes of the market-status message class and generating appropriate phrases as output was explored. The networks were trained using the back-propagation algorithm and the set of 113 phrasal lexicon entries and their semantic attributes as training pairs. The preliminary results of those experiments are described here.

Even the limited problem of generating phrases for a single class of messages is quite complex. Learning to associate appropriate words or morphemes with specific semantic attributes, or *sememes* as they have been referred to in the linguistic literature, is just one of the subproblems involved. This subproblem is complicated by the need to select morphemes or affixes to take care of such details as verb tense and agreement. Linearizing selected words, morphemes and affixes into syntactically well-formed sequences is another subproblem. All these are further complicated by synonymy and a many-to-many correspondences between sememes and morphemes. For example, the phrases 'was swept into a broad and steep decline' and 'trembled' are synonymous, at least with respect to the sememes in ANA's phrasal lexicon. In the first case there is a partial one-to-one correspondence between sememes and words; the direction attribute maps into the noun 'decline', the scope attribute maps into the adjective 'broad', and the degree attribute maps into the adjective 'steep'. In the second case the mapping is many-to-one; all three attributes map into the verb 'trembled'. Given these complexities, it would seem unlikely that a single network could be trained to sort out all these complexities and recognize the inherent regularities of the domain based on such a small sample of training pairs. But perhaps the sample is large enough to capture the regularities involved in the separate subtasks of associating sememes with morphemes and linearizing morphemes. To test this hypothesis two separate networks were implemented, a sememe-to-morpheme network and a morpheme-ordering network.

4. A SEMEME-TO-MORPHEME NETWORK

A number of sememe-to-morpheme networks were devised and trained. One network which achieved a performance rate of approximately 75 percent acceptable output is described here in detail. Most of the discussion to follow centers on that network because the flaws in its performance were informative. Analysis of those flaws suggested ways to revise and improve the network's behavior, and the results of some of those revisions are briefly discussed also.

The first sememe-to-morpheme network to achieve acceptable output consisted of 168 nodes — 56 input units, 40 hidden units, and 72 output units — with a total of 5,232 weighted links connecting the nodes (56*40 + 40*72 + 40 + 72). The 56 input units formed a vector representing eight semantic attributes in a quasi-distributed fashion which will be described shortly. There were 72 morphemes in the phrases of the training set, including 68 base forms of words such as 'advance', 'high' and 'sharp' and four suffixes such as '-ed', '-er', '-ly' and '-ing'. So the 72 output units formed a vector in which each morpheme was represented locally, i.e., by a single node. The task of the network, given a set of specific sememes as input, was to activate a set of morphemes as output that could comprise an appropriate phrase for the sememes. The order of the morphemes was not relevant for this network. (Imposing valid syntactic order on the morphemes was the task of the network described in the next section.) In fact, morphemes would be read off in alphabetic order as output of this network.

Finding an appropriate encoding to represent input-output patterns to a network is somewhat of an art. This is also true when it comes to determining the optimum number of hidden nodes as well as the optimum range of values for the learning and momentum factors. In this network the number of hidden nodes was arbitrarily set at 40. A similar network with 60 hidden nodes was tried but produced no significant differences in output, but another network with only 12 hidden units did not learn as well. Initially, the momentum factor was kept at .9, and the learning factor was kept under .3 because higher values resulted in oscillation of the error measure. The local encoding scheme chosen for the output was straightforward. Each output node represented a single morpheme, so the target node for a morpheme was turned on if the morpheme occurred in the phrase and left off otherwise. To turn on a target node its value was set at .9; otherwise it remained at 0. Since no phrase consisted of more than 18 morphemes, no more than 18 of the 72 nodes in the target morpheme vector could be activated at one time.

The simplest encoding scheme for the input sememes would make use of a vector comprised of six units, one for each sememe. A numeric value could be chosen for each potential value of each sememe. For example, the direction sememe has two potential values (direction = 'up', 'down'), so 'up' might be encoded as 1 and 'down' might be encoded as 0. The degree sememe has four potential values (degree = 'great', 'moderate', 'small', 'unchanged'), so 'great' might be encoded as 1, 'moderate' as .5, 'small' as .2, and 'unchanged' as .1. In fact, encodings for all values of all six sememes were chosen to fall within the range of 1 to .1 (e.g., 'up'=1, 'down'=.1). But the input encoding was complicated by the fact that the phrases in the training set are not unique with respect to sememe vectors. For example, the phrases 'closed out the day with a modest gain' and 'ended moderately higher' have identical input sememes. This poses a problem for training in that the weights cannot be expected to converge to activate a single set of morphemes if they are receiving contradictory feedback from synonymous phrases with different morphemes. (In an actual trial the network oscillated wildly.) To get around this problem two additional sememes were added to each training pair. These sememes were assigned random values that were kept constant throughout training. Thus, an eight-unit input vector was required. Finally, the input encoding was further complicated by the fact that each sememe was represented not by a single unit but by a group of seven identical units, forming the quasi-distributed representation mentioned earlier. The seven-unit representation was a historical accident, serving no theoretical purpose. Such a representation might have practical value in the situation where redundancy was required in that the performance of the system would degrade gracefully as input units were damaged or lost.

The sememe-to-morpheme net was trained by presenting repeated sweeps of all 113 phrasal lexicon training pairs and applying the back-propagation algorithm to update the weights on every presentation. After 6200 learning sweeps of 113 pairs each, which consumed about five days of continuous processing averaging about 75 percent of a DEC VAX 8600 processor, the weights were converging at rate of less than .0001 point per training sweep, so the training procedure was halted. Then the sememes for each of the 113 phrases were presented to the network. It took 9 seconds of real time for the network to compute and print the output for all 113 input vectors. Examining the output showed that the network had produced a completely accurate choice of morphemes for 75 percent of the input sememes, a partially accurate selection of morphemes for 20 percent, and an inaccurate selection for 5 percent of the input sememes. A closer look at the output and the behavior of the network follows.

First, we examine two instances of actual network input and output in some detail. Given the following input sememes and target morphemes:

(1) Input sememes: verb-type:process, time:nil, direction:up, degree:nil, scope:nil, duration:nil
     Target morphemes: 'advance', '-ed'
     Output morphemes: advance, -ed, (gain, stage)
     The network generated the following activity on the 72 output nodes:
         activation of .8 on the node for 'advance',
         activation of .9 on the node for '-ed',
         activation of .3 on the node for 'stage',
         activation of .2 on the node for 'gain',
         and activation of 0 on all other nodes.

Given another input-target pair:

(2) Input sememes: verb-type:process, time:close, direction:up, degree:nil, scope:broad, duration:nil
     Target morphemes: 'close', '-ed', 'broad', '-ly', 'high', '-er'
     Output morphemes: broad, close, high, -ed, -er, -ly, (advance)
     The network generated the following activity on the 72 output nodes:
         activation of .9 on each of the nodes representing the morphemes 'broad', 'close',
         high', '-ed', '-er', and '-ly',
         activation of .5 on the morpheme for 'advance',
         and activation of zero on all the remaining nodes.

Both of these instances were counted as completely accurate instances of morpheme selection by the network.

Other examples counted as completely accurate include the following (only morphemes whose activation was greater than .75 or between .25 and .75 are mentioned, the latter being shown in parentheses):

(3) Input sememes: verb-type:process, time:nil, direction:up, degree:moderate, scope:nil, and duration:nil
    Target phrase: 'staged a moderate advance'
    Output morphemes: a, gain, modest, post, -ed

(4) Input sememes: verb-type:process, time:close, direction:down, degree:nil, scope:broad, and duration:nil
    Target phrase: 'closed broadly lower'
    Output morphemes: broad, close, day, low, out, the, with, -ed, (-er, -ly)

(5) Input sememes: verb-type:process, time:nil, direction:up, degree:great, scope:nil, and duration:nil
    Target phrase: 'soared'
    Output morphemes: (a, gain), post, sharp, -ed

(6) Input sememes: verb-type:process, time:nil, direction:down degree:great, scope:broad, and duration:nil
    Target phrase: 'trembled'
    Output morphemes: a, and, be, broad, decline, into, -ed, (send, steep, sweep)

(7) Input sememes: verb-type:process, time:nil, direction:up degree:great, scope:broad, and duration:nil
    Target phrase: 'was catapulted sharply and broadly higher'
    Output morphemes: and, be, broad, catapult, sharp, -ed, (high).

The results thus far are encouraging, not only because the network has learned to associate appropriate morphemes with corresponding groups of semantic attributes, but also because there appears to be evidence of synonymy and collocation relations. Synonymy is evidenced in examples (2), (3), (5), and (6) above. In (2), activation for the morpheme 'advance' must come from the same source as activation for the morpheme 'high', presumably from the sememe 'up'. In (3), the target morpheme 'moderate' is clearly synonymous with the activated morpheme 'modest'. Indeed, the two phrases 'staged a moderate advance' and 'posted a modest gain' are synonymous. In (5), the target phrase 'soared' is clearly synonymous with the phrase formed by the activated morphemes 'posted a sharp gain'. And in (6), where the morphemes 'send' and 'sweep' both receive activations of .6, the network seems to recognize the equivalence of those terms in the phrase 'was (sent/swept) into a broad and steep decline'. Furthermore, both versions are synonymous with the phrase 'trembled'.

Collocation relations are apparent in (1) and (4). In (1), it is likely that the activation on the node for the term 'stage' comes from the fact that the network has seen the phrase 'staged an advance' before. Similarly, in (4), although the target phrase is simply 'closed broadly lower', the terms 'out the day' receive activation simply because the network has seen them occur in conjunction with 'closed' so frequently in the phrase 'closed out the day ...'. This phenomenon demonstrates the capacity of the network to exploit its broad bandwidth parallel processing capacity to generate whole phrases non-serially, and to seemingly store and access both whole phrases and their constituent individual morphemes simultaneously.

Roughly 20 percent of the network's output morpheme selections were incomplete. Some examples include the following.

(8) Input sememes: verb-type:process, time:close, direction:down, degree:nil, scope:narrow, and duration:nil
    Target phrase: 'closed out the day with a narrow decline'
    Output morphemes: close, the, -ed, (day, out)

(9) Input sememes: verb-type:process, time:close, direction:up, degree:small, scope:nil, and duration:nil
Target phrase: 'closed out the day with a slight gain'
Output morphemes: a, close, the, -ed, (day, plus, with)

(10) Input sememes: verb-type:process, time:close, direction:down degree:small, scope:nil, and duration:nil
Target phrase: 'closed out the day with a slight loss'
Output morphemes: a, close, day, out, the, with, -ed, (small).

In example (8) neither the sememe 'narrow' nor the sememe 'down' is realized in any of the activated morphemes. Similarly, in (9) the sememe 'small' is overlooked. And in (10) the sememe 'down' is again ignored.

In 5 percent of cases the network appeared to be just plain confused; at least there were no obvious reasons for the poor choices it made. Two examples from this category are the following.

(11) Input sememes: verb-type:process, time:nil, direction:down degree:moderate, scope:nil, and duration:nil Target phrase: 'lost some ground'
Output morphemes: a, gain, loss, post, -ed

(12) Input sememes: verb-type:process, time:nil, direction:down degree:nil, scope:broad, and duration:nil
Target phrase: 'slipped into a broad decline'
Output morphemes: a, advance, broad, decline, out, the, with, -ed, (close, suffer).

One hypothesis for the network's failures may be that the input encoding scheme did not facilitate learning. The sememes 'narrow', down', and small' were all represented by .1 values on the input nodes. It may be that .1 is not sufficiently distinguishable from 0, which is the value used to encode 'nil' for a given attribute, thus leading the network to conflate the two. This suggests that a more effective encoding scheme might use values of -1 and 1 rather than 0 and 1 for input. When -1 and 1 encoding scheme was tried using a local representation of 8 nodes for input instead of 56 the network displayed a significant improvement in learning. Furthermore, this new scheme made it possible to increase the value of eta to .5 and decrease the value of alpha to .1, thus reducing the number of cycles needed to converge to about 2500 without leading to oscillation. But the tightest learning was achieved using an encoding of -1 and 1 on an input vector of 16 nodes. Under this encoding each value (e.g., 'up', 'down', 'great', 'moderate', 'small', 'unchanged', 'broad', 'narrow', etc.) was represented by a single node. When 'down' was set to 1, 'up' was set to -1 and vice versa, and 0 was reserved for the value 'nil'. Given this encoding scheme and configuration the network converged in under 1500 cycles and produced nearly flawless output. No synonym substitutions were made and only nine morphemes were missed out of the total of 674 morphemes in the training phrases.

5. A MORPHEME-TO-PHRASE NETWORK

In another set of experiments the capacity for a network to learn to linearize morphemes into valid syntactic strings was explored. Once again, the back-propagation algorithm and the 113 phrasal lexicon pairs were used to train a network. In this case, the morphemes that appeared in each phrase were presented to the network in alphabetical order, and the network's task was to output those morphemes in valid syntactic order. As was the case in the previous experiments, the networks that did not achieve flawless performance were informative. The details of one partially successful morpheme-to-phrase network and a brief description of one wholly successful network follow.

The same local representation of 72 morpheme nodes that served as output of the previous network served as input to this network. For output, some representation scheme had to be devised to capture both the identity and the position of each morpheme in a phrase. One straightforward way to accomplish that would be to use a local encoding scheme consisting of 18 times 72, or 1296 units. (No phrase was longer than 18 morphemes.) Each sequential bank of 72 units would represent one morpheme position in an output phrase; only one unit in each bank would be turned on to represent the target morpheme for that position. However, this scheme was initially rejected due to its processing time requirements. A network this size, 72 input nodes by 80 hidden nodes by 1296 output nodes, would contain 110,816 weights. That is about 20 times the size of the sememe networks of the previous experiments, and those smaller networks had been taking five days of processor time to converge. So a number of smaller networks based on distributed representation schemes were tried. After a few different schemes were tried and failed, a somewhat arbitrary distributed representational scheme succeeded in generating some interesting results. In that scheme 18 groups of 7 units each, for a total of 126 output nodes, were used. Each 7-unit group represented a single morpheme, and a morpheme's sequential position in a phrase was indicated by its sequential position in the array of 18 groups. Seven units were required to assign a unique binary code to each of the 72 morphemes. The particular code assigned to an individual morpheme was simply the binary equivalent of the morpheme's ordinal number after alphabetic sorting. As in the case of the poor choice of encoding for sememes, this arbitrary choice of codes for morphemes had some unhealthy but interesting consequences.

When one of the phrasal lexicon entries was presented to the network for training, the input nodes corresponding to the morphemes that appeared in the phrase were activated with values of .9. The remaining input nodes were left at zero. At the same time, the target array to be used for comparison was instantiated with values of .9 and 0 according to the binary code for each morpheme in the phrase. So for example, the phrase 'closed broadly higher', contains the following morphemes which are shown with their ordinal numbers and binary codes:

```
close 8 0001000
-ed 67 1000011
broad 5 0000101
-ly 70 1000110
high 21 0010101
-er 68 1000100
```

This phrase would result in the instantiation of the following target array:
000.9000 .90000.9.9 0000.90.9 .9000.9.90 00.90.90.9 .9000.900 0000000 0000000 0000000 000...

In addition to the 72 input nodes and 126 output nodes, the morpheme-to-phrase network also contained 60 hidden nodes yielding 12,066 weighted connections. It was trained using an eta value of .2 and an alpha value of .9. After a training period of 5000 sweeps of 113 training pairs each the network had achieved a performance of 100 percent perfect output for noiseless input. Noiseless input means that input activation levels consisted of only .9's and zeros, as in training. So for example, the following input-output morphemes were observed:

(13) Input morphemes: be up -ed
    Output phrase: be -ed up

(14) Input morphemes: be downhill push -ed
    Output phrase: be -ed push -ed downhill

(15) Input morphemes: and be broad catapult high sharp -ed -er -ly
    Output phrase: be -ed catapult -ed sharp -ly and broad -ly high -er.

This network was then tested using the morpheme activation output from the sememe-to-morpheme network. Recall that the output of the sememe-to-morpheme network was noisy in that perfect activation levels of .9 were not always achieved and extra morpheme nodes sometimes received activation while target morphemes nodes sometimes received little or no activation. In response to this input, the morpheme-to-phrase net produced 25 syntactically well-formed responses and 35 nearly well-formed responses. 14 responses were semantically inverted and the remaining 39 responses were garbled.

The following examples demonstrate the network's capacity to generate semantically well-formed phrases under noisy input conditions.

(16) Input morphemes: advance -ed (gain stage)
Output phrase: advanced -ed

(17) Input morphemes: a lose -ed
Output phrase: post -ed a lose

(18) Input morphemes: a close day out the with -ed (small)
Output phrase: close -ed out the day with a small decline.

Example (6) demonstrates the network's ability to filter out unnecessary input. Examples (17) and (18) demonstrate its ability to compensate for missing and weak input. In (17), although there was no activation on the input node for the morpheme 'post', that morpheme was generated as output to complete the phrase. In (18), the morpheme 'small' is generated despite the fact that its input activation was low, and somewhat more mysteriously, the critical term 'decline' was supplied despite the fact that there was no activation for it at all.

The partially formed output samples provide some insight into the arbitrary encoding scheme.

(19) Input morphemes: a close day out the with -ed (heavy lose sharp)
Output phrase: close -ed out the day with a and lose

(20) Input morphemes: post sharp -ed (a gain)
Output phrase: post -ed a downhill gain.

The use of the word 'and' in the adjective position in 19) is a conspicious error. Given that the morphemes 'heavy' and 'sharp' both received some activation on input, one would like to see either of the phrases 'a heavy loss' or 'a sharp loss' generated as output. The source of the error becomes apparent when one examines the binary codes for the terms 'heavy', 'sharp', and 'and', which are 0010100, 0101100 and 0000100 respectively. In order to generate the morpheme 'heavy' the network would have needed to generate sufficient activation on both the 4 bit and the 16 bit. Similarly, in order to generate the morpheme 'sharp' the network would have had to generate sufficient activation on the 4 bit, the 8 bit and the 32 bit. But because the network was receiving weak input activation on both terms, there was only enough strength to turn on the 4 bit, which is in fact the binary code for the morpheme 'and'.

A similar error occurred in 20). The phrase 'downhill gain' is anomalous. In fact, what is wanted is the phrase 'sharp gain', but because the binary code for 'sharp' is 0101100 and the binary code for 'downhill' is 0001100, the error was a matter of one unflipped bit. These errors suggest that an encoding scheme with more hamming distance between terms is desirable. But what is really needed is an encoding scheme that captures some of the semantic and linguistic categories of the terms, so that if an error is made the resultant term is still within the same semantic or linguistic category. Furthermore, it would be nice if such an encoding scheme could be learned by the system rather than manually designed. This is perhaps the most interesting open research problem related to this work.

One example of a semantic inversion made by the network is the following:

21) Input morphemes: a advance gain -ed
Output phrase: produce -ed a lose.

This error may (or may not) be related to the fact that the binary code for the morpheme 'lose' turns on the 16 bit and the 8 bit and the binary code for the morpheme 'gain' turns on the 16 bit and the 1 bit, but the binary code for the morpheme 'advance' turns on only the 2 bit, so who knows what the network was doing here.

Examples of some seemingly aphasic output include the following:

(22) Input morphemes: a and be broad decline into -ed (send sweep)
Output phrase: be -ed a -ed catapult a and and broad close

(23) Input morphemes: and be broad catapult sharp -ed (high)
Output phrase: be -ed advance yet and and broad and gain.

The simplest alternative to the arbitrary distributed encoding problem would be to use the 1296 unit local encoding scheme described earlier. This was actually tried when additional processing power became available. A Convex vector processing machine provided a factor of 10 speedup of the network training programs (with no changes to the code whatsoever). So the local encoding network described earlier was configured and trained. It achieved perfect output for noiseless input in under 1500 cycles. When given noisy input, the local encoding network did not make any of the arbitrary substitution errors made by the distributed encoding network. Like the distributed encdong network, it did filter out extraneous input morphemes, but unlike the distributed encoding network, the local encoding network did not supply missing morphemes to complete a phrase. Further analysis is required to determine what accounts for this difference.

6. CONCLUSIONS

The behavior of the networks described here are encouraging, particularly the ability of the sememe-to-morpheme network to learn synonym classes and collocations and the ability of the morpheme-to-phrase net to learn word order. But the experiments reported here are very preliminary. They serve to help define some of the problems for future research in connectionist text generation. Some follow-up experiments suggested by these experiments include:

(a) training the morpheme-to-phrase network on noisy data,
(b) experimenting with better encoding schemes for sememes and morphemes,
(c) training a network to learn an encoding schemes for sememe and morphemes,
(d) implementing a data-to-morpheme network.

Although connectionist research in general is in its infancy, the virtues of the connectionist paradigm make it a viable methodology for exploring many of the problems of text generation.

ACKNOWLEDGEMENTS

This work was inspired by the works of Hopfield, Hinton, Sejnowski and Rosenberg. It was greatly facilitated by the resources at Bellcore, by the helpful discussions my colleagues there provided, especially Steve Hanson, Bob Allen, David Burr, Tom Landauer, Josh Alspector, Louis Gomez, Scott Deerwester and David Copp, and by the support of my managers, Don Walker and Michael Lesk.

REFERENCES

Ackley, D.H., Hinton, G.E. & Sejnowski, T.J. (1985) A Learning Algorithm for Boltzmann Machines. *Cognitive Science, 9*, 147-169.

Anderson, J.A. (1983) Cognitive and Psychological Computation with Neural Models. *IEEE Transactions on Systems, Man and Cybernetics, 13*, 799-815.

Appelt, D.E. (1983) TELEGRAM In: *Proceedings of the 21st Annual Meeting of the Association for Computational Linguistics*. Cambridge, Mass.

Becker, J. (1975) The Phrasal Lexicon. In: *Proceedings of the Conference on Theoretical Issues in Natural Language Processing (TINLAP Workshop)*. Cambridge, Mass.

Bienkowski, M.A. (1986) *A Computational Model for Extemporaneous Elaborations*. CSL Report 1. Cognitive Science Laboratory, Princeton University.

Bock, J.K. (1982) Towards a cognitive psychology of syntax. *Psychological Review, 89*, 1-47.

Conklin, E.J. & McDonald, D.D. (1982) Salience as a Simplifying Metaphor for Natural Language Generation. In: *Proceedings of the National Conference on Artificial Intelligence —AAAI-82*. Pittsburgh, Pennsylvania.

Cumming, S. (1986) The Lexicon in Text Generation. In: *Proceedings of the First International Workshop on Automating the Lexicon*. Pisa.

Danlos, L. (1984) Conceptual and Linguistic Decisions in Generation. In: *Proceedings of the 10th International Conference on Computational Linguistics*. Stanford.

Dell, G.S. (1985) Positive Feedback in Hierarchical Connectionist Models. Applications to Language Production. *Cognitive Science, 9*, 3-23.

Feldman, J.A. & Ballard, D.H. (1982) Connectionist Models and their Properties. *Cognitive Science, 6*, 205-254.

Gigley, H.M. (1983) HOPE — AI and the Dynamic Process of Language Behavior. *Cognition and Brain Theory, 6*, 39-87.

Hinton, G.E. & Sejnowski, T.J. (1986) *Learning and Relearning in Boltzmann Machines*. In: J.L. McClelland & D.E. Rumelhart (Eds.) *Parallel Distributed Processing: Explorations in the Microstructure of Cognition, Volume 1*. Cambridge, Mass.:MIT Press.

Hinton, G.E. (1981) Implementing Semantic Networks in Parallel Hardware. In: G.E. Hinton & J.A. Anderson (Eds.) *Parallel Models of Associative Memory*. Hillsdale: Erlbaum.

Hinton, G.E. & Sejnowski, T.J. (1985) A Learning Algorithm for Boltzmann Machines. *Cognitive Science, 9*, 147-169.

Hopfield, J.J. (1982) Neural networks and physical systems with emergent collective computational abilities.In: *Proceedings of the National Academy of Sciences, Biophysics 79*, 2554-2558.

Hovy, E.H. (1985) Integrating Text Planning and Production in Generation. In: *Proceedings of the National Conference on Artificial Intelligence — AAAI-85*. Los Angeles, California.

Jacobs, P. (1985) PHRED: A Generator for Natural Language Interfaces. In: *Computational Linguistics, 11*, 219-242.

Jones, M.A. & Driscoll, A. (1985) Movement in Active Production Networks. In: *Proceedings of the 23rd Annual Meeting of the Association for Computational Linguistics*, Chicago.

Kempen, G. (1977) Conceptualizing and Formulating in Sentence Production. In: S. Rosenberg (Ed.) *Sentence Production: Developments in Research and Theory* . Hillsdale: NJ, Lawrence Erlbaum.

Kempen, G. & Hoenkamp, E. (forthcoming) An Incremental Procedural Grammar for Sentence Formulation. *Cognitive Science*.

Kukich, K. (1983) The Design of a Knowledge-Based Report Generator. In: *Proceedings of the 21st Annual Meeting of the Association for Computational Linguistics*. Cambridge, Mass.

Kukich, K. (1983) *Knowledge-Based Report Generation: A Knowledge Engineering Approach to Natural Language Report Generation*. Doctoral Dissertation, University of Pittsburgh.

Kukich, K. (1985) The Feasibility of Automatic Natural Language Report Generation. In: *Proceedings of the Eighteenth Hawaii International Conference on System Sciences*.

Kukich, K. (in press) Fluency in Natural Language Reports. In: L. Bolc & D. McDonald (Eds.) *Natural Language Generation Systems*. Berlin: Springer.

Mann, W.C. (1983) An Overview of the Nigel Text Generation Grammar. In: *Proceedings of the 21st Annual Meeting of the Association for Computational Linguistics*. Cambridge, Mass.

McClelland, J.L. & Rumelhart, D.E. (1981) An Interactive Activation Model of Context Effects in Letter Perception. *Psychological Review, 88*, 375-407.

McDonald, D.D. (1981) Language Production. In: *Proceedings of the 19th Annual meeting of the Association for Computational Linguistics*.

McKeown, K.R. (1982) *Generating Natural Language Text in Response to Questions about Datastructure*. Ph.D. Thesis, University of Pennsylvania, Computer and Information Science Department.

Minsky, M. & Papert, S. (1969) *Perceptrons*. Cambridge, Mass.: MIT Press.

Reilly, R.G. (1984) A Connectionist Model of Some Aspects of Anaphor Resolution. In: *Proceedings of the 10th International Conference on Computational Linguistics,* Stanford.

Rumelhart, D.E., Hinton, G.E. & Williams, R.J. (1986) Learning Internal Representations by Error Propagation. In: J.L. McClelland & D.E. Rumelhart (Eds.) *Parallel Distributed Processing: Explorations in the Microstructure of Cognition*. Cambridge, Mass.: MIT Press.

Rumelhart, D.E. & McClelland, J.L. (1982) An Interactive Activation Model of Context Effects in Letter Perception. *Psychological Review, 89*, 60-94.

Rumelhart, D.E. & McClelland, J.L. (1986) On Learning the Past Tenses of English Verbs. In: J.L. McClelland & D.E. Rumelhart (Eds.) *Parallel Distributed Processing: Explorations in the Microstructure of Cognition*. Cambridge, Mass.: MIT Press.

Sejnowski, T.J. & Rosenberg, C.R. (1986) *NETtalk: A Parallel Network that Learns to Read Aloud*. Technical Report JHU/EECS-86/01. The Johns Hopkins University Electrical Engineering and Computer Science Department, Baltimore MD.

Selman, B. (1985) *Rule-Based Processing in a Connectionist System for Natural Language Understanding*. *CSRI-168* Computer Systems Research Institute, University of Toronto. Toronto, Canada.

Waltz, D.L. & Pollack, J.B. (1985) Massively Parallel Parsing. *Cognitive Science, 9*, 51-74.

Chapter 27

THE GENERATION OF TENSE

Veronika Ehrich

TABLE OF CONTENTS

1. Introduction
2. Types of temporal meaning and temporal expressions
3. Interactions between temporal expressions
3.1 Lexical aspect and tense
3.2 Interactions between tense and adverbs
3.3 Temporal adverbs and inherent aspect
4. The generation of tense in simple sentences

1. INTRODUCTION

In this chapter I am concerned with the question of how speakers convey temporal meaning in actual speech. More specifically, I will be dealing with speakers' choice of tense forms contributing appropriately to the linguistic formulation of the intended message. Although tense marking of the verb is obligatory in all Indo-European languages, tense is not the only linguistic means for conveying temporal information in these languages, nor is the meaning of the tenses the only type of temporal information contributing to the temporal reference of an utterance. Therefore, I will first present an overview of different types or categories of temporal meaning and relate these to certain categories of linguistic expressions (Section 1). In Section 2, I will present some observations about the interaction between tense, lexical aspect and temporal adverbs in German. Finally, in Section 3, I will discuss some of the constraints that these interactions impose on a language production system which is functioning at well-defined levels of processing (conceptual, functional, positional) and is characterized by specific processing properties like modularity, incrementality and linearity.

2. TYPES OF TEMPORAL MEANING AND TEMPORAL EXPRESSIONS

Temporal information is information about situations. Situations can belong to different *categories*, they can be seen from different points of view, or *aspects*, they bear different *relations* to each other, and they occupy certain *positions* within a given frame of reference.

(i) *Category*. A given situation can be seen as an activity or a state, an act or an event, an action or a process. Activities and states span extended periods in time and do not lead to specific results. They are temporally open, or 'unbound'. Acts and events may or may not lead to results, they do not span extended periods in time but are condensed to just one point 'in time'. Actions and processes span extended, but closed periods in time and are defined by the resultant states to which they lead. The main parameters for categorial distinctions of situations are durativity (+DUR), resultativity (+RES) and intentionality (+INT; cf. Figure 1).

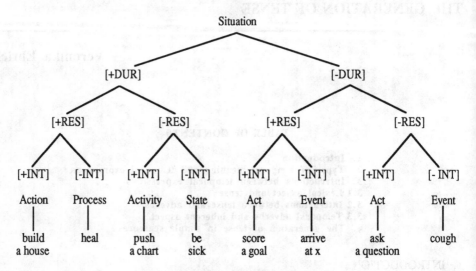

Figure 1. Categories of Situations

(ii) *Aspect*. A situation can be seen from the inside or from the outside. The internal perspective presents the view of the participant involved in some ongoing state of affairs of which he grasps only a partial view 'on line'. The external perspective presents a given situation as a whole with its beginning, progress and end. Seen from an internal point of view a situation is ascribed duration whereas seen from an external point of view, a situation is seen as temporally closed. Both categorial and aspectual information are about duration and temporal closure. And in both cases this information is dependent on the perspective from which a given situation is seen. Categorial information, however, represents a conventionally frozen or 'canonical' perspective, whereas aspectual information represents the actual and sometimes even personal perspective.

(iii) *Relation*. A given situation e may precede or succeed, overlap or coincide with a second situation e' ($e<e'$; $e>e'$, $e\infty e'$; e,e'). Temporal precedence and overlap can be taken as basic relations that hold between situations (as in Kamp's, 1979, theory) or they can be based on the part/whole relationship ('$\sqsubset$') which hold between connected regions (as in recent proposals by Bartsch, 1983,1985).

(iv) A situation can be assigned a *position*, which definitely locates it within a given frame of reference like the calender system. The '23rd of August' opens a definite slot within which a certain event (e.g. my departure to France) is to be located.

Situations have internal and external properties. Internal properties determine the situation type e, they specify the participants $x_1...x_n$ involved in e and the relation F holding between them. External properties determine the space/time region or 'location' L being covered by the situation in question.

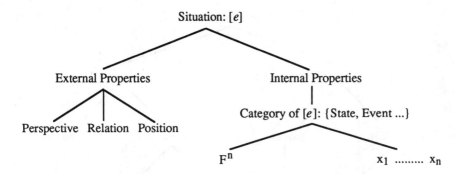

Figure 2. External and Internal Properties of Situations

Relational and positional information is information about the temporal location of a given situation. Duration and closure of situations (conveyed by categorial and perspectival information) are usually not seen as strictly temporal properties. They do, however, determine the relational potential of a given situation. For instance, if e is an act or an event, that is, if e is nondurative and temporally closed, whereas e' is an activity or a state and thus durative and temporally open, then e' may include e but not vice versa. Moreover, since open situations *per definitionem* do not have beginnings or ends, it is impossible to order them with respect to other situations in terms of temporal precedence or succession.

In Germanic languages, categorial distinctions are lexically encoded as parts of the inherent word meaning of verbs, the so-called 'lexical' or 'inherent' aspect (*Aktionsarten* in terms of traditional grammar). We can distinguish four of them: *durative verbs* denoting activities and states, *durative-resultative verbs* denoting actions and processes (Vendler's, 1967, accomplishments), *resultative verbs* denoting non-durative acts and events, which lead to certain results (Vendler's achievements), and *semelfactive verbs* denoting nondurative and nonresultative acts and events.

Aspectual information is morphologically encoded by *aspect markers* on the verb. The *imperfective aspect* gives expression to the internal perspective, whereas the *perfective aspect* encodes the external perspective (cf. Comrie, 1976).

Relational information is also morphologically encoded, by tense morphemes or particles attached to the verb. Tense temporally relates the situation e denoted by the verb to the speaking event u. If e precedes u, the verb will be marked by a Past Tense morpheme, if u precedes e a Future Tense will be chosen, if neither e precedes u nor vice-versa, we get a Present Tense marker on the verb (which may be ø).

The position of situations is referred to by temporal adverbs like *on the 23rd of August*. The calender system referred to by this expression is, of course, not the only frame of reference which may locate a given event. Actually, speakers often make use of a more implicit (contextually bound) frame of reference, either set up by previous discourse and referred to by anaphors or by the discourse situation being referred to by deictics. Accordingly, one can distinguish the following subcategories of temporal adverbs (cf. Figure 3): calendarics vs. non-calendarics, indexicals vs. non-indexicals, deictics vs. anaphors. (For different sub-categorizations of temporal adverbs, see Kamp & Rohrer, 1983; Oversteegen, 1987; Smith, 1980, 1981.)

Figure 4 is a schema of the form/meaning relationship for verbs in German. This schema is oversimplified in several respects:

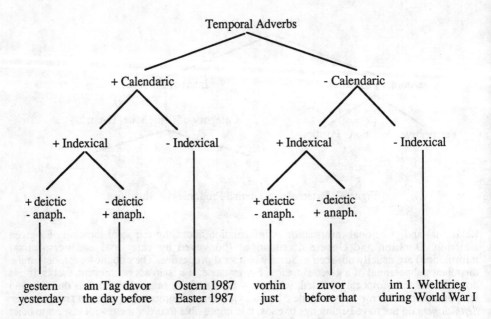

Figure 3. Subcategorization of Temporal Adverbs

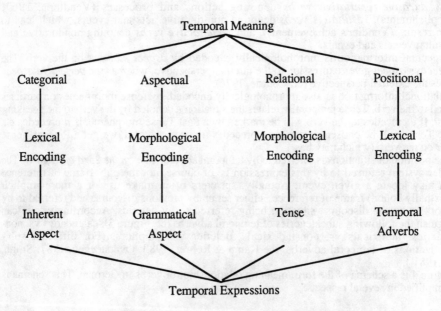

Figure 4. The Form/Meaning Relationship for Verbs (in German)

1. Lexical aspect can be encoded grammatically through the selection of certain function words within a verb phrase. It has often been noted (Verkuyl, 1972; Ullmer-Ehrich, 1977; Dowty, 1979) that what is called 'lexical' aspect very often depends on the nominal complement of the verb and is thus grammatical in nature. Thus, *eat* is an activity word [+DUR,-RES] but *eat the cake* is an action word [+DUR, +RES], whereas *eat cake* again denotes an activity.

(1) a. He has been eating for hours
     b. He has been eating the cake for hours
     c. He has been eating cake for hours

These observations seem to indicate that we are dealing not just with strictly lexical properties of verbs but with semantic properties of full verb phrases being generated by the lexical meaning of the constituent verbs on the one hand in combination with the grammatical meaning of function words such as prepositions and quantifiers on the other hand.

2. Aspect and Tense are not always encoded by different morphemes. In fact, it is one of the central assumptions of the present chapter that, as far as German is concerned, aspect and tense converge in the verb inflection. For instance, the Present Perfect denotes a previous situation, as does the Past Tense, cf. (2) and (3):

(2) Hans ist zurückgekommen
     John has come back

(3) Hans kam zurück
     John came back

However, if referred to by the Present Perfect, the situation in question is seen as having an impact on the present state of affairs, which is why inference (2') holds.

(2') Hans ist zurückgekommen   Hans ist zurück
$$\supset$$
      John has come back   John is back

The Past Tense is not bound to the present in this way. Accordingly, an inference corresponding to the one in (2') cannot be drawn.

(3') Hans kam zurück   Hans ist zurück
$$\not\supset$$
      John came back   John is back

In other words, Perfect and Past express different views of a given situation, or, to put it differently, they express different 'aspects'. The Past Tense regards a previous event from an internal point of view, the Present Perfect takes an external point of view in binding a previous situation to the state of affairs resulting out of it.

3. The relation between some event e and the speaking event u is not the only relevant temporal relation. In coherent discourse, one usually speaks about more than just one event. Hence, speakers also have to specify the temporal relations holding between various narrated events. We will thus distinguish two kinds of temporal relations, (i) the deictic relation between a narrated event e_j and the speaking event u, (ii) the anaphoric relation between two (or more) narrated events e_j and e_i (cf. Figure 5).

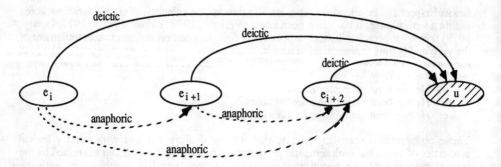

Figure 5. Deictic (——) and anaphoric (------) temporal relations

3. INTERACTIONS BETWEEN TEMPORAL EXPRESSIONS

At both sentence and discourse levels, different types of temporal information interact with each other in conveying the temporal reference of an utterance. I will first outline some of these interactions and then try to draw some consequences for models of language generation.

3.1 Lexical aspect and tense

Lexical properties, whether defining the Aktionsarten inherent to verbs ('lexical aspect') or generated as parts of verb phrase meanings, have important effects on how grammatical tense is to be interpreted. The Present Tense in each of the sentences (4) through (6) can be considered as referring to some time span which includes the time of speaking. In (4), however, the Present Tense has a second interpretation, which probably is the preferred one. In this interpretation, the Present Tense refers to the future.

(4) a. John is coming to Nijmegen
                                                   [-DUR, +RES]
     b. Mary is leaving Paris

(5) a. The baby is crying
                                                   [+DUR, -RES]
     b. The bell is ringing

(6) a. Mary is writing a letter
                                                   [+DUR, +RES]
     b. John is knitting a sweater

These differences in tense and aspect interpretation have consequences with espect to the choice of temporal adverbs: (4), for instance, allows for adverbial attributes with future time reference, whereas (5) and (6) do not.

(4') a.   John is coming to Nijmegen next week
      b.   Mary is leaving Paris quite soon
(5') a. * The baby is crying soon
      b. * The bell is ringing soon
(6') a. * Mary is writing a letter tomorrow
      b. * John is knitting a sweater next week

A language like German, which does not have an obligatory Imperfective Aspect marking, shows similar distinctions. The Present Tense of the resultative, nondurative verbs in (7) is ambiguous between a 'present' and a 'future' reading, the latter probably being the preferred one here, too. The sentences in (8), on the other hand, do not have a future reading.

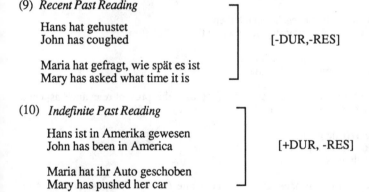

(7) a.   Hans kommt nach Nijmegen·
          John comes to Nijmegen

     b.   Ich schicke Maria ein Päckchen   [-DUR,+ RES]
          I am sending Mary a parcel

     c.   Du verlierst deinen Schlüssel
          You lose your key
          You are losing your key

(8) a.   Das Baby weint
          The baby is crying

     b.   Es klingelt   [+DUR,-RES]
          (The bell) is ringing

     c.   Hans schläft
          John is sleeping

In spoken German, unlike English, reference to past events is usually encoded with the Present Perfect. Depending on the durativity of the verb, however, the Perfect is to be interpreted as recent past (9) or as indefinite past (10).

(9) *Recent Past Reading*

     Hans hat gehustet
     John has coughed   [-DUR,-RES]

     Maria hat gefragt, wie spät es ist
     Mary has asked what time it is

(10) *Indefinite Past Reading*

     Hans ist in Amerika gewesen
     John has been in America   [+DUR, -RES]

     Maria hat ihr Auto geschoben
     Mary has pushed her car

In traditional grammar, the meaning of the Present Perfect is analyzed in terms of 'completion' ('Vollendete Gegenwart'), which is to say that a situation referred to by means of the Present Perfect is understood as being completed by the time the utterance takes place. Comrie argues against this position, pointing to the fact that the Present Perfect may be used with reference even to future events. According to his own analysis, the Present Perfect expresses 'Present Relevance'. I would like to suggest a combination of both analyses: The Present Perfect expresses completion *and* present relevance. Completion of a given situation is related to some reference point r, and r may coincide either with the speaking event u or with that situation e' which results from the completion of e. In other words, 'present relevance' can be given either directly (by coincidence of r and u) or indirectly by coincidence of r and e' with inclusion of u in e'.

The latter case is instantiated by the Present Perfect of resultative verbs (cf. 11):

(11) *Present State Reading*

    a. Maria hat Hans geheiratet   [-DUR,+RES]
    b. Maria hat den Brief geschrieben   [+DUR,+RES]

In these cases, the Present Perfect does not necessarily refer to a recent past. All that is required is that the resulting state *e'* still holds. Hence, (11a) would be inappropriate if Mary had divorced John before the time at which the utterance was made.

3.2 Interactions between tense and adverbs

In German, Temporal Adverbs may shift the basic temporal meaning of a given tense. The Present Tense, for instance, may be used with reference to the future irrespective of the inherent aspect of the verb, provided that the verb is temporally specified by an adverb with appropriate temporal reference. The German analogues to the anomalous English examples above (5'a, 6'a) are therefore perfectly acceptable (cf. 12-13).

(12)   Das Baby weint gleich   (+DUR,-RES)
(13)   Maria schreibt den Brief morgen   (+DUR,+RES)

Similarly, the Present Perfect may be used in reference to either a past or a future event. Sentence (14a) has two different interpretations, (14b, c) accordingly. Sentence (14b) refers to a future, (14c) to a past event.

(14) a. Maria hat den Brief gleich geschrieben
        Mary has written the letter immediately

      b. Maria wird den Brief gleich geschrieben haben
        Mary will have written the letter in just a moment

      c. Maria schrieb den Brief gleich (nachdem...)
        Mary wrote the letter immediately (after...)

In combination with anterior adverbs, the Present Perfect loses the 'present relevance' aspect of its meaning but keeps the completion aspect (cf. 15-17):

(15)   Hans hat vorige Woche gehustet
(16)   Hans ist 1969 in Amerika gewesen
(17)   Hans hat 1972 geheiratet

The past referred to by (15) is not necessarily a recent one (cf. 9). The past of (16) is not indefinite, but definite (cf. 10). Because of the durativity of the verb, however, it remains indeterminate, whether John spent all of 1969 in America or only part of the year. (17) assigns a definite period in time to the event *e* of Mary's marriage with John (cf. 11). Because of the nondurativity of the verb, it is clear that *e* does not span *over*, but only falls *into* that period. But it is left open whether, at utterance time, the state *e'* resulting from *e* still holds or not. The bare Perfect (11-13) binds event time (E) to speaking time (S). Temporal Adverbs suspend this binding and link E directly to a position T within a given frame of reference.

Temporal Adverbials subcategorize into deictics and anaphorics (see Figure 3 above). Strict deictics like *tomorrow*, *a week ago*, *in an hour* must be connected to either the actual speaking event, as in (18), or to some fictitious speaking event, as in (19) (so-called 'inner speech').

(18)   Mary is coming tomorrow

(19)   John cleaned the house. Mary was coming tomorrow and would be upset about the mess otherwise.

Anaphorics like *the following day, a week before that* or *after an hour* cannot be bound by the speaking event (20a) but must be linked to some reference point in previous discourse (20b); they may, however, replace deictics in inner speech (21) (so-called 'Erlebte Rede').

(20)   a. * Mary is coming back the following day.
      b.   John cleaned the house. The following day, Mary came back and was quite pleased.
(21)   John cleaned the house. Mary was coming the following day and would be upset about the mess otherwise.

Certain adverbs can be used in either way, as deictics or as anaphorics. There is, however, a restriction as to the tense with which they combine in different uses. German *bald* ('soon'), for instance, in combination with the Present Tense or the Present Perfect (22, 23), only permits a deictic interpretation and denotes a time posterior to the speaking time in this interpretation.

(22)   John kommt bald
        John comes soon

        John wird bald kommen
        John will come soon

(23)   Maria hat das Problem bald gelöst
        Mary has solved the problem soon

        Maria wird das Problem bald gelöst haben
        Mary will soon have solved the problem

In combination with the Past Tense or the Past Perfect, however, *bald* can only have an anaphoric interpretation, and in this case it denotes a time which is posterior to some previously introduced reference time *r* but still lies in the past, seen from the point of view of the speaking event. Wich is why the equivalences stated in (22) and (23) do not have analogues in (24) and (25).

(24)   ...*r*   Hans kam bald
            Hans wird bald kommen

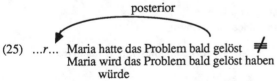

(25)   ...*r*... Maria hatte das Problem bald gelöst
           Maria wird das Problem bald gelöst haben
           würde

3.3 Temporal adverbs and inherent aspect

Different adverbs also bear different restrictions on the inherent aspect of the verb with which they combine. *Gestern* combines with any Aktionsart, but *zur Zeit* combines only with duratives and semelfactives, which then get an iterative reading:

(26) a.   Hans arbeitet zur Zeit
           John is working at present

      b.   Maria löst das Problem zur Zeit
           Mary is solving the problem at present

      c.   Hans hustet zur Zeit (iterative)
           John is coughing at present

      d. * Maria kommt zur Zeit an
           Mary is arriving at present

Heute, again, combines with any Aktionsart. However, the Present Tense in combination with *heute* not only may but must be interpreted as 'future' for resultative verbs, whereas it has to be understood as 'present' if the verb is nondurative.

(27) a. Hans kommt heute

          John is coming today   (S < E)

      b. Maria schreibt den Brief heute
                                                       (S < E)
          Mary is writing the letter today

(28) a. Hans arbeitet heute
                                                       (S,E)
          John is working today

      b. Hans hustet heute
                                                       (S,E iterative)
          John is coughing today

Seit can combine with the Present or Past Tense of nonresultative verbs only.

(29) a. Das Baby weint(e) seit dem Mittag
          The baby has (had) been crying since noon

      b. Maria schreibt (schrieb) seit dem Morgen an dem Brief
          Mary has (had) been writing on the letter since this morning

(30) a. * Hans kommt seit einer Minute
          John has been coming for a minute

      b. * Maria schreibt den Brief seit dem Morgen
          Mary has been writing the letter since this morning

However, together with the Present Perfect, *seit* + *x* also combines with resultatives:

(31) a. Maria hat den Brief seit einer Woche geschrieben
          Mary has had the letter written for a week

      b. Hans hat den Gipfel seit gestern erreicht
          John has been at the summit since yesterday

In this case, the adverbial temporally specifies the state which results from the event denoted by the verb. This can also be achieved by direct reference to the result in question:

(32) a. Der Brief ist seit einer Woche geschrieben
         The letter has been written for a week

      b. Der Gipfel ist seit gestern erreicht
         The summit has been reached since yesterday

In (32a, b) the main verb has the form of a so-called 'state passive' (*Zustandspassiv*). Actually, the combination of *seit* + *x* with a Present Perfect resultative verb is only possible if the verb in question has a state passive.

(33) a. * Hans hat Maria seit einem Monat *ge*heiratet
      b. * Maria ist seit einem Monat *ge*heiratet
      c.   Maria ist seit einem Monat *ver*heiratet

(34) a. * Ich habe dir das Buch seit einer Woche gegeben
         I have had the book given to you for a week

      b. * Das Buch ist dir seit einer Woche gegeben
         The book has been given to you for a week

4. THE GENERATION OF TENSE IN SIMPLE SENTENCES

Language generation theories conceive of human speech as the output of a highly specialized information system which has certain processing characteristics and is functioning at various well-defined levels of representation. Like any information processing system it can be designed in various ways, that is with different built-in processing characteristics (cf. Figure 6). It can be either (i) modular or interactive, (ii) sequential or discontinuous, (iii) serial or parallel, (iv) linear or projective. A system is modular (Figure 6A) if no level-n-information is input to level n-i, interactive otherwise. A system is sequential if no level-n-information is passed over to a non-adjacent level n + i (with i $\geq$ 2), discontinuous otherwise (Figure 6B). A system is serial, if all level-n-information must have been generated before it generates any level-n+1-information (Figure 6C), whereas it is parallel if it can work at different levels at the same time. A model is incremental, if it is nonserial (i.e. parallel) and sequential. In an incremental model, every bit of information generated at level n will be passed over to level n + 1 as soon as possible, even when the system is still working at level n (Figure 6D). A linear system, finally, generates all level-n-information strictly from left to right, whereas a projective system may generate different bits of information in nonadjacent positions (Figure 6E).

Information processing models can be compared in terms of the 'degrees of freedom' they permit. Modular, sequential and/or serial models are more strictly constrained than their interactive, discontinuous and/or parallel counterparts. From a methodological point of view, stricter models are preferable because their predictions can be falsified more easily. From the point of view of a realistic psychology they may still be (partly) inappropriate. The human mind is simply not an arbitrary processing system but rather one constrained by fundamental biological determinants, which are not *per se* isomorphic to methodological constraints. Under the assumption that the human mind is an information processing system, psychologically realistic theories, therefore, have to delineate its actual processing characteristics and explain how these constrain (different types of) human behavior. Psychological theories of language generation, more specifically, deal with the question of how linguistic information is processed in accordance with the general processing characteristics of the mind. Kempen & Hoenkamp (in press), for instance, assume that the language processor is modular, incremental and projective. In other words, they choose stricter processing constraints as far as modularity and sequentality are concerned but allow for weaker constraints with respect to seriality and linearity.

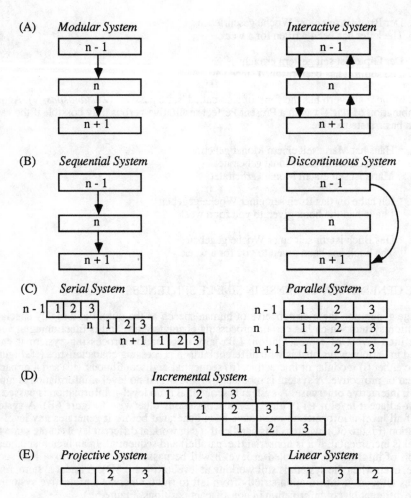

Figure 6. Information Systems with Different Processing Characteristics

Apart from the processing characteristics of a language generating system, a theory of language generation has to define the different *levels* of representation at which linguistic information is processed and the *format* or ('language') in which that information is represented at a given level. Language production theories, however different they are in detail, commonly assume three levels of representation: a level of thought (or a conceptual level), a level of linguistic encoding, and a level of articulation (cf. Garrett 1980). Speakers generate a message at the first level, give it a linguistic form at the second level and articulate this at the third level. On the message level, speakers generate concepts and define relations holding beween them. The level of linguistic encoding is usually seen as being composed of two sublevels. At the first, 'functional' level, concepts (generated at the conceptual level) are mapped onto lexical items ('lemmata'), which are specified for their semantic and syntactic but not for their phonological properties. Relations between concepts, generated at the message level, are mapped onto syntactic structures at the functional level, providing for categorial information such as 'is an NP' and functional information such as 'is a subject'. At the second, so-called 'positional' level, lexical words ('lemmata') are mapped onto phonologically shaped word forms.

The question now arises, where tense is generated: (i) together with verb-inherent aspect and temporal adverbs at the functional level, or (ii) postfunctionally at the positional level, that is, after all lexical information — about verb-inherent aspect and temporal adverbs — has been specified. The answer to this question has important implications with respect to the processing characteristics the system can be supposed to have. For instance, the system must be discontinuous if tense is generated postfunctionally, because in this case, message information gets passed over to a nonadjacent level. If, in addition to this, the system is serial, all relevant lexical information will be available before any tense is chosen. This seems to be of some advantage, because — as has been shown above — the interpretation of a given tense form is dependent on the inherent aspect of the verb. Hence, if the speaker-intended temporal reference is 'future' and no position-specifying adverb has been generated, the tense generator may choose a Present Tense for nondurative, resultative, but not for durative or nonresultative verbs (cf. examples (7) and (8) above). In other words, the range of possible choices between alternative tense forms is narrowed down if tense is chosen only after all lexical information is available. However, as we have seen above, what is sometimes called 'lexical aspect' very often is not purely lexical but depends on grammatical properties of the entire VP. Thus, in a model where function words like prepositions or quantifiers are generated on a positional level, information about lexical aspect very often is postfunctional itself and then interacts with tense information at the same level. So, whereas the Present Tense may be used to refer to the future in case (35), it does not have a future reading in (36); the latter differs from the former only by the insertion of the preposition *an*.

(35)   Hans schreibt den Brief bestimmt noch
        I'm sure John is still writing the letter

(36)   Hans schreibt an dem Brief bestimmt noch
        I'm sure John is still working on writing the letter

Hence, seen from the point of view of a desirable reduction of choices between alternative tense forms, a model where temporal information is specified on two subsequent levels is of no theoretical advantage in comparison with a model where all relevant information is specified on the same — i.e., the functional — level. A one-level hypothesis, moreover, has the methodological advantage of being more strictly constrained in terms of sequentiality: All temporal information that has been generated on the message level is passed on to the subsequent functional level, and no discontinuous processing is required.

I will now give some rules for tense/adverb selection in German. The list is restricted to the Present Tense and the Present Perfect and remains incomplete even in this restricted domain. For instance, nothing will be said about the 'Historical Present' or about the 'Double Perfect'.

RI *Future Reference*

1. (a) Use the Present Tense (↑) or the Future Tense (↓) in reference to future situations.
   (b) Choose the Future Tense whenever (i) the verb is nonresultative and (ii) no position-specifying adverb is available.
2. (a) Specify the position of the situation by means of a posterior adverb.
   (b) Leave the position unspecified only in cases where it is given by previous utterances or where (i) the verb is resultative or (ii) the Future Tense is chosen.

RII *Present Reference*

1. Choose the Present Tense in reference to situations which overlap temporally with the speaking situation.

2. Choose the Present Perfect in reference to present situations only if
   (i)   the situation is a state
   (ii) the agent of the state causing event is to be thematized
   (iii) the verb is resultative and
   (iv) has a corresponding state passive form.

RIII *Past Reference*

1. Choose the Present Perfect in reference to past situations.
   (a) Specify the position of the situation in question by means of an anterior verb
   (b) Leave the position unspecified only in cases where the situation in question is an event/act which is either
   (i) recent or
   (ii) temporally bound.

The arrows in rule RI-1a point to the conventionally preferred choice: In German, future reference is most commonly expressed with the Present Tense (↑), the Future Tense (↓) is always possible but it is used only in particular contexts. Rules RI-2a and RIII-2a indicate that, by default, the position of a past or future situation is given overt expression with a temporal adverb. Rules RI-2b and RIII-2b state exceptions to the default rule.

In the remaining part of this chapter, I will discuss some processing problems connected with Rule RI. The opposition between default and exception cases in this rule raises the question as to the level at which the decision about tense or the overt specification of positional information is made: the message level or the functional-level. If it is a message-level decision whether the position is to be specified or not, this decision would have to be made in terms of functional-level grammatical or lexical choices (i.e., tense choice, as in RI-2bi, or choice of lexical aspect, as in RI-2bii). This assumption is, however, incompatible with the modularity hypothesis, which does not allow for message-level decisions (level n) to be made dependent on functional-level (level n+1) decisions. As far as lexical aspect is concerned, the problem can be solved quite easily: we only need to reformulate Rule RI-2bi in terms of situation types. Rule RI-2b would then read as follows:

(R1-2b') Leave the position unspecified only in cases where the situation is temporally bound.

This reformulation does not, however, cover the interdependency between position-specification and tense-selection rules (RI-1b, RI-2bii). As far as this problem is concerned, two alternative solutions seem to offer themselves: We may either assume that tense selection is a message-level decision, or consider position specification as a matter of linguistic encoding rather than message construction. Both alternatives are rather dissatisfying: The first one makes message construction dependent on rather idiosyncratic features of a given language's tense system, the second one implies that information which has been made available at the message level is not made use of at the linguistic level. In order to dispense with this dilemma, I will assume that both message-level and functional-level representations are given a rather abstract format. More specifically, I will assume that abstract information about the location and the categorial type of situations is copied onto the linguistic level immediately after the corresponding message-level representation has been generated. (We may call this the *incrementality assumption.*) Grammatical choices (tense selection) and lexical choices (selection of inherent aspect) are then made at the functional level of linguistic encoding on the basis of this abstract information.

Categorial distinctions are represented by abstract features such as durativity, resultativity and intentionality (cf. Figure 1 above). Locational information is represented in terms of Reichenbach's (1947) threefold distinction between Event Time (E), Speaking Time (S) and Reference Time (R). E is the time of the narrated event e, S is the time of the speaking event u and R is the location of the reference point from which a given situation is seen. Three types of temporal relations can be distinguished: (i) the *intrinsic* relation between E and R which is determined by the perspective a speaker is taking, (ii) the *deictic* relation between R and S and (iii) the *ordering* relation between E and S. Once (i) and (ii) are given, (iii) can be inferred. The messages to be constructed for *Hans kommt (gleich)* or *Das Baby weint (gleich)* will now have the format shown in Figures 7a and 8a. At the level of linguistic encoding, abstract information about temporal location and situation type is copied to the highest projection of V, from where it gets passed down to the head phrases of the lower projections. The functional level representation will then have the format shown in Figures 7b and 8b.

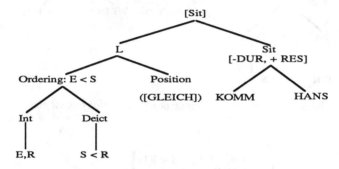

Figure 7a. Message Representation for *Hans kommt (gleich)*

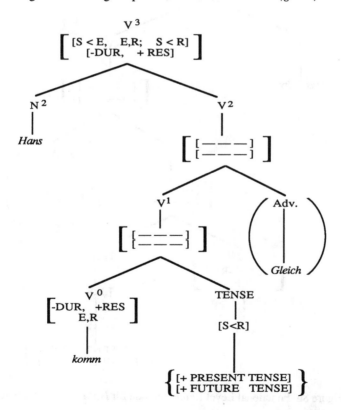

Figure 7b. Functional Level Representation for *Hans kommt (gleich)*

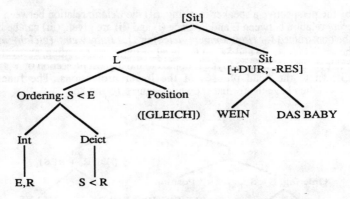

Figure 8a. Message Representation for *Das Baby weint gleich*

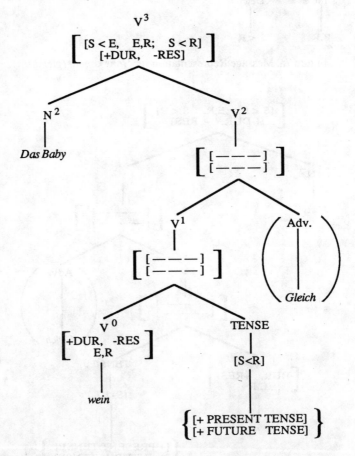

Figure 8b. Functional Level Representation for *Das Baby weint (gleich)*

The dotted lines in Figures 7b en 8b symbolize head feature bundles inherited from higher V-nodes. Lexical features (durativity, resultativity) are passed down to V⁰. Grammatical-tense features split at the V⁰-level. The 'instrinsic-relation' feature (i.e., the relation between E and R) is passed down to V⁰. The 'deictic-relation' feature (i.e., the relation between S and R) is passed down to the TENSE Category introduced as sister node of V⁰. TENSE expands into a Tense Marker which is computed on the basis of feature information in accordance with the tense selection rules (RI to RIII) stated above. In our case, the Tense Category specified as [S < R] may expand into either the Tense Marker [+PRESENT TENSE] or the Tense Marker [+FUTURE TENSE]. The latter *may* always be chosen, although it is not the preferred tense. It *must* be chosen, in case the verb is [-RES] and the position is left unspecified (RI-2b). Note that at the linguistic level, temporal information is represented in different ways: as (i) *a Tense Feature Bundle* of the higher V-projection, as (ii) a Category TENSE attached to V⁰, as (iii) *a Tense Marker* dominated by TENSE and, finally, at the positional level, as (iv) *a Tense Morpheme* with a specific phonological shape.

So far, the discussion has centered around structural properties of temporal information at the levels both of message construction and linguistic encoding. Sentence production is, however, a process in time at each of these levels. The remaining part of the chapter will therefore be devoted to some issues concerning the *on-line* generation of tense in simple sentences.

It can be taken for granted that a sentence production system has to meet certain word-order constraints (in almost all languages). This brings us to the question whether the order of the steps to be taken in the production process is determined by the order of the words to be generated. A simplistic model would proceed according to the following principle: If the word order to be obtained is AB, the order of steps to be taken also is AB. A system working according to this principle would be strictly linear. Given the incrementality hypothesis, such a model would imply that the order of the steps taken at the message level were dependent on the order of the steps at the functional level. This implication is, however, incompatible with the modularity hypothesis. Hence, if we are to maintain modularity and incrementality, we have to give up strict linearity in favor of a projective system. This is not to say that at the message level the order of the steps is necessarily indeterminate. Message generation may work according to certain ordering principles, as long as the principles are imposed by level-inherent constraints rather than level-transcendent ones. We may, for instance, assume that external and internal properties of situations are always generated *en bloc*, which is to say that the system specifies *all* of the external properties of a situation before (or after) it gets to any of its internal properties. At the level of linguistic encoding, the order of the steps is determined by message-level order on the one hand and structural constraints of linguistic form on the other hand. If we assume that at the message level external properties of situations are in fact specified first, the system will not run into trouble. It will immediately create a node V^max at the linguistic level (according to the incrementality assumption) and pass the relevant temporal information over to this node, from where it may run down the syntactic tree in the way described above. If, on the other hand, internal information is conceptualized first, it will also have to be lexicalized first, that is, before the linguistic encoder has access to any tense-relevant information. Suppose the linguistic encoder has already created the lemmata *Hans* and *komm* or *Das Baby* and *wein*. In this case it would have to come up with the tense specification next. If, at this point, ordering information (E<S, E,R, S<R) is available at the message level, a TENSE category can be created and attached to V⁰. The relevant ordering features will then be assigned to V⁰ (E,R) and TENSE (S<R). At this point, tense selection has to take place, because it is impossible to send the verb off to the positional level otherwise (according to the incrementality assumption). However, if the verb is *weinen*, a modular system will have to 'wait' until the adverb *gleich* comes in, since if no adverb were to follow, it would have to select FUTURE TENSE. Hence, the incrementality of the system will be delayed at this point, which may cause disfluencies in speech. Alternatively, the system might select a Present Tense, because this is the preferred selection anyway, and then decide to add an adverb to the message created so far, because it would otherwise not have expressed the intended temporal meaning. In this case, the message level decision would be made on the basis of linguistic level decisions. This may increase the fluency of the ultimate speech output, but at the cost of the modularity of the process.

In psycholinguistics, very little is known about the actual properties of the sentence production process. It is, for instance, far from clear whether message generation operates according to pre-established ordering principles and, if so, whether these principles are dependent on structural constraints imposed by the encoding language. It may very well be the case that speakers of, say, VSO and SOV languages, because of their linguistic knowledge, apply different ordering strategies when they generate the content of what they are going to communicate. Thorough empirical research is necessary before questions like these can be approached and ultimately be given a convincing answer.

REFERENCES

Bartsch, R. (1983) Over de semantiek van nominalsaties. *Glot, 6,* 1-29.

Bartsch, R. (1985) *On Aspectual Properties of Dutch and German Nominalizations.* Paper, Universiteit van Amsterdam.

Barwise, J. & J. Perry (1983) *Situations and Attitudes.* Cambridge, Mass.: MIT Press.

Comrie, B. (1976) *Aspect. An Introduction to the Study of Verbal Aspect and Related Problems.* Cambridge: Cambridge University Press.

Cooper, R. (1983) *Tense and Discourse Location in Situation Semantics* . Paper, University of Wisconsin, Madison.

Dowty, D.R. (1979) *Word Meaning and Montague Grammar. The Semantics of Verbs and Times in Generative Semantics and Montague PTQ.* Dordrecht: Reidel.

Garrett, M.F. (1980) Levels of Processing in Sentence Production. In: B. Butterworth (Ed.) *Language Production, Vol. 1.* London: Academic Press.

Hornstein, N. (1977) Towards a Theory of Tense. *Linguistic Inquiry, 8,* 521-557.

Kamp, H. (1979) Events, Instants and Temporal Reference. In: A. von Stechov & R. Bäuerle (Eds.) *Semantics from Different Points of View.* Berlin: Springer.

Kamp, H. & Rohrer, C. (1983) Tense in texts. In: R. Bäuerle, C. Schwarze & A. von Stechow (Eds.) *Meaning, use and interpretation of language.* Berlin: De Gruyter.

Kempen, G. & Hoenkamp, E. (in press) An Incremental Procedural Grammar for Sentence Formulation. *Cognitive Science.*

Matthiessen, C. (1983) Choosing Primary Tense in English. *Studies in Language, 7,* 369-429.

Oversteegen, E. (1987) Temporal Adverbials in the Two Track Theory of Time. In: V. Ehrich & H. Vater (Eds.) *Temporalsemantik.* Tübingen: Niemeyer.

Reichenbach, H. (1947) *Elements of symbolic logic.* Toronto: Macmillan.

Smith, C.C. (1978) The Syntax and Interpretation of Temporal Expressions in English. *Linguistics and Philosophy, 2,* 43-100.

Smith, C.C. (1981) Semantic and Syntactic Constraints on Temporal Interpretation. In: P.J. Tedeschia & A. Zaenen (Eds.) *Syntax and Semantics, Vol. 14.* New York: Academic Press.

Ullmer-Ehrich, V. (1977) *Zur Syntax und Semantik von Substantivierungen im Deutschen.* Kronberg/Ts: Scriptor.

Vendler, Z. (1967) Verbs and Times. In: Z. Vendler (Ed.) *Linguistics and Philosohphy* . Ithaca: Cornell University Press.

Verkuyl, H.J. (1972) *On the Compositional Nature of the Aspects.* Dordrecht: Reidel. (Foundations of Language Supplementary Series, Vol. 15.)

Chapter 28

PERCEPTUAL FACTORS AND WORD ORDER IN EVENT DESCRIPTIONS

Giovanni B. Flores d'Arcais

TABLE OF CONTENTS

1. Introduction
2. The relation between perception and description
3. Perceptual factors and order of mention
3.1 Set-up of the experiments
4. The experiments
4.1 Experiment 1: the effect of object size
4.2 Experiment 2: the effect of object size and movement pattern
4.3 Discussion of Experiments 1 and 2
4.4 Experiment 3: naming an object and describing an event
4.5 Discussion of Experiment 3
5. Conclusion

1. INTRODUCTION

To describe an object, a scene or an event is one of the most common functions of language. This paper represents a contribution to the study of effects of the perceptual organization which results from the exposure to objects, scenes or events on the production of descriptive language. In the present study an attempt was made to isolate effects of the figural properties of the objects or events to be described on linguistic variables of the utterances produced, in particular, on the preference for a given *word order* in the sentences produced.

Let us begin with a brief outline of the process which presumably takes place between the presentation to an observer of a simple visual event and the moment at which the observer begins producing a descriptive utterance. This process can be devided into a series of stages. (a) In a first phase, the observer has to encode the event perceptually in a *perceptual code*. The format of this code is not of concern here, and it is likely to be modality-specific. (b) This code is interfaced with a *conceptual representation* of a more abstract character, which constitutes the memory representation of the object, configuration or event. Although the format of this conceptual representation should be rather abstract, it may be affected somewhat by the structure of the perceptual code, in the sense that the internal structure of the conceptual representation could reflect at least some properties of the perceptual organization.

In order to produce a verbal description of the object, event, or configuration, the speaker has to select and organize elements from the conceptual representation in such a way that these meet one of the obvious constraints of language, namely its temporal 'left-to-right' organization. This requires (c) a process of *selection* of the elements or attributes to be described, and then (d) a process of *linearization* of these elements in an array. Once a *conceptual array* has been made at this stage, the organized and linearized material is ready to be interfaced with a syntactic structure, that is, it can be used in the process of (e) *formulating* a structure ready for output. At some point (f) the appropriate *lexical entries* have to be selected and accessed, and morphological decisions have to be made. After these stages, (g) a *phonological* representation has to be constructed, and finally, (h) an *articulatory program* has to be released and executed.

Notice that although these stages are described here as sequential, no claim is made about their seriality. While at least some seriality is very likely to be involved in the process going from perception to description, it is also probable that at least some of the subprocesses described overlap, in part or totally, or that the sequence is different from the one just described (e.g. f 'before' e). For example, it has been shown (Lindsley, 1976) that a speaker begins articulating a sentence once he or she has planned a constituent of it and before having finished a plan concerning the whole sentence structure. It is possible that the various subprocesses just outlined are organized in cascades. These different stages or phases can be further specified or combined in more comprehensive stages. The phases described have been reduced to three stages in many models of sentence production (e.g. Schlesinger, 1977; Danks, 1976; Kempen, 1977). For example, Kempen (1977) distinguishes three stages of *conceptualization, formulation* and and *articulation.*

The extent to which the operations described for these various stages correspond to distinct psychological processes is of course very difficult to determine, both theoretically and empirically. A given perceptual organization can affect the conceptual representation, and this can affect processes at the later stages. Alternatively, the perceptual code can directly affect the stage of linearization and that of formulation. Still, it is possible to try to relate certain stages to the end result of the process empirically. For example, it is possible to relate the stage of perceptual encoding to the stage of producing the actual form of the sentence. Such an attempt has been made in previous work (Flores d'Arcais, 1975, 1980 a, b) and in the experiments reported here. The notion underlying this work is that the perceptual representation puts some constraints on the stages of formulation of a descriptive sentence, for example by requiring the selection of certain syntactic forms, or by giving priority to the choice of a given lexical unit. Thus, characteristics of the perceptual organization (e.g., one object is more likely to be seen as figure against a background) are taken to affect the choice of a syntactic construction or lexical selection in descriptive language.

In my previous studies (just listed) *figural* properties of the visual events given for description were varied, and the effects on some structural and lexical variables of the descriptive sentences were observed, such as choice of active and of passive sentences, word order, and preferred order of clauses. In the present study I investigate how perceptual organization affects the order of mention of the objects involved in simple events in the sentences uttered to describe these events.

2. THE RELATION BETWEEN PERCEPTION AND DESCRIPTION

In this area there has been surprisingly little work. Something is known about the way context or manipulation of the speaker's attention might affect structural variables in linguistic production. For example, Tannenbaum & Williams (1968) gave their subjects a picture to be described, together with a preamble, namely a paragraph designed to direct the subjects' attention to some specific aspects of a picture (e.g., to the actor or the object acted upon) and observed how this affected latencies in producing active or passive sentences as a description of the picture.

Related to the same problem are some interesting demonstrations by Osgood (1971) and a later series of experiments (Osgood & Bock, 1977). In this ingenious work, Osgood tried to show how manipulation of properties of the event, such as the context in which one object is presented or the previous linguistic behavior of the subjects, can affect linguistic variables in description, such as the choice of the definite article. For example, the first time an object was presented to a number of observers, these were likely to use the indefinite article *a*, and when the same object was reintroduced again afterwards, the definite article *the* was almost invariably selected.

My own previous work went in somewhat the same direction. In a first study (Flores d'Arcais, 1975) I tried to examine the influence of certain figural characteristics of simple pictures on the ease of production of active or passive sentences. The notion proposed was that the choice of the active or passive voice is in part dependent on whether one of the two objects depicted is *focused* on. Once an object has been conceptualized as the *topic* or *focus* of the situation to be described, there would be a strong tendency to produce a sentence in which the topicalized object took the first surface position. This, in turn, would influence the ease of producing a sentence in the active or in the passive voice.

The figural properties tested in these experiments were the *direction* of the action, the *localization* (left/right) and the *size* of the object. The results showed that it is easier (takes less time) to start uttering a sentence when the *first word* used refers to (a) the object on the left or (b) the larger object; and (c) when the 'action' takes place from left to right.

In another series of experiments carried out by Levelt, Maassen and myself (e.g. Levelt & Maassen, 1981; Flores d'Arcais, 1980a,b and unpublished work), an attempt has been made to isolate experimentally two phases of the production of descriptive sentences, namely a stage of perceptual coding and a stage of formulation. The experiments consisted in the presentation of events involving a simple movement of two objects. The events could be described using a *conjunctive* statement such as 'The triangle and the square move upwards' or a *disjunctive* sentence 'The circle moves upwards and the triangle moves downwards'. The results supported the distinction between two independent and probably additive stages of perceptual coding and of formulation. Visually more complex movements took longer to describe, and disjunctive sentences were easier to produce (as shown by a shorter latency before the start of the utterances). A series of experiments aimed specifically to test various hypotheses about the difference in production ease of the two types of sentences, conjunctive and disjunctive. The conclusion was that the difference found between the two sentence types is most likely to be explained in terms of the difficulty of lexically accessing the nouns which refer to the two objects in the two types of descriptive sentences. In a third study (Flores d'Arcais & Joustra, 1979), I investigated the effect of the order of two distinct events on the choice between two-clause sentences with temporal subordinating conjunctions (*before* or *after*).

Thus, in the first study, some figural characteristics of simple pictures, namely *localization*, *size* and *direction of the action*, affected the ease of uttering an active or a passive sentence as a description of the pictures. In the second study it was found that stimulus complexity affects a stage of perceptual representation and that this stage of information processing is independent of another stage, responsible for the process of linguistic formulation of the sentence uttered as a description of the visual event. In the third study the order of the events was shown to have an effect on the choice between complex sentence types.

3. PERCEPTUAL FACTORS AND ORDER OF MENTION

The general purpose of the experiments carried out in the present study was still an attempt to see to what extent structural variables in descriptive language are dependent on the perceptual representation. The previous experiments had shown that ease of production of various types of sentences is sensitive to different perceptual variables. Certain structural characteristics of the sentences, such as the order of the words within a simple sentence, seem to be partly dependent on perceptual properties of the objects or events to be described. The effect of these properties might be rather weak, but it seems clear that they put certain restrictions on the selection of linguistic variables in the sentences produced.

The work of the present study concentrated on the effect of perceptual factors on a particular linguistic variable, namely *word order* within the descriptive statements. Within a sentence, word order is the result of several constraints. First, there are constraints from the *grammar*: In a language which does not possess surface cases or other devices such as prefixes or suffixes to mark grammatical relations, a typical way to inform the hearer about grammatical realtions is word order. 'The boy kicks the girl' means something different than 'The girl kicks the boy', while in languages which include cases and also allow a relative freedom of order, categories of subject and object would be marked by cases and word order would have little or no importance for marking grammatical relations. (Cf. the two perfectly equivalent Latin expressions 'puer amat puellam' and 'puellam amat puer'.) At any rate, grammar exerts several constraints on the order of words or larger syntactic units within the sentence.

Second, there probably are *conceptual* constraints: the order in which elements of a situation are organized at the conceptual level is likely to be nonrandom: The way in which the elements of the configuration to be described are organized at the conceptual level is likely to place constraints for the stage of linearization. It is on this type of constraint that I have tried to focus in the present work. Of course, there are other constraints, such as phonological or rhythmic constraints or even some of a more pragmatic character. These reflect variables such as the intended meaning of the speaker or the reference to a previously mentioned object or event. For example, the speaker is likely to put emphasis on the new rather than the 'given' object or event, with effects on the selection of lexical units for output.

As was pointed out in the introduction, in the process of producing a sentence, at the level of the *linearization* process , a selection has to take place among the conceptualized material in order to produce something like a conceptual array, namely an *ordered* abstract structure which will then result in the actual linguistic string ready for articulation. The selection among the conceptualized events or objects is likely to be sensitive to several factors. For example, if an inanimate and an animate object are involved in an interaction, the animate object may have a higher probability of being topicalized and consequently selected first in the conceptual array.

In the present study, I presented the subjects with simple events and requested them to give a verbal description. According to the view held here, the object or the part of the event which has been topicalized in the conceptual array should tend to be located early at the level of the formulator. In this way, perceptual coding would affect the order of mention of the elements or objects of the visual event in the descriptive sentence. A preference for a given order of mention should reflect a differential organization of the conceptual structure underlying the sentence. Production of a sentence with an order which reflects the way in which objects are conceptually represented should be easier, and, among other things, result in shorter production latencies.

3.1 Set-up of experiments

The subjects were presented with two objects clearly different in size, a large one A and a small one B. In the first experiment, the small object was inside the large one, and in the second the two objects were next to each other. In the second experiment the two objects followed each other in their displacement on the display, toward the left or towards the right. In the third experiment, both conditions occurred. Thus, the figural variables considered were the *size* of the objects, the *relative localization* (one object within the other or side by side) and the spatial *position* of the objects in performing the action (one 'leading', the other 'following' the other).

Let us briefly consider the possible effects of these three factors. In each case, one object should be likely to be 'localized' or 'isolated' perceptually more easily. The perceptually isolated object is likely to be preferred for selection in the conceptual array, and in turn, this should affect the ease of producing a sentence with the topicalized or focused object in first position. Consider first the effect of size. The results of a previous study (Flores d'Arcais, 1975) would allow the prediction that the larger object tends to be preferred for early selection in the conceptual array and its name would tend to take an early position in the formulation. This would result in a preference for early mention of the large object. On the other hand, when the two objects are presented one within the other, it could be expected that the configuration would allow a perceptual coding in terms of figure and ground, and this could affect the ease of uttering a sentence with the name of the smaller object, localized as figure, in first position. Finally, on the basis of the previous study (Flores d'Arcais, 1975) we would expect that the object which 'leads' in movement should also be likely to be topicalized more easily, and therefore would tend to be put in first position in the sentence.

Each of these three factors should be expected to have an effect (a) on the preference for a sentence in which either the large, the inside or the 'leading' object would be mentioned in the first position; and (b) on the latency before starting to utter the sentences selected in this way. Of course, these three factors could act with different strength. The effect of size was tested in both experiments, the effect of figure versus ground in the second. Thus, the effect of size was contrasted with that of figure/ground organization across the two experiments. Leading versus following was tested in the second experiment.

The complexity of the movement might also differentially affect the ease of accessing the different lexical terms. This factor has also been tested in Experiment 1 and 2.

4. THE EXPERIMENTS

The experimental events consisted of simple movements of two figures, a large one and a small one. The figures used in each event were two of the following three: a triangle, a circle and a square; and each of these three could be either the large or the small figure. In Experiment 1 the small figure was inside the large one, in Experiment 2 the two figures moved next to each other, and in Experiment 3 both conditions occurred. Both figures were displaced in the same direction. The two figures could 'perform' in their displacement either the same, or a different action, selected out of three different types of movement: (a) a simple horizontal displacement toward the left or the right (MOVE); (b) a jumping displacement consisting of a combination of a relatively slow bouncing with horizontal displacement (BOUNCE); and (c) a combination of a quick vertical alternation with a horizontal displacement (VIBRATE). I will call MOVE a *simple* movement, and the other two actions (BOUNCE and VIBRATE) *complex* movements.

4.1 Experiment 1: the effect of object size

Materials, Method and Subjects. The two figures of the event moved independently one inside the other. The event was presented on a display and at the end of the event the Ss were given either a *cue word* — referring to one of the two objects — or the instruction DESCRIBE, meaning that they were to give a free description of the event. In addition there were catch trials which included a *verification* task: The Ss were presented with a sentence which could be either a correct or an incorrect description of the event previously given, with the task being to verify or falsify the statement with the word RIGHT or WRONG. The Subjects were 24 paid volunteer students at the University of Leyden. All descriptions produced in this experiment as well as in the following ones were in Dutch. The results in the free-description situations, which included a total of 96 trials, consisted of (a) the frequencies of use of a given word order (in one case the large object could have been described first, in the other case the small object; e.g. 'the triangle bounces and the square moves'); and (b) the latency in uttering each of the statements. The frequency of use of sentence types in the 'forced' trials with the cue word, the corresponding latencies, and the latencies obtained in the verification trials were not used for the present analysis.

Results. For the purpose of analysis we considered the following four input conditions separately:

(a) Both the large and the small figure perform the simple action.
(b) The large figure performs the simple action and the small figure one of the two complex actions.
(c) The large figure performs a complex movement and the small one the simple movement.
(d) Both figures perform a complex movement.

Table 1 reports the proportion of sentences produced in which the large figure was mentioned first; Table 2 gives the corresponding latencies. An analysis of variance was carried out on the arc sine transformations of the individual scores (for the proportion of cases in which the first word referred to the large object). Given unequal N's, the average latencies before starting to utter a sentence for the four conditions were compared using pairwise t-tests.

The main results are the following. First, as shown in Table 1, Subjects prefer to describe the event by naming the large object first; this difference is large and very significant (F=34.155; 1,23 d.f.; $p < .001$). Second, as shown in Table 2, when subjects decide to start describing the small figure first, they are in general significantly faster. (Of the five comparisons made, four t values were significant, ranging from 4.13 to 1.97 with d.f. > 30.) Thus, there is an interesting trade-off between preference for a given form of description and latency; this will be commented on in section 4.3. Inspection of the averages based on the different types of figure (triangle, circle and square) considered separately, and an analysis of variance on these data, showed the effects to be independent of the type of figure involved in the action: These averages did not differ significantly.

Table 1. Proportion of sentences produced with the larger object mentioned first, for the various types of movements in Experiment 1.

	Movement type of objects			
Same			Different	
Simple	Complex		Simple	Complex
.77	.69		.79	.83

Table 2. Latencies (ms) between signal and begin of the descriptive sentence, for the different types of movements in Experiment 1.

	Movement type of objects				
Object mentioned first	Same		Different		Average
	Simple	Complex	Simple	Complex	
Large	1022	1004	1026	1051	1025
Small	945	979	958	999	968

4.2 Experiment 2: the effect of object size and movement pattern

Materials, Method and Subjects. This experiment was essentially identical in design to Experiment 1, with the important difference that the two figures were side by side without ever coming into contact with each other. Either both figures moved from left to right or both moved from right to left, and the actions were the same as in the first experiment. Two out of the three figures — a square, a circle and a triangle — were the objects of the events: one was always a *large* one, the other a *small* one. Twenty-four paid volunteer studented at Leyden University took part in this experiment.

Results. The data set used consists of the proportion of sentences with the large object mentioned in first position, and the corresponding latencies. The results are presented in Tables 3 and 4. An analysis of variance was carried out on the arc-sine transformed proportions of sentences produced with the large figure mentioned first.

The results show two effects. First, there is an overall effect corresponding to the one found in Experiment 1, namely a tendency to mention the large figure first ($F=23.401$; 1,23 d.f.; $p < 001$). Another effect is the tendency to mention first the object which *precedes* the other in the movement ($F=37.166$; 1,23 d.f.; $p < .001$). These two effects interact: in the events where the small figure has the lead, the preference for mentioning the large figure first is reduced ($F=5.229$; 1,23 d.f.; $p < .05$). In addition the results show another effect: The figure which performs a *complex* movement tends to be selected more often for mention in first position. This effect also interacts with the previous two factors ($F=6.117$; 1,23 d.f.; $p < .02$).

Table 3. Proportion of sentences produced with larger object mentioned first, for the various types of movements in Experiment 2.

	Movement type of objects				
Figure leading in Movement	Same			Different	
	Simple	Complex		Simple	Complex
Large	.83	.77		.75	.89
Small	.48	.51		.40	.60

Table 4. Latencies (ms) between the signal and the begin of the descriptive sentence, for the different types of movements in Experiment 2.

		Movement type of objects				
Figure leading	Figure mentioned first	Same		Different		Average
		Simple	Complex	Simple	Complex	
Large	Large	1022	977	1039	1040	1020
	Small	952	1021	973	1039	992
Small	Large	1002	1093	1098	1057	1061
	Small	952	994	1003	980	983

The latencies show the same pattern as found in Experiment 1. When the small figure has been selected to be mentioned first, the descriptive sentence is uttered with a shorter latency.

Given the large range in the number of responses produced for each category (15 to 122), it was not appropriate to carry out an analysis of variance on the latency data. Individual comparisons were therefore made with Student's t. Among the several significant differences, we consider the following (all with d.f. > 30). The latencies are significantly shorter when one of the following is mentioned first in the sentence: (a) the small figure (significant t values between 3.42 and 1.95): (b) the small figure when it *precedes* the large in the movement (significant t values between 2.91 and 1.82); (c) the small figure which performs a *complex* action, while the large one performs a simple action (significant t's between 2.13 and 1.89). In this Experiment, as in Experiment 1, the effects do not seem to depend on the specific figures involved in the action.

4.3 Discussion of Experiments 1 and 2

The results of the first two experiments are consistent. There is a preference for mentioning first the larger of the two objects. Further, there is a tendency to mention first the object which has the lead in the movement. Third, there is a tendency to mention first the figure which performs a complex action.

It seems likely that the two objects are differentially coded perceptually and that the large one is coded more easily as the *topic* of the event. An unexpected result was the absence of any difference in the preference for a sentence form or in the latency when one of the two figures was inside of the other, as compared to the condition where they were presented next to each other. As noted before, in the stimulus situation used in Experiment 1 we had expected a figure/ground organization of the configuration which, in turn, could have affected the choice of one of the two objects for mention. We had expected the object represented as 'figure' to be coded preferentially as the 'topic' and this should have resulted in this object being mentioned first (cf. Clark & Chase, 1974). The perfect correspondence of the results of Experiments 1 and 2 indicate that it was in each case the larger object that was more easily topicalized. Another interesting result was the shorter latencies when the objects performed a complex action, as opposed to a simple action. This difference can be explained as due to the perceptual 'saliency' of the complex movement. The preferences for giving first mention to the large object and to the object which preceeds the other in the movement are consistent with previous results, see Flores d'Arcais, 1975.

An interesting result was the trade-off between the speed of initiating an utterance and the choice of the object to be mentioned first. Most subjects preferred to begin the sentence by naming the large object in first position. However, when they produced a sentence by mentioning the smaller figure first, they were faster. How can this fact be interpreted?

To account for this trade-off, one could hypothesize a differential effect in perceptually coding the picture and the event which is to be described. The larger object would be coded more easily perceptually, and this would affect early lexical selection. On the other hand, the smaller object, which could be coded as figure against ground, would tend more strongly to become the topic of the conceptual representation related to the abstract linguistic representation produced at the formulation level, and therefore it would be easier to start a sentence by mentioning it first. If this hypothesis has some value, it would imply the existence of two perceptual codes which affect the process of sentence production, namely one concerned with the coding of the object, the other with the coding of the event. This hypothesis has important theoretical consequences for the general approach we have taken and it has been tested further in another experiment.

4.4 Experiment 3: naming an object and describing an event

The previous experiments have shown an interesting trade-off between preference for mentioning one of the two objects and the latency in uttering a sentence with the name of one of the two objects in the first position. A speaker tends to prefer to utter a sentence by mentioning first the name of the larger object. On the other hand, when the first object mentioned in the sentence is the small object, the sentence is produced more rapidly.

This difference could be interpreted by postulating two distinct perceptual codes for the event. The first would concern coding of the objects involved in the event, the other the event itself. With the first type of coding, the large object would tend to be coded first, yielding an abstract representation along the lines of 'There is a large triangle and a small circle'. On the other hand, the small object would be located more easily with respect to the large one in the coding of the event, and the conceptual representation would be something like 'The circle is moving on the triangle, and the triangle is bouncing'. The first process would be related to the accessing of a lexical item, namely the term for the larger object. The second process would be related to the formulation of a sentence. Thus coding of the object would relate to choice of a lexical item, and preference for one sentence type would reflect this choice. Coding the event would be directly related to the process of sentence formulation.

The present experiment required the Subjects to perform one of the following two operations: In one condition they were requested to name the object which performed a given action, in the second condition they had to produce a sentence beginning with a probe word. The probe given to the Subjects was the name of one of the two objects involved in the event.

Thus, in the first condition the Subjects had only to mention the name of the object which performed the action mentioned in a question. The two objects performed two different actions (e.g. one 'bouncing' and the other 'vibrating', and the Subject was asked which object performed one of the two actions (e.g. 'Which one is bouncing?'). In the second condition the Subject was given a cue word referring to one of the two objects of the event (e.g. 'The triangle') and had to produce a sentence using the probe word in first position. By the above reasoning, in the first condition it should be easier to mention the large object: It should take less time to answer to the question when the large object performed the designated action. In the second condition, on the other hand, it should be easier to utter the descriptive sentence starting with the smaller object; when the probe correponds to the smaller object, then, the production latency should be lower.

Materials, Method and Subjects. The materials for the experiment were the same as in Experiments 1 and 2. The two objects involved in the event were the same, and so were the actions performed. In contrast to the first two experiments, in each event every object performed a *different* action. The relative position of the two objects, one inside the other or the two next to each other, which distinguished Experiment 1 from Experiment 2, was varied within this experiment and became another factor in the design.

As mentioned above, the Subject was requested to perform one of the two following tasks cued at the end of the event, after the objects had disappeared: (a) Name one of the two objects, as an answer to a question which appeared on the display at the end of the event (e.g. 'Which one is bouncing?'). (b) Produce a descriptive sentence beginning with a probe word presented on the display at the end of the event (for example 'The triangle'). (c) A series of catch trials, as in the previous experiments, included a verification task. The subject was instructed to respond as fast as possible. The latency of the response was measured from the onset of the question/probe word on the display. The events, together with the question or the probe word which indicated which of the two tasks had to be performed, were presented in random alternation, intermixed with catch trials. In the analysis, however, the data obtained for each of the two tasks was considered separately. The designs of these two subexperiments were then as follows:

(1) *Object naming task*: (a) Relation between the two objects (small object inside vs. outside the large one); (b) Object to be mentioned (large vs. small).
(2) *Sentence production task*: (a) Relation between the two objects (small object inside vs. outside large one); (b) Probe word referring to large vs. small object.

Sixteen students at the University of Leyden took part in the experiment as paid volunteer Subjects.

Results. The data consisted of the latencies for mentioning the object as a response to the question or for beginning the descriptive sentence. There were very few error responses (fewer than 5%); these were omitted from the analysis. The average latencies for the two conditions are reported in Table 5.

Consider, first, the task of mentioning the object in answer to the question (Table 5a). The large object was mentioned significantly faster than the small one ($F= 6.79$; 1,15 d.f.; $p<.05$). Inspection of the data also shows another tendency. When the small object is displaced inside the large one, it is mentioned relatively faster. This effect does not reach significance, however, (interaction $F=3.12$; 1,15 d.f.; $p<.10$).

A different pattern emerges from the latencies for producing a description of the event starting with the probe word (Table 5b). When the probe word corresponds to the larger object, it takes significantly longer to begin the descriptive sentence ($F=9.43$; 1,15 d.f.; $p<.01$). The interaction this time is marginally significant ($F=4.49$; 1,15 d.f.; $p<.055$), indicating a small effect of the relative positions of the two objects.

Table 5. Average latencies (ms) (a) in naming an object as response to the question and (b) in initiating a descriptive sentence with the given probe (Experiment 3).

(a) Object naming task

Object referred to by question	Relation of small to large object	
	Inside	Outside
Large	651	639
Small	667	678

(b) Sentence production task

Object to be mentioned first	Relation of small to large object	
	Inside	Outside
Large	924	912
Small	873	887

4.5 Discussion of Experiment 3

The results are consistent with those of the first two experiments. When the object to be mentioned is the large one, naming latencies are shorter. Thus, when an event involving two objects of different sizes is presented for description, it seems easier to access the lexical information corresponding to the larger of two objects. When a description of the event involving two objects of different sizes has to be produced, on the other hand, and the Subject is requested to begin by mentioning the smaller object, the sentence production latency is shorter. In other words, it seems easier to describe an event by mentioning first the action performed by the small object. The data thus seem to speak in favor of the hypothesized distinction between two different aspects of the perceptual coding process which is related to the process of sentence formulation.

The data also show a small effect of the relative position of the two objects. When the small figure is inside the large one, it seems relatively easier to mention it first. In this condition, moreover, the latencies for beginning the sentence which describe the event are the shortest. Both these results speak for an additional effect of a perceptual figure/ground organization of the two objects which interacts with the two effects which showed up in the present experiment, namely the tendency to mention the larger object first and the tendency to find it easy to begin a descriptive sentence with the smaller object in first position.

5. CONCLUSION

The results of the three experiments reported in this chapter lead to two principal conclusions about the formulation of descriptive language. A property of the objects to be described, namely their relative size, affects the ease of identifying the object: The larger object is identified faster. The preference for producing sentences in which the larger object is mentioned first can be taken to be dependent on this difference. At the same time, it is easier to produce a sentence in which the action performed by the smaller object is mentioned first. Together, these findings seem to indicate an interesting distinction between two processes, one related to accessing the lexical unit corresponding to a single object and the other responsible for the formulation of the descriptive sentence.

REFERENCES

Clark, H.H. & Chase, W.G. (1974) Perceptual coding strategies in the formation and verification of descriptions. *Memory and Cognition, 2,* 101-111.
Danks, J.H. (1977) Producing ideas and sentences. In: S. Rosenberg (Ed.) *Sentence production.* Hillsdale (N.J.): Erlbaum.
Flores d'Arcais, G.B. (1975) Some perceptual determinants of sentence construction. In: G.B. Flores d'Arcais (Ed.) *Studies in perception.* Milano-Firenze: Martello-Giunti.
Flores d'Arcais, G.B. (1980a) Organizzazione percettiva e struttura linguistica nella descrizione di un evento. In: *XVIII Congress of the Italian Psychological Society: Atti della Divisione Ricerca di Base in Psicologia,* 331-333. Palermo: S.I.P.S.
Flores d'Arcais, G.B. (1980b) *Perception and language.* Paper, Tokyo University.
Flores d'Arcais, G.B. & Joustra, J. (1979) The expression of temporal order in descriptive language. *Italian Journal of Psychology, 6,* 203-223.
Kempen, G. (1977) On conceptualizing and formulating in sentence production. In: S. Rosenberg (Ed.) *Sentence production.* Hillsdale (N.J.): Erlbaum.
Levelt, W.J.M. & Maassen, B. (1981) Lexical search and order of mention in sentence production. In: W. Klein & W.J.M. Levelt (Eds.) *Crossing the boundaries in linguistics .* Dordrecht: Reidel.
Lindsley, J.R. (1976) Producing simple utterances: Details of the planning process. *Journal of Psycholinguistic Research, 5,* 331-354.
Osgood, C.E. (1971) Where do sentences come from? In: D.D. Steinberg & L.A. Jakobovits (Eds.) *Semantics: An interdisciplinary reader in philosophy, linguistics and psychology.* London: Cambridge University Press.
Osgood, C.E. & Bock, J.K. (1977) Salience and sentencing: Some production principles. In: S. Rosenberg, (Ed.) *Sentence production.* Hillsdale, N.J.: Erlbaum.
Schlesinger, I.M. (1977) *Production and comprehension of utterances.* Hillsdale, N.J.: Erlbaum.
Tannenbaum P.H. & Williams, F. (1968) Generation of active and passive sentences as a function of subject or object focus. *Journal of Verbal Learning and Verbal Behavior, 7,* 246-250.

Chapter 29

METACOMMENTS IN TEXT GENERATION

Bengt Sigurd

TABLE OF CONTENTS

1. Syntactic types of metacomments
2. Which words can be metacommented?
3. Functional types of metacomments
4. Metacomments in the grammar
5. Metacomments in text generation

The following paragraph illustrates the concept of *metacomments*, i.e. comments on the words chosen by the speaker.

> *It is not, frankly speaking, always easy to, as the expression goes, express oneself. Often one does not find 'the proper word' and must, so to speak, be satisfied with whatever one can — how shall I put it? — get hold of. The speaker often makes mistakes — to put it mildly.*

To my knowledge, metacomments have not yet been included systematically in any computerized text (or speech) generation system, and their special status in the text has not been discussed much by linguists. (For some studies, see list of references.) One reason why metacomments have not been focused on by computational linguists may be that metacomments typically belong to spontaneous speech, whereas text generation systems generally try to simulate written text. Expert systems try to simulate dialogue, but designers of expert systems have, so far, only touched on the problems of metacomments. An exception is Clippinger (1978), who discussed a system which simulates a person who, while participating in a dialogue, produces some metacomments. One reason why metacomments have not been discussed by text generation linguists may be that computerized text generation systems are still in their infancy. Designers of text generation systems often seem to be quite happy if they manage to produce grammatical sentences from facts stored in a data base (cf. Kempen, 1987). Metacomments belong to the higher stylistic layers of language. Still, they will have to be handled, at least in sophisticated text and speech generation systems. They are also interesting from theoretical points of view and they shed light on the complex process of speech production, as I hope to show in this paper.

In the introductory paragraph, the phrase *frankly speaking* indicates that the speaker intends to be more open than is usually the case in speaking. He is warning that he is going to break the conventions of communication in some way. The words *as the expression goes* indicate that he is using a well-established combination of words, not a fresh one. The quotation marks around the words *the proper word* have a similar function. Finally, the phrase *to put it mildly* is a warning that the speaker is using a euphemism and not telling the whole truth.

Thinking about metacomments, you will realize that they could be used in many situations; some individuals, in fact, use metacomments a lot. Some even overuse them, developing the bad habit of interspersing their speech with metacomments as a way of filling in empty pauses and keeping the floor. Some persons add metacomments in writing, as they are untrained in writing and feel uncertain about words. Some persons add metacomments because of an academic ambition to express themselves precisely and unambiguously — and a desire to show it. This motivation to avoid misunderstandings is also a good reason why computerized text generation systems should be able to insert metacomments in the text. (See the Proceedings of COLING84 for several papers about misunderstandings.)

Metacomments are also quite common as return signals, back channel items, in dialogue. The frequent back channel item *OK* only indicates that you have understood. If you say *Fine* you say that you like (the contents of) the utterance. If you say *precisely* or *exactly* or — in British English — *quite*, you seem to comment on the wording just as much as on the content. If a speaker says *Chernobyl was the Waterloo of nuclear industry* the partner may say *Exactly*, as he thinks the word *Waterloo* is just right. On another occasion the partner may say *to put it mildly*, thereby indicating that the words were not strong enough.

Metacomments highlight the difference between the meaning of words and the intended meaning. They also focus on the author behind the text, which most computer systems try to avoid. When a person is simulated by the computer, as in the famous program Eliza and many games, the result is often somewhat bizarre.

This paper will present a survey of English (and some Swedish) metacomments and their respective functions. The problem of integrating metacomments in a computerized text or speech generation system will also be discussed.

1. SYNTACTIC TYPES OF METACOMMENTS

The following is a brief summary of metacomments in English. (Some of the comments have also been discussed in the literature referred to.)

1. Adverb + participle of verb of speaking. Examples: *frankly, roughly, loosely, mildly, metaphorically, strictly, technically + speaking/spoken, expressed, formulated*. The combinations have different stylistic values/acceptability and some are more like fixed phrases or idiomatic expressions than others. The adverb may occur before or after the participle in some cases. The participle may in some cases be left out, e.g. *frankly (speaking)*. Note that the participles *writing/written* are never used, even when the comment is produced in writing. Swedish has equivalents, e.g. *ärligt talat* (frankly spoken), but only the past participle of the equivalent of *speak (tala)* is used (which reveals that Swedes comment on the choice of words after it has occurred, not in the act).

2. Prepositional phrase (+ participle of verb of speaking). Examples: *(expressed) in one word, in brief, in short, in simple words. The performance was (in one word) a disaster (in one word)*.

3. *To* + infinitive + adverb or prepositional phrase according to 1 or 2. Examples: *The performance was, to speak openly, a disaster. Her song is, to put it mildly, disturbing*.

4. *If + I/one may/can* + verb of speaking. Examples: *The performance was, if one may say so, a disaster. The disease is, if one may use a strong word, lethal*.

5. *So to speak/say*. An idiomatic phrase. Examples: *The ship is, so to say, a wreck. The boat is, so to speak, a powder box*.

6. *As they say/one says/it is said, as the expression goes*. Example: *The building is, as they say, a tourist trap*.

7. *So-called*. Example: *The ship is a so-called copra schooner*. The Swedish equivalent, *så kallad/kallat*, is much more common, both in speech and writing. The Swedish phrase may sometimes (with the neuter form *kallat*) be added after the word(s) commented on: *Bilen var en kupé, så kallat*. (The car was a so-called coupé). The existence of a well-established and very frequent abbreviation, *s.k.*, proves the importance of this little metacomment in Swedish.

8. Quotation marks (' '). This metacomment is special, as it consists of graphic markers and is thus primarily restricted to writing. The author often has a choice surrounding either one or several words with quotes. In our demonstration text above we may use quotes around the word *proper*, the combination *proper word* or the whole noun phrase *the proper word*,

but clearly the word *proper* is the central word. There exists a nonverbal — and spoken — equivalent in speech, namely the gestures with two raised fingers. Often the speaker also pronounces the words *quote* and *unquote*. This way of metacommenting by quotation marks has been borrowed into Swedish (and probably into several other languages), in particular in academic circles. Of course, quotation marks are used primarily when rendering what somebody else has said or written (i.e., in direct speech). But a secondary use has developed where the function of the quotation marks is to indicate that the speaker does not take full responsibility for the word. Untrained writers feel tempted to use this possibility very often, as they are afraid they may be using the words incorrectly; the term *scare quote* has been used to denote this usage.

9. Expressions such as *a kind of, sort of*. Examples: *The ship was a kind of torpedo boat, The airplane made some sort of landing maneuver*. These expressions are used excessively by some persons in spontaneous speech (cf. Aijmer, 1984). There are Swedish equivalents, e.g., *nå(go)n slags, nå(go)n sorts* (some kind/sort of).

10. *As it were, in a/some way*. Example: *The speedboat made a U-turn, as it were*. There are Swedish equivalents as *liksom, på något sätt* (in some way).

11. Words such as *real(ly), typical(ly), exact(ly), genuine(ly), perfect(ly)*, which comment on how well the object, action or event is covered by the word(s) chosen. Examples: *The ship is a typical brigg, The computer is a real IBM PC*. The examples in 9 deal with the cases on the periphery of the meaning of the word, while the words in 11 illustrate prototypical cases. Lakoff(1975) has taken a special interest in such words (which he calls *hedges*).

12. Questions inserted almost anywhere in the utterance, typically indicating hesitation. Examples: *How shall I put it? What is it called? The food was —What is the word I am looking for? — exquisite*. In speech such expressions co-occur with various hesitation phenomena.

2. WHAT WORDS CAN BE METACOMMENTED?

Every word can clearly be quoted as having been said by somebody else, but not every word can be metacommented. This can be seen by trying to surround random words in a text by quotation marks, as in *The ship made 'a' turn 'to' the left 'and' hit 'the' diving submarine. Then 'it' 'made' a 'turn' to the 'right'*. It seems clear that the so-called grammatical words cannot — and need not — be metacommented, only so called lexical words (full words).

It is, in fact, hard to imagine any secondary or metaphorical sense of grammatical words. They are seemingly inserted automatically by the grammatical machinery and do not leave the speaker any choice. When metacommented, they are also stressed in an unnatural way. It may indeed sometimes be hard to imagine any deviant meaning for a lexical word, too, e.g. for the word *'right '*.

As a corollary of these observations we may note that adverbial comments such as *technically speaking*, and *to say the least* are always interpreted as referring to a lexical word, never a grammatical word in the sentence.

Metacomments, notably quotation marks, raise fundamental linguistic and semiotic issues. The phenomena in the outer or inner world which we want to denote or refer to by words are often deviant from the definitions in dictionaries and from the prototypes we have in our minds; they are often borderline cases. When we want to talk about a certain kind of modern clothing we may hesitate to call it a *shirt*, as it is too long, but *dress* may not seem proper either. In such a case *a sort of shirt* or *'shirt'* may do the job. If we want to refer to a freighter rebuilt as a destroyer, we may use the words *the 'destroyer'* in order to remind the reader that it is not a 'real' destroyer. But we cannot use quotation marks around every word that denotes an object of reality which is somewhat deviant or marginal. It seems, in fact, to be a fundamental — and necessary — property of natural language to allow for a fairly loose application of words, stretching the meaning to cover new cases and not being too specific.

3. FUNCTIONAL TYPES OF METACOMMENTS

The basis of metacomment use is a kind of Gricean maxim: Use the words in a conventional way. If you feel you deviate too much or run the risk of being misunderstood or offensive, etc., insert a metacomment! The flow chart in Figure 1 indicates some different types of metacomments and the conditions for choosing among them.

The flow chart assumes that the system is first trying to match a set of features in the world (a reality pattern) with sets of features corresponding to the meanings of the words (lexical patterns). We may think of the patterns as lists or networks where some features or links are more important than others and some must be obligatory. All criteria need not be met; a certain deviance or fuzziness is accepted, as noted above. But if a certain borderline is crossed, it is reasonable to insert quotation marks or words such as *a kind of, some sort of,* or *as it were,* as indicated by the first diamond of the flow chart.

Even if a word fits the first set of criteria, there may be reasons to add a metacomment. If the word may be offensive to the addressee or to the audience, the speaker may still retain it, if he adds a metacomment such as *frankly speaking, to be straightforward,* or *if you allow the expression.* Alternatively, the author may choose another expression which is not offensive. It is then proper to insert a metacomment to warn the audience that a euphemism has been used.

How to find a euphemism is an interesting problem, but it will not be tackled in detail in this paper. There seem to be certain rules which can be applied in at least some cases. Instead of saying that a substance is dangerous, one may say that it is *not very healthy* or *not too good for you.* These expressions illustrate a productive process where a euphemism is created by taking the antonym and adding a *diminisher,* such as *less, not very,* or *not too* (cf. the paper by Jameson in this volume).

An expert system is a special kind of text generation system, where the system tries to simulate the answers of an expert in a field. There must often be situations where the expert has to choose between a technical term and a nontechnical expression, which may be slightly inaccurate, but comprehensible to the user, normally a layman. This is clearly a place for a metacomment. Finding an ordinary word or a simple expression as a substitute for the technical term may not be easy. This problem is clearly related to the problem of giving good explanations in an expert system. The two kinds of metacomments under discussion are illustrated in the figure by the metacomments: *technically speaking* and *to put it simply.*

A special metacomment which has to do with the fit of the meaning of a word to the intended meaning is illustrated by the last diamond of the diagram. If the object in the real world is a prototypical case, there are often reasons to say so. A doctor — or an expert system simulating a doctor — may want to tell the patient that the case diagnosed is a textbook example, which does away with any hesitation. He can do that by adding a metacomment such as: *typical, genuine, real, textbook.*

Important types of metacomments can be referred to by the following names:

1. Vagueness warning: *kind of, as it were*
2. Malphemism warning: *frankly (speaking)*
3. Euphemism warning: *to put it mildly*
4. Expert warning: *technically speaking*
5. Layman warning: *to put it in simple words*
6. Distance note: *so-called, ''*
7. Prototype note: *typical, genuine*
8. Hesitism: *How shall I put it? What is the word?*

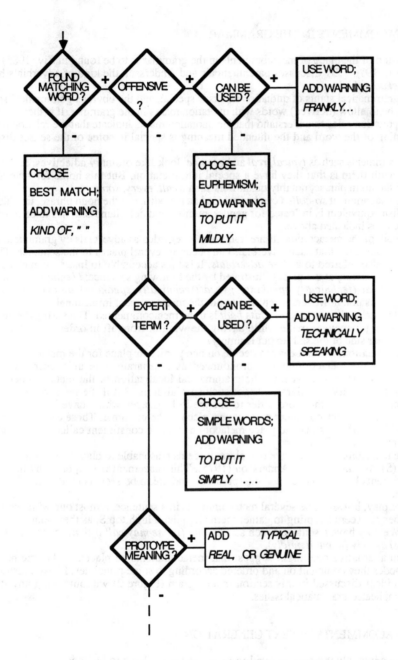

Figure 1. Some criteria used when choosing words and adding metacomments

4. METACOMMENTS IN THE GRAMMAR

A discussion of the place of metacomments in the grammar is to be found in Ziv (1985) and in
Andersson (1976). Ziv discusses parentheticals and Andersson the kind of adverbials he calls
speech act adverbials.

The grammatical status of quotation marks is special, and the obvious grammatical solution
seems to be to allow (derived) words with quotation marks in the grammar. It is then the task of
the interpretation rules to understand that the quotation marks indicate that the relation between
the meaning of the word and the intended meaning is special in some of the senses discussed
above.

Metacomments such as *typical, real* and *genuine* look like ordinary adjectives, and the only
problem with them is that they have a special interpretation. But this holds for several other
words in the noun phrase, notably quantifiers such as *all, every, some*.

The metacomment *so-called* can be included as a modifier in the noun phrase, in which case
its Swedish equivalent is inflected for gender, number and definiteness. It has to be interpreted
along the lines indicated above.

The bulk of the metacomments are traditionally regarded as adverbials by grammarians, who
have often observed that such adverbials can occur at several places in the sentence. They are
sometimes also referred to as *free adverbials*. It is thus acceptable to insert the metacomment
technically speaking at the places illustrated by the following sentence: *(Technically speaking)
the white boat (technically speaking) gybed (technically speaking) quickly (technically
speaking)*. It is not, however, acceptable to put the metacomment immediately after *the,* unless
the word *white* or the expression *white boat* is to be metacommented. The verb *gybe* denotes a
special sailing maneuver made while having the wind in from aft in order to get the wind in
from the other side of the sail (to put it simply).

In this situation, it is not easy to decide on one particular place for the metacomment to be
generated. If the metacomment is pronounced as a separate tone unit, corresponding to
separation by commas in writing, the grammatical localization of the metacomment can be
relegated to a separate minigrammar for such special units. But if the metacomment is more
integrated and causes the word order to change in languages which have inversion, such as
Swedish, then the metacomment must have a place in the grammar. These cases are discussed
by Ziv (1985), who hesitates to place metacomments in a constituent called *tail* in functional
grammar.

If the metacomment is to have one place, it seems reasonable to place it under a top node of
its own (S), as suggested by Andersson (1975). This placement is supported by the fact that
metacomments have a 'speech act' interpretation and are to be seen as modifiers of the whole
sentence.

There may, however, be several metacomments in a sentence, almost one with every word,
and it does not seem tempting to gather them all under a high top S, as they relate to different
words. We may have a sentence such as *The ship (if one may call it that), gybed (technically
speaking) quickly (to put it mildly)*.

As an alternative one might suggest that metacomments be placed in the tree beside the
lexical nodes they comment on and ordered according to some principles. I have illustrated the
different ideas discussed in this section in a diagram (Figure 2) without taking any stand on
these complicated grammatical issues.

5. METACOMMENTS IN TEXT GENERATION

Metacomments which are integrated in the noun phrase have to be generated with the other
words in the noun phrase. But the metacomments which can appear freely almost at any place in
the sentence, can be generated in a different way. They can be produced in a special, secondary
metachannel and brought down from there at certain points in the production process and
inserted in the primary (matrix) sentence. This approach agrees well with the fact that
metacomments often are pronounced as separate units in a monotone, often low, pitch
corresponding to the commas or dashes which often surround metacomments in writing. The

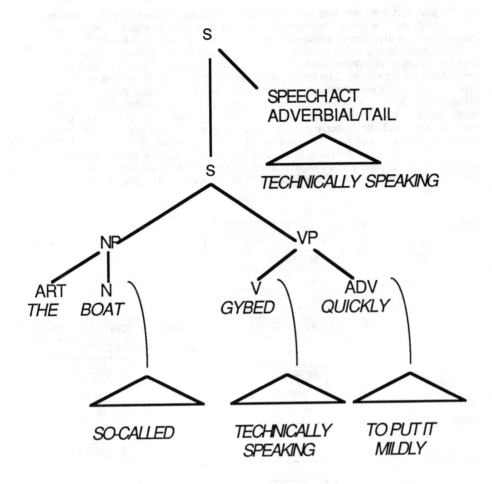

Figure 2. Alternative placements of metacomments in the syntactic tree

isolation of a metacomment may be full or partial. The special prosodic features in speech, and the special graphic markers in writing, certainly help the listener or reader to identify the metacomments and interpret them according to the special principles outlined in this paper. This two-channel model of speech production may be illustrated as follows.

METACHANNEL: *TECHNICALLY SPEAKING*

PRIMARY CHANNEL: *THE BOAT GYBED*

The metacomment *technically speaking* is stored in the metachannel during the generation process, when the word *gybed* is chosen, and it may be brought down from that channel at various points in the production process, e.g. before the whole sentence (*Technically speaking the boat gybed*), before the finite verb *gybed* (*The boat — technically speaking — gybed*), or after the whole sentence (*The boat gybed, technically speaking*) . Several metacomments may be pending in the metachannel to be brought down and integrated in the primary channel at suitable points. It is an interesting empirical task to find out, by the study of spontaneous texts or by experiments, where metacomments are generally placed, which prosodic and graphic markers they get in different positions, how several metacomments are handled, etc.

The generation of a metacomment (like the insertion of a metacomment in the metachannel) may be triggered at several decision points in the process of text production. Typically metacomments are triggered by lexical items, as outlined above. If the system, e.g., finds that *gybe* is suitable for the situation, it should consult the user model to find out whether the listener/reader has marine knowledge. If the addressee can thus be expected to understand the word, nothing has to be added, but if he probably does not understand the word, a metacomment would be proper, e.g. *to use a marine term*. The addressee can then be satisfied at least temporarily — one does not have to understand all words precisely at once, it may be possible to find out the meaning later. The system may also be more helpful and add an explanation or a simpler term. The generation of explanations or substitutes by a computer can make use of explanations and definitions which can be found in dictionaries and encyclopedias.

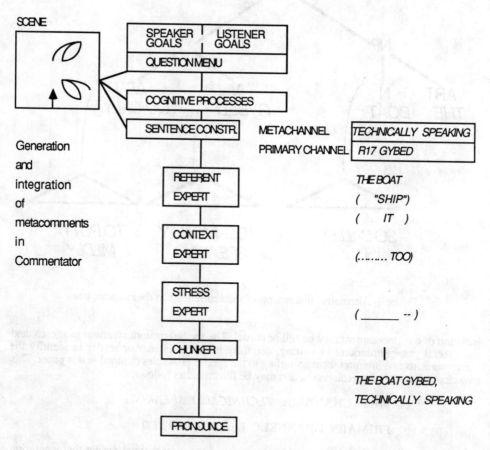

Figure 3

What remains is to implement the ideas of this paper in an advanced text or speech generation system. Some of the problems and solutions can be made more concrete if we consider how metacomments could be generated in the text and speech generation system Commentator (Sigurd, 1983, 1984). The system Commentator is designed to look at a scene (screen) — or rather get coordinate values — and comment on the localization and movements of certain objects (e.g. persons, ships) in front of a gate (or a harbour). The comments can be produced in writing or in speech — via a speech synthesizer — and constitute a coherent text with the correct pronouns, certain connecting adverbials, varying pitch and stress, etc. The system cuts the speech to be uttered into chunks separated by pauses of different duration, and it can easily be made to place metacomments in separate chunks and give them a special monotone prosody. Typical sentences uttered by Commentator are: *The destroyer is to the right of the submarine. It is approaching the submarine. It is approaching the harbour too, but is not close to it. Now the destroyer has reached the submarine.* It does not seem natural to metacomment any of the fundamental predicates, such as *right, approach, close, reach.* But the movements of the objects may often fall outside the prototypical patterns for existing words and in such cases there are reasons to use metacomments to go with the words chosen as best. The movement may, e.g., not be perfectly covered by the term *zigzag* or *circle*, but one of these words may still be the best choice. It is then reasonable to use the word while adding a metacomment.

The generation of the metacomment *technically speaking* in Commentator is illustrated in Figure 3. It is assumed that Commentator can identify the movements of the boat, the positions of the sails and the direction of the wind and arrive at the conclusion that the word *gybe* would be proper. As *gybed* is marked as a technical term in the lexicon the comment *technically speaking* is placed in the metachannel while the construction of the sentence proceeds. The reference expert decides on a proper reference expression, maybe *ship* or *it*. The context expert decides whether to insert an adverb such as *too*. The stress expert decides whether the stress should be changed, e.g., some words de-stressed because the same words were used in the preceding sentence. The chunker decides how big the chunks are that should be pronounced, and puts the metacomment in sentence-final position in this case.

Handling the full range of metacomments discussed in this paper requires a complex interplay between the various modules of the text or speech generation system. How this should be brought about is an important issue for future research.

REFERENCES

Aijmer, K. (1984) 'Sort of' and 'kind of' in English conversation. *Studia Linguistica (Lund)* 38, 118-128.
Andersson, L-G. (1975-1976) Talaktsadverbial. *Nysvenska Studier,* 55-56, 25-46.
Clippinger, J. (1978) *Meaning and discourse : A computer model of psychoanalytic speech and cognition.* Baltimore MD: Johns Hopkins University Press.
Kempen, G. (1987) Language generation systems. In: I.Batori (Eds.) *Computational linguistics. An international handbook of computer oriented language research and applications.* Berlin/New York: de Gruyter.
Lakoff, G. (1975) Hedges: A study in meaning criteria and the logic of fuzzy concepts. In: D. Hockney (Eds.) *Contemporary research in philosophical logic and linguistic semantics.* Dordrecht: Reidel.
Quirk, R., Greenbaum, S., Leech, G. & Svartvik, J. (1985) *A comprehensive grammar of the English language.* London: Longman.
Sigurd, B. (1983) Commentator: a computer model of verbal production. *Linguistics, 20,* 611-632.
Sigurd, B. (1984) Computer simulation of spontaneous speech production. *Proceedings of the Tenth International Conference on Computational Linguistics (COLING-84),* Stanford.
Sigurd, B. (1986) Computer simulation of dialogue and communication. In: F. Karlsson (Ed.) *Papers from the fifth Scandinavian Conference of Computational Linguistics.* Helsinki: Department of Linguistics.
Ziv, Y. (1985) Parentheticals and functional grammar. In: A.M. Bolkestein, C. de Groot & J.L. Mackenzie (Eds.) *Syntax and pragmatics in functional grammar.* Dordrecht: Foris.

Name Index

Abelson, R.P. *8*
Ackley, D.H. *409*
Aijmer, K. *455*
Allgayer, J. *74*
Allwood, J. *336*
Anderson, J.A. *411*
Anderson, J.R. *264*
Anderson, R. *66*
Andersson, L.-G. *458*
Appelt, D.E. *4, 7, 63, 68, 131, 177, 184-5, 219-20, 228, 243, 298, 374, 397, 406*
Arens, Y. *261*
Baars, B.J. *351, 358*
Badecker, W. *390*
Bader, L. *383*
Badler, N.I., *130*
Baker, S. *5*
Baldwin, J.M. *360*
Ballard, D.H. *407*
Balota, D.A., *354*
Barwise, J. *160, 163*
Bastian, J. *360*
Bates, M. *159*
Becker, J.D. *140, 407*
Berndt, R. *383, 389*
Bienkowski, M.A. *406*
Birk, G.B. *5*
Birk, N.P. *5*
Block, R. *344*
Bobrow, D.G. *51, 220*
Bock, J.K. *351, 354, 356, 358-61, 365, 372, 406, 442*
Boomer, D.S. *353*
Bartsch, R. *424*
Bassie, S. *220*
Brachman, R.J. *51, 72, 220, 264*
Bree, D.S., *91*
Bresnan, J. *355*
Bronnenberg, W.J. *335*
Brown, J.S. *46*
Brown, R. *354*
Bühler, K. *4*
Bunt, H.C. *333-4, 336, 338, 340-2*
Burani, C. *61*
Burton, R.R. *46*
Busemann, S. *127, 135*

Butterworth, B. *384*
Camden, C.T. *351*
Caramazza, A. *383, 390*
Carnap, R. *4*
Carr, T.H. *354*
Castelfranchi, C. *61*
Chafe, W. *266*
Charniak, E. *8*
Chase, W.G. *448*
Chomsky, N. *163*
Chumbley, J.I. *354*
Clark, E.V. *354, 380*
Clark, H.H. *354, 380, 448*
Clippinger, J. *453*
Cohen, P.R. *4, 63-4, 68-9, 185*
Cohen, R. *92*
Collier, R. *99*
Collins, A. *46, 185, 187*
Comrie, B. *359, 425, 429*
Conklin, J.D. *120, 130, 176*
Cook, W. *266*
Cottrell, G.W. *408*
Cowan, G. *5*
Cumming, S. *407*
Cutler, A. *354, 356-7*
Danes, F. *271*
Danks, J.H. *442*
Danlos, L. *171, 194, 200, 202, 206-7, 215-17, 219, 406*
Davey, A. *119, 168, 180, 254, 256, 272, 279*
Dell, G.S. *351, 355, 357-61, 397, 408*
Derr, M.A. *46, 171*
De Smedt, K. *183*
Devescovi, A. *61*
Dik, S.C. *255, 258, 266, 307, 309, 314-6, 318, 323, 326-8, 331*
Dominic, J.F. *183*
Donellan, K.S. *63*
Dowty, D.R. *427*
Driscoll, A. *411*
Dukes, W.F. *360*
Emele, M. *135*
Emerard, F. *217*
Fawcett, R.P. *4, 255, 259*
Fay, D. *354, 356-7*
Feldman, J.A. *407*

464

Ferguson, C.A. *380*
Fikes, R. *51*
Fillmore, C.J. *122*
Fleck, M.M. *293*
Flores d'Arcais, G.B. *442-4, 448*
Flower, L.S. *185-7*
Ford, C. *85*
Fox, B. *85*
Frederiksen, C.H. *183*
Friederici, A.D. *383*
Friedman, J. *159, 315*
Friendly, M. *357*
Fries, P.H. *271*
Fromkin, V.A. *351-4, 358, 360*
Garrett, M.F. *351-5, 358, 365, 387, 397, 434*
Gawron, J.M. *222*
Gazdar, G. *4, 222, 242, 248, 339*
Gentner, D. *185, 187*
Gigley, H.M. *384, 408*
Givon, T. *273*
Goldman, N.M. *128, 165, 175, 402*
Goodglass, H. *380, 387, 389-90*
Goodman, B. *68*
Goody, E. *10*
Grashey, P. *384*
Gregg, L.W. *183*
Gregory, M. *4*
Grewendorf, G. *24*
Grice, H.P. *4, 19-20, 23, 30, 120, 403, 456*
Grimes, J.E. *98*
Gross, M. *204, 214*
Grosz, B.J. *4, 51, 75*
Habel, C. *74*
Halliday, M.A.K. *4, 253-5, 258-62, 266, 268-9, 271-4, 279, 297-9*
Hanakata, K, *133*
Handa, K, *150*
Harley, T.A. *355, 357*
Harrah, D. *24, 37*
Harris, Z. *202*
Hasan, R. *259, 271-4*
Hawkins, S. *372*
Hayes, J.R. *185-7*
Heeschen, C. *380-3*
Henderson, A. *51*
Hill, A.S. *5*
Hindle, D. *293*
Hintikka, J. *24*
Hinton, G.E. *407, 409, 411*
Hirst, G. *202, 323*
Hobbs, J. *98-9*

Hoenkamp, E. *123, 360, 366, 384, 398-9, 401-3, 406, 433*
Hoeppner, W. *74, 128, 130*
Hopcroft, J. *280*
Hopfield, J.J. *407*
Hopper, P. *260, 262, 269*
Horacek, H. *344*
Hovy, E.H. *7, 10, 12-3, 20, 29, 130, 184-5, 259, 406*
Huijbers, P. *354, 397*
Hull, H.R. *5*
Humes, A. *188*
Huttenlocher, J. *354*
Isahara, H. *150*
Ishizaki, S. *150*
Isserlin, H. *381*
Jackson, J.H. *378-9*
Jacobs, P. *130, 185, 193, 203, 219-20, 224, 226, 259, 406*
Jakobson, R. *4*
James, C.T. *360*
Jameson, A. *4, 74, 128*
Janssen, T.M.V. *315*
Johnson-Laird, P.N. *118, 402*
Jones, M.A. *411*
Joshi, A.K. *235-6, 238, 374*
Joustra, J. *443*
Kamp, H. *64, 424-5*
Kaplan, E. *380, 387, 389*
Kaplan, R.M. *251, 355*
Karlin, R.F. *71*
Karttunen, L. *251*
Kasper, R. *298*
Katz, J.J. *4*
Kay, M. *298, 331, 371, 374*
Keenan, E.L. *359, 372*
Kehl, W. *147*
Keijser, A. *380, 390*
Keil, F.C. *360*
Kelly, M.H. *360*
Kempen, G. *183, 185-6, 194, 214, 354, 360, 366, 369, 373, 375, 384, 397-9, 406, 433, 442, 453*
King, J. *222*
Klein, J.M.E. *222, 242, 248, 339*
Kleist, K. *379*
Kobsa, A. *72*
Kolk, H.H.J. *378, 380-4, 387-90*
Kosslyn, S.M. *117, 122*
Kroch, A. *238*
Kronfeld, A. *66*
Kubicek, L.F. *354*
Kukich, K. *97, 219, 406-7*

Kuroda, S. *130*
Kwee, T.-L. *307, 322*
Labov, W. *100*
Lakoff, G. *455*
Lakoff, R. *10, 37*
Lamping, J. *222*
Langacker, R. *225*
Langley, P.W. *384*
Laporte, E. *217*
Laubsch, J. *133*
Laver, J.D.M. *353*
Lebowitz, M. *99*
Lenneberg, E.H. *384*
Lesniewski, A. *133*
Levelt, W.J.M. *123, 354-7, 361, 373,
    397, 402-3, 443*
Levesque, H. *63-4, 69*
Linde, C. *100*
Lindsley, J.R. *442*
Loebner, E. *222*
Longacre, R.L. *266*
Loomis, R.S. *5*
Luckhardt, H.D. *159*
Luria, A.R. *384*
Maassen, B. *355-6, 361, 397, 443*
MacKay, D.G. *353, 358*
Malone, T. *51*
Mann, W.C. *7, 48-9, 85, 87, 90-2, 97-
    9, 120-1, 130, 140, 169, 178-9, 188-
    9, 219, 254-6, 269, 271, 279-80, 294-
    5, 299, 406*
Marcus, M.P. *293*
Marshall, J.C. *381*
Martin, J.R. *74, 91, 266, 271, 273*
Matthews, K. *52, 62*
Matthiessen, C. *85, 92, 179, 255-7, 259,
    261, 279-80, 294-5, 299*
Mazzucchi, A. *389-90*
McCauley, C. *354*
McCawley, J.D. *23*
McClelland, J.L. *149, 408, 411*
McCoy, K.F. *46, 52, 97-8*
McDermott, D.V. *8*
McDonald, D.D. *7, 46, 120, 129-30,
    137, 166, 169, 170, 176, 183-5, 188-
    9, 206, 219, 233, 245, 374, 406*
McKeown, K.R. *12, 46, 48-9, 52, 56,
    92, 97-9, 107-8, 114, 120, 130, 168,
    171, 181, 194, 219, 228, 243, 271,
    331, 406*
McNeill, D. *354*
McPherson, E. *5*
Meehan, J. *130*

Menn, L. *389-90*
Miceli, G. *389*
Miller, G.A. *118, 402-3*
Minsky, M. *409*
Momma, S. *135*
Montague, R. *342*
Moon, D. *137*
Moore, J. *130, 178, 220, 261*
Morizono, A. *130*
Morris, C.W. *4*
Motley, M.T. *351, 358*
Nebel, B. *172, 255*
Neumann, B. *118, 121*
Newcombe, F.C. *384*
Newell, A. *220*
Nilsson, N. *295-6*
Nold, E.W. *187*
Noordman, L.G.M. *403*
Novak, H.-J. *118-9, 121*
Okada, N. *130*
Oldfield, R.C. *354*
Olson, D.R. *122*
Ortony, A. *66*
Osgood, C.E. *442,*
Oversteegen, E. *425*
Paivio, A. *357*
Papert, S. *409*
Paris, C.L. *99, 114*
Parmelee, C.M. *354*
Patten, T. *256, 286, 291, 293, 295, 297*
Paulson, A. *222*
Payne, L.V. *5*
Pearl, J. *149*
Perlmutter, D.M. *359*
Perrault, C.R. *63, 68, 185*
Perry, J. *160, 163*
Peters, P.S. *355*
Pijls, F. *214*
Piot, M. *211*
Pollack, J.B. *408*
Postal, P.M. *359*
Pullum, G.K. *222, 242, 248, 339, 359*
Pustejovsky, J.D. *7, 137, 170, 172,
    183, 233, 245, 374*
Quirk, R. *210*
Rau, L. *220*
Reich, P.A. *351, 355, 357-8, 360-1*
Reichenbach, H. *436*
Reichman, R. *48-9, 75*
Reilly, R.G. *408*
Reiter, R. *128*
Reithinger, N. *76*
Riesbeck, C.K. *8*

Ritchie, G. *298*
Ritchie, R.W. *355*
Robinson, M.L. *5*
Rochester, S.R. *74, 273*
Rohrer, C. *425*
Rohrman, N. *360*
Rosenberg, C.R. *411*
Rösner, D. *127, 133-4, 138, 140*
Rubin, D.C. *357*
Rumelhart, D.E. *149, 407-8, 411*
Sag, I.A. *222, 242, 248, 339*
Saussure, F. de *395-7*
Scardamalia, M. *187*
Schank, R.C. *8, 12,150, 259*
Schlesinger, I.M. *442*
Schmauks, D. *71, 77-8*
Schmolze, J.G. *72, 220, 264*
Schreuder, R. *123, 402-3*
Schriefers, H. *354, 357, 397, 399, 402*
Schwitalla, J. *20*
Searle, J. *63*
Sejnowski, T.J. *407, 409, 411*
Shallice, T. *384*
Shepherd, H.R. *98*
Shieber, S.M. *243, 330*
Shopen, T. *380*
Sidner, C.L. *4, 51, 75*
Sigurd, B. *460*
Siklossy, L. *33*
Simmons, R. *171, 175*
Slocum, J. *171, 175*
Small, S.L. *408*
Smit, R.A. *91*
Smith, C.C. *425*
Sondheimer, N. *172, 255*
Sperber, R.D. *354*
Steinberg, E.R. *183*
Stefik, M. *185*
Stemberger, J.P. *351-3, 355, 358-9*
Stevens, A.L. *46*
Straker, D.Y. *11*
Strunk, W. *5*
Sugiyama, K. *134*
Swartout, W.R. *4, 183*
Tallal, P. *384*
Tannenbaum, P.H. *442*
Thesingh, J.C. *341*
Thompson, J.G. *360*
Thompson, S.A. *48-9, 85, 90-2, 140, 169, 260, 262, 269*
Tou, F. *51*
Tsotsos, J.K. *123, 130*
Tsuji, S. *130*

Tversky, A. *52-3*
Tzeng, O.J.L. *384*
Uchida, H. *134*
Ullman, J. *280*
Ullmer-Ehrich, V. *427*
Van Bakel, J. *330*
Van de Kerkhof, M.M. *384*
Van der Korst, B. *309, 314*
Van der Sloot, K. *341*
Van Dijk, T.A. *35*
Van Grunsven, M.F. *378, 380-1, 383-4, 387-90*
Van Katwijk, A.F.V. *338*
Van Wijk, C. *365, 369, 373*
Vaughan, M. *137, 183, 188-9*
Vendler, Z. *425*
Verkuyl, H.J. *427*
Vijay-Shanker, K. *238, 374*
Von Hahn, W. *74, 128*
Von Monakow, C. *384*
Von Stockert, T.R. *383*
Wahlster, W. *74, 128, 130*
Waltz, D.L. *408*
Wang, W.S.Y. *384*
Warren, R.K. *351, 359-60, 372*
Wason, P.C. *187*
Wasow, T. *222*
Weathers, W. *5*
Webber, B.L. *64*
Weber, G. *122, 130*
Weiner, J. *97*
Weinreb, D. *137*
Weydt, H. *37*
White, E.B. *5*
Wilensky, R. *220*
Williams, F. *442*
Williams, R.J. *51, 407, 409*
Willis, H. *5*
Winchester, O. *5*
Wingfield, A. *354*
Winograd, T. *51, 195, 197, 206, 220, 256, 279, 334*
Wish, M. *56*
Wodehouse, P.G. *3*
Wong, H.K.T. *75*
Woods, W. *107*
Woolf, B.P. *46*
Yazdani, M. *183, 188*
Yuille, J.C. *130*
Ziv, Y. *458*